The Complete Warrior's Mindset Collection (Vol. 6)

On War, Maxims of Napoleon & Frederick the Great's Instructions — Foundations of Modern Military Thought

A Modern Translation

Adapted for the Contemporary Reader

Carl von Clausewitz | Napoleon Bonaparte
Frederick the Great

Translated by Tim Zengerink

Table Of Contents

Preface - Message to the Reader

What If You Could Help Rebuild the Greatest Library in Human History?

Thousands of years ago, the Library of Alexandria stood as the crown jewel of human achievement — a sanctuary where the collected wisdom of every known civilization was gathered, preserved, and shared freely.

And then, it was lost.

Through fire, conquest, and the slow erosion of time, humanity lost not just books — but ideas, dreams, discoveries, and stories that could have changed the world forever.

Today, the Library of Alexandria lives again — and you are invited to be a part of its restoration.

Our mission is simple yet profound:

To rebuild the greatest library the world has ever known, and to translate all timeless works into every language and dialect, so that no seeker of knowledge is ever left behind again.

By joining our movement to rebuild the modern Library of Alexandria, you become part of an unprecedented mission:

- **Unlimited Access to the Greatest Audiobooks & eBooks Ever Written:**

  Instantly explore thousands of legendary works—Plato, Shakespeare, Jane Austen, Leo Tolstoy, and countless more. All instantly available to read or listen, placing a complete literary universe at your fingertips.

- **Beautiful Paperback & Deluxe Editions at Printing Cost**

  Own any title as an elegant paperback, deluxe hardcover, or stunning collectible boxset—offered to you at true printing cost, delivered straight to your door. Build your personal Library of Alexandria, crafted for beauty, built for durability, and worthy of proud display.

- **Fresh Translations for Modern Readers—in Every Language & Dialect**

  Enjoy timeless masterpieces reimagined in clear, contemporary language—no more outdated phrases or obscure references. Alongside the original versions, we're tirelessly translating these classics into every language and dialect imaginable, ensuring accessibility and understanding across cultures and generations.

- **Join a Global Renaissance of Literature & Knowledge**

  You directly support expanding our library, publishing deluxe editions at true cost, translating works into all global languages, and bringing humanity's greatest stories to people everywhere. By joining today, you're not just preserving a legacy of masterpieces; you set in motion a powerful wave of literary accessibility.

Become a Torchbearer of Knowledge.

Join us for free now at **LibraryofAlexandria.com**

Together, we will ensure that the light of human wisdom never fades again.

With gratitude and a shared love of knowledge,
The Modern Library of Alexandria Team

Visit:

www.libraryofalexandria.com

Or scan the code below:

Introduction

Masters of Modern Strategy: The Warrior as Thinker, Leader, and Builder of Power

The evolution of warfare across centuries is not only a tale of new weapons and larger armies—it is a history of thought. Behind every campaign, every decisive battle, and every sustained empire lies the strategic vision of minds capable of reading uncertainty, leading men under fire, and adapting ideas to the realities of their time. The Complete Warrior's Mindset Collection (Vol. 6) gathers the intellectual legacies of three of the most influential commanders in modern history—Carl von Clausewitz, Napoleon Bonaparte, and Frederick the Great—each of whom not only fought wars, but theorized them.

This volume features excerpts from Clausewitz's On War, Napoleon's Maxims of War, and Frederick's Instructions to His Generals. Together, they provide the foundation of modern military theory and leadership. But more than that, they reveal what it means to think strategically—not just on the battlefield, but in life, politics, and decision-making under pressure.

Clausewitz gives us a philosophy of war as a continuation of politics by other means, with a depth of abstraction that transcends any one conflict. Napoleon condenses battlefield experience into aphorisms of clarity and brilliance, drawn from victories and near defeats alike. Frederick articulates the moral, organizational, and logistical expectations of commanders, emphasizing order, initiative, and responsibility.

Each speaks to different elements of the warrior's mindset: Clausewitz focuses on theory and fog; Napoleon on boldness and momentum; Frederick on structure and judgment. Their works are as vital to modern strategists and leaders as they were to their contemporaries. This introduction will explore their individual contributions, how they interrelate, and what enduring lessons they hold for those who would lead, build, or battle with purpose.

Clausewitz: Friction, Uncertainty, and the Theory of Total War

Carl von Clausewitz (1780–1831), a Prussian officer and scholar, wrote On War after decades of military service during the Napoleonic era. Left incomplete at his death, the text remains one of the most influential works in the history of strategy. It is not a manual of tactics, but a profound investigation into the nature of war itself.

Clausewitz begins with a now-famous assertion: "War is merely the continuation of policy by other means." This redefinition is not rhetorical—it is foundational. War, for Clausewitz, is not an isolated act, but embedded in political objectives. It is never autonomous. Understanding this relationship is crucial for any leader, strategist, or nation.

He identifies three dominant forces in war: violence and hatred, chance and uncertainty, and reason and policy. These correspond to the people, the army, and the government. A great commander must harmonize these elements in every engagement. He must navigate chaos, rally emotion, and remain anchored in rational aims.

Perhaps Clausewitz's most important concepts are friction and the fog of war. Friction refers to the accumulation of small obstacles that make even simple plans difficult. The fog of war describes the lack of clarity and reliable information in combat. Both phenomena demand adaptability, initiative, and psychological resilience.

Clausewitz also introduces the idea of the culminating point—the moment beyond which continued offensive operations become counterproductive. Recognizing this point is key to sustaining strategic advantage. He warns against overreaching, not from cowardice, but from disciplined awareness of limits.

For the warrior-mind, Clausewitz offers the highest order of strategic thought. He prepares the leader not just to fight, but to understand conflict at its most abstract and political levels. His message is clear: to lead well, one must think deeply.

Napoleon: Action, Timing, and the Principles of Command

Napoleon Bonaparte (1769–1821) was not only one of history's greatest military commanders—he was also a relentless student and teacher of war. His Maxims of War, compiled from his reflections and battlefield notes, provide a condensed philosophy of operational excellence.

Unlike Clausewitz's theory, Napoleon's style is direct, sharp, and drawn from lived experience. His maxims cover every aspect of leadership: movement, morale, deception, logistics, and decision-making. What unites them is a reverence for initiative and a contempt for hesitation.

One of his core beliefs is that war is the realm of movement. In his view, the force that strikes first and hardest often prevails. "The art of war," he writes, "consists in a well-reasoned and extremely circumspect defensive, followed by a rapid and audacious attack." For Napoleon, timing is everything.

Another key theme is the psychological dimension of warfare. Napoleon understood that morale, perception, and the personal presence of a commander could tilt the balance of battle. He believed in decisive leadership, in the power of example, and in using fear and confidence as tools.

His maxims also emphasize concentration of force, economy of effort, and unity of command. These principles form the basis of modern operational doctrine. Yet Napoleon's genius was not just in theory—it was in recognizing when to break the rules. His victories stemmed not from formulas, but from judgment refined by instinct and observation.

To the modern warrior, Napoleon offers not philosophical abstraction, but tactical lucidity. He shows that leadership is about rhythm—about when to wait, when to feint, and when to strike. His writings train the reader to think in lines of force, moments of opening, and the fragile morale of both friend and foe.

Frederick the Great:
Discipline, Structure, and the Moral Economy of War

Frederick II of Prussia (1712–1786), known as Frederick the Great, brought order and enlightenment to the military traditions of his time. His Instructions to His Generals is not merely a technical guide—it is a code of ethics, expectations, and institutional clarity.

Frederick believed that war required forethought, logistical precision, and moral clarity. His generals were expected not only to obey orders but to demonstrate judgment under fire. His instructions cover formation management, discipline, supply systems, and the importance of always being prepared for the unexpected.

Unlike Napoleon's aggressive dynamism, Frederick favored calculated maneuver and defensive depth. He taught that the greatest victories often came from letting the enemy overextend and then responding with organized violence. He also emphasized intelligence and reconnaissance, warning against rashness and praising methodical movement.

What stands out most in Frederick's writing is his concern for the ethics of command. He believed in meritocracy, demanded honesty among officers, and expected restraint in victory. He held that commanders must care for their men and punish only with reason. He saw military leadership as a form of stewardship—not vanity.

Frederick's clarity, moderation, and attention to human detail make him a valuable voice for today's leaders. He shows that greatness is not only about brilliance, but about systems that sustain performance. His disciplined ethos teaches the warrior to think in terms of structure, continuity, and the long-term cohesion of force.

The Synthesis of Strategic Thought: Theory, Tactics, and Temperament

Clausewitz, Napoleon, and Frederick represent three dimensions of warrior mastery:

- Clausewitz offers a map of war's inner structure: its political nature, its fog, and its logic.
- Napoleon provides the tempo, instinct, and audacity needed for tactical dominance.
- Frederick brings institutional wisdom, restraint, and operational discipline to strategic execution.

Together, they form a complete curriculum. They show that the warrior's mind must be at once philosophical and practical, daring and composed, visionary and precise. They also share one essential value: responsibility. To lead is to bear the weight of consequences—for men, for missions, and for the world that follows.

None of these figures advocate for endless war. Each understands its cost. But they also knew that war, once chosen or imposed, must be met with full presence of mind, mastery of self, and unity of command.

For the modern strategist—military, political, or personal—these texts offer a mirror. They challenge you not only to act, but to understand; not only to decide, but to reflect; not only to win, but to deserve victory.

Welcome to The Complete Warrior's Mindset Collection (Vol. 6). May Clausewitz sharpen your thinking, Napoleon ignite your courage, and Frederick discipline your command—so that you lead with clarity, execute with excellence, and endure with principle in any theater of life.

On War

General Carl von Clausewitz

Foreword

The Germans interpret their national colors—black, red, and white—with the phrase "Durch Nacht und Blut zur licht" ("Through night and blood to light"). This saying captures the profound symbolism of the red in their flag, representing struggle, sacrifice, and the passage from darkness to enlightenment. Few works convey this concept as powerfully as Clausewitz's deep and philosophical analysis of "War." In his writings, war is unveiled in its raw essence: the exertion of force to achieve political ends, bound only by the law of expediency. This interpretation provides a key insight into German political aims, essential for understanding the complexities of Europe's modern landscape. Clausewitz's ideas have shaped the political framework not just of Germany but of the continent, tracing a logical path from the Napoleonic era and Waterloo to the present.

Just as Darwin illuminated the driving principles of biology, Clausewitz laid bare the life-histories of nations, establishing "the survival of the fittest" as an unspoken law of international relations decades before Darwin's theory was introduced. As T.H. Huxley later observed, this "fittest" is not necessarily the ethically "best." Both Darwin and Clausewitz approached their subjects not with moral judgments but with a recognition of natural forces. For them, struggle was neither moral nor immoral but simply a condition of life, much like famine or disease. Understanding war as an innate force has profoundly influenced European thought, especially after events like Königgrätz and Sedan, which reinforced the necessity of military readiness. Thus, today, Europe stands as an armed camp, with peace maintained solely through a balance of power. This equilibrium will hold only as long as all forces remain equal; when that shifts, so too will the peace.

The desirability of this balance of forces may be debated, as I discuss at length in "War and the World's Life." But no one would welcome a return to a period of relentless conflict. Yet with each passing year, pressures on the existing state of equilibrium increase as populations grow, creating an inevitable push toward a point of rupture. This tension is leading to a pressure along the line of least resistance, where, sooner or later, an eruption seems unavoidable.

The recent Hague Conference highlights a critical reality: no responsible government in Europe desires to be the point of rupture. War is recognized for its heavy toll, and nations would prefer peace over the responsibilities that conflict brings. Yet, in Britain, we appear dangerously unaware of Europe's dominant sentiment, dismantling our defenses at a time when such actions make us vulnerable to potential invasion. European leaders do not thank us for this self-inflicted weakening of our position, for most would prefer to live out their years in peace rather than risk the liabilities of war. However, the dissemination of Clausewitzian principles has fostered an underlying tension—a kind of societal pressure cooker among nations. It resembles water heated above its boiling point under pressure: a force that could erupt without warning and beyond control.

This state of "molecular tension," as Clausewitz would describe it, leaves Europe in a precarious balance. And though every responsible leader desires to avoid war, they are also aware that, given the right circumstances, the collective pressures of their governed populations might lead to an uncontrollable explosion. Thus, while no one seeks war, the very conditions Clausewitz foresaw—a volatile equilibrium at the mercy of political and social pressures—remain as relevant as ever.

The situation can be likened to an ordinary steam boiler, which steadily delivers pressure to its engines as long as its structure remains intact. But if any breach appears in its casing—if the boiling water is suddenly released from restraint—then, in an instant, the entire mass will explode into vapor, unleashing a force so powerful that no manmade barrier can withstand it.

Similarly, the ultimate consequences of defeat are impossible to predict. The only way to avoid these consequences is to ensure victory, and, following Clausewitz's principles, victory can be guaranteed only by establishing in peacetime an organized system that can mobilize every available man, horse, and weapon (or ship and cannon in the case of a naval war) as swiftly as possible and with maximum force to the decisive field of conflict. This principle, leading to the well-known doctrine by Von der Goltz, provides an explanation for President Kruger's actions in 1899: "The statesman who, knowing his forces are prepared and seeing war as inevitable, hesitates to strike first is guilty of a crime against his country."

Our failure to maintain this readiness lies in the fact that our representatives—elected by popular vote—lack a grasp of this cause-and-effect chain. As a result, our attempts to achieve lasting peace through a balanced approach of efficiency and cost-effectiveness in national defense have failed.

To those unacquainted with the sway of Clausewitz's ideas on the thought patterns of Europe, this assessment may seem exaggerated. However, M. Gustave Le Bon's study of the psychology of crowds reveals the profound influence of these ideas. I do not suggest that Clausewitz's works have been systematically studied or fully grasped in any army—not even the Prussian—but his theories form the fundamental basis for every European military drill regulation, save for our own. Over two or three years, half the male population of every continental nation is drilled according to these principles, embedding a responsiveness to his core ideas. Those who understand this latent, synchronized mindset can provoke a powerful reaction by simply activating the "chords" of these precepts, often overwhelming any other ethical or ideological appeal that might lack this preconditioning.

Germany's recent political shifts illustrate this phenomenon. Socialist leaders in that country lack the expertise of their rulers in crowd dynamics. Long before this, in 1893, the government implemented policies to curb the Socialist movement within useful bounds. The Socialists were free to challenge capital as long as they did not disrupt military discipline. This tolerance was pragmatic; the government knew that unchecked dominance by employers would be detrimental to state loyalty, as men with nothing to lose would hardly be willing to die for their country. However, when Socialist activities began to interfere with military order, the government acted decisively, and the Socialists suffered significant losses in elections.

If a nation can evoke such a profound response in an internal matter—where the immediate interests of the majority might seem aligned with the Socialists—consider how much more potent this response would be when directed outward, against an external threat. In such cases, the "obvious interest" of the people naturally aligns with that of the state. For a statesman to disregard the immense "thought wave" generated by a trained, unified crowd of seven million men, prepared to rally to their leader's command, would be a betrayal as severe as one who fails to strike when his army stands ready for immediate engagement.

The current state of near-immediate readiness among European armies can be traced directly to the spread of Clausewitz's ideas. Each force has been organized according to a uniform standard, making this readiness directly proportional to the sense of duty that motivates each army. In places where dedication and willingness to sacrifice are weak, troops are unprepared and lack efficiency. In contrast, in Prussia, where these values have been ingrained through a century of rigorous training, soldiers are primed for action with the utmost precision. They are so well-prepared that, should Prussia turn its attention to any neighbor, the sheer speed of their advance would almost certainly secure victory in the first confrontation, long before the opponent could reorganize or strengthen their defenses.

An example illustrates this: in 1887, Germany nearly went to war with France and Russia. At that critical juncture, Germany's unparalleled efficiency, driven by this deeply rooted duty—an attribute that surely ranks among humanity's finest—meant that she could have subdued France within six weeks. After just a fortnight, Germany could have begun shifting troops from the Rhine to the Niemen. This situation could very well recur. But had France and Russia received even a ten-day advance notice, Germany's plan would have been foiled. France alone might have forced Germany to deploy her full strength solely to counter her forces.

However, there are still those in England, largely ignorant of Germany's interpretation of Napoleonic principles, who naively assume Germany would set aside the advantages gained from a century of disciplined effort and readiness for the delays of a Court of Arbitration. These politicians expect Germany to waste the edge her readiness provides by following outdated diplomatic customs such as recalling ambassadors and issuing formal ultimatums.

Interestingly, many of today's politicians have acquired their wealth through business, a form of competition not unlike war, as Clausewitz observed. Did these business leaders send their competitors a courtesy notice before launching strategies to outmaneuver them? Did Andrew Carnegie, the famed peace advocate, notify rivals of his moves while building the Steel Trust, accumulating wealth at the expense of competitors? Certainly not. So why would the leaders of a powerful nation, entrusted with safeguarding the well-being of their citizens, willingly risk their hard-won strategic advantage? A nation's leaders, like directors safeguarding the interests of shareholders, must act decisively when the stakes are this high. Generations of sacrifice, patriotism, and strategic foresight have put Germany in a position of readiness that should not be squandered on the procedural delays of traditional diplomacy.

Though recent studies by the French General Staff into Napoleon's records have shown that Clausewitz may not have fully grasped the exact details of Napoleon's strategic method, it's widely acknowledged that he captured the core spirit of it—the spirit that remains central to modern military strategy. Despite changes brought about by advances in communication, logistics, and even the mechanics of warfare itself, Clausewitz's insights into the essence of war still hold true. In fact, with these modern innovations, this spirit of strategy has only grown in importance, for improved communication allows leaders today a degree of control over vast forces that would have been unimaginable in Clausewitz's time.

It's true that weapons now allow for combat over greater distances, but this doesn't change the nature of war itself. Killing remains a constant; what has shifted is our capacity to concentrate firepower, now twentyfold what could be achieved in Napoleon's era. Where Napoleon was limited by terrain, today's leaders can apply intense fire on any position regardless of the ground. For instance, at the Battle of St. Privat-Gravelotte in 1870, the Germans concentrated massive artillery fire in a way that would have been impossible in Napoleon's time. With today's technology, leaders could focus even more overwhelming fire on a single point, and redirect it seamlessly across a front as needed.

These changes in tactics and technology, however, do not alter the truth of the nature of war as Clausewitz presented it—a truth that every soldier and leader should understand deeply. The core elements of war—

death, wounds, suffering, and hardship—are as present today as they were a century ago, and they elicit the same response from soldiers as they did then. This fundamental reaction is something that a great commander must grasp and be prepared to manage. As technological advancements continue, the burden increasingly falls on the character and resilience of the leader, who must steel himself against the raw and visceral pressures of the battlefield.

For those who aspire to lead, preparing for these responsibilities requires a mental fortitude and a profound understanding of their role. In this context, few pieces of advice are as timeless and inspiring as Krishna's counsel to Arjuna in the Mahabharata, spoken centuries ago when Arjuna hesitated at the prospect of leading his forces into battle:

"This Life within all living things, my Prince,
Hides beyond harm. Scorn thou to suffer, then,
For that which cannot suffer. Do thy part!
Be mindful of thy name, and tremble not.
Nought better can betide a martial soul
Than lawful war. Happy the warrior
To whom comes joy of battle...
But if thou shunn'st
This honourable field—a Kshittriya—
If, knowing thy duty and thy task, thou bidd'st
Duty and task go by—that shall be sin!
And those to come shall speak thee infamy
From age to age. But infamy is worse
For men of noble blood to bear than death!
Therefore arise, thou Son of Kunti! Brace
Thine arm for conflict; nerve thy heart to meet,
As things alike to thee, pleasure or pain,
Profit or ruin, victory or defeat.
So minded, gird thee to the fight, for so
Thou shalt not sin!"

COL. F. N. MAUDE, C.B., late R.E.

Brief Memoir of General Clausewitz

General Carl von Clausewitz, author of the work presented here, was born in 1780 in the small town of Burg, near Magdeburg. He began his military career young, enlisting as a Fahnenjunker (ensign) in the Prussian Army in 1792. Clausewitz quickly found himself on the front lines, participating in the campaigns of 1793-94 along the Rhine. This early exposure to war shaped his perception of military life, sparking his interest in studying the science and discipline behind military engagements. After this period of active service, Clausewitz took time to immerse himself in formal military studies, enrolling in the Military School in Berlin in 1801. During his tenure at this institution, which lasted until 1803, Clausewitz drew the attention of General Gerhard von Scharnhorst, a highly respected figure who headed the school at the time. Scharnhorst's support became a defining influence on Clausewitz's career, giving him opportunities that would shape his legacy. This admiration was mutual, with Clausewitz's writings reflecting an enduring respect and appreciation for Scharnhorst's vision and strategic acumen.

Clausewitz's career soon accelerated. In 1806, he served as an aide-de-camp to Prince Augustus of Prussia. However, the Prussian Army faced a crushing defeat at the hands of Napoleon, and Clausewitz, injured and captured, found himself a prisoner in France. His captivity offered him time to deepen his study of warfare, reflecting on its larger purpose and strategic considerations. Upon his return to Prussia, Clausewitz joined General Scharnhorst's staff, working closely on the substantial reorganization of the Prussian military—a task born out of necessity after the humiliating losses of 1806. This period was crucial, for it refined Clausewitz's understanding of the larger, systemic issues in military structures and strategic thought. He was also selected as a military instructor to the Crown Prince, later Frederick William IV, a position that underscored his growing reputation as a thinker in military circles.

In 1812, along with several other Prussian officers, Clausewitz entered Russian service, initially working as an aide-de-camp to General Phul. His talents were soon recognized, and he became involved with Wittgenstein's army, where his diplomatic skill came to the fore. Clausewitz was instrumental in negotiating the notable Tauroggen Convention with General Ludwig York. The circumstances surrounding this convention underscored his adaptability and insight. Sent to York's headquarters with two letters—one from General d'Auvray, Chief of Staff to Wittgenstein, to General Diebitsch, detailing maneuvers to isolate York's forces from Marshal Macdonald; and another, an intercepted letter from Macdonald to the Duke of Bassano—Clausewitz was tasked with encouraging York to break with the French. The situation was tense, as York, commanding Prussian forces allied with the French, hesitated over the potential risks and political repercussions of defection.

Clausewitz's approach was diplomatic yet firm. When he entered York's chambers, York's response was initially defensive. The general warned him to "stay back," saying, "Your damned Cossacks let a letter from Macdonald slip through, ordering me to march to Piktrepohnen. Your troops aren't advancing; you're too weak. I must march; negotiations are over." Clausewitz, undeterred, requested a candle to present his letters and diplomatically insisted, "Your Excellency would not wish me to leave without completing my duty." York eventually relented, lighting candles and summoning Colonel von Roeder, his Chief of Staff, to review the documents. After a tense silence, York's demeanor shifted as he asked Clausewitz, "Do you believe in the sincerity of General d'Auvray's letter—that Wittgenstein's troops will truly be in place on the 31st?" Clausewitz confidently replied, "I trust the letter's sincerity, based on my knowledge of d'Auvray and Wittgenstein's headquarters, though, as Your Excellency knows, in war plans may not always go as drawn."

After moments of deep thought, York extended his hand to Clausewitz, saying, "You have me. Tell General Diebitsch to meet me at Poschenen Mill tomorrow at 8 A.M. I am committed to breaking with the French." The significance of this statement was profound; York had made a fateful decision to defect. But his resolve did not stop there—York declared, "I won't do this halfway. I'll bring Massenbach as well." Calling in an officer from Massenbach's cavalry, York paced the room in a manner reminiscent of Schiller's Wallenstein, demanding, "What's the mood in your regiments?" The officer, visibly moved, passionately affirmed that his men shared York's desire to free themselves from the French alliance.

Clausewitz's handling of this negotiation demonstrates his strategic calm and persuasive ability, qualities that aligned with his broader philosophy of war. This episode reveals his skill not only in strategic operations but in the delicate diplomacy often needed to sway opinion in tense situations. His poise and determination helped turn a critical tide, one that would have significant ramifications on the broader war effort. Clausewitz's experiences, such as the Tauroggen Convention, solidified his place among the military intellectuals of his time, informing the deep, reflective analysis found in his later work On War. Through both action and reflection, he sought to illuminate the complexities of military strategy and the nuances of leadership. This depth of understanding remains at the heart of his contributions to military theory, emphasizing the importance of rigorous preparation, adaptability, and a strategic vision in the face of shifting alliances and uncertain outcomes.

"You young ones may talk; but my older head is shaking on my shoulders," the General replied, hinting at the wisdom that comes from experience. This line, drawn from Clausewitz's Campaign in Russia in 1812, reflects the cautionary voice of a seasoned soldier facing the brutal realities of warfare.

Following the conclusion of the Russian campaign, Clausewitz remained with the Russian military, though now he was assigned as a staff officer with Blücher's headquarters up until the Armistice of 1813. The following year, he took on the role of Chief of Staff to General Walmoden's Russo-German Corps, part of the Army of the North under Bernadotte. Clausewitz's name appears frequently in the annals of this campaign, particularly in his role during the Battle of Goehrde, where his strategic insights were recognized.

In 1815, Clausewitz returned to Prussian service, assuming the position of Chief of Staff to Thielman's corps, which was engaged in skirmishes with Grouchy's forces at Wavre on June 18. Once peace was restored, he received a command on the Rhine. By 1818, he had risen to Major-General and taken on the prestigious role of Director of the Berlin Military Academy, the very institution where he had once been a student.

Clausewitz's career continued to advance, and in 1830, he was appointed Inspector of Artillery at Breslau, only to be shortly afterward assigned as Chief of Staff to the Army of Observation on the Polish frontier, under the command of Marshal Gneisenau. This last assignment brought him into daily contact with General Brandt, who later recorded his impressions of Clausewitz's character and intellectual depth. Brandt recounts how, on one occasion at Marshal Gneisenau's table in Posen, the conversation turned to a rather absurd sermon given by a priest. This prompted a broader discussion on the role of the church and its oversight, eventually leading to theological topics. Brandt, speaking for himself, remarked that he considered theology a "historical process, a moment in the evolution of humankind." The remark sparked a lively debate, especially with Clausewitz, who Brandt believed would have been sympathetic to his views given his studies under Kiesewetter, a Kantian philosopher. However, Clausewitz, though acquainted with Kant's philosophy in a simplified form, took a contrasting stance, defending his point with rigor, showing how his philosophical grounding shaped his approach to thought and analysis.

Brandt goes on to highlight Clausewitz's extraordinary ability to reason through military strategy, describing how he meticulously analyzed marches, calculated timing, and identified decisive points on the battlefield. Although fate denied Clausewitz the opportunity to showcase his skills in a high command, Brandt believed that he would have excelled as a strategist on a grand scale. As a battlefield leader, however, Brandt thought Clausewitz might have struggled due to a "lack of experience in command," which limited his ability to inspire troops with the same force as others might.

After the dissolution of the Army of Observation, Clausewitz returned to Breslau. Tragically, only a few days after his arrival, he fell ill with cholera, likely contracted during his service along the Polish frontier. He passed away in November 1831.

Clausewitz's intellectual legacy was preserved in his extensive writings, which were published posthumously in nine volumes. However, it is his seminal work on war, encapsulated in three volumes, that cemented his reputation as one of history's most influential military theorists. In the current English translation, the translator humbly acknowledges any imperfections in rendering this complex text, but hopes to bring Clausewitz's ideas more vividly to English readers. The translator believes that the significance of Clausewitz's work remains as pertinent today as it was at the time of its original publication, especially in matters concerning national and strategic interests.

J. J. GRAHAM (Col.)

Book I. On the Nature of War

Chapter I. What is War?

1. Introduction.

We intend to begin by examining each individual component of our topic, analyzing them as separate elements. Afterward, we will explore each major section or branch, delving into its specific aspects and unique contributions. Finally, we will approach the subject as a unified whole, assessing it in all its interconnected relations. This progression, from simple to complex, allows us to build a solid foundation of understanding that will inform the larger picture. However, it is essential to start with an overarching perspective on the nature of the entire subject. Such a foundational view ensures that, even when focusing on distinct parts, we continuously bear in mind how each part relates to the whole, providing a cohesive and comprehensive understanding throughout

2. Definition.

We shall avoid delving into the complex definitions of war as they are commonly presented by theorists. Instead, we will focus on its fundamental essence by likening it to a duel. In essence, war is nothing more than a duel on a vast scale. To conceptualize the endless individual confrontations that collectively comprise a war, we might imagine two wrestlers, each attempting to overpower the other through sheer physical force, aiming to compel their opponent to submit to their will. Each seeks to disable the other, rendering further resistance impossible.

Thus, war is fundamentally an act of force designed to make our adversary comply with our demands. This use of force is armed with the tools of art and science, which intensify its impact. While there are certain self-imposed limits, almost negligible and known as the customs of international law, these restrictions do not significantly weaken its intrinsic power. Force—specifically physical force, as moral force presupposes the concepts of state and law—is, therefore, the primary means, and the enforced submission of the enemy to our will is the end goal. To achieve this fully, the enemy must be disarmed; thus, disarmament becomes the immediate objective in theory, supplanting the broader objective as a practical focus for hostilities.

3. Utmost Use of Force.

One might think, particularly from a humanitarian perspective, that there exists an artful way to subdue an enemy with minimal bloodshed, and that this should ideally be the direction of military strategy. However appealing this notion may seem, it is a misconception that must be entirely dismissed. In matters as severe as war, errors born of goodwill are particularly dangerous. Since using maximum physical power does not rule out the involvement of intelligence, it follows that the side wielding force without restraint and without undue concern for bloodshed gains an advantage over an opponent who uses less intensity. The former will then set the terms, compelling the latter to escalate to the same extremes, limited only by the counteracting force each side can summon.

This reality must be confronted directly, for ignoring the brutal nature of war or turning away in horror is, in effect, to misunderstand its essence and, in doing so, risk acting against one's own best interests.

If wars between civilized nations appear less brutal and devastating than those fought by savages, this distinction emerges from the social structures within states and the diplomatic relationships between them. War stems from this social condition, and, as a result, is shaped and restrained by it. However, these limitations are not inherent to war itself; they are merely conditions imposed upon it. Therefore, inserting a principle of moderation into the nature of war itself would be entirely misguided.

Two fundamental motivations drive people to war: primal hostility and deliberate antagonism. In defining war, we've focused on the latter since it is the most universally applicable. It's challenging to imagine the most intense, instinctive hostility without also picturing it accompanied by deliberate intent to harm. Conversely, intentional hostility can often exist without extreme animosity or any form of passionate hatred. Among primitive cultures, actions are usually rooted in emotions, while in advanced societies, they are often influenced by rational considerations. This difference, however, is a byproduct of societal factors, norms, and institutions and is not universally applicable, as even the most advanced societies can harbor intense, passionate animosities against one another.

This analysis reveals the error in assuming that a civilized nation's war could be purely a calculated decision, detached from emotion and driven solely by governmental rationale. The notion that future wars might evolve to a point where armies and combatants would no longer be necessary—replaced by the symbolic manipulation of influence alone—veers into absurdity. Such a theory began to gain traction before the realities of the latest wars proved it false. War, being an act of force, is inevitably tied to emotion. Even if it is not initially born from emotional fervor, it invariably arouses such emotions, depending not on civilization's level but on the stakes involved and the conflict's duration.

If, in practice, civilized nations do not execute prisoners or indiscriminately devastate towns, it is because they've learned more effective ways to exert power—thanks to advances in weaponry and tactics—than resorting to instinctual violence. The discovery of gunpowder and the continual evolution of firearms show that the core intent to destroy the opponent remains unchanged by civilization's progress.

Thus, we reaffirm that war is an act of force driven to its maximum limits. As one side imposes its will upon the other, this prompts a cycle of escalation, where both sides engage in a reciprocal action that naturally drives them toward extremes. This is the first mutual intensification, and the first true extreme, encountered in the nature of war.

4. The Aim is to Disarm the Enemy.

We've already noted that the ultimate aim in war is to disarm the enemy, and now we'll argue that this goal, at least in theory, is essential. To compel an opponent to comply with our demands, we must place him in circumstances so burdensome that they outweigh the concessions we seek. This oppressive state cannot be merely temporary; if it appears fleeting, the enemy may resist in hopes of eventual relief. Therefore, any changes brought about through the continuation of war should worsen his situation, driving him closer to submission rather than allowing a momentary escape.

The most debilitating condition an adversary can face is complete disarmament. So, to secure our objective, we must either thoroughly disarm him or bring him to a state where that threat looms unmistakably close. Hence, the aim in warfare, whether we define it as the enemy's disarmament or defeat, must always remain centered on this principle.

War is fundamentally a clash between two active, opposing forces—each exerting their own will and resisting the other. It's not simply one side's action on a passive opponent, for endurance alone does not constitute warfare. Therefore, our aims apply to both sides. This creates another cycle of reciprocal action: as long as my opponent is undefeated, he retains the potential to defeat me. If he succeeds, I'll lose command of my position and face his terms as he once faced mine. This is the second reciprocal escalation, and it leads to a further extreme in the nature of conflict.

5. Utmost Exertion of Powers.

To successfully defeat the enemy, we must calibrate our efforts in line with his capacity for resistance. This resistance is defined by the combination of two interdependent factors: the sum of available resources and the intensity of his will to fight. While the sum of resources can be somewhat quantified—often linked to troop numbers and material supplies—the strength of will is much harder to gauge. It hinges on the motivations driving the enemy, and these can only be roughly estimated.

Once we have a sense of the enemy's combined power, we then assess our own resources, determining how best to achieve a decisive advantage. If possible, we bolster our strength to secure a clear preponderance. But if our resources are limited, we must still maximize them to tip the balance in our favor. However, the enemy is engaged in the same process—striving to match or exceed our preparations, leading to a continuous escalation of forces on both sides. This process of reciprocal intensification drives each side closer to the limits of its capacity, pulling both toward an extreme state of mobilization. This is the third cycle of reciprocal escalation, pushing each side further into a third level of extremity.

6. Modification In the Reality.

In examining war in its pure, theoretical form, the mind is naturally drawn toward extreme conclusions. Left unrestrained, each force in war follows its own inherent laws, creating a mutual escalation that pushes both sides toward absolute extremes. If we were to strictly apply this pure theoretical view, setting absolute goals and exhausting all resources in pursuit, it would become a chain of logic, spiraling toward an idealized outcome that exists only in theory. A rigid insistence on reaching the extreme would result in little more than a hypothetical, disconnected from practical reality—a "law on paper," rather than a guide adaptable to the real world.

Even if we could measure this ultimate escalation of force with precision, it's improbable that people would willingly adhere to such a theoretical ideal. The human mind resists purely logical extremes, especially when they entail a clear overspend of resources and energies that contravene other state principles. Often, the sacrifices required would far exceed the practical worth of the objective, making it unreachable because willpower isn't fueled by theoretical abstractions.

But a shift occurs when we move from theoretical constructs to real-world contexts. In theory, each side relentlessly strives for perfection and, ideally, attains it. But in reality, this approach would only hold if:

1. War existed as a self-contained act, erupting spontaneously without any connection to the states' prior relationships or historical context.
2. It relied on a single, isolated solution or a few simultaneous actions to reach its conclusion.
3. War itself provided a complete, final outcome without subsequent influence from anticipated political consequences.

Each of these criteria, rarely if ever fulfilled, illustrates the distance between theoretical extremes and the nuanced, interconnected nature of real-world warfare.

7. War Is Never an Isolated Act.

Considering the first point, the adversaries in war are not abstract entities or unknowable forces to one another, even regarding that non-material aspect of resistance—the will. This will is not an enigma; its future potential can largely be anticipated by observing its current state. War rarely erupts without warning; it doesn't reach full intensity in an instant. Consequently, each side can gauge the other's character and capability through past actions and existing conduct, rather than basing judgment solely on the idealized version of what the adversary "should be" or "should do" under perfect conditions.

Human beings, constrained by their imperfect nature, inevitably fall short of any absolute standard. These limitations influence both sides of a conflict and introduce an element of unpredictability, which acts as a natural moderating factor, softening the rigid application of theoretical extremes. Thus, in real warfare, each party operates with a nuanced understanding, shaped by the tangible evidence of the other's strengths, weaknesses, and temperament rather than any idealized abstraction.

8. War Does Not Consist of a Single Instantaneous Blow.

Expanding on the second point, we explore the implications of a war that is drawn out over a sequence of actions, as opposed to one resolved in a single, all-encompassing stroke. If warfare were to culminate in one decisive act or a group of simultaneous actions, then, logically, every aspect of preparation would veer toward absolute extremes. This would be because any shortfall or omission in preparation could not be corrected once events are underway, leaving no room to recover or adjust. In this scenario, the most reliable guide for planning would be the visible preparations and mobilizations of the enemy, as all other factors would fall into the realm of speculation. However, if a war instead unfolds through a succession of actions and engagements, each preceding engagement could inform the next, thus grounding future strategy in a real-world assessment rather than an abstract notion of perfection or completion. In this way, reality tempers the abstract by substituting tangible experiences for mere hypothetical extremes.

If, however, all possible resources for conflict were raised in an instant and applied in a single engagement, the entire course of a war would indeed hinge on that solitary outcome. An adverse result in such a case would deplete the available means to such a degree that subsequent engagements would be nearly impossible to mount; thus, all subsequent actions would essentially prolong the initial engagement rather than initiating distinct new confrontations. Yet, we've already seen that even in preparation, the realities of the world intervene to keep pure theoretical abstractions at bay, limiting both sides from reaching the absolute heights of mobilization. This mutual interaction between opponents thus keeps each side from fully committing all resources to any one action, and all forces are not poured into a single event.

Furthermore, even if one were to attempt a total, all-encompassing mobilization of forces, the nature of these resources and their varied applications makes it inherently impractical to bring everything to bear at the same time. Military power includes not only troops already on active duty but also the national territory, its physical attributes, population, and potential allies. While it might be possible to mobilize all deployable troops at once, the entire country and all its geographic and strategic assets—its fortresses, rivers, mountains, and population—cannot be activated simultaneously. This is only feasible in cases where the country is so compact that the entire terrain could be engaged from the start of hostilities. Additionally, the contribution of allies, a resource largely dependent on diplomatic relations, is often not accessible immediately. Allies may enter the conflict only after it has begun, and as the conflict evolves, they may even step in to balance the scales of power as the situation demands.

This portion of the resistance—which cannot be mobilized instantly and often represents a substantial part of the nation's power—frequently proves more significant than one might initially assume, sometimes balancing the odds even after a powerful initial strike has been made. We will delve into this idea further later on. For now, it suffices to illustrate that a complete, simultaneous concentration of all forces in a single moment is not only impractical but contrary to the essence of warfare.

That said, this reality of warfare does not lessen the urgency of preparing adequately for the first decisive encounter; any unfavorable initial result would put one at a substantial disadvantage, and though not always conclusive, the impact of the first engagement is significant, influencing subsequent events in proportion to the scale of its outcome. Nevertheless, the possibility of later success can incline a strategist to reserve some portion of strength rather than risk everything on one engagement, as the mind naturally resists expending all resources without the assurance of immediate victory. This reluctance leads each side to withhold some forces, preventing the first encounter from achieving the intensity it might otherwise have had if no future opportunities existed. When one side exercises such caution, it becomes, in effect, a signal to the other side that they too can limit their efforts. This dynamic, whereby each opponent's hesitation effectively moderates the ambitions of the other, creates a reciprocal influence that gradually tempers the tendency toward extreme actions, resulting in a more measured approach to warfare.

9. The Result in War Is Never Absolute.

Finally, we must recognize that even a decisive outcome in a war seldom represents an absolute end for the defeated nation. Often, the vanquished state perceives the loss not as a permanent condition but as a temporary setback that future diplomatic or political maneuvers could amend. This perspective alone is enough to soften the intensity and reduce the absolute tension typically associated with total defeat, as both sides may assume that the consequences of defeat could be reversed over time through political or strategic adjustments.

10. The Probabilities of Real Life Take the Place of The Conceptions of The Extreme and The Absolute.

As a result, war becomes disengaged from the strict and relentless pursuit of extremes. If neither side seeks nor fears an ultimate extremity, then the extent of effort expended can be adjusted by judgment, relying instead on probabilities and practical considerations derived from real-world situations. In place of the extreme ideals of all-out effort or uncompromising absolutes, leaders are required to exercise discernment based on the probable courses of action of their opponent. This shift makes the course of war more adaptable to circumstances and grounded in the dynamics of reality, as each state's government and unique context provide the necessary elements for evaluating likely outcomes.

At this stage, what had been abstract concepts of an "ideal adversary" or a "perfect state" recede, replaced by real, specific states and governing bodies with their own distinct characteristics, challenges, and limitations. The decision-making process begins to reflect realistic expectations, with each belligerent gauging the adversary's intentions through a law of probability, observing their conduct, their political situation, and the context in which they operate, then taking action based on those insights.

11. The Political Object Now Reappears.

With these realities in mind, we cannot avoid revisiting the original political objective that war seeks to fulfill. Earlier, in pursuing the concept of war as an extreme act, the notion of outright disarmament and total subjugation overshadowed the political aim. Now, as the pressure to reach extremes relaxes, the political objective naturally reclaims its importance. If war involves weighing probabilities and is fundamentally grounded in actual players and specific relationships, then the political purpose—the underlying reason for war—becomes essential to every calculation. This objective, being the ultimate motive, frames and directs the nature and scope of the military engagement.

A belligerent's political aim, however modest or grand, will correlate directly with the level of resistance they expect to face. A minor political aim typically implies a smaller commitment of forces from both sides, as each state appraises its goals and prepares to limit its costs. Similarly, if our political objective is relatively insignificant, our willingness to compromise or abandon it will be correspondingly high. In this sense, the intensity of the military effort is proportionate to the perceived value of the political outcome; the less vital the objective, the more flexible both parties are likely to be in conceding or modifying it.

The interplay of real-world factors—political objectives, resource availability, and the finite nature of human will—ultimately defines the course of war far more than theoretical absolutes. It is this dynamic, blending practical limitations with strategic aspirations, that shapes and contains war within a realistic, probabilistic framework rather than one of unbounded extremism.

Thus, the political objective, as the foundational motive behind a war, becomes the measure by which the aim of military action and the scope of effort are determined. While it is not, in itself, an absolute yardstick, its value lies in its effect on the belligerent states involved. War, after all, operates within the realm of real-world stakes, not in theoretical absolutes. The same political goal might stir vastly different reactions depending on the specific nations involved or even on the same nation at different times. Therefore, we can only use the political objective as a gauge by examining how it impacts the masses it seeks to mobilize, which in turn demands that we consider the character of those masses.

It's clear that the response to a political objective can vary tremendously, depending on whether these masses are infused with a passionate energy or are relatively indifferent. Sometimes, this interplay can transform a minor political objective into a dramatic escalation. For example, when there exists a profound animosity between two states, even a minor cause might spark a conflict far more intense than the original issue might seem to warrant, causing what appears to be a mere spark to set off a complete conflagration.

This principle applies both to the effort that each state will invest in the pursuit of its political goal and to the ultimate objective that military action should pursue. In some cases, the political objective itself might be the direct goal of the military, such as the annexation of a province. In other scenarios, however, the political aim might not align directly with military action; in those instances, military strategy might aim to secure an equivalent outcome that can serve as leverage when negotiating peace. Here, too, understanding the specific character and motivations of the states involved is vital, for there are situations in which the military equivalent required to ensure the political objective must be disproportionately greater than the objective itself.

The extent to which the political objective dictates the standard of military aim and the level of exertion depends greatly on the nature of the masses involved. When there is little hostility or other divisive sentiment between two states, the political objective may itself largely determine the direction of military strategy. In such cases, the war effort might closely reflect the political motive, diminishing proportionately as the objective's importance decreases, especially when the political motive is the dominant consideration.

This perspective allows us to understand how, without contradiction, wars may range across an entire spectrum of intensity and purpose, from all-out warfare aimed at annihilation to limited engagements, such as maintaining a mere army of observation. These variations bring us to a further dimension of inquiry—a question which will require deeper exploration in our subsequent discussion.

12. A Suspension in The Action of War Unexplained by Anything Said as Yet.

No matter how minimal the political stakes, limited the means, or small the scope of the military objective, can the course of military action afford any true pause? This question probes the essence of warfare and illuminates its inner workings.

Every endeavor has a natural duration, a time required for its completion, which may extend or compress depending on how swiftly the action unfolds. This speed depends on the actor's disposition and abilities, with some individuals or armies working more methodically and others advancing with greater haste. Importantly, a slower pace does not indicate a deliberate intent to prolong; rather, it reflects the inherent time they need to maintain effectiveness. This duration is a function of subjective factors and defines the "length" of the action itself.

Given this, if we accept that each phase of a military campaign requires a specific length of time, then any delay beyond that—any hiatus in hostilities—might initially seem counterintuitive or even counterproductive. It's essential, however, to remember that this discussion pertains not to the progress of any one party in isolation but to the ongoing rhythm of the entire campaign.

In the interplay of forces, halts may seem inconsistent with the drive towards victory. Nonetheless, as we scrutinize these intervals, we must remain aware of the broader strategic context, recognizing that delays or pauses might sometimes serve deeper strategic purposes, aligning with the overall momentum of war even if they seem momentarily at odds with its direct, kinetic thrust. Thus, within the whole course of the war effort, understanding these seemingly idle moments as part of a larger calculation becomes essential to grasping the nuanced flow of military operations.

13. There Is Only One Cause Which Can Suspend the Action, And This Seems to Be Only Possible on One Side in Any Case.

When two adversaries arm themselves for conflict, it signifies a mutual animosity compelling each to readiness. As long as these parties remain armed—continuing the conflict in a suspended state, rather than seeking peace—this animosity endures. It can only be set aside, temporarily, by one shared motive: awaiting a more favorable moment to act. At first glance, this strategic pause appears to benefit only one side; logically, the advantage of waiting for the right moment must inherently disadvantage the other. If one party stands to gain by delaying action, then the other logically gains by pressing forward.

A situation of perfectly balanced forces does not in itself produce a pause in hostilities, as the side with the clearer objective (typically the aggressor) has an intrinsic reason to keep advancing. Suppose, hypothetically, that each side's motives and available resources align to create a sort of "equilibrium," with one side motivated by a strong desire for action but equipped with limited means, while the other lacks a pressing need to act despite having ample resources. Even here, unless the two sides choose peace, this so-called equilibrium remains a fleeting state. Either side would eventually be compelled to disrupt it, for this type of balance only stalls until an anticipated shift arises—favoring one party over the other. Thus, the logic of equilibrium itself doesn't sustain a cessation of action; rather, it invariably gives way to a tactical pause in anticipation of a more opportune moment.

Consider a scenario where one state pursues a specific objective, say, the conquest of a region from the adversary, which serves its political aims and opens the door to possible peace talks. After achieving this conquest, the first state may no longer feel compelled to act and thus pauses, its aim essentially accomplished. Should the opponent find this new state of affairs acceptable, peace could follow naturally; if not, the opponent must move to counter. Suppose, however, that in a matter of weeks, the second state will be better prepared for action; it has a sound basis for delaying its response until then.

Yet, the rational course for the first state—the one that achieved its objective—is now to act immediately, preempting the delay that would only serve its rival's interests. This interplay assumes that each side possesses thorough awareness of the other's intentions and resources. In practice, the decision to suspend or press forward hinges on constantly changing calculations of advantage, where each side is continuously probing for the right moment to best serve its own objectives.

14. Thus A Continuance of Action Will Ensue Which Will Advance Towards A Climax.

If we imagine that the actions in war could maintain an unbroken continuity, the result would drive the conflict increasingly toward the extreme. Constant, uninterrupted activity would intensify emotions and inject a heightened level of passion and elemental force into the overall conflict. This incessant momentum would lead to a more rigid continuity in operations, creating a tighter cause-and-effect relationship between each event. Consequently, every action would gain greater significance, making each decision or move fraught with higher stakes and more danger.

In reality, however, war rarely unfolds in such a seamless, unceasing manner. Historical records show that extended periods of inaction often occupy much of the time spent in many wars, with actual hostilities or maneuvers accounting for only a fraction of the overall period. This intermittent pace suggests that such pauses are not simply deviations from the norm; they are inherent possibilities within the nature of war. Thus, periods of inactivity do not contradict the logic of war itself but instead represent an alternative mode within its framework. The existence of these pauses in activity prompts us to understand why and how they occur, rather than dismiss them as anomalies.

15. Here, Therefore, The Principle of Polarity Is Brought into Requisition.

This brings us to the concept of polarity in war, a principle that becomes essential here. Since we assume the interests of each commander to be diametrically opposed, we arrive at a true state of polarity. We will explore this concept in greater detail in another chapter, but for now, a preliminary explanation will suffice.

The principle of polarity is relevant when it can be understood within a single, unified context where the opposing elements—positive and negative—completely negate each other. In a battle, each side strives for victory, which embodies true polarity; one side's victory is intrinsically the other side's defeat. However, when we consider two distinct things connected by a shared relationship that exists outside their direct control, it is not the entities themselves that exhibit polarity but rather their relationship to one another.

In war, these relationships can be nuanced, yet they fundamentally operate in a polarized manner, shaping each side's actions in accordance with the larger, often complex, strategic interplay.

16. Attack And Defence Are Things Differing in Kind and of Unequal Force. Polarity Is, Therefore, Not Applicable to Them.

If war consisted of only one approach—namely, a continuous offensive where no defense existed—or, put another way, if the difference between attack and defense was simply that one side held a proactive purpose while the other did not, and both employed identical tactics, then each success on one side would directly translate to a loss on the other. In this case, true polarity would be evident, as every gain on one side would inherently result in an equivalent loss on the opposing side.

However, war does not operate through a single, undifferentiated approach. Instead, it encompasses two distinct forms: attack and defense, each of which is fundamentally different in nature and often of unequal strength—a point we will discuss in greater detail later. Therefore, the concept of polarity does not reside in the nature of attack or defense itself but rather in the shared outcome they are directed toward: the final decision or resolution.

In this sense, if one commander is motivated to delay a decisive engagement, the opposing commander has a vested interest in accelerating it, but each desires the same type of resolution, only at different times. For instance, if Commander A believes that it is advantageous to postpone the attack by a month, Commander B would prefer to have it happen immediately. This forms a direct opposition in their interests. However, this does not necessarily imply that Commander B's best move is to initiate an attack on A right away. The concept of polarity here involves their opposing desires regarding timing rather than suggesting that their ideal actions would mirror each other. In essence, this polarity of interests reveals that while both commanders are aligned in seeking a definitive outcome, they are divided in how, and more specifically, when that outcome should be achieved.

17. The Effect of Polarity Is Often Destroyed by the Superiority of The Defence Over the Attack, And Thus the Suspension of Action in War Is Explained.

If we acknowledge that the defensive position holds a natural strength over the offensive, a question follows: does the benefit of postponing a decision equal the inherent strength of the defensive form? If the advantage of delay does not outweigh the power of defense, it cannot effectively counterbalance this inherent strength, and thus may not meaningfully impact the progress of war.

This leads us to understand that the driving force of opposing interests—one side desiring immediate action, the other preferring delay—may diminish if it's countered by the strength of the defensive position. In other words, the potential advantage gained from delaying a decision might be negated by the inherent power of defense, rendering the impulse to act immediately ineffective.

Consequently, if the side that would benefit from immediate action is too weak to abandon the defensive advantage, it may have no choice but to accept the less favorable future prospects. For this side, it may still be preferable to face a defensive battle later, even under unfavorable conditions, than to assume the offensive now or to concede peace prematurely. This understanding highlights the substantial superiority of the defensive strategy (when properly understood), which is likely far greater than it initially appears.

From this, we can infer that many of the periods of inactivity common in war are explained by this very dynamic. The inherent strength of the defensive position can absorb and nullify the motives for offensive action, leading to pauses in conflict. This pattern, which experience has repeatedly shown, becomes more pronounced when the motives for action are weaker; thus, the stronger the defensive advantage, the more frequent the halts in warfare. In summary, the greater disparity between the strengths of offense and defense, the more likely action is to be tempered, resulting in intervals of inaction.

(This analysis reflects an era before the impact of long-range weapons, which would later alter these considerations.)

18 A Second Ground Consists in The Imperfect Knowledge of Circumstances.

Another significant factor that can interrupt the flow of action in warfare is a limited or incomplete understanding of the overall situation. Each commander has full knowledge only of his own position; the details of his opponent's situation are known indirectly, typically through reports that can be unreliable or fragmented. This incomplete information may lead him to misjudge the enemy's strength or intentions, sometimes mistakenly attributing the power of initiative to the adversary when, in fact, it lies within his own grasp. Such a misjudgment based on partial information may, therefore, result in a choice to delay action under the assumption that the opponent has the upper hand, though the reality may be otherwise.

This gap in understanding could equally drive premature action as much as it might prompt unwarranted inaction. Hence, incomplete knowledge alone doesn't strictly delay or accelerate action, but it stands as one of the natural factors that could lead to pauses in combat without causing a fundamental conflict in logic. When we consider human nature's tendency to overestimate the enemy's capabilities rather than underestimate them, this imperfect grasp of information generally leads commanders toward caution, favoring delay over reckless engagement. Thus, incomplete insight into the adversary's situation often serves to restrain action in war, influencing how principles are applied and decisions made.

The possibility of a pause in warfare introduces a new dynamic, wherein the element of time blends into the conduct of war. This delay tempers the immediate influence of risk, while also allowing additional opportunities to correct or recover any lost balance of power. When the driving passion and intensity of war are high, actions tend to be more immediate, and periods of inactivity are brief. Conversely, when the animating force of war is weaker, these pauses lengthen, as the strength of motivation inherently bolsters the willpower necessary to sustain momentum. Thus, the more powerful the underlying motives, the more readily a commander will maintain an active stance, while less intense motivations will naturally produce extended pauses in the theater of war.

19. Frequent Periods of Inaction in War Remove It Further from The Absolute and Make It Still More a Calculation of Probabilities.

The slower the tempo of action in war, the more frequent and extended the pauses become, which allows greater opportunity for rectifying mistakes. This, in turn, emboldens a commander in making calculations and judgments; he will be more inclined to temper his strategies, resisting the urge to pursue absolute extremes, and instead rely on estimations of probability and educated guesses. Consequently, as the pace of war slows, a commander has more leeway to approach each unique situation in a manner suited to its specific demands, basing his plans on the practical realities and variables at hand rather than an uncompromising pursuit of maximum force.

20. Therefore, The Element of Chance Only is Wanting to Make of War A Game, And in That Element It Is Least of All Deficient.

From the discussion above, it's evident that war, in its very nature, becomes a matter of calculating probabilities. Yet, there remains one additional factor that fully transforms war into something resembling a game, and that factor is chance. Few human endeavors are as closely and consistently bound to the workings of chance as war. With this element, the unforeseen and the accidental, luck also takes on a significant role, shaping outcomes in ways that are impossible to fully predict or control. In this way, war weaves in the unpredictable, turning each decision and maneuver into a gamble influenced by the unknowable twists of fortune.

21. War Is a Game Both Objectively and Subjectively.

Looking at the subjective aspects of war—the human conditions and psychological factors influencing it—reveals even more clearly how much it resembles a game. The defining environment for military actions is one steeped in danger. In the face of this ever-present threat, what mental quality comes forward first? It is courage. Courage and careful calculation can indeed coexist, but they are distinct mental traits, each unique in nature. Boldness, reliance on luck, daring, and even recklessness are expressions of courage, but they often lean into the unpredictable because that is their element.

Thus, right from the beginning, we see that war does not rest on any fixed, mathematical certainty. It's a constant interplay of possibilities, chances, good fortune, and misfortune. These elements interweave like a complex web of both coarse and delicate threads, and in doing so, they turn war into perhaps the most uncertain of all human endeavors, akin to a high-stakes game of chance.

22. How This Accords Best with The Human Mind in General.

Our intellect naturally seeks clarity and certainty, yet our minds are often drawn to the allure of uncertainty. Instead of rigidly following the structured path of philosophical investigation and logical reasoning—ultimately leading us into unfamiliar spaces where we feel like strangers—it sometimes prefers to dwell within the imaginative realm of chance and fortune. In this domain, instead of existing under the constraints of necessity, it revels in a wealth of possibilities. Energized by these open-ended prospects, courage takes flight, and the thrill of risk and daring finds its element, much like a fearless swimmer diving headlong into the swift current.

Should theory dismiss these nuances, content with absolute conclusions and rigid rules, it risks losing practical relevance. Theory, therefore, must account for the human element, recognizing the roles of courage, boldness, and even a certain recklessness. The Art of War deals not with static entities but with living, moral forces, which means it can never be entirely absolute or definitive. This reality creates space for chance to influence both significant and minor outcomes. Just as randomness has a place in warfare, so too must courage and self-assurance occupy a proportional presence to meet it. When these qualities are present in ample measure, the leeway for what is unpredictable and unforeseen can also expand.

Thus, courage and self-confidence are not just incidental but essential qualities in warfare, and theory must, therefore, allow room for all levels and expressions of these fundamental military virtues. Wisdom and prudence still hold value, but in the context of warfare, they are measured by a different standard—one that appreciates the calculated yet daring nature of military action.

23. War Is Always a Serious Means for A Serious Object. Its More Particular Definition.

Such is the essence of War, the role of the Commander who conducts it, and the framework of theory that shapes it. Yet, War is far more than a mere game or a pursuit of thrill, fortune, or adventurous wins; it is not a venture fueled solely by uninhibited passion or free-spirited enthusiasm. Instead, War is a formidable instrument for a serious purpose, one that integrates and transforms elements of fortune, the fluctuations of passion, bursts of courage, imaginative leaps, and even the intensity of zeal—all of which serve as attributes of this complex tool.

In modern societies—especially those that are civilized and well-organized—the waging of War is always rooted in a political context and ignited by a political purpose. Thus, War is essentially a political act. If War were, in its purest form, an unrestrained and absolute force, as we conceptualized in theory, then the moment it was brought into play by political forces, it would exist autonomously, pushing policy aside entirely and following only its own rigid laws. It would be like a detonated explosive—unable to be steered, bound solely to the course predetermined by its prior setup. This has been a common perspective whenever policy and military action appear to be out of sync, often leading to a false separation of the two. But in reality, this view is fundamentally mistaken. War, as it manifests in the actual world, is not an unending release of force spent in a single moment. Instead, it is a gradual release of power that never unfolds with complete intensity or uniformity.

The forces at play in War are not always fully exerted or released at a single instant; rather, they pulse, waxing and waning. Sometimes they surge enough to overcome inertia or resistance, while at other times they are insufficient to create immediate impact. Thus, War proceeds with varying intensity, alternating between periods of forceful engagement and relative calm. This pulsation of effort, from fierce escalation to quieter moments, allows War to exhaust its power over time, thereby creating space for external influences to shape its course. Because of this, War can be guided and influenced, directed by a rational intelligence that operates not in isolation but with adaptability to the course of conflict.

Reflecting on War's origin in political intent, it naturally follows that the purpose which called it into being must continue to be its highest and most foundational consideration. However, the political aim does not dictate War's course as an authoritarian ruler might; it must adapt to the means through which it is expressed. Changes in the means or circumstances of warfare can lead to modifications in political objectives, yet these objectives retain precedence. Policy, therefore, remains intertwined with the entirety of War's action, persistently shaping its progression to the extent that the unleashed forces of War permit.

24. War Is a Mere Continuation of Policy by Other Means.

Thus, we recognize that War is not simply a political act in itself; it is also a tangible extension of political strategy—a continuation of political dialogue and negotiation, executed through alternative means. Everything in War beyond its intrinsic nature as a political tool pertains to the specific characteristics of the methods it employs. Political objectives must naturally align with these methods, and both the general principles of military strategy and the Commander's judgment in any given situation may demand this alignment. This requirement is by no means insignificant, as it involves reconciling the fundamental nature of War with the intended political outcomes.

While these demands of War can, at times, greatly influence and even alter political objectives on a case-by-case basis, we must always see these changes as adjustments to the original political intent rather than replacements for it. War remains a means, and politics, with its goals and purposes, is the end. In our understanding, the means—War—must necessarily encompass and serve the ultimate political objective.

25. Diversity In the Nature of Wars.

The stronger and more compelling the motives driving a War, the more it permeates the life and identity of an entire people. When the motivations are intense and emotions are highly charged, the War moves closer to an idealized form, marked by an uncompromising drive to overcome and destroy the enemy. In such cases, military and political aims align more closely, making the War seem more purely military, less entangled with broader political nuances. Conversely, when motives are less powerful and tensions more subdued, the path of military action diverges further from the political objectives. Here, the nature of War becomes more restrained, redirecting it from an abstract ideal and giving it a more political appearance.

To avoid misunderstandings, it's essential to clarify that this "natural direction of War" refers only to the philosophical or logically deduced form, not to the energy of forces actively clashing. These real forces, driven by emotions and passions, may sometimes escalate beyond control, yet even in such cases, they will usually remain under political direction. In reality, contradictions between military action and political goals are rare, as sustained, intense exertion typically implies a grand strategic purpose aligning with both elements. If the aim is modest, the emotional intensity among the masses will also likely be subdued, often requiring encouragement rather than restraint to reach even limited objectives.

26. They May All Be Regarded as Political Acts.

Returning to the central theme, we see that while some types of War seem to minimize the role of political influence, and in others, politics appears prominent and active, both are equally political in nature. If we view State policy as the guiding intelligence of the State itself, then it must account for all external conditions, including those arising from situations that demand a large-scale War. This comprehensive view means that, whether or not War visibly bears a political face, it is still fundamentally tied to the State's policy as part of its larger strategic calculus.

However, if we think of policy not as the objective analysis of broader circumstances but rather as a stereotype of cunning—an excessively cautious, often deceitful maneuvering that avoids outright force—then we might mistakenly assume that certain types of War serve policy more than others. This perception arises when politics is reduced to something cautious or evasive, creating the illusion that some Wars are more policy-driven simply because they align with this more conventional and passive form of statecraft.

27. Influence of This View on The Right Understanding of Military History, And on The Foundations of Theory.

We observe, then, first and foremost, that War, in any scenario, must be viewed as an extension and instrument of political policy, inseparably linked to the motives and decisions guiding the State. Only by adopting this perspective can one align with the lessons of military history, which consistently reinforces this relationship. Without it, one risks reading history incorrectly or, at best, only partially understanding the true drivers of military engagements. This perspective unlocks the full meaning behind historical conflicts, clarifying how Wars adapt their character in response to the varied motives and unique conditions that bring them into existence.

The primary responsibility of both the Statesman and the General, and indeed their most profound exercise of judgment, is to correctly understand the specific nature of the War they face. It is critical that they avoid perceiving or attempting to mold War into something it cannot inherently be. This understanding forms the foundation of strategy, representing the most essential question in planning any military endeavor.

For now, we stop here, satisfied to have established the central viewpoint that will guide our study of War and its theoretical framework. We will revisit and delve deeper into these principles when we explore the formation of a War plan, where this foundation will be applied in practical terms.

28. Result For Theory.

War, then, is not only like a chameleon, adapting its character slightly with each specific situation, but it also forms a unique and complex trinity, embodying three distinct but interwoven elements. These elements are: the primal violence and animosity that stem from instinctual hatred, which often drives it blindly; the element of chance and probability, which allows the unfolding of individual talents and courage within the dynamic scope of possibilities; and finally, the calculated, subordinated aspect of War as a tool of political policy, which aligns it with reason and intentional design.

Each of these aspects aligns closely with a particular sphere. The raw, instinctual passion relates more closely to the people, whose underlying tensions fuel the initial momentum of War. The element of courage and skill—directed within the framework of chance and the uncertainties of War—corresponds to the General and the Army. Meanwhile, the political aim, which shapes the broader, strategic objectives of the conflict, falls under the responsibility of the Government alone.

These three guiding forces, which each act as law-givers in their own right, are firmly embedded within the very nature of War yet remain variable, shifting in degree from one conflict to the next. Any theoretical approach that ignores one of these aspects or attempts to impose a rigid structure upon their relationships would fall short, diverging so significantly from reality that it would lose relevance altogether.

The challenge, therefore, lies in establishing a theoretical balance between these three guiding forces, like a point evenly pulled by three equal attractions. How to achieve this delicate equilibrium is something we will explore further in the section dedicated to the "Theory of War." For now, the framework we've defined provides a crucial initial perspective, allowing us to discern these broad elements of War and begin forming a structured understanding of its underlying principles.

Chapter II. Ends and Means in War

With the previous chapter establishing the complex and changeable nature of War, we turn now to how this nature influences both the objectives and the methods employed in warfare. When we consider the main target of War, which serves to achieve the political objective, we find that it, too, varies as much as the political aim itself and the specific conditions of the conflict.

If we focus on the pure concept of War—viewing it as a means to compel the enemy to submit to our will through force—we would conclude that the political objective lies outside War's immediate scope. For, if the ultimate aim of War is to use violence to enforce our will, the entire effort must revolve around neutralizing the enemy, specifically by rendering them defenseless. While this purely abstract goal often translates into real-world strategies, it is not the only form War may take.

Within this framework, we need to consider three primary objectives, each encompassing distinct elements that must be addressed: the enemy's military power, the territory in question, and the enemy's will to continue.

1. Military Power: The military forces of the adversary must be degraded to a point where they are no longer capable of sustaining the fight. This is what we mean when we refer to "destroying the enemy's military power" in the context of War—it signifies a degradation or neutralization rather than total annihilation.

2. Territory: Control over the territory is crucial, as the resources and population of a region can produce new forces that prolong resistance. Therefore, conquering the land itself is a vital element in limiting the enemy's ability to recover and rearm.

3. Will of the Enemy: Even after achieving dominance over both military power and territory, the War does not truly end until the enemy's will to fight is subdued. This means that either the enemy's government and its allies must be compelled to accept peace terms, or its people must be willing to submit to our terms. Without this, despite full occupation, there remains the risk of renewed hostilities, either from within the occupied territory or from external allies. Though the risk of renewed conflict could arise even after formal peace is declared, this merely underscores the fact that some Wars do not inherently resolve all issues or guarantee enduring peace.

In short, while the destruction of forces and control over territory are essential to victory, the resolution of War requires subduing the opponent's will, either through government acquiescence or the people's acceptance of new terms.

Even after peace is achieved, some latent sparks of conflict often remain that might otherwise have continued to smolder. However, the conclusion of peace generally dissipates these tensions, cooling passions and turning many minds towards rebuilding and renewal. In every society, there exists a substantial number who inherently favor peace, and once peace is secured, they withdraw support from the possibility of renewed resistance. Thus, regardless of potential future flare-ups, peace represents a substantial end, signaling the conclusion of the War's business.

In the abstract sense, War aims to achieve peace by first neutralizing the enemy's military forces, then subduing the territory, and finally positioning ourselves in such a way that the enemy feels compelled to negotiate peace. Typically, these objectives unfold in tandem, with military defeat and territorial conquest reinforcing each other, as the loss of land also depletes the enemy's available forces. However, this sequence is not fixed; in some cases, the enemy may retreat across vast distances, preserving their military power even as we gain control of significant or entire portions of their territory.

In reality, complete disarmament or defeat of the enemy, the ideal objective deduced from theoretical conceptions of War, is rarely reached and is not a requisite for peace. Peace agreements often occur before one side is wholly disarmed, sometimes even before the balance of power shifts significantly. Historical examples abound where treaties were established without complete military dominance. A decisive victory becomes especially impractical when fighting an opponent who possesses a significant advantage in strength. In such scenarios, pursuing absolute defeat is often little more than an unrealistic ideal, particularly if the opposing force is markedly superior.

The reason the abstract goal of disarmament seldom aligns with real-life War lies in the fundamental differences between War in theory and War in practice. If War conformed strictly to theory, combat between states with vastly unequal strength would seem nonsensical or impossible, as their power disparity would discourage any engagement. Real-life Wars often arise between states with stark power imbalances precisely because War in practice deviates significantly from its theoretical conception.

Two key factors can lead a nation to concede short of defeat: first, a low probability of success, and second, the excessive cost of achieving victory. As we have seen, War cannot adhere solely to logical rigor but must factor in probabilities. The weaker the motives and the lower the passions, the more likely War will be influenced by such probabilities. In cases of lesser passions and motivations, even a weak probability of success for the adversary might be enough to secure peace without necessitating a prolonged campaign to annihilate the opponent.

If one side foresees this from the outset, it is natural for them to aim merely for this probable outcome rather than expending vast time and resources attempting the total destruction of the enemy's forces. This approach reflects the nuances of War in reality—a realm where absolute outcomes are often set aside for practical solutions based on probability, cost, and the reasonable pursuit of peace.

An even more fundamental factor influencing the decision to pursue peace is the assessment of the resources already expended and the resources still required. Since War is not driven by mere impulse but is guided by political objectives, the worth of these objectives sets a limit on the sacrifices deemed acceptable to achieve them. This calculation includes both the magnitude of the expenditure and the duration over which these sacrifices must be sustained. Thus, when the required investment in the War reaches a point where it outweighs the value of the political objective, the objective itself must be relinquished, and peace becomes the inevitable outcome.

In Wars where neither side has the power to completely disarm the other, the inclination toward peace on each side will vary in proportion to both the likelihood of achieving future success and the scale of continued sacrifices. If both sides experience equally strong motivations toward peace, they will meet somewhere along the line of their political differences. However, if one side has stronger motivations to cease hostilities, peace can still be reached, but generally to the advantage of the side with less incentive to end the conflict. Here, we set aside the distinction between positive and negative objectives, though this difference is crucial and will be explored later, as the original political objectives may shift significantly throughout the War due to unfolding events and outcomes.

This leads to a crucial question: how can we alter the probability of success in our favor? Primarily, by employing the same methods as when our aim is outright victory—through the depletion of the enemy's military forces and the occupation of their territories. However, these methods take on new meanings here, as they do not always imply a strategy of total conquest. For instance, when we engage the enemy's Army, it matters greatly whether our intention is to follow up an initial victory with relentless strikes until their forces are entirely broken or to stop at a single significant victory. A solitary, strategic victory might serve to undermine the enemy's confidence, demonstrate our superiority, and provoke apprehension about future engagements. In this scenario, we would limit our objective to diminishing the enemy's forces just enough to achieve these psychological and strategic advantages.

Similarly, the capture of enemy territory serves a different purpose if our aim is not to destroy their Army outright. In a campaign of complete conquest, territorial gains are secondary, emerging naturally as a consequence of the enemy's military defeat. To seize territory before neutralizing the enemy's forces would traditionally be seen as a necessary drawback. But if we are not striving for total destruction and recognize that the enemy seeks to avoid a decisive engagement, occupying a vulnerable or poorly defended province may be advantageous on its own. This action alone could instill enough anxiety about potential losses to prompt the enemy to seek peace, essentially serving as a more efficient path toward our goal.

Additionally, we encounter unique strategies for shaping the likelihood of success without directly targeting the enemy's Army, namely through expeditions and maneuvers that align with broader political goals. If there are specific operations likely to dissolve the enemy's alliances, make them ineffective, or attract new alliances to our side, or even stimulate support from political factions sympathetic to our cause, these actions can substantially increase our prospects for success. In certain cases, these politically oriented measures could be more effective than confronting the enemy's forces directly, offering a more direct route toward our aims.

A second, equally important question is how to influence the enemy's endurance, essentially raising the cost of their success. When we consider methods of prolonging or intensifying the strain on the enemy's resources, we enter the domain of strategic attrition. By elevating the cost of their continued efforts—through disrupting supply lines, targeting critical infrastructure, or drawing them into engagements that drain their resources or morale—we make their objective harder and more expensive to attain. In doing so, we can force them to weigh the continued expense of the War against the diminishing returns of their political aims. Such tactics make it increasingly appealing for the enemy to seek a peace agreement rather than pressing on with an increasingly costly campaign.

The enemy's expenditure in terms of strength consists chiefly in the depletion of his forces, which occurs through the destruction of his troops by our actions, and in the loss of his territories, resulting from our conquests. Here, it is crucial to recognize that the meaning of these measures is not fixed across all scenarios; each has a different significance depending on the broader objectives. While these variations in impact may seem subtle, even minor nuances often decisively influence the selection of our methods for applying force. Our aim here is merely to show that, given certain conditions, it's entirely feasible to achieve our goals in various ways without any inherent contradictions or errors.

Beyond these two primary means, there are three additional and distinct methods for directly escalating the enemy's resource drain. The first of these methods is invasion, understood here as the occupation of enemy territory not necessarily to retain control over it but rather to impose contributions or wreak widespread damage. The aim, in this case, is not the conquest of territory per se, nor the direct defeat of the enemy's armed forces, but rather to inflict harm on the enemy in general.

The second approach is to direct our efforts toward those targets where our actions would cause the enemy the most harm. This could involve choosing between two potential courses of action, one that aligns with the goal of defeating the enemy's Army, while the other might offer greater advantage if a direct defeat isn't feasible. Common language might frame the first as primarily military and the second as political, but from the highest vantage point, both are equally military in nature. Their suitability depends solely on the circumstances at hand.

The third and most extensive approach, due to its frequent applicability, is exhausting the enemy. The term "wearing out" precisely conveys the concept, suggesting a steady depletion of the enemy's physical resources and will through prolonged effort. This "wearing down" is not merely a figure of speech but accurately represents a progressive weakening.

If our strategy focuses on defeating the enemy through prolonged conflict, we should aim for the smallest possible objectives, as the nature of sustained effort means that the larger the objective, the greater the required resource commitment. The smallest conceivable objective is simply passive resistance—engagement without any active intent. In this way, our resources achieve their maximum value, and the likelihood of success increases. However, this passive approach cannot reach the level of absolute inaction, as mere endurance alone does not constitute fighting; the essence of defense is an active engagement where enough of the enemy's power is diminished that he abandons his aims. This is our goal in every individual action, and it is what defines the negative nature of the defensive stance.

Admittedly, this negative objective in each act may not yield as decisive an impact as a successful offensive action would in the same circumstances. However, it has a key advantage: it offers a greater chance of success, even if each action is less potent in isolation. The shortfall in impact from individual defensive acts is compensated for over time, with the contest's duration playing a pivotal role. Hence, the negative approach, which forms the basis of a purely defensive strategy, is also the most natural way to overcome the enemy through sustained effort—that is, by gradually wearing him down.

Here lies the foundational distinction between Offensive and Defensive strategies, a distinction that exerts its influence throughout the entire realm of warfare. For now, we cannot delve too deeply into this concept, but we note that from the notion of a defensive, negative purpose, all the advantages and stronger forms of combat that characterize the Defensive position are derived. In this structure, we see the philosophical law at play: the greater the certainty of success, the more achievable the aim. This is a principle we will revisit in detail later.

If this negative approach—essentially the focus of all resources into a purely defensive state—provides a contest advantage sufficient to balance any numerical superiority on the opponent's side, then simply maintaining the conflict over time may be enough to gradually wear down the adversary's resources. This attrition can eventually reduce the enemy's strength to a level where their political aims no longer justify the ongoing conflict, compelling them to abandon their objectives. Thus, this strategy of wearing down the opponent applies to many situations in which the weaker force stands firm against a stronger one.

Frederick the Great during the Seven Years' War is a prime example. Although he could never muster the strength to entirely overthrow the Austrian monarchy, had he attempted a direct assault similar to that of Charles XII, he would undoubtedly have been crushed. Instead, Frederick's skillful application of resource conservation over seven grueling years demonstrated to the coalition against him that their drain of resources was far greater than they initially anticipated, eventually leading to peace.

This demonstrates that there are indeed numerous paths to achieving one's objectives in war. Complete domination over the enemy is not required in every scenario. The destruction of the enemy's military force, conquest or simple occupation of territory, direct incursions aimed at political targets, and even a strategy of passive defense, waiting for the opponent to make their move—each of these can serve as a valid means to compel the enemy's will, depending on the unique circumstances that suggest the viability of one approach over another.

Moreover, a whole array of even shorter, more direct methods—often termed arguments ad hominem—could be added to this toolkit. These are moments of strategic intuition or bold decision-making that break conventional frameworks and cannot be easily classified. In every field of human activity, these flashes of individual initiative transcend formal methods; they are especially potent in war, where the personal qualities of leaders hold immense sway in both political and military spheres. Recognizing this, we should avoid over-categorizing these influences, as doing so risks pedantic excess. With these factors in mind, the potential paths to reach the ultimate aim in war indeed become limitless.

To avoid undervaluing these varied methods as mere exceptions or diminishing their impact on warfare's conduct, we must remember the vast diversity of political objectives that can ignite a war. There is a vast spectrum between a life-or-death struggle for a nation's existence and a war undertaken out of obligation due to a weak alliance. Within this range are countless gradations that surface in real-world conflicts. Disregarding any one of these nuances would be equivalent to rejecting the whole spectrum, and that would mean ignoring the complexity of real-world scenarios entirely.

These, then, are the broader considerations linked to the purpose pursued in war. Now, let us turn to the means by which it is pursued.

Fundamentally, there is only one true means: Combat. However diverse combat may appear in its forms, however far it may stray from the rough expression of hatred and animosity evident in a direct hand-to-hand clash, and however many elements might emerge in war that don't involve actual combat, the essence of war remains rooted in the confrontation. All effects in war, at their core, trace back to this act of fighting.

This principle holds true even amidst the complex diversity of reality in war. Everything that happens in warfare is enacted through armed forces. Therefore, where the forces of war—armed soldiers—are deployed, the foundational concept of combat must necessarily underlie all actions.

Accordingly, everything related to military forces, including their creation, maintenance, and application, falls within the realm of military activity. While creating and sustaining these forces are critical, they are ultimately just means; the actual application of these forces remains the core objective.

In warfare, we're not dealing with isolated individual conflicts, but rather with a structured whole made up of many different components. Within this vast structure, we can identify two types of units: those defined by participants (e.g., battalions, brigades) and those defined by purpose (specific objectives of each engagement). Each unit, whether it's an entire division or a small detachment, organizes itself into successive tiers of units, each becoming part of a higher command structure. Every engagement between these units forms its own distinct conflict, with a specific goal or "combat unit."

Since combat underpins the entire application of military force, the organization of armed forces ultimately revolves around organizing and coordinating a set of these combat actions. Consequently, every military activity is either directly or indirectly tied to combat. Soldiers are recruited, equipped, trained, and sustained all for the singular purpose of being prepared to fight at the critical time and place.

If every strand of military action ultimately converges in combat, then understanding and directing this combat sequence is the essence of military strategy. From this sequencing and its execution alone stem the concrete results of war; they are never generated solely from the conditions established beforehand. Within each combat encounter, the focus is on the destruction of the enemy's forces, as this forms the heart of the concept of combat itself. This destruction of enemy combat strength is, therefore, typically a means to achieve the larger objective of each engagement.

The primary aim of any particular combat might simply be the elimination of enemy forces, but this is not universally necessary. Depending on the broader political aims and the multiple objectives within a war, individual battles might focus on other goals altogether. When, as we have seen, defeating the enemy is not the only path to achieving the political objective, other tactical goals can become the focus of specific wartime actions and therefore of individual battles.

Furthermore, even battles where the primary objective is the destruction of enemy forces don't always have to prioritize that destruction directly. When we consider the multitude of components within a large military force and the varied circumstances that influence its deployment, it's evident that the combat of such a force demands a multifaceted structure. This complexity includes subordinating units to larger formations and defining objectives at different levels. Certain units may have objectives that do not explicitly involve the destruction of enemy forces, though they contribute to this end in an indirect way.

For example, when a battalion is ordered to capture a strategic hill or bridge, the immediate goal is securing the position itself, while the destruction of enemy forces involved becomes secondary. If simply demonstrating a strong presence suffices to make the enemy retreat, the objective is still achieved. However, this hill or bridge is only strategically significant as it facilitates further attrition against the enemy.

On the battlefield, this concept holds; however, on a broader scale across the entire theater of war, where entire states or nations oppose one another, the range of possible relationships and combinations grows exponentially. The diversity of strategies multiplies as does the hierarchy of objectives, each feeding into the next and positioning the initial tactics even farther from the ultimate objective. Thus, as the theater widens, so too does the chain of means that bridge each intermediate aim with the final goal, stretching the direct link from action to objective.

In warfare, there are numerous instances where the main objective of a confrontation is not necessarily to achieve total destruction of the opposing forces. Often, the destruction of enemy forces is not the end goal but rather a secondary means to fulfill a larger, more strategic purpose. In these cases, the act of combat itself becomes less about the complete annihilation of the enemy and more about measuring the relative strengths and outcomes. The engagement becomes valuable primarily for its immediate results and strategic decision-making, rather than for inflicting maximal casualties on the opposing forces.

This approach to combat reveals how a straightforward comparison of power between mismatched forces can substitute for direct confrontation. When one side recognizes a significant disadvantage, it may elect to retreat or reposition, effectively acknowledging its inferiority without a drawn-out battle. This strategic dynamic shows how an entire campaign might unfold with minimal violent engagements; by preparing to fight or displaying the intent to engage, a commander can force advantageous responses or deter enemy actions. These calculated maneuvers serve campaign objectives and contribute meaningfully to the overall strategy, sometimes without major engagements.

Historical campaigns offer many examples of this strategic approach, where commanders achieved substantial outcomes by relying on posturing, threat, and limited engagements rather than constant, large-scale battles. Whether all of these historical cases were successful or whether the commanders deserved the praise they received is open to debate. However, the effectiveness of achieving strategic objectives without relying solely on sustained battles is undeniable.

Though battle remains the primary means of exerting power in war, its flexibility allows for a variety of strategic applications, depending on the objectives. At first glance, the singular reliance on battle as a method might seem restrictive. However, this reliance is actually the element that unifies the study of war, providing a continuous thread that binds together all aspects of military action and strategy. This unity enables us to analyze warfare as a cohesive whole, where battle remains the ultimate reference point for understanding the full scope of military efforts.

In considering the role of destruction in war, it becomes clear that destroying the enemy's force is a crucial objective, though not necessarily the only goal in every context. Circumstances often dictate whether the total destruction of the enemy's forces is indispensable, merely advantageous, or simply one of many available approaches. Still, the destruction of the enemy's military capabilities forms the foundational core of warfare. Every tactical decision, every strategic maneuver, fundamentally relies on the assumption that should a full clash of arms arise, the intention would be to secure a decisive outcome. Much like a cash payment that finalizes a financial transaction, direct confrontation seals the underlying intent of military action, confirming that battle, or at least the potential for it, remains inseparable from the practice of war.

Thus, if victory in battle is the basis for all other strategic combinations, then it follows that any major enemy success could unravel even the most well-laid plans, whether directly related to that victory or not. Each significant military triumph has the power to destabilize previous accomplishments and cause broader repercussions across the strategic landscape, similar to how water seeks a level in connected vessels. The effects of one victory extend beyond the immediate result, shifting the entire balance and forcing all prior and future actions to adjust to the new reality.

For this reason, the destruction of the enemy's armed forces consistently stands out as the paramount, most decisive method in warfare. It represents the most effective and influential means to an end, surpassing all other options and establishing itself as the essential tool upon which the outcomes of military operations ultimately rest.

Only under conditions of assumed equality, where both forces have equivalent strength and resources, can we regard the destruction of the enemy's forces as a decisive factor for victory. It would be a serious misjudgment to assume that a reckless offensive can always trump measured skill and strategic caution. A hasty or poorly executed attack could backfire, leading to our own forces' loss rather than the enemy's. Hence, when we speak of the efficacy of destruction, we refer to the end—the strategic aim—rather than the means employed to reach it. Our comparison here is between outcomes achieved by focused efforts toward different objectives.

When we speak of destroying the enemy's armed forces, it's crucial to recognize that this encompasses not only the physical aspect but also the psychological, or moral, force. Both dimensions—moral and physical—are inherently intertwined at every level, influencing each other even in minor engagements. After a major success or decisive victory, this moral dimension has a fluid nature that can easily permeate through and influence all subsequent operations, amplifying the effect of each move toward further goals.

The value of targeting the destruction of the enemy's armed forces lies in its unparalleled efficacy. Yet, this method also entails higher costs and risks. The direct costs are evident, as greater efforts to weaken the enemy inevitably result in higher attrition of our own forces, assuming all else is equal. Additionally, if a high-stakes engagement aimed at annihilating the enemy fails, the consequences can be more severe, with potential repercussions that could compromise our own position. Other approaches, by comparison, are often less costly when successful and carry fewer risks if unsuccessful. Yet, the viability of these methods is limited to situations where the enemy does not actively pursue a decisive military confrontation. If the adversary does seek a conclusive victory through major force, we must adjust our strategy to respond in kind, regardless of our initial objectives.

In such cases, the outcome hinges on the ensuing high-stakes conflict. If our preparations had been aligned toward multiple objectives rather than a single decisive encounter, we might face a disadvantage because our resources and plans were distributed across various aims rather than focused singularly on overwhelming the enemy's forces. In essence, when one belligerent commits to seeking victory by a decisive battle while the other pursues alternative objectives, the former gains an advantage due to their unwavering focus. Therefore, when aiming to avoid direct confrontation, one should do so under the assumption that the opponent has similarly refrained from preparing for a decisive battle.

Our earlier discussion on alternative objectives refers to other positive aims that can be pursued in warfare, rather than the pure defensive strategy aimed at wearing down the enemy. In the defensive posture, there is no distinct positive objective; instead, resources are directed solely to countering the opponent's actions rather than achieving any separate goals.

Next, we must address the converse of destroying the enemy's forces: preserving our own. These two priorities—destruction and preservation—are interdependent, continually influencing each other and forming two aspects of a single strategy. However, their effects diverge when one emphasis dominates over the other. An offensive aimed at eradicating enemy forces carries a positive objective, with the ultimate aim of subjugating the opponent. Conversely, preserving our forces is a negative objective, focused on thwarting the adversary's plans, extending the conflict's duration, and causing the enemy to deplete their resources.

Pursuing a positive objective naturally leads to offensive acts of destruction, whereas aiming to preserve one's forces necessitates a reactive stance, awaiting the enemy's moves. In this latter approach, the emphasis is on defense, with the primary goal being to withstand the adversary's offensives until they expend their resources.

How far this sense of anticipation should go and can be taken is something we'll examine more closely in the theory of attack and defense, where we return to the starting point. For now, let's simply say that waiting is not just about passively enduring. In the actions that come with it, aiming to destroy the enemy's armed forces involved in this conflict may still be our goal, just as much as any other objective. It would, therefore, be a serious mistake in basic thinking to assume that by choosing this approach, we can't aim to destroy the enemy's forces and must instead prefer a peaceful outcome without bloodshed. The advantage of this defensive strategy may certainly lead to that result, but only with the risk that it might not be the most sensible choice, as that decision depends on factors that are not within our control but instead depend on our opponent's actions. Thus, this other bloodless approach cannot at all be seen as the natural way to satisfy our strong desire to protect our forces; on the contrary, when circumstances aren't favorable, this path could lead to total ruin. Many generals have made this mistake and have been defeated because of it.

The only clear result of the advantage that comes from this defensive strategy is that it delays the final decision, meaning that the side on defense can wait for the right moment. The outcome is usually that the action is postponed as much as possible in terms of both time and distance, in so far as distance is connected to it. When the moment arrives where further delay is no longer possible without terrible consequences, then the advantage of the defensive approach is exhausted, and the effort to destroy the enemy's forces, which had been held back by a balance of forces, emerges again, unchanged and ready.

In the earlier reflections, we have seen, therefore, that there are multiple ways to reach the goal, that is, to achieve the political objective; yet, the only real way to get there is combat, and thus everything must obey the supreme law of decision through arms. Where one side demands this decision, the other side cannot refuse it, as it is a form of justice that must be answered. Therefore, a country that tries any other approach must ensure its opponent will not respond with force, or else it may lose its case in this ultimate judgment. Therefore, among all the goals that can be pursued in war, destroying the enemy's armed forces always appears as the one that overrules all others.

What can be achieved through different strategies in war will only become clear in time, and we'll learn this little by little. Here, we only acknowledge that such strategies are possible, as they show the gap between theory and reality and the effects of unique circumstances. But we couldn't avoid immediately showing that the bloody path to resolve the crisis, the drive to destroy the enemy's forces, is the true essence of war. When political aims are minor, motivations weak, and the overall energy low, a cautious commander might try various methods, hoping to slip skillfully into peace without major crises or bloody battles by using his enemy's weaknesses on the battlefield and in the government. We can't judge him if his approach is based on strong reasoning and proves successful. Still, he must remember that he is walking a dangerous road where the "God of War" could take him by surprise. He must always keep his eyes on the enemy, so he doesn't find himself defending with a blunt rapier if his enemy raises a sharp sword.

The results that come from the nature of War, how its goals and methods interact, and how, in the realities of practice, it sometimes strays more or less from its strict original idea, moving back and forth, yet always remaining bound by that strict idea as though by a supreme law: all of this we must keep in view and remember constantly as we examine each of the following topics. Only by doing so can we truly understand their real connections and correct significance, and avoid getting endlessly caught up in the most obvious contradictions with reality, and eventually with ourselves.

Chapter III. The Genius of War

Every specific calling in life, if one is to pursue it successfully, requires unique qualities of mind and character. When these qualities are of a high level and show themselves through exceptional accomplishments, the mind that possesses them is often called GENIUS. We are well aware that this word has many meanings that vary greatly in scope and nature, and that, with several of these meanings, it is challenging to define the essence of Genius. However, since we do not claim to be philosophers or linguists, we shall stick to the meaning used in everyday language, where "genius" refers to a very high mental ability in certain fields.

We want to pause here for a moment on this power and dignity of the mind to affirm its place and explain more thoroughly what the concept means. Yet, we won't linger on that (genius) which earns its title through remarkable talent, on genius in the strict sense of the term, which is a concept without clear boundaries. Instead, we aim to consider every shared tendency of mental and moral qualities toward the work of War, with all these common traits forming what we can regard as the ESSENCE OF MILITARY GENIUS. We say "common," because military genius consists precisely of not just a single quality related to War, like courage, while other traits of mind and character may be missing or turned in ways that are unhelpful in War. Instead, it is A HARMONIOUS UNION OF QUALITIES, where one quality may stand out more than others, but none can be in opposition.

If every soldier needed to be at least somewhat gifted with military genius, our armies would be very weak; for, as it demands a specific inclination of mental abilities, military genius can only rarely be found when the intellect of a nation is engaged and developed in various ways. The fewer the professions a Nation follows, the more the military occupation dominates, and thus the more military genius will appear. But this affects only how often it is found, not the degree of it, since the level of military genius depends on the general state of education and intellectual culture in the country. If we observe a fierce, warlike people, we find that a warlike spirit is more common among individuals than it would be among a civilized people; in the former case, nearly every warrior possesses it, while in the latter, the masses are driven by it out of necessity rather than choice. Yet, among less civilized people, we seldom find a truly great General, and almost never what we would call a genuine military genius, as such genius requires an intellectual development not achievable in a primitive state.

Of course, a civilized nation can also be inclined toward war and have a strong military culture; and the more general this is, the more military spirit can be found among individuals in its armies. As this tendency coincides with a higher level of civilization, it is from such nations that the most remarkable military achievements have come, as shown by examples like the Romans and the French. The greatest military names in these and in other nations known for war come from periods of higher culture.

From this, we can conclude how significant the role of intellectual abilities is in outstanding military genius. We will now look at this aspect more closely.

War belongs to the realm of danger, and therefore courage, above all else, is the primary quality of a soldier. Courage exists in two forms: first, physical courage, or bravery in the face of personal danger, and second, moral courage, or bravery in accepting responsibility, whether before the judgment of external authorities or of the inner force, the conscience. Here, we speak only of the first.

Courage in the face of personal danger, in turn, has two forms. First, it may come from a lack of fear of danger, whether due to an individual's natural makeup, a disregard for death, or simply habit; in any of these cases, it can be seen as a lasting condition. Second, courage may come from positive motivations, like personal pride, patriotism, or enthusiasm of any kind. In this case, courage is not so much a regular state as it is a sudden drive.

We can imagine that these two kinds of courage work in different ways. The first type is more reliable because it has become like a second nature, never abandoning the person; the second type often pushes them further. In the first type, there is more steadiness; in the second, more daring. The first keeps a cooler head, while the second can sometimes sharpen one's judgment but often confuses it. Together, the two create the most complete form of courage.

War is the realm of physical effort and hardship. To avoid being completely overcome by these, a certain toughness of body and mind is needed, which, whether natural or learned, creates a level of indifference to them. With these qualities, under the guidance of just a reasonable mind, a person becomes a suitable tool for War; and these are the traits frequently found among wild and semi-civilized groups. If we go further in examining what War demands of a person, we see that the powers of reason take a greater role.

War is the realm of uncertainty: three-quarters of the things upon which action in War depends are hidden, to some degree, in great uncertainty. In such cases, a sharp and insightful mind is needed above all, to discover the truth through the instinct of its judgment.

An average mind might sometimes stumble upon the truth by luck; extraordinary courage may, at other times, make up for a lack of such insight; but in most cases, the average outcome will reveal the limits of a lacking understanding.

War is also the realm of chance. In no other area of human activity is there so much allowance for this intruder, because none is in constant contact with it from all sides like War. Chance adds to the uncertainty of every situation and disrupts the course of events.

Due to this uncertainty in all information and assumptions, and this constant intrusion of chance, a person acting in War often finds that things are different from their expectations; and this must inevitably affect their plans, or at least the assumptions linked to those plans. If this influence becomes so great that it makes the original plan completely useless, then, typically, a new plan must replace it; but often, in the heat of action, the necessary information is missing, as circumstances demand immediate decisions, allowing no time to seek out new information and often not enough time even for careful thought.

But more often, a correction of just one assumption and new knowledge of unforeseen events do not completely overturn our plans but only cause hesitation. Our knowledge of the situation has grown, yet instead of decreasing, our uncertainty has only increased. This happens because we do not gain all our understanding at once but bit by bit; thus, our decisions are constantly challenged by new experiences, and the mind, if we may put it this way, must always be "on guard."

Now, if one is to safely navigate this constant clash with the unexpected, two qualities are essential: first, a mind that, even amid thick darkness, has some faint inner light to guide it toward the truth, and second, the courage to follow this dim light. The first quality is captured by the French phrase coup d'œil. The second is resolution.

Since battle is the primary focus of War and time and space are crucial factors—especially when cavalry, with their swift movements, was the main force—this idea of quick, accurate decision-making originally applied to evaluating these two factors. Thus, an expression arose to describe this quality, one that suggests simply a correct judgment made by sight. Many teachers of the Art of War then defined coup d'œil with this limited meaning. But it's undeniable that all skillful decisions made in the heat of action soon came to be understood by this phrase, such as choosing the right place to strike, and so on. Thus, coup d'œil often refers not just to the physical eye but even more to the mental eye. Naturally, both the phrase and its meaning are more at home in tactics, but it should not be absent from strategy, where quick decisions are also often needed.

If we strip away the overly figurative and narrow meanings from this concept, it simply means the quick recognition of a truth that an ordinary mind either cannot see or can only see after long study and thought.

Resolution is an act of courage in individual cases, and when it becomes a regular feature, it is a trait of character. But here, we are not speaking of courage in the face of physical danger but rather in the face of responsibility—in a way, against moral danger. This has often been called courage d'esprit because it comes from the understanding; however, it is not an action of the intellect for that reason alone—it is an action of feeling. Mere intelligence does not equate to courage, as we often see the cleverest people lack resolution. The mind must first stir the feeling of courage, which it must then guide and sustain, as in urgent moments, a person is moved more by feelings than by thoughts.

We have assigned to resolution the role of dispelling the torments of doubt and the risks of delay when there aren't strong enough reasons to act as guidance. Due to the careless use of language that is common, this term is often applied to simple tendencies toward daring, bravery, boldness, or even recklessness. But when there are enough motives within a person, whether objective or subjective, true or false, we have no right to speak of their resolution; for, in doing so, we take on their perspective and bring in doubts they do not have.

Here, it is only a question of strength versus weakness. We're not particular enough to argue over this slight misuse of language; our point here is simply to prevent misunderstandings.

This resolution, which overcomes the state of doubt, can only be brought about by the intellect and, in fact, by a unique inclination of the mind. We argue that merely having a sharp intellect and the necessary emotions is not enough to create resolution. Some individuals possess the clearest insight into the most complex problems and do not shy away from responsibility, yet, in challenging situations, they cannot arrive at a decision. Their courage and wisdom function independently of one another; they don't support each other, and as a result, they don't produce resolution.

The precursor to resolution is an action of the mind that reveals the necessity of taking a risk, thus influencing the will. This unique tendency of the mind, which conquers every other fear by the fear of wavering or indecision, is what creates resolution in strong minds. Therefore, in our view, people with limited intelligence can never be resolute. They may act without hesitation in confusing situations, but in such cases, they act without thought. Now, of course, when someone acts without thought, they cannot be in conflict with themselves due to doubt, and this type of action may sometimes lead to the right result; however, as we've said before, it is the average outcome that signifies the presence of military genius.

If this claim seems unusual to anyone who knows many a resolute cavalry officer who is not a deep thinker, we must remind them that what we're discussing here is a specific mental tendency, not a high level of intellectual power.

We believe, then, that resolution owes its existence to a particular direction of the mind, a tendency belonging more to a strong mind than to a brilliant one. To support this view on the nature of resolution, we can add that there are numerous cases of people who have shown the greatest resolution in lower ranks, only to lose it in higher positions. While they are required to make decisions, they also see the risks of making a wrong choice. As they are faced with unfamiliar circumstances, their mind loses its initial strength, and they become all the more hesitant as they realize the danger of the indecision into which they have fallen and the more they have been accustomed to acting spontaneously.

From coup d'œil and resolution, it's natural to discuss a related quality, presence of mind, which must play a major role in the unpredictable world of War, as it is essentially a significant victory over the unexpected. Just as we admire presence of mind in a quick-witted response to an unexpected remark, we also admire it in a prompt solution to sudden danger. Neither the reply nor the solution needs to be extraordinary on its own as long as it hits the mark; something that would seem ordinary if carefully thought out may make a striking impression when it's an instant reaction of the mind. The term "presence of mind" aptly describes the speed and readiness of the mind's response.

Whether this admirable quality should be attributed more to a person's mental agility or their emotional steadiness depends on the specific case, though neither quality can be completely absent. A sharp retort points more to a quick mind, while a quick solution to sudden danger suggests more clearly a balanced spirit.

If we take an overall view of the four elements that make up the environment in which War operates—danger, physical effort, uncertainty, and chance—it's easy to see that a powerful mind and understanding are needed to navigate safely and successfully among these opposing forces. This strength, depending on the different circumstances, is described by military writers and historians as energy, firmness, steadfastness, strength of mind, and strength of character. All these expressions of heroic nature might seem to represent one and the same willpower, adapted to different situations. However, while these qualities are closely related, they are not identical, and it is useful for us to examine a little more carefully the workings of the mind in relation to them.

First, to clarify this idea, it's important to note that the force, burden, or resistance that brings out the power of the General's mind is only partially due to the enemy's actions, resistance, or direct opposition. The enemy's actions only impact the General directly in terms of his personal safety without disrupting his role as a Commander. For instance, if the enemy resists for four hours instead of two, then the Commander faces personal danger for four hours instead of two; yet, this amount of time in danger becomes less significant the higher the Commander's rank. For someone at the position of Commander-in-Chief, it means very little.

Second, although the enemy's resistance directly impacts the Commander by causing losses that come with extended opposition—and although the responsibility for these losses tests and challenges his willpower—this is by no means the heaviest burden he bears. This burden is lighter because he only has himself to answer to. The other consequences of the enemy's resistance affect his soldiers directly, and these effects, in turn, impact him through his men.

As long as his soldiers, full of confidence, fight with zeal and spirit, the Commander rarely needs to show great energy of will in pursuing his goals. But as soon as challenges arise—as they always do when major stakes are involved—the situation no longer runs smoothly like a well-oiled machine; instead, the machine itself begins to resist, and overcoming this requires a powerful will from the Commander. This resistance doesn't necessarily mean outright disobedience or complaints, though these are common enough among individuals; rather, it is the overall feeling of the collapse of both physical and moral strength. The Commander faces not only the painful sight of bloodshed but also the internal and external struggle against the sense of exhaustion and fear that his soldiers pass on to him, directly or indirectly, along with their emotions, worries, and wishes.

As more soldiers lose their strength and can no longer be rallied by their own will, the whole weight of this inertia begins to rest on the Commander's Will. Through the spark within him, through the light of his spirit, he must ignite again the flame of purpose and the light of hope in others. To the extent that he succeeds in this, he stands above the masses and remains their leader; when that influence fades, and his spirit can no longer rekindle the spirit in others, then the masses pull him down with them, sinking into a base state driven by the instinct to avoid danger and devoid of pride.

These are the burdens that a military Commander's courage and intelligence must overcome if he wishes to make his name renowned. These pressures increase with the size of the forces he commands, and therefore, to match the weight of these challenges, the Commander's strength must grow in proportion to the height of his position.

Energy in action reflects the strength of the motivation that drives the action, whether this motivation comes from a rational conviction or from an impulse. However, the latter—an impulse—is almost always present wherever great strength is to manifest.

Among all the noble feelings that fill the human heart in the stirring chaos of battle, none, we must acknowledge, are as powerful and enduring as the soul's thirst for honor and fame, which the German language unfortunately downplays with the terms Ehrgeiz (greed for honor) and Ruhmsucht (hankering after glory), attaching negative connotations. Certainly, in War, the misuse of these high aspirations can lead humanity to its most shocking horrors, yet, by origin, these are among the noblest feelings inherent to human nature, and in War, they are the enlivening spirit that animates the vast body of an army. Although other feelings may have a broader influence, and many of them—such as love of country, fanaticism, revenge, and all types of enthusiasm—may seem loftier, the thirst for honor and fame remains essential.

These other feelings may inspire the large masses more generally and may even stir them more strongly, but they do not instill in a Leader the desire to surpass others, which is a necessary quality for a person in that position if he is to distinguish himself. Unlike the thirst for honor, these other motivations do not make the military effort personally significant to the Leader, who seeks to maximize its value; it is as if he plows with labor, sows with care, to reap abundantly. Through these ambitions, from Commanders at the highest levels to those in the lowest ranks, this kind of energy, this spirit of competition, and these driving forces, the actions of armies are chiefly energized and succeed.

As for the highest Commanders, we may ask: Has there ever been a great Leader without a love for honor, or can we even imagine such a person?

Firmness refers to the resilience of the will when facing a single, powerful impact, while staunchness applies to enduring a series of impacts. Although the two are closely related and are often used interchangeably, there is still a clear difference between them. Firmness against a single strong blow may simply come from the strength of a feeling, while staunchness must be more closely supported by reason, as the longer an action lasts, the more systematic reflection is involved, and it is partly from this that staunchness draws its power.

If we now turn to strength of mind or soul, the first question to ask is: What are we to understand by these terms?

Clearly, strength of mind is not about intense displays of emotion or easily triggered passions, as this would contradict all common uses of language. Rather, it is the ability to listen to reason even in the height of extreme emotion, amid the storm of the most intense passions. Should this ability rely on intellectual strength alone? We doubt it. The fact that some people with remarkable intellect struggle to control themselves doesn't necessarily prove otherwise, as one could argue that it may require a powerful, rather than merely broad, intellect. However, we believe we are closer to the truth in suggesting that the ability to submit to the control of the intellect, even in moments of the strongest emotional turmoil—that power we call self-command—has its roots in the heart itself.

In reality, it is another feeling, which in strong minds balances the passionate impulses without suppressing them; and only through this balance does the intellect gain mastery. This balancing force is nothing but a sense of human dignity, the noblest form of pride, a deep-seated desire of the soul to act at all times as a being of understanding and reason. Thus, we may say that a strong mind is one that maintains its equilibrium even amid the most violent emotional surges.

If we take a look at the range of human characters in terms of feeling, we first find people with very little excitability, often described as phlegmatic or indifferent. Second, we see those who are highly excitable but whose feelings still remain within certain bounds, thus considered emotional yet level-headed. Third, there are those who are easily stirred, whose feelings flare up quickly and fiercely, like gunpowder, but do not last. Fourth and finally, there are those who are not easily moved by minor causes and who generally cannot be roused suddenly, but only gradually; their feelings grow powerful and tend to last much longer. These are people with strong, deep-seated passions.

This difference in character likely lies close to the boundary of the physical forces driving human behavior and belongs to that hybrid realm we call the nervous system, which appears partly physical, partly spiritual. With our limited understanding, we won't go further into this mysterious area. But it is important for us to spend a moment considering the effects these different types of natures have on action in War, and to determine how far a strong mind can be expected from each.

Phlegmatic people are not easily disturbed from their calm state, but we cannot assume that there is strength of mind where there is no visible sign of strength at all. Still, it must be admitted that such people do possess a particular suitability for War, due to their steady calmness. They often lack a positive motivation for action, or the drive that leads to activity, and therefore may lack initiative, but they are unlikely to throw things into disarray.

The second type is distinguished by their tendency to act impulsively over small matters, but they become easily overwhelmed by significant events. People of this type may show great energy when assisting an individual in distress, but in response to the suffering of an entire nation, they tend to despair rather than take action. Such people are not lacking in either energy or steadiness in War; however, they will rarely accomplish anything truly significant unless motivated by great intellectual strength, and it is uncommon for a strong, independent mind to accompany this type of character.

Intense, volatile emotions are not well suited to practical life, and so they are not particularly useful in War. They certainly have the advantage of strong impulses, but these cannot sustain them for long. At the same time, if this excitability in such people channels into courage or a sense of honor, they may still prove valuable in lower ranks in War, as the responsibilities in these positions are generally shorter in duration. Here, one brave decision, one burst of soul-driven force, may be sufficient. A courageous assault, a spirited battle cry, is the work of a few moments, while a determined fight on the battlefield lasts a day, and a campaign takes a year.

Due to the quick movement of their emotions, it is doubly difficult for men of this temperament to maintain mental balance; as a result, they frequently lose composure, which is the most disadvantageous trait in their nature for the conduct of War. However, it would contradict experience to claim that very excitable individuals can never maintain a steady balance, even under the most intense excitement. Why should they lack the sense of self-respect, since they are usually noble in character? This feeling is rarely absent in them, but it often doesn't have time to take effect. After an emotional outburst, they tend to suffer most from an inner sense of shame. Yet, if they have, through education, self-awareness, and life experience, learned over time to be cautious, so that in moments of strong excitement, they can sense early on the counteracting force within themselves, then even such men may possess great mental strength.

Finally, those who are slow to be moved, but whose emotions are therefore more profound, resemble a steady red heat as opposed to a flickering flame. Such men are best suited, with their massive strength, to overcome the tremendous obstacles we might use figuratively to describe the challenges of command in War. Their emotional impact is like the movement of a massive object—slower, but more unstoppable.

Although these individuals are less likely than the former to be suddenly overwhelmed by their feelings and embarrassed afterward, it would still be against experience to believe they can never lose their calm or be overtaken by uncontrollable passion. On the contrary, this is bound to occur whenever the noble pride of self-control is missing, or whenever it is insufficiently strong. This is seen most frequently in people of noble spirit in less developed societies, where the low level of intellectual development tends to give way to the dominance of passions. However, even among the most cultured groups in civilized states, life is full of examples of this sort—of individuals swept away by the intensity of their passions, much like the legendary poacher who was chained to a stag in the forest.

Thus, we repeat: a strong mind is not merely one that can feel intense excitement, but one that can maintain calm under the most powerful excitement, so that, despite the storm within, perception and judgment remain free to act—like a compass needle on a ship tossed by a storm.

By strength of character or simply character, we mean the persistence of conviction, whether that conviction is the result of our own thoughts or those of others, and whether these convictions are principles, opinions, sudden inspirations, or any insights of the mind. But this type of firmness cannot exist if a person's views are constantly shifting. Such changes don't need to be caused by outside influences; they may arise from the continuous workings of one's own mind, which in this case would reveal a fundamental inconsistency. Clearly, we would not say of a person who changes his views at every turn, regardless of the reasons for the change, that he possesses character. Therefore, only those can truly be said to have this quality whose convictions remain steady—either because these convictions are deeply rooted and inherently stable, or, as in the case of more passive individuals, because they lack mental activity and thus have few reasons to change; or lastly, because of a deliberate act of will, guided by a strong principle of the mind, which resists changing opinion up to a certain point.

In War, because of the many powerful impressions the mind encounters and the uncertainty surrounding all knowledge and understanding, more factors arise to distract a person from their chosen path and to make them doubt themselves and others than in any other human activity.

The painful sight of danger and suffering easily allows emotions to take precedence over the rational convictions of the mind; and in the murky atmosphere that envelops everything, gaining a deep and clear understanding is so challenging that a change of opinion is more understandable and more forgivable. At all times, we are left acting on mere guesses or approximations of the truth. This is why differences in opinion are more pronounced in War than anywhere else, and the flood of impressions countering one's own convictions is constant. Even the most imperturbable mind is rarely immune to this, as these impressions are powerful and simultaneously affect both the intellect and the emotions.

When judgment is clear and profound, only general principles and viewpoints from a high perspective can emerge; on these principles, the opinion formed in each particular situation anchors itself, so to speak. But remaining committed to these prior reflections, despite the overwhelming current of opinions and events that the present brings, is precisely where the difficulty lies. Between the specific situation and the overarching principle, there is often a broad gap that cannot always be bridged by a clear line of reasoning, and where a certain confidence in oneself and a dose of skepticism are useful.

In such cases, nothing but a strict guiding principle can help—one that overrides reflection and immediately controls it: this principle is, in all uncertain cases, to hold firmly to the initial opinion and not to abandon it unless a clear conviction forces a change. We must have unwavering belief in the superior authority of tried and tested principles and not forget, under the blinding influence of immediate events, that these have lesser value. By this preference for initial convictions in uncertain situations, and by holding to them, our actions gain the stability and consistency that define what we call character.

It's easy to see how crucial a balanced mind is to strength of character, and thus people with strong minds generally exhibit a lot of character.

Force of character leads us to a related but flawed version of it—OBSTINACY.

In specific cases, it is often very difficult to distinguish where one ends and the other begins; yet, it doesn't seem hard to grasp the difference in theory.

Obstinacy is not a failure of the intellect; we use the term to mean a resistance against our better judgment, and it would be contradictory to blame this on the intellect, as the intellect is the source of judgment. Obstinacy is A FLAW OF THE EMOTIONS or heart. This rigidity of will, this intolerance for opposition, stems solely from a particular kind of egotism, which values above all other satisfactions the pleasure of directing both oneself and others solely according to one's own mind. We might call it a type of vanity, though it is clearly something more. Vanity is content with mere appearance, but obstinacy thrives on the enjoyment of the reality itself.

Thus, we say that force of character turns into obstinacy whenever the resistance to opposing viewpoints arises not from stronger convictions or reliance on a trustworthy principle, but from a feeling of opposition. Although this definition, as we've already admitted, may not be particularly helpful in practice, it does prevent us from mistaking obstinacy for an intensified form of force of character, as obstinacy is something fundamentally different. It is certainly related to force of character and closely aligned with it, yet it is not an intensification; in fact, some highly obstinate individuals, due to a lack of understanding, exhibit very little actual force of character.

Having examined these high qualities of a great military Commander and those attributes where heart and mind work in concert, we now turn to a specific aspect of military activity which may be seen as the most defining, if not the most critical, and which requires only the mental faculties without relying on emotional strength. This is the connection between War and terrain, or ground.

Firstly, this connection is an enduring condition of War, as it's impossible to imagine modern Armies carrying out any operation outside of a defined area. Secondly, it is of the utmost importance, as it can shape, and sometimes completely transform, the impact of all forces involved. Thirdly, while this connection may sometimes relate to the smallest details of the local terrain, it may also involve vast expanses of territory.

In this way, the relationship between War and terrain creates a distinct effect. If we think of other human activities related to land and space, like gardening, farming, building, hydraulic works, mining, hunting, or forestry, they are all confined within relatively limited areas that can be explored with sufficient precision. But the Commander in War must conduct operations over a corresponding area that he cannot directly observe, one that even the most diligent efforts cannot fully explore, and one that, due to constant changes, he can rarely understand completely.

Certainly, the enemy is usually in a similar situation; yet, firstly, the fact that the difficulty applies to both does not make it any less challenging, and any Commander who can overcome it through talent and experience will hold a significant advantage. Secondly, the notion that both sides face equal difficulty is only a theoretical assumption, rarely seen in practice, as one of the two opponents (typically the defender) generally has a much better understanding of the terrain than the other.

This unique challenge can only be overcome by a specific natural talent, often referred to—though too narrowly—as Ortsinn, or sense of locality. This is the ability to form a quick and accurate mental image of a landscape and, as a result, to always know one's precise location within it. Clearly, this is an act of imagination. This perception is shaped partly by what the eye physically sees and partly by the mind, which fills in the gaps using knowledge and experience, forming a complete picture from the scattered elements visible to the eye. For this picture to emerge clearly to the intellect as a coherent mental map, and for it to become fixed with details that never fragment again, can only be achieved through the mental faculty we call imagination.

If a great poet or painter should feel offended that we expect such work from their muse, or if they roll their eyes at the thought of a sharp gamekeeper excelling in imagination, we are quick to clarify that we refer to imagination here in a limited sense—as performing a rather mundane role. Yet, however small this role may seem, it still requires that natural talent, for without it, one would struggle to visualize things with the clarity of the visible world. We readily admit that a good memory is highly helpful here, but whether memory is an independent mental faculty in this context or merely the product of imagination's power to better preserve these images, we leave undecided, as it is often difficult to separate these two faculties from each other.

There's no denying that experience and sharp mental acuity play an important role in this skill. Puysegur, the renowned Quartermaster-General under the famous Luxemburg, used to say that he initially had little confidence in himself in this regard, as he would often lose his way when sent to retrieve the parole from a distance.

It is natural that the need for this talent grows with rank. If a hussar or rifleman leading a patrol must know all the main and side roads well, and if a few markers and a limited capacity for observation suffice for this task, then the leader of an Army must be familiar with the general geography of an entire province or country. He must always keep in mind the layout of the roads, rivers, and hills without losing sight of the finer "sense of locality" (Ortsinn). No doubt, he benefits greatly from general information, maps, books, reports, and from the specific insights of his Staff; however, if he himself possesses a talent for quickly and clearly forming an internal image of a landscape, it gives his actions a more assured and confident quality, frees him from a certain mental helplessness, and makes him less reliant on others.

If this talent can indeed be credited to imagination, then it is almost the only service that military work demands from that unpredictable muse, whose influence is generally more harmful than helpful in other respects.

We believe we have now covered the different expressions of mental and emotional strength that military work requires of human nature. Intelligence appears as an essential force throughout; hence, we can understand why the work of War, though plain and straightforward in its outward results, cannot be conducted successfully by those lacking distinguished mental abilities.

With this perspective, we need no longer view familiar concepts, like outflanking an enemy position—which has been done countless times—or a hundred other similar strategies, as the products of great genius.

Certainly, people often see the straightforward, honest soldier as the complete opposite of a reflective man, full of ideas and inventions, or as the opposite of a brilliant mind adorned with every kind of refined education. This contrast is not without truth, but it doesn't imply that the soldier's value lies solely in his courage or that no special mental energy or ability is needed to make someone what is known as a true soldier. We must once again emphasize that it is very common to hear of men losing their vigor after being promoted to a position they feel unprepared for; but we also remind readers that we are discussing distinguished achievements—those that earn a person renown within their field of activity. Each level of command in War thus forms its own level of required ability and corresponding fame and honor.

A vast gap exists between a General—that is, someone in charge of an entire War or a specific theater of War—and his Second in Command. The reason for this is simple: the latter operates under the direct oversight of a higher authority, meaning he is limited to a smaller sphere of independent thought. This is why common opinion believes that only high positions require exceptional talent and that an ordinary level of ability suffices for anything below that level. It is also why people tend to view a subordinate General, who has grown old in service and whose focus on routine duties has resulted in a certain narrowness of mind, as a man of limited intellect, and, though they respect his bravery, they often find amusement in his simplicity.

Our aim is not to secure a better reputation for these brave men, as that would neither improve their effectiveness nor greatly enhance their happiness. We only wish to depict things as they are and to disprove the notion that an unthinking fighter can achieve distinction in War.

Since we consider remarkable talent essential for those aiming to gain distinction, even in lower ranks, it naturally follows that we hold in high regard those who achieve recognition as a Second in Command of an Army. Their apparent simplicity, especially when compared to a well-rounded scholar, a quick-thinking businessman, or a statesman, should not mislead us about the superior nature of their intellectual activity. Occasionally, individuals carry over the reputation earned in a lower role into a higher one without truly deserving it in their new position; if they are not heavily employed and thus not frequently exposed to situations that might reveal their weaknesses, the judgment of others does not always make a clear distinction as to how much credit is truly due to them. Thus, such individuals often contribute to an undervaluation of the qualities needed to excel in certain positions.

For each rank, from the lowest up, to render notable services in War requires a specific kind of genius. However, the title of genius is generally reserved by history and posterity's judgment for those minds that have excelled at the highest level, that of Commanders-in-Chief. The reason for this is that, in this position, the demands on reasoning and intellectual abilities are generally far greater.

To lead an entire War or its major actions—what we call campaigns—to a successful end requires a deep understanding of State policy at the highest levels. Here, the conduct of the War and the policy of the State intersect, and the General becomes, simultaneously, a Statesman.

We do not call Charles XII a great genius because he could not make his military power serve a higher judgment and wisdom, nor could he achieve a truly glorious purpose with it. Likewise, we do not grant that title to Henry IV of France, as he did not live long enough to resolve the relations between different states through his military efforts and to engage in that higher realm where noble sentiments and a chivalrous spirit are less about conquering an external enemy than about resolving internal discord.

To help the reader appreciate all that a General must comprehend and judge correctly in an instant, we refer back to the first chapter. We say the General becomes a Statesman, yet he must still remain a General. He must consider all aspects of the State on one hand, and on the other, he must have a precise understanding of what he can achieve with the resources at his disposal.

Since the diverse and undefined nature of all conditions in War brings numerous factors into consideration, most of which can only be assessed by probability, if the Commander does not approach them with a mind that has an instinctive grasp of truth, his thoughts and views will become confused, and his judgment will end up bewildered. In this regard, Buonaparte was correct when he remarked that many issues a General must decide on would be problems worthy of mathematical analysis on par with those tackled by Newton or Euler.

What is required from the higher faculties of the mind here is a sense of unity and a judgment expanded to such an extent that it gives the mind an extraordinary ability to see, one that effortlessly dispels a thousand vague ideas which an ordinary intellect would only uncover with great effort, exhausting itself in the process. However, this higher mental activity, this genius-like insight, would still not make its mark in history if not supported by the qualities of temperament and character we previously discussed.

Truth alone is a weak motivator for action in humans; thus, there is always a significant gap between knowing and doing, between theory and practice. A person is driven most forcefully by their emotions and finds the strongest support, if we may use that term, in the qualities of heart and mind we have described as resolution, firmness, perseverance, and force of character.

If, however, this elevated state of heart and mind in the General did not manifest itself in the broad effects that stem from it, and if it could only be accepted on faith, it would rarely become part of history.

Everything known about the sequence of events in War is generally straightforward and often has a uniform appearance; merely recounting such events does not reveal the difficulties that had to be overcome. Only occasionally, through the memoirs of Generals or those close to them, or through a specific historical inquiry into a particular circumstance, do some of the many threads that make up the entire picture come to light. The reflections, doubts, and internal struggles that precede the execution of significant actions are often intentionally concealed for political reasons, or they fade from memory because they were viewed as mere scaffolding, necessary only until the building was completed.

Finally, without attempting a precise definition of the higher faculties of the soul, if we accept a distinction within the intellectual faculties themselves, based on the common ideas established by language, and ask ourselves what type of mind most closely resembles military genius, then a look at the subject, as well as experience, would suggest that in times of War we would rather entrust the welfare of our families, the honor, and the safety of our country to minds that are searching rather than inventive, broad in scope rather than narrowly specialized, and cool-headed rather than impulsive.

Chapter IV. Of Danger in War

Typically, before we truly understand what danger is, we imagine it to be more alluring than frightening. In the intoxication of enthusiasm, as we charge toward the enemy—who then cares about bullets or about men falling? To throw oneself, for a brief moment blinded by excitement, against cold death, uncertain whether we or others will escape it, all this near the golden gates of victory, close to the rich rewards that ambition craves—can this be difficult? It will not be difficult, nor will it even seem so. But such moments—though not a single heartbeat's work, as some believe, but more like a doctor's draught, diluted and spoiled by the passage of time—are rare.

Let us join the novice as he heads to the battlefield. As we approach, the sound of cannon fire grows clearer and soon gives way to the ominous whistling of shells, which naturally draws the attention of the inexperienced. Balls begin to hit the ground close to us, some in front, some behind. We hurry to the hill where the General and his numerous staff stand. Here, the frequent impact of cannonballs and the bursting of shells bring the reality of life to bear, contrasting sharply with the youthful fantasies of the imagination. Suddenly, someone we know falls; a shell lands among the crowd, causing some involuntary movements. We begin to feel less at ease and less composed; even the bravest among us will feel, to some extent, unsettled.

Now, let us take another step closer into the battle that rages before us like a staged drama. We arrive at the position of the nearest Division General. Here, one cannonball follows another, and the roar of our own guns adds to the confusion. From the Division General, we move to the Brigadier. He, a man known for his bravery, carefully keeps himself behind a rise in the ground, a building, or a tree—a clear sign of the mounting danger. Grape shot rattles off the roofs and fields; cannonballs howl above and slice through the air in all directions, soon accompanied by the frequent whistling of musket balls. One more step towards the troops, to the stalwart infantry that has held its ground under this heavy fire for hours. Here, the air is filled with the hissing of bullets, their proximity marked by a quick, sharp sound as they pass just an inch from the ear, the head, or the chest.

Adding to all this, the sight of the wounded and the fallen tugs at the heart with a wave of compassion and pity. The young soldier cannot advance through these various levels of danger without sensing that reason does not operate here in the same medium, nor is it refracted in the same way as it is in contemplative thought. Indeed, he would have to be an extraordinary person not to lose the ability to make immediate decisions under these initial impressions. It is true that habit quickly dulls these effects; within half an hour, we begin to feel more or less indifferent to what's happening around us. But an ordinary character never quite achieves complete calm or the natural resilience of mind; thus, we see once again that ordinary qualities are insufficient—a truth that only becomes more apparent the greater the scope of responsibility.

Enthusiastic courage, stoic bravery, natural fearlessness, strong ambition, or a long familiarity with danger—all these are essential if the impact of such a resistant medium is not to fall far short of what, in the quiet of a study, might appear to be merely the standard.

Danger in War is part of its friction; an accurate understanding of its influence is essential for clarity of perception, and so we bring it to attention here.

Chapter V. Of Bodily Exertion in War

If only those enduring frostbite, wilting under intense heat and thirst, or collapsing from hunger and fatigue were allowed to give opinions on events in War, we might indeed have fewer judgments that are correct objectively; yet these judgments would at least be subjectively accurate, containing within them the true relation between the observer and the situation. We can observe this through the humble, often subdued or even despondent opinions expressed by those who have directly witnessed or been involved in adverse events. This response, in our view, indicates the powerful effect of physical fatigue and the extent to which it should be considered when forming opinions.

Among the many things in War that defy precise measurement, physical exertion stands out. Provided there is no unnecessary waste, it amplifies all other forces, yet no one can definitively say to what extent it can be pushed. What's notable, however, is that just as only a strong arm can fully draw the archer's bow, so in War, it is only through a great, guiding spirit that we can bring out the full latent strength of an Army. For there is a difference when an Army, beset by misfortune and surrounded by danger, collapses like a crumbling wall, where survival hinges on extreme physical exertion; and when a victorious Army, driven solely by pride, is moved entirely at the will of its Commander. The same level of effort that might elicit pity in the first scenario commands admiration in the second, as maintaining it is far more challenging.

Here, we reveal to the untrained eye one of those factors that silently restrain mental actions and secretly drain the soul's strength.

Although the primary focus here is the extreme effort a Commander requires from his Army or a leader demands from his followers—that is, the spirit needed to call for it and the skill to elicit it—the personal physical effort of Generals and the Chief Commander must also be considered. Having pursued our analysis of War conscientiously to this point, we must also acknowledge the significance of this minor yet essential aspect.

We have discussed physical exertion here, primarily because, like danger, it is a core source of friction in War, and its indeterminate nature makes it like an elastic force whose resistance, much like friction, is notoriously hard to quantify.

To prevent misuse of these reflections on the many factors that heighten the challenges of War, nature has equipped our judgment with a safeguard: our sensibilities. Just as an individual cannot justify referencing personal limitations when insulted or mistreated, but may do so after successfully defending himself or avenging the affront, so too will neither a Commander nor an Army diminish the shame of a dishonorable defeat by highlighting the danger, distress, or exertions involved—factors that would instead amplify the glory of a victory. Thus, our feelings, which ultimately reflect a more refined form of judgment, prevent us from doing what, according to reason alone, might seem a fair assessment.

Chapter VI. Information in War

By the term "information," we refer to all knowledge we have about the enemy and his country; it is, therefore, the foundation of all our thoughts and actions. If we consider the nature of this foundation—its unreliability, its ever-changing character—we soon realize what a precarious structure War is, and how easily it could collapse, burying us beneath its ruins. For although every manual tells us to trust only certain information and to always remain suspicious, this is merely comforting book advice, the kind of instruction system-writers and compendium authors fall back on when they have nothing more insightful to offer.

Much of the information gathered in War is contradictory, an even greater portion is false, and the vast majority is, at best, uncertain. An officer, therefore, needs a certain power of discernment, which only knowledge of people, practical experience, and sound judgment can provide. The law of probability must serve as his guide. This is no minor challenge, even for initial plans developed in the calm of a study, outside the immediate chaos of War; but it becomes immensely more difficult when, in the thick of War, reports arrive one after another. It's fortunate if these reports contradict each other to the extent that they balance out and prompt further investigation. It is much worse for the inexperienced if chance does not provide this balance and instead one report supports another, reinforcing, exaggerating, and completing a picture with vivid new details until urgent necessity forces a hasty decision that will soon be revealed as foolish, as the reports turn out to be falsehoods, exaggerations, and errors.

In brief, most reports are inaccurate, and human timidity amplifies lies and misinformation. Generally, people are more inclined to believe the bad than the good. There's a tendency to exaggerate the bad to some degree, and though the resulting alarms subside on their own, like waves, they often rise again for no apparent reason. Relying on his own sound judgment, the Commander must stand firm, like a rock against which the sea breaks in vain. This role is not easy; anyone who is not naturally resilient or well-trained by experience in War, with a mature sense of judgment, would do well to counterbalance his own natural inclinations by leaning slightly away from fear and toward hope; only then might he retain his equilibrium.

This difficulty in accurately perceiving things is one of the greatest sources of friction in War, as it often makes reality differ greatly from expectation. Sensory impressions carry more weight than abstract ideas formed through careful reflection, and this discrepancy is so powerful that no major undertaking has ever been executed without the Commander having to suppress new doubts at the very moment he begins his work. Ordinary men who rely on others' suggestions often become indecisive on the spot, believing that circumstances differ from what they anticipated, and this view gains strength as they continue to yield to others' opinions.

Even those who have designed their own plans often find, upon seeing things firsthand, that they doubt their decisions. A firm reliance on oneself must shield the Commander from the apparent pressures of the moment; his initial conviction will ultimately prove correct when the immediate, terrifying scenery that fate has thrust onto the stage of War is drawn back, revealing a wider horizon. This is one of the significant divides between conception and execution.

Chapter VII. Friction in War

As long as we lack firsthand experience with War, it is impossible to understand where the difficulties lie that are so often discussed, or what it is that the genius and extraordinary mental powers required of a General truly accomplish. Everything appears so simple; the essential areas of knowledge seem so straightforward, and all the necessary decisions seem so minor that, by comparison, even the simplest problem in higher mathematics takes on a kind of scientific dignity. But if we have seen War, then all becomes clear. Yet, even then, it is still exceedingly difficult to explain exactly what brings about this change, to define this unseen yet entirely effective factor.

Everything in War is very simple, but even the simplest thing is hard to do. These difficulties pile up and create a friction that no one who hasn't seen War can fully imagine. Imagine, for example, a traveler who, toward evening, hopes to complete the final two legs of his day's journey—four or five leagues with post-horses, along a main road; it seems like nothing. But upon reaching the next-to-last station, he finds there are no horses, or only poor ones; then he encounters a hilly region, rough roads, and a dark night. After much effort, he finally reaches the next station, only to find poor accommodations awaiting him. So it is in War;

due to an endless array of minor circumstances that cannot be adequately captured on paper, things fall short, and expectations are not met. A strong, iron will can overcome this friction; it can crush obstacles but often crushes the machine itself in the process. This outcome is something we will often see. Like an obelisk toward which the main streets of a city converge, the strong will of a determined spirit stands out prominently in the heart of the Art of War.

Friction is the only concept that, in a general sense, captures what sets real War apart from War on paper. The military apparatus, the Army and all that relates to it, is actually straightforward, which makes it appear easy to manage. But consider that no part of it is a single, solid piece; instead, it is made up of individuals, each introducing its own friction in every direction. Theoretically, everything seems fine: the commander of a battalion is responsible for carrying out orders; and because the battalion is bound together by discipline into a cohesive unit, with a leader who should be zealous and reliable, the mechanism appears to turn smoothly on an iron pin with minimal friction. But reality is different, and in War, all the exaggerations and falsehoods in such a concept reveal themselves immediately. The battalion is still made up of many individuals, of whom the most inconsequential, if circumstances align, can cause delay or even disruption. The dangers inherent in War and the physical strain it demands amplify these issues so significantly that they may be considered its greatest sources of friction.

This immense friction, which is not concentrated at a few specific points as it is in mechanics, instead permeates every part and intersects with chance, allowing for events that could not have been anticipated, as they often arise by chance. Take, for example, the weather: a fog may prevent the enemy from being spotted in time, a battery from firing at the right moment, or a report from reaching the General; similarly, rain can delay a battalion's arrival because it had to march perhaps eight hours instead of three; or it may keep the cavalry from charging effectively because they are bogged down in heavy ground.

These examples are just a few specific incidents offered to help illustrate, allowing the reader to better follow the author, for entire volumes could be written on these challenges. To avoid this, and still provide a clear sense of the countless minor obstacles one faces in War, we might continue piling up illustrations—if we weren't afraid of becoming tedious. But for those who have already understood, we ask them to permit us to add just a few more.

Activity in War is like movement in a resistant medium. Just as a person submerged in water cannot perform with ease and precision even the most natural, basic movement—walking—so in War, without exceptional ability, one cannot even maintain an average level of performance. This is why the well-versed theorist resembles a swimming instructor who, on dry land, teaches movements that are required in water. To those who forget about the water, these movements might seem absurd and comical. This is also why theorists who have never themselves plunged into War or who lack the ability to generalize from their experience often appear impractical or even ridiculous because they merely teach what everyone already knows—how to walk.

Furthermore, every War is filled with unique situations and, at the same time, is like an unexplored sea full of hidden reefs the General might sense but has never seen, and around which he must navigate in the dark. If a headwind arises, meaning a significant and unforeseen event works against him, then the highest degree of skill, quick decision-making, and energy are needed. Yet, to those watching from afar, everything seems to proceed with the utmost ease. This awareness of friction is a major part of the experience in War, so often spoken of and so crucial in a competent General. The best General is certainly not the one who is most preoccupied with friction or most intimidated by it (this includes the class of overly cautious Generals, of which there are many among the experienced). However, a General must recognize friction to overcome it where possible and to avoid expecting a level of precision in results that friction itself makes unattainable.

Moreover, friction cannot be learned in theory, and if it could, it would still lack that seasoned judgment known as tact, which is more necessary in dealing with a multitude of small, varied challenges than in major, decisive situations where one's judgment can be supplemented by consulting others. Just as a worldly person, through instinctive tact honed by habit, speaks, acts, and moves appropriately for each occasion, so too does the experienced officer in War make decisions and take action—large and small, with every pulse of War, as we might say—in a manner suited to each specific situation. Through experience and practice, he instinctively knows when a certain course of action will not work. Thus, he avoids situations that might compromise him, as repeated missteps in War erode all foundations of trust and become extremely dangerous.

It is this friction, as we term it here, that turns what seems simple in War into something difficult in practice. As we proceed, we will encounter this topic frequently, and it will become clear that, besides experience and a strong will, there are numerous other rare qualities of mind required to make a person a truly skilled General.

Chapter VIII. Concluding Remarks, Book I

The elements we have discussed that come together in the atmosphere of War, creating a resistant medium for every activity, are danger, physical exertion, information, and friction. In their obstructive effects, these elements can collectively be understood as general friction. So, is there any kind of "oil" that might reduce this friction? There is only one, and it is not always available at the will of the Commander or his Army: it is the habituation of an Army to War.

Habit strengthens the body for great exertion, the mind for facing great danger, and the judgment for withstanding initial impressions. Through habit, a valuable attentiveness develops across every rank, from the hussar and rifleman up to the Division General, thereby easing the work of the Chief Commander.

Just as the human eye adapts in a dark room, widening its pupil to take in the small amount of light, gradually recognizing shapes and finally becoming familiar with them, so too does the experienced soldier become accustomed to the challenges of War, while the novice encounters only pitch darkness.

No General can instantly instill this habituation to War in his Army, and maneuvers in peace are only a weak substitute, weak when compared to true War experience, but not weak in comparison to other Armies where training is limited to mere mechanical routines. Structuring exercises in peacetime to incorporate some of these elements of friction—so that judgment, attentiveness, and even decision-making of individual leaders are tested—is far more important than many believe, particularly those lacking experience. It is crucial that soldiers of every rank do not encounter situations in War that would otherwise surprise or bewilder them if seen for the first time. If they have encountered these situations even once before, they will be at least halfway familiar with them. This concept extends even to physical hardship; exercises are less about conditioning the body than conditioning the mind.

In War, the young soldier is often quick to interpret unusual hardships as signs of errors, confusion, or disorder in the leadership, leading to distress and discouragement. This would not occur if he had been prepared for it through peacetime exercises.

Another, narrower but still significant, way to build War habituation in peacetime is to recruit experienced officers from foreign armies. Peace seldom prevails over all of Europe, and never over the entire world. A state that has enjoyed prolonged peace should seek to secure officers who have proven themselves in various theaters of War or send its own officers to these places to gain practical lessons in War.

Although the number of such officers may seem small compared to the whole, their impact is noticeable.(*)

Their experience, their natural abilities, and the mark of their character influence their subordinates and peers. Even if they cannot be placed in top command positions, they can still serve as valuable resources—people who know the terrain and can be consulted in specific situations.

Book II. On the Theory of War

Chapter I. Branches of the Art of War

War, in its literal sense, is fighting, for only fighting is the active principle within the broader range of activities we term War. Fighting is a contest of strength between moral and physical forces, conducted through the latter. That the moral aspect cannot be omitted is obvious, for mental states always have a decisive impact on the forces employed in War.

The necessity of fighting soon led people to invent special means to gain an advantage; as a result, the methods of fighting have undergone significant changes. However, regardless of how it is carried out, the essence of fighting remains unchanged, and it is fighting that defines War.

From the outset, these inventions included weapons and equipment for individual fighters. These must be provided and mastered before War begins. They are made to fit the nature of combat, thus shaped by it; however, it's clear that the activities involved in creating these tools differ from the act of fighting itself—they are merely preparations, not the combat itself. That arming and equipping are not essential to the concept of fighting is evident, as mere hand-to-hand struggle is also fighting.

Fighting determines all aspects of arms and equipment, and these, in turn, influence the methods of fighting; there is, therefore, a reciprocal influence between the two.

Nonetheless, the fight itself remains a distinct activity, especially as it operates within a unique element—the element of danger.

If ever there was a need to distinguish between two types of activities, it is here; and to appreciate the importance of this distinction, we need only recall how often exceptional competence in one area has proved to be mere pedantry in the other.

It is not difficult to conceptually separate one activity from the other if we view the armed and equipped fighting forces as a given means, the effective use of which requires only an understanding of their general capabilities.

Thus, the Art of War, in its proper sense, is the art of using given means in combat, and we can best refer to this as the "Conduct of War." In a broader sense, however, all activities that exist because of War—including the entire formation of troops, meaning their recruitment, arming, equipping, and training—also belong to the Art of War.

For a sound theory, it is crucial to separate these two types of activities, as it is easy to see that if each act of War begins with the preparation of military forces and assumes fully organized forces as a prerequisite, then the theory would only apply in rare cases where the available force precisely meets those conditions. On the other hand, if we want a theory suitable for most situations, one that will not be completely useless in any situation, it must be based on the means most commonly available and should focus solely on their actual results.

The conduct of War is, therefore, the organization and management of the fighting. If this fighting were a single act, there would be no need for further division. But the fight consists of a greater or lesser number of individual, self-contained acts, which we call combats, as shown in the first chapter of the first book, and these combats form new units. From this arises two distinct activities: the organization and management of these individual combats in themselves, and the combination of them with each other, aimed toward the ultimate objective of the War. The first is called tactics, and the second, strategy.

This division into tactics and strategy is now widely accepted, and people generally know which category to assign to a particular fact, even if they don't fully understand the basis for this classification. However, when such divisions are consistently applied in practice, they must have a substantial foundation. We have sought this foundation and might say it is the common usage of the majority that led us to it. Conversely, we view the arbitrary, forced definitions of these concepts imposed by some writers as inconsistent with how these terms are generally understood.

According to our classification, therefore, tactics is the theory of using military forces in combat, while strategy is the theory of using combats to achieve the objective of the War.

The precise way to define an individual or independent combat, the conditions that define this unit, will become clear only when we examine the nature of combat itself. For now, we can simply state that, in terms of space—that is, in simultaneous combats—the unit extends as far as personal command reaches; in terms of time—that is, in combats occurring in close succession—it extends to the point where the crisis in each combat is entirely resolved.

That ambiguous cases may arise—cases, for instance, where several combats could also be viewed as a single one—does not undermine the validity of our distinction, for this is true of all distinctions between real things that vary along a continuous spectrum. Thus, there will certainly be activities in War that, without any change in perspective, could be considered both strategic and tactical; examples include very extended positions resembling a chain of posts or the preparations for crossing a river at multiple points.

Our classification addresses only the use of military force. Yet, in War, there are numerous activities that support this use, though they are distinct from it, sometimes closely related, sometimes less so. All these activities pertain to the maintenance of military force. Just as its creation and training precede its use, so too is its maintenance a necessary condition. But, strictly speaking, all activities associated with it are essentially preparatory for combat; they are no more than tasks closely aligned with the action, so interwoven with the fighting that they fluctuate in importance alongside the use of the forces.

Therefore, we are justified in excluding these activities, along with other preparatory actions, from the Art of War in its strictest sense—from the actual conduct of War. And we must do so if we are to adhere to the foundational principle of all theory: the elimination of unrelated elements. Who would include in the true "conduct of War" the entire array of logistics and administration, just because they operate in constant interaction with the use of troops, when they are fundamentally distinct from it?

In the third chapter of our first book, we noted that since the fight or combat is the only directly effective action, all other activities ultimately converge upon it and are thus encompassed by it. By this, we meant that these other activities each have an objective which, according to their own particular laws, they must aim to achieve. Here, we must examine this concept more closely.

The activities outside of combat involve a variety of elements.

One group of these elements is, in a certain respect, part of the combat itself, sharing its nature, while also serving in another respect to maintain the military force. The other group pertains purely to sustenance and only exerts a limited influence on combat through its effects, as a result of reciprocal interaction. The elements that relate to combat include marches, camps, and cantonments, for they involve different arrangements of troops, and where troops are concerned, the concept of combat is always present.

The other elements, which relate solely to maintenance, include subsistence, care of the sick, and supply and repair of arms and equipment.

Marches are completely integrated with the use of troops. Marching during combat, generally referred to as maneuvering, does not necessarily involve the use of weapons, yet it is so inextricably tied to combat that it forms an essential part of what we call a combat. On the other hand, marching outside of combat is simply the execution of a strategic plan. The strategic plan determines when, where, and with what forces a battle is to take place, and marching is the only means to carry that plan into action.

Marching outside of combat is therefore a tool of strategy, though not exclusively a matter of strategy, as the marching force could encounter combat at any moment. Hence, its execution must follow both tactical and strategic principles. For example, directing a column to march along a particular side of a river or mountain branch is a strategic choice, as it implies the intention to engage on that specific side should combat arise during the march.

Conversely, if a column marches along a ridge instead of through a valley, or divides into multiple columns for easier movement, these are tactical choices, as they pertain to how troops will be employed in the expected combat.

The specific marching formation always relates to combat-readiness and is thus tactical in nature; it is simply the initial or preparatory arrangement for a potential battle.

Since marching is the means by which strategy deploys its active elements—namely, combats—and since these combats often only reveal themselves through their outcomes rather than in detailed action, it is understandable that theory sometimes confuses the tool for the effective principle. Thus, we may hear of a "decisive, skillful march," referring to the combat combinations that the march facilitated. This shift in meaning is natural, and conciseness is often desirable enough to excuse it, but we must remember the full implication of this concept to avoid falling into error.

We make a mistake of this kind when we attribute an independent power to strategic combinations, separate from tactical outcomes. We read about marches and maneuvers executed, objectives achieved, and yet hear not a word about combat, leading to the erroneous conclusion that there are methods in War to defeat the enemy without fighting. We cannot fully demonstrate the far-reaching impact of this error until later.

However, although a march can be seen as an integral part of the combat, it still contains certain aspects that don't belong to combat and are therefore neither tactical nor strategic. These include all arrangements related only to troop accommodations, such as bridge construction, road-making, and so on. These activities are merely conditions; in many circumstances, they are closely connected to the troops and may nearly merge with them, as in the case of constructing a bridge in the presence of the enemy. Yet, by nature, these are activities whose theory does not fall within the theory of the conduct of War.

Camps, which refer to any arrangement of troops in a concentrated, battle-ready position as opposed to cantonments or quarters, represent a state of rest, thus of recovery. But camps are also the strategic positioning of troops for battle at a chosen location, and in the way they are established, they contain the foundational lines of the battle, a condition that underpins any defensive engagement. Therefore, they are essential parts of both strategy and tactics.

Cantonments replace camps to better refresh the troops. Like camps, they are strategic in terms of location and scope, and tactical in their internal organization, designed for readiness to fight.

The occupation of camps and cantonments usually serves not only to recuperate the troops but may also have other aims, such as covering a particular area or holding a position. Yet, the primary purpose can also be solely recuperation. We remind readers that strategy can pursue a wide range of objectives, as any apparent advantage may be the goal of a battle, and preserving the force with which War is conducted often becomes the purpose of its smaller combinations.

Thus, if in such cases strategy focuses only on troop maintenance, we do not leave the realm of strategy for that reason, as we are still dealing with the deployment of military force; every positioning of that force on any point of the theater of War is indeed a deployment.

However, if maintaining troops in camp or quarters involves activities that don't employ armed forces—such as building huts, pitching tents, or providing supplies and medical services—these do not fall within the realm of strategy or tactics.

Even entrenchments, which, by their location and preparation, are clearly part of the battle's order and thus tactical, do not belong to the theory of the conduct of War concerning their construction. The knowledge and skill required for such work are inherent in a well-organized Army; the theory of combat presumes these qualities.

Among the areas that relate purely to maintaining an armed force, since none of these are directly involved in combat, victualling the troops takes precedence, as it must be done almost daily and for each individual. For this reason, it permeates the elements of strategy that shape military action. We specify "elements of strategy" because, during a battle, troop subsistence rarely influences the plan, though it is conceivable. Thus, the care for troop subsistence primarily interacts with strategy, and it's common for the main strategic elements of a campaign or War to be mapped out with a view toward provisioning. Yet, despite how frequently and significantly these supply considerations affect strategy, subsisting the troops remains entirely separate from using the troops and impacts the latter only indirectly, through its outcomes.

The other branches of administrative activity we mentioned stand even farther from troop utilization. The care of the sick and wounded, as essential as it is for the Army's welfare, directly affects only a small portion of the individuals within it, thus exerting only a limited and indirect influence on the employment of the rest. The replenishment and replacement of weapons and equipment, except for those routine activities essential to maintaining troop readiness, occurs only periodically and therefore seldom impacts strategic plans.

However, we must avoid a misunderstanding here. In certain cases, these factors can indeed be decisive. The distance to hospitals and supply depots, for example, could easily become the sole basis for crucial strategic decisions. We neither wish to deny nor downplay this. But we are not focusing here on the specific circumstances of an individual case; rather, we are dealing with abstract theory. Our point is that such influence is too rare to warrant giving the theories of medical care or supply replenishment the same theoretical importance as victualling, making it unnecessary to incorporate these various approaches into the theory of the conduct of War.

If we've grasped the results of these reflections, then the activities associated with War divide into two primary categories: those that are merely preparations for War and the War itself. This distinction must also be reflected in theory.

The knowledge and skills applied in preparing for War encompass the creation, discipline, and maintenance of all military forces. We won't specify terms for these activities, but they include artillery, fortifications, elementary tactics, the entire organization and administration of the various armed forces, and so forth. In contrast, the theory of War itself deals with using these prepared resources to achieve the aims of War. It only requires the end results of these preparations—that is, an understanding of the primary characteristics of the resources to be used. We refer to this as "The Art of War" in a limited sense, or the "Theory of the Conduct of War," or the "Theory of the Employment of Armed Forces"—all of which signify the same concept to us.

Thus, this theory will address the combat as the actual confrontation; marches, camps, and cantonments will be treated as elements closely linked to it. The subsistence of the troops will be considered only as one of many external conditions, in terms of its impact, not as an activity related to combat.

Viewed in this more specific sense, the Art of War splits further into two major components: tactics and strategy. Tactics is concerned with the precise form, structure, and execution of individual combats, focusing on the arrangement and direct actions of troops within each engagement. Strategy, on the other hand, is concerned with the higher purpose and utility of those combats as they contribute to the overarching objectives of a campaign or War. Both tactics and strategy are inherently connected to the surrounding circumstances—such as marches, camps, and cantonments—but only through the lens of combat itself. These circumstances are either tactical or strategic depending on whether they relate to the specific organization and form of the battle, or to its broader significance and purpose within the War.

It is likely that some readers may view this rigorous separation between tactics and strategy—two activities so closely intertwined in both concept and execution—as unnecessary, perhaps even excessively meticulous, given that it doesn't directly influence the practical conduct of War on the battlefield. We acknowledge this perspective and agree that it would be overly pedantic to expect this theoretical distinction to yield direct, measurable effects in real-time combat situations. After all, soldiers on the battlefield are unlikely to pause and consider where tactics end and strategy begins.

Nevertheless, it is essential to recognize that the foremost task of any theory is to clarify and untangle complex concepts and ideas that may otherwise remain jumbled, intertwined, and ultimately confusing. Only by establishing a clear and precise understanding of names, terms, and concepts can we proceed with clarity and efficiency in our exploration of War, ensuring that both author and reader interpret each concept from a shared, consistent perspective. Without such clarity, misunderstandings easily arise, leading to differences in interpretation that can complicate both study and practical application.

Tactics and strategy, while interconnected and often overlapping in time and space, remain fundamentally different kinds of activities. The inner principles, relationships, and dynamics between these two aspects of War cannot be fully understood or appreciated until we establish a clear definition of each activity, examining how they interact and diverge. Tactics is the granular, immediate application of force in combat, grounded in the present and dealing with specific movements, formations, and maneuvers. Strategy, in contrast, is the broader, forward-looking plan, the deliberate orchestration of those combats toward achieving a higher purpose that often transcends the immediate context of the individual engagement.

Anyone who finds this distinction unimportant or irrelevant may simply dismiss all theoretical considerations as unnecessary. Alternatively, they may not have yet experienced the frustration and limitations imposed by the vague, contradictory, and often perplexing ideas that arise in the absence of a structured perspective. Without such clarity, we encounter discussions on the conduct of War that lack focus, meander without purpose, and fail to produce satisfactory results, frequently drifting into tedious or fantastical realms, or otherwise remaining ambiguous and disconnected from reality. These discussions often fail to add meaningful insight, largely because the spirit of scientific inquiry has historically overlooked these topics, leaving the study of War without the structured foundation that other fields have long developed.

Chapter II. On the Theory of War

1. The First Conception of the "Art of War" Was Merely the Preparation of The Armed Forces.

In the past, the term "Art of War" or "Science of War" referred exclusively to the combined body of knowledge and practical skills focused on material aspects. It encompassed the design, preparation, and handling of weapons, the construction of fortifications and defensive structures, the organization of an army, and the mechanics of its movements. These areas of knowledge and expertise aimed to create an armed force capable of engaging in War. All of this related solely to material aspects and involved a single-sided focus on technique, essentially an activity that progressed through stages, from simpler tasks to increasingly refined mechanical skills.

This understanding of the Art of War related to War itself in much the same way as a sword-maker's craft relates to the skill of wielding the sword. The actual use of this force in moments of danger, the continuous interplay of mental and emotional energies in pursuit of specific objectives, and the complex dynamics of applying these forces under ever-changing conditions—these aspects had not yet even been considered.

2. True War First Appears in the Art of Sieges.

In the art of sieges, we first see an element of intellectual guidance over combat, a glimpse of the mind's influence on the physical forces under its command. However, this influence generally took form in new physical constructs, such as approaches, trenches, counter-approaches, and batteries, with each advance in intellectual strategy resulting in a tangible creation of this sort. The intellectual process served primarily as a framework to arrange these material innovations in a coherent sequence. Because this type of warfare offered limited ways for intellect to manifest beyond these tangible structures, nearly everything needed in siege warfare was achieved through such physical means.

3. Then Tactics Tried to Find Its Way in The Same Direction.

Later, tactics sought to shape its mechanical components into a coherent system based on the unique qualities of its tools. This approach aimed to bring forces to the battlefield in a structured manner; yet, instead of fostering flexible mental engagement, it created an Army resembling an automaton. With rigid formations and strict orders of battle, the Army was designed to move only in response to commands, its actions unfolding like the mechanisms of clockwork.

4. The Real Conduct of War Only Made Its Appearance Incidentally and Incognito.

The actual conduct of War—that is, the practical use of prepared resources tailored to the specific demands of each situation—was not originally considered a suitable subject for theoretical study. Instead, it was thought best left to individual talent and intuition. Gradually, as War evolved from the close, chaotic encounters of the Middle Ages into a more regular and systematic practice, sporadic reflections on this topic began to emerge. These insights, however, mostly appeared incidentally within memoirs and narratives, somewhat in disguise and without formal recognition.

5. Reflections On Military Events Brought About the Want of a Theory.

As contemplation on War steadily grew, and as the study of its history increasingly took on a critical perspective, there arose a pressing need for established principles and rules. Such foundations were needed to anchor the inevitable debates surrounding military events, allowing the conflict of opinions to converge around a single focal point. The swirl of conflicting views, which lacked a central guiding principle or any discernible structure, had become unsettling and unsatisfactory to those seeking a clearer understanding.

6. Endeavours To Establish A Positive Theory.

Thus, there emerged an effort to create maxims, rules, and even entire systems to guide the conduct of War. This approach aimed at achieving a concrete, positive objective, without fully considering the endless challenges that the conduct of War presents. As we have shown, the conduct of War has no clear boundaries in any direction, while every system, by nature, imposes fixed limits and structured synthesis. This results in an unresolvable conflict between such theories and the realities of practice.

7. Limitation To Material Objects.

Theorists quickly recognized the complexity of the subject and believed they were justified in sidestepping it by focusing their maxims and systems solely on material aspects and one-sided activities. Their aim was to achieve results that, like those in the science of preparing for War, would be entirely certain and concrete. Therefore, they limited their focus to elements that could be quantified and made calculable.8. SUPERIORITY OF NUMBERS.

Superiority in numbers, as a material condition, was selected from among the factors contributing to victory because it could be calculated mathematically by considering combinations of time and space. The idea was to disregard all other factors by assuming they would be equal on both sides, thus neutralizing each other. This approach would have been useful as a preliminary step to understand this one factor in isolation. However, to treat numerical superiority as an absolute rule, viewing the entire Art of War as simply achieving a formula of bringing larger forces to a given point at a given time, proved too narrow a focus and was ultimately overturned by the complexities of real-world circumstances.

9. Victualling of Troops.

Another theoretical school attempted to systematize a different material element by making the subsistence of troops, based on a predefined organizational structure of the Army, the primary guiding principle in higher-level conduct of War. This approach did yield clear numerical guidelines, but these figures relied heavily on a series of arbitrary calculations and thus could not withstand the demands of practical application.

10. Base.

A resourceful author attempted to condense a wide range of objectives into a single concept, termed a BASE, which encompassed numerous aspects, including some connections with intangible forces. This list included the subsistence of troops, maintaining their numbers and equipment, securing lines of communication with the homeland, and, ultimately, ensuring a safe route for retreat if necessary. Initially, he proposed that this concept of a base should replace each of these individual elements; then he aimed to replace the base itself with its length or extent; and finally, he introduced the angle formed between the army and this base. All of this was done to yield a purely geometric outcome, which proved entirely impractical. This impracticality was inevitable, given that each substitution involved compromises, omitting critical aspects contained within the original concept.

The idea of a base is indeed a valuable strategic necessity, and credit is due to anyone who has introduced it thoughtfully. However, using it in the way described above is inadmissible, leading only to narrow conclusions that push theorists in an illogical direction—namely, toward an overemphasis on the decisive impact of an enveloping form of attack.

11. Interior Lines.

In response to this misguided approach, another geometric principle, known as the concept of interior lines, was elevated as the new guiding rule. While this principle is grounded in a solid truth—that combat is the only truly effective means in War—its purely geometric nature renders it yet another example of a narrow, one-sided theory that ultimately lacks the practical dominance required to succeed in the complexities of real-world warfare.

12. All These Attempts Are Open to Objection.

All these theoretical efforts should be regarded as valuable advancements in the analytical realm, moving closer to truth by breaking down components of War. However, in their synthetical aspect—when it comes to practical precepts and rules—they prove largely ineffective.

They seek fixed quantities and precise measurements, while in War, nearly everything is variable, requiring calculations with ever-shifting factors.

These theories focus only on material forces, yet every military action is infused with intelligent forces and the impact of human decision-making.

They consider only one side's actions, while War is a constant interplay of reciprocal actions, where the effects are always mutual and intertwined.

13. As A Rule, They Exclude Genius.

Everything beyond what this limited philosophy—born of narrow perspectives—could grasp was considered outside the realm of science and left to the domain of genius, which RISES ABOVE RULES.

Pity the warrior who is content to crawl through this barren landscape of rules, rules that genius finds too confining, over which it stands superior, and might even mock! Whatever genius accomplishes should serve as the highest rule, and theory can do no better than to explain how and why this is so.

Pity, too, the theory that sets itself in opposition to the creative mind! No degree of humility can bridge this contradiction, and the humbler it tries to be, the sooner it will be driven from practical life by ridicule and scorn.

14. The Difficulty of Theory as Soon as Moral Quantities Come into Consideration.

Every theory becomes immeasurably more complex the moment it enters the realm of moral factors. Architecture and painting, for example, operate confidently as long as they deal purely with physical materials;

there is little dispute over the mechanical or optical principles involved. But as soon as moral elements come into play—as soon as feelings, impressions, and emotional responses are involved—the entire framework of rules dissolves into a set of ambiguous ideas.

Medicine, for the most part, is concerned only with physical phenomena; its focus is the human body, an organism in constant change, never identical from one moment to the next. This inherent variability makes medical practice challenging and places the physician's judgment above the theoretical science itself. Yet, how much more challenging the task becomes if a moral dimension is introduced! And how much higher regard we must have for the physician of the mind, who must grapple not only with physical, but also with deeply intangible, moral effects.

15. The Moral Quantities Must Not Be Excluded in War.

In War, one's actions are never directed solely at physical targets; they are always simultaneously aimed at the intelligent force that animates these physical elements, and separating the two is impossible.

This intelligent force, however, is only visible to the inner eye—the mind's perception—and this varies from person to person and even within the same person at different times.

Since danger pervades every aspect of War, it is mainly courage, the awareness of one's own power, that influences judgment. Courage, in a sense, acts as a lens through which all perceptions must pass before they reach the understanding.

Yet, despite these subjective variations, we cannot deny that these factors attain a certain objective value through accumulated experience.

Everyone understands the moral impact of a surprise attack or an assault from the flank or rear. Everyone sees the enemy as less courageous the moment he retreats and feels emboldened in pursuit compared to when being pursued. Every commander judges the opposing general based on their reputation, age, and experience, shaping their actions accordingly. Each person carefully observes the spirit and morale of both their own forces and those of the enemy. All these effects, and others rooted in human psychology, are consistently observed, recur frequently, and therefore can be reasonably treated as real factors in their own right. What use would we have for any theory that ignored them?

Experience, then, is essential in validating these insights. No theory, and no General, should dabble in philosophical or psychological speculations beyond this point.

16. Principal Difficulty of a Theory for The Conduct of War.

To fully grasp the complexity of formulating a theory for the conduct of War, and thereby identify the essential characteristics such a theory must have, we need to examine more closely the primary factors that define the nature of activity in War.

17. First Specialty. —Moral Forces and Their Effects. (Hostile Feeling.)

The first of these specialities consists in the moral forces and effects.

Combat, in its essence, originates as an expression of hostile feeling, but in large-scale conflicts—what we call Wars—this hostility often reduces itself to a merely hostile perspective, with little innate personal animosity between individuals on opposite sides. Still, no combat occurs without some level of hostile feeling emerging. National hatred, which is a common aspect in our Wars, often serves as a substitute for direct personal enmity, filling the individual with a sense of opposition to their counterpart.

Even where this national hatred is absent and no personal hostility exists at first, the act of combat itself tends to ignite hostile feelings. When someone commits an act of violence against us under the command of their superior, it is human nature to feel an urge to retaliate against that individual rather than against the distant authority who ordered it. This response, whether we call it human or animal, is simply the reality of our nature. Theorists are often inclined to view combat as a purely abstract test of strength, detached from emotional involvement. But this is one of many oversights in theory, as it fails to acknowledge the consequences of neglecting these emotional forces.

Beyond the natural hostile feelings stirred up by the combat itself, there are other emotions that, while not essential to combat, easily merge with it due to their affinity—ambition, the desire for power, enthusiasm of all kinds, and so forth.

18. The Impressions of Danger. (Courage.)

Finally, combat introduces the element of danger, an environment in which all actions in War must exist and operate, much like a bird in the air or a fish in water. The effects of danger impact the feelings, either directly—by instinct—or indirectly, through rational thought. In the first case, danger instinctively triggers the impulse to escape; if escape is not possible, it leads to feelings of fear and anxiety. When this reaction is absent, it is replaced by courage, which serves as a counterbalance to that instinct.

However, courage is not a product of rational calculation; it is a feeling just like fear. While fear is concerned with physical survival, courage is focused on moral resilience. Courage, then, can be considered a higher instinct. Yet, precisely because courage is noble in nature, it resists being used as a passive tool that responds exactly as prescribed. Courage, therefore, is not simply a counterweight to danger to neutralize its effects; rather, it is a unique force in its own right.

19. Extent of the Influence of Danger.

To fully understand the influence of danger on the main participants in War, we must recognize that its reach extends beyond the immediate physical danger of the moment. Danger dominates the individual not only by posing a direct threat but also by endangering everything entrusted to them. It weighs heavily not only in the moments when it is physically present but also through the power of imagination in all other moments connected to the present situation. Furthermore, danger influences not just by itself but also indirectly through the weight of responsibility, which amplifies its effect tenfold on the mind of the commander.

Who could give counsel or make a decision about a significant battle without feeling their mind affected—if not unsettled—by the immense danger and responsibility that such a critical decision entails? Indeed, we can say that action in War, as long as it is genuine action and not a mere state of being, is never truly free from the sphere of danger.

20. Other Powers of Feeling.

If we consider the intense emotions stirred by hostility and danger as unique to War, we do not, for that reason, exclude other feelings that accompany individuals throughout life. These emotions, too, will often find their place in War. It is true that many small, petty actions driven by human passions tend to fade away in the seriousness of warfare; but this is generally true only for those in lower ranks who, constantly propelled from one state of danger and exertion to the next, lose sight of life's other concerns. These individuals often grow unaccustomed to deceit, recognizing its futility in the face of death, and attain a soldierly simplicity of character that has long symbolized the military profession.

In higher ranks, however, the situation differs. The higher a person's position, the more they must remain aware of everything around them. With this come diverse interests from many directions and a wide range of passionate forces, both good and bad. Envy and generosity, pride and humility, fierceness and compassion—all may emerge as active forces in this vast and complex drama.

21. Peculiarity of Mind.

The unique qualities of the mind in the chief commander, along with their emotional traits, hold great significance. From an imaginative, impulsive, and inexperienced mind, one should expect very different decisions than from a calm, thoughtful, and wise understanding.

The variety in mental individuality produces a diversity of approaches to reach the goal.

This broad diversity in mental character, especially influential in the higher ranks where it becomes more pronounced, is what primarily accounts for the numerous ways of achieving the objectives we discussed in the first book. It also contributes to the prominent role that probabilities and chance play in shaping the course of events, as each individual's unique mental attributes shape how they navigate War's uncertain paths.

23. Second Peculiarity. —Living Reaction.

The second unique aspect of War is the dynamic, living reaction and the reciprocal interactions that arise from it. Here, we are not speaking about the difficulty of estimating this reaction, as that falls under the challenge previously mentioned of treating moral forces as measurable quantities. Instead, we mean that the very nature of reciprocal action resists any attempt to implement a rigid plan.

The impact that any decision or measure has on the enemy is among the clearest of all action-based insights. However, every theory must rely on broad categories or groups of phenomena, and it cannot account for each truly unique case on its own—that responsibility is left to personal judgment and talent. Therefore, it is natural that in War, a realm where plans are based on general conditions yet frequently disrupted by unexpected or unusual events, more must be entrusted to individual talent, and there is less reliance on a theoretical guide than in most other fields.

24. Third Peculiarity. —Uncertainty of All Data.

Lastly, the profound uncertainty of all information in War poses a unique challenge, as every action must, to some extent, be planned in a state of near-darkness. This limited visibility often distorts reality, much like fog or moonlight, making things appear exaggerated or giving them an unnatural form.

What this faint light fails to reveal must either be uncovered by talent or left to chance. Once again, therefore, it is talent—or the favor of fortune—that must be relied upon in the absence of clear, objective knowledge.

25. Positive Theory Is Impossible.

With materials of this nature, we can only conclude that it is entirely impossible to build a theory for the Art of War that would act like a rigid scaffolding, providing the commander with complete external support on all sides. In every instance where he must rely on his own talent, he would find himself beyond the reach of this theoretical scaffolding and, in fact, often in direct opposition to it. No matter how comprehensive the theory might be, the outcome would always be the same as we described earlier: talent and genius operate outside the confines of fixed rules, and theory stands in contrast to the unpredictable realities of War.

26. Means Left by Which a Theory Is Possible (The Difficulties Are Not Everywhere Equally Great).

Two approaches offer a way out of this difficulty. First, the challenges we have described in the nature of military action do not apply equally to everyone, regardless of rank. In the lower ranks, the emphasis lies more on the spirit of self-sacrifice, while the obstacles facing understanding and judgment are vastly reduced. The scope of events is narrower; goals and means are fewer, and the information is often more concrete, generally involving what is directly visible. However, as we move up the ranks, these difficulties grow, reaching their peak at the level of the Commander-in-Chief, where nearly everything must be left to individual genius.

Additionally, in keeping with the nature of the subject, these challenges vary according to their specific focus: they diminish when results are grounded in the physical world and increase as they shift into the moral realm, where they become motivations influencing the will. Therefore, it is easier to establish theoretical guidelines for organizing and conducting a battle than for determining how to leverage the outcomes of that battle. In the former, physical weapons clash, and although the mind is present, the demands of the material world must still be respected. However, when it comes to the broader effects of battles, where material outcomes become motives, we deal solely with the moral dimension. Simply put, it is easier to form a theory for tactics than for strategy.

27. Theory Must Be of The Nature of Observations Not of Doctrine.

The second possibility for a theory lies in the understanding that it does not need to serve as a direct guide for action. Generally speaking, whenever an activity frequently deals with the same objectives, ends, and means, even if there are minor adjustments and variations, it becomes something that can be examined analytically by the reasoning mind. Such examination is the core purpose of every theory and gives it a legitimate claim to that name. Theory, in this sense, is an analytical study of the subject, leading to precise understanding; and, if combined with experience—such as military history in our case—it fosters a thorough familiarity with it.

The closer theory comes to this goal, the more it shifts from objective knowledge to the subjective skill required in action, thereby enhancing practical effectiveness when personal talent is the only deciding factor. This benefit will reflect directly in the development of talent itself. If theory explores the components of War; if it distinguishes what initially seems blurred together; if it thoroughly explains the properties of various means; if it reveals their likely effects; if it clarifies the nature of goals; if it sheds the light of critical analysis across the entire field of War—then it has achieved its main purpose. It becomes a valuable guide for anyone seeking to learn about War from books, illuminating the path, helping them move forward, developing their judgment, and guarding them against mistakes.

If a knowledgeable person spends years dedicated to clarifying a complex topic, they will likely understand it better than someone attempting to master it quickly. Theory exists so that each generation does not have to clear the same ground and struggle through the subject from scratch but can find the material organized and illuminated. Its role is to educate the future leader's mind in War, or better yet, to assist in their self-education, but not to accompany them onto the battlefield. Just as a wise mentor shapes and enlightens a young mind without leading them through every step of their life, so too should theory play its role.

If principles and guidelines naturally emerge from the insights that theory offers—if the truth takes on this crystalline form—then theory should not resist this inherent mental process. Instead, theory should highlight these principles if they complete the structure of thought. But this should be done to fulfill a philosophical need for clarity, showing where ideas converge, rather than to create a rigid formula for battlefield use. Even these principles and guidelines are more valuable in shaping the general outline of one's habitual thought processes than as fixed markers for immediate action.

28. By This Point of View Theory Becomes Possible and Ceases to Be i Contradiction to Practice.

Viewing theory in this way opens up the possibility of a satisfying and useful framework for the conduct of War—one that never conflicts with reality. It only requires a rational approach to harmonize theory with action, so that the absurd gap between theory and practice, so often caused by unreasonable theories that ignore common sense, is finally closed. Such a harmony would prevent the misuse of this gap by those who, due to narrow-mindedness and ignorance, use it as an excuse to yield to their own natural limitations.

29. Theory Therefore Considers the Nature of Ends and Means—Ends and Means in Tactics.

Theory must therefore take into account the nature of both the means and the ends.

In tactics, the means are the trained, armed forces engaged in the struggle, and the goal is victory. The exact definition of victory will be better explained when we examine the combat itself. For now, we define victory simply as forcing the enemy to withdraw from the battlefield. This victory then allows strategy to achieve the objective for which the combat was undertaken, giving the combat its unique significance. This intended purpose does influence the nature of the victory itself. A victory aimed at weakening the enemy's forces is different from one intended solely to secure a particular position.

Thus, the purpose of a combat can meaningfully shape how it is prepared and conducted, making it a factor that tactics must consider.

30. Circumstances Which Always Attend the Application of The Means.

Since certain conditions consistently accompany combat and can significantly impact its outcome, they must be factored into the use of armed forces.

These conditions include the terrain of the battlefield, the time of day, and the weather.

31. Locality.

The terrain, which we will discuss further under "Country and Ground," could theoretically have no influence if combat took place on an entirely flat, uncultivated plain. In the vast steppes, such a scenario might be possible; however, in the cultivated landscapes of Europe, this is nearly an imaginary notion. Thus, a battle between civilized nations, in which terrain has no impact, is almost inconceivable.

32. Time of Day.

The time of day affects combat through the distinction between day and night; however, its influence goes beyond these divisions, as each combat has a certain duration, with large battles often lasting for many hours. When preparing for a major battle, it is notably different whether it begins in the morning or toward evening. That said, there are certainly many battles where the time of day is relatively unimportant, and in most cases, its influence is only minor.

33. Weather.

Weather has an even rarer impact on the outcome of combat, and it usually plays a role only through the presence of fog.

34. End And Means in Strategy.

Strategy primarily relies on victory—meaning the tactical outcome—as a tool to achieve its objective, ultimately aiming at factors that lead directly to peace. In using these means toward its goal, strategy is also influenced by various circumstances that can impact its effectiveness to varying degrees.

35. Circumstances Which Attend the Application of The Means of Strategy.

These circumstances include the country and terrain, with the former encompassing the entire theater of war along with its territory and population. Additionally, both the time of day and the season of the year play a role; finally, the weather, especially any extreme conditions, such as severe frost, can be influential.

36. These Form New Means.

By integrating these elements with the outcomes of combat, strategy assigns a unique significance to each result—and therefore to the combat itself—by aligning it with a specific objective. However, when this objective does not directly lead to peace and instead serves as an intermediate aim, it is to be considered merely a means to an end. In strategy, we can thus regard the results of combats or victories, in their various forms, as means to achieve broader goals.

For instance, the capture of a position is a result of combat tied specifically to terrain. But it is not only individual combats with distinct goals that serve as means; any overarching objective we pursue by coordinating multiple battles toward a shared goal also acts as a means. A winter campaign, for example, represents such a coordinated effort adapted to the season.

Thus, as primary objectives, only those elements remain which can be assumed to lead directly to peace. Theory examines all these ends and means, evaluating their effects and their interconnections.

37. Strategy Deduces Only from Experience the Ends and Means to Be Examined.

The first question is: How does strategy arrive at a complete list of these objectives? If a philosophical analysis were undertaken to achieve a perfect, absolute list, it would inevitably become entangled in the very complexities that both the practice and theory of War must avoid. Instead, strategy turns to experience, focusing on combinations demonstrated by military history. This approach admittedly produces only a limited theory, applicable primarily to scenarios that have historical precedent. However, this limitation is unavoidable since, in all cases, theory must either draw from or compare itself against historical examples to substantiate its points.

Moreover, this limitation is largely theoretical rather than practical. A key advantage of this approach is that theory remains grounded, avoiding overly complex or abstract ideas, and remains firmly practical in its applications.

38. How Far the Analysis of The Means Should Be Carried.

Another question arises: How far should theory delve into analyzing the means? Clearly, it should go only as far as the individual elements are practically relevant in their own distinct forms. For instance, understanding the range and impact of different weapons is critical to tactics; however, knowing their exact construction, although related to these effects, is unnecessary. Conducting War is not about producing powder and cannon from raw materials like charcoal, sulfur, saltpeter, copper, and tin; rather, the elements War considers are finished arms and their operational effects.

Strategy, likewise, uses maps without concerning itself with the technicalities of triangulations. It does not investigate the division of a country into departments and provinces or how people are educated and governed to maximize military effectiveness. Instead, it takes these conditions as they exist within the European States and observes where such diverse conditions may have a significant impact on War.

39. Great Simplification of The Knowledge Required.

It is clear that, by this approach, the number of topics theory must address is significantly simplified, and the knowledge required for the conduct of War is greatly reduced. The vast array of information and technical skills that support War in general—and that are essential before an army is fully equipped and ready for the field—converge into a few key results before reaching the ultimate goal of their efforts in actual combat. This process is like the way the many streams of a country merge into rivers before flowing into the sea. Only those activities that flow directly into the "sea of War" need to be understood by the one responsible for conducting its operations.

40. This Explains the Rapid Growth of Great Generals, And Why a General Is Not a Man of Learning.

The conclusion we have reached is so essential that any other outcome would have made us question the validity of our reasoning. This understanding explains why individuals often succeed in War, even in high-ranking and supreme command positions, despite having previously worked in completely unrelated fields. Indeed, history shows that the most distinguished generals rarely come from the ranks of highly educated or scholarly officers; rather, they have typically been individuals who, due to their circumstances, could not have acquired an extensive amount of knowledge. Consequently, those who have thought it necessary—or even beneficial—to train a future general by teaching every fine detail have often been dismissed as impractical pedants.

It is easy to see how such an approach can be detrimental, as the human mind is shaped by the knowledge it absorbs and the direction given to its ideas. Only exposure to what is significant can elevate the mind; focusing on minor details only narrows it, unless the mind itself instinctively rejects such minutiae as unworthy.

41. Former Contradictions.

Because the essential simplicity of knowledge required for War was overlooked and instead entangled with a mass of secondary sciences and arts, the resulting clear disconnect from real-life events could only be explained by attributing everything to "genius"—a quality seen as needing no theory and for which no theory could be formulated.

42. On This Account All Use of Knowledge Was Denied, And Everything Ascribed to Natural Talents.

People who were guided more by common sense recognized the vast gap between a true genius and a scholarly pedant, and they became, in a way, free-thinkers. They dismissed belief in theory entirely, claiming that conducting War was a natural human function performed better or worse depending on the inherent talent one possesses. While it's true that these individuals came closer to the truth than those who valued misguided knowledge, it is also clear that this view is itself somewhat exaggerated.

No activity of human understanding can occur without a certain set of ideas; these ideas are not, for the most part, innate but acquired and form the foundation of one's knowledge. The real question, then, is what kind of ideas should be cultivated? We believe this question is answered if we say they should focus on the actual elements one must engage with in War.

43. The Knowledge Must Be Made Suitable to The Position.

Within the military field itself, the knowledge required varies according to the Commander's position. A lower-ranking officer will focus on smaller, more limited objectives, while a higher-ranking Commander must address broader, more comprehensive ones. There have been Field Marshals who might not have excelled as leaders of a cavalry regiment, and vice versa.

44. The Knowledge in War Is Very Simple, But Not, At the Same Time, Very Easy.

Although the knowledge required in War is straightforward—concerned with relatively few topics and addressing these only at their ultimate results—the skill in execution is not necessarily simple. We discussed in the first book the general challenges of military action, excluding those that demand courage alone. Additionally, while mental activity may be relatively simple at lower levels, the complexity grows with rank; at the highest level, that of the Commander-in-Chief, it becomes one of the most difficult tasks the human mind can face.

45. of The Nature of This Knowledge.

An Army Commander does not need to be a learned historian or public figure, but he must understand higher affairs of State, know how to assess deep-seated traditions, recognize the interests involved, evaluate current issues, and understand the character of key figures. He does not need to be a keen judge of human nature or a sharp evaluator of character traits, but he must be familiar with the personalities, feelings, habits, common faults, and tendencies of those he commands. He doesn't need to know the construction of a carriage or the harness details of a battery horse, but he must be able to accurately calculate the time required for a column to march under various conditions.

The essential knowledge required for success in high-level military command is distinguished by its reliance on an intuitive, almost instinctive talent. This talent is necessary to distill the essence from life's diverse experiences—like bees extracting nectar from flowers. Such knowledge, crucial to the art of War, isn't simply a matter of studying theories or even learning through guided practice. It demands a unique intellectual capacity that allows one to discern critical patterns and insights. This understanding is cultivated not just through traditional study and reflection but also through lived experience, which fosters judgment and intuition. While life itself may not produce scientific geniuses like Newton or Euler, it can nonetheless nurture extraordinary minds adept at mastering the calculations of War, exemplified by military leaders like Condé or Frederick. These individuals possess the keen mental agility required to handle the nuances of command on the battlefield.

Therefore, to affirm the intellectual merit of military activity, we do not need to resort to untruths or mere academic formalities that obscure rather than reveal its nature. Indeed, history shows us that no genuinely great and distinguished commander has ever been hampered by a limited or narrow mind. Yet, numerous examples exist of individuals who, despite performing with notable distinction in lower ranks, could not meet the demands of the highest roles due to insufficient intellectual capacity. Naturally, even among those who hold the esteemed position of Commander-in-Chief, capabilities vary according to their individual talents and the extent of authority and responsibility they command. It is clear that different levels of command require knowledge that differs in depth, with higher ranks requiring a far more comprehensive, adaptive approach than is necessary for lower ranks.

46. Science Must Become Art.

A unique and essential condition for understanding the conduct of War is that this knowledge must pass fully into one's mind, transforming from something objective into something deeply personal and intrinsic. In most other arts or practical fields, a person can rely on knowledge learned once, even if they no longer engage with its core spirit or principles on a daily basis, and can reference external sources as needed. For instance, an architect calculating the strength of a pier uses established data and applies rules that he might execute almost mechanically. The conclusions he draws may not even feel like a product of his intellect, as he may rely heavily on external guides and calculations.

But in War, this approach is impossible. The moral uncertainties, the constantly changing scenarios, and the relentless pace of decisions require a commander to carry within himself an internalized framework of knowledge that he can call upon at any moment. There is no time to consult external formulas or theoretical guides when so much is at stake. Every decision must come from a deep, internalized understanding. The commander must be prepared at each heartbeat, able to rely on his mental foundation to produce intuitive, timely decisions.

This is the reason why those who are skilled in War seem to act with ease, as though their decisions require little effort, and why observers often attribute their success to "natural talent." By "natural talent," however, we mean an ability that has been painstakingly shaped through observation, study, and countless experiences, transforming acquired knowledge into a part of their intuitive faculties. When knowledge is fully assimilated and blended with one's mental life, it ceases to be a mere collection of facts or rules and instead becomes a source of genuine power.

Through these reflections, we believe we have illuminated the true nature of a theory for the conduct of War, outlining a path to its solution. When examining the two domains of War—tactics and strategy—the latter undoubtedly poses the greater challenges for theory. This is because tactics is confined to a specific, well-defined area of operation, with a focused set of objectives, whereas strategy, with its direct aim of achieving peace, opens a vast and fluid field of possibilities. The Commander-in-Chief must, by necessity, navigate these ultimate strategic goals with clarity and foresight. As a result, the strategic domain, where he operates, demands an understanding of complex variables and unforeseeable outcomes, making it exceptionally challenging.

Theory, therefore, particularly at the highest level of command, must often limit itself to basic principles and guiding insights rather than attempting to prescribe exact steps. This approach allows theory to offer the Commander an enhanced perspective that aids him in aligning his actions with sound judgment rather than binding him to rigid rules that may conflict with reality. Theory should serve to guide and strengthen his understanding, allowing him to act with greater confidence and consistency, without forcing him to go against his instincts or internal judgments simply to adhere to an abstract, "objective" principle.

In this way, a well-constructed theory of War can be both practical and insightful, serving as a support to the Commander's intellect and enhancing his natural abilities without encumbering him with inflexible doctrines or rigid systems. It is a framework that respects the fluid nature of War, helping the Commander remain true to his understanding and enabling him to execute decisions effectively in the face of ever-shifting challenges.

Chapter III. Art or Science of War

1.—Usage Still Unsettled (Power and Knowledge. Science When Mere Knowing; Art, When Doing, Is the Object.)

The choice between these terms seems to be The question remains unresolved, and there doesn't seem to be a consensus on the true basis for deciding it, though the solution is, in fact, straightforward. As we have already clarified elsewhere, "knowing" is not the same as "doing." These two concepts are so distinct from one another that confusing them would overlook an essential difference. "Doing," or the act of carrying out, cannot simply be captured within the pages of a book, and thus, we can argue that a book should never be titled as an "Art" because it cannot fully embody the execution of what it attempts to instruct. However, due to established conventions, we often group the requisite knowledge for practicing an art under the term "theory of art," or simply "art." For instance, the Art of Building includes various fields of knowledge necessary to construct a building effectively, though these individual fields may themselves be complete sciences.

Therefore, it is reasonable to maintain this convention, referring to such knowledge collectively as "Art" when the objective is to enable someone to "do" or "be capable of doing," as seen in terms like the Art of

Building. Conversely, we use "Science" when pure knowledge is the primary objective, as in the Sciences of Mathematics or Astronomy. It follows logically that some complete sciences will be included within the scope of many arts, and this overlap should not confuse us. However, it's worth noting that even the purest of sciences contains an element of "Art." In Mathematics, for instance, the practical application of figures and algebra represents an art. This is but one example among many.

The fundamental reason for this blurring between science and art is that, while the distinction between knowledge and ability is clear in the abstract, it becomes harder to identify a strict dividing line between them within individuals. Knowledge and ability, while distinctly different in concept, often intermingle when put into practice, making it challenging to isolate them completely within human action.

2. Difficulty of Separating Perception from Judgment. (Art of War.)

Indeed, all forms of thinking are inherently forms of Art. The logician marks a distinction when determining where the process of pure cognition, or acquiring factual premises, ends, and where judgment—an active interpretation or decision—begins. It is precisely at this juncture that Art enters, for judgment itself is an artful act, reliant on insight and discernment rather than mere data accumulation. Furthermore, even the mind's initial perception and organization of information is another layer of judgment, and thus also a form of Art. And, if we take this line of thinking even further, the sensory perception of reality—how we experience and categorize our sensory input—is also tied to judgment and therefore infused with Art.

In sum, it is impossible to imagine a human being with only the faculty for cognition, devoid of any judgment, or vice versa; this interdependence means that Art and Science can never be entirely separated. The more these abstract elements of understanding manifest as concrete actions and expressions in the world, the more we may distinguish their realms: Art concerns itself with creation, with producing something anew, whereas Science occupies itself with the processes of inquiry, analysis, and understanding. Thus, in light of this intertwined nature, it is indeed more suitable to speak of the "Art of War" rather than the "Science of War," as War's goals and execution involve creative application more than rigid scientific certainty.

Having established this conceptual framework, we now assert that, in the strictest sense, War is neither truly an Art nor a Science. Relying on the assumption that it must be categorized as either has misled thinkers into viewing War alongside traditional arts or sciences, giving rise to flawed analogies that have obstructed true understanding. This miscategorization has been noted previously, prompting some to suggest that War might instead be viewed as a type of "handicraft." Yet, classifying War as a mere handicraft does more harm than good, for a handicraft is essentially an elementary or limited art, bound by rigid, well-defined rules.

Historically, the Art of War did indeed follow a regimented, almost mechanical approach for a time—as seen during the era of the Condottieri, the mercenary leaders of Renaissance Italy. But this development stemmed less from the intrinsic nature of War than from external pressures. Military history itself illustrates how, during that period, the practice of War strayed far from its natural course and was constrained by external, rather than organic, influences. This divergence underlines the reality that War cannot, in truth, be confined by the rigidities of handicraft, or by the strict categories of art or science.

3. War Is Part of The Intercourse of The Human Race.

In light of this, we assert that War does not truly belong to the realm of Arts and Sciences; instead, it finds its place within the broader sphere of social life and interaction. War is fundamentally a struggle of significant, conflicting interests that are ultimately resolved through bloodshed, setting it apart from other forms of human conflict only by its recourse to violence. Rather than forcing War into comparisons with any traditional Art, it would be more appropriate to view it as akin to competitive business activities—a battlefield of human motives, aspirations, and strategies, each party striving to overcome the other. Business competition, after all, represents a clash of interests that involves careful maneuvers and a keen sense of positioning, though without the physical violence of War.

War is even more closely aligned with the realm of State policy, which itself can be seen as a grand-scale version of business competition, where the stakes and players are magnified. State policy is, in fact, the very environment from which War arises; it is the fertile ground in which the roots of War take shape, where its form begins to emerge in latent, undeveloped outlines. In a way, War within State policy can be compared to the traits of a living organism existing in its earliest, embryonic form. Just as every quality of a living being is implicit in its embryo, so too are the qualities and potentialities of War concealed within the sphere of policy, waiting to materialize in response to the broader forces at play.

In this regard, the analogy between War and the dynamics of policy has only grown more relevant since Clausewitz's time. Today, as State priorities increasingly focus on developing infrastructure and fostering economic competition, the connection between War and State policy has tightened. Modern States are intensely focused on cultivating their economic systems, building trade networks, and advancing technological dominance—all of which heighten the likelihood of conflict. While conferences like those held at The Hague aim to prevent wars, such gatherings only delay the inevitable tensions that accompany great nations competing for global influence. Thus, War, as it emerges from the crucible of State interests, is less an art to be perfected than an extension of a larger social and political drama, driven by human ambition and the complex interplay of global power dynamics.

4. Difference.

The fundamental distinction lies in the fact that War is not an exercise of will imposed upon lifeless matter, as seen in the mechanical Arts, nor is it a force directed toward a living but compliant subject, like the human mind and emotions in the expressive or ideal Arts. Rather, War is a direct confrontation with a living and actively resisting opponent. The inapplicability of Arts and Sciences categories to such an activity is immediately evident. This also clarifies why attempts to derive rigid laws from War, akin to those applicable to the physical world, have consistently led to misconceptions and misunderstandings.

Despite this, some theorists persist in modeling War on the principles of the mechanical Arts, as though it could be directed through a formulaic set of rules. Imitating the ideal Arts was never really an option, as they too often disregard strict rules and remain fluid, with established principles proving to be temporary or flawed. These principles are continually eroded and reshaped by shifting social currents, opinions, and cultural norms. As a result, a rigid theoretical approach to War grounded in universal rules has been continually proven inadequate and out of place.

Whether a dynamic, living confrontation such as War can ever be governed by overarching laws, and whether those laws can provide valuable guidance, will be explored in this book. However, it is self-evident that this subject—like any that falls within human comprehension—can be illuminated and made somewhat transparent by analytical thought. This possibility of clarifying War's intrinsic relationships and core principles is, in itself, sufficient to support the creation of a theory.

Chapter IV. Methodicism

To clarify our perspective on the concepts of method and methodology, which hold substantial importance in War, let us briefly examine the logical structure through which the realm of action is guided and controlled, much like the roles of orderly officials in a well-organized administration.

In its broadest sense, Law applies to both understanding and action and holds a subjective or even arbitrary quality in its literal interpretation, representing the underlying framework governing our interactions with the world and external objects. As an element of understanding, Law reflects the interrelations and outcomes between objects; when tied to the will, it functions as a driver of actions, essentially equivalent to a command or prohibition.

Principle, by contrast, is akin to a law for action but lacks strict rigidity. It embodies the spirit and essence of law, granting judgment more latitude in cases where the unique complexities of reality defy strict application. Thus, principles act as guiding stars for action, allowing the individual to determine when and where they apply by recognizing instances where they fall short. Principles become a genuine aid because of this flexibility.

Principles are termed objective when derived from universal truths and thus hold equal relevance to all; they are subjective, often termed maxims, when they involve personal nuances, making them particularly valuable only to the individual who holds them.

Rule often parallels Law, yet retains flexibility in application. We might say "no rule without exceptions," suggesting freedom in application that contrasts with the rigidity of Law, where exceptions are less tolerable.

In another sense, Rule acts as a tool for uncovering hidden truths through specific signs that can then apply the intended law to the broader truth. For instance, all gaming rules, shortcuts in mathematics, and similar tools serve to extract truth from a single, readily accessible indicator.

Directions and instructions serve as specific guidelines influencing numerous minor factors too varied and minor to fall under universal laws. These assist by adjusting conduct to fit a wide array of secondary elements, maintaining adherence to overarching objectives.

Method, on the other hand, is a chosen, recurrent approach selected from multiple possible paths of action. Methodicism involves relying on predetermined methods instead of broader principles or detailed instructions, requiring that the cases it addresses share essential similarities. Since no two situations are identical, Methodicism ideally covers as many scenarios as possible based on probable resemblance.

Methodicism does not rest on specific premises; rather, it relies on the most common circumstances to establish an average truth. Through consistent application, Methodicism gradually acquires a mechanical quality, eventually producing right outcomes as if by instinct rather than deliberate choice.

The concept of law in the context of understanding War isn't essential because the varied and unpredictable occurrences of War lack the type of consistent regularity that would benefit from strict definitions of law. Where straightforward explanations are adequate, adopting more complex terminology only introduces unnecessary complication and a tone of artificial sophistication. Moreover, the idea of law governing action is unsuited for War theory because the highly variable and diverse nature of combat lacks any universally consistent principles deserving the name of law.

However, concepts such as principles, rules, prescriptions, and methods are indispensable for a theory of War. They form the foundation of coherent doctrines, where truths can be effectively solidified into clear guidelines. Since tactics is the part of military conduct where theory can most closely approach positive doctrine, these concepts appear most frequently in tactical thinking.

For instance, tactical principles might include maxims like: not deploying cavalry against unbroken infantry except in dire circumstances, only using firearms within effective range, or conserving strength for the climactic engagement. While these principles don't apply absolutely in every instance, they should remain in the commander's mind to ensure the advantages they offer aren't overlooked when relevant.

In cases where a commander's judgment about an opponent's movements or intentions derives from specific observable signs, we refer to this as a rule. For example, noticing unusual cooking activities in the enemy's camp might signal an impending movement. Or, the intentional exposure of certain units may signal a false attack. Here, specific observations lead directly to conclusions, making it possible to derive meaning from isolated clues and interpret them as indicators of broader intent.

An actionable rule, for example, might suggest that if an enemy begins limbering up artillery during combat, it indicates a withdrawal and prompts an aggressive advance. This tactic hinges on the understanding that such a movement typically implies the enemy's readiness to abandon the field, thus creating an opportunity to press the advantage when the opponent is least prepared to resist.

Regulations and methods bring preparatory theories directly into the conduct of War by embedding them as active guiding principles within disciplined troops. Instructions on formations, drills, and field maneuvers are built on regulations and methods; regulations are more prominent in drill manuals, while methods prevail in field instructions. In practice, the actual conduct of War incorporates these as accepted standards of behavior, so theory treats them as foundational practices that influence the course of action.

For those tactical decisions allowing flexibility, there can be no rigid regulations or absolute directives because such impositions would undermine freedom of action. However, methods—meaning standard ways of performing recurring tasks—are useful and can be included in War theory as guiding principles, provided they're not misrepresented as universally applicable systems. Instead, they should be seen as practical approaches that offer a useful framework or shortcut, adaptable according to situational needs, while remaining under the commander's discretion.

The frequent reliance on method in War becomes clearly essential and, indeed, unavoidable when we consider the numerous uncertainties involved. Often, decisions must be based on guesses or incomplete information, as each side is unable to know all the variables influencing the other's strategies. Even if these variables were fully known, time constraints and the sheer scope of possible responses usually prevent either side from carrying out extensive, tailored countermeasures. Therefore, many actions in War are ultimately based on probabilities, a limited range of potential outcomes, and methods that can address general needs rather than specific details.

The scope of any military event is made up of countless small factors, each of which, theoretically, should be accounted for. Since this is often impractical, many assumptions must be made about their cumulative effects, allowing for decisions to be made on what is most likely or broadly applicable. Furthermore, as we move down the chain of command, the number of officers increases. Therefore, at lower ranks, less is left to individual discretion, as frontline officers primarily rely on existing regulations and their personal experience. Here, methodical processes are critical, not only as a foundation for their decision-making but also as a safeguard against reckless or erroneous judgments, which can have especially high costs in these ranks.

Beyond necessity, method also brings real benefits. Repetition of a standard method improves the overall performance of the military apparatus, creating a smooth and efficient machine. Troops become more accurate, coordinated, and responsive, and the natural friction that arises in any coordinated movement decreases, making for more reliable execution.

Thus, the importance of method grows as one moves down the ranks and becomes less essential as one ascends to higher command levels. At lower levels, method acts as a guide for actions that are routine or limited in scope; at higher levels, however, its value declines. Method is suited to tactics more than strategy, as the latter operates on broader scales with complex interdependencies and unique scenarios requiring judgment rather than formulaic responses. War, in its essence, is not composed of a multitude of tiny occurrences that even out over time. Instead, it consists of singular, crucial events that require bespoke responses. War is less like a vast field of identical stalks to be uniformly mowed and more like a forest of unique, towering trees, each demanding a tailored approach.

The suitability of method within military operations is not dictated solely by rank but is shaped by the scope and nature of the decisions being made. Higher levels in the chain of command are typically focused on overarching objectives, making method a less applicable tool. For instance, predefined orders of battle or rigid formations for advance guards and outposts can restrict both the General and his subordinates. While a General may have developed these methods himself and can adapt them to circumstances, they are more appropriately grounded in theory due to the general characteristics of troops and equipment.

However, any method that seeks to prescribe comprehensive, pre-made plans for entire wars or campaigns as if from an automated process is fundamentally flawed. Such rigid plans cannot account for the complexity and unpredictability inherent in real conflict, and their application in such high-level planning is not only impractical but counterproductive. In War, adaptive thinking is paramount, and while method serves as a valuable tool within certain bounds, it must yield to strategy and creativity in the highest and most complex echelons of command.

As long as a coherent and robust theory for the conduct of War remains absent, there is a risk that method, or standardized approaches to action, will overextend its influence even into the highest spheres of command. Many of those occupying high command positions may not have had opportunities for deep study or engagement with broader strategic principles and higher state interests. Consequently, when faced with the convoluted and inconsistent writings of theorists or critics, they often rely on their inherent good sense, which in turn rejects these ambiguous prescriptions. However, having no foundation beyond their own direct experiences, they fall back on what experience alone provides: the imitation of methods historically used by notable commanders.

This reliance on imitation has led to recurring patterns of action, transforming methods into a kind of standard approach. We see this in Frederick the Great's Generals, who frequently employed the oblique order of battle, or in the French Revolution's Generals, who preferred turning movements with extended battle lines, and finally in Napoleon's commanders, who aggressively advanced in massed formations. The repeated application of these approaches exemplifies how imitation can elevate method to a near-standard in high military operations.

An improved and accessible theory could transform how commanders in the highest ranks approach War by fostering an independent capacity for analysis and judgment. Rather than relying on imitation, commanders would develop methods grounded in principles derived from well-founded theories. Imitating a great commander's methods is tempting, yet there is inevitably something subjective in the way each one conducts War. Each leader brings a unique perspective and style, which does not always align with that of those who would emulate them.

However, eliminating this individual flair or "methodicism" entirely from military conduct would neither be feasible nor advisable. Such individuality reflects the general character of a particular War, which often arises from distinctive circumstances. Theory cannot always predict or accommodate these specific factors that shape each conflict. For instance, the Wars of the French Revolution had an unmistakable, unique approach influenced by the period's spirit—a mode of conduct that no theory could have accurately forecast or encapsulated.

The problem arises when a method, initially effective in a specific context, outlasts its usefulness as circumstances shift subtly but significantly. Theory, aided by critical analysis, should strive to prevent the persistence of outdated practices by shedding light on their limitations and the evolving nature of War. The consequences of failing to adapt can be severe, as vividly illustrated by the Prussian Generals in 1806. They adhered stubbornly to the outdated oblique order of Frederick the Great, oblivious to the changing dynamics of warfare. This approach, instead of yielding strategic advantages, led to catastrophic results at Saalfeld and Jena, where Generals Prince Louis, Tauentzien, Grawert, and Ruechel essentially hastened the destruction of Hohenlohe's army. Here, methodicism, worn out and detached from the reality of contemporary tactics, resulted in one of the most disastrous collapses ever experienced by an army in battle.

In sum, an enlightened theory could serve as a preventive tool against outdated methodologies, fostering adaptability in the face of changing circumstances and ensuring that commanders at every level rely not on mechanical imitation but on informed, situationally responsive strategies.

Chapter V. Criticism

The impact of theoretical principles on practical life is most effectively achieved through criticism rather than direct instruction. Criticism allows abstract truths to engage with real events, bringing theoretical concepts closer to life and refining one's understanding through their repeated application. This highlights the need to establish a clear standpoint for criticism alongside theory itself.

In historical narration, which typically outlines events in chronological order and sometimes examines their immediate causes, we distinguish between simple narration and the CRITICAL. Within this CRITICAL examination, we identify three distinct mental operations:

1. Historical Verification: This is the rigorous investigation and clarification of uncertain facts. It falls within historical research and stands separate from theoretical inquiry.

2. Tracing Causes and Effects: This is the essential part of critical inquiry, in which effects are traced back to their causes. This process is invaluable for theory because any theoretical point that relies on experience for validation or explanation must be understood in terms of these causal connections.

3.*Evaluating the Means Used: This is criticism in the strict sense, where we assess the methods and choices made, incorporating praise or blame. Here, theory informs historical understanding and the lessons derived from it.

In these last two critical processes, much depends on dissecting events down to their fundamental elements—reaching undoubted truths rather than resting on subjective assumptions or partial explanations.

However, this cause-effect tracing often encounters significant challenges, particularly in situations where real causes are unknown or ambiguous. War, where details are frequently obscured and motives of key actors are often intentionally hidden or quickly forgotten, presents an extreme case. The nature of war events necessitates that critical narration must advance alongside historical investigation. Yet, even with diligent inquiry, gaps between cause and effect can remain, making it unjustifiable to treat known causes as the definite origins of observed effects. Theory can only demand that such investigations are rigorous; if a full connection cannot be drawn, they should stop short without forcing conclusions. Issues arise only when explanations are stretched to fit the known facts, thereby ascribing undue significance to them.

Another inherent challenge in critical inquiry is that war events rarely arise from a single cause. Instead, they result from multiple factors, which means an unbiased approach alone is insufficient. Critical analysis must also weigh each contributing cause appropriately, necessitating a deeper investigation into each factor's nature. This process can lead into the proper domain of theory, where each element's significance is examined.

In sum, effective critical inquiry in the context of war requires a balanced, cautious approach, one that acknowledges both the complexity of events and the limits of our knowledge. By avoiding forced conclusions and accepting that not all outcomes are fully explainable, criticism becomes a valuable tool for developing theory without falling prey to over-simplified or misleading interpretations.

In critically analyzing methods used in war, we encounter the essential question: What specific outcomes did these chosen methods produce, and were these outcomes anticipated by those in command? This inquiry naturally turns us to the unique effects each method or tool brings to the conduct of war, requiring us to examine their intrinsic nature. In this way, we enter the realm of theoretical investigation since to critique meaningfully is to assess each element against fundamental principles. Effective criticism, therefore, hinges on reaching objective truths, avoiding the pitfall of settling on arbitrary propositions that others could just as easily dispute or counter with equally unfounded assertions. A debate overflowing with such contradictions yields no solid conclusions and thus lacks educational value.

The necessity of analyzing both the causes and the methods used in war brings us inevitably into the domain of theory, a field concerned with universal truths that apply beyond specific cases. Whenever a solid theoretical foundation is available, criticism can build upon it, pausing in its analysis when it reaches a logical conclusion derived from established principles. However, when no such theoretical basis is available, the analysis must delve deeper into the original elements. This pursuit can lead the historian or critic into an overwhelming labyrinth of details, necessitating boundaries for practicality. However, such limitations may arise arbitrarily, and even if they seem reasonable to the critic, they might lack objective justification or fall short of convincing others who demand a broader perspective.

Thus, a well-founded theory serves as the essential cornerstone for effective criticism. Without it, criticism cannot reach that instructive stage where it serves as a demonstration—a clear, irrefutable presentation of insights derived from understanding. But it would be misguided to expect a theory capable of addressing every abstract truth so comprehensively that criticism could simply assign each case to a pre-defined category without further interpretation. Such a rigid expectation would be overly pedantic, hindering criticism from reaching a meaningful engagement with each unique circumstance. Instead, the same spirit of inquiry that generates theory must also guide criticism, allowing it the flexibility to extend beyond the strict boundaries of established doctrine. In this way, criticism can illuminate specific points relevant to the unique demands of each case.

On the other hand, criticism would lose its essential purpose if it became a mechanical exercise in theory application. All positive conclusions reached through theoretical inquiry—be they principles, rules, or methods—tend to lose their universality and absolute truth the more rigidly they are treated as unchanging doctrines. They exist as flexible tools for use when suitable, with the final decision about their application always left to the judgment of those analyzing or conducting the action. These theoretical principles should guide criticism not as fixed, immutable standards, but as aids to judgment. As such, they provide a foundation but must allow for the context-specific interpretations each unique scenario demands.

To illustrate, consider a well-established tactical principle stating that cavalry should generally be placed behind infantry rather than in line with it. It would be shortsighted to condemn every deviation from this principle automatically. Instead, criticism must examine the specific reasoning behind any deviation, reserving the right to invoke the principle only if the justification proves insufficient. Similarly, theory may assert that divided attacks often decrease the probability of success, but it would be unreasonable to attribute every failed operation to a divided attack without closely examining the connection. Equally, we cannot dismiss this theoretical principle entirely if we see a divided attack succeed in a particular case. Criticism's responsibility to investigate cannot permit either a simplistic condemnation or an unquestioning endorsement.

Consequently, criticism rests on the analytical foundation laid by theory. The conclusions that theory has reached do not need to be repeatedly demonstrated by criticism, for theory has already validated them in its process. This allows criticism to draw upon these established insights as a framework, interpreting each new situation in a way that respects the truths derived from theory but also accommodates the nuanced judgments each unique case demands.

Criticism that operates with this dual commitment—to theoretical insight on one hand and to the specific circumstances of each case on the other—achieves a balance that makes it not only a force of judgment but also a force for deeper understanding. This approach demands from the critic an ability to apply theoretical principles wisely, using them to shed light on new circumstances without allowing them to become rigid dictates. In this way, criticism not only evaluates but also evolves, moving theory forward as it adapts its principles to the ever-changing reality of war and its complex dynamics.

This role of criticism, which involves scrutinizing whether specific actions led to anticipated outcomes and if chosen strategies achieved their intended objectives, seems straightforward when causes and effects, means and goals, are closely aligned. For instance, if an army is caught by surprise and is therefore unable to mobilize its forces or resources in an organized and strategic manner, the impact of that surprise is immediate and unambiguous. Or, if military theory asserts that a convergent attack is intended to generate a larger yet less predictable impact, then the critical question is whether the commander's primary goal was indeed to achieve this high-stakes outcome. If so, then the convergent strategy aligns well with the objective. However, if the intent behind this approach was to secure a more predictable victory, not rooted in any unique situation but based solely on the general qualities of a convergent attack—as has often been the case—then this reveals a fundamental misunderstanding of the strategy's nature, constituting a critical error.

In these cases, where we deal with immediate consequences and straightforward objectives, the process of military analysis and critique is relatively straightforward. One can engage in such examination by isolating these elements from the broader campaign and focusing solely on their specific impacts. Yet, war is far from isolated; it is a tapestry of interconnected actions, each one rippling across the whole. Any action, no matter how seemingly minor, has repercussions that extend to the overarching objectives of a campaign, subtly influencing or modifying the ultimate outcome. Similarly, each strategic decision, however narrow in its immediate scope, inevitably resonates with broader goals.

Thus, we can trace the effects of a cause as far as the sequence of meaningful events continues, and we cannot confine our analysis solely to whether a particular strategy achieved an immediate objective. Instead, we must also consider each short-term goal as a stepping stone toward higher objectives, following this chain upward until we arrive at a fundamental goal that no longer requires validation—often, in the case of pivotal or conclusive decisions, this ultimate objective is peace itself. With each step up this hierarchy, a new perspective emerges, potentially altering our judgment of strategies that may have seemed sound at a lower level but require reassessment from a broader view.

In the critical analysis of a military action, investigating causes and evaluating means relative to ends must proceed in tandem. Identifying root causes enables us to uncover the aspects truly worth examining. This recursive movement up and down the chain of cause and effect presents substantial challenges; the further removed a cause is from the immediate event, the greater the array of other influencing factors that must be simultaneously considered, understood in terms of their roles, and ultimately disentangled. The greater the significance of an event, the more complex the interplay of individual forces and conditions shaping it becomes. For example, if we understand why a particular battle was lost, we also gain insight into a part of the larger reasons behind the repercussions this loss had on the entire war. However, this represents only a fraction of the whole, as additional causes will also shape the final outcome to varying degrees.

This complexity is equally present when we assess strategies and their relation to higher objectives. The loftier the objective, the more numerous and interdependent the strategies employed to achieve it must be. The final objective of the war is a culmination of all simultaneous army actions, making it necessary for the analysis to encompass not only what each unit has done but also what each could have done to contribute.

Consequently, this can open a broad field of inquiry, one in which it is easy to become disoriented, given that we are often forced to rely on a series of informed assumptions. These assumptions cover various factors that may not be immediately observable but almost certainly played a role and, therefore, cannot be ignored.

In this intricate process, the critic must avoid becoming lost in speculative hypotheses while simultaneously navigating the reality that not all conditions and causes will be visible in concrete form. Instead, critique demands a delicate balance between objective examination of concrete events and the interpretive reconstruction of plausible but unseen factors. Through this dual lens, the critic seeks not only to unravel the specific results of each action but to understand how each choice, however indirect, contributed to the ultimate aims. Thus, criticism in war requires a methodical yet adaptive approach, continually shifting focus from the narrow and immediate to the broad and cumulative, illuminating how individual actions fit within the broader tapestry of military objectives.

When, in 1797, Buonaparte led the Army of Italy from the Tagliamento towards the Archduke Charles, his primary goal was to compel the Archduke into a decisive engagement before reinforcements from the Rhine could strengthen the Austrian forces. If we examine only this immediate objective, the choice of strategy appears sound and well-justified by the outcome. With his overwhelming numerical superiority, Buonaparte pressed forward, meeting only token resistance as the Archduke, recognizing his disadvantage, quickly retreated and relinquished control of the Norican Alps passages.

This favorable outcome presented Buonaparte with fresh strategic opportunities. He could now consider pushing into the Austrian heartland, potentially facilitating coordination with the Rhine armies under Moreau and Hoche and opening communication lines. From Buonaparte's immediate perspective, this course of action seemed reasonable. However, if we adopt the vantage of the French Directory, which had a broader overview and could assess that the Rhine armies would not be campaign-ready for another six weeks, Buonaparte's maneuver over the Norican Alps appears more precarious. Should Austria have drawn substantial reinforcements from their forces on the Rhine to support the Archduke in Styria, Buonaparte's Army of Italy could have been severely outmatched, possibly jeopardizing not just his campaign but the entire war effort. This awareness likely influenced Buonaparte's swift readiness to sign the Leoben armistice when he reached Villach, sensing the inherent risk in an unchecked advance.

If we elevate our critical analysis further, acknowledging that Austria lacked reserves between the Archduke's forces and Vienna, Buonaparte's advance takes on an entirely new strategic significance. The very capital of Austria lay vulnerable. Assuming Buonaparte recognized that Vienna was effectively unguarded and understood he still held a numerical advantage over the Archduke, his offensive into Austrian territory becomes purposeful, contingent on the value Austria placed on the security of its capital. Should the Austrian government deem the loss of Vienna intolerable, even considering peace terms to avoid this outcome, the advance carries the highest strategic value. If Buonaparte had any credible indication of this, our analysis could reasonably end here. But if this response from Austria was speculative, then our critical perspective must broaden further, considering what might have occurred if the Austrian leadership had chosen to abandon Vienna and withdraw into the more extensive reaches of their empire.

To pursue this question, we must examine the projected movements of the Rhine armies on both sides, considering the numerical superiority held by the French forces—130,000 to Austria's 80,000—suggesting that, all else being equal, France could expect a favorable outcome. This line of inquiry then raises the question of the Directory's potential response to a French victory: Would they push their success to the farthest Austrian frontiers, striving for the total collapse of Austria's power? Or would they consider a more restrained approach, perhaps annexing territories to secure a peace accord? Evaluating the probable results of each scenario enables us to gauge the likely decisions of the Directory.

Should our critical exploration reveal that France's forces were insufficient for a full subjugation of Austria, and thus at risk of an eventual reversal of positions, the implications for the Army of Italy's actions would be profound. Even partial territorial gains might strain French resources, positioning them in precarious strategic conditions. This consideration likely influenced Buonaparte, despite his awareness of the Archduke's weakened state, to pursue peace at Campo Formio, a treaty that, while exacting considerable concessions, stopped short of overly burdensome terms for Austria.

The French government could not have reasonably predicted the comparatively moderate terms of Campo Formio. Therefore, if their advance was based on more than mere ambition, two major considerations must have shaped their judgment. First, they may have evaluated Austria's sensitivity to the looming outcomes and weighed whether, despite favorable odds, Austria would deem the sacrifices of ongoing war acceptable or if a face-saving peace might avert such sacrifices. Second, there was the possibility that Austria, rather than rationally analyzing their position, would instead be thoroughly demoralized by their recent setbacks, capitulating to the French in a gesture of resignation.

In each of these scenarios, critical evaluation demands we look not only at the immediate cause-and-effect relationship between action and outcome but also at how successive levels of strategic ambition interact, creating a chain of considerations that extends all the way to the overarching political aims and the terms of eventual peace.

The matter under examination here is far from an abstract debate; rather, it addresses a vital, grounded issue frequently encountered when leaders consider the merits of pursuing a war to its utmost limits. This question, with its undeniable gravity, often acts as a powerful check on the willingness to adopt extreme measures, given the significant risks associated with such pursuits.

The second consideration is equally critical because, in war, we engage not with distant, idealized concepts but with immediate, concrete realities that must be accounted for consistently. Even Napoleon himself was keenly aware of the powerful fear his very presence instilled—a psychological weapon he wielded to considerable effect. His reliance on this psychological edge even led him to push boldly toward Moscow; but on that occasion, his calculations led him to a costly misjudgment. By 1812, the dread of Napoleon had been eroded by years of relentless, exhaustive warfare that had strained his forces and depleted his resources. In 1797, however, this dread was fresh and potent, and the knowledge of how to resist such a colossal pressure was not yet widely understood or embedded in the psyche of his adversaries. Nevertheless, Napoleon's boldness in 1797 might still have brought about negative outcomes had he not, with what seemed almost an instinctive caution, opted to sign the Treaty of Campo Formio—a peace of moderate terms that avoided potentially disastrous escalations.

These reflections, when brought together, reveal the vast scope, complexity, and nuanced character of any fully developed critical examination of strategic choices, especially when those choices are significant enough to sway the fate of entire campaigns or wars. Such an analysis underscores that in addition to a deep theoretical understanding, an innate talent for strategic insight is crucial in evaluating military decisions. This innate talent is especially necessary when it comes to untangling the web of interrelated events and isolating the connections that genuinely impact the outcome, while disregarding the overwhelming number of irrelevant or secondary factors.

Moreover, talent plays an indispensable role in another way within critical assessments. Effective criticism should not limit itself to assessing decisions that were made; it must also evaluate potential alternative courses of action, weighing the choices that could have been taken under the circumstances. This process of generating alternatives relies not merely on dissecting the options that were selected but on proposing new possibilities—an imaginative leap that requires a kind of creative thought beyond the scope of pure analysis. Even when there may be only a limited number of realistic alternatives, the exercise of identifying those that were not chosen calls for an inventive quality that cannot be substituted by standard theoretical methodologies, depending instead on the critic's natural creativity and insight.

While it may be exaggerated to credit even the most simple maneuvers, like turning a position, as supreme acts of genius, the ability to imagine alternative strategies demonstrates a vital capacity for independent thought and creativity in criticism, and this capacity significantly elevates the value of the critical examination. Take, for example, Napoleon's actions on July 30, 1796. Faced with the siege of Mantua, he chose to break it off temporarily, assembling his forces to intercept the Austrian army, which was approaching in separate columns to relieve the besieged fortress. This maneuver resulted in a series of resounding victories, which were later replicated on an even grander scale during repeated attempts to lift the siege. The success of these actions has earned widespread admiration and acclaim.

However, this decision by Napoleon meant abandoning the siege entirely, as there was no practical means of preserving the siege artillery, which could not be replaced in the ongoing campaign. Mantua was reduced to a mere blockade, and, despite Napoleon's battlefield successes, the city—whose defenses might have fallen swiftly had the siege persisted—held out for an additional six months.

Critics have generally accepted this drawback as an inevitable consequence, with no better solution proposed, dismissing the idea of holding off a relief force from entrenched defensive lines as outdated, a tactic long since abandoned. Yet in the era of Louis XIV, this approach had been used with notable success; only the force of shifting military fashions seems to explain its absence from consideration in this instance. Had the idea of this defense strategy even been briefly entertained, further scrutiny might have shown that a well-entrenched force of 40,000 elite infantry under Napoleon's command could have held the lines around Mantua against the 50,000 troops under Wurmser, with little risk of a direct assault.

Exploring this option fully is beyond our current scope, but enough has been said to suggest that such a course merited serious consideration. Whether Napoleon himself ever entertained the idea remains uncertain, as neither his memoirs nor contemporary sources offer any insight on the matter. Nor has it been addressed in critical literature, suggesting that the concept itself may have simply faded from the collective military consciousness of the time. The notion of resurrecting this approach is hardly revolutionary, as it comes naturally to those willing to challenge prevailing orthodoxies. Nevertheless, it is essential for such ideas to be revisited and included in an evaluation, where they can be compared against the actual choices made by Napoleon. No matter the outcome of such a comparison, the task of criticism is to ensure all realistic possibilities are brought to the table and thoroughly evaluated.

In conclusion, the value of this kind of expansive, multi-dimensional criticism lies in its capacity to deepen our understanding of strategic decisions, providing a comprehensive perspective that enriches our grasp of both the successes and potential alternatives in complex military contexts. It requires a balance of practical judgment, theoretical knowledge, and an imaginative openness to all viable options, embodying a critical ideal that enhances not only our knowledge of history but also the strategic acumen with which we approach future challenges.

When Buonaparte, in February 1814, after securing victories at Etoges, Champ-Aubert, and Montmirail, decided to turn away from Blücher's army and instead confront Schwartzenberg, defeating his forces at Montereau and Mormant, he was met with universal admiration. Observers applauded Buonaparte's tactical ingenuity, recognizing his skill in concentrating his forces to exploit the errors of his adversaries, who had unwisely dispersed their troops. This rapid and calculated shift, in which he directed his full strength alternately toward one opponent and then another, was seen as a masterstroke of command. Although these dynamic maneuvers ultimately did not stave off his defeat, it has generally been viewed that Buonaparte's failure to alter the campaign's outcome was beyond his control, rather than a result of any flaw in his approach.

However, few have paused to consider an alternative question: what might have transpired if, rather than diverting his efforts from Blücher to engage Schwartzenberg, Buonaparte had instead launched a second, sustained attack on Blücher, driving him toward the Rhine? We are convinced that such a choice would have fundamentally altered the campaign's trajectory. Indeed, we believe that, faced with Buonaparte's relentless pursuit, the Allied forces would likely have abandoned their advance on Paris, retreating instead beyond the Rhine. While we do not insist that others share our conviction, anyone versed in the principles of strategy will recognize, at the very mention of this alternative course, that it holds significant potential and should be considered seriously within a critical analysis.

In this instance, the evidence necessary to support this alternative is readily apparent; yet, much like the previous example, it has often been ignored due to the prevalence of narrow perspectives and a lack of independent judgment. The tendency to adopt fixed, one-sided views without entertaining possible alternatives has precluded the exploration of other viable options.

From the necessity of proposing better alternatives than those criticized has emerged a common form of criticism—one that simply points to other options without sufficiently proving their advantages over the original choice. This approach, merely suggesting an improvement without fully demonstrating its merit, fails to convince all audiences. As a result, a chorus of competing views arises, with different critics each proposing alternatives, leading to an ongoing debate that lacks any established foundation upon which a reasoned discourse can be built. Such unfocused exchanges have filled military literature with a plethora of disjointed opinions and arguments.

The form of demonstration we advocate is essential, especially when the superiority of an alternative is not immediately obvious and open to question. This demonstration should include a thorough examination of each approach on its own merits and then an evaluation of how well each aligns with the intended goal. By tracing the reasoning back to core principles, debate can be resolved—or at least refined into new insights—while the typical cycle of pros and cons merely leaves arguments perpetually at odds, each canceling the other out in a fruitless stalemate.

For instance, if we were to substantiate our belief that the continued pursuit of Blücher would have proven more effective than diverting attention to Schwartzenberg, we would ground our reasoning in a series of foundational truths, clearly illustrating that the course we propose aligns more closely with Buonaparte's strategic goals than the alternative he actually chose.

1. Advantage of Maintaining Direction: Generally, it is strategically wiser to concentrate efforts in a single direction, as diversions often waste valuable time and reduce the cumulative pressure on the enemy. By continuing strikes in one direction, especially where the enemy's morale is already compromised due to prior losses, the probability of further successes increases. In doing so, none of the advantage already secured is dissipated or rendered inactive, maximizing the impact of each subsequent blow.

2. Priority of Targeting Blücher: Although numerically weaker than Schwartzenberg, Blücher's aggressive and enterprising nature made him a far more critical adversary. His persistence posed a unique threat, effectively acting as the central force that encouraged and drew other Allied forces into action. Therefore, neutralizing Blücher would weaken the cohesion and morale of the opposing forces more substantially than focusing on Schwartzenberg.

3. Impact of Blücher's Losses: The extent of Blücher's casualties amounted almost to a decisive defeat, giving Buonaparte a clear upper hand. This advantage made Blücher's retreat to the Rhine highly probable, especially since he had limited reinforcements waiting there. Consequently, a focused pursuit of Blücher would likely result in pushing him back across the Rhine, removing him from the immediate theater and yielding a crucial strategic victory.

4. Psychological Impact on Schwartzenberg's Staff: No other action could generate the same psychological effect as a concentrated blow against Blücher, whose defeat would resonate dramatically through Allied ranks. For Schwartzenberg's weak and indecisive staff, this would appear formidable, stoking fear and hesitation. While recent setbacks against Buonaparte—like the defeats of the Crown Prince of Württemberg at Montereau and Count Wittgenstein at Mormant—were certainly known to them, such incidents occurred closer to home. In contrast, devastating news of Blücher's rout, stretching along the Marne and across to the Rhine, would have arrived more indirectly, amplifying its impact through escalating rumors. Indeed, the intense maneuvers Buonaparte later attempted at Vitry in March sought to play on these very fears, aiming to sway the Allies with the threat of a strategic envelopment. However, this was attempted under markedly different conditions, following his defeats at Laon and Arcis, and when Blücher, by then commanding 100,000 men, was already in closer communication with Schwartzenberg.

The analysis demonstrates that a concerted effort against Blücher could have yielded more sustainable advantages for Buonaparte, influencing not only the military balance but also the broader strategic environment.

There are, without a doubt, individuals who may still remain unconvinced by the preceding arguments. Nevertheless, they cannot counter by claiming that "while Buonaparte threatened Schwartzenberg's base with his advance toward the Rhine, Schwartzenberg simultaneously jeopardized Buonaparte's communications with Paris," as the previous points make clear that Schwartzenberg would likely not have considered advancing on Paris at all.

To further clarify using the campaign of 1796 as an example: Buonaparte saw the course he pursued as the most certain means of defeating the Austrian forces. However, assuming that was indeed the case, the resulting victory would have been largely superficial, with minimal practical effect on the fall of Mantua. The approach we might have advocated would, in our view, have offered a much more reliable means of preventing Mantua's relief. Yet, even if we hypothetically accept Buonaparte's perspective—that his method was more assured of success—the question then narrows to a choice between achieving a somewhat more certain but less impactful victory on one hand, and a victory of greater potential significance, though perhaps less certain, on the other.

Framed in this way, boldness would naturally lean toward the second option. It suggests a readiness to choose a riskier but vastly more meaningful outcome, rather than settling for the security of a safer yet ultimately less valuable victory. This consideration, unfortunately, may have been overlooked in Buonaparte's decision, which might have appeared justifiable only at a glance. While Buonaparte was far from lacking in boldness, it is likely that he did not grasp the full implications of his decision as thoroughly as we might now with the benefit of hindsight.

In analyzing the selection of military strategies, it is also essential for the critic to draw on examples from military history, as experience is a far more reliable guide in the art of war than any abstract or philosophical theory. However, the use of historical examples is bound by certain conditions, which merit a separate examination in their own right. Unfortunately, these conditions are so often disregarded that references to history typically serve only to muddy the understanding rather than clarify it.

One final and critical point remains: how far should a critic, when evaluating specific military decisions, leverage a broad perspective and the knowledge of outcomes that only hindsight allows? Should a critic not, at times, put aside this retrospective view in order to better approximate the actual circumstances and pressures that surrounded the chief actor at the time? This question is crucial, for it determines the scope and boundaries of informed critique. Knowing when to consider or ignore outcomes, and to place oneself as much as possible in the moment of decision, is essential to assessing events with the fairness they deserve.

When criticism evaluates actions, offering either praise or censure, it should aim to place itself as closely as possible in the mindset of the person who acted, trying to gather all available knowledge that person had and understanding the motives that guided them. At the same time, it should disregard what the actor could not have known, especially the final outcome. Yet, this ideal remains unattainable because the precise conditions and circumstances that led to a decision can never be reconstructed in the exact way they were perceived by the original decision-maker. Numerous smaller factors, which may have subtly influenced the outcome, often go unnoticed, and some subjective motivations remain forever hidden.

Such subjective factors might only come to light through personal memoirs or insights from the actor's closest confidants; even then, they are often selectively presented or even misrepresented. Thus, criticism must inevitably forgo a portion of the context that was real and immediate to those being criticized.

At the same time, the challenge of ignoring what criticism now knows in hindsight is significant, especially regarding elements that are truly central to understanding events. Ignoring irrelevant or accidental circumstances is relatively easy, but when it comes to fundamental information, it becomes exceedingly difficult—almost impossible.

Let us first consider the impact of knowing the final outcome. When a result arises from a combination of factors rather than mere chance, it becomes nearly impossible for a critic to disregard this knowledge entirely. For this outcome colors the interpretation of the events leading up to it, often illuminating facets that may have been overlooked otherwise. Indeed, military history, with its repository of outcomes and consequences, is itself a resource for criticism, enhancing understanding through the lens of final results. Therefore, even if a critic attempts to disregard outcomes in certain cases, achieving total impartiality is impractical.

This challenge of hindsight bias extends not only to outcomes but also to prior events and data that form the basis of decisions. Criticism typically has access to a wider array of facts than the individuals involved had at the time of action. It might seem straightforward to exclude these additional insights, but this is more complex than it appears. Much of the knowledge regarding prior events is grounded not only in concrete data but also in speculation and assumptions that filled gaps in real-time information. Where information was lacking, supposition filled the void, often guiding actions as though these conjectures were confirmed facts.

In the realm of criticism, when it possesses concrete knowledge of previous and concurrent events, can it genuinely avoid being influenced by this knowledge? For instance, when examining what was unknown to the actor at the moment of action, the critic inevitably considers what they themselves might have deemed probable in similar circumstances. Just as it's challenging to disregard knowledge of outcomes, it is equally difficult to ignore additional contextual knowledge about prior and concurrent events, for both create an inevitable lens through which actions and decisions are judged.

Thus, the task of criticism, while aiming for an objective analysis of decisions in their own context, cannot wholly disregard the advantage of hindsight. Instead, it must strive to balance this understanding with a cautious and empathetic approximation of what the person acting saw, felt, and understood, knowing that the ultimate fairness of judgment lies somewhere between full detachment and the wisdom of hindsight.

When a critic seeks to evaluate a particular act, assigning either praise or blame, they can only partially step into the perspective of the individual responsible for that action. In some cases, this can be done effectively enough to serve practical purposes, but in other instances, the gap between the critic's understanding and the actor's perspective is far wider, and it's essential never to lose sight of this reality.

Complete alignment between critic and actor, however, is neither feasible nor desirable. In military affairs, as in any field requiring skill, a natural aptitude, or talent, is indispensable. This talent varies in degree and can sometimes surpass that of the critic, particularly when dealing with figures of extraordinary ability, such as Frederick or Buonaparte. As a result, if criticism is to offer insights even in cases involving remarkable talent, it must use the broader perspective that hindsight affords, rather than treating the solution devised by a great general as though it were a mere calculation. Through the unfolding of events and the precise convergence of circumstances, criticism can acknowledge the profound impact of genius and recognize the unique combination of factors that such genius might have intuitively grasped.

For any act of genius, however small, it is crucial for criticism to assume an elevated standpoint, integrating objective bases for judgment that allow the critic to minimize personal bias and avoid using their own limited understanding as a universal standard. This higher ground ensures that the critic's assessment, informed by the full context, does not come across as a presumptuous emulation of the individual's own talent. Instead, this elevated perspective prevents the critic from presenting their insights as though they inherently possess the wisdom evident only after careful study of the event.

Despite this, it is easy to fall into the trap of vanity, where critics may unconsciously assume a tone implying that their grasp of the event's intricacies comes from personal expertise. Such an assumption, though deceptive, is a pitfall critics may slip into, often resulting in disapproval from readers who detect these airs of superiority. Furthermore, even if the critic has no such overblown claims, failing to clarify this can still lead readers to misconstrue their tone as one of overconfidence, sparking accusations of deficient critical judgment.

Thus, when a critic identifies a miscalculation made by a Frederick or a Buonaparte, it does not imply that they themselves would have avoided the same mistake. Indeed, the critic may readily admit that, in the shoes of such great commanders, they might have erred even more. Rather, their judgment arises from viewing the misstep within the broader flow of events, forming an opinion based on the result rather than any claim of superior insight.

This perspective represents a judgment shaped by the event's outcome and the resulting chain of circumstances. Yet, there's another, distinct influence that the outcome itself exerts on judgment, which involves evaluating the soundness of a decision solely by its result. This could be called "judgment according to the result." At first glance, this method seems questionable, yet it is not entirely inappropriate.

Evaluating actions solely by their outcomes may appear superficial or even unjust because it might disregard the nuanced factors underlying a decision. However, in cases where there is an absence of visible strategy, or when other aspects of judgment are less applicable, the final result can sometimes serve as a useful, if simplified, measure. In fact, even a decision that seems unwise at first may later be validated by its outcomes, revealing an unforeseen acumen on the part of the decision-maker.

In the end, a result-oriented approach in criticism has value, provided it is tempered with the acknowledgment that the outcome alone does not define an action's merit. It can reveal insights about decision-making but must be balanced against a deeper understanding of the decision's context, intentions, and immediate pressures.

When Buonaparte advanced towards Moscow in 1812, the entire success of his campaign hinged on whether the capture of the Russian capital and the events leading up to it would coerce Emperor Alexander into negotiating peace. Buonaparte's strategy rested on an assumption that had served him well in prior campaigns: the decisive capture of a critical city or battlefield would force a political settlement, as it had with the Emperor Francis after Austerlitz in 1805 and Wagram in 1809, and with Alexander himself after Friedland in 1807. However, should Alexander remain resolute, refusing to negotiate despite the occupation of Moscow, then Buonaparte's venture would inevitably collapse into a strategic defeat, forcing a withdrawal with little to show for his efforts.

In this context, it's important to set aside certain aspects of the campaign. We'll bypass, for instance, any detailed analysis of Buonaparte's maneuvering en route to Moscow, as well as the potential missed opportunities that might have induced Alexander to negotiate peace earlier. Similarly, we won't delve into the disastrous conditions of his retreat or question whether some aspects of the campaign's design led directly to its tragic end. Nevertheless, even if the campaign leading up to Moscow had been flawless, a fundamental uncertainty would still have loomed: Would the capture of Moscow compel Alexander to peace, or would it not?

Without peace, any return from Moscow, regardless of how meticulously it was executed, would still mark a strategic failure. Thus, even in a best-case scenario devoid of catastrophe, Buonaparte's campaign would have ended as a disappointing and costly venture. Had Alexander indeed signed a disadvantageous peace, this campaign might have joined Austerlitz, Friedland, and Wagram as another feather in Buonaparte's cap. But the success of those earlier campaigns too was ultimately contingent on securing peace; had the Emperor Francis or Alexander refused to capitulate, those campaigns might have led to calamities not unlike those witnessed in 1812. Hence, despite Buonaparte's extraordinary military prowess, skillful maneuvers, and relentless energy, his campaign in Russia ultimately depended upon a single question—one which can only be posed to fate itself: Would Alexander make peace?

In contemplating the 1812 campaign, it would be unjust to retroactively invalidate the earlier campaigns of 1805, 1807, and 1809 simply because their outcomes were different. To argue that they were fundamentally reckless undertakings, whose results were contrary to natural order, and that in 1812 strategic reality finally asserted itself, would be a limited and unwarranted judgment. Such a view overlooks the complex, unpredictable human dimensions of political decisions, an intricate web of influences that no one can fully foresee, and which ultimately guided the defeated sovereigns' choices.

Even more unreasonable would be to claim that the Russian campaign deserved the same success as Buonaparte's prior victories and that its failure was the result of some deviation from the natural order. We cannot dismiss Alexander's determination as an aberration or a wholly unpredictable factor. Indeed, the Russian Emperor's steadfastness was one of those variables that, though uncertain, was not beyond the realm of possibility in Buonaparte's grand calculations. Thus, while fate can be fickle, it was not unjust in 1812—it was merely different, an outcome shaped by real and enduring human resolve rather than the supposed whims of chance.

What could be more reasonable than to suggest that, in 1805, 1807, and 1809, Buonaparte accurately gauged his adversaries, while in 1812 he misjudged Alexander's resolve? In those earlier campaigns, his judgment was sound; in the latter, he erred. And in both instances, we evaluate his decisions by the outcome.

All actions in war are aimed at likely outcomes, rather than certainties. Since absolute certainty is impossible, some element must always be left to fate—or, as some might prefer to call it, chance. The goal, naturally, is to minimize reliance on chance as much as possible within each individual situation. Yet it would be a fundamental error to assume that we should always favor the option with the least reliance on chance, as the entirety of theoretical analysis on the nature of war demonstrates. Indeed, there are moments when extreme audacity is the highest wisdom.

In war, whatever portion is left to chance seems to remove both merit and responsibility from the actor. And yet, we feel an undeniable satisfaction when the anticipated outcome aligns with expectations, and a corresponding disappointment when it doesn't. Beyond this, the judgment we make based purely on outcome reflects something less tangible: a mysterious sense that seems to link the commander's genius with fortune. This sentiment gives us pleasure, especially when a commander achieves consistent success, as it suggests an almost invisible thread between skill and fortune that goes beyond mere luck. It is no wonder that success in war feels more substantial and noble than the mere luck of a gambler. This sense of admiration grows with each repeated victory or defeat, helping to explain why we take pleasure in following a successful commander's journey if they have not otherwise compromised our interest in their behalf.

In light of these deep, elusive qualities, criticism—having already weighed all within the bounds of human reasoning—must ultimately allow the results themselves to speak for those areas where hidden, complex factors evade clear understanding. Criticism should, therefore, protect the "silent judgment" that results pronounce from both the clamor of shallow opinions and from those who might misuse such ultimate judgments to serve base interpretations.

This reliance on outcome serves to reveal what human reasoning alone cannot foresee, and it applies most directly to judgments of intellect and mental faculties. These elements, being deeply personal and linked to will, tend to resist any objective evaluation, which is why we must rely on results to speak for them. Whether it is courage or fear that ultimately determines action, there is often no objective basis through which sagacity or calculation could anticipate the likely result.

At this point, it is worth addressing the medium of criticism itself—its language. The language of criticism is intertwined with the nature of action in war, as criticism represents the deliberation that ideally precedes wartime decisions. For this reason, it is essential that the language used in criticism mirrors the tone and precision that would characterize genuine deliberation in the conduct of war. Without this alignment, criticism risks losing its relevance and practical value, failing to engage with the realities of military life. Only when criticism maintains this authenticity in tone and structure does it gain credibility, ensuring it serves as a useful tool within the world of real-world command and action.

In our reflections on the theory of war, we stated that its role is to shape and prepare the mind of a Commander for war, guiding his intellectual development rather than providing rigid doctrines or systems he could employ as mental crutches. The true value lies not in scientific formulas or pre-determined systems to aid decisions in particular cases, nor in truths constructed as indirect systems to be followed, but rather in fostering a natural, intuitive grasp of strategic reality. Therefore, the approach should be similarly direct and insightful in any critical examination.

Certainly, where demonstrating the full nature of a concept would be overly exhaustive, criticism may turn to foundational truths established by theory. However, as a Commander internalizes these theoretical truths more from habitual understanding than from adhering to rigid rules, so too must criticism apply such principles. It should not treat theory as an external code or absolute formula, but rather illuminate the logic within each truth, while deferring only the most detailed proof to theory itself. This approach avoids shrouded, ambiguous language and instead advances clearly, with a visible and coherent chain of reasoning.

This ideal of transparent, grounded criticism may not always be fully achievable, but it should remain the standard for all critical examination. Criticism should therefore minimize complex scientific forms and avoid constructing its own form of rigid, "truth apparatus." Rather, it should be guided by natural, impartial insight. Unfortunately, this principle has seldom governed critical inquiries in practice. Instead, critical works often reveal a certain intellectual vanity—an inclination to dazzle through displays of complex ideas rather than fostering true understanding.

A recurrent flaw in criticism is the clumsy and unwarranted application of rigid, narrow systems as if they were codified laws. These systems, when treated as infallible guidelines, are fundamentally inadequate, as they cannot encompass the full complexity and unpredictability of war. Criticism becomes clearer and more valuable when it exposes these systems' one-sidedness, highlighting that their application lacks the flexibility required in real-world situations. Once the limitations of such narrow systems are understood, critical judgments grounded in them are diminished in credibility. Since the number of conceivable systems is finite, these one-sided frameworks, while flawed, are a lesser concern in the broader landscape of military criticism.

In striving toward this clearer, more adaptable form of criticism, the emphasis should be on straightforward insights that speak directly to the dynamics of war. This does not simply improve the quality of analysis but fosters a more genuine understanding, preparing Commanders to face unpredictable realities with a mind that is perceptive, flexible, and grounded in the true spirit of warfare.

An even greater fault lies in the excessive use of technical terms, scientific jargon, and metaphors, which systems often bring along like the unruly baggage of an army scattered across a battlefield. Critics who haven't fully embraced a system—perhaps because they haven't found one they agree with, or simply haven't mastered one—often resort to fragments of these systems. They wield these fragments like rulers, measuring a General's supposed errors by borrowed snippets of theory. Many can't reason effectively without such fragments of "scientific" military thought, using these bits of theory or metaphor as mere ornamental flourishes in their narratives.

It is in the nature of such terms that they lose meaning—and if they ever had any, it vanishes—when taken out of their original system and used as general axioms or shorthand. These technical phrases and metaphors, instead of clarifying, tend to obscure, becoming dark points in the discourse where writer and reader lose mutual understanding. Worse still, these phrases are often empty shells with little substance. When writers rely on such vagueness, they seldom know clearly what they mean, instead clinging to ambiguous ideas that would dissolve if articulated plainly.

Another critical flaw is the misuse of historical examples and the ostentatious display of erudition. We have already discussed the role of military history and will further explore our stance on the proper use of examples and history in separate chapters. Here, we should note that one historical incident briefly mentioned can support multiple, even contradictory, views. When unrelated facts are gathered across distant times and places, heaped together as if they form a coherent argument, they often only cloud judgment and confuse the understanding rather than providing any meaningful proof. In such cases, when examined, these supposed "facts" frequently turn out to be mere trinkets, serving as little more than a showcase of the critic's knowledge rather than adding any substance.

What can practical life gain from these obscure, often misleading, confused, and arbitrary interpretations? So little that theory, presented in this convoluted way, has long stood as the opposite of practice. This approach often becomes an object of ridicule among soldiers whose skills in the field are unquestioned.

This divide would not exist if theory had kept itself to simple language and practical approaches, addressing only as much as could truly be established. If theory, avoiding false airs and unnecessary displays of scientific rigor or historical allusions, had focused on essentials, it would not have fallen into irrelevance.

Theory, in that case, would be able to go hand-in-hand with those leading in the field, complementing rather than obstructing the natural genius required for effective command.

Chapter VI. On Examples

Historical examples clarify and provide the most compelling form of proof in empirical sciences, a truth that holds especially for the Art of War. General Scharnhorst, whose handbook remains one of the finest texts on real warfare, emphasized the importance of historical examples, expertly weaving them into his analyses. Had he survived beyond the war in which he fell, his planned fourth installment on artillery would have provided even more evidence of his discerning and insightful approach to experience-based study. Yet, while Scharnhorst's approach is a model of how historical examples should be applied, many theoretical writers often misuse them in ways that are both unsatisfying and logically inconsistent. This misuse calls for a clear distinction between the correct and incorrect application of historical examples.

Military knowledge, as it underpins the Art of War, belongs to the category of empirical sciences. Even when these insights are drawn from the inherent qualities of things, our understanding of their true nature emerges largely from experience. Moreover, when applied practically, these insights are influenced by so many variable circumstances that the resulting effects can seldom be predicted from theoretical assumptions alone. For instance, consider gunpowder, a central agent in military operations; though its fundamental effects on the battlefield were discovered through direct experience, to this day, experiments continue to refine our understanding of its impact. We may know, hypothetically, that an iron cannonball propelled at a velocity of 1000 feet per second can decimate anything in its path. But the sheer number of surrounding factors that influence this impact—factors learned only through experience—reveals the depth of empirical knowledge required to grasp its full effect.

The Art of War requires a blend of both physical and moral considerations, especially in understanding the psychological impact of weaponry and tactics. In the Middle Ages, for example, firearms were rudimentary in design, so their physical effects were much weaker than today's standards. Yet, their psychological impact was enormous, instilling fear in ways that vastly outpaced their mechanical efficacy. One can only truly appreciate the transformative power of experience by witnessing firsthand the unyielding resilience of one of Buonaparte's seasoned battalions, standing firm under relentless cannon fire. These troops, hardened by continuous exposure to danger and emboldened by a string of victories, had developed an intrinsic strength that defies mere theory. Conversely, we know that in modern Europe, some troops still lack such resilience; a few well-aimed cannon shots would suffice to disperse them.

Only through history and lived experience can we fully understand both the practical and psychological effects of warfare. Examples from history, when properly applied, become indispensable guides to appreciating the realities and complexities of military action, illustrating not only the physical mechanics of war but also the moral resilience it demands.

In empirical sciences, including the theory of the Art of War, historical proof cannot consistently verify every proposition; proving every tactical truth through history alone would be challenging. When a particular method proves effective in warfare, it often becomes widely adopted. Nations emulate one another, the tactic gains popularity, and its practical value is generally accepted, establishing itself in theory. In these cases, theory points broadly to experience as its source, yet rarely relies on individual historical instances to assert its truth.

However, when historical evidence aims to refute an established method, confirm a questionable idea, or justify a novel approach, specific historical examples are crucial for validation. Examining these examples more closely reveals four main purposes that historical proofs can serve.

1. Clarifying a Concept: In abstract discussions, ideas are often challenging to understand or can be misinterpreted. When an author is concerned that a concept may not be clear, historical examples provide tangible illustrations, illuminating the concept and ensuring readers grasp the intended meaning.

2.*Illustrating Applicatio*: Examples show how an idea unfolds in real-world conditions, highlighting nuances that general theories may not fully capture. The discrepancies between theory and practice often lie in these finer details, which historical examples help bring to light.

3. Supporting a Statemen*: Citing a particular historical event can substantiate an argument, especially if the goal is simply to prove a fact or effect's feasibility. This does not demand an exhaustive historical account but merely a reference to a recognized event to validate a point. For instance, if one claims that fortified positions can succeed under certain conditions, mentioning the fortified position at Bunzelwitz in 1761 suffices as credible support.

4. Formulating Theory: Through examining and synthesizing detailed historical cases, one can derive theoretical principles, grounded in historical testimony itself. Here, history provides not only examples but the primary evidence for theoretical development.

For the first purpose—clarifying concepts—only a brief reference to the historical case is needed, as the example serves mainly to elucidate part of an idea. Strict historical accuracy is not crucial in this case; in fact, a hypothetical scenario might suffice, though historical examples are generally preferable as they connect theory more closely with real-life experience.

In the second case, where the purpose is to demonstrate the application of a concept, a more thorough recounting of events is necessary. Yet again, absolute historical precision is secondary to conveying the idea's practical implications, and the same considerations about hypothetical cases apply as with the first.

For the third purpose—substantiating an assertion—the mere mention of a verified fact is often adequate. For instance, if the argument is about the effectiveness of fortified positions, the Bunzelwitz position becomes an appropriate historical citation.

These methods underscore how historical examples can be employed thoughtfully within military theory: whether for illustration, application, or formal proof, each approach aligns the example with the critical intent of theory. Thus, while examples cannot prove every military truth, they effectively bridge abstract ideas with the observable realities that are essential to the practice of war.

When historical cases are used to illustrate or prove an abstract military truth, they must be scrutinized with precision, breaking down each relevant detail thoroughly to bring the truth vividly to life for the reader. Without a careful examination of each pertinent aspect of a historical example, the argument weakens, and we find ourselves relying on multiple cases to compensate for what one well-detailed example could have demonstrated alone. This approach assumes that, in aggregating numerous cases, the finer details that we cannot provide will balance each other out over a broader set of examples.

Consider, for example, if we intend to argue that positioning cavalry behind rather than alongside infantry is more effective or that an enveloping movement using widely separated columns is highly risky without a clear advantage in numbers, both on the battlefield (tactically) and across a campaign (strategically). In the first case, it would not suffice to mention a few lost battles with cavalry on the flanks and a few victorious battles with cavalry stationed behind infantry; and in the second, we cannot simply refer to the battles of Rivoli and Wagram or the failed Austrian offensive in Italy in 1796, nor the similar French attempt in Germany that same year. For each example, we must demonstrate how these tactical or strategic formations significantly impacted the outcomes by carefully tracing events. Only then can we discern whether these particular setups are genuinely flawed; this clarity is essential because condemning such approaches outright would overlook situations in which they may indeed be effective.

In cases where it is impractical to delve deeply into specific examples, the lacking demonstrative strength may be partially compensated by citing several cases; however, this method is fraught with pitfalls and is often misused. Instead of one well-examined example, several cases are briefly mentioned, giving an impression of substantial evidence. However, there are situations where even a dozen examples would be inconclusive, particularly if the tactic in question is commonplace. In such cases, it would be equally easy to compile a dozen other instances yielding opposite results. For instance, one might cite numerous failed battles where the losing side used separate converging columns, yet one could also list an equal number of victories using the same tactic. Clearly, this approach does not lead to a meaningful conclusion.

Through careful reflection on these distinctions, it becomes apparent just how easily historical examples can be misinterpreted or misused. They are most effective when meticulously analyzed to reveal the relationship between strategy and outcome, making it clear when certain methods should be adapted and when they might yield unfavorable results. The critical factor in this process is not just in the quantity of examples but in the depth and clarity of each example's analysis, ensuring that the historical evidence presented genuinely supports the theoretical principle it is meant to illustrate.

When an event is only superficially examined instead of being thoroughly dissected in all its components, it resembles an object seen from afar, where details are blurred, making the whole appear uniform on all sides without distinguishing its essential features. Such distant views often lead to conflicting interpretations, as the event lacks the clarity needed for a definitive understanding. Because of this ambiguity, the same historical event has been used to substantiate opposing perspectives. For instance, some regard Daun's campaigns as masterpieces of prudence and strategic acumen, while others see them as the embodiment of hesitancy and lack of boldness. Similarly, Buonaparte's audacious 1797 march across the Noric Alps can be painted as either a daring masterstroke or as reckless impetuosity. His setback in 1812 might be explained by critics as either the result of excessive energy or a lack thereof. Such contradictory interpretations abound, highlighting how partial understandings can yield irreconcilable opinions, and in cases where two perspectives are in opposition, one is inherently flawed.

Feuquieres, in his memoirs, deserves credit for providing an abundance of examples. He preserved numerous historical details that would otherwise have faded from memory and was one of the first to link abstract theoretical ideas directly with the practical conduct of war. In this way, the examples he presented serve as tangible illustrations of his theories. However, even with his sometimes detailed recounting, he often fails to show that his conclusions naturally stem from the inner workings of these historical events. Thus, while the examples may be illuminating, they do not always convincingly support the theories he seeks to advance.

Another challenge arising from superficial treatment of historical events is that readers may lack prior knowledge of the events or may not recall enough of them to fully grasp the author's arguments. This lack of context leaves them with only two choices: to accept the conclusions without understanding or to remain unconvinced.

One of the primary difficulties in using historical events as illustrations lies in reconstructing them for readers in a way that allows those events to serve as concrete proofs. Frequently, authors lack the necessary materials, time, or space to render events with sufficient detail for this purpose. Nevertheless, we argue that when advancing a novel or uncertain theory, a single thoroughly examined example can be far more enlightening than a handful of examples covered only superficially. The problem with these shallow narratives goes beyond the fact that they are unconvincing as proofs. The larger issue is that authors who take such a cursory approach to history often lack deep familiarity with the material. This superficial treatment spawns numerous inaccurate interpretations and theories that might never have surfaced if the author had rigorously connected each aspect of the events with the broader outcomes they are intended to support.

Acknowledging these difficulties and simultaneously recognizing the necessity of using historical examples, we conclude that recent military history is naturally the most suitable field for drawing such examples. Contemporary history is not only more reliably documented but is also typically more detailed, providing a more solid foundation for meaningful analysis. Recent events allow for better access to primary sources and nuanced perspectives, enabling authors to present a clearer, more comprehensive view that is essential for establishing well-grounded theoretical arguments.

In ancient times, the conditions surrounding warfare, as well as the methods used to conduct it, were significantly different from those of today. Consequently, the events from those periods hold limited practical or theoretical value for modern study. Additionally, just like any history, the nuances of military history tend to fade over time. Smaller details, once vibrant and revealing, gradually disappear, leaving only the broad strokes and dominant themes. This process is similar to an old painting that has lost its fine brushstrokes and color vibrancy, resulting in exaggerated proportions that can skew our understanding of the original work.

Looking at warfare's current state, it's clear that only wars from the Austrian succession onward—those conducted with weaponry and tactics reasonably close to the present day—still offer us substantial lessons. Despite the many changes, large and small, that have reshaped military tactics and technology, these conflicts remain relevant. In contrast, the War of the Spanish Succession, where firearms had not yet evolved to a high level of efficiency and cavalry still dominated the battlefield, offers far less practical insight. The further back we go, the less practical military history becomes, as the records of these wars are scant in detail and often only broadly illustrative. Warfare from ancient times, then, is the least valuable of all.

However, the diminished value of ancient military history is not entirely without exceptions. This limitation applies mainly to areas reliant on precise details or those heavily altered by evolving methods of warfare. While we may lack specifics on tactics in battles between the Swiss and Austrians or between the Burgundians and French, these campaigns unmistakably marked a crucial shift, displaying for the first time the superiority of a well-trained infantry over even the finest cavalry. Similarly, examining the era of the

Condottieri reveals how closely the method of waging war was tied to the instruments at hand; at no time were forces used in warfare so sharply distinguished as a specialized, standalone class, separate from the general populace. The approach of the Romans during the Second Punic War, in which they attacked Carthaginian territories in Spain and Africa while Hannibal occupied Italy, offers a wealth of insight, as we know enough about the political and military dynamics involved to analyze this form of indirect defense in its larger context.

Nevertheless, as we delve deeper into specifics that deviate from these broader strategic frameworks, we find fewer applicable examples from ancient history. Not only do we lack the means to evaluate similar events accurately, but these earlier examples are often rendered obsolete by modern warfare's unique characteristics. Regrettably, it remains fashionable for many historians to draw on these distant examples. Although we won't speculate on how much of this trend might stem from vanity or pretentiousness, we frequently detect a lack of genuine intent to educate and persuade. Instead, such references are often mere decorative flourishes used to mask gaps or conceal weaknesses in the argument.

Teaching the art of war solely through historical examples, as Feuquieres once suggested, would undoubtedly be a monumental achievement. Yet, for anyone considering this endeavor, the task would be a lifetime's work. To approach it adequately, one would first need years of hands-on experience in the field to gain the essential understanding of actual warfare. Those driven by ambition to take on such a noble task must prepare themselves as if embarking on a spiritual journey: dedicating all their time, sparing no effort, and braving any obstacles of rank or authority. Rising above personal vanity, free from bias or self-censorship, they must, in the spirit of the French code, commit to "the Truth, the whole Truth, and nothing but the Truth."

Book III. Of Strategy in General

Chapter I. Strategy

In the second chapter of the second book, Strategy is defined as "the employment of the battle as the means towards the attainment of the object of the War." At its core, Strategy concerns itself directly with the battle, but to fully understand this role, the theory of Strategy must also examine the instrument of action—the armed force—along with its primary connections and influences. This is essential because the battle both depends on this force and, in turn, affects it. Thus, Strategy must possess a deep understanding of the battle itself, particularly in terms of the range of possible outcomes and the critical mental and moral factors that shape the battle's effectiveness.

Strategy, then, is the art of employing battle to achieve the ultimate goal of the War. Its purpose is to provide direction to all military operations, aligning them with the larger objective of the War. To this end, Strategy is responsible for outlining a coherent plan that connects a series of actions, which together aim for decisive resolution. This involves creating plans for individual campaigns and guiding the specific battles within each campaign. Since many of these actions must rely on conjectures—some of which inevitably prove to be incorrect—and because countless details can't be fully anticipated in advance, Strategy must remain actively engaged with the Army on the field. It is there to manage situations as they arise and make necessary adjustments to the overarching plan, which is an ongoing necessity in War. Strategy, therefore, can never truly release its grip on the unfolding situation.

Yet historically, Strategy was often conceived as something to be conducted from the cabinet, removed from the immediacy of the battlefield. This view implies that Strategy could function separately from the Army, which would only be feasible if the cabinet were close enough to serve as the Army's primary headquarters.

In this respect, theory plays an essential role in guiding Strategy, not by prescribing rigid rules but by illuminating the essential aspects and relationships that contribute to sound planning. Theory helps reveal whatever principles or guidelines may be discernible, enabling Strategy to operate with a structured understanding of complex situations.

Reflecting on how deeply War intersects with matters of vast importance, it becomes clear that its successful orchestration demands an exceptional breadth of understanding. A Prince or General who can skillfully organize the War effort to fit both the objective and available resources, achieving a balance where nothing is excessive or deficient, displays the ultimate testament of strategic genius. The impact of such talent, however, is often not as visible in the creation of innovative tactics that capture immediate attention but rather in the lasting success of the entire campaign. It is the quiet realization of every unspoken assumption and the seamless coordination of every element that warrants admiration. This harmony is only visible in the overall outcome. Observers who, in analyzing the final result, fail to detect the subtleties of this harmony are likely to misplace their search for genius, seeking it in bold displays rather than in the cohesive and balanced execution of strategic vision.

The tools and methods of Strategy are, in reality, extraordinarily straightforward and consistently applied. They are so widely recognized through repeated use that it seems almost absurd to common sense when critics inflate these basic concepts into proofs of unmatched genius. The act of flanking an enemy—a maneuver employed countless times—is often held up as a sign of unprecedented brilliance or profound insight, even as evidence of the broadest expertise. Could anything be more absurd? (*)

(*) This passage critiques theorists like Lloyd and Bülow and the numerous writers from the 18th century whose rigid, formulaic views have left an enduring legacy, especially in England—ED.

Adding to the irony, these same critics often dismiss moral forces entirely from the realm of theory, focusing solely on material forces. By doing so, they reduce Strategy to a few simple calculations of equilibrium, superiority, time, and space, dictated by lines and angles alone. If Strategy truly amounted to nothing more than this, it would hardly pose an intellectual challenge worthy of a schoolchild.

Yet, let's concede this much: the aim is not to solve scientific formulas or puzzles. The relationships between material forces are indeed straightforward; it's the moral forces that complicate matters. However, these moral forces come into significant play only in the higher reaches of Strategy, where it meets political science—indeed, where the two become inseparable. Here, moral factors largely determine what and how much should be pursued in War, rather than dictating how actions should be executed. In the practical tactics of War, both large and small, moral elements tend to narrow down to just a few manageable aspects.

In this way, Strategy remains uncomplicated in structure, yet this simplicity doesn't make it any easier to practice. Once a State has established its objectives for War, the general course of action becomes clear. But following that course without being thrown off track by a multitude of fluctuating influences requires not only clarity and stability of mind but an extraordinary strength of character. Out of a thousand men who each display exceptional qualities—whether insight, intellect, boldness, or strength of will—only a rare few possess the blend of virtues necessary to rise above mediocrity and excel in the path of a true military leader.

It may seem unusual, but for those familiar with the demands of war, it is clear that a significantly greater strength of will is often required to make a strategic decision than to act in tactics. In tactical situations, the immediacy of events creates a sense of urgency; a Commander finds themselves caught in a swift current of unfolding actions, where hesitation can lead to devastating consequences. Driven by the pace of the moment, they suppress fears and press forward, carried by the very momentum of the situation. Strategy, however, operates at a more deliberate pace, which permits space for doubts and second-guessing, for external objections and internal misgivings. Because events are perceived indirectly, through conjecture and estimation rather than firsthand experience, convictions in Strategy lack the compelling force they acquire in the immediacy of tactics. The result is often that when decisive action is required, many Generals find themselves immobilized by uncertainty.

Reflecting on history, consider Frederick the Great's 1760 campaign, often praised as a masterpiece of strategic maneuvering and celebrated for its sophisticated marches. Critics highlight his alternating attempts to flank Daun, moving first against one side, then the other. Yet, viewed plainly, without excessive admiration, there is nothing overwhelmingly profound in these maneuvers themselves. What commands respect is not the maneuvers as isolated acts, but the insight of the King in keeping his ambitions finely attuned to his actual resources. He pursued a great objective with strictly limited means, committing only to what was essential to achieve his purpose. This wisdom is visible not just in this campaign but consistently across his three wars.

Frederick's overarching aim was the preservation of Silesia within the bounds of a secure and enduring peace. As the ruler of a relatively modest state, advanced in certain administrative aspects but otherwise unremarkable, he could neither attempt the conquests of an Alexander nor follow the reckless course of Charles XII, which had led that monarch to ruin. Thus, Frederick's conduct throughout these wars displays a balanced, calculated force—a power tightly controlled and punctuated by bursts of daring in critical moments, only to return to a steady pace in accordance with nuanced political considerations. Neither vanity, glory, nor revenge could sway him from his calculated path, and it was this consistent adherence to purpose that ultimately brought him victory.

These words barely begin to capture the depth of Frederick's genius in navigating the delicate balance between ambition and pragmatism. To fully appreciate his mastery, one must study the extraordinary outcome of his efforts and the precise choices he made that allowed him to survive insurmountable odds. In the 1760 campaign—and indeed in every campaign we study—it was his ability to maintain equilibrium against overwhelming forces while incurring only minimal losses that defines his brilliance. This trait, his unerring capacity to gauge the limits of his power and the clarity to act within them, remains the hallmark of his genius.

Another aspect worth highlighting is the immense difficulty in execution. Strategically, turning an enemy's flank, keeping a concentrated force, or relying on swift, well-coordinated movements to leverage a smaller force are concepts that may be easy to grasp in theory. In fact, such strategies are so straightforward in concept that it's tempting to view them as mere basics, nothing extraordinary. But if a General tries to execute them as Frederick the Great did, the complexity reveals itself. Even years later, observers and historians spoke of the perils involved in Frederick's chosen camps and movements, which seemed hazardous, even reckless, at the time. For the King, however, the perceived risk was mitigated by his understanding of Daun's system, his army's formation and deployment, his cautious nature, and his personal responsibilities. Frederick knew he could make such choices because his understanding and character allowed him to see security where others saw only danger.

To appreciate fully the King's decision-making, it's essential to recognize the determination, boldness, and strength of will he possessed. Frederick wasn't blindly risking everything; he understood the intricacies of his opponents and had the confidence to navigate risks that many would avoid. Even thirty years after the events, people still marveled at his daring. How many other Generals, facing similar circumstances, would have dared to consider these seemingly straightforward strategic decisions as truly viable?

Moreover, Frederick's constant movement presented its own challenges. Throughout the campaign, his army was in nearly perpetual motion. Twice they traversed rugged cross-roads, from the Elbe to Silesia, pursued by Lascy's forces, ready for battle at any moment. The King's soldiers needed an exceptionally high level of organizational skill, and coordinating such movements demanded monumental exertion. Even with countless supply wagons trailing them, maintaining adequate provisions proved difficult. For eight days before the Battle of Leignitz, his troops marched, alternately filing left and right before the enemy, enduring significant fatigue and deprivations.

Imagine the stress of maintaining unity and morale under these conditions. These operations were not conducted without "friction," to use a metaphor from mechanical engineering. Just as a machine wears down with use, so did Frederick's forces. As they endured hunger and thirst, their suffering was evident, both to the King and his Generals. Frederick's command would be tested not only by the need for sound decisions but by the weight of witnessing the sacrifices he demanded from his men. Ordinary leaders would hesitate to demand such sacrifices, fearing the inevitable breakdown in morale, discipline, and, ultimately, military cohesion. Yet, his soldiers bore these hardships largely due to an unshakable belief in Frederick's genius and leadership.

These are the true marvels we should honor—the execution, not merely the ideas. No one can truly grasp this counterbalance in action without firsthand experience. Those who know war solely through reading or peacetime drills may not fully appreciate this dynamic. Thus, we urge such individuals to trust our accounts of this aspect of war, knowing they may lack the experiential insight to envision it fully.

To clarify our perspective, we close this chapter with a preview of our approach to strategy. We'll examine key elements of both moral and material considerations in war, exploring each individually before progressing to more complex, interconnected aspects. Finally, we'll look at how these elements coalesce into a cohesive plan for war or an entire campaign, unveiling the intricate architecture that underlies military strategy.

Observation.

In an earlier draft of the second book, the author left some notes intended for use in revising the first chapter of that book. Since that revision was never completed, these endorsed passages are presented here in their entirety for their intended insight and emphasis.

To begin, when armed forces gather at a specific location, a battle at that spot becomes feasible; however, this mere potential for conflict does not mean that a battle will necessarily ensue. Can this potential, then, be treated as something actual and, by extension, something effective? Indeed, it can. While the battle itself may not materialize, the possibility alone carries real consequences. The effects of this possibility—whatever they might ultimately be—cannot fail to manifest in some tangible way.

This latent potential has the power to shape decisions and actions, to stir both hope and dread, and, by virtue of its presence, influences the trajectory of subsequent events. Whether or not a battle physically takes place, the anticipation alone reverberates through the strategic landscape, altering the decisions of commanders, the morale of troops, and the political calculations behind the scenes. This possibility is thus imbued with its own form of reality, one that exerts a silent but potent influence on the course of a campaign.

1. Possible Combats Are on Account of Their Results to Be Looked Upon as Real Ones.

If a detachment is dispatched to intercept a retreating enemy, and that enemy surrenders without further resistance, it is the very presence and implied threat of combat from our pursuing force that compels their submission. Similarly, if a segment of our Army seizes an undefended enemy province, thereby cutting off a substantial source of the enemy's reinforcements or supplies, it is the potential battle—implicitly promised if the enemy attempts to reclaim the lost province—that solidifies our control over it.

In these examples, the mere potential of a battle is enough to produce real results, equating it to an actual event in strategic impact. If, however, the enemy deploys a superior force in response, compelling our troops to abandon their objectives without a fight, our initial plans may have failed, but the offered battle still exerted an effect: it drew the enemy's resources and attention to that position. Even in cases where the maneuver backfires and weakens our position, the implications of these potential engagements function similarly to the outcomes of lost battles, forcing shifts in power and resources.

From this perspective, the degradation of the enemy's military strength and the undermining of their power fundamentally stem from battles—whether these engagements transpire or remain as impending threats. It is through this immediate or anticipated clash of forces that the enemy is compelled to yield ground, resources, or strategic advantage, demonstrating that a battle's mere possibility can carry substantial influence.

2. Twofold Object of The Combat.

These effects manifest in two distinct ways: direct and indirect. They are considered indirect if they involve objectives beyond the immediate destruction of the enemy's forces—objectives that, while not focused on force destruction, contribute to it in an indirect yet potentially even more powerful manner. Securing control over provinces, towns, fortresses, roads, bridges, or supply depots might serve as the immediate goal of a confrontation, but these objectives are never the ultimate purpose. Such elements can only be seen as stepping stones toward achieving a greater level of dominance. They are means to eventually compel the enemy into a position where accepting battle would be entirely untenable.

Thus, these intermediary goals—whether capturing territories, securing strategic positions, or denying resources—function solely as stages in a larger strategic framework. They provide incremental advantages that ultimately contribute to the overarching objective: creating conditions for a decisive engagement where the enemy's defeat becomes inevitable. These goals should always be understood as transitional elements leading toward the core aim of debilitating the enemy's power, rather than as endpoints in and of themselves.

3. Example.

In 1814, the capture of Napoleon's capital, Paris, effectively achieved the primary objective of the War. The political divisions rooted in Paris quickly became active forces, creating a dramatic internal rift that led to the rapid disintegration of the Emperor's power. Yet, when assessing this situation, the key perspective is that the internal discord within Paris severely reduced Napoleon's military strength and defensive capabilities. Consequently, this decline amplified the Allies' superiority to the extent that any meaningful resistance from Napoleon became impossible. It was this decisive imbalance that ultimately secured peace with France.

If we imagine, however, that at this pivotal moment, the Allies' forces had been similarly weakened by external factors, the strategic advantage would have dissipated, nullifying the impact of capturing Paris and its broader significance. This hypothetical serves to underscore the crucial nature of maintaining force superiority at all costs.

We have traced this line of reasoning to highlight that this perspective is the fundamental and accurate way to understand the situation and to appreciate its strategic significance. Ultimately, this analysis always circles back to the essential question: what outcomes—whether advantageous or disadvantageous—could result from the potential engagements, large or small, that each side might initiate at any given moment? When considering a campaign plan, this query remains the definitive criterion for guiding strategic decisions and determining the best course of action right from the campaign's inception.

4. When This View Is Not Taken, Then A False Value Is Given to Other Things.

If we do not train ourselves to perceive War—and each individual campaign within it—as a continuous sequence of battles, each leading logically to the next, we risk misinterpreting the significance of isolated achievements, such as seizing a geographical location or occupying an undefended province. When such an acquisition is viewed as a standalone success, rather than as one moment in an ongoing sequence of strategic events, it may be mistakenly perceived as a permanent gain. This flawed perspective can prevent us from questioning whether holding this position may, in fact, lead to future disadvantages. History often reveals the recurrence of such oversights.

War resembles commerce in that a merchant cannot isolate the profit from a single transaction as a separate, secure gain. Instead, every profit remains subject to the dynamics of the entire business venture. Similarly, in War, no single victory or gain can be evaluated in isolation from the overall outcome; only the sum total of victories, losses, and maneuvers determines whether each action was advantageous or detrimental.

If the strategist maintains their focus on the anticipated series of engagements, they keep their perspective aligned with the true nature of War. This mindset cultivates a momentum of force that infuses actions with the necessary urgency, ensuring that plans are executed with the decisiveness and vigor appropriate to the demands of War—unhampered by distractions or minor setbacks.

(*) This chapter critiques the theories held by the Austrian Staff in 1814 and lays the groundwork for the Prussian General Staff's modern doctrine.

Chapter II. Elements of Strategy

The factors shaping the use of combat within Strategy can be logically divided into several distinct categories, such as moral, physical, mathematical, geographical, and logistical considerations. The first category encompasses all that can be derived from the moral qualities and psychological effects in warfare, while the second involves the tangible military strength, including troop numbers, organizational structure, and the balance among infantry, artillery, and cavalry forces. The mathematical category includes the angles formed by lines of operation, as well as concentric and eccentric movements to the extent that their geometrical aspects contribute to strategic calculation. The geographical category involves natural and man-made features like high ground, rivers, forests, and road networks. Lastly, the logistical category pertains to all factors concerning the provision and maintenance of supply lines.

Separating these categories in our analysis clarifies each one's relative importance and allows us to quickly assign each element its appropriate weight. For instance, we may recognize that the strategic value of a base of operations, considering only its position relative to operational lines, relies far less on the pure geometric angle than on the quality and accessibility of the surrounding terrain and roads.

However, attempting to dissect Strategy solely through these separate elements would be a misguided approach. In each military operation, these elements are intertwined and rarely exist in isolation. Treating them independently would reduce the analysis to a lifeless, overly technical exercise, one that, like a dream of endless, futile construction, would continually fail to bridge the gap between theoretical abstractions and the complex reality of warfare. May every strategist be spared from such a misguided undertaking! Instead, we should strive to address warfare holistically, refraining from unnecessary dissection except where it may clarify a particular point or insight that arises not from theoretical speculation but from direct engagement with the total reality of war.

Chapter III. Moral Forces

We must revisit this topic, briefly mentioned in the third chapter of the second book, because the moral forces hold a central place in the nature of War, acting as the intangible spirit that infuses its entire essence. These forces latch on most readily and harmoniously to the Will, which not only initiates but guides all the diverse powers in War, merging with it almost as if into a single, flowing stream, given that Will itself is a moral force. Unfortunately, these forces defy detailed book analysis; they resist classification, cannot be quantified, and must be both observed and experienced to be understood.

The spirit and other moral qualities driving an Army, its General, the Government, and even public opinion in the provinces where War unfolds, as well as the moral impact of a victory or defeat, vary enormously in their character. Depending on how these forces align with our objectives and circumstances, their influence can manifest in several distinct ways.

While it may seem impossible to capture these elements fully in theoretical writing, they are as much a part of the theory of the Art of War as any other component. It would be a shallow perspective to frame principles and rules without regard for moral forces and then, as soon as these forces assert themselves, to classify them as exceptions and thereby, in a way, codify these exceptions as rules themselves. Or, worse, to invoke "genius" to explain anything that doesn't fit the rigid framework—this implies that rules were crafted only for those lacking insight, or that the rules themselves may be little more than folly.

Even if military theory serves only as a reminder of these forces, emphasizing the need to acknowledge their full value and ensure they are accounted for, it has extended its reach to the domain of the immaterial. By establishing this broader perspective, it preemptively calls into question any defense based solely on physical forces alone. For in truth, the physical and moral forces are inseparably blended in War; they cannot be separated like metals by a refining process. Any rule relating to physical forces must incorporate the influence of moral forces to avoid resulting in overly cautious or overly broad pronouncements that miss the true nature of War.

Even the most straightforward theories have unknowingly strayed into this moral domain; for example, the effects of victory are impossible to fully explain without considering the moral impressions left behind. Therefore, most of the elements we explore in this book are a blend of both physical and moral causes and effects. We might even say that the physical forces are just the wooden handle, while the moral forces are the precious metal, the shining, honed edge of the weapon itself.

The strength and impact of moral forces in War, often beyond belief, are most vividly illustrated through history. This is where the General finds the richest and most sustaining food for the mind. Yet, it is not through methodical demonstrations, in-depth critiques, or scholarly treatises that one draws the essence of knowledge from history. Rather, it is through sentiments, broad impressions, and sudden sparks of insight that the seeds of understanding are planted and nourish the intellect.

Attempting a systematic study of the main moral elements in War—detailing each with the rigor of a devoted scholar and cataloging their potential benefits and drawbacks—would risk falling into the predictable and mundane. In dissecting such aspects, we might inadvertently lose sight of the living spirit of the subject, which often escapes when reduced to mere analysis. What remains then are facts and observations that nearly everyone knows already. For this reason, we choose a different approach, embracing an intentionally fragmented, impressionistic perspective. We aim here to emphasize the significance of these moral forces in a broad sense and to capture the spirit in which the ideas presented in this book were conceived, rather than exhausting each element in exhaustive detail.

Chapter IV. The Chief Moral Powers

The core elements defining success in War include The Talents of the Commander, The Military Virtue of the Army, and Its National Spirit. Determining which of these is most crucial is an elusive task, as both the potency of each and their impact relative to one another are complex and hard to gauge in general terms. Instead, the soundest approach is to acknowledge the inherent power of each, avoiding the common pitfall of devaluing one in favor of another, as human judgment often swings whimsically between extremes. History itself offers ample proof of the irrefutable significance of each of these elements.

In recent times, European armies have, to a large extent, achieved parity in terms of discipline and readiness. Moreover, the art of warfare has—much as philosophers might say—evolved into a broadly shared method among armies, reducing the likelihood of unique, individual techniques of command (such as Frederick the Great's famed oblique order) appearing with regularity. Thus, under present conditions, the significance of National Spirit and an army's sustained exposure to War has likely increased. However, should a long period of peace return, the situation could change once again.

The national spirit within an army—manifesting as enthusiasm, fanaticism, belief, or collective opinion—is especially potent in mountainous campaigns, where each soldier often operates independently. Consequently, mountainous terrains are ideally suited for armies comprising local levies or patriotic militias.

Conversely, an army's discipline and cohesiveness, forged through rigorous training and producing a resilient courage that binds soldiers together as though they were cast in iron, become particularly advantageous in open fields, where unified formations excel.

Meanwhile, the talent of a General shines brightest in diverse, rolling landscapes. In mountainous regions, where individual sections are dispersed, a General's capacity to direct all units is often stretched beyond practical limits. In flat plains, by contrast, conditions are more straightforward, limiting the complexity of maneuvers that showcase strategic genius.

These correlations, or "elective affinities," should therefore be regarded as guiding principles when planning military campaigns. The interplay between the commander's talents, the army's disciplined courage, and the ardent spirit inspired by national pride will always bear significantly on the path to victory, particularly when aligned with the natural advantages of the chosen terrain.

Chapter V. Military Virtue of an Army

This spirit of military virtue is something apart from mere bravery or an enthusiasm for warfare. While bravery is indeed an essential component, much as a natural gift unique to some individuals, it also becomes cultivated in the soldier, refined through habit and immersion within the larger framework of an Army. Yet, this courage must differ from individual bravery—it must shed the wild impulse for unchecked action and raw displays of strength. Instead, it must transform into a disciplined force, shaped by obedience, order, method, and an awareness of the structure it serves. Likewise, a passion for the profession of arms can certainly animate the military virtue within an Army, lending it fervor and zeal, yet it remains distinct from that core virtue itself.

War, as a distinct vocation, maintains its own identity regardless of the general relevance it may hold or the broad call to arms that could encompass nearly an entire male population. Even so, it continues to stand separate from the other vocations of human life. To internalize the very nature and ethos of this pursuit, to understand, harness, and integrate the driving forces that fuel it, to become immersed in its unique character, cultivating confidence and skill through repeated engagement—to move fully from one's civilian self into the role assigned by War—this is what constitutes the military virtue in each soldier.

No matter the efforts to blend the soldier and citizen into a single role, nor the attempts to nationalize warfare, nor the belief that modern warfare has distanced itself from the days of the Condottieri, the distinct identity of the military profession will persist. So long as this distinct identity remains, those who practice it will inevitably view themselves as members of a particular order or guild, wherein the "Spirit of War" finds its most faithful expression through its unique rules, customs, and culture. Indeed, this esprit de corps, or corporate spirit, is not only natural but essential to cultivate within any Army. It represents the shared unity of purpose among soldiers and a foundation upon which military virtue crystallizes and binds.

An Army that retains its formation under relentless fire, that remains unshaken by phantom fears and resolute in the face of real danger, that contests each inch of ground even under the most intense pressure, whose pride in its victories is matched by unyielding obedience, respect for, and trust in its leaders, even when shadowed by the demoralization of defeat; an Army with soldiers physically hardened and inured to hardships, like seasoned athletes; an Army that views its labor as a pathway to victory rather than a burden overhanging its standards; an Army that is constantly reminded of its values by the simple creed of the honor of its arms—such an Army embodies the true essence of military virtue.

This unity of purpose, physical resilience, and steadfast morale make up the heart of the military spirit, forming an indomitable force bound by duty and honor. It is this spirit that drives an Army forward through the trials of War, creating a bond that transcends mere loyalty, binding soldiers to one another, to their leaders, and to their mission. The true military spirit, therefore, lies not only in the courage to face an enemy but in the disciplined commitment to remain strong, respectful, and undeterred, no matter the adversity. This spirit of duty and honor, where individual valor is tempered by collective discipline and unity, stands as the foundation of any Army that aspires to greatness.

Soldiers may exhibit tremendous bravery, as did the Vendéans, or accomplish remarkable feats, like the Swiss, Americans, or Spaniards, yet this does not necessarily mean they possess military virtue in the fullest sense. Similarly, a Commander might lead standing armies to victory, as Eugene and Marlborough did, without truly harnessing or benefiting from this distinct moral quality within his forces. Therefore, it is critical not to assume that no victory is possible without military virtue, or that it alone is the determining factor in every success. Highlighting this point helps bring clarity to our understanding of military virtue as a specific moral force—it is not an all-encompassing element of military achievement, but rather a powerful, calculable force that can be present or absent, much like any physical instrument in warfare.

With this concept defined, let us consider both the influence military virtue has and the means by which it can be cultivated within an Army. Military virtue serves for individual units much like the genius of a Commander does for the entirety of an army. The General directs the overarching course of action, but cannot steer each segment or part individually. When the General's direct guidance does not reach down to every part, it is military virtue that steps in to lead these segments, maintaining cohesion and focus.

Generals are chosen for their exceptional abilities and have often earned their roles through recognized talent, while the leaders of larger divisions have typically been rigorously tested over time. Yet this rigorous vetting tends to lessen as we move down the ranks, resulting in a gradual decline in the reliability of individual talents. Military virtue is meant to bridge this gap; where individual skill or experience may be lacking, the collective moral strength should take its place. This military virtue arises naturally in populations with certain characteristics: bravery, adaptability, endurance, and enthusiasm for the tasks of war.

These qualities, rooted in a people's character, bolster an Army's spirit and strength when forged into the discipline and purpose of military virtue. A force enriched by this virtue becomes more resilient, more cohesive, and able to act with a unity that transcends individual differences in skill or experience. It enables a well-led Army to move as one, with each part contributing to the whole, guided by a shared sense of duty and honor that empowers soldiers beyond mere bravery or individual valor. Military virtue thus emerges as a critical asset—not indispensable to every victory but a formidable power that, when cultivated, can turn even ordinary forces into something extraordinary.

The role of military virtue, as distinct from other qualities, reveals some key insights about its specific place within various types of forces, leading to these deductions:

1. Military virtue is primarily a characteristic of standing armies, and these established forces benefit from it the most. In situations involving national uprisings, however, the same purpose is often served by natural qualities such as patriotism and the instinct to defend one's land. These inherent qualities emerge and strengthen more rapidly within irregular forces or local militias than the disciplined military virtue found in standing armies.

2. When standing armies face each other, they may function effectively even with limited military virtue, as the structured nature of their engagements compensates for this. However, when a standing army confronts a national insurrection, the need for military virtue becomes pronounced. In these circumstances, troops are frequently more dispersed, and each division operates with greater autonomy. The cohesion that military virtue provides thus becomes vital. Conversely, in situations where an army can remain concentrated, the General's strategic guidance plays a larger role, compensating for any lack of collective military spirit. As a result, the need for military virtue intensifies in proportion to the complexity of the theater of operations and the necessity for forces to operate independently.

These insights provide practical guidance: if an army lacks this fundamental military virtue, then simplifying war objectives and operations should be prioritized to avoid complex maneuvers that demand extensive independence from each unit. Further, organizational strength must be reinforced to compensate for any deficiency in military virtue. Relying solely on a standing army's structure does not ensure genuine cohesion; only a truly disciplined and mission-driven force can embody the unity and resilience crucial on the battlefield.

The military virtue of an army stands as one of the most critical moral forces in warfare. When absent, its role is sometimes filled by other factors, such as superior generalship or widespread public enthusiasm, but otherwise, the results of the army's efforts often fall short of expectations. The profound impact of military virtue is evident throughout history: the Macedonians under Alexander, the Roman legions under Caesar, the Spanish infantry under Alexander Farnese, the Swedes under Gustavus Adolphus and Charles XII, the Prussians under Frederick the Great, and the French under Napoleon. To ignore this historical evidence is to overlook how the remarkable successes of these leaders and their triumphs in dire circumstances were achievable only with armies that embodied this virtue.

This indomitable spirit can originate from only two sources, and both are required in combination: the first is a series of campaigns crowned with great victories, and the second is a level of army activity that sometimes reaches the utmost intensity. Through this dual process, the soldier gradually learns his own strengths, ultimately achieving a refined self-assurance essential for enduring and succeeding in the most challenging of military campaigns.

The more a General consistently demands from his troops, the greater confidence he can have that those demands will be met. Soldiers take as much pride in conquering hardship as they do in confronting danger. Thus, it is only within the continuous activity and relentless exertion of military life that the spirit of true military virtue can flourish, though it must also be nurtured by the glow of victory. Once this spirit is established, it becomes a resilient force, able to withstand even the harshest misfortunes, defeats, or prolonged periods of peace, albeit for a limited time. This resilient spirit, however, is fostered only in war and under the guidance of truly exceptional Generals; yet, once firmly rooted, it can endure across generations, even under moderate commanders and through extended peaceful intervals.

We should be careful not to confuse the noble, cohesive spirit of battle-hardened veteran troops, who bear the marks of war and have fully acclimated to its demands, with the superficial self-esteem often found in a standing army bound together by little more than regulations and drill routines. While steady discipline and strict adherence to orders can uphold a certain degree of military virtue, they cannot produce its essence. These qualities, though valuable, cannot stand on their own; they function like a fragile structure that, like glass cooled too quickly, can shatter with a single crack. An army built in peacetime might possess order, discipline, and a measure of pride, but these are not sufficient to create lasting unity and fortitude in the field. Under the slightest strain, even the highest morale can quickly shift to discouragement, or in some cases, outright panic, as in the French expression sauve que peut (every man for himself).

An army lacking deeply rooted military virtue can only accomplish great things under exceptional leadership—it cannot rely on itself alone. Such forces must be led with extraordinary care, gradually strengthened through both victory and shared hardships until they develop a sturdier armor of experience. Thus, it is essential not to conflate an army's spirit, rooted in a lasting, unified commitment to the cause, with the passing mood or temper that may shift with circumstances or setbacks.

Chapter VI. Boldness

In discussing boldness within the spectrum of strategic powers, we find it naturally opposing foresight and prudence, as previously examined in relation to the certainty of outcomes. Here, it becomes clear that theory cannot rightfully impose limits on boldness through its analytical framework or theoretical "laws." Boldness, this noble force that elevates the human spirit above daunting threats, must be recognized as a dynamic and essential element inherent to warfare. In truth, what other field of human endeavor would give boldness such a rightful home if not in War?

From the lowliest driver and drummer to the commanding General, boldness is the most noble of virtues. It is the very steel that sharpens and brings brilliance to the weapon of war. Indeed, in the realm of warfare, boldness has earned its own unique privileges. Beyond the calculable results of distance, timing, and quantity, we must grant boldness a "margin of effect," a certain latitude whereby it taps into and magnifies the weaknesses of opponents—when boldness truly dominates, it becomes a force of creation. This claim can be supported logically: whenever boldness confronts hesitation, the probability tilts naturally in its favor. Hesitation reveals an imbalance, a wavering that boldness can exploit and, in effect, convert to its own advantage.

Only when boldness meets with equally resolute and cautious foresight—foresight that is, in a sense, as powerful and daring in its way as boldness itself—does it encounter genuine resistance. Even so, such balanced confrontations are rare. Out of all the so-called cautious individuals we encounter, the majority lean toward prudence more out of an innate sense of fear than any true wisdom or discernment. Thus, while boldness may at times encounter obstacles, it retains a profound, almost instinctive advantage in the face of timidity.

In the collective actions of large armies, boldness is a vital force that enhances rather than detracts from other strengths. This is because the grand machinery of massed forces operates under a unifying will—an external, rational control guided by the structural discipline and commands that bind it together. Within this disciplined framework, boldness among the ranks acts like a compressed spring, ready to release its energy precisely when required.

As rank increases, boldness must evolve and pair with a reflective and purposeful mind. It can no longer be a raw outburst of passion, as it shifts from personal sacrifice to the responsibility for the safety and success of others, the whole force under command. Where regulations and routines shape the conduct of the lower ranks, the General must rely on judgment and reflection, as his boldness without purpose can readily turn into missteps. Yet even when misguided, boldness retains an admirable quality that sets it apart from other flaws. Armies that exhibit signs of untimely, fervent boldness reveal a deep-rooted strength, the excess growth of a fertile ground of martial spirit. Even foolhardiness, a reckless boldness without a clear goal, speaks to the same powerful force of feeling—a passion that lacks only the guidance of reason.

Still, when boldness descends into disobedience, defying orders or showing disregard for the established chain of command, it must be curbed. This is not because boldness itself is undesirable, but because the act of defiance threatens the central tenet of military success: obedience. In warfare, nothing carries greater weight than the discipline that obedience enforces, as it ensures cohesion and unity of purpose across the ranks.

Most will agree that, when measured equally in other qualities, over-caution leads to far more failures than boldness ever does. It may seem logical to assume that a clear objective would inspire and fortify boldness, thus reducing its inherent merit by making it less spontaneous; however, the reality often defies this assumption. The introduction of reason tempers the emotional drive behind boldness, often curtailing its intensity. Hence, as commanders advance in rank, boldness becomes increasingly rare. Whether or not a leader's understanding and judgment grow with promotion, the weight of external pressures and responsibilities increases with rank. These burdens frequently cloud a commander's mind and overwhelm less capable individuals with doubt and hesitation.

This dynamic is captured in the French proverb, "Tel brille au second qui s'éclipse au premier" ("He who shines in a secondary role is overshadowed in the first"). Many generals who appear unremarkable or indecisive when placed in supreme command were known earlier in their careers for their boldness and decisiveness. History offers numerous examples of such leaders, including Beaulieu, Benedek, Bazaine, Buller, Melas, and Mack, each showing that boldness can be a fleeting quality when untempered by experience and preparation for the responsibilities of high command.

When boldness arises from necessity, we must distinguish its varying levels of intensity. If danger is imminent, and one's actions are driven by an immediate need to escape a dire consequence, then we can admire the resolution displayed, though it still holds value. For example, if a young man leaps across a wide ravine to demonstrate his riding skill, his act is bold; but if he makes the same leap to escape a pursuing enemy, it is better described as resolute. The farther the necessity lies from the actual point of action, however, the greater the number of factors the mind must process to arrive at that choice, which means that the perceived necessity detracts less from the boldness of the act. Consider Frederick the Great: when he saw that war was unavoidable in 1756 and knew he had to strike first to avoid destruction, his decision to begin the war himself was, without a doubt, very bold. Few in his position would have had the will to act so decisively.

While strategy mainly concerns generals or high-ranking commanders, boldness in all ranks remains crucial, as it amplifies other military virtues within an army. With a bold force, many operations become possible that would otherwise be inconceivable in an army lacking this quality. Therefore, boldness should be nourished throughout the ranks, even if the central focus here is the boldness of the General. The higher one rises in command, the more intellect, insight, and strategic thinking dominate. As a result, boldness—a characteristic of the emotions—is often subdued, which is why it's so rare to find boldness combined with high command. Yet, when it does appear, it should be all the more admired. Boldness guided by superior intelligence marks the hero—not because it dares the impossible, but because it rigorously adheres to higher judgment and genius, calculating and acting with a speed born of instinct. When boldness expands the reach of a leader's vision, this expanded view produces outcomes that are accurate and wise, albeit riskier. In contrast, an average person, especially one who is naturally cautious, may reach careful conclusions at a distance from risk. However, as danger and responsibility press in, even the most cautious person loses the capacity to maintain clear sight of the broader situation and, often, their power to make a final decision.

It is nearly impossible to imagine a distinguished General who lacks boldness; this is not a trait one acquires but an innate power that serves as the foundation of a successful military career. The extent to which this power has been refined by experience and tempered by life shapes the leader as they reach a position of command. The greater the remaining capacity for boldness, the more powerful the mind, and the higher it soars. Risk will continue to grow, but so will the purpose and the goals. Whether the action stems from a distant and unavoidable necessity, as with Frederick, or is driven by grand ambition, as with Alexander, both demand boldness, albeit from different sources. Frederick's calculated approach might captivate the intellect, while Alexander's ambitious exploits stir the imagination.

The spirit of boldness can develop within an army either because it is inherent in the people or because a successful war led by competent generals has fostered it. In the latter scenario, however, the spirit of boldness cannot be present at the outset but must instead develop through sustained effort and victory. In our era, war remains almost the only means to cultivate this quality within a people, especially under bold leadership. Only through war can a nation counteract the comfort-seeking tendencies that can weaken the spirit, a decline often seen in prosperous societies focused on commercial growth.

For a nation to hold a robust political position, it must maintain a strong character and proficiency in war, allowing each to reinforce the other in a dynamic cycle. This fusion of character and military competence underlies a lasting national strength and provides a sturdy foundation upon which to navigate the complexities of the political landscape.

Chapter VII. Perseverance

The reader may come to this text expecting angles and lines, those hallmarks of scientific rigor, yet instead finds a cast of characters and forces drawn from everyday life, people as familiar as those encountered on any street. And yet, despite this divergence from mathematical precision, the author sees no need to introduce even a hint more mathematical reasoning than the subject demands. War, by its very nature, defies the tidy expectations and neat calculations that a formulaic approach might offer. In War, more than any other field, events play out unpredictably, often defying initial assumptions and transforming drastically upon closer inspection.

Consider the calm focus of an architect, who watches as each beam and stone rises in perfect alignment with the original design. Even the doctor, though contending with complex variables, possesses enough mastery over his tools and medicines to wield them with confidence. But for the Commander, the leader of a vast army, this level of certainty is unattainable. Instead, they find themselves swept into a storm of true and false reports, mistakes arising from fear or negligence, and a host of setbacks: contradictions to their orders, whether born from errors or sound judgments, ill will, genuine or misguided senses of duty, and the fatigue of the troops. Moreover, they must face accidents that no one could have foreseen, becoming subject to countless impressions—most discouraging, some offering slight encouragement. Over time, however, seasoned commanders acquire the intuition, or tact, to weigh and judge these incidents quickly. Those with high courage and resilience stand firm against this unrelenting storm of challenges as steadfastly as a rock withstands the pounding of waves. Anyone who wavers under these pressures would find themselves incapable of completing even the simplest mission.

Thus, perseverance becomes one of the most essential traits in the pursuit of a set objective, especially in the absence of a compelling reason to abandon it. Perseverance alone becomes the stabilizing counterbalance, standing firm against the thousand reasons to give up. Nearly every celebrated accomplishment in War has been achieved through immense toil, continuous effort, and the endurance of physical and mental hardships. The strain of war consistently threatens the soldier's will, ready to exploit any moment of weakness or exhaustion. Success, then, depends on an unbreakable will, an unyielding force of resolve that drives forward through adversity, standing as a testament to human tenacity and determination, inspiring admiration in the present and generations to come.

Chapter VIII. Superiority of Numbers

This principle of achieving victory applies universally in both tactics and strategy, and it deserves a thorough examination starting from its most general aspects. Here, we can consider it through the following perspective:

In Strategy, the choice of location, timing, and the numerical strength for battle is established. Through these three elements—place, time, and force—Strategy wields a substantial influence over the outcome of the encounter. Once tactics engages in the battle, and the dust settles with either victory or defeat, Strategy then seeks to exploit the outcome to advance the broader objective of the war. Typically, this ultimate objective lies at a considerable distance, rarely positioned near at hand. Numerous intermediate goals, each serving as a means to support the larger end, become essential stepping stones in reaching this ultimate objective. These goals vary considerably in their practical nature, and in each conflict, the overarching purpose may differ greatly. We will explore these matters in greater depth as we examine individual objectives and their strategic interplay; it is not our intention here to attempt a comprehensive catalog of them, even if that were feasible. Consequently, we defer further exploration of how battle outcomes are utilized strategically until later.

The way in which Strategy influences a battle's outcome is multi-faceted. As Strategy defines place, time, and force, it can implement each aspect in various ways, each exerting a different impact on both the battle's immediate result and its subsequent ramifications. Consequently, our understanding will evolve gradually as we delve into specific applications and situations that shape strategic influence.

If we isolate the combat from all modifying factors arising from its immediate objectives or circumstances and disregard the inherent bravery of troops, which we consider a constant, we are left with the pure concept of combat: a battle devoid of specific form, characterized solely by the number of participants. Within this framework, it is numerical strength alone that dictates the likelihood of victory. However, arriving at this point after stripping away so many other contributing factors highlights an essential truth: numerical superiority in battle is just one component in the pursuit of victory. Thus, having superior numbers does not, on its own, guarantee victory, nor even necessarily comprise the main advantage; its importance varies considerably depending on the additional circumstances in play.

Yet, the influence of numerical superiority has its degrees. One can envision forces being double, triple, or quadruple the size of their opposition, and it becomes clear that, as this advantage scales, it will eventually dominate all other factors. Ultimately, the sheer weight of numerical strength, when amplified to such extremes, becomes a force that can overtake and overwhelm everything else.

From this perspective, we acknowledge that numerical superiority is indeed a critical element in determining the outcome of a battle. However, this advantage must be substantial enough to offset all other contributing factors. Consequently, a fundamental strategic principle emerges: concentrate the largest possible number of troops at the decisive point. By doing so, whether or not our forces prove sufficient, we have maximized the potential of our available means. This principle is foundational in Strategy, universal in its application, and relevant across all historical contexts, whether for Greeks against Persians, English against Mahrattas, or French against Germans.

Yet, to refine our understanding, we should consider Europe's contemporary military dynamics, where armies are more uniformly matched in equipment, organization, and tactical proficiency. Only two factors—military spirit and the skill of Generals—create meaningful distinctions, and these qualities fluctuate with time and circumstance. Reviewing Europe's modern military history, we find few instances comparable to the likes of Marathon. Frederick the Great did triumph at Leuthen with about 30,000 men against 80,000 Austrians and at Rosbach with 25,000 men against a 50,000-strong coalition. These, however, are rare exceptions of victories achieved against forces more than double in size. Charles XII's victory at Narva doesn't offer an apt comparison, as the Russians then were yet unfamiliar with European tactics and standards, and too little is known of the battle's details.

Napoleon, at Dresden, faced 120,000 men against 220,000, less than double his own force. At Kollin, Frederick's attempt with 30,000 against 50,000 Austrians failed, as did Napoleon's efforts at Leipzig, where his 160,000 faced an Allied force of 280,000. These cases suggest that, in Europe's current military landscape, it is nearly impossible for even the most gifted General to achieve victory against an adversary with twice their numbers. This insight leads us to believe that, in both small and large battles, a substantial numerical advantage—often less than two-to-one—generally ensures victory, even if other factors are less favorable. Admittedly, extreme geographical obstacles, such as a narrow pass, might prevent even a force ten times greater from succeeding, but such situations fall outside the scope of typical battle.

Therefore, we conclude that in comparable circumstances, superior numbers at the decisive point are paramount. This principle applies generally, as strength at this point depends on both the army's absolute size and the General's skill in deploying it effectively.

Thus, the initial rule is to field the largest possible army. This might sound straightforward, yet it has not always been prioritized. To illustrate, in many detailed eighteenth-century war histories, the size of the armies is scarcely mentioned, if noted at all. And where it is, it receives no particular emphasis. In fact, it wasn't until Tempelhof, in his account of the Seven Years' War, that consistent data on army strength began to appear—though even he handled it somewhat superficially.

Even in Massenbach's extensive critiques of the Prussian campaigns of 1793-94 in the Vosges, we find abundant discussion of geographical features—hills, valleys, roads, and paths—yet hardly a word on the relative strength of forces. This omission reflects a curious idea once held by many critical historians, who believed there existed an ideal army size—a supposed "normal strength" beyond which additional forces would become more of a hindrance than a benefit. For instance, both Tempelhof and Montalembert hinted at this notion, with Tempelhof touching on it in his early writings and Montalembert raising it in his correspondence about the Russian plans in 1759.

Additionally, there are numerous examples where not all available forces were fully committed to a battle or a campaign simply because numerical superiority wasn't valued as highly as it should have been. The Prussians at Jena in 1806 and Wellington at Waterloo serve as notable examples where such miscalculations occurred.

If we firmly embrace the principle that a decisive numerical advantage can drive almost any outcome, this conviction should shape our approach to war preparations. We should aim to field the largest force possible, thereby either securing our own advantage or, at the very least, preventing the enemy from gaining one. This approach addresses the necessity of mobilizing the greatest absolute force at our disposal for any given war effort.

While it's true that determining this absolute force level falls under the government's purview, setting it is an integral part of the overarching strategy. Still, the General who leads these forces often has little influence over this initial determination. Whether due to a lack of input or limitations on resources, he is usually left to accept the forces as given and must find ways to make them count.

In situations where achieving outright numerical superiority is out of reach, the alternative is to create a relative advantage at decisive points through skillful deployment of available resources. At this stage, the art of calculating space and time becomes fundamental. This focus on timing and spatial calculation has, over time, come to represent much of what people believe defines the essence of military strategy. Some even attribute an almost unique mental acuity to master strategists in this area, as if they possessed an inherent sense of time and space.

However, while calculations of time and space are foundational to strategy and provide the daily basis for its practical execution, they are neither the most complex nor the most determinative factor in achieving victory.

If we take a straightforward look at military history, we find relatively few cases in which errors in calculating time and space alone led to significant losses, especially in strategic planning. When we try to explain every victory of an active, decisive commander—like Frederick the Great or Napoleon—through the mere technicalities of coordinating time and space, we run the risk of entangling ourselves in overly conventional thinking. Clarity and productive use of ideas demand that we accurately name and identify the true forces at play.

What actually characterizes the victories of such commanders lies in their keen understanding of their opponents (such as Daun or Schwarzenberg), their audacity in leaving only minor detachments in place temporarily, their energy in forced marches, their boldness in swift assaults, and the intense focus that truly great leaders summon in moments of critical danger. These qualities drive such outcomes, rather than a precise, sterile calculation of time and space.

Even the seemingly interconnected success—where triumphs like those at Rosbach and Montmirail catalyze victories at Leuthen and Montereau, as seen with commanders on the defensive—are, if we are exact, relatively rare historical occurrences. Far more commonly, the real strength of relative superiority lies in concentrating an overwhelming force at critical points. This success is rooted in accurately identifying those critical points, directing forces effectively from the outset, and decisively prioritizing critical engagements over less essential ones. Frederick the Great and Napoleon exemplify this approach with exceptional clarity.

With this in mind, we can recognize that numerical superiority holds a foundational place as a goal, something to be pursued as much as possible and prioritized in strategic calculations. However, considering it as an absolute prerequisite for victory would misunderstand its role. We are not implying that overwhelming numbers alone assure success. Instead, the core principle is to maximize available force whenever feasible, while the ultimate decision—whether to engage or withdraw—must rest on a comprehensive view of the situation.

In England, perhaps because of our lack of experience with invasion and the unique nature of colonial conflicts, we have yet to fully grasp the strategic importance of numerical superiority. We continue to cling to the notion of an "adequate" army size, a concept Clausewitz himself has critiqued sharply.

Chapter IX. The Surprise

From what we covered in the last chapter—the overall goal of gaining a relative advantage—comes another goal that is equally important: the element of surprise against the enemy. This goal is the foundation for nearly every plan, since without surprise, having the upper hand at the crucial moment isn't possible.

Surprise, then, isn't just a way to gain strength in numbers; it also stands as a powerful tactic on its own because of its psychological impact. When a surprise works well, it causes confusion and a drop in morale within the enemy's ranks, and there are countless examples, big and small, of how much success grows when this happens. Here, we're not just talking about the specific surprises that come with an attack but the goal to surprise the enemy in general, especially by how forces are positioned, which applies just as much to defense, where surprise is crucial.

We say that every plan without exception relies on surprise to some extent, although the amount varies depending on the type of operation and other factors.

This difference, in fact, comes from the unique qualities of the army, its commander, and even the government leading the war.

Keeping plans secret and acting quickly are the two main parts of this strategy, and they both rely on the government and Commander-in-Chief having strong willpower and the army having a high sense of duty. But with weak discipline or poor leadership, surprise is unlikely to succeed. And while this goal is common and necessary in war, and it's true that it always has some effect, it's also true that it rarely works to a remarkable degree because of its nature. We would misunderstand its power if we thought it could achieve a lot on its own. In theory, it holds a lot of promise; in reality, it often runs into obstacles and fails to move forward smoothly.

Surprise is much easier to achieve in tactics for a very simple reason: distances and time frames are smaller. So, in strategy, it's easier to use surprise the closer plans are to tactical actions, but it's much harder the more those plans move toward political goals.

Preparing for a war often takes several months; gathering an army in its main locations usually requires setting up depots and supply centers and making long marches, the purpose of which will eventually become clear enough.

It's a rare occurrence for one country to surprise another with a sudden declaration of war or by repositioning large military forces in an unforeseen direction. In the 1600s and 1700s, during an era when warfare centered largely around sieges, the idea of surrounding a fortified stronghold unexpectedly was a common goal. In fact, this tactic became a distinctive and crucial element in the art of warfare during those times. However, even back then, despite the focus on this type of surprise, it was seldom successfully achieved.

For events that can be organized within a day or two, the idea of a surprise is far more conceivable. In these cases, it's often feasible to move faster than the enemy expects, allowing a force to seize control of a strategic position, a territory, or a key route. But while such minor surprises are easier to plan and carry out, they generally lack significant impact. It becomes clear that the greater the potential effect of a surprise maneuver, the harder it becomes to put it into action. Some might believe that surprises on a small scale—such as seizing a position, taking control of a road, or even securing a crucial supply route—could lead to bigger outcomes like securing a victory in battle or capturing a major supply center. But this expectation, although it can be imagined, doesn't often find support in historical evidence. In fact, there are very few instances in recorded history where these smaller surprises have led to truly substantial results. It's reasonable, then, to conclude that there are inherent challenges that make it difficult for these minor surprises to have large-scale successes.

Of course, for anyone seeking insight from history on such matters, it's wise not to rely too heavily on the standard phrases, favored examples, or narrow interpretations of certain historians and critics. Rather, it's more valuable to examine the facts of history directly and see them with one's own eyes. For instance, consider a particular moment in the Silesian campaign of 1761, a campaign that has since achieved a certain level of historical prominence. Specifically, it was on July 22nd, a day that Frederick the Great is said to have outmaneuvered Laudon near Neisse, securing the route to Nossen. This move supposedly thwarted the planned alliance of Austrian and Russian forces in Upper Silesia, and it's believed that Frederick's maneuver earned him a valuable four-week advantage in the campaign. But anyone who carefully reads the key historical accounts of this campaign and examines this event objectively might not find this action as important as it's often portrayed. The impact of Frederick's maneuver on July 22nd, after closer examination, may not carry the weight that history sometimes assigns to it. The logic often used to explain its significance is fraught with contradictions. Additionally, Laudon's decisions during this well-known period of maneuvers are, in many ways, puzzling. So, one might question how anyone with a desire for truth and clarity could fully accept the traditional accounts of this event without hesitation.

In sum, while small, tactical surprises may achieve short-term goals or limited gains, expecting them to lead to sweeping, game-changing outcomes is usually unrealistic. And historical records themselves remind us to remain cautious when drawing conclusions from surprise tactics alone.

(*) Tempelhof, The Veteran, Frederick the Great. Also see (Clausewitz) "Hinterlassene Werke," vol. x., p. 158. When we anticipate major successes in a campaign based on the element of surprise, we tend to envision intense activity, swift decisions, and forced marches as the tools to achieve them. However, even with these efforts at the highest levels, they may not yield the desired outcome. Examples from Generals renowned for their skill in these tactics—like Frederick the Great and Napoleon Bonaparte—demonstrate this reality. Take Frederick, who left Dresden unexpectedly in July 1760, aiming to catch Lascy off guard, only to pivot back towards Dresden without any real gain. Instead of achieving his goal, this entire episode left him in a worse position, as he lost the fortress of Glatz during this time.

Similarly, in 1813, Napoleon twice pivoted unexpectedly from Dresden to attack Blücher—without mentioning his advance into Bohemia from Upper Lusatia—yet neither attempt met his objectives. These were ineffective moves that cost him valuable time and strength and could have put him in jeopardy in Dresden.

Thus, the success of a surprise doesn't always hinge solely on the Commander's energy, activity, or decisiveness. Instead, it requires additional favorable conditions, which are rare and usually beyond the Commander's direct control. Frederick and Napoleon each offer telling examples of this point. Napoleon's famed maneuver against Blücher's Army in February 1814, when Blücher's forces were isolated from the main Grand Army and advancing along the Marne, demonstrates a surprising move with remarkable results. In that instance, Napoleon achieved more in two days than one could normally expect from a surprise maneuver. Blücher's Army, stretched over a distance requiring a three-day march, was struck in segments, suffering losses akin to a defeat in a major battle. The surprise was complete, as Blücher would have organized his forces differently had he anticipated Napoleon's proximity. This success was largely due to Blücher's oversight; Napoleon didn't know all the specifics and thus benefited from an element of chance in his favor.

(*) Blücher believed his march was shielded by Pahlen's Cossacks, who, unbeknownst to him, had been withdrawn by the Grand Army Headquarters under Schwartzenberg without warning.

It was the same with the battle at Liegnitz in 1760. Frederick the Great won a remarkable victory by shifting his position during the night, just after he had settled on it. This move took Laudon completely by surprise, costing him 70 pieces of artillery and 10,000 men. Although Frederick had adopted the tactic of frequently changing his direction to either avoid battle or throw off his opponents' plans, the King himself noted that he changed positions on the night of August 14-15 not specifically to confuse the enemy, but simply because he wasn't satisfied with the location he'd chosen. Thus, chance played a significant role here, too; without the lucky timing of the attack, the overnight position change, and the challenging terrain, the outcome wouldn't have been the same.

Even in the broader sphere of Strategy, there are examples of surprises that led to major successes. Take, for instance, the impressive marches of the Great Elector against the Swedes, from Franconia to Pomerania and from Brandenburg to the Pregel River in 1757, or Bonaparte's famous crossing of the Alps in 1800. In Bonaparte's case, an entire army surrendered its strategic hold by capitulation; similarly, in 1757, another army was nearly forced to yield both its strategic ground and itself. Lastly, Frederick the Great's unexpected invasion of Silesia also serves as an example of a surprise attack with significant impact. Such events produced powerful results but are rare in history—unless we mistake them for situations where a state, like Saxony in 1756 or Russia in 1812, simply failed to prepare in time due to lack of activity or energy.

One essential observation remains. A surprise can only be effective when it is imposed by the side setting the terms of engagement. And it's the side that is acting from a place of strength that establishes those terms. If we surprise the enemy with a poor decision, we might end up facing significant losses rather than benefits. In such cases, the enemy doesn't even need to react to the surprise; the mistake itself provides the means to counter the attack. Generally, since offensive action involves more proactive movements, surprises are more naturally suited to the attacker. However, this isn't always the case, as we'll see later. Mutual surprises can occur between both the offensive and defensive, and in these cases, the advantage goes to the side whose strategy is better timed and more effective.

Ideally, this should be how it works, yet practical reality doesn't follow this model precisely, for a straightforward reason. The psychological impact of a surprise often transforms an otherwise poor situation into a favorable one for the side that manages to surprise, and it can prevent the other side from making effective decisions. In such situations, not only the chief commander but each individual leader on the surprised side is affected. A surprise disrupts unity, allowing the individual judgment of each leader to emerge more readily.

Much depends on the overall balance of power and morale between the two sides. When one side possesses a strong moral advantage, intimidating and overpowering the other, it can use surprise tactics more effectively, even benefiting from situations where failure might otherwise seem inevitable.

Chapter X. Stratagem

Stratagem involves a hidden motive and thus stands in opposition to straightforward dealings, just as wit differs from direct reasoning. It has little to do with persuasion, personal gain, or outright force, but closely aligns with deceit, as both aim to keep their intentions concealed. Stratagem itself can be seen as a type of deception, although it differs from typical deceit in that it does not involve breaking any explicit promises. The one using stratagem leaves it to the other party to make their own errors in judgment, which, eventually accumulating into one critical mistake, suddenly reveal the real situation. In this way, just as wit is a clever handling of ideas, stratagem is a clever handling of actions.

At first glance, it might seem that Strategy derived its name appropriately from stratagem, and that even with all the real and apparent shifts in how wars have been waged since the time of the Greeks, this term still captures the essence of Strategy. If we leave the actual execution of battle—the physical combat itself—to tactics, and view Strategy as the art of using these encounters with skill, then besides the inherent forces of character, such as intense ambition or an unbreakable will, no personal trait seems as naturally suited to guide strategic activity as stratagem. The constant drive toward surprise that we discussed earlier hints at this connection, as every attempt at surprise contains at least a touch of stratagem.

However, as much as we might like to imagine commanders in war outwitting each other with stealth, agility, and clever ruses, we have to acknowledge that these traits rarely show up prominently in historical accounts and have seldom managed to emerge amidst the many surrounding factors and conditions.

The reason for this is fairly clear, and it almost parallels what we discussed in the previous section. Strategy, unlike daily life, has no room for actions that consist merely of words—statements, declarations, and the like. In everyday situations, such words are inexpensive and are often the primary tools with which a cunning person can mislead others. In war, however, what resembles these verbal tricks—like false plans, misleading orders, or purposely planted rumors—generally have limited impact in the broader scope of Strategy. These actions are used only in specific cases that present themselves, meaning they don't arise naturally from the commander's own strategy.

Moreover, for a deception to reach the level of appearing as a real battle plan and to convincingly mislead the enemy, significant time and resources are required. The greater the intended impression, the larger the effort and time spent. Since armies rarely have the luxury to invest such time and effort for mere deception, very few "demonstrations" in Strategy achieve their intended goals. In fact, committing large numbers of troops to a mere feint for too long is risky, as the forces might ultimately be needed elsewhere at a decisive moment, especially if the trick fails.

The main leader in a war is generally well aware of this hard truth and has little interest in engaging in tactical tricks for show. The grave seriousness of necessity pushes everything toward direct action, leaving little room for games. In essence, the movements on the strategic chessboard lack the quickness and adaptability essential to true stratagem.

From this, we conclude that a sharp and perceptive mind is more essential and beneficial to a General than craftiness, though craftiness can be advantageous as long as it doesn't come at the cost of necessary qualities of character—a compromise that is all too common.

Yet, as strategic resources dwindle and forces weaken, they become more suited for employing stratagem. For those who find themselves powerless and vulnerable, with all other prudence and insight failing them, stratagem emerges as a final option. The more dire and desperate their situation, the more they are driven to one bold, decisive strike, and the more naturally stratagem aligns with this approach. When freed from any need to calculate further or to plan for what comes next, boldness and stratagem can reinforce each other. Together, they focus even a faint glimmer of hope into a sharp, concentrated point—one that just might ignite into something much greater.

Chapter XI. Assembly of Forces in Space

The best approach in Strategy is to be as strong as possible—first in general and then at the decisive point. Thus, beyond the initial effort that creates the Army, a task not always handled by the General, there's no law more urgent or straightforward in Strategy than to keep forces united. No portion should be separated from the main body unless absolutely necessary. This is a principle we stand by and view as a reliable guide. Over time, we will understand what valid reasons might justify a detachment of forces, and we'll see that this principle's impact varies depending on the aims and resources of each War.

It may seem unbelievable, yet history has seen countless instances where troops were divided or separated simply because of a vague adherence to conventional practice, without any clear reasoning. When the principle of keeping forces concentrated is understood as the rule, with every division as an exception needing a strong justification, not only is such pointless division avoided, but many flawed reasons for dividing forces are also prevented from taking hold.

Chapter XII. Assembly of Forces in Time

Here, we are dealing with an idea that often appears misleading in real-life situations. To clarify it, we need to define and explain it carefully, and we ask for a brief analysis to do so.

War can be thought of as the collision of two opposing forces. Naturally, this would mean that the stronger force not only destroys the other but also drives it forward in its own momentum. This suggests that all forces intended for the collision should be applied at once as a fundamental rule of War.

In reality, this holds true, but only when the battle acts like a mechanical collision. When the battle becomes an ongoing, mutual struggle of destructive forces, we can indeed imagine using forces in stages. This is especially the case in tactics, mainly due to the central role of firearms, but also for other reasons. For instance, if 1,000 soldiers face 500 in a gunfight, the total damage depends on the size of both forces; the side with 1,000 will fire twice as many shots as the side with 500, yet more shots will likely hit the 1,000 soldiers than the 500, since they are assumed to be in tighter formations.

If we suppose the number of hits is double, both sides would suffer similar losses. Out of the 500, there might be 200 casualties, and similarly, out of the 1,000. Now, if the side with 500 had held back another 500, keeping them out of the line of fire, both sides would have 800 soldiers still fit for action. However, one side would have 500 fresh soldiers with full ammunition and high morale, while the other side would have 800 who are somewhat disordered, low on ammunition, and physically drained.

The assumption that 1,000 soldiers would suffer twice the losses that 500 would isn't accurate. The additional loss the side with the reserve troops faces should be considered a downside of their original arrangement. Furthermore, it's likely that the side with 1,000 soldiers would initially have an advantage by pushing back the opponent and forcing them to retreat. Now, whether these initial benefits balance out the downside of ending with 800 somewhat disordered troops against an opponent who isn't much weaker in number and has 500 completely fresh soldiers, is not something we can resolve with more analysis; here, we must turn to experience. Few seasoned officers would disagree that, in most cases, the advantage goes to the side with fresh troops in reserve.

In this way it becomes evident how the employment of too many forces in combat may be disadvantageous; for whatever advantages the superiority may give in the first moment, we may have to pay dearly for in the next.

But this danger only endures as long as the disorder, the state of confusion and weakness lasts, in a word, up to the crisis which every combat brings with it even for the conqueror. Within the duration of this relaxed state of exhaustion, the appearance of a proportionate number of fresh troops is decisive.

But when this disordering effect of victory stops, and therefore only the moral superiority remains which every victory gives, then it is no longer possible for fresh troops to restore the combat, they would only be carried along in the general movement; a beaten Army cannot be brought back to victory a day after by means of a strong reserve. Here we find ourselves at the source of a highly material difference between tactics and strategy.

The tactical results, the results within the four corners of the battle, and before its close, lie for the most part within the limits of that period of disorder and weakness. But the strategic result, that is to say, the result of the total combat, of the victories realised, let them be small or great, lies completely (beyond) outside of that period. It is only when the results of partial combats have bound themselves together into an independent whole, that the strategic result appears, but then, the state of crisis is over, the forces have resumed their original form, and are now only weakened to the extent of those actually destroyed (placed hors de combat).

The consequence of this difference is, that tactics can make a continued use of forces, Strategy only a simultaneous one.(*)

(*) See chaps. xiii., and xiv., Book III and chap. xxix. Book V.—TR.

If I cannot, in tactics, decide all by the first success, if I have to fear the next moment, it follows of itself that I employ only so much of my force for the success of the first moment as appears sufficient for that object, and keep the rest beyond the reach of fire or conflict of any kind, in order to be able to oppose fresh troops to fresh, or with such to overcome those that are exhausted. But it is not so in Strategy. Partly, as we have just shown, it has not so much reason to fear a reaction after a success realised, because with that success the crisis stops; partly all the forces strategically employed are not necessarily weakened. Only so much of them as have been tactically in conflict with the enemy's force, that is, engaged in partial combat, are weakened by it; consequently, only so much as was unavoidably necessary, but by no means all which was strategically in conflict with the enemy, unless tactics has expended them unnecessarily. Corps which, on account of the general superiority in numbers, have either been little or not at all engaged, whose presence alone has assisted in the result, are after the decision the same as they were before, and for new enterprises as efficient as if they had been entirely inactive. How greatly such corps which thus constitute our excess may contribute to the total success is evident in itself; indeed, it is not difficult to see how they may even diminish considerably the loss of the forces engaged in tactical, conflict on our side.

If, therefore, in Strategy the loss does not increase with the number of the troops employed, but is often diminished by it, and if, as a natural consequence, the decision in our favor is, by that means, the more certain, then it follows naturally that in Strategy we can never employ too many forces, and consequently also that they must be applied simultaneously to the immediate purpose.

But we must vindicate this proposition upon another ground. We have hitherto only spoken of the combat itself; it is the real activity in War, but men, time, and space, which appear as the elements of this activity, must, at the same time, be kept in view, and the results of their influence brought into consideration also.

Fatigue, exertion, and privation constitute in War a special principle of destruction, not essentially belonging to contest, but more or less inseparably bound up with it, and certainly one which especially belongs to Strategy. They no doubt exist in tactics as well, and perhaps there in the highest degree; but as the duration of the tactical acts is shorter, therefore the small effects of exertion and privation on them can come but little into consideration. But in Strategy on the other hand, where time and space, are on a larger scale, their influence is not only always very considerable, but often quite decisive. It is not at all uncommon for a victorious Army to lose many more by sickness than on the field of battle.

If, therefore, we look at this sphere of destruction in Strategy in the same manner as we have considered that of fire and close combat in tactics, then we may well imagine that everything which comes within its vortex will, at the end of the campaign or of any other strategic period, be reduced to a state of weakness, which makes the arrival of a fresh force decisive. We might therefore conclude that there is a motive in the one case as well as the other to strive for the first success with as few forces as possible, in order to keep up this fresh force for the last.

In order to estimate exactly this conclusion, which, in many cases in practice, will have a great appearance of truth, we must direct our attention to the separate ideas which it contains. In the first place, we must not confuse the notion of reinforcement with that of fresh unused troops. There are few campaigns at the end of which an increase of force is not earnestly desired by the conqueror as well as the conquered, and indeed should appear decisive; but that is not the point here, for that increase of force could not be necessary if the force had been so much larger at the first. But it would be contrary to all experience to suppose that an Army coming fresh into the field is to be esteemed higher in point of moral value than an Army already in the field, just as a tactical reserve is more to be esteemed than a body of troops which has been already severely handled in the fight. Just as much as an unfortunate campaign lowers the courage and moral powers of an Army, a successful one raises these elements in their value. In the generality of cases, therefore, these influences are compensated, and then there remains over and above as clear gain the habituation to War. We should besides look more here to successful than to unsuccessful campaigns, because when the greater probability of the latter may be seen beforehand, without doubt forces are wanted, and, therefore, the reserving a portion for future use is out of the question.

This point being settled, then the question is, Do the losses which a force sustains through fatigues and privations increase in proportion to the size of the force, as is the case in a combat? And to that we answer "No."

The fatigues of War result in a great measure from the dangers with which every moment of the act of War is more or less impregnated. To encounter these dangers at all points, to proceed onwards with security in the execution of one's plans, gives employment to a multitude of agencies which make up the tactical and strategic service of the Army. This service is more difficult the weaker an Army is, and easier as its numerical superiority over that of the enemy increases. Who can doubt this? A campaign against a much weaker enemy will therefore cost smaller efforts than against one just as strong or stronger.

So much for the fatigues. It is somewhat different with the privations; they consist chiefly of two things, the want of food, and the want of shelter for the troops, either in quarters or in suitable camps. Both these wants will no doubt be greater in proportion as the number of men on one spot is greater. But does not the superiority in force afford also the best means of spreading out and finding more room, and therefore more means of subsistence and shelter?

If Buonaparte, in his invasion of Russia in 1812, concentrated his Army in great masses upon one single road in a manner never heard of before, and thus caused privations equally unparalleled, we must ascribe it to his maxim that it is impossible to be too strong at the decisive point. Whether in this instance he did not strain the principle too far is a question which would be out of place here; but it is certain that, if he had made a point of avoiding the distress which was by that means brought about, he had only to advance on a greater breadth of front. Room was not wanted for the purpose in Russia, and in very few cases can it be wanted. Therefore, from this no ground can be deduced to prove that the simultaneous employment of very superior forces must produce greater weakening. But now, supposing that in spite of the general relief afforded by setting apart a portion of the Army, wind and weather and the toils of War had produced a diminution even on the part which as a spare force had been reserved for later use, still we must take a comprehensive general view of the whole, and therefore ask, Will this diminution of force suffice to counterbalance the gain in forces, which we, through our superiority in numbers, may be able to make in more ways than one?

But there still remains a most important point to be noticed. In a partial combat, the force required to obtain a great result can be approximately estimated without much difficulty, and, consequently, we can form an idea of what is superfluous. In Strategy this may be said to be impossible, because the strategic result has no such well-defined object and no such circumscribed limits as the tactical. Thus what can be looked upon in tactics as an excess of power, must be regarded in Strategy as a means to give expansion to success, if opportunity offers for it; with the magnitude of the success the gain in force increases at the same time, and in this way the superiority of numbers may soon reach a point which the most careful economy of forces could never have attained.

By means of his enormous numerical superiority, Buonaparte was enabled to reach Moscow in 1812, and to take that central capital. Had he by means of this superiority succeeded in completely defeating the Russian Army, he would, in all probability, have concluded a peace in Moscow which in any other way was much less attainable. This example is used to explain the idea, not to prove it, which would require a circumstantial demonstration, for which this is not the place.(*)

(*) Compare Book VII., second edition, p. 56.

All these reflections bear merely upon the idea of a successive employment of forces, and not upon the conception of a reserve properly so called, which they, no doubt, come in contact with throughout, but which, as we shall see in the following chapter, is connected with some other considerations.

What we desire to establish here is, that if in tactics the military force through the mere duration of actual employment suffers a diminution of power, if time, therefore, appears as a factor in the result, this is not the case in Strategy in a material degree. The destructive effects which are also produced upon the forces in Strategy by time, are partly diminished through their mass, partly made good in other ways, and, therefore, in Strategy it cannot be an object to make time an ally on its own account by bringing troops successively into action.

We say on "its own account," for the influence which time, on account of other circumstances which it brings about but which are different from itself can have, indeed must necessarily have, for one of the two parties, is quite another thing, is anything but indifferent or unimportant, and will be the subject of consideration hereafter.

The rule which we have been seeking to set forth is, therefore, that all forces which are available and destined for a strategic object should be simultaneously applied to it; and this application will be so much the more complete the more everything is compressed into one act and into one movement.

But still there is in Strategy a renewal of effort and a persistent action which, as a chief means towards the ultimate success, is more particularly not to be overlooked, it is the continual development of new forces. This is also the subject of another chapter, and we only refer to it here in order to prevent the reader from having something in view of which we have not been speaking.

We now turn to a subject very closely connected with our present considerations, which must be settled before full light can be thrown on the whole, we mean the strategic reserve.

Chapter XIII. Strategic Reserve

A reserve has two distinct purposes: first, to extend and renew the battle, and second, to provide support in case of unexpected developments. The first purpose suggests the benefit of deploying forces gradually, which doesn't apply to Strategy. For instance, when a unit is dispatched to reinforce a position that's close to falling, it falls under the second purpose since the need for reinforcement couldn't have been fully anticipated. But a unit positioned at the rear specifically to prolong the fight would essentially be a tactical reserve, under the command of the lead General and not a strategic one.

However, in Strategy, the need for a reserve to handle unforeseen situations does exist, especially when unexpected events could arise. In tactics, where the enemy's moves are often revealed only through direct observation—and may be obscured by every forest, slope, or fold in the landscape—preparedness for unexpected events is essential. Reserves can then be deployed to bolster areas that suddenly appear too weak and to adjust the formation of forces to align more effectively with the enemy's movements.

Such cases also arise in Strategy, given that strategic decisions are closely tied to tactical developments. Often in Strategy, actions are based on what is observed directly, on unconfirmed reports arriving periodically, or on immediate combat outcomes. As a result, a core aspect of strategic command is to hold forces in reserve according to the level of unpredictability for future events.

This is particularly true in defensive scenarios, and especially in defending natural barriers like rivers or hills, where surprises are frequent and necessary. Yet, this unpredictability lessens as strategic operations move further away from immediate tactical demands and diminish almost entirely as they align more closely with political concerns.

For instance, the enemy's precise direction in battle can only be seen firsthand; the point at which he plans to cross a river becomes clear from last-minute preparations; and the route for invading a country is often reported by the newspapers before the first shot is fired. The larger the operation, the less likely it is to be a surprise. Factors like time and distance become so extensive, and the circumstances leading to the action so public and unchangeable, that the upcoming event is either revealed well in advance or can be predicted with reasonable accuracy.

Conversely, the value of a reserve in these broader strategic situations, even if available, tends to be less impactful the more the action assumes a generalized form.

We've observed that the outcome of a smaller battle, by itself, doesn't hold much weight; each individual combat only finds true significance when seen as part of the larger battle's outcome. Yet, even this decision in the full-scale battle is not absolute and varies in importance, depending on how critical the defeated force was to the overall strength. For example, a defeat of one division can be offset by a victory achieved by the whole army. Even a lost battle for an entire army can be balanced, or even turned to advantage, by a more decisive victory soon after, as seen in the two-day Battle of Kulm on August 29 and 30, 1813. There's no room for doubt here; however, it is equally clear that each victory's impact is far greater when it affects a larger, essential part of the enemy's forces, making future chances of recovery much slimmer. We will go over this progression in more detail elsewhere, but it's enough here to highlight its unquestionable importance.

If we add a third consideration to this idea, which is that in tactics, where forces are used steadily, the overall result is often delayed until the action is fully complete, while in Strategy, where forces are often used all at once, the main outcome can usually be felt from the very start. From these three points alone, we can clearly see why strategic reserves become progressively unnecessary, increasingly irrelevant, and even risky as their intended use becomes broader and more generalized.

It's not hard to pinpoint the moment when strategic reserves become an unrealistic concept: it's the moment of the SUPREME DECISION. All available forces must be used in this crucial phase, and keeping any reserve solely for use after this moment goes against all logic.

In tactics, reserves allow for both countering unexpected enemy maneuvers and addressing unforeseen combat outcomes if things go poorly; in contrast, Strategy, at least when it concerns the most decisive outcome, cannot rely on these options. Typically, Strategy can only make up for losses at one position by achieving gains elsewhere, occasionally by repositioning troops, but planning for such reversals with reserves in advance has no place in strategic planning.

We've called the idea of a strategic reserve that does not support the main outcome absurd. We would not have gone into such detail on this topic in these chapters if this idea did not often appear in different forms, presented as sound, sensible thinking. One person sees this reserve as the peak of strategic insight and foresight; another dismisses it outright, along with the concept of any reserve, which extends even to tactical reserves. This mix-up of ideas influences reality, and to witness a remarkable example of this confusion, we only need to recall that in 1806 Prussia left a reserve of 20,000 men stationed in the Mark under Prince Eugene of Württemberg—who could not possibly reach the Saale in time to be useful—and that another 25,000 troops remained in East and South Prussia, only meant to be activated later as a reserve.

With such examples, we cannot be accused of merely battling with illusions.

Chapter XIV. Economy of Forces

The path of reasoning, as we've discussed, rarely fits neatly into strict principles or defined opinions, much like a mathematical line. There's always some flexibility. But this applies to all practical skills in life. In art, for example, we don't define beauty with exact measurements; lines of grace can't be traced by formulas. So, in War, the person in command quickly learns that they must rely on a refined sense of judgment—one that, based on natural insight and sharpened through reflection, instinctively grasps the right decision. They realize that sometimes the guiding rule must be simplified down to a few core principles that become their compass, while at other times, a particular approach becomes their solid ground for action.

One essential guiding point is this: maintaining the coordination of all available forces, or, in simpler terms, making sure no part of the force is left idle. If there are troops where the enemy isn't fully engaging them, or if a part of the force is kept marching, inactive while the enemy is fighting, then the forces are being mismanaged. In this sense, leaving forces unused is worse than using them inefficiently. When action is necessary, the first priority is for every part of the force to act because even activity with less clear purpose still engages and wears down part of the enemy's resources, while troops kept entirely idle lose their effectiveness for that moment. This principle is clearly connected with the ideas in the last three sections; it's the same essential truth, viewed from a broader perspective and condensed into one clear idea.

Chapter XV. Geometrical Element

The extent to which the geometric element, or form, in the arrangement of military forces can become a central principle is most evident in the art of fortification, where geometry dictates both major and minor details. Geometry also plays a large role in tactics. It serves as the foundation of basic tactics, or the theory of moving troops; but in field fortification, as well as in the theory of positions and their attack, its lines and angles act like rulers that often determine the outcome. Some aspects have been misused in the past, and some were trivial; yet, in today's tactics, where surrounding the enemy is a key goal in every combat, the geometric element has gained renewed importance in a simple yet consistently applied way. Even so, in tactics, where everything is more fluid and where moral forces, individual actions, and chance weigh more heavily than in siege warfare, the geometric element can never reach the same level of dominance. Its role is even less in Strategy; certainly, in Strategy, the arrangement of troops, along with the shapes of countries and territories, holds significance, but the geometric element is not decisive, as it is in fortifications, nor is it as crucial as in tactics. How this influence presents itself can only be demonstrated gradually in those instances where it clearly emerges. Here, our aim is to highlight the difference between tactics and Strategy concerning its impact.

In tactics, time and space quickly narrow to their smallest possible limits. If a troop formation is attacked from the flank or rear, it soon reaches a point where retreat is no longer possible; such a position nears an absolute inability to continue the fight, requiring it to break free or avoid such a situation entirely. This adds great effectiveness to all strategies designed to create such circumstances, mostly due to the anxiety it creates for the enemy about possible outcomes. For this reason, the geometric arrangement of forces is a key factor in achieving tactical success.

In Strategy, this concept appears only faintly, due to the larger time and space scales. We don't engage one theater of war with another directly, and sometimes weeks or even months may pass before a strategic move intended to encircle the enemy can be completed. Additionally, the distances involved are so vast that even with the best planning, the chance of perfectly targeting the desired point is low.

In Strategy, the opportunity for such combinations—that is, those based on the geometric element—is much narrower, and for this reason, any advantage gained at a particular point has a much stronger impact. Once an advantage is secured, it has ample time to develop fully before it is interrupted or entirely negated by any opposing efforts. Thus, we confidently regard it as an established truth that, in Strategy, the quantity and scale of victorious battles matter more than the shape of the overarching lines that connect them.

However, an opposing view has been popular in modern theory, claiming that by emphasizing geometric form, greater importance could be attributed to Strategy. Since Strategy was thought to involve higher mental functions, it was hoped this perspective would elevate the nature of War and, as some argued—by substituting new ideas—make it appear more scientific. We consider it a fundamental duty of any thorough theory to clearly expose such misconceptions. Since the geometric element often serves as the foundational concept in these theories, we have emphasized this point to make its implications unmistakable.

Chapter XVI. On the Suspension of the Act in War

If one considers War as an act of mutual In considering the idea of destruction, we typically picture both sides moving forward in some way, each one aiming to gain an advantage; however, when we focus on the present, it's almost inevitable that one side will appear to be preparing or waiting, while the other is making the actual advance. This difference occurs because conditions between two opposing forces are rarely, if ever, exactly the same, and as time progresses, circumstances are bound to shift. As a result, at any given moment, one side will likely hold a slight advantage over the other. Now, if both commanders are fully aware of this disparity, it logically follows that the side with the more favorable position has a clear motivation to act, while the opposing commander would have an equally compelling reason to wait. Therefore, it's unusual to find both sides equally inclined to advance at the same time, just as it is improbable that it would serve both of their interests to remain passive simultaneously. This opposition of interests regarding movement versus waiting does not stem from any general principle of polarity, and thus does not contradict the argument we presented in the fifth chapter. Rather, it arises because both commanders are reacting to the same situational factor—the likelihood of either improving or worsening their respective positions through any forthcoming actions.

But let's suppose, for the sake of argument, that both sides somehow find themselves in an almost perfectly balanced state where neither side has a stronger advantage, or, let's consider that each commander might mistakenly believe the situation to be even, due to limited or imperfect knowledge of the opponent's position. Even in such cases, differences in their political objectives prevent the two sides from remaining entirely inactive for long. From a political standpoint, at least one of the opposing forces must be seen as the aggressor, because it is virtually impossible for a war to break out if both sides' intentions are purely defensive. Politically, the aggressor pursues an active, positive objective, while the defender's purpose is primarily reactive and, therefore, negative. This distinction means that, even in scenarios where both forces are evenly matched or equally uncertain about the other's circumstances, it falls to the aggressor to take action, driven by the need to fulfill a positive aim. Thus, the responsibility to move forward lies on the aggressor, as only through direct action can they achieve the objective that initially led them to initiate the conflict.

From this perspective, any pause in warfare goes against its very nature; two armies, as incompatible forces, should continuously strive to eliminate each other, just as fire and water don't reach a state of balance but instead act upon one another until one of them is gone. Imagine two wrestlers, locked together, yet not making a single move for hours—that would be unnatural. In the same way, action in war should, ideally, progress without pause, like a clock that ticks down in steady motion. Yet, despite the wild and intense nature of war, it is still held back by human limitations. This paradox—that people deliberately create and step into dangers they simultaneously fear—should not be surprising to anyone.

When we glance at military history as a whole, we often observe the opposite of a relentless drive toward a goal. In fact, it appears that standing still or doing nothing is often the standard state for an army engaged in war, while taking action is the exception. This might lead one to question whether our understanding of constant motion in war is even accurate. However, though this tendency toward inaction can be seen broadly in history, recent campaigns stand out as proof that ongoing action is possible. The wars of the French Revolution, and especially the campaigns led by Napoleon, clearly demonstrate the concept in practice. In these campaigns, war was carried out with an intensity that pushed it to its natural limits. So, this level of continuous action is indeed possible—and if it's possible, it follows that it must also be necessary.

How else could anyone justify the tremendous use of resources in warfare if action weren't the primary goal? A baker heats his oven only when he has bread to bake; a horse is only harnessed when there's a journey to undertake; so why engage in the immense efforts of war if the only objective is to provoke similar efforts in the enemy?

Thus, the general principle that action should be constant is validated. Now, let's look at some of its inherent modifications—those that stem from the nature of war itself, apart from any specific circumstances.

Here, we should take note of three factors that naturally counterbalance this principle, slowing down what would otherwise be an unchecked drive forward.

The first factor, which consistently leads to delays and serves as a slowing principle, is the natural tendency toward hesitation and lack of resolve within the human mind. This is akin to a form of inertia within the moral world, driven not by attraction but by repulsion—that is, by fear of danger and the weight of responsibility.

In the intense, heated environment of War, people who are usually steady and dependable can seem to become sluggish, weighed down by hesitation. To keep things moving continuously, a stronger push, repeated frequently, is necessary. The mere thought of the goal they've set out to achieve is rarely enough to overcome this inner resistance. If there isn't a leader with a natural drive for war—a person who thrives in its challenges, as a fish does in water—or if the pressure of some significant responsibility isn't driving them forward, then the common tendency will be to hold back, to pause, and rarely to advance.

The second factor is the limited nature of human understanding and judgment, which becomes even more pronounced in War. Here, people rarely have a clear idea of their own position from one moment to the next, let alone an accurate perception of the enemy's position, which is usually shrouded in secrecy. This uncertainty often leads both sides to see the same objective as advantageous, even though, in reality, it benefits one side more than the other. Because of this, both sides may believe it wise to hold back and wait, as discussed in the fifth chapter of the second book.

The third factor, acting like a gear that locks up periodically to bring things to a halt, is the inherent advantage of defensive positioning. One side may feel too weak to attack the other, but that doesn't mean that the other side feels strong enough to launch an attack either. When shifting from defense to offense, not only is the added strength of a defensive stance lost, but this advantage also transfers to the opponent. Put simply, the advantage difference between offense and defense can be represented by twice the defensive advantage, which explains how both sides might, simultaneously, feel too weak to attack each other and may truly be so.

Thus, even during active military engagements, careful planning and the fear of taking on excessive risk manage to find a foothold, allowing them to moderate and rein in the natural intensity of war. Yet, these factors alone—even if their effects are not exaggerated—don't fully account for the prolonged stretches of inactivity common in the wars of earlier times. In many of those wars, fought over relatively minor stakes, this inactivity filled nine-tenths of the time that troops were deployed.

The primary reason for this tendency towards long pauses lies in the balance of demands and the general outlook of each side, as discussed in the chapter on the essence and purpose of War. In such wars, the influence of minor political interests or the lack of a strong will to act decisively made War a kind of "half-

and-half" affair, lacking full commitment. A war might function as nothing more than an armed neutrality, or as a show of strength to boost negotiations. Often, it was an effort to gain small advantages with minimal effort while waiting for favorable conditions, or a burdensome treaty obligation carried out with minimal enthusiasm.

In cases like these, where the driving interest is weak and the spirit of hostility low, where there's little urgency to act and not much to fear from the enemy, there are no strong motives urging cabinets to take big risks. This led to a restrained form of war in which the real fighting spirit was chained down, and War became a tame, hesitant endeavor.

The more War becomes drained of its vitality in this way, the less its theory retains the solid principles and foundations necessary for logical reasoning. The essential factors decrease, and the accidental ones grow, shifting the nature of War. However, even in this type of warfare, there's a certain cleverness at play—perhaps more varied and widespread than in the more intense form of War. What was once a high-stakes game played with gold coins now resembles a business transaction with small change. On this battleground, where War drags on with minor maneuvers, skirmishes at outposts that seem half-hearted, and elaborate plans that come to nothing, where positions are taken and abandoned, leaving only faint traces of purpose and sense, here—on this field—many theorists see the true Art of War. They celebrate these feints, parries, and superficial skirmishes of earlier wars as the ultimate goal of military theory, viewing them as proof of the mind's triumph over brute force. To them, modern Wars are merely barbaric brawls, devoid of meaning or lessons, and as steps backward into chaos.

This perspective is as superficial as the minor skirmishes it romanticizes. Certainly, when great forces and passions are absent, it's easier for a skillful hand to display finesse; but isn't commanding great forces a higher exercise of the intellect in itself? Doesn't this conventional war of tactics and tricks belong to the broader and more demanding conduct of large-scale conflict? Doesn't it serve the same role as the agile movements on a ship compared to the motion of the ship itself? Such tactics can only succeed as long as the enemy follows the same unspoken rules. But how long can we rely on the enemy respecting those outdated customs? Did not the French Revolution catch us off guard, shattering our established system of War from Chalons to Moscow? And didn't Frederick the Great do the same to the Austrians, who were unprepared and secure in their traditional methods, shaking their entire monarchy to its core?

Woe to the government that faces a determined enemy with only a half-hearted policy and an outdated military system. Against an opponent who acts like a force of nature, recognizing no law but that of its own strength, every lack of energy or effort tilts the scales in the enemy's favor. Switching from these sparring tactics to the mindset of a true fighter isn't easy, and even a light blow may bring the whole structure crashing down.

The sum of all these factors is that the active phases of a campaign rarely proceed in a smooth, uninterrupted line. Instead, they move in bursts, with periods of tension and observation between the bloody clashes. During these pauses, both sides typically fall into a defensive stance. However, when one side pursues a higher purpose, it tends to favor offense, keeping itself in a generally advancing posture, which naturally affects how it proceeds.

Chapter XVII. On the Character of Modern War

The close attention given to the modern character of War deeply affects all strategic planning. Since Buonaparte's fortune and audacity overturned established methods and led to near-immediate devastation of major Powers; since the Spanish, with their fierce resistance, demonstrated the powerful effect of a nation's general mobilization and large-scale insurgent actions despite their internal weaknesses; since Russia, in the campaign of 1812, taught us that a vast Empire is not easily conquered (a truth that should have been clear before), and revealed that the likelihood of ultimate victory doesn't necessarily lessen as battles, cities, and territories fall—a belief that diplomats had once held unquestionable, causing them to rush into inadequate temporary peace deals. In fact, Russia showed that a nation often grows strongest within its homeland's depths, when the invader's strength is depleted, and how tremendous the force is when the defense shifts powerfully to offense. Additionally, since Prussia (in 1813) showed how rapid efforts can multiply an Army six times through a militia, equally effective abroad as at home—since all of these historical moments revealed just how influential a nation's heart and will can be in amplifying both political and military strength. Finally, since governments have recognized all of these powerful tools, it is unlikely they will leave them idle in future Wars, whether their existence is at risk or they are spurred by ambition.

It's clear that a War fought with the full strength of each nation on both sides requires a fundamentally different approach than one calculated solely on the strength and arrangements of standing Armies. Standing Armies once resembled fleets, with land forces and sea forces operating in isolation from the larger framework of the State, giving the art of land warfare a resemblance to naval tactics—a connection that no longer exists.

Chapter XVIII. Tension and Rest

The Dynamic Law of War

As we previously examined in the sixteenth chapter, most past campaigns included a considerable portion of time devoted to pauses and inactive phases rather than constant combat or forward movement. Although, as emphasized in the last chapter, the nature of War has evolved significantly, with the current approach showing a marked increase in active engagement, it remains undeniable that intervals of rest will inevitably punctuate periods of action. This reality prompts a closer examination of these two contrasting phases in War—moments of rest and moments of tension and action.

When action pauses and neither side pushes forward with a definite initiative, a state of rest settles over the conflict, producing a kind of equilibrium. But this is not merely a physical balance of forces; it's an equilibrium in the broadest sense, encompassing a wide range of factors—moral, strategic, political, and even economic elements—all of which contribute to this delicate balance. As soon as one side formulates a new objective, however, and takes the first active steps toward realizing it, whether through initial preparations or by moving forces, a tension immediately emerges if the opposing side resists. This tension can persist for extended periods, driven by each side's desire to assert dominance, until a decisive event—the confrontation or battle—takes place. It is only through this event that a decision is reached: either one side abandons its objective or the other side is forced to concede it.

This critical decision is grounded in both the physical contest and the calculated strategies developed on each side. Once a decision is made, a movement in one direction or another ensues, with one side advancing and the other often forced into retreat or withdrawal. Yet, such movement is not endless; it typically exhausts itself either when the advancing side encounters enough resistance from its own logistical challenges or when the defending side builds up sufficient counterforce to halt or divert the progression. At this point, the forward motion loses momentum, and the campaign may either enter another resting phase, where no side actively seeks major gains, or it may transition into a renewed state of tension, where both sides await a decisive outcome before making further moves. Often, this renewed state of tension results in another decision, which might reverse the direction of movement as one side recalibrates to advance or withdraw once more.

This distinction—among equilibrium, tension, and motion—might appear somewhat abstract, but it holds essential value in practical terms. In a state of rest and equilibrium, either side may still undertake various activities as opportunities arise, which do not aim for sweeping changes but serve to create small advantages. These actions may even include notable confrontations or skirmishes, perhaps even full-scale battles, yet they are fundamentally different in nature and yield different consequences compared to actions taken in a state of high tension.

In a state of tension, however, the effects of any resulting decision are typically greater. This is because such a decision is backed by a stronger resolve and a more intense urgency on both sides. Everything has been prepared and focused on achieving a critical movement, creating a charged situation in which the decision resembles the force of a well-timed and carefully prepared explosive, releasing a powerful impact. On the other hand, events of a similar scale that take place within a resting or equilibrium phase resemble a mass of powder scattered in the open air, unable to reach the same concentrated level of effect due to a lack of unified focus and tension driving the action.

Thus, understanding the underlying nature of these two states—equilibrium with rest and tension with movement—offers insights that can guide the strategic choices in War, clarifying why some decisions yield immediate, forceful results while others have a more muted impact, leaving the broader course of conflict temporarily unchanged.

Simultaneously, it's natural to view the state of tension in various intensities, with each degree moving gradually closer to a state of rest, so that, at the end, only a slight difference may remain between them. The real value of these reflections leads to the conclusion that any action taken during a state of tension has far greater significance and potential for impactful results than if the same action were taken during a state of equilibrium. This importance increases exponentially as the tension reaches its highest levels.

For example, the cannonade at Valmy on September 20, 1792, had a much larger impact than the Battle of Hochkirch on October 14, 1758. In an area where the enemy retreats because he lacks the strength to defend it, we can secure our position differently than we would if the enemy had withdrawn with the intention of preparing for a decisive confrontation under more favorable conditions. Similarly, during a strategic offensive, a misstep, an ill-chosen position, or even a minor faulty maneuver could have immediate, decisive consequences; however, in a state of equilibrium, such mistakes would need to be glaringly obvious to provoke significant enemy activity.

As we previously mentioned, many past wars were marked, for the most part, by prolonged periods of equilibrium. Tensions, when they did arise, were often brief and had relatively weak effects, resulting in limited achievements. Events from these wars often amounted to little more than elaborate displays, sometimes staged to celebrate a royal occasion (as at Hochkirch), to satisfy national pride (as at Kunersdorf), or to gratify a commander's personal ambition (such as at Freiberg).

It is essential for a commander to fully comprehend these states, possessing the insight to act in harmony with their demands. We learned during the 1806 campaign just how crucial this understanding can be. In that campaign, the intensity of the situation demanded a focus on supreme resolution, where the commander's full attention should have been devoted solely to that final decisive outcome. Yet, in the midst of that intense pressure, measures were proposed—and some partially enacted—like reconnaissance missions toward Franconia, which at best would have offered only a slight shift in a state of equilibrium. These misguided plans diverted the army's efforts from what truly mattered, resulting in the oversight of the essential actions required to succeed.

This theoretical distinction is also vital as we further develop our approach. Everything we discuss regarding the balance of attack and defense, and the completion of this dual nature of combat, revolves around the heightened state of tension and movement. All actions that occur during a state of equilibrium should only be seen as secondary, as that critical period of crisis is the essence of War itself, while equilibrium merely serves as its shadow.

Book IV. The Combat

Chapter I. Introductory

In the previous book, we explored the essential elements that drive War. Now, we turn our focus to the combat itself, which serves as the actual force of action in Warfare. Combat, with its physical and moral effects, at times embodies the main goal of an entire campaign in straightforward or more intricate ways. Thus, in this core activity and its impacts, we expect these elements of War to reappear.

The structure of combat falls within the scope of tactics, and we will only touch on it here in a broad sense to understand its role as a whole. In practice, smaller, more immediate objectives often shape the specific character of each combat. We will not delve into these particular details until later. However, these unique aspects are typically minor when compared to the general traits of a combat, making most combats quite similar to one another. To avoid redundancy at each step, we find it necessary to examine the general nature of combat now before delving into its specific applications.

Therefore, in the next chapter, we will briefly outline the characteristics of the modern battle in its tactical flow, as this understanding forms the basis of our concept of what a battle truly entails.

Chapter II. Character of a Modern Battle

Given the way we've defined tactics and strategy, it naturally follows that if the nature of tactics changes, that change will impact strategy as well. If the tactical actions in one situation differ entirely from those in another, then strategy must change too, to stay consistent and make sense. Therefore, it's essential to understand what a large-scale battle looks like in its current form before we continue studying its role in strategy.

So, what typically happens now in a major battle? We organize ourselves in large formations, positioned closely alongside or behind one another. We deploy only a relatively small part of the total force, letting it wear itself out in extended firefights that last several hours, only occasionally interrupted and shifted by isolated bayonet charges or cavalry attacks. When this front line has burned through much of its energy and is reduced to almost nothing but ash, it is pulled back and replaced by a fresh group.

In this way, the battle, based on an altered principle, smolders gradually like damp gunpowder. When nightfall demands a halt, as neither side can see any longer nor wishes to rely on the luck of fighting blindly, each side assesses its remaining forces that can still be considered effective, meaning those units that haven't yet burned out entirely like dormant volcanoes. They take stock of ground gained or lost, check the security of their rear, and tally their impressions of courage or cowardice, skill or error, both in their own ranks and the enemy's. These observations are summed up into a single overall impression that drives the decision either to leave the field or resume the fight the following day.

This description isn't meant to be a perfect picture of a modern battle but rather to convey its overall atmosphere, applicable to both offensive and defensive actions. The unique elements given by specific objectives, terrain, and other factors can be added to this depiction without changing its essence.

Modern battles take on this form not by chance; they do so because both sides are closely matched in military organization and knowledge of warfare, and because the raw force driven by significant national interests has burst through artificial constraints, following a more natural course. Given these two conditions, battles are bound to retain this nature.

This general view of the modern battle will prove helpful as we move forward, especially when we need to assess the importance of individual elements like strength or terrain. It applies particularly to major, decisive battles or those close in scale. While smaller skirmishes have shifted in the same direction, they have done so to a lesser degree. Examining these details falls under tactics, though we'll have the chance later on to clarify this by providing a few specific examples.

Chapter III. The Combat in General

Combat is the true expression of warlike action; all other elements serve merely as support, tools in the grand pursuit. It is essential, therefore, that we take a thorough and thoughtful look at the nature of combat itself. At its core, combat means to fight, with the primary goal being either the destruction or capture of the enemy. The enemy, in each specific engagement, is the armed force standing in opposition to us, a force positioned to defend, resist, or retaliate against our own. This concept is straightforward, yet it requires further exploration and expansion, as there are layers of complexity woven into its simplest form.

Imagine, if you will, the State and its military as a unified whole, a single organism whose intent and purpose align under a common banner. With this perspective, one could easily view war as a single vast engagement, one immense confrontation where everything is directed at a single target. In the rudimentary circumstances of primitive societies, war could indeed take this simple shape, a singular clash with straightforward outcomes. But in the context of modern warfare, a war is composed of countless engagements—some large, others small—unfolding either simultaneously or in succession. This fragmentation of action into distinct, individual events arises from the many complex relationships and factors that fuel our wars today.

This segmentation becomes even more apparent when we consider that the ultimate purpose of war—its political objective—is rarely, if ever, straightforward. Even if this political goal were singular and easily defined, it would still be tied to a multitude of other considerations, all of which must be addressed and accounted for. Thus, it becomes impossible to achieve this overarching purpose through just one single, decisive act. Instead, a series of actions, varying in scale and significance, must be carried out, each contributing to the greater aim. These distinct actions each serve as a piece of the greater whole, each with its own purpose and relevance in the larger scheme, binding them together into a continuous and interconnected effort.

It is important to remember, as we have already discussed, that every act of strategy can ultimately be traced back to the concept of a combat encounter. Strategic actions draw upon military power, and at their core lies the implicit notion of fighting. For this reason, we can reduce any military operation in Strategy to its most basic unit, the single combat, focusing specifically on the goals of each individual encounter. As we progress, we will uncover the specific objectives of these various combats by examining the factors that create and drive them. For now, it is sufficient to recognize that each combat, no matter how great or small, carries with it a unique objective that supports the larger mission. Therefore, the defeat or capture of the enemy in each instance must be seen not as the ultimate end but as the means to attain that particular goal, a step that furthers us along the path to fulfilling our overarching objective.

In this way, combat is more than just confrontation; it is a deliberate pursuit with layered purposes that collectively shape the course of a campaign. The destruction or conquest of opposing forces is, fundamentally, only a vehicle for achieving the specific aims embedded within each encounter, each battle woven into the strategic tapestry of war.

However, this outcome is valid only in terms of its structure, and it's significant mainly because of the logical links between ideas themselves; in fact, we only pursue this concept so we can promptly set it aside. What does it mean to "overcome" the enemy? It's invariably about weakening their military force—whether that's by killing, wounding, or otherwise reducing their ability to fight, whether entirely or simply enough that they can't continue. Thus, when we ignore specific objectives tied to individual combats, we can consider the complete or partial defeat of the enemy as the sole purpose of any confrontation.

Now, we argue that in most cases, especially in large-scale battles, the unique objective defining each battle—tying it to the broader goals—is merely a minor variation of this overall purpose or an additional aim aligned with it. While this secondary aim can be significant enough to differentiate the battle, it remains relatively minor compared to the overarching goal. Consequently, if only this secondary aim is achieved, a limited part of the combat's purpose is fulfilled. If this view holds true, then we see that framing the enemy's defeat as merely a means to an end, with some separate objective always being the true aim, is correct in a technical sense but could mislead us if we forget that breaking the enemy's power is central to that aim. This so-called objective is merely a slight variant of it. Losing sight of this fact led to severely mistaken ideas before the most recent wars, creating theoretical trends and fragmented systems that considered themselves advanced and skillful precisely because they minimized reliance on the real tool of war—weakening the enemy's force.

Such a system could only take hold because it was based on additional incorrect assumptions, replacing the necessity of overpowering the enemy with other concepts, ascribing to them an influence they didn't genuinely possess. We'll address these misconceptions wherever necessary, but discussing combat itself requires us to acknowledge the genuine importance it holds and to caution against the errors that arise from following an idea merely for its technical correctness.

Now, how can we demonstrate that in most cases, particularly those of highest importance, the core aim is indeed the destruction of the enemy's army? How do we tackle the very refined idea that suggests it's possible, by using a calculated, indirect approach, to achieve a greater impact on the enemy with less direct combat? This theory suggests that through minor but highly targeted strikes, one could cause a breakdown in the enemy's capabilities or impose control over their choices, thus creating a faster path to victory. Undoubtedly, a win at one location can carry more weight than a win at another. There is also a strategic organization of battles, which, in effect, is the science of arranging them in relation to one another. We do not deny this. But we argue that the direct defeat of the enemy's forces remains essential everywhere. Our point here is solely to emphasize the overwhelming importance of this destructive principle.

It's crucial to remember that we are discussing Strategy here, not tactics. Therefore, we are not considering tactical maneuvers that might allow us to inflict substantial damage on the enemy at a minimal cost to ourselves. By "direct destruction," we mean the tangible tactical outcomes on the battlefield. Our assertion, then, is that only significant tactical successes can lead to meaningful strategic results. Put another way, tactical victories are central to conducting a successful war.

To support this view, we point to a straightforward fact: the time required for any elaborate, complex plan. The question of whether a simple attack or a more detailed, carefully prepared one yields a greater outcome often favors the latter, assuming the enemy stays entirely passive. However, every carefully planned attack requires preparation time, and a counterattack by the enemy could disrupt the entire plan. If the enemy decides on a more straightforward attack, one that can be executed faster, they seize the initiative and undermine our larger strategy. Thus, in addition to weighing the advantages of a complex attack, we must also consider the risks we face during its setup, opting for simplicity whenever there's a chance that the enemy will disrupt our plan. If that's the case, we may need to choose a more straightforward, faster approach and adjust our goals accordingly to align with the enemy's character, behavior, and other surrounding factors.

When we step away from the weak pull of theoretical ideas and focus on real-life applications, it becomes evident that a bold, confident, and determined opponent will not allow us the luxury of time for complex, intricate schemes. Ironically, it is against such an enemy that we would most need skill. This, in our view, makes the case clear: simple and direct approaches have the advantage over complex, indirect ones.

Our belief, then, is not that the simplest strike is always the best, but rather that we shouldn't aim too high for the time we have to act, as this principle will naturally lead us toward direct confrontation, especially when faced with a formidable enemy. Instead of striving to outmaneuver the enemy through overly complex strategies, we should focus on staying ahead of them with greater simplicity in our plans.

If we look to the core reasoning behind these contrasting ideas, we see that one is based on skill, and the other on courage. It's tempting to think that a moderate amount of bravery combined with high skill could achieve more than great bravery with moderate skill. But unless we stretch this relationship to an illogical extreme, there's no basis for saying that skill should have such an advantage over courage in a setting ruled by risk—where courage is truly meant to shine.

Following this abstract view, we would add that real-world experience strongly supports this stance; in fact, it's the very source of these insights. Anyone who studies history with an open mind will see that of all military virtues, decisive energy in action has consistently been the greatest contributor to the honor and success of armed forces.

As for how we justify focusing on destroying the enemy's strength as the primary objective, not only across the entire war but also in each individual battle, and how this principle fits all the various forms and requirements born from the conditions of war—these points will be covered later. For now, our only aim is to assert its broad significance, after which we return to discussing the combat itself.

Chapter IV. The Combat in General (continuation)

In the previous section, we showed that defeating the enemy is the true purpose of combat, and we tried to prove this by taking a closer look at the idea, showing that this is true in most cases, especially in the most important battles, because destroying the enemy's army is always the main goal in war. Other goals that may be mixed in with this idea of destroying the enemy's forces—and may have a greater or lesser influence on the outcome—we'll discuss in general terms in the next section and understand better as we go on. Here, though, we separate the fight from any other purpose, focusing only on defeating the enemy as the complete and sufficient goal of any combat.

What, then, do we mean by the destruction of the enemy's army? It means a reduction in their forces that is relatively greater than the losses on our own side. If we have a large advantage in numbers over the enemy, then naturally, if both sides lose the same amount, it's a smaller loss for us than for them and, therefore, can be considered a gain. Since here we are considering the fight apart from any other goals, we must also exclude situations where combat is only used indirectly to lead to a greater destruction of the enemy's forces; therefore, only that direct gain achieved through the mutual process of destruction is to be considered as the goal, for this is an absolute gain, which continues throughout the campaign and, in the end, will always add up as a pure profit. But any other type of victory over our opponent would either have a reason in different goals, which we've completely excluded here, or would only give a temporary relative advantage. An example will make this clear.

If, through a smart arrangement of our forces, we've put the opponent in such a difficult situation that he cannot continue the fight without risk, and after some resistance, he retreats, then we could say we have defeated him in that area. But if we have spent just as much of our own resources as the enemy to achieve this, then when we total up the campaign's results, there's no gain from this victory, if such an outcome can even be called a victory. So, defeating the enemy—putting them in a position where they must abandon the fight—doesn't count as a true gain on its own, and for that reason, it cannot be defined as the goal. This leaves, as we said, only the direct gain made in the process of destruction. This includes not only the losses suffered during the fight but also those that occur after the retreat of the defeated side as a direct result of the same battle.

From experience, it's understood that the physical losses sustained during a battle rarely show a significant difference between the victorious side and the defeated side. In fact, these losses are often very similar or even identical, with no clear advantage on either side. Occasionally, the side that ultimately wins might even sustain greater losses than the side that loses. However, the most crucial and impactful losses for the defeated side don't generally start until the retreat. It's during the retreat, a phase that the victorious side does not endure, that the defeated army begins to suffer its heaviest and most decisive losses.

As the defeated troops attempt to withdraw, scattered groups of weakened battalions, already in disarray, become easy targets for the enemy's cavalry, which cuts them down as they flee. The ground is littered with exhausted soldiers, unable to continue moving. Cannons that have been damaged and shattered caissons are left abandoned, their use now forfeited. Other essential equipment, bogged down by rough or muddy roads, can't be moved quickly enough and inevitably falls into the enemy's hands. During the night, with visibility low and organization weakened, countless soldiers get lost and stumble into enemy territory, where they are quickly captured, unable to defend themselves. In this way, victory often transforms from a mere decision of who won into a physical, visible reality with each loss the defeated suffer in their retreat. Though this may seem contradictory at first glance, it is understandable when examined in the following light.

Both sides, throughout the battle, face not only physical losses in terms of men and equipment, but they also suffer significant losses in morale. Morale is affected deeply during combat; it can be shaken, worn down, or even completely broken. When considering the aftermath of a battle, it's essential to look beyond the loss of soldiers, horses, or artillery pieces and to factor in the collapse of order, courage, confidence, and cohesion, along with the loss of any clear plan or strategic alignment. All of these elements together are what determine if a fight can or should be continued. In the end, it's the morale that plays the most critical role, and in situations where both sides experience similar physical losses, it is morale alone that often dictates the outcome of the conflict.

While it's difficult to assess physical losses accurately during the intensity of battle, it's easier to gauge the impact on morale. Two primary indicators help reveal this impact on morale. First is the loss of the battlefield itself—the ground on which the fight has taken place. The second indicator is the level of superiority achieved by the enemy's forces. If we have used up our reserves more quickly than the enemy, if we've spent more resources just to stay on equal footing, this tells us a great deal about the enemy's moral advantage. Such a situation often stirs a certain bitterness in the heart of the commander, who may even begin to feel disappointed in his troops. The real, underlying issue, however, lies in the troops themselves. Soldiers who have been actively engaged for long periods grow weary, both physically and mentally. Their energy becomes depleted, and their motivation or morale diminishes, almost as if they have burned out like dying embers. Their ammunition dwindles, their numbers shrink, and they're left exhausted, with possibly even their courage in tatters. So, this once-unified force, which had moved with purpose before the battle, has now become something entirely different due to the strain of combat; thus, we can often measure the loss of morale by examining how many reserves had to be deployed, as if using a ruler to assess their diminishing strength.

The loss of the ground where the battle took place and the depletion of fresh reserves are usually the main reasons that compel a retreat, though it's important to note that other factors may also play a role. These can include the need to keep various sections of the army aligned with one another, the overarching plan for the campaign, and other strategic considerations.

Every battle, therefore, is a brutal test of both physical and moral strength, an ordeal that wears down both body and spirit. The side that emerges victorious is the one that has the greatest amount of both physical resources and morale left at the end. During the battle, the loss of morale is the chief cause of a decision, and after that decision is reached, this loss in morale continues to grow until it reaches its peak by the time the battle is over. This moment marks a crucial opportunity for the victor, who should use this time to press every advantage and limit the enemy's forces as much as possible, for that is the true goal of engaging in battle in the first place. For the defeated, the total loss of order and discipline can make any further resistance by isolated groups more damaging than helpful, as they will only face punishment and losses in attempting to continue. The collective spirit of the troops is broken; the original drive, the rush to win or avoid losing, which had once helped them push through danger, has now faded. Now, danger no longer feels like a test of bravery; instead, it feels like a relentless punishment to be endured. Thus, at the very first moment of defeat, the losing side's morale is weakened and dulled, and they lose the strength to respond to danger with any kind of defiance.

However, this phase does not last forever. The morale of the defeated begins to recover slowly. Order starts to be restored, courage resurfaces, and in most cases, only a small part of the initial advantage remains for the victorious side, sometimes none at all. On rare occasions, the defeated side's frustration and desire for revenge may even turn the situation in the opposite direction, leading to unexpected resistance or hostility. Meanwhile, however, the tangible gains made by the victorious side—the lives lost, the wounded and captured soldiers, and the cannons seized—remain as permanent, unchangeable factors in the victor's favor. These concrete, measurable gains cannot simply disappear from the record and will remain as enduring marks of the battle's outcome.

The losses in a battle consist more in killed and wounded; those after the battle, more in artillery taken and prisoners. The first the conqueror shares with the conquered, more or less, but the second not; and for that reason they usually only take place on one side of the conflict, at least, they are considerably in excess on one side.

Artillery and prisoners are therefore at all times regarded as the true trophies of victory, as well as its measure, because through these things its extent is declared beyond a doubt. Even the degree of moral superiority may be better judged of by them than by any other relation, especially if the number of killed and wounded is compared therewith; and here arises a new power increasing the moral effects.

We have said that the moral forces, beaten to the ground in the battle and in the immediately succeeding movements, recover themselves gradually, and often bear no traces of injury; this is the case with small divisions of the whole, less frequently with large divisions; it may, however, also be the case with the main Army, but seldom or never in the State or Government to which the Army belongs. These estimate the situation more impartially, and from a more elevated point of view, and recognise in the number of trophies taken by the enemy, and their relation to the number of killed and wounded, only too easily and well, the measure of their own weakness and inefficiency.

In point of fact, the lost balance of moral power must not be treated lightly because it has no absolute value, and because it does not of necessity appear in all cases in the amount of the results at the final close; it may become of such excessive weight as to bring down everything with an irresistible force. On that account it may often become a great aim of the operations of which we shall speak elsewhere. Here we have still to examine some of its fundamental relations.

The moral effect of a victory increases, not merely in proportion to the extent of the forces engaged, but in a progressive ratio—that is to say, not only in extent, but also in its intensity. In a beaten detachment order is easily restored. As a single frozen limb is easily revived by the rest of the body, so the courage of a defeated detachment is easily raised again by the courage of the rest of the Army as soon as it rejoins it. If, therefore, the effects of a small victory are not completely done away with, still they are partly lost to the enemy. This is not the case if the Army itself sustains a great defeat; then one with the other fall together. A great fire attains quite a different heat from several small ones.

Another relation which determines the moral value of a victory is the numerical relation of the forces which have been in conflict with each other. To beat many with few is not only a double success, but shows also a greater, especially a more general superiority, which the conquered must always be fearful of encountering again. At the same time this influence is in reality hardly observable in such a case. In the moment of real action, the notions of the actual strength of the enemy are generally so uncertain, the estimate of our own commonly so incorrect, that the party superior in numbers either does not admit the disproportion, or is very far from admitting the full truth, owing to which, he evades almost entirely the moral disadvantages which would spring from it. It is only hereafter in history that the truth, long suppressed through ignorance, vanity, or a wise discretion, makes its appearance, and then it certainly casts a lustre on the Army and its Leader, but it can then do nothing more by its moral influence for events long past.

If prisoners and captured guns are those things by which the victory principally gains substance, its true crystallisations, then the plan of the battle should have those things specially in view; the destruction of the enemy by death and wounds appears here merely as a means to an end.

How far this may influence the dispositions in the battle is not an affair of Strategy, but the decision to fight the battle is in intimate connection with it, as is shown by the direction given to our forces, and their general grouping, whether we threaten the enemy's flank or rear, or he threatens ours. On this point, the number of prisoners and captured guns depends very much, and it is a point which, in many cases, tactics alone cannot satisfy, particularly if the strategic relations are too much in opposition to it.

The risk of having to fight on two sides, and the still more dangerous position of having no line of retreat left open, paralyse the movements and the power of resistance; further, in case of defeat, they increase the loss, often raising it to its extreme point, that is, to destruction. Therefore, the rear being endangered makes defeat more probable, and, at the same time, more decisive.

From this arises, in the whole conduct of the War, especially in great and small combats, a perfect instinct to secure our own line of retreat and to seize that of the enemy; this follows from the conception of victory, which, as we have seen, is something beyond mere slaughter.

In this effort we see, therefore, the first immediate purpose in the combat, and one which is quite universal. No combat is imaginable in which this effort, either in its double or single form, does not go hand in hand with the plain and simple stroke of force. Even the smallest troop will not throw itself upon its enemy without thinking of its line of retreat, and, in most cases, it will have an eye upon that of the enemy also.

We should have to digress to show how often this instinct is prevented from going the direct road, how often it must yield to the difficulties arising from more important considerations: we shall, therefore, rest contented with affirming it to be a general natural law of the combat.

It is, therefore, active; presses everywhere with its natural weight, and so becomes the pivot on which almost all tactical and strategic manœuvres turn.

If we now take a look at the conception of victory as a whole, we find in it three elements:—

1. The greater loss of the enemy in physical power.
2. In moral power.
3. His open avowal of this by the relinquishment of his intentions.

The returns made up on each side of losses in killed and wounded, are never exact, seldom truthful, and in most cases, full of intentional misrepresentations. Even the statement of the number of trophies is seldom to be quite depended on; consequently, when it is not considerable it may also cast a doubt even on the reality of the victory. Of the loss in moral forces there is no reliable measure, except in the trophies: therefore, in many cases, the giving up the contest is the only real evidence of the victory. It is, therefore, to be regarded as a confession of inferiority—as the lowering of the flag, by which, in this particular instance, right and superiority are conceded to the enemy, and this degree of humiliation and disgrace, which, however, must be distinguished from all the other moral consequences of the loss of equilibrium, is an essential part of the victory. It is this part alone which acts upon the public opinion outside the Army, upon the people and the Government in both belligerent States, and upon all others in any way concerned.

But renouncement of the general object is not quite identical with quitting the field of battle, even when the battle has been very obstinate and long kept up; no one says of advanced posts, when they retire after an obstinate combat, that they have given up their object; even in combats aimed at the destruction of the enemy's Army, the retreat from the battlefield is not always to be regarded as a relinquishment of this aim, as for instance, in retreats planned beforehand, in which the ground is disputed foot by foot; all this belongs to that part of our subject where we shall speak of the separate object of the combat; here we only wish to draw attention to the fact that in most cases the giving up of the object is very difficult to distinguish from the retirement from the battlefield, and that the impression produced by the latter, both in and out of the Army, is not to be treated lightly.

For Generals and Armies whose reputation is not made, this is in itself one of the difficulties in many operations, justified by circumstances when a succession of combats, each ending in retreat, may appear as a succession of defeats, without being so in reality, and when that appearance may exercise a very depressing influence. It is impossible for the retreating General by making known his real intentions to prevent the moral effect spreading to the public and his troops, for to do that with effect he must disclose his plans completely, which of course would run counter to his principal interests to too great a degree.

In order to draw attention to the special importance of this conception of victory we shall only refer to the battle of Soor,(*) the trophies from which were not important (a few thousand prisoners and twenty guns), and where Frederick proclaimed his victory by remaining for five days after on the field of battle, although his retreat into Silesia had been previously determined on, and was a measure natural to his whole situation. According to his own account, he thought he would hasten a peace by the moral effect of his victory. Now although a couple of other successes were likewise required, namely, the battle at Katholisch Hennersdorf, in Lusatia, and the battle of Kesseldorf, before this peace took place, still we cannot say that the moral effect of the battle of Soor was nil.

(*) Soor, or Sohr, Sept. 30, 1745; Hennersdorf, Nov. 23, 1745; Kealteldorf, Dec. 15, 1745, all in the Second Silesian War.

If it is chiefly the moral force which is shaken by defeat, and if the number of trophies reaped by the enemy mounts up to an unusual height, then the lost combat becomes a rout, but this is not the necessary consequence of every victory. A rout only sets in when the moral force of the defeated is very severely shaken then there often ensues a complete incapability of further resistance, and the whole action consists of giving way, that is of flight.

Jena and Belle Alliance were routs, but not so Borodino.

Although without pedantry we can here give no single line of separation, because the difference between the things is one of degrees, yet still the retention of the conception is essential as a central point to give clearness to our theoretical ideas and it is a want in our terminology that for a victory over the enemy tantamount to a rout, and a conquest of the enemy only tantamount to a simple victory, there is only one and the same word to use.

Chapter V. On the Signification of the Combat

In the previous section, we examined combat in its pure form, viewing it as a small-scale representation of the entire war. Now, we turn to consider how combat connects with other aspects of the broader conflict. Our first question is: what, precisely, is the significance of a combat?

Since war is essentially a mutual act of destruction, the most straightforward answer, both in theory and perhaps in practice, would seem to be that all forces from each side come together in a single, massive effort, culminating in a single, overwhelming clash. There is certainly much truth to this notion, and it would seem reasonable to adhere to it, thereby treating smaller combats merely as necessary losses—like wood shavings from a carpenter's plane. However, the matter is not quite so simple.

The natural occurrence of multiple combats results from dividing forces, which is to be expected, and so the immediate objectives of individual combats are best understood through the concept of force division. However, these objectives, and with them, the whole variety of combats, can be broadly grouped into certain categories, and understanding these categories will help clarify our observations.

Destroying the enemy's forces is, in truth, the goal behind all combats; nevertheless, other objectives may be present, and at times, these secondary objectives may become the dominant ones. Thus, we must distinguish between combats where destroying the enemy's forces is the primary aim and those where it serves more as a means to another end. The destruction of enemy forces, control of a location, or control of a valuable asset might each serve as the general motivation for combat. This motivation could stem from a single aim or a combination of several, although typically one of these remains the primary purpose.

The two main forms of war—offensive and defensive, which we will discuss soon—do not alter the first of these motivations, but they do influence the other two. Therefore, if we organize these objectives in a structured way, they would be represented as follows:

Offensive. Defensive.

1. Destruction of the enemy's forces
2. Defense of a location

3. Defense of a specific objective

However, these motivations do not seem to entirely cover all possible purposes of combat when we consider that there are also actions such as reconnaissance and demonstrations, where none of these three objectives is the true aim of the engagement. For this reason, it becomes necessary to include a fourth category. In strict terms, reconnaissance actions designed to expose the enemy's position, alarms intended to exhaust the enemy, and demonstrations meant to keep the enemy pinned to one point or to lure him elsewhere are all objectives achieved indirectly and under the guise of one of the three main objectives listed above, often the second. For instance, an enemy intending reconnaissance must deploy forces as though the aim is to attack, defeat, or drive us away. However, this apparent purpose is not the actual one, and our current concern is with the real objective. Therefore, to the previous three objectives of offensive action, we must add a fourth: to lead the enemy to a false conclusion. The possibility of offensive actions toward this end naturally follows from the very nature of warfare.

At the same time, we should recognize that the defense of a location can take two forms: it may be absolute, where the location must be held at all costs, or it may be relative, where the defense is only necessary for a certain duration. This temporary defense occurs frequently in engagements involving advanced posts and rear guards.

It's evident that the purpose behind a combat significantly affects the preliminary arrangements. We proceed differently if the aim is simply to push an enemy post from its position than if the goal is to fully defeat it. Similarly, our approach differs if we aim to defend a location to the last from what it would be if we only needed to hold the enemy off for a time. In the first case, little attention is given to the line of retreat; in the second, the retreat becomes the primary consideration.

These reflections properly fall under the realm of tactics and are mentioned here only as examples to clarify our discussion. The strategic significance of the various objectives in combat will be detailed in the chapters that address each of these goals specifically. For now, a few general observations are in order. First, the importance of each objective generally declines in the order in which they appear above, meaning that the first objective should always dominate in a major battle. Finally, the last two objectives in a defensive engagement are, in truth, without productive results—they are purely negative goals, meaning they can only contribute indirectly by supporting something else that is positive. Therefore, a strategic position where such engagements are frequent is typically a sign of weakness in the overall situation.

Chapter VI. Duration of Combat

When we move beyond examining combat in isolation and instead view it in connection to the broader elements of war, its duration takes on a critical importance. The length of time a battle lasts can be thought of, in some sense, as a secondary measure of success. For the side that emerges victorious, the ideal outcome would be a swift and efficient resolution, where the objective is achieved quickly. For the side that faces defeat, a prolonged battle becomes valuable, as the longer they can sustain the engagement, the more they can mitigate their loss. Thus, a quick victory demonstrates a superior strength or advantage, while a delayed decision provides some compensation for the defeated, as it reflects a level of resistance against the opponent's efforts.

This general concept of combat duration becomes especially relevant in those battles where the goal is one of relative defense. In these cases, the success of the operation often rests entirely on the ability to maintain the engagement over a specified period, which is why we classify duration as one of the strategic elements in warfare. In some defensive engagements, where the primary purpose is to delay or hold off the enemy for a time, the result may not depend on immediate victory or defeat but rather on the sheer persistence of resistance.

The duration of a battle is inherently influenced by several essential factors. These factors include the absolute size of the forces engaged, the balance and variety of unit types on each side, and the specific nature of the terrain. A larger force of, say, twenty thousand men does not wear down or exhaust itself against an enemy as quickly as a force of two thousand, as the sheer number of troops adds to the overall endurance of the engagement. Similarly, facing an enemy with two or three times the strength reduces the length of time one can hold out compared to facing an equally sized opponent. Additionally, certain types of units impact the duration differently—cavalry encounters, for instance, tend to be resolved much more quickly than infantry skirmishes. A battle involving only infantry may conclude sooner than one in which artillery plays a role, as the presence of artillery adds another layer of complexity and firepower, prolonging the struggle. Terrain also exerts its influence—progress through hilly or forested regions is naturally slower and more challenging than on flat, open ground. Each of these factors interacts to shape how long a battle can be sustained before reaching a conclusion.

From this, it follows that in order to achieve a specific goal through the length of a combat engagement, one must account for the force strength, the composition of units across the three main arms (infantry, cavalry, and artillery), and the strategic position relative to the terrain. While this principle is crucial, what matters most to us here is the practical insight gained from experience on this topic. Historical examples have provided us with rough estimations of combat duration under various circumstances, helping us understand the effects of these elements in practice.

For instance, an average division of 8,000 to 10,000 troops, composed of all arms, can typically withstand an opponent of considerably superior numbers for several hours, provided the terrain does not overly favor the attacker. Even when faced with a relatively moderate or negligible numerical disadvantage, a division can hold the line for a good portion of the day, often for about half a day. When this force is part of a larger corps comprising three or four divisions, it can extend the engagement to roughly twice that duration. If an army consists of 80,000 to 100,000 troops, this timeframe stretches further, allowing resistance to continue for three or even four times as long. These large-scale formations, or masses, can thus be expected to operate independently over extended periods without the need for smaller, isolated skirmishes, provided that within this time frame, reinforcements or additional forces can arrive to join the fray. These arriving forces can shift the battle, converging with the original engagement and steering the outcome into a single, unified direction that integrates with the progress and results of the ongoing combat.

These approximations of combat duration are rooted in accumulated experience, yet it is equally critical to refine our understanding of the decisive moment in battle—the turning point when victory or defeat is essentially determined. This point of decision, along with the ultimate conclusion of the engagement, forms a fundamental aspect of our study of combat. In the same way that the duration of a battle informs us about the endurance and resilience of each side, the moment of decision helps us recognize the pivotal factors that determine the course and conclusion of the conflict.

Chapter VII. Decision of the Combat

No battle is determined by a single, instantaneous event, even though every battle reaches moments of critical tension that influence the final outcome. The loss of a battle, therefore, is a gradual process, with each phase contributing to a shift in the balance. However, within every combat, there exists a crucial moment (*).

(*) Within the context of the weaponry available at that time.

This moment holds supreme importance, as the entire strategy of a large-scale battle hinges on accurately judging this point: How long can a given force sustain its resistance? Misjudging this timing can cause the entire maneuver based on it to unravel—as exemplified by Kouroupatkin's failure at Liao-Yang in September 1904. There comes a point in any engagement where it may be considered decisively concluded, such that any further fighting would essentially constitute a new battle rather than a continuation of the previous one. Developing a clear sense of this decisive moment is crucial, as it enables commanders to determine whether reinforcements could still effectively turn the tide of combat.

Too often, fresh forces are sent into battles that are beyond recovery, resulting in needless losses. Conversely, there are occasions when opportunities to secure a decisive outcome are overlooked due to inaction at a critical time. The following examples illustrate this point with absolute clarity:

In 1806, at the Battle of Jena, the Prince of Hohenlohe, commanding 35,000 troops, engaged an opposing force of 60,000 to 70,000 under Napoleon. When Hohenlohe's army was defeated, it was not merely beaten but so utterly scattered that it essentially dissolved. Despite this, General Rüchel attempted to re-engage with a reserve of 12,000 troops, only to see his forces dispersed just as quickly.

In contrast, on the same day at Auerstadt, another Prussian force held out in combat. Facing Marshal Davout's army of 28,000 with a force of 25,000, the Prussians maintained resistance until midday. Although they had not gained ground, they had also not been destroyed and had even inflicted losses on an enemy hampered by insufficient cavalry. However, by failing to deploy a reserve force of 18,000 under General Kalkreuth, they missed an opportunity to tip the battle's outcome decisively in their favor. Given the situation, with those additional reserves, it would have been nearly impossible for the Prussians to lose.

Each combat can be seen as an integrated whole, in which the outcomes of smaller engagements combine to produce an overall result. The ultimate decision of the combat lies within this cumulative outcome. It's important to note that this conclusion does not necessarily mean a clear-cut victory, as defined in previous discussions, since the necessary preparations may not have been made, or the opportunity may be absent if the enemy retreats prematurely. In most cases, even after prolonged resistance, the decision occurs before the combat reaches a level of success that would fully satisfy the idea of a total victory

We therefore pose the question: When is the moment of decision in a battle—specifically, the point beyond which an additional effective, though reasonably proportionate, force could no longer reverse a disadvantageous situation?

Leaving aside false attacks, which by their nature lack a decisive outcome, we consider the following scenarios:

1. When the goal of the battle is the capture of a movable object, the loss of that object always constitutes the decisive moment.
2. If holding ground is the objective, the decision generally occurs with the loss of that ground. However, this is not always the case, as certain types of terrain—those with unique defensive advantages—tend to hold greater significance. Terrain that may be strategically important but easy to traverse can sometimes be recaptured with minimal risk, meaning the loss of such ground doesn't always equate to a final decision.
3. In all other situations, where these two conditions have not already determined the battle's outcome—particularly when the primary objective is the destruction of the enemy's forces—the decision comes at the point when the victor no longer perceives themselves as being in a fragmented or partially incapacitated state. In other words, it's the moment when the incremental use of forces, discussed in Chapter 12 of Book 3, ceases to offer further advantage.

This understanding forms the basis for the strategic unity of a battle, which we've addressed in this section.

In a battle where the attacker maintains almost complete order and effectiveness—or, at most, has lost control over only a small segment of his forces—while the opposing side is largely disorganized, the possibility of reversing the outcome becomes minimal. When the attacker has preserved his structure and morale while the defender's forces are scattered or fragmented, the chances of any reversal are slim. Likewise, once the defeated side has managed to recover its own organization and effectiveness, the likelihood of a successful counter by the previously disadvantaged side diminishes even further.

The smaller the portion of a force actively engaged in combat, and the larger the reserve held back, the less likely it becomes that any newly arriving enemy force could regain control or force the attacker into retreat. A commander who skillfully applies the principle of preserving combat strength and effectively uses reserves to create a strong moral impact on the enemy builds the surest foundation for victory. Notably, Napoleon and the French forces during his campaigns displayed mastery in this approach, demonstrating how the calculated use of reserves, even in close quarters, could tip the psychological and tactical scales toward victory.

Moreover, the point at which the victor's forces emerge from the intense crisis phase and return to their original, organized state generally occurs faster when smaller units are involved. For example, a small cavalry picket pursuing the enemy in a galloping charge can return to its proper formation within a few minutes, effectively ending the crisis phase. A full cavalry regiment, however, requires more time to regroup and reestablish its order. This process takes even longer with infantry, especially if they are dispersed in single lines as skirmishers. In such cases, returning to a cohesive formation is a slower, more gradual process. For larger formations like divisions that combine different types of units—infantry, cavalry, and artillery—the challenge of reorganizing after combat is even greater. When divisions scatter in various directions during an engagement, the result is a loss of formation order, often complicated further as each segment may lose track of the others' exact positions.

Consequently, the time required for the victorious commander to gather his forces, restore formation, and reestablish some degree of operational order increases with the total size of the force. This process is much like resetting a "battle workshop," where the instruments and tools—representing troops and divisions—are reorganized to function effectively once more. The larger the force, the more extensive the effort needed to regroup and bring the different parts back into an organized and cohesive whole.

If the victory is achieved at night, the reorganization process takes even longer, as darkness complicates visibility, communication, and coordination among units. The arrival of nightfall acts as a shield, often protecting retreating forces from immediate pursuit and buying them time to reorganize or escape. Given these factors, it's rare for a night attack to yield a clear and successful result, as conditions do not typically favor coordinated advances in the dark. However, exceptions exist, such as the night assault at Laon on March 10, 1814, where York successfully launched a night attack on Marmont's corps. This rare example illustrates how, under the right circumstances, a night operation can produce an effective result. Similarly, densely wooded or rugged terrain serves as a natural barrier, affording protection against an immediate counterattack. Such terrain hinders swift movement and clear sight lines, making it challenging for a pursuer to press an advantage. In these cases, both night and rough terrain serve as obstacles, not only making a renewed engagement more complex but also reducing the possibility of the battle simply continuing in a straightforward manner.

Up to this point, we have been considering the arrival of reinforcements for the losing side primarily as an increase in force that typically arrives directly from the rear. This scenario is the most common, where fresh troops enter the battle from behind the main front, reinforcing the existing line. However, the dynamics of the situation shift markedly if these new forces approach from a different direction. A new line of attack introduced from a separate angle creates fresh opportunities and challenges, as it introduces an unexpected element into the existing flow of the battle.

The effect of flank or rear attacks, as it pertains to strategy, will be covered in detail elsewhere. Here, we focus on their role in restoring a battle, which is primarily a tactical issue. It's relevant here because we're discussing tactical outcomes, so our observations naturally extend somewhat into tactical territory.

Attacking the enemy's flank or rear can greatly amplify the impact of an assault; however, this result is far from guaranteed, as such maneuvers can sometimes weaken rather than strengthen the overall effect. The particular circumstances of each battle largely determine whether a flank or rear attack will be advantageous, just as they do with any other tactic. Yet, for our purposes, two points about these attacks are especially significant. First, attacks on the flank or rear usually have a greater effect on the outcome after a decision has been reached than on the decision itself. When it comes to salvaging a lost battle, securing a favorable decision is the primary aim, not merely increasing the magnitude of success. From this perspective, one might argue that a reinforcing force arriving to restore the fight would be more helpful if it directly joined our main force rather than approaching the enemy's flank or rear, separated from our own troops. There are cases where this is indeed true; however, in the majority of situations, the opposite holds, and this relates to the second point of importance.

The second point is the moral impact of the surprise, which generally favors a reinforcement arriving to turn the tide. The effect of a surprise is almost always intensified when it comes from an unexpected direction, such as the enemy's flank or rear. An opponent who is deeply engaged in the heat of battle, scattered and in extended formations, is less capable of responding effectively to such a maneuver. It's easy to see how an attack from the flank or rear, which might have limited effect at the start of the battle when forces are more concentrated and prepared for such surprises, gains considerable weight if it occurs in the battle's final stages, where formations are already strained and disordered.

We must therefore acknowledge that, in most situations, reinforcements arriving from the enemy's flank or rear will be more impactful, like adding weight to the end of a long lever. Under these conditions, a smaller force might succeed in turning the tide with an attack on the flank or rear where it would be insufficient in a direct engagement. In such scenarios, the impact of moral forces can become overwhelmingly dominant, to the extent that outcomes defy precise calculation. This is the ideal situation for boldness and daring.

When deciding in uncertain situations whether a battle that has turned unfavorable can still be salvaged, attention must be given to these factors and the interplay of all supporting elements. Each of these factors should be weighed carefully.

If the engagement is still ongoing when the reinforcements arrive, the renewed fight merges seamlessly with the original one, creating a unified outcome where the earlier disadvantage is effectively erased. In this case, both engagements blend into a single result, making the previous setback irrelevant to the final tally. However, if the battle has already been decided, the initial result stands on its own, and the arrival of new forces initiates a separate engagement. When the reinforcements lack sufficient strength to match the enemy independently, a favorable outcome from this second engagement is unlikely. However, if the reinforcements are powerful enough to engage the enemy without considering the earlier defeat, they may succeed in winning this second combat, potentially compensating for or even outweighing the initial loss. Nevertheless, even with a favorable outcome in the second engagement, the effects of the first defeat will not entirely vanish from the account.

In the Battle of Kunersdorf (*), Frederick the Great initially seized the left flank of the Russian position, capturing seventy artillery pieces in the process. However, by the end of the battle, both the captured position and the artillery were lost, effectively nullifying the gains from the initial success. If it had been possible to consolidate the initial victory and delay the second phase of the battle until the following day, then even if Frederick had ultimately lost, the achievements of the first engagement would still have partially offset the losses of the second.

(*) August 12, 1759.

But when a battle that is unfolding unfavorably is halted and turned around before reaching its conclusion, the initial disadvantage doesn't merely vanish; it also lays the groundwork for a more decisive victory. Consider the tactical unfolding of a battle: until the final outcome is reached, all successes in separate engagements remain unresolved decisions. These partial victories can not only be erased by the final outcome but can be entirely reversed. As our forces endure losses, the enemy is also expending resources and weakening their own position, bringing them closer to a critical state. Thus, when our fresh forces enter the battle, their advantage becomes even more pronounced. If we then manage to turn the overall outcome in our favor—taking back the battlefield and recovering all captured assets—then every sacrifice the enemy made to secure these gains becomes a clear benefit to us, and our earlier losses become the stepping stone to a larger triumph. The enemy's most impressive achievements, which they would have valued highly if victorious, turn instead to a source of regret for their wasted efforts. This transformation—where victory brings a glow to all gains and defeat tarnishes them—is the powerful shift that victory and defeat impose on the same elements of a battle.

Therefore, even if we are overwhelmingly stronger and could defeat the enemy in a subsequent engagement, it is generally wiser to interrupt a losing battle, if it's proportionately important, and alter its direction rather than to simply plan on a second engagement later.

Field Marshal Daun demonstrated this approach in 1760 when he attempted to aid General Laudon during the Battle of Leignitz while it was still underway. When this effort failed, he chose not to engage Frederick in a second battle the following day, despite having ample resources to do so.

For these reasons, significant skirmishes involving advance guards that occur prior to a main battle should generally be regarded as unavoidable drawbacks, and when avoidable, should be avoided (*).

(*) This viewpoint contrasts with Napoleon's strategy, who believed in vigorously engaging with the advance guard to anchor the enemy's focus and "paralyze his independent will." Napoleon's approach highlights a fundamental strategic concept later recognized by the French General Staff: in August 1870, von Moltke's failure to firmly fix the enemy's attention in this manner led him into several precarious situations, from which he was saved only by Bazaine's inaction and the decisive initiatives of subordinates like von Alvensleben. [See works by Bonnal, Foch, et al.—Editor]

Another conclusion remains to be addressed.

When one side loses a pitched battle, this loss alone does not justify immediately deciding on a new battle. The decision to re-engage must be based on different factors. However, there is a significant counterpoint to this: the moral impulse of anger and a desire for revenge. This feeling permeates from the highest-ranking field marshal to the youngest drummer boy; troops are rarely more motivated than when they have the opportunity to erase a stain on their honor. This, however, presumes that the proportion of the force that suffered defeat isn't so large that this sentiment becomes overshadowed by a sense of helplessness.

Consequently, there is a natural tendency to harness this morale boost to recover from the defeat promptly, leading to a desire for another battle if circumstances allow. In such situations, this second engagement is almost invariably an offensive one, as the defeated side seeks to reassert itself.

There are numerous examples in the history of secondary battles where such retaliatory engagements occurred, driven by the immediate need to redeem a loss. However, major battles generally involve a wider array of decisive factors, making it less common for a single desire for retaliation to serve as the primary motivation for engagement.

Such a feeling must certainly have driven the noble Blücher and his third corps back to the field on February 14, 1814, despite the defeat his other two corps had suffered three days earlier at Montmirail. Had he known that he would confront Napoleon himself, overwhelming logic would have likely urged him to delay his revenge to another day. Instead, Blücher believed he would find Marmont and expected the satisfaction of honorable retribution. However, rather than reaping the rewards of his resolve, he suffered the consequences of a flawed assumption.

The distances between forces intended to fight in coordination depend heavily on the duration of the combat and the timing of its decision. When positioning masses to fight together within the same battle, this arrangement could be considered a tactical setup, provided that the forces are placed closely enough that separate engagements are unlikely, and the entire area they occupy can be treated as a single strategic point. However, war often presents situations where forces meant to unite for one battle must be placed far enough apart that the possibility of separate engagements remains. In such cases, while uniting for a single combined action is still the primary goal, the arrangement itself is strategic in nature rather than purely tactical.

Strategic dispositions of this type include marches conducted in separate masses or columns, the formation of advance guards and flanking columns, and the placement of reserves meant to support multiple strategic points rather than just one. Additionally, these arrangements cover the concentration of multiple corps that may be stationed in widely dispersed cantonments, among others. The need for such dispositions arises frequently, making them a necessary component of strategy. We might think of these arrangements as the "small change" in the strategic economy of war, while the major battles—and all engagements of similar importance—are like the gold and silver currency.

Chapter VIII. Mutual Understanding as to a Battle

A battle cannot unfold unless both sides consent to engage; this idea, which underpins the concept of a duel, has given rise to certain expressions in historical writing that often lead to ambiguous or even misleading interpretations.

Many historical accounts describe situations where one commander has "offered battle" to the other, only for the opposing commander to "decline" the offer. However, unlike a duel, which is a simple and direct encounter based purely on the mutual desire to engage, a battle is a far more complex event. Its basis is not merely the shared wish of two sides to fight, but rather the broader objectives attached to the battle, which serve larger strategic purposes. These objectives are, in turn, part of an even greater scheme, as every war, seen as a single "combat unit," operates under overarching political objectives and constraints determined by a higher authority. Thus, the simple urge to defeat the opposing commander falls into a secondary role, or even vanishes as a motivation in and of itself, acting merely as the means to fulfill the higher intentions that drive the engagement.

In the ancient world and during the early days of standing armies, the notion of offering battle to the enemy held a weightier meaning than it does in the present day. Ancient warfare was organized with the understanding that two sides would measure their strength in the open field, where they could face each other without significant impediments. The entire art of war was centered around the organization and arrangement of the army, referred to as the "order of battle." At this time, the concept of offering battle was significant, as warfare was often approached with a view to arranging armies in set formations that could clash on open, unobstructed terrain.

In this context, armies commonly entrenched themselves in fortified camps, where the position was often regarded as unassailable or highly defensible. A battle could only commence once the enemy left their fortified position, moved into open terrain, and essentially "entered the lists," as in a formal duel. This setup required both sides to be willing to fight under similar, largely agreed-upon conditions, and prevented attacks on the entrenched camp from being a viable option in many cases. For example, when we read that Hannibal "offered battle" to Fabius in vain, it simply indicates that Fabius chose not to fight openly, as this didn't align with his strategic intentions. This choice tells us nothing about Hannibal's physical or moral superiority over his opponent; it merely shows that he sought an open battle, while Fabius refrained.

A similar dynamic applied in the early period of modern armies, especially in large-scale battles. When these battles occurred, commanders brought large numbers of troops together into one massive formation and arranged them in a pre-established order of battle that required relatively open, level ground to be effective. This type of arrangement was neither well-suited for offensive maneuvers nor for defending in rugged, confined, or mountainous terrain. Because of these limitations, defending forces often had the option of avoiding battle if they positioned themselves in a difficult location, as the attacking army would be unable to operate effectively under such conditions. Although this approach to battle gradually evolved, these dynamics remained relevant through the early modern period and up until the First Silesian War.

It wasn't until the Seven Years' War that commanders increasingly began to undertake attacks on forces positioned in challenging terrain. The gradual shift toward engaging in broken or otherwise restrictive terrain began to reshape the art of battle. While advantageous ground continued to provide significant defensive benefits, it no longer served as a total barrier to the attacking army, as had often been the case in earlier warfare. Before this change, commanders were highly restricted in their options, with fortified or difficult terrain often being seen as a "magic circle" that protected defending forces by deterring attackers. Over time, however, the expansion of tactical flexibility and the adaptation of armies to a wider range of conditions reduced the effectiveness of terrain as an absolute shield against engagement, marking a significant development in the conduct of warfare.

In the past thirty years, warfare has advanced significantly in this respect, and now there is nothing to prevent a general who sincerely seeks to resolve matters through battle from doing so. He can actively search out his enemy and launch an attack; if he chooses not to, he cannot reasonably claim that he intended to fight. The expression "he offered battle, which his opponent did not accept" now means nothing more than that the circumstances didn't seem favorable enough to warrant a battle. In essence, this expression no longer fully conveys what it once did and now serves as little more than a cover for this admission.

It remains true that the defensive side cannot entirely avoid the possibility of a battle, but it is still within their power to sidestep it by giving up their position and the role that position carries. However, such a retreat acts as a partial victory for the attacking side and is, in itself, an acknowledgment of the attacker's current advantage. Therefore, the traditional notion of a formal challenge, or a "cartel of defiance," can no longer justify the inactivity of a general whose responsibility is to press forward—in other words, the offensive side. As long as the defender holds their position without retreating, they must be credited with the willingness to fight, and they can rightly claim to have "offered" battle if they are not directly attacked, though this may already be understood implicitly.

On the other hand, a commander who both wishes to retreat and has the means to do so cannot be easily forced into a battle. Since the benefits of a retreat by the defending side are often insufficient in themselves to meet the attacker's objectives, and since achieving a decisive victory may be urgently needed, the few available methods of forcing such a reluctant opponent into a battle must be carefully identified and skillfully executed.

The main methods for compelling an enemy to stand and fight are, first, to surround them, cutting off any feasible retreat so that battle becomes either inevitable or, at the very least, more favorable than a highly dangerous retreat; and second, to surprise the opponent. This second approach was once frequently necessary due to the extreme difficulty of maneuvering troops into position, but in the modern era, it has become far less effective.

Given the increased flexibility and maneuverability of contemporary troops, commanders today do not hesitate to initiate a retreat, even in full view of the enemy, as only specific natural obstacles, such as difficult or rugged terrain, can cause genuine problems for an organized retreat.

An example of this kind of situation is found in the Battle of Neresheim, fought by Archduke Charles against Moreau in the Rauhe Alp on August 11, 1796. Here, the archduke engaged in battle primarily to make his retreat easier, although we must admit that the renowned general and writer's own reasoning in this case remains somewhat challenging to interpret fully.

The Battle of Rosbach also serves as an example, assuming we believe that the commander of the allied army did not truly intend to initiate an attack against Frederick the Great.

Regarding the Battle of Soor, the King himself stated that this battle occurred because he considered it dangerous to retreat within the enemy's view; yet, at the same time, he provided additional reasons to justify the choice to engage in battle.

Overall, aside from cases of organized night attacks, such instances will always be rare. Those situations in which an enemy is genuinely compelled to fight by being nearly surrounded will typically only involve individual corps, as seen with Mortier's corps at Dürrenstein in 1809 or Vandamme's at Kulm in 1813.

Chapter IX. The Battle (*)

(*) Clausewitz still uses the term "die Hauptschlacht," whereas modern terminology prefers simply "die Schlacht" to describe the decisive action within an entire campaign. Engagements that arise from the collision of troops as they move toward the strategic climax of each segment of the campaign are now referred to as "Treffen," meaning "engagements," or "Gefecht," meaning "combat" or "action." In technical terms, Gravelotte qualifies as a "Schlacht," or "battle," while Spicheren, Woerth, Borny, and even Vionville are considered only "Treffen."

Its Decision

What is a battle? It is the conflict of the main forces, not a minor skirmish over a secondary objective, nor a mere attempt that is abandoned when we recognize that the goal is out of reach. A battle is a struggle waged with all available forces to achieve a decisive victory.

While additional objectives may be involved alongside the main goal, and the nature of the battle may take on various aspects depending on the circumstances that lead to it, the battle itself is still part of a larger whole. But because the essence of war is conflict, and the battle represents the clash of the main armies, it must be considered the true center of gravity in war. Thus, unlike all other encounters, a battle is distinct in that it is arranged and undertaken with the specific goal of securing a decisive victory.

This focus influences how a battle is decided, the impact of the victory it contains, and the importance theory assigns to it as a means to an end. For these reasons, we give it particular attention, and before addressing any special objectives that may accompany it, we recognize that these do not fundamentally change the character of a true battle.

When a battle occurs primarily on its own merit, the elements of its outcome must be found within itself; in other words, the effort for victory must continue as long as any possibility or hope remains. A battle, then, should not be abandoned due to secondary factors but only if the forces involved appear to be entirely inadequate.

How, then, do we describe the precise moment of decision?

If a structured formation and cohesion of the army are the primary conditions under which the bravery of the troops can secure a victory—as was the case for much of modern military history—then the breakdown of that formation signals the decision. A defeated wing, falling out of formation, determines the fate of everything connected to it. In cases where the strength of the defense lies in a close union between the army and the terrain, with the land and its obstacles becoming part of the army itself, the capture of a critical point in this terrain marks the decision. When the key to the position is lost, it can no longer be defended, and the battle cannot continue.

In both scenarios, the defeated armies resemble the broken strings of an instrument, rendered incapable of performing their function.

Both the geometric and geographic principles that once held armies in fixed, rigid formations—creating a kind of "crystallized tension" that limited the use of available forces—have now, to a large extent, lost their predominant influence. Armies may still be drawn up in a particular order when entering battle, but this arrangement no longer determines the outcome as it once did. Similarly, obstacles in the landscape, which were once relied upon to fortify positions and provide strongholds, are still used to reinforce defense but no longer serve as the only foundation upon which a battle position depends.

Earlier in this book, we attempted to provide an overview of the modern battle's nature. According to our understanding, the "order of battle" now serves simply as a useful arrangement for deploying forces effectively. The conduct of battle has become a process of gradual attrition, a steady wearing down of both sides as they expend their forces against each other, each aiming to exhaust the other first.

As a result, the decision to withdraw from a battle comes about more directly than in other types of engagements from the comparison of fresh reserves that each side has remaining. These reserves are significant because they alone retain their full morale and fighting spirit, unlike the exhausted and battered battalions that have already been through the intense conditions of battle. These battle-worn units, having been "burned out" by the harshness of combat, simply cannot be compared to the vigor of fresh reserves. Lost ground also plays a role, as we have pointed out elsewhere, by serving as a rough gauge of lost morale and a clear indicator of the toll the battle has taken. Thus, while lost ground represents less an actual loss of forces and more a symbol of weakening morale, the state of fresh reserves becomes the primary measure that each commander must carefully monitor and weigh.

Generally, a battle leans in one direction from the very beginning, but this shift is often subtle, remaining almost imperceptible for some time. Sometimes, this initial tendency is firmly established by the preparations made in advance, and a commander who begins a battle under such adverse conditions without recognizing the disadvantage shows a lack of discernment. Even in cases where no clear advantage exists at the start, the natural course of a battle more often resembles a gradual and continuous shift in balance rather than a swinging, back-and-forth exchange of advantages. This shift starts subtly but grows steadily more visible and stronger with each phase of the battle. This slow but steady disturbance of equilibrium stands in contrast to the dramatic, alternating gains and losses that some imagine, often based on exaggerated or misleading accounts.

Whether the equilibrium remains stable for a considerable time or whether it swings briefly to one side before tipping back, it is a near certainty that in most battles, the defeated commander foresees the approaching end well before a formal retreat is ordered. Sudden, critical events that unexpectedly shift the outcome are far less common than many accounts suggest; they are more a matter of how people retrospectively color and dramatize their lost battles, seeking to give special emphasis to moments they believe altered the tide.

In making this case, we rely on the insights of those experienced in war, who, if impartial, would likely confirm this perspective to readers without personal familiarity with battle. To explore the deeper, tactical necessities behind this gradual tipping process would take us well into the field of tactics, which is beyond the current discussion. Here, our concern is only with the outcomes and the lasting results of these dynamics within the broader strategy of war.

When we say that the defeated general usually foresees the unfavorable outcome of a battle some time before deciding to abandon it, we acknowledge that there are exceptions; otherwise, we would be proposing a contradiction. If, at every moment that a battle takes on a decisive direction, it were already deemed lost, then no additional forces would logically be used to reverse it, and this decisive shift could not persist for any significant period before retreating. Certainly, there are instances in which battles that seemed firmly decided for one side ended in victory for the other, but such occurrences are rare and not the norm. These exceptional cases, however, are considered by any general faced with adversity, who must hold out hope for them as long as a reversal remains possible. He hopes that with greater efforts, by summoning the remaining morale, by pushing his own limits, or by the intervention of a lucky break, the tide may turn. He will pursue this possibility as far as his courage and judgment allow. We will return to this topic, but first, we need to clarify what signs indicate that the balance is tipping.

The final outcome of a battle is composed of the cumulative results of each of the smaller engagements within it, but the outcome of each separate clash is determined by several factors.

First, there is the effect of morale in the minds of leading officers. If a division general watches his battalions being forced to give way, it will affect his behavior and his reports, which in turn influence the decisions of the Commander-in-Chief. Thus, even partial defeats that appear to be recovered still impact the overall outcome, as their impression adds up in the mind of the Commander, often unconsciously and against his will.

Second, there is the faster depletion of troops, which is observable even in the relatively orderly and slow-paced nature of our battles compared to the rapid shock tactics of earlier times.

Third, there is the loss of ground.

These elements act as a sort of compass for the general, giving him a sense of where the battle is headed. If whole batteries have been captured without taking any from the enemy; if battalions have been routed by enemy cavalry while those of the enemy remain as impenetrable masses; if the line of fire across his formation involuntarily wavers from point to point; if repeated attempts to capture specific positions have failed, with assaulting battalions repeatedly scattered by well-aimed volleys of grapeshot and canister; if his artillery's response grows feeble against that of the enemy; if battalions under fire begin to diminish at an alarming rate as uninjured troops flee alongside the wounded; if entire divisions are cut off and captured due to the breakdown of the battle plan; if the line of retreat itself becomes threatened—then the Commander can gauge the direction in which his battle is headed. The longer this negative trend continues, the more pronounced it becomes, making it increasingly difficult to reverse the situation and bringing him closer to the moment when he must concede the battle.

We will now make a few observations on this critical moment of decision.

We have stated repeatedly that the final outcome of a battle often hinges on the relative number of fresh reserves available in the last stages. When a commander sees his opponent has a decisive advantage in reserves, he will generally resolve to retreat. A defining feature of modern battles is that setbacks and losses sustained throughout can be counterbalanced by fresh forces, as the modern arrangement of battle lines and the methods of bringing troops into action allow for the use of reserves almost universally and in any position. Thus, as long as a commander who is facing a disadvantage still has a significant advantage in reserves, he will continue to fight. However, the moment his reserves begin to fall below those of his opponent, the outcome is effectively decided. At this point, his actions are governed partly by immediate circumstances and partly by his own courage and determination, which may sometimes border on reckless stubbornness.

How a commander accurately assesses the remaining reserves on both sides is a matter of practical, intuitive skill, which falls beyond our present discussion; we are concerned only with the conclusions he draws. Yet, even this realization is not the moment of decision itself, as it arises gradually rather than as a single, immediate turning point. Instead, it serves as a general motivation toward resolution, while the decision itself typically requires additional immediate causes. Two primary factors frequently trigger this final decision: the increasing risk of retreat and the onset of nightfall.

When each new phase of the battle makes retreat increasingly hazardous and when reserves are so depleted that they no longer suffice to create breathing room, a commander has no choice but to yield to the inevitable. By conducting a well-managed retreat, he can save what would otherwise be lost through further delay, which might end in a rout or disaster.

Nightfall, as a rule, brings most battles to a close because night engagements rarely promise any advantage unless under very specific circumstances. Additionally, night offers a better opportunity for retreat than daytime, so a commander facing an unavoidable or probable withdrawal will prefer to use the cover of night to manage it effectively.

Aside from these two primary and usual causes, there are numerous other factors that are more unique to each battle and still have an impact on the final decision. As the balance of a battle increasingly tips toward one side, each partial outcome exerts a stronger influence, hastening the decision to retreat. For instance, the loss of a single battery or a successful charge by a couple of cavalry regiments might catalyze a decision that had already been in the making.

In concluding this discussion, we must pause to consider the internal conflict between the commander's courage and his reason. On one hand, the pride of a confident conqueror, the unyielding determination of a naturally stubborn spirit, and the intense resolve of noble feelings may refuse to abandon the battlefield, as doing so would mean a blow to honor. Yet, on the other hand, reason advises him not to risk everything, to avoid staking all on a losing fight, and to save enough strength for an orderly retreat. While courage and tenacity are invaluable in war, and while there is little hope for victory if one is unwilling to seek it through all possible means, there comes a point where persistence is no longer strategic but rather sheer, desperate folly—a point at which no rational observer could approve further resistance.

In one of history's most famous battles, the Battle of Waterloo, Napoleon committed his last reserve to a fight that was beyond recovery. He spent his final resource, and, ultimately, as a defeated man, he lost not only the battlefield but also his crown.

Chapter X. Effects of Victory

Depending on our perspective, we might be equally surprised by the extraordinary outcomes of some great battles as by the lack of significant results in others. Let us consider for a moment the nature of the effects brought about by a major victory.

Three distinct types of impact can be recognized here: the effect on the immediate instrument itself, namely, the generals and their armies; the effect on the states involved in the war; and the particular results of these impacts as they influence the further course of the campaign.

If we think only of the minor differences that often separate victor from vanquished—such as the number of killed, wounded, captured soldiers, or the artillery lost on the battlefield—the far-reaching consequences that emerge from these seemingly insignificant figures can be perplexing. Yet, typically, these outcomes unfold quite naturally.

In the seventh chapter, we noted that the magnitude of a victory increases not simply in proportion to the size of the vanquished force but at an even greater rate. The moral effects of a major battle are significantly more pronounced for the defeated side than for the victor; this greater impact leads to further losses in physical strength, which in turn amplify the moral toll, creating a cycle of mutual reinforcement. It is on this moral effect that we must place particular emphasis. It moves in opposite directions for each side: it drains the energies and spirit of the defeated while simultaneously elevating the strength and confidence of the victor. However, its main impact lies on the side of the vanquished, where it directly causes new losses and aligns naturally with the very nature of war, with its dangers, physical exhaustion, difficulties, and all the hardships associated with combat. As such, it combines with these war-related burdens, intensifying them. Meanwhile, for the conqueror, these same hardships act as weights that drive his courage to even greater heights.

As a result, we see that the defeated side often sinks far below the initial equilibrium line, while the victor's morale rises only moderately above it. Therefore, when we speak of the effects of victory, we mostly refer to those manifesting within the defeated army. This effect is more intense in a significant combat than in a minor engagement, and in a great battle, it becomes much more pronounced. The great battle is fought purely for the sake of achieving victory, pursued with the utmost commitment and resources. At this precise moment and place, the entire war's plan, along with every strategy and future hope, converges here, and it is as if destiny itself arrives to provide a decisive answer. This sense of urgency and high tension extends from the commander throughout the entire army down to even the most junior wagon driver—diminishing in intensity, yet still present at every level.

By its very nature, a great battle is never a mere unplanned or routine action but a grand, decisive act, standing apart from ordinary efforts and heightening the tension of every mind involved. The higher the emotional tension surrounding the outcome, the more powerful the impact of that outcome when it arrives.

The moral impact of victory in our modern battles is even greater than it was in earlier times of military history. If these battles represent, as we've described, an intense contest of strength to its fullest extent, then it is the total of these forces—both physical and moral—that must play a decisive role, more so than any specific arrangements or the whims of luck.

A single mistake can be corrected in a future engagement; we might even hope for a better chance of good fortune next time. But the combined weight of moral and physical power isn't easily changed, and thus, a victory gained through such total effort holds a greater sense of permanence. Though likely very few people involved in a battle—whether in the army or outside of it—consciously consider this difference, the experience of battle itself instills a strong conviction in all who are present. And when reports on the battle are made public, even if they're colored by particular interpretations of certain events, they still convey to the broader world that the victory's causes are grounded more in general strength than in isolated factors.

Anyone who has not personally witnessed the loss of a major battle will likely find it hard to form a fully vivid or accurate picture of it. Abstract descriptions of specific incidents simply cannot compare to the comprehensive reality of a lost battle. Let us linger a moment over this scene.

The first impression that grips both the imagination and the intellect is the dwindling of once-massive forces; then, there is the gradual loss of ground, which occurs to some degree in almost every battle, even for the attacker, if his efforts do not succeed entirely. Next comes the breakdown of the original formations, as units are intermingled and reorganized in disarray. The looming danger of retreat—visible in nearly all battles to some extent—is often felt acutely, sometimes more strongly, sometimes less, but almost always present. Then, the retreat begins, usually at night or, at the very least, continuing through the night.

On this initial march, the army must immediately leave behind a number of soldiers—exhausted, scattered, or simply unable to go on. These are often the bravest troops, those who fought at the front lines and held out the longest. The feeling of defeat, which might have been limited to high-ranking officers on the battlefield, now spreads through every rank, down to the common soldiers. It's worsened by the haunting realization of having left behind so many valiant comrades who were, until moments ago, indispensable allies in the fight. Distrust begins to build toward the commander, whom subordinates, to varying degrees, blame for the wasted efforts they made in battle.

This feeling of defeat is no distant or imagined idea that might be overcome—it's a raw and undeniable truth that the enemy is stronger. The reasons for this truth may have been hidden before, subtle enough to go unnoticed. Or perhaps these weaknesses were faintly suspected but countered with hope for luck, trust in fortune, a sense of fate, or sheer determination. Now, these hopes have proven inadequate, and the harsh truth is unavoidable, undeniable, and absolute.

All these feelings differ greatly from panic, which rarely follows a defeat in an army fortified by military discipline and virtue, and only occasionally in less disciplined armies. These emotions arise even in the best of armies; although experience in war, a history of victories, and strong confidence in a commander may lessen their impact slightly, these feelings are never entirely absent in the immediate aftermath of a loss. They are not simply the result of losing trophies of war, which are often captured later and whose loss may not be widely known right away. Therefore, these feelings will emerge even when the tide turns gradually, and they form a predictable effect of victory in every instance.

We've noted that trophies intensify these feelings.

Clearly, an army in this state is weakened as an instrument of war. When reduced to a point where it faces added struggles from the regular challenges of warfare, it cannot realistically be expected to regain what has been lost through sheer renewed effort. Prior to the battle, there was either a real or presumed balance between the two sides; that balance has now shifted, and external support is needed to restore it. Every attempt without such reinforcement can only result in further setbacks.

Thus, even a modest victory by the primary army must result in a continued downward shift for the defeated side until external factors intervene. If these factors are distant, and the victorious commander is a determined leader seeking fame and driven by ambitious goals, then only an exceptional commander, with an army embodying genuine military spirit forged through extensive campaigns, could withstand the relentless tide of success, tempering its impact with small but repeated acts of resistance, until the momentum of victory finally subsides upon reaching its goal.

Now, as for the impact of defeat on the nation and government beyond the army—it is a sudden collapse of hopes stretched to their limits, a collapse of all confidence. In the vacuum left behind, fear enters with its corrosive power, spreading widely and completing the loss of spirit. This effect is like a true shock to the nerves, as though one of the two fighters were struck by an electric jolt from the other's victory. However varied in degree, this effect is always present to some extent. Rather than each individual stepping forward with resolve to repair the damage, many hesitate, believing their efforts will be futile, doubting when they should charge forward; others fall into discouragement, letting their will fade, and leave everything to chance.

The subsequent course of the war and the results of this victory depend partly on the character and talent of the victorious general but even more on the specific circumstances surrounding the victory and where they lead. Without boldness and a willingness to take risks on the part of the leader, even the most dazzling victory will produce little substantial success, and its force will be quickly spent if circumstances offer strong, resilient opposition. Imagine how differently Frederick the Great might have exploited Daun's victory at Kollin, or the alternative consequences if France had held the victory at Leuthen instead of Prussia!

The conditions that allow us to anticipate great outcomes from a major victory will become clearer when we address the specific topics to which these results are connected. Then, it will be possible to explain the apparent imbalance between the scale of a victory and its results—a difference that is often too quickly blamed on a lack of vigor in the victor. Here, focusing on the great battle itself, we will simply state that the effects we have described are a natural and inevitable consequence of victory, growing in intensity with the strength of the victory itself. These effects become even more significant when the entire force of the army is concentrated on this victory, when the full military power of the nation is invested in that army, and when the state relies on this military power.

Yet, we might ask, should theory accept this effect of victory as absolutely unavoidable? Should it not, instead, seek out countermeasures capable of neutralizing these effects? It seems natural to respond affirmatively; however, may we avoid the misguided path of many theories that give birth to a mutually destructive Pro et Contra. Certainly, the impact of victory is necessary, as it is grounded in the inherent nature of war and persists even if we attempt to counteract it—just as a cannonball's motion is inherently downward, even if it is fired in an opposite direction to offset some of this natural force.

All warfare presupposes human vulnerability, and it is against this that it is directed.

Therefore, when we later discuss what actions might be taken after the loss of a major battle—when we assess the resources still available even in the most dire of situations, and when we suggest that everything might still be recovered—we do not mean to imply that the effects of such a defeat can be entirely undone. The resources used to repair a disaster could otherwise have been applied toward achieving positive goals, which applies equally to moral and physical resources.

A separate question is whether the loss of a major battle might awaken forces that otherwise would never have emerged. This is certainly possible and has indeed been the case for several nations throughout history. However, inspiring this intensified response falls outside the boundaries of military strategy, which can only consider it as a potential factor.

If there are instances where the outcomes of a victory take on a destructive nature due to the reactionary forces it stimulates—though such cases are certainly rare—then it must be equally acknowledged that the impact of the same victory can vary depending on the character of the people or state that has been defeated.

Chapter XI. The Use of the Battle

Whatever specific form warfare may take in individual situations, and whatever we might later find necessary to acknowledge about its conduct, we need only return to the fundamental concept of war to understand the following principles:

1. The destruction of the enemy's military forces is the primary aim of warfare, and it is through decisive, direct action that this objective is pursued.

2. This destruction of enemy forces must be achieved primarily through battle.

3. Only large, comprehensive battles can yield substantial results.

4. The results are maximized when individual combats coalesce into one major battle.

5. It is only in a large-scale battle that the Commander-in-Chief takes direct command, and naturally, he places greater confidence in his own leadership than in that of his subordinates.From these truths a double law follows, the parts of which mutually support each other; namely, that the destruction of the enemy's military force is to be sought for principally by great battles, and their results; and that the chief object of great battles must be the destruction of the enemy's military force.

Undoubtedly, the principle of annihilation appears to some extent in other forms of combat. Admittedly, there are instances in which, due to highly favorable conditions, even a minor engagement has led to disproportionately high destruction of enemy forces, as seen in examples like Maxen. Conversely, in a larger battle, the capture or defense of a single strategic point may assume extraordinary importance, overshadowing the broader destruction of enemy forces as the immediate objective. Yet, as a general rule, it remains a core truth that battles are undertaken primarily with the aim of destroying the enemy's army, and that this ultimate destruction can be effectively achieved only through the means of a battle.

The battle, therefore, can be seen as the concentrated essence of war—the very focal point of effort within an entire war or campaign. Just as the sun's rays converge in the focus of a concave mirror, creating a point of intense heat and energy, so too do the forces, circumstances, and energies of war concentrate within the great battle, for one ultimate and unified exertion.

The very assembly of troops into a cohesive whole, a practice evident in nearly every war, reflects the intention to deliver a decisive strike with this amassed force, either proactively as the assailant or reactively as the defender under the enemy's pressure. When this decisive action does not occur, it indicates that other moderating or delaying factors have interwoven themselves into the original motivations for hostility, thereby diminishing, transforming, or completely restraining the movement toward battle. Even in such instances of mutual restraint, a situation common to many wars, the idea of a potential battle remains ever-present in the minds of both sides, serving as a distant focal point in the formation of their plans. The more seriously the war is prosecuted, the more it embodies the mutual release of hostilities, a relentless effort to overpower the opponent. Thus, the more seriously war is pursued, the more will all actions lead toward that inevitable and deadly encounter, and the greater the battle's significance becomes.

Typically, when the objective is significant and positive, meaning it involves substantial stakes for the enemy, battle arises naturally as the most straightforward and effective means. For this reason, it is also the most advantageous course of action, as will be elaborated further, and generally, when a battle is avoided purely out of reluctance to face its decisive nature, it tends to incur subsequent penalties.

These positive objectives generally belong to the offensive side, making the battle a more natural instrument for the attacker. Yet, without delving too deeply into the precise distinctions between offense and defense here, it must still be noted that even for the defender, in the majority of cases, there is no more effective option for addressing the critical demands of the situation or solving the complex problem at hand.

The battle is, without a doubt, the bloodiest method of resolution. While it does not solely involve mutual slaughter and its primary effect is often more a blow to the enemy's morale than to the actual number of troops, as we will explore in the following chapter, bloodshed is nonetheless its unavoidable cost, and slaughter remains its nature as well as its name. (*) This violent aspect can cause the humanity in any general's mind to recoil.

(*) "Schlacht," derived from "schlachten," meaning "to slaughter."

But the spirit of a person feels an even deeper tremor at the thought of committing everything to a single, decisive blow. In one precise point of space and time, all action is concentrated, and at such a moment, an unclear feeling may arise, as if within this confined space all one's strength might not fully unfold, as if simply having more time could somehow give an advantage—even though time itself offers nothing concrete. This is purely an illusion, yet even as an illusion, it has weight. The same human frailty that affects us in every significant decision is felt even more intensely by a general when he must risk such monumental stakes on a single moment's decision.

For this reason, statesmen and generals across history have often tried to avoid the decisive battle, attempting instead to achieve their goals without resorting to it or, when necessary, subtly abandoning those goals altogether. Historians and theorists have then sought to find, in these campaigns, alternative elements that they have upheld as equivalents to, or even more advanced forms of, decision-making than direct battle. Thus, in modern times, it came close to being accepted that battle was an unfortunate error within the framework of war—a severe, regrettable episode that a carefully planned and rational campaign would never need. Only those generals who could manage to wage war without shedding blood were seen as truly worthy of honors, while the theory of war—a subject suited, it seemed, only to the contemplation of philosophers—was especially directed toward teaching these methods.

However, contemporary events have shattered this illusion, though it is always possible that it will reemerge in the future, tempting those in power into strategies that indulge human frailty and therefore resonate closely with human nature. Perhaps, in time, the campaigns and battles of Buonaparte may be seen as nothing but primitive acts of barbarity and foolishness, leading people once again to appreciate the dress-swords of outdated, rigid institutions and formalities. If theory can issue a warning against this potential misstep, it will provide a valuable service to those who heed its voice. May we contribute in some way to supporting those in our own nation who have the authority to speak on these matters, guiding them into this field of study and encouraging them to examine it with an open mind.

Not only does the fundamental concept of war urge us to seek a decisive outcome through a major battle, but history supports this as well. Since the earliest times, only great victories have led to truly significant success for the offensive side in its fullest sense and for the defensive side in a relatively satisfactory manner. Even Buonaparte would never have witnessed the triumph at Ulm, singular in its nature, had he recoiled from spilling blood; rather, this victory was a natural outcome of his earlier campaigns. It is not only the bold, the rash, or the overly ambitious generals who have sought to conclude their campaigns with the substantial risk of a decisive battle; the fortunate and successful commanders have done so as well. Their achievements provide a powerful answer to this profound question.

Let us put aside the notion of generals who achieve victory without bloodshed. If the sight of a bloody conflict is horrifying, it is all the more reason to respect the serious nature of war itself, not to dull the sword we carry, bit by bit, out of a sense of humanity—lest we find ourselves disarmed when someone else steps in wielding a sharp blade, ready to sever the very limbs from our body.

A great battle is indeed a major decision within a campaign or war, though not necessarily the only one required to determine its course. Instances where a single, decisive battle has determined the outcome of an entire campaign are more common in modern warfare, but cases where one battle decides the entire war remain exceptional.

The lasting impact of a decisive battle does not rely solely on the battle itself—that is, on the size of the forces engaged or the intensity of the victory. Instead, it also depends on numerous other factors, including the balance of military power between the opposing sides and the relationships between the states to which these forces belong. When the bulk of the available forces is committed to a battle, it naturally brings about a major decision, the extent of which can often be foreseen in some respects, though not fully. Even if it is not the only decision in a war, it is the first and, as such, influences every subsequent decision. Therefore, a deliberately planned large-scale battle—considered within the broader strategic context—is typically the primary instrument and focal point of an entire military plan.

The more a general embraces the true spirit of war and the competitive nature of battle, the more convinced he becomes that he must and will conquer. Such a general will strive to bring all possible forces to bear in the first battle, hoping and aiming to secure victory there and then. Buonaparte rarely embarked on a campaign without intending to overcome his enemy immediately in the initial battle. Similarly, Frederick the Great, albeit in a more confined setting and with somewhat lesser stakes, held a similar conviction when he led a small army to free his rear from the grasp of Russian or Imperial forces.

The significance of the decision yielded by a great battle depends, as we have noted, partly on the size of the forces engaged and partly on the extent of the victory achieved.

How a general may amplify the importance of a battle regarding force size is self-evident. Notably, as the importance of the great battle increases, so does the number of decisions connected to it, and thus generals who, confident in their own abilities, sought bold, decisive outcomes, have typically managed to engage the majority of their forces in the main battle without overlooking other crucial points.

The consequences, or more accurately, the effectiveness of a victory, hinge primarily on four key factors:

1. The tactical formation chosen as the order of battle.
2. The characteristics of the terrain.
3. The balance between the types of forces—infantry, cavalry, and artillery—within each army.
4. The comparative overall strength of the two opposing armies.

A battle with both armies aligned in parallel formation, without any attempt to attack the enemy's flank, is less likely to produce substantial success compared to a battle where the defeated army is forced to change its orientation or is outflanked. When a defeated army is turned or compelled to shift its front significantly, the disruption in its formation allows for a deeper impact, which intensifies the victory. In contrast, when the battle takes place in broken, rugged, or hilly terrain, the effects are generally reduced because the landscape diffuses the power of each blow, dispersing forces and diminishing the overall intensity of the engagement.

If the defeated army's cavalry is as strong as, or even stronger than, that of the victor, the results of the battle will also be limited, as the pursuit of the retreating forces becomes less effective. Cavalry typically plays a crucial role in pressing the advantage during the aftermath of a battle, exploiting the enemy's disarray. Without this advantage, the opportunity to maximize the victory is greatly diminished, and much of the intended impact is lost.

Moreover, it's easy to see that if the victor holds a numerical advantage and skillfully uses it to turn the enemy's flank or force a reorientation of their line, the outcome will be more decisive than if the victorious side were outnumbered. Superior numbers allow the conqueror to apply pressure at critical points, creating broader disruption in the enemy's ranks. The Battle of Leuthen, it's true, offers a notable exception to this principle—where Frederick the Great achieved a decisive victory despite being outnumbered. Still, as the saying goes, "no rule without an exception."

In these various ways, a commander can shape the battle to have a more decisive character. Of course, in doing so, he opens himself to increased risk, but this is the inevitable price of pursuing such ambitious results. War operates under a moral dynamic that rewards boldness, and commanders seeking decisive victories must recognize and embrace this reality.

There is nothing in warfare that compares in significance to the great battle. It is the pinnacle of strategic achievement to prepare the conditions for such an event, to select the optimal time and place, to position the troops effectively, and finally, to make the most of the victory achieved. While these are crucial, they need not be extraordinarily complex or mysterious; rather, the essentials are relatively straightforward. This process doesn't demand advanced or intricate planning so much as it requires sharp judgment, vigor, steady determination, and a youthful spirit of initiative—heroic qualities that theory can describe but never fully instill. It requires little of what books can teach and much that, if teachable at all, must reach a general through experience, inspiration, or other means beyond mere words on a page.

The drive toward a great battle—a confident, deliberate approach to it—must come from an internal sense of strength and an understanding of necessity. In other words, it must stem from innate bravery and insights refined by encounters with the weightiest of life's challenges. Great examples from history serve as the best teachers, but it is unfortunate when theoretical prejudices obscure these lessons, for even the light of knowledge can be bent and colored by clouds of misconception. It is the duty of theory to dispel such misconceptions, for the flawed reasoning of one generation can be corrected by pure reason in another.

Chapter XII. Strategic Means of Utilising Victory

The more challenging task—preparing perfectly for a victory—remains largely unrecognized, an understated effort that is truly the realm of Strategy, even if it seldom receives the praise it deserves. The public glory often lies in making the most of a victory already achieved. Questions regarding the specific aims of a battle, how these aims tie into the larger framework of a war, where the course of victory might lead depending on circumstances, and where its peak impact lies—these are all matters that we will examine in detail later. However, one principle holds true in every case: without a pursuit, no victory can achieve significant effect. Whatever the scope of success, it must extend at least into some immediate pursuit beyond the initial gains, which is essential to complete the victory itself. To avoid reiterating this point, we will explore now the fundamental role of pursuit as the critical extension of victory.

The pursuit of a retreating army begins at the precise moment the enemy ceases resistance and leaves their position. Until this point, any movement toward the enemy is simply part of the battle's progression. Usually, even if the victory appears certain at this juncture, it remains modest in scale and would amount to little without a pursuit on the same day. It is during this initial pursuit phase, as previously noted, that the tangible trophies of victory—such as captives, arms, and supplies—are often gathered.

When armies enter battle, both sides typically suffer from physical fatigue due to the urgent nature of the preceding movements. The intense exertion of a large-scale conflict then pushes this exhaustion further; consequently, the victorious army is often nearly as disorganized and depleted as the defeated one. It needs time to regroup, collect stragglers, and resupply troops low on ammunition. These activities place even the victorious army in a state of crisis similar to what we discussed before. Should the defeated force be only a fraction of the enemy's overall army, or if it can expect reinforcements soon, the victor may face a real risk of being caught unprepared and suffering a costly reversal. In such cases, this concern alone may quickly curtail or significantly limit the pursuit. Even when no immediate reinforcement is anticipated, the victor's exhaustion still places natural constraints on the intensity of the pursuit. Although there may be no fear of losing the victory entirely, further engagements could reduce the gains already achieved.

At this critical moment, the physical needs and limitations of the entire army weigh heavily on the commander's decision. The thousands of troops under his command urgently require rest, sustenance, and relief from the hazards of battle; only a small portion have the mental clarity and vigor to look beyond immediate needs and consider the long-term effects of a sustained pursuit, which might appear to most as mere "extras" to victory—a kind of luxury in the triumph. Yet, these thousands, by way of the military hierarchy, have an indirect influence on the general's decisions. Through their officers, their collective exhaustion and needs are conveyed all the way up to the commander's own consciousness. Furthermore, the commander himself, worn by mental and physical fatigue, may experience a natural decline in alertness and drive. These human limitations, purely incidental to the nature of warfare, mean that commanders often achieve less in pursuit than they might otherwise have accomplished. In many cases, whatever additional pursuit is carried out stems from the thirst for glory, the energetic resolve, or, perhaps, the steely determination of the general.

Such factors help explain why so many generals pursue victory cautiously, even when they have the advantage of superior numbers. Generally, the first phase of pursuit is limited to the day of the victory itself, extending through the night that follows. By the end of this period, the need for rest imposes a natural halt on the advancing forces.

This initial pursuit naturally unfolds in varying degrees of intensity.

The first level occurs when cavalry alone is used. In this case, the pursuit often consists more of keeping the enemy alert and under observation than of truly pressuring them, as even minor terrain obstacles can typically halt the advance. Cavalry can be highly effective against scattered groups of demoralized soldiers, but when facing the main body of a retreating army, it returns to its role as a support force. The retreating army can position fresh reserves to protect its withdrawal, and at any minor obstacle, a combination of arms can allow it to make a successful stand. The exception to this is when an army is in a state of complete disarray and is fleeing in chaos.

The second level of pursuit occurs when a strong advance guard made up of all arms leads the chase, with a majority of cavalry. This type of pursuit usually drives the enemy back to the nearest position where their rearguard can take a strong stance or to the next available position large enough for the entire army to regroup. Finding such positions may not be immediate, so the pursuit may continue for a bit further. Generally, however, it does not extend beyond a mile or two, as the advance guard would otherwise lack sufficient support from the main body.

The third and most intense degree of pursuit takes place when the victorious army itself continues to advance as far as its physical limits will allow. In this scenario, the defeated army will often abandon ordinary defensive positions as soon as the victor shows intent to press the attack or attempt an outflanking maneuver. The rearguard, in turn, is even less likely to engage in a firm resistance, favoring retreat instead.

In all three scenarios, the onset of night usually brings an end to the pursuit if it falls before the conclusion of the action. Cases where the pursuit continues through the night are rare and reflect an exceptional level of determination.

Night fighting is inherently unpredictable, with much left to chance, and at the end of a battle, the normal organization and order within an army are bound to be disrupted. Therefore, it is understandable why both generals are usually reluctant to continue operations under such difficult conditions. Unless the enemy's army is utterly shattered, or the victor possesses an unusual superiority in morale and organization, any pursuit through the night leaves much to fate. Even the most daring generals avoid such gambles when possible, as it seldom benefits anyone. Thus, in general, nightfall concludes the pursuit, especially when the battle is resolved just as darkness approaches.

When this pause occurs, it provides the defeated side with a brief but critical opportunity. Either they can halt, regroup, and reorganize immediately, or, if they choose to retreat under cover of night, they gain a head start. This break significantly improves the state of the defeated army: much of the disarray is corrected, ammunition is replenished, and a fresh formation is restored. Any engagement that follows is now a new battle rather than a mere continuation of the prior pursuit, and though it may offer limited prospects of success, it still represents a renewed clash rather than a straightforward rounding up of scattered remnants by the victor.

When the victor is able to continue the pursuit through the night, even if only with a strong advance guard composed of all branches of the military, the impact of the victory is dramatically amplified. Examples of this can be seen in the battles of Leuthen and La Belle Alliance (Waterloo), where such persistent pursuit magnified the effects of the initial victory.

The tactical pursuit that follows the decisive moment of battle plays a critical role in maximizing the victory's outcome, and it is worth examining here to highlight the difference in impact that such a pursuit can create. This initial chase, up to the nearest point where the enemy might find temporary refuge, belongs almost as a right to any conqueror. It is generally independent of any broader strategic plans, which may indeed limit some of the positive outcomes of a victory obtained with the main army but cannot negate this first wave of pursuit. Cases where it might be entirely impractical to carry out even this initial pursuit are conceivable only under the most unusual circumstances, making them exceptions that have little bearing on the general principles of warfare.

It's also essential to acknowledge that the conduct of modern warfare has expanded the potential scope for decisive action. In earlier wars, where objectives and resources were narrower, many unnecessary and artificial constraints affected the conduct of battle, especially concerning the pursuit phase. Generals of the past held an almost ceremonial notion of the "Honor of Victory," believing that once the decision was secured, further destruction of the enemy was unnecessary, even viewing it as cruelty. For these commanders, breaking the enemy's force was only one of many options in warfare rather than the core objective, making it natural to sheath their swords the moment the enemy submitted. This perspective, even if not the only factor guiding their decisions, reinforced a tendency to end hostilities once victory was in sight. Consequently, arguments about the exhaustion of forces or the physical impracticality of prolonging the fight were readily accepted and given greater weight.

Certainly, conserving one's fighting force is essential, especially if it is the only tool at hand and future challenges lie ahead. The offensive does eventually exhaust its resources. However, this older calculation was misguided, as the additional losses incurred through pursuit were typically minor compared to those inflicted on the enemy. Such a viewpoint could only exist in a context where military force itself was not seen as the lifeblood of victory.

Thus, in past conflicts, only true military giants—figures like Charles XII, Marlborough, Eugene, and Frederick the Great—followed their victories with vigorous pursuit when the victory was substantial enough, whereas most other generals were content to hold the battlefield. In modern warfare, the intensified urgency and significance of conflicts have largely removed these old restrictions, making pursuit an essential part of securing victory. As a result, the scale of trophies, captured materials, and prisoners has increased, becoming the expected outcome rather than the exception. Cases in modern warfare where pursuit does not follow have become rare exceptions, typically explained by unusual circumstances.

For instance, at battles like Gorschen and Bautzen, it was only the superior numbers of the enemy's cavalry that prevented a total rout. At Gross Beeren and Dennewitz, the lack of pursuit was due to the unwillingness of Bernadotte, the Crown Prince of Sweden, to follow through. Similarly, at Laon, Field Marshal Blücher's personal health—at seventy years old, weakened and temporarily confined due to an eye injury—was a significant factor preventing a full pursuit.

In this way, we see how the vigor of pursuit after a battle has become a defining element in the way modern wars are conducted and a powerful tool for amplifying the outcomes of a hard-won victory.

Borodino provides a striking example for this discussion, and we feel compelled to address it further—not only because the circumstances cannot be reduced to a simple critique of Buonaparte's decisions, but also because it might otherwise seem as though this battle, and many other similar cases, belong to the rare category where strategic conditions restrain the general's hand from the outset. French authors and ardent admirers of Buonaparte—such as Vaudancourt, Chambray, and Ségur—have criticized him for not using his final reserves to drive the Russian army completely off the field, transforming what was essentially a defeated opponent into a scattered, routed force. They argue that a complete rout would have reshaped the Russian loss into an irrevocable catastrophe.

To delve into the complex positions of both armies would take us too far afield, but one crucial point is clear: when Buonaparte crossed the Niemen, his army numbered 300,000 strong. By the time of Borodino, this same force had dwindled to 120,000. He was keenly aware that he might be left with insufficient troops to reach Moscow—the key to his entire campaign. The victory he achieved at Borodino almost guaranteed him access to the Russian capital, as it seemed unlikely the Russians could rally for another full-scale battle within a week. Buonaparte believed that in Moscow, he would find peace negotiations, and while a complete dismantling of the Russian army would have made this outcome more certain, his foremost concern was to reach Moscow with a formidable enough force to command authority over the city, and by extension, the Russian government.

As history shows, the strength he brought to Moscow was insufficient for these aims, yet it would have been weaker still had he scattered his own troops in an attempt to completely shatter the Russians. Understanding this balance, Buonaparte's decision was, in our view, entirely justified. This example, however, does not fit with those cases where broader strategic concerns prevent a general from fully exploiting a victory, for at Borodino, there was never a question of simple pursuit. By four o'clock in the afternoon, Buonaparte's victory was clear, but the Russians still held much of the battlefield and were unwilling to withdraw. Had he ordered another attack, the Russians would have fiercely resisted, likely resulting in a total Russian defeat, but at great additional cost to the French.

Therefore, we can place Borodino among those battles, like Bautzen, that remained partially unresolved. In Bautzen, the defeated side chose to withdraw sooner, whereas at Borodino, the victor settled for a partial victory—not because he doubted his ability to fully defeat the Russians, but because he could not afford the further sacrifices needed to achieve it.

Returning now to our main topic, the takeaway regarding this initial phase of pursuit is that the vigor with which it is executed largely determines the full value of a victory. This pursuit is not merely an addendum but a continuation of the victory, and in some cases, it is even more consequential than the victory itself. Strategy, as it converges here with tactics to reap the benefits of success, exerts its authority by calling for this essential extension of victory.

Beyond this immediate pursuit, however, the true trajectory of victory begins—a course set into motion by the momentum of initial success. As previously noted, this momentum is shaped by further strategic factors that we will address in detail later. For now, it's important to highlight the universal aspects of pursuit, so as to provide a foundational understanding without need for repetition in future discussions.

In the extended stages of pursuit, three levels of intensity can be observed: a simple pursuit, a more aggressive or hard pursuit, and finally, a parallel march aimed at intercepting the enemy.

The first level, a simple following or pursuit, forces the enemy to keep retreating until they find a position where they feel ready to risk another battle. This kind of pursuit allows the victor to capture whatever the enemy cannot manage to carry with them—this includes sick or wounded soldiers, exhausted troops, baggage, supply carts, and various other materials. However, this straightforward following does not necessarily escalate the disorder within the enemy's ranks; it simply capitalizes on the immediate spoils left behind by their retreat.

If, instead of merely occupying the ground the enemy abandons each day, the pursuing force structures its actions so that each day they drive forward, disrupting any attempts by the enemy's rear-guard to establish a stand, this type of approach has a much more significant impact on the retreating army. By forcing the enemy to hasten their retreat, this constant pressure creates a persistent sense of flight and escalates disarray among the ranks. Nothing deflates a soldier's morale quite like hearing the enemy's cannon fire again just as they are about to settle down for much-needed rest after a forced march. When this pressure is maintained day after day, it can lead the entire army to a breaking point, potentially causing a total collapse. The cumulative effect of feeling compelled to act in response to the victor's dictates, without the ability to resist, cannot help but severely impact the morale of the retreating forces.

This effect reaches its peak when the enemy is forced to undertake night marches. For example, if the victor's forces move in at sunset, dislodging the enemy from a recently chosen camp—whether for the main body or the rear-guard—the defeated army is then left with two unappealing options. They must either retreat through the night or shift their position further back under the cover of darkness, both of which lead to severe exhaustion and disrupted operations. Meanwhile, the pursuing force can rest overnight without any disruption, giving them a distinct advantage.

The planning of these pursuits—especially the timing of marches and the choice of halting positions—depends on many situational factors, such as the army's supply lines, natural terrain obstacles, large urban centers, and other strategic considerations. It would be overly simplistic, or even pedantic, to attempt a purely mathematical model of how a pursuer might dictate the retreating enemy's movements to the point of compelling them into night marches while enjoying rest themselves. Nonetheless, with careful planning, pursuit marches can be organized with this objective in mind, significantly increasing the pressure and effectiveness of the pursuit.

Yet, this approach is rarely implemented, as it poses a substantial challenge to the pursuing army. Following a fixed daily routine—marching early, halting by midday, tending to logistics, and resting at night—is far more convenient. On the other hand, adapting one's movements entirely to the enemy's timetable requires staying in a high state of readiness, often delaying decisions until the last moment. Such a strategy might involve marching at irregular hours, sometimes in the morning, sometimes at night, continuously operating within sight of the enemy, exchanging cannon fire, and coordinating maneuvers to flank and outmaneuver the enemy. All this tactical maneuvering is costly and places a heavy burden on the pursuing force. Given that war is rife with hardships, armies are generally reluctant to adopt methods that impose additional strain if they are not deemed absolutely essential.

These observations apply not only to entire armies but also to advance guards, which commonly undertake such pursuits. For these reasons, the second, more intense level of pursuit—continuously pressing the enemy—is relatively rare. Even in Napoleon's 1812 Russian campaign, such a rigorous pursuit was seldom practiced, as the arduous conditions of the campaign threatened to drain the French forces before they could achieve their goals. Conversely, in other campaigns, the French were known for their vigor and persistence in pursuit, often achieving notable results through their relentless pursuit efforts.

Finally, the third and most powerful form of pursuit is a parallel march toward the main objective of the retreating army. When an army has been defeated, it will often have a strategic destination behind it, whether close or distant, that it aims to reach as a priority. This destination could be a critical point that, if missed, would endanger its further retreat, such as a narrow pass or defile. Alternatively, the location might be of high strategic importance, like a major city, supply depot, or critical fortification that the retreating army needs to secure before the victor arrives. Or, it could be a point where the retreating force expects to gain renewed defensive strength by occupying favorable terrain or merging with other military units.

If the victor moves toward this crucial point along a parallel or lateral route, it can escalate the enemy's retreat, possibly pushing them into a state of chaotic haste or even outright flight. The retreating force has only a few options to counter this kind of pressure.

The first and boldest option is for the defeated army to turn and confront the victor head-on in a surprising counterattack. This approach requires a daring commander and a resilient army—one that has been beaten but is still intact and able to mount a strong resistance. Such a move is only feasible in rare situations, where the army's morale and structure remain relatively unbroken despite the recent loss.

The second option is to accelerate the retreat, but this plays into the victor's hands, often pushing the defeated troops to extreme limits. Such forced haste can lead to severe consequences, with significant losses among stragglers, abandoned equipment, broken artillery, and disorganized supply trains.

The third and least favorable option is for the retreating army to veer off in a different direction, making a wide detour to avoid the nearest interception point and attempt to march at a safer distance from the pursuing force. This strategy aims to relieve some of the urgency in the retreat, hopefully reducing the immediate pressure on the army. However, this option often proves disastrous, much like an insolvent debtor taking on new loans to address old debts. While there are scenarios where this approach might be the best or only choice, and instances where it has even been successful, it is generally a poor strategy that introduces new risks and prolongs the army's vulnerability. Frequently, this choice is driven not by strategic clarity but by an undesirable motive—the fear of further confrontation. This fear can lead the commander to avoid any potential encounters with the enemy, which can worsen the army's predicament.

A commander who falls into this trap risks deepening the crisis for his army. No matter how much the morale of the force may have declined or how justified his concerns about facing the enemy may seem, anxiously dodging every chance of engagement only amplifies the issues at hand. For example, had Napoleon in 1813 avoided the Battle of Hanau and tried to cross the Rhine at Mannheim or Coblenz instead, he would not have brought back the 30,000 to 40,000 men he managed to save. The Bavarians had blocked his path to the Rhine, yet by making a resolute stand at Hanau and employing a skillful use of artillery, Napoleon's troops shattered the Bavarian resistance, enabling his army to reach its objective and cross the Rhine.

Small, calculated combats, particularly when the defeated army can use defensive positions to its advantage, play an essential role in reviving the morale of a retreating force. These measured, well-planned encounters allow the retreating troops to recover a sense of cohesion and strength, proving to themselves that they can still hold their ground under the right circumstances. Rather than avoiding every skirmish, the commander's resolve to engage in smaller defensive actions can become the first step toward rebuilding the fighting spirit of his army.

The extraordinary impact of even the smallest victories on the morale of an army is astonishing; however, for most generals, embracing this strategy requires immense self-control. The alternative—evading all encounters—initially appears so much easier that it naturally tends to be preferred. Yet, ironically, this approach often serves the pursuer's objectives best, leading to the complete disintegration of the retreating force. It's worth emphasizing, though, that our focus here is on an entire army in retreat, not on a single division that has been cut off and is attempting to rejoin its main force through a detour. In such cases, the conditions are entirely different, and success for the detached unit is not uncommon.

One critical factor for the success of this "race" between two forces is that a division of the pursuing army should advance along the same path taken by the retreating enemy. This not only enables the pursuer to pick up stragglers but also maintains the psychological impact of a constant enemy presence, which can be a powerful force in sapping the morale of the retreating troops. Blücher, despite his otherwise commendable pursuit after the Battle of La Belle Alliance, missed this crucial detail, lessening the pressure on the retreating forces.

These demanding marches inevitably affect both the pursuer and the pursued, and they are ill-advised if the retreating army can regroup with another significant force, if it is led by a skilled and determined commander, or if its forces have not yet been thoroughly weakened and prepared for destruction. However, when conditions favor such an approach, it acts with overwhelming power. The losses within the beaten army due to sickness, fatigue, and demoralization mount disproportionately; the constant anxiety over impending disaster saps the army's spirit, making any kind of organized defense nearly impossible. Under these conditions, the retreating army may see thousands of soldiers surrender daily without further resistance.

During these rare phases of uninterrupted success, the victorious commander should not hesitate to divide his forces strategically, extending the reach of destruction. This allows him to pull every nearby resource into his sweep: isolating enemy detachments, capturing forts unprepared for immediate defense, occupying large towns, and so on. This aggressive expansion can continue until circumstances change, and the more the victor dares in this manner, the longer it will take for a new balance of power to emerge.

History is full of examples where decisive victories were followed by relentless and highly effective pursuits that led to remarkable outcomes. Napoleon's campaigns offer plenty of cases in point: the battle of Jena in 1806, where the Prussian army was shattered and pursued relentlessly; Ratisbonne in 1809, where a decisive victory forced a hasty retreat and further losses; Leipzig in 1813, where coalition forces pursued Napoleon's weakened army out of Germany; and finally, La Belle Alliance in 1815, where a sustained pursuit solidified the victory at Waterloo. These examples showcase how grand victories, when coupled with vigorous and well-executed pursuits, often lead to sweeping strategic successes.

Chapter XIII. Retreat After a Lost Battle

In a lost battle, an army's power is significantly damaged—its morale even more so than its physical strength. A second confrontation, unless supported by new favorable conditions, would likely lead to utter defeat or even total destruction. This is a basic military principle. The usual course is to continue the retreat until a balance of forces is reestablished. This balance might come through reinforcements, the shelter of strong fortifications, natural defensive advantages in the terrain, or a separation of the enemy's forces. The speed at which this equilibrium is reached depends not only on the magnitude of losses and the extent of the defeat but even more on the character and persistence of the opponent. There are countless examples of armies rallying a short distance from the battlefield despite no change in their circumstances. Often, this can be attributed to the adversary's own lack of resolve or to an insufficient advantage gained in the battle to have a lasting impact.

Taking advantage of such weaknesses or oversights by the enemy, and not surrendering a single inch more than absolutely necessary, is essential. A slow, determined retreat that involves constant resistance and bold counterstrokes wherever the enemy attempts to overextend their advantage is crucial for maintaining whatever remains of the army's morale. The most skilled generals and battle-hardened armies have always made their retreats resemble that of a wounded lion, striking back as they withdraw. This method is undeniably sound, and it represents the best approach in theory.

It is true that, when abandoning a hazardous position, time-wasting formalities have sometimes been observed, which can add unnecessary risk. In such critical moments, speed is vital, and experienced commanders recognize this as a crucial rule. But this should not be confused with the orderly withdrawal after a lost battle. Those who try to rush a retreat with a few hasty marches to regain stability often make a grave error. The initial movements should be as measured as possible, adhering to the principle of never letting the enemy dictate the pace. This approach inevitably requires fierce fighting with the enemy in close pursuit, but the benefit justifies the cost. Without it, the retreat can quickly accelerate into a panicked flight, resulting in greater losses from stragglers than from rear-guard actions. Moreover, this loss of order further erodes the already fragile spirit of resistance.

To conduct such a retreat effectively, a strong rear-guard is essential. This force should consist of seasoned troops under the command of a fearless general, ready to support the main army at critical moments. Skillful use of the terrain, with carefully placed ambuscades, especially where the enemy's advance guard becomes overconfident, is also necessary. In short, a retreat should resemble a series of small, carefully staged battles, each intended to slow the enemy and extract a price for every inch gained.

The difficulty of an organized retreat naturally depends on how favorable or unfavorable the conditions were at the time of the battle, as well as the intensity with which the battle was fought. The battles of Jena and La Belle Alliance illustrate how, when every last soldier is used against a strong enemy, any hope for a controlled retreat can be utterly lost.

There have occasionally been proposals(*) suggesting that an army retreat in divided segments or even along diverging paths. However, we are not referring to separations that are merely for logistical ease, where the overall concentration of forces is maintained and still allows for unified action; rather, we address here any division that disrupts unity, which is highly dangerous, fundamentally flawed, and thus a major mistake. After a defeat, the army is already weakened and in a state of disorganization; the primary and immediate need is to consolidate, regaining order, morale, and a sense of collective security through this unity. The notion of splitting into separate groups to harass the enemy on both flanks while they pursue their victory is a bizarre concept. It might work to intimidate a timid and overly cautious enemy, but unless such a response is assured, such a strategy is better avoided.

If the strategic situation following a battle requires flanks to be protected by detachments, then such measures should be strictly limited to what is unavoidable. This division of forces should always be viewed as an undesirable necessity rather than a sound tactic, and it is rare that any army is in a position to implement it immediately after a defeat.

For instance, when Frederick the Great, following his defeat at the Battle of Kollin(*), was forced to retreat and abandon the siege of Prague, he organized his withdrawal in three columns—not out of tactical preference but due to the positioning of his forces and the urgent need to protect Saxony. Similarly, after the Battle of Brienne(), Napoleon sent Marmont back to cover the Aube River while he himself moved towards Troyes on the Seine. This division avoided disaster only because the Allies, rather than pursuing in a concentrated force, also split up—Blücher moved towards the Marne, and Schwartzenberg advanced with excessive caution out of fear that his forces would be too weak on their own.

(*) Reference here is made to the military theories of Lloyd, Bülow, and others.

(*) June 19, 1757.

() January 30, 1814.

Chapter XIV. Night Fighting

The way to handle combat at night, and all the details that come with it, is really a tactical matter, but here we'll look at it as a complete strategy that stands out as a unique tool in warfare. Essentially, any attack at night is just an intense kind of surprise. At first glance, a night attack seems like a big advantage for the attacker. We assume the enemy will be caught off guard, while the attacker is fully prepared for whatever may come. What an imbalance! We imagine the enemy in total confusion, while the attacker only has to gather up the rewards of his advantage. This leads to endless plans for night attacks from those who don't actually lead them or bear the responsibility, yet in reality, these attacks seldom occur.

These ideal plans are usually based on the idea that the attacker knows the defender's layout because it was prepared in advance and could not have gone unnoticed during scouting and questioning; on the other hand, the attacker's plans, being made only at the last moment, are unknown to the enemy. But the second part of that idea isn't always completely true, and the first part is even less so. If we aren't close enough to fully observe the enemy's every move, as the Austrians did with Frederick the Great before the Battle of Hochkirch (1758), then what we know about the enemy's position will always be incomplete. This information comes from scouts, patrols, prisoners, and spies—sources that can't always be trusted because the information is often outdated, and the enemy's position may have changed.

Additionally, with the tactics and ways of setting up camp used in the past, it was much easier to study the enemy's position than it is now. A line of tents is much simpler to recognize than a line of huts or a bivouac, and a camp stretched out in a line across the front is also easier to understand than a layout with Divisions in columns, as is often done today. We may be able to observe the ground where a Division is camped in this way, but still not gain an accurate picture of it.

However, just knowing the position isn't enough. It's also crucial to understand the steps the defender might take during the combat, and these are not just random actions. These steps make night attacks even harder in modern warfare than in the past because the defender now has an advantage of time in preparing for attacks. In our battles, the defender's position is less permanent than it used to be, so the defender is now better equipped to surprise his opponent with unexpected counterattacks than he could in the past.

From this, we can conclude that the attacker in a night combat feels the disadvantage of not being able to see as much as the defender does. This shared limitation means that only particular reasons can make a night attack advisable. Usually, these reasons are relevant to smaller or secondary parts of an army rather than the main body. It follows that night attacks, as a rule, tend to occur with smaller, secondary combats rather than with large-scale battles.

In some cases, it may be possible to attack a segment of the enemy's army with a significantly larger force, aiming to surround it entirely. This allows for the possibility of capturing the entire segment or inflicting serious losses through a lopsided battle, assuming other circumstances are in our favor. However, such a plan can only succeed if it's a true surprise, because no isolated part of the enemy's force would willingly engage in an uneven fight. Instead, they would likely retreat. But achieving a surprise on such a meaningful scale, especially outside of very close terrain, is something that can typically only happen at night. So, if we want to take advantage of poor positioning on the enemy's part, we must use the night, at least to prepare and approach, even if the main combat itself doesn't begin until dawn. This is the principle behind many smaller nighttime raids against outposts and small groups, where the essential goal is to use superior numbers and an encircling approach to trap the enemy in such a disadvantageous position that they can't escape without taking significant losses.

As the size of the target group grows, so does the difficulty of success, since a larger force has more resources within itself to hold out in battle until reinforcements can arrive. Therefore, it's not practical to make an entire enemy army the target of such an attack under normal conditions. Even though a full army doesn't have reinforcements waiting elsewhere, it still holds enough internal strength to defend itself from attacks on multiple fronts, especially in today's warfare, where everyone is prepared from the start for this common type of flanking maneuver. Whether the enemy can attack us from multiple directions successfully depends not on the element of surprise but on completely different conditions. Without going into the nature of these factors here, we can simply note that flanking an opponent involves both high potential rewards and equally high risks. Therefore, unless particular circumstances strongly support such a plan, only a substantial advantage in numbers can justify attempting it. Such a superior force would be the same amount of force we would apply against just a portion of the enemy's army.

Turning and surrounding a small section of the enemy, especially under the cover of darkness, is also more feasible for another reason: even if we commit considerable resources to such an action, we're only risking a portion of our army. That's more manageable than risking the entire force on a single large gamble. Besides, the remaining part—or possibly the entire force—can act as a support or fallback point for the section involved in the attack, which greatly reduces the risk of the operation.

Not only does this risk factor limit night missions to smaller units, but the execution's challenges do, too. Since surprise is at the core of these operations, stealth in approach is essential to carry them out. This stealth is far easier to achieve with small groups than with large ones and moving entire columns from an army in secret is rarely practical. Therefore, these night operations are generally focused on small outposts and can only realistically target larger groups if they are poorly defended, as in the case of Frederick the Great's attack at Hochkirch.

In recent times, with the faster pace and increased intensity of warfare, it has often happened that armies have set up camp close to one another without establishing an extensive system of outposts. Such proximity usually occurs during the final stages of a campaign, when the pressure for a decision is highest. However, at these times, both sides are often more prepared for battle. In contrast, in earlier wars, it was common for armies to camp within sight of one another to mutually monitor each other's movements over a longer period. Frederick the Great, for example, frequently camped near Austrian forces for weeks, close enough that they could have easily exchanged cannon fire.

However, this practice, which was much more favorable to night attacks, has largely been abandoned in recent warfare. Armies today are no longer as self-sustaining in terms of supplies and encampment needs, so they generally keep a day's march between themselves and the enemy. If we focus specifically on night attacks at the scale of an entire army, it becomes clear that reasons for such actions rarely present themselves. When they do, they typically fall into one of a few specific categories.

1. A very rare instance of either extreme negligence or boldness in the enemy's ranks, balanced by a significant edge in morale on our side, though such situations are infrequent.

2. A situation in which the enemy's army is already panicked or, in general, where our moral strength is so superior that it effectively substitutes for strategic oversight during the engagement.

3. An attempt to break through an enemy army of superior size that has us surrounded, where the element of surprise is essential, and the aim is solely to create a path through, allowing a far greater concentration of force.

4. Finally, when facing dire circumstances, where our forces are heavily outmatched by the enemy's, making a daring, high-risk move our only hope of success.

However, in all these cases, there is still the requirement that the enemy's army is within sight and lacks a forward defense line.

As for the majority of night engagements, these are usually conducted so as to conclude by dawn. The initial approach and first wave of attack are carried out under the cover of night, allowing the attacker to take advantage of the disarray they create in the enemy ranks. Engagements of this sort, where the attack itself doesn't begin until dawn and the night is used solely for positioning, are not truly considered night combats.

Book V. Military Forces

Chapter I. General Scheme

We will examine military forces in the following aspects:

1. In terms of their numbers and structural organization.

2. In the conditions that define them outside of actual combat.

3. Regarding the requirements for their upkeep; and finally,

4. In their broader connections to the land and terrain.

This book, therefore, will focus on elements related to an army that serve as essential preconditions for combat but do not involve combat itself. These aspects are interconnected with combat and influence it, so they often reappear when we discuss the application of combat. Nonetheless, we must first explore each of these elements independently to understand its essence and unique characteristics.

Chapter II. Theatre of War, Army, Campaign

The nature of these elements does not allow for a perfectly precise definition of the three essential factors representing space, mass, and time in war. Still, to avoid misunderstandings, we should clarify the usual meaning of these terms, which we will generally follow.

1. Theatre of War.

This term denotes properly such a portion of this term refers to a defined section of the area where war occurs, with boundaries that are secured in a way that gives it a form of independence. This security might come from fortifications, significant natural obstacles, or simply a substantial distance separating it from other active regions within the war zone. Such a section is not just a part of the whole but functions as a complete, self-contained unit. Changes happening in other parts of the war zone have only indirect effects on it. To illustrate, imagine a forward movement occurring in one area, while in another, a retreat takes place, or one part is held defensively while an offensive is underway elsewhere. This well-defined concept cannot be universally applied; however, it helps outline distinctions in planning and action.

2. Army.

With the concept of a Theatre of War established, defining an Army becomes straightforward: it's essentially the body of troops operating within a particular Theatre of War. However, this definition doesn't entirely capture the common understanding of the term. For instance, in 1815, Blücher and Wellington each commanded a separate army, despite both being in the same Theatre of War. The chief command is thus another key identifier in defining an Army. Ideally, a single command should control a given Theatre of War, granting the commander the necessary independence to act effectively within that domain.

Absolute troop numbers alone don't determine what constitutes an Army, as it might seem at first glance. When multiple armies operate under one command within a single Theatre of War, they are referred to as Armies, not due to their size but based on arrangements that predate the conflict (e.g., the Silesian Army, the Army of the North, in 1813). If a large force were divided into corps within one Theatre, we wouldn't typically split them into separate Armies—doing so would go against the conventional meaning of the term. Likewise, while it would seem pedantic to call every independent band of irregular troops in a remote province an Army, no one was surprised when people referred to the Vendean forces in the Revolutionary War as the Vendean Army, despite its modest size.

In general, the concepts of an Army and a Theatre of War go hand in hand, naturally encompassing one another.

3. Campaign.

Although the sum of all military events in every Theatre of War within a given year is often referred to as a Campaign, it is more accurate and typical to use this term to describe the operations in a single Theatre of War. It's even less appropriate to associate a Campaign solely with the span of one year, as wars no longer naturally divide into yearly Campaigns marked by prolonged winter breaks. However, since events in a Theatre of War naturally form distinct chapters—such as when the direct impact of a major event subsides, and fresh strategies start to unfold—it makes sense to consider these natural divisions when dividing a year (or Campaign) into comprehensive sections of action. For instance, no one would define the Campaign of 1812 as ending at Memel, where the armies were positioned on January 1st, nor would they classify the French retreat across the Elbe as part of the 1813 Campaign, as that phase was clearly a continuation of the retreat from Moscow.

The inability to provide these concepts with greater clarity is of little concern since they aren't meant to serve as rigid philosophical definitions or foundations for strict assertions. Rather, they are simply tools to bring added clarity and accuracy to the terminology we use.

Chapter III. Relation of Power

In the eighth chapter of the third book, we discussed how superior numbers in battles bring an advantage, from which follows the broader strategic importance of numerical superiority. This establishes the basic importance of the balance of power, and here we will delve into a few more specific points on the topic.

A thorough review of modern military history brings us to conclude that numerical superiority is increasingly decisive, and that gathering the largest possible forces for decisive engagements is more essential than ever. Though courage and a resilient spirit have always amplified an army's physical strength, and will undoubtedly continue to do so, historical records show that certain eras have seen superior organization and equipment grant one side a significant moral edge. Other periods have been marked by exceptional mobility as a powerful advantage, or by new tactical systems that temporarily transformed battle outcomes. Some commanders have leveraged an acute understanding of terrain, general strategic principles, or innovative methods to gain substantial advantages, but this approach has also receded, and wars today seem to unfold in simpler, more straightforward ways.

If we set aside prior beliefs and examine the evidence from recent wars, we notice only faint echoes of these once-influential factors, whether over the course of a full campaign or in decisive engagements—meaning, the grand battles. For more on the term "great battle" itself, we refer to the second chapter of the previous book.

Today, armies are so aligned in terms of arms, gear, and training that few notable differences remain between the most and the least equipped forces in these respects. Although a slight distinction might exist due to the technical skill within specialized units, it generally means that one side may innovate a new device or approach, which the other side quickly adopts. Even among lower-ranking generals and leaders of corps and divisions, ideas and methods within their scope are broadly uniform across the board. This uniformity has reached a point where, apart from the skill of the commander-in-chief—a factor largely subject to chance, as it is not closely tied to the nation's or army's general level of training—experience in combat is often the sole remaining variable that can decisively separate one force from another. Therefore, as these various factors edge toward equality, the importance of raw numbers becomes increasingly pronounced.

The character of modern battles reflects this newfound equilibrium. Take, for example, the Battle of Borodino, where the French, considered the preeminent army of the time, faced the Russians, who lagged behind in several aspects of organization and specialized training. Throughout this intense and protracted battle, there was little evidence of one side outmaneuvering the other through superior strategy or intellect. Instead, the battle represented a straightforward clash of two forces in which brute strength was the deciding factor. Since both sides were relatively evenly matched, the outcome became a matter of incremental advantage, ultimately tipping toward the side with the most determined commander and the most battle-seasoned troops.

We choose Borodino as an example here, as it uniquely involved two almost equally sized armies, a balance rarely found in battles, thereby emphasizing how modern warfare has evolved into direct tests of strength when other distinctions diminish.

We do not argue that all battles follow this exact pattern, but it reflects the prevailing nature of most conflicts. In battles where forces measure their strength against one another slowly and with care, any numerical advantage must, of course, make the outcome more certain for the larger side. Indeed, if we look through the records of modern military history, we rarely find cases where a smaller army has defeated another twice its own size, something which was once not unheard of. Even Napoleon, considered one of the most outstanding generals of recent times, only achieved his great victories with an army that was either superior in numbers or at least very close to his opponent's in size—Dresden in 1813 being the one notable exception. When he faced a stronger opponent, as at Leipzig, Brienne, Laon, and Waterloo, he faced defeat.

In strategic planning, the total strength of an army is usually a fixed number that a commander cannot easily alter. But this doesn't imply that fighting a war with an obviously smaller force is impossible. War isn't always a matter of choice in state policy, and it becomes even less so when there's a significant disparity in forces. As a result, practically any balance of power is possible in war, and it would be a peculiar theory indeed that abandoned its purpose precisely where it was most needed.

Although military theory would certainly prefer an evenly matched force, it cannot dictate that a highly imbalanced one is useless. There can be no set limitations on this. The smaller the force, the more modest its objectives must be, and the shorter the time it can likely endure. In these respects, a weaker force has room to give ground, so to speak. We can only discuss the ways that force size influences the conduct of war as they arise within each specific situation, yet it is essential here to establish this broad perspective, though we'll add one more point to round it out.

The further an army falls behind its opponent in strength, the more tension it must sustain within its forces and the greater its energy must be as it faces danger. If this energy falters, giving way to despair rather than heroic resolve, then indeed, even the best military strategies cannot salvage the situation.

When this heightened determination is combined with prudent restraint in its aims, we see a display of impressive actions balanced with caution, as in the campaigns of Frederick the Great. However, the less effect this caution and moderation can have, the more the army must rely on pure resolve and intense exertion. When the imbalance of forces becomes so severe that no adjustment to the army's objectives could reasonably protect it from a potential disaster, or when the likely duration of danger is such that even the utmost careful use of resources cannot bring it to its goal, the focus must shift to consolidating all available energy for one final, decisive blow. The army, encircled on all sides, with little hope from sources that seem unlikely to help, will place its last confidence in the strength that courage in the face of desperation can bring and will treat the boldest actions as the wisest. In this situation, the commander will use all forms of cunning and daring available; and if success doesn't come, they may at least find in an honorable defeat the foundation for future triumph.

Chapter IV. Relation of the Three Arms

We will focus here on the three primary military branches: Infantry, Cavalry, and Artillery. Though this analysis is generally more applicable to tactics, it's essential to delve into it here to clarify each arm's unique capabilities within combat.

Combat itself is essentially of two main types, each fundamentally distinct from the other. First, there is the "destructive principle of fire," which emphasizes impact from a distance, and second, there is the "personal combat," or close-range engagement, where fighting happens face-to-face. This close combat has two forms, which we could call absolute in nature: one, being attack, characterized by forward movement, and the other, defense, which relies on standing firm.

Each of these branches has distinct strengths aligned with one of these fundamental types of combat. Artillery, for instance, operates exclusively within the destructive principle of fire. Its purpose is purely to inflict damage at a distance, using the impact of fire to break down opposing forces. It doesn't engage directly with the enemy; it affects the enemy without direct confrontation. Cavalry, on the other hand, is designed for personal combat and performs exclusively in that arena. Its strength lies in its capacity for direct attack, taking advantage of the ability to cover ground rapidly to overtake or confront enemies head-on. However, it lacks the firm defensive quality necessary for standing ground, being designed for speed and maneuverability rather than holding position. Infantry is unique because it effectively combines both principles of combat—possessing firepower but also the essential capacity to engage in close, hand-to-hand combat, whether advancing or defending.

When we examine these arms based on the nature of close combat, Infantry, with its balance between firmness and some degree of mobility, is uniquely equipped to both hold a defensive position and advance on an enemy. Infantry's ability to remain steadfast and "rooted" when necessary makes it invaluable in defense while still allowing some level of movement for attack. Cavalry, meanwhile, excels in attack, given its speed, but is limited in a defensive role since it lacks the means to "stand firm" and hold territory.

This inherent division of essential combat qualities among different branches of the military establishes Infantry's superiority in terms of flexibility and general usefulness. Infantry alone is equipped with all three essential combat qualities, allowing it to engage in both forms of combat and to shift effectively between attack and defense. From this, we can see that the most effective deployment of military power comes from a strategic combination of these three branches, where each arm's strengths can be enhanced to balance out its limitations. Infantry forms the backbone of this structure by uniting the essential principles of fire, movement, and firmness, while Cavalry and Artillery can be deployed to reinforce these principles as needed.

In modern warfare, the "destructive principle of fire" has proven to be overwhelmingly effective, with artillery playing an increasingly powerful role in battle outcomes. Still, hand-to-hand combat or the threat of close combat remains the ultimate foundation of warfare, making a force that relies solely on artillery, for example, inadequate in practice. While it's technically possible to have an army composed only of Cavalry, its utility would be limited due to its lack of defensive capacity and the challenges it would face in prolonged engagements. An army of Infantry, however, is not only conceivable but, in fact, would be the most resilient of the three because it encompasses all critical combat attributes.

Thus, if we were to rank these three branches in terms of their standalone or independent value, Infantry would come first, followed by Cavalry, and then Artillery. However, this order shifts when we consider the three arms working together as a unified force. Given that the destructive capacity of fire from artillery is exceptionally impactful, an army entirely without Cavalry would be weakened, but far less so than one that lacked Artillery altogether. This is due to the higher importance of firepower over sheer maneuverability in most modern engagements. In essence, while each branch brings unique strengths, Infantry's versatility remains the core of effective military force, with Artillery's firepower as a vital component in any combined strategy.

An army made up solely of infantry would undoubtedly face challenges against a fully equipped force with all three branches—infantry, cavalry, and artillery. Yet, if the infantry's numbers were proportionately increased to make up for its lack of cavalry, it could adjust its tactics and still operate effectively. Its limited cavalry would indeed create certain disadvantages: for instance, its outpost operations would become more challenging, it would struggle to chase down a retreating enemy with much vigor, and any retreat it had to make would demand greater effort and resilience. But these issues, though inconvenient, wouldn't necessarily render it powerless on the battlefield.

When such an infantry-based army opposes an enemy consisting only of infantry and cavalry, it would still maintain a fair advantage. In contrast, it is difficult to imagine that an opposing force made up exclusively of infantry and cavalry could effectively hold its ground against an army equipped with all three arms, including artillery. This is because the balance and varied strengths that artillery brings in combined-arms strategy would be a distinct advantage.

It's essential to note that these insights into the relative value of each military branch are based on general patterns in warfare, where one situation might offset another over time. Thus, the principles discussed here aren't intended to apply rigidly to every specific scenario of combat. For instance, a battalion positioned on outpost duty or conducting a retreat might, in certain cases, prefer to have a squadron of cavalry rather than a couple of artillery guns. Similarly, a cavalry detachment supported by horse artillery, tasked with swiftly pursuing or intercepting a fleeing enemy, would not need the support of infantry to fulfill its objective effectively.

To summarize, these considerations reveal several essential conclusions about the relative utility of each arm.

1. Infantry is the most self-sufficient of the three arms, capable of operating effectively even without immediate support from other branches.
2. Artillery lacks the capacity for independent action, as it generally relies on the other arms for protection and support in both offense and defense.
3. Among the three, infantry is the backbone of any combined force, holding the central role in both sustaining positions and engaging in direct combat.
4. Cavalry, while valuable for specific tasks like reconnaissance, pursuit, and quick engagements, is the branch that an army can most afford to function without, especially if other forces are increased proportionally.
5. A well-balanced combination of all three arms—infantry, artillery, and cavalry—provides the most formidable and adaptable force, offering flexibility across various terrains, situations, and tactical needs.

If the combination of the three arms—infantry, cavalry, and artillery—yields the most strength, it's only natural to wonder what the ideal ratio of each would be. However, determining this ideal balance is nearly impossible due to the many variables involved.

In theory, if we could accurately calculate the cost of organizing, provisioning, and maintaining each arm, alongside the effectiveness each provides in combat, we would arrive at a precise answer for the best proportion. Yet, this remains largely hypothetical. To begin with, calculating the total cost is complex. While the financial expenses of training, equipping, and sustaining each arm might be straightforward to tabulate, assigning a quantitative value to the lives of soldiers involved introduces a factor beyond simple arithmetic—a moral and practical calculation that most would find impossible to quantify.

Moreover, each arm relies heavily on different resources within a state: infantry mainly draws from the population, cavalry requires an abundant supply of horses, and artillery demands considerable financial resources for equipment and maintenance. These separate demands mirror a state's varying strengths or weaknesses in population, resources, and economy at different times in history. Indeed, if we observe the military evolution of different nations, we see that their reliance on each arm often reflects these distinct resources rather than any calculated ratio of combat effectiveness.

Yet, for practical reasons, some form of comparative standard is useful, so we rely on the cost in money alone as the one measurable factor. For simplicity, let's assume that a squadron of 150 horsemen, an infantry battalion of 800 soldiers, and an artillery battery with eight six-pounders would all incur roughly the same expenses to organize, train, and maintain.

Assessing the combat effectiveness of each arm relative to the others is even more challenging. If the destructive potential of each arm were the only consideration, then a comparison might be achievable. However, each arm serves a distinct purpose within the military structure, fulfilling roles that often complement rather than replace each other. The effectiveness of each arm can vary depending on changes in the conduct of war, adjustments in battlefield tactics, and other operational factors that can alter the relative importance of any one arm without necessarily diminishing its role. Therefore, these diverse uses make it difficult to pin down an exact, lasting proportion.

In short, while the ideal balance of the three arms would strengthen an army's combat readiness, determining that balance remains elusive, shaped as it is by shifting factors that vary with the resources, needs, and aims of each specific war and nation.

We often hear people claim that experience provides clear guidance on the ideal balance among the three arms of the military—infantry, cavalry, and artillery—and that military history offers ample evidence on the subject. Yet, any such claims are usually little more than speculative talk, lacking a foundation based on essential principles. Consequently, while the concept of an ideal ratio between the three arms is imaginable, it remains elusive—a theoretical "x" that cannot be precisely calculated and remains, at best, an abstract ideal rather than an actionable formula. However, it is possible to assess the effects of having a significant advantage or disadvantage in a specific arm compared to the enemy's corresponding arm.

Artillery, for example, amplifies the destructive power of an army through its firepower and thus considerably increases an army's impact on the battlefield. But it is also the least mobile of the three arms, which can make an army more cumbersome. Artillery requires additional support, as it cannot engage in close combat effectively. If artillery becomes too plentiful, it may not be adequately protected by other troops and could be captured by the enemy. Additionally, artillery has a unique vulnerability because its primary assets—guns and carriages—can quickly be repurposed by the enemy if captured.

Cavalry, by contrast, enhances the army's mobility and pace. When cavalry is limited, the tempo of battle slows, as infantry must conduct many tasks on foot. This lack of speed can hinder the swift, decisive exploitation of victory—reaping the benefits with a "sickle" rather than a "scythe," so to speak. While an overabundance of cavalry does not directly weaken combat power in the way that artillery can, it poses logistical challenges. Feeding a large cavalry force is resource-intensive, and, strategically, it might be more effective to have the same expenditure support a larger infantry force instead of an excessive number of cavalry.

These effects from the dominance of one arm over others are crucial considerations in military art, especially as commanders rarely have control over the proportion of forces they inherit; by the time a general receives his command, the balance among infantry, cavalry, and artillery is often already set.

To envision how an imbalance among these arms shapes the character of warfare, one can consider the following scenarios:

An excess of artillery generally leads to more cautious, defensive strategies. With a heavy artillery presence, a force is likely to seek strong defensive positions, using natural barriers like mountains or rugged terrain to protect their artillery assets. Such an approach positions the army to wait out the enemy, allowing them to approach and incur losses. A campaign dominated by artillery takes on a slow, measured character, marked by strategic patience and restrained movements.

A disproportionate amount of cavalry, however, creates a more agile and flexible style of warfare, where rapid advances and strategic positioning take precedence. Cavalry can extend the operational reach of the army, maintaining a high tempo of engagement and the capability for fast maneuvers, even if it may lack the brute strength of artillery in fixed positions. Meanwhile, an army composed predominantly of infantry takes on a different style entirely, leaning toward endurance-based engagements and adaptable, multi-phase operations that capitalize on both offensive and defensive opportunities.

In each case, the balance—or imbalance—among the three arms significantly influences not only the tactics but the entire operational approach of the campaign. The combination of these forces shapes the spirit of the conflict, turning it into a highly tailored and adaptive dance that reflects the unique strengths and constraints of each arm.

Conversely, if an army lacks sufficient artillery, its strategy will lean towards offensive, mobile, and active operations. Marching, endurance, and exertion become its distinctive weapons, and the war assumes a more diverse, vibrant, and rugged character, with numerous smaller skirmishes substituting for major events. A shortage of artillery pushes the army to rely on agility and resilience, keeping campaigns lively, dynamic, and continuously evolving.

When an army has an abundance of cavalry, it favors expansive plains and adopts wide-ranging maneuvers. Cavalry's mobility allows it to operate at a distance from the enemy, giving the army rest and logistical advantages without affording the same to its opponent. This surplus of cavalry enables more aggressive and daring moves, such as extensive flanking operations or surprise maneuvers, as it commands a broader operational space. In cases where diversions or invasions serve as genuine auxiliary strategies, an ample cavalry force greatly enhances these efforts, allowing the army to execute complex and wide-reaching plans.

In contrast, a pronounced shortage of cavalry reduces an army's mobility without compensating with increased firepower, as an excess of artillery might. This deficiency leads the army to adopt a methodical, cautious approach. The primary tactics emphasize maintaining close proximity to the enemy to monitor movements precisely, avoiding rapid or hasty advances, and instead pressing forward steadily with concentrated forces. Such an army will naturally favor defensive operations and rugged terrain to counterbalance its limited cavalry. When offense is necessary, the focus is on taking the most direct route to the enemy's central forces, aiming for slow but steady advances.

These distinct forms of warfare—shaped by a dominance or deficiency in any one of the three arms—rarely dictate the complete direction of a military campaign on their own. Critical decisions, such as choosing between strategic offense or defense, selecting the theater of war, or deciding on a major battle, are usually determined by broader, more fundamental considerations. If such a preponderance does guide major decisions, it may suggest an undue emphasis on secondary factors. However, even with these primary considerations settled, the balance of arms influences how they are executed: prudence and patience may mark the offensive, while boldness and audacity can infuse the defensive.

Moreover, the character of a war itself can significantly affect the proportions of the three arms. In a national or militia-driven war with widespread civilian enlistment (Landsturm), infantry naturally becomes predominant. Here, a shortage of equipment is more common than a shortage of men, and because available resources are allocated to essentials, it is conceivable that for every artillery battery of eight guns, two or three infantry battalions might be mustered.

For a weaker state facing a far more powerful adversary without the option of mass enlistment, increasing its artillery is the fastest way to enhance its army's effectiveness. Artillery saves manpower while intensifying the core destructive element of military force. Such a state is also likely to operate within a confined theater, making the stationary, powerful artillery arm more suitable. Frederick the Great adopted this approach during the latter part of the Seven Years' War, reinforcing his artillery to offset his manpower disadvantage.

Lastly, cavalry is the arm of rapid movement and critical decision-making. Its expansion beyond typical proportions is especially valuable when the conflict spans vast territories, where multiple expeditions and decisive, far-reaching operations are essential. Napoleon Bonaparte exemplified this strategy by building up his cavalry for swift, decisive blows across multiple theaters.

The offensive and defensive aspects of war, on their own, don't necessarily impact the ideal proportion of cavalry within an army. This becomes clearer as we delve into each strategic approach. Generally, both attackers and defenders cover similar ground in a campaign and often share comparable aims, as evidenced by the campaign of 1812. It's a common belief that, in the Middle Ages, cavalry vastly outnumbered infantry and that its prevalence has diminished since then. However, this idea is somewhat mistaken. If we examine historical records from the Middle Ages, we find that while cavalry held immense value, the overall numerical balance may not have been drastically different from more recent periods. Numerous armies of the Crusades, for instance, were heavily composed of foot soldiers, and large bodies of infantry accompanied German Emperors on their expeditions to Rome.

The real distinction lies in the role and value placed on cavalry at that time. Cavalry represented the elite—often the social and military "flower" of the army. Although outnumbered by infantry, it was considered the dominant arm of war, with infantry seen as secondary. Thus, infantry's lower regard often led to the misconception that there were far fewer foot soldiers. It's true that minor raids or incursions in regions like

France, Germany, and Italy sometimes involved forces comprised entirely of cavalry, as it was considered the more decisive arm. However, in larger conflicts, mixed forces were far more typical.

This arrangement began to shift as the feudal system declined, and armies increasingly relied on recruited and paid soldiers. As wars started to depend more on finances and enlistment—as during the Thirty Years' War and Louis XIV's campaigns—the trend of employing vast, often ineffective infantry ranks was curtailed. Some speculated that warfare might eventually rely solely on cavalry, but just as infantry numbers seemed poised to dwindle, advances in firearms elevated their significance. These advancements ensured that infantry retained, and even strengthened, its numerical dominance over cavalry. Around this period, if infantry numbers were low, the balance was roughly equal between infantry and cavalry; if high, infantry outnumbered cavalry three to one.

The reduced role of cavalry became more pronounced as firearms continued to improve, not only in the technology of the weapons themselves but also in the tactical skills developed to employ them. For example, by the Battle of Mollwitz, the Prussian army had achieved such precision in infantry firepower that further enhancement was largely unnecessary. Additionally, infantry's use in broken terrain and as skirmishers became more refined, further solidifying its combat role.

In our view, while the number of cavalry units has not radically changed, the significance attached to them has evolved considerably. This may seem contradictory, but it is quite logical when considering the context. In the Middle Ages, although infantry may have constituted a larger share of the army, this was not due to its effectiveness relative to cavalry. Instead, infantry filled out the ranks simply because only the wealthiest could afford to serve as cavalry. Thus, infantry was often a last resort rather than a prized unit type, and if the army had been able to increase its cavalry numbers freely, it likely would have.

Even as cavalry's overall importance in warfare has diminished, it has retained enough utility to maintain a steady numerical ratio with infantry—one that reflects historical norms rather than any strict numerical reduction.

Since at least the wars of the Austrian Succession, the ratio of cavalry to infantry has remained remarkably consistent, with cavalry typically making up about one-fourth, one-fifth, or one-sixth of the total force. This long-standing balance suggests that these ratios may meet the inherent demands of military operations. However, we're not entirely convinced that this is simply a natural equilibrium. There are reasons to believe other factors have influenced these ratios. Austria and Russia, for instance, maintained large cavalry forces, partly because their political systems retained elements of Tartar military traditions. For Napoleon, cavalry numbers were indispensable for his vast campaigns, and since his conscription system had stretched the limits of recruitment, adding cavalry was a means to strengthen his army without requiring as many men.

Frederick the Great, on the other hand, focused intensely on conserving manpower and resources. Given his limited population base, he saw the necessity of maintaining his army's numbers by recruiting from outside his small territories. Since maintaining a complete cavalry force demanded fewer soldiers than infantry, it fit Frederick's needs better, especially since his campaigns relied heavily on army mobility. By the end of the Seven Years' War, Frederick's army still showed a cavalry-to-infantry ratio close to one-fourth, despite his deliberate prioritization of cavalry in his forces.

It's worth noting that armies with low cavalry counts sometimes still achieved victories. The Battle of Grossgörschen is an interesting example. Napoleon's French army numbered about 100,000, with only 5,000 cavalry and 90,000 infantry, while the Allies had 70,000 soldiers, with a substantial 25,000 of them cavalry and only 40,000 infantry. Though the Allies had 20,000 more cavalry, Napoleon won due to his advantage in infantry. This raises the question: would he have fared any worse if his infantry force had been even larger? Despite the Allied cavalry's strength showing its value in limiting Napoleon's trophies after the battle, the outcome underscores that winning the battle itself often remains the primary goal.

Given these observations, we hesitate to view the established proportion of cavalry to infantry as an inherent balance dictated by their respective combat values. Instead, it seems likely that the relative numbers of these arms will continue to shift over time, and we might eventually see cavalry becoming a much smaller component in military forces.

With artillery, advancements over time have naturally led to more guns on the battlefield, especially as technology has allowed artillery to become lighter and more effective. However, since Frederick the Great's era, the ratio of artillery to infantry has stayed close to two or three guns per thousand soldiers at the start of campaigns. As campaigns progress, artillery attrition rates tend to be lower than those of infantry, so by the campaign's end, the ratio can increase to three, four, or even five guns per thousand troops. Whether this ratio should increase even further without compromising overall war strategy is something only future experiences in combat can definitively reveal.

The key insights we draw from these considerations include the following:

1. Infantry remains the primary arm, with cavalry and artillery as supportive forces.
2. Through exceptional command skill and strong infantry numbers, an army may partially offset a lack of the other two arms. The stronger and better-trained the infantry, the easier it becomes to compensate.
3. Dispensing with artillery is harder than doing without cavalry, as artillery forms the core destructive force that integrates closely with infantry combat.
4. Given artillery's unmatched destructive power and cavalry's relatively limited effect, an ongoing strategic question remains: How much artillery can be effectively used, and what minimal cavalry proportion is essential?

Chapter V. Order of Battle of an Army

The order of battle refers to the arrangement and formation of various military arms into distinct sections or segments of the entire army. This order of battle, which becomes the structural and strategic foundation for the entire campaign or war, establishes a consistent norm for arranging and employing the army's sections. It combines both arithmetic and geometric principles—arithmetic in the division of units and geometry in the layout of formations.

The arithmetic aspect begins with the permanent peace-time organization of the army, which establishes individual units like battalions, squadrons, and batteries. These smaller units are then combined into larger groupings, forming more significant structures up to the level of the whole army, tailored to meet the prevailing conditions. The geometric aspect arises from foundational tactics learned and practiced during peace, providing the framework within which these units are arranged. When war begins, these tactical arrangements merge with the practical needs of combat, linking the peace-time training with the large-scale demands of battlefield engagements and determining the general formation that will guide the army's actions.

This structured approach has been a constant practice whenever large armies have mobilized for war. There have even been times when this orderly arrangement was considered a central feature of the battle itself. During the seventeenth and eighteenth centuries, when advancements in infantry firearms led to a surge in the number of infantrymen and permitted longer, thinner battle lines, the order of battle became simpler in structure yet more complicated to execute. Back then, cavalry was commonly stationed on the wings of an army, where it could avoid enemy fire and had ample space for maneuver. Consequently, the entire army formed a tightly bound, indivisible entity. This rigid unity meant that if the army were split down the center, it became like an earthworm severed in two—the wings might still retain some mobility, yet the central command and coordination would be lost. The army's structure was thus tightly interlocked, making any attempt to divide portions of it feel like a temporary disbanding and reassembling.

Movement across the terrain was equally complex. The marching formations of the whole army often disrupted the regularity of its battle formation, so if an enemy was nearby, march formations had to be meticulously planned. Each wing and line had to keep precise distances from each other, often requiring troops to push through challenging landscapes to maintain formation. These carefully structured, close formations often meant armies would have to stealthily advance upon the enemy's position to avoid detection and risk.

A significant shift occurred in the latter half of the eighteenth century, when military leaders realized that cavalry could be effectively positioned behind the army rather than exclusively on the wings. By allowing cavalry to take on broader roles beyond mere flanking or one-on-one cavalry skirmishes, the whole structure of the army became more flexible. The army's front, or battle line, was no longer strictly dependent on the fixed position of its cavalry. Instead, the army could now be constructed from interchangeable parts, each segment consistent with the next, capable of being separated and recombined without compromising the overall order of battle. This new fluidity gave rise to the development of the corps system, where each corps included a balanced combination of all arms—infantry, cavalry, and artillery. Although military thinkers had long recognized the need for such flexibility, it only became feasible with these changes.

This evolution in military formation closely relates to the concept of combat because, in the past, a single battle often represented the entirety of the war effort and battle itself has always been its most critical element. Still, while the order of battle is largely a tactical concern—dealing with the arrangement and coordination of troops in preparation for combat—this development illustrates how tactics, by structuring the army into adaptable units, laid a solid groundwork for broader strategic planning.

The larger an army grows, the more it spreads across vast areas, leading to increasingly complex interactions between its various sections. This widening in scope significantly expands the field of strategy, and therefore, the order of battle—as we have defined it—must engage in a dynamic relationship with strategy. This interaction is most apparent where tactics and strategy converge, particularly during moments when the general arrangement of troops transitions into specific battle formations.

Let us examine three strategic elements: division, combination of arms, and order of battle (disposition).

1. Division.

In a strategic context, it is less about the exact size of a division or corps, and more about determining how many divisions or corps are ideal within an army. An army split into three sections is often challenging to manage, but two sections are even more problematic, as such a configuration can nearly paralyze the chief command by limiting maneuver options.

Establishing the size of larger or smaller units—whether on basic tactical grounds or more advanced strategic considerations—offers considerable room for subjective judgment. Numerous reasoning methods have been applied, each with its own peculiarities. However, the practical need to break an independent army into several parts is clear and gives valid strategic reasons for deciding on the number and strength of an army's major sections. Meanwhile, tactics can dictate the strength of smaller units, such as companies or battalions, without directly impacting the larger strategic plan.

It is almost unimaginable to have an independent fighting body without at least three distinct parts—one to advance, another to cover the rear, and a central main force. Four parts are even more practical, as the center, or main body, should ideally be the strongest section, with smaller flanking sections on each side. This configuration can scale to eight parts, which often proves to be the most functional arrangement for an army.

For example, a well-balanced structure for a full army could include a dedicated advance guard, three sections for the main body (typically a right wing, a central section, and a left wing), two units held in reserve, and two additional sections to send to the right and left flanks as needed. Although it would be excessive to regard these exact numbers as a rigid rule, they do represent one of the most effective and commonly used arrangements in strategic operations, offering a blend of flexibility and strength that is often practical on the battlefield.

Certainly, at first glance, it might appear that commanding an army (or any large organized body) could be streamlined with only three or four subordinate leaders. This limited hierarchy might simplify the dissemination of orders and give the commander-in-chief clearer oversight. However, this convenience is offset by significant drawbacks. The first drawback lies in the way orders travel through a hierarchy. When orders pass down a longer chain of command—where corps commanders serve as intermediaries between division leaders and the commander-in-chief—they often lose some of their immediacy, precision, and impact. Orders become slower, less forceful, and may suffer in accuracy as they travel through each additional layer of command. The second drawback is subtler but critical: the commander's influence and control weaken as the autonomy of each subordinate increases. If, for example, a commander oversees 100,000 troops organized into eight divisions, they wield a more concentrated and direct power than if that same force were split into just three large corps. In large part, this is because each corps leader begins to see their unit as a self-contained entity, resisting any redistribution or reallocation of troops under their command. These commanders develop a sense of "ownership" over their corps and are generally reluctant to allow the temporary or permanent reassignment of forces to other parts of the army. With even minimal experience in wartime logistics and organization, one can quickly recognize how this protective tendency can hinder overall strategic flexibility.

That said, it is equally problematic to have an excessive number of divisions, as this can lead to confusion and logistical chaos. Managing as many as eight divisions is already challenging from a single headquarters; ten divisions would be the upper limit for practical coordination. For smaller divisions, where communication options are fewer and less immediate, a reduced target number of four or five divisions is more effective. This balance ensures that orders remain clear and actionable, preventing the formation of an unwieldy structure.

However, if an army's structure demands larger brigades, thus making it impractical to organize within the typical five or ten-unit model, then establishing corps d'armée becomes necessary. However, it is essential to remember that creating a corps introduces a new level of command, potentially diluting the commander-in-chief's direct authority and overall control.

So, what precisely constitutes an excessively large brigade? Generally, brigades are structured between 2,000 and 5,000 troops, with 5,000 marking an upper limit. Two primary reasons dictate this cap: first, a brigade is designed to be a unit led directly by a single commander, ideally within the audible range of the commander's voice. Second, larger infantry brigades require artillery support, which then forms a specialized, combined-arms division. This threshold ensures that brigades remain manageable and sufficiently supported while maintaining operational flexibility.

It is beyond our scope to delve into the tactical nuances of how the three main arms—infantry, cavalry, and artillery—should ideally be distributed, nor is it necessary to debate at which troop strength these combined arms should come together, whether within 8,000 to 12,000-man divisions or larger 20,000 to 30,000-man corps. However, it's nearly indisputable that combining all three arms creates a self-sufficient division. For divisions expected to operate independently, this combined-arms structure becomes even more advantageous, enhancing their capacity for effective, autonomous action.

For example, consider an army of 200,000 troops, organized into ten divisions, each consisting of five brigades. In this arrangement, each brigade would contain 4,000 troops. This organization appears balanced and proportional. Alternatively, the army could be divided into five corps, each with four divisions, and each division comprising four brigades. In this configuration, each brigade would have approximately 2,500 troops. However, the first structure, with its higher number of divisions and stronger brigades, is more straightforward. Additionally, the second arrangement introduces yet another level of rank hierarchy, requires twice as many commanders to relay orders to fewer overall divisions and weakens each brigade's strength. With the smaller brigades totaling eighty, versus only fifty in the initial model, the simplicity and effectiveness of the first approach become apparent. Each of these factors—clarity of command, the strength of units, and logistical efficiency—favors the larger initial setup, not merely for the ease of dispatching orders to fewer commanders but for the overall coherence it brings to army management.

For smaller armies, the introduction of a corps structure is even less practical, as it complicates the chain of command without offering commensurate benefits in strategic or operational capability.

This abstract perspective provides a foundation for considering army structure, though, in practice, specific situations can justify deviating from general principles. For example, even though directing eight or ten divisions in open, level terrain is feasible, maintaining this coordination across a vast, mountainous region might be practically unworkable. Similarly, when a large river splits an army into two parts, establishing a separate commander for each half becomes essential for effective leadership. Many other factors—such as terrain, climate, and local resistance—can exert a decisive influence, making it necessary to adapt the structure accordingly. This flexibility is critical, as there are countless unique conditions where standard guidelines may prove insufficient or even obstructive.

Yet, despite the necessity for adaptability, experience suggests that these fundamental principles are remarkably resilient. More often than one might expect, these abstract foundations hold up in real-world scenarios, prevailing over circumstances that would seem to call for exceptions. Instead of constantly overturning these basic rules, commanders frequently find that they provide a reliable framework for structuring and maneuvering forces.

To clarify the intent behind these considerations, we will arrange the critical points in a straightforward outline to illustrate how each element contributes to the broader objective. By "numbers" or "parts of a whole," we refer only to the primary divisions of an army—the direct, foundational separations. With this in mind, we state the following:

1. When an entire force is divided into too few sections, it becomes cumbersome to manage effectively, making coordination more challenging.
2. If the divisions within a larger force are excessively large, the influence and authority of the commanding leader are diluted, as direct control over each part becomes more difficult to maintain.
3. Each additional layer or step in the chain of command through which an order must travel weakens that order in two significant ways: first, the order loses some of its clarity and impact as it moves through each successive level; second, the delay in relaying the order grows, extending the time it takes to implement it, which can hinder swift, decisive action.

These principles emphasize the importance of balance in structuring command: too few divisions can lead to rigidity, overly large parts reduce centralized control, and excessive layers slow down communication and reduce command effectiveness.

The main point of these considerations is to illustrate that the number of co-equal divisions within an army should be maximized to improve flexibility and responsiveness, while the hierarchical steps between command and action should be minimized to maintain clarity and speed. However, it's practical to limit an army's co-ordinate divisions to around eight to ten, and those in subordinate corps to four or six, to ensure smooth and manageable oversight.

2. Combination of Arms.

In strategic terms, the integration of infantry, cavalry, and artillery within an army's structure primarily concerns those segments expected to operate in detached positions where they may face independent combat. Naturally, the largest and most robust divisions are generally best suited for detachment because they embody a self-sustaining combination of arms. This independence means they are equipped to adapt to various tactical challenges without needing immediate reinforcements.

From a strict strategic perspective, only the largest sections, like army corps (or divisions if corps aren't available), need a permanent blend of all three arms, with smaller divisions arranged based on immediate tactical circumstances. But as armies grow—often to 30,000 or 40,000 per corps—it's clear that such large formations benefit from an internal combination of arms within smaller divisions. Anyone familiar with field operations understands the complications and delays that arise when reinforcements from other sections are necessary to bring in cavalry to aid infantry, adding confusion, miscommunication, and critical time delays.

The finer details—such as the exact arrangement and proportion of the arms, the depth to which this combination should extend within smaller units, and the reserve size for each arm—are tactical decisions, falling under the purview of battlefield command.

3. The Disposition.

Deciding how to position various parts of an army in relation to one another is largely a tactical concern, focusing specifically on preparing for battle. While there are strategic elements involved in determining how and where to place forces, these decisions are generally dictated by the demands of the immediate situation, rather than adhering to a fixed "order of battle."

Thus, the order of battle pertains to the structured arrangement of an army, organizing it into a cohesive unit ready for combat. Each part of this mass can be strategically or tactically allocated as needed and then returned to its position, thus maintaining an organized and reliable framework. This structured arrangement establishes a predictable rhythm and operational consistency, creating a steady foundation for carrying out the "methodical beat" of military action—a concept previously discussed as a core feature of disciplined warfare.

Chapter VI. General Disposition of an Army

The time gap between assembling the military forces and the moment when strategy has led the army to the decisive point—where every unit has been assigned its position and role by tactics—often stretches quite long. This same gap occurs from one major turning point to the next. In earlier times, such pauses were barely considered a part of war at all. For instance, consider how General Luxemburg organized his camps and marches. Luxemburg is well-known for his camps and marches, making him a representative figure of his time, and his methods are well-documented in the Histoire de la Flandre militaire, unlike other generals of that era.

Camps were typically set up with their backs to a river, swamp, or deep valley—a setup that would be seen as risky today. Where the enemy was located rarely influenced the direction the army faced, and often, the rear of the camp was turned toward the enemy while the front pointed homeward. This arrangement, which seems unimaginable today, only makes sense if we consider that the comfort of the troops was the main priority, almost as though being in camp meant taking a break from war itself. It was a bit like going backstage, where troops could relax. The custom of having a barrier at the rear was about the only form of security back then, but even this approach conflicted with the idea of fighting a battle in that exact spot. Yet, there was little fear of being forced to fight while camped, since battles at the time were typically arranged more like duels, with each side meeting at a mutually convenient spot.

Armies in those days, due in part to their large number of cavalry—which had begun to lose its former glory but was still viewed, especially by the French, as the key arm—and due in part to the heavy structure of their formations, couldn't fight in all kinds of terrain. When an army was positioned in rugged or broken terrain, it was almost like being on neutral ground. Since these armies could barely operate in rough country, it was often preferable to go out to meet an opponent seeking battle. While Luxemburg's battles at Fleurus, Steinkirk, and Neerwinden took a different approach, this shift in thinking had just begun with his leadership and hadn't yet influenced how camps were set up. Innovations in warfare generally start with changes to critical matters, then gradually affect other practices. The phrase "il va à la guerre," used when a scout left to observe the enemy, shows how far camping was from being considered true combat.

Marching was handled in a similarly detached manner. The artillery often separated from the rest of the army, taking different, safer routes whenever possible. Cavalry on either wing would usually alternate taking the right side of the formation, so each group had the honor of marching on the right in turn.

Currently (especially since the Silesian wars), the circumstances in which an army operates outside of battle have become so closely linked to the act of fighting itself that these two states are now deeply interconnected, making it impossible to view them independently. In earlier campaigns, the battle was viewed as the core tool, while everything outside the fight was merely a supporting structure—like a weapon where the blade is steel but the handle is a separate piece of wood glued on, forming a single whole but comprised of mismatched parts. Now, however, we might imagine battle as the sharp edge and the non-combat situations as the blade's spine, both crafted from one unified piece of metal, where the boundary between steel and iron is no longer clear.

This out-of-battle state is shaped both by the organizational standards and regulations brought by the army from peacetime and by the tactical and strategic adjustments made in the moment. There are three primary situations in which an army may find itself outside of active combat: stationed in quarters, moving on a march, or set up in a camp. All three of these states are relevant to both tactics and strategy. They overlap frequently in many aspects, so much so that tactical and strategic considerations often blend together, leading to decisions that serve both purposes at once.

Before addressing any specific objectives related to an army's activities outside combat, we should consider these three situations in general terms. However, it's crucial first to assess the overall arrangement of the forces, as this overarching structure plays a defining role in camps, cantonments, and marches.

When we examine the general arrangement of forces without a particular objective in mind, we can only imagine them as a cohesive unit, designed to function as a single whole prepared to fight as one. Any variation from this unified form would suggest a distinct, specific purpose. Thus, we arrive at the concept of an army, whether large or small, organized as a complete entity.

Moreover, when there is no immediate objective, the sole purpose that remains is the preservation of the army itself, including its security. To meet this essential goal, the army must be organized to sustain itself comfortably and be able to regroup easily when preparing for combat. From these requirements, two primary conditions emerge as essential: the ability for the army to exist without undue hardship and the capacity to concentrate its forces swiftly for battle. Out of these conditions, several desirable points arise that apply directly to the basic needs and security of the army.

1. Ease in securing provisions for the army.
2. Readiness in arranging adequate shelter for the troops.
3. Ensuring that the rear is well-protected.
4. Having clear, open terrain directly ahead.
5. Positioning the army in rugged or varied terrain for advantage.

6. Access to strategic points of support.

7. A well-organized and effective distribution of troops across the area.

Our explanation of these points is detailed as follows:

The first two considerations guide us to choose areas that are well-developed, with large towns and good road networks. These factors influence our overall strategic decisions rather than specific actions.

Concerning rear security, more information is provided in the chapter on lines of communication. Here, it is essential to note that the core of the army's position should ideally align perpendicularly with the main line of retreat linked to the position.

As for the fourth point, while an army cannot survey an entire expanse ahead of it with the clarity it has over the ground immediately in front, it relies on advanced guards, scouts, patrols, spies, and other reconnaissance resources for a strategic view. These efforts become less demanding in an open landscape compared to a terrain filled with obstacles. This is in contrast with the fifth point, where a broken landscape ahead would necessitate additional reconnaissance efforts.

Strategic support points, or points d'appui, differ significantly from tactical ones. In strategy, the army does not need to be in direct contact with these points, and, more importantly, these points must be extensive. Since strategy operates within a larger scale of time and space, support points like coastlines or major rivers—when within a mile or so—serve as strategic anchors because they effectively limit the enemy's ability to outflank the army on a grand scale. The enemy would be restricted from undertaking marches that span miles or require days in such areas. Conversely, for strategic purposes, smaller obstacles, such as a lake with a circumference of just a few miles, provide limited impediment. Large fortresses also serve as strategic support points, especially when they offer significant potential for broader offensive maneuvers.

The organization of the army into separate groups or sections may align with either specific objectives or general operational requirements. Here, we are discussing the latter.

The first general requirement involves positioning an advanced guard and other units to keep watch on enemy movements. For very large armies, a second necessity is to station reserves a few miles behind the main force, creating a secondary position. Finally, the two wings of the army often necessitate distinct deployment of particular corps to protect them.

This wing protection does not imply deploying units solely to shield the spaces around the army's flanks, preventing enemy encroachment on perceived "weak points." Such an idea is illogical, as the enemy's wings would likewise be vulnerable in any attempt to outflank our own. Instead, the wings of an army are not inherently weak, but they hold particular strategic value. When an army's strength is inferior, its wings could indeed become exposed areas if the opponent's forces are stronger or if their lines of communication are better secured.

In most situations, the wings are critical not due to inherent weakness but because their defense demands more complex maneuvers and additional time for preparation than that of the front. Consequently, it is generally essential to fortify the wings against unexpected enemy advances by placing more substantial forces on them. By increasing these forces, even if they only offer light resistance, the time required for the enemy to apply pressure increases. The stronger the forces on the wings, the more the enemy must commit to reveal their plans, allowing the desired outcome to be achieved. Following this, any additional actions will depend on the broader strategy at hand. Therefore, corps placed on the wings act as extended forward guards to delay enemy approaches on the flanks and afford time for necessary countermeasures.

If these corps are intended to regroup with the main body without necessitating a simultaneous retreat from the main force, they must naturally be positioned slightly ahead of the main line. This forward positioning allows them to fall back onto the main body without pulling back directly from the flanks of the established position. This arrangement provides the flexibility to withdraw in an organized fashion even without the pressure of a serious engagement.

Out of these subjective considerations, which relate to the internal structure and organization of the army, emerges a practical framework for deployment. This framework typically comprises four or five distinct parts, depending on whether the reserve remains integrated with the main body or operates separately. Just as the overall availability of food and shelter for the troops influences the choice of a main position, these factors also contribute significantly to determining the placement of the separate divisions. They are balanced alongside other strategic concerns, aiming to meet all logistical needs while still adhering to military objectives.

In most instances, organizing the army into five separate corps resolves the primary challenges of subsistence and billeting. With this arrangement, few adjustments are needed for supplying the troops or housing them adequately across the designated space.

It remains to consider the appropriate distances at which these separated corps can be placed to allow for effective mutual support and the ability to concentrate forces for battle as needed. The chapter on combat duration and decision-making offers insight here, clarifying that no absolute distance fits every scenario. Instead, general guidelines are provided, as variations in factors like relative army strength, weaponry, and terrain significantly impact practical distances.

The positioning of an advanced guard is relatively straightforward; as it withdraws, it naturally falls back towards the main body of the army. It can generally be stationed a long day's march away without risking an independent, isolated battle. However, it shouldn't advance farther than necessary for the army's security, since greater distance increases the toll on the advanced guard as it retreats.

For corps stationed on the flanks, it's helpful to remember that a division of approximately 8,000 to 10,000 troops can usually sustain combat for several hours, sometimes even half a day, before the engagement is resolved. This means such a division can be placed a few leagues or a mile or two away without undue concern. Larger corps of three or four divisions can manage up to a day's march or around three or four miles in distance.

From this general arrangement of the main body into four or five divisions, each at a carefully measured distance, a standard, almost mechanical method for dividing an army has evolved—applicable when there are no overriding strategic reasons to deviate from this typical structure.

Though each part of the army is organized with the capacity to handle an independent combat if necessary, it's essential to understand that the goal of dividing an army is not to fight in isolated segments. Instead, this division is largely a temporary necessity, allowing the army to function and survive in a way that aligns with the passage of time and the demands of strategy. When the enemy moves closer and seeks a decisive engagement, the purpose of these scattered divisions becomes irrelevant. At this point, everything converges towards the single, unified purpose of battle, and the temporary distribution of forces loses its function.

As soon as battle begins, considerations like quarters and supplies become secondary; observing the enemy from various directions and positioning along the flanks has served its purpose in delaying their advance through partial resistance. Now, the entire focus converges into one unified force—the main battle effort. The true mark of strategic expertise lies in the ability to manage army dispositions as a temporary means to an end, treating these divisions as necessary, albeit inconvenient, while prioritizing unity and cohesion in battle.

Chapter VII. Advanced Guard and Out-Posts

These two bodies—advanced guards and outposts—are among those elements in military structure that blend tactical and strategic functions. On one hand, they provide the immediate framework needed for organizing battle and implementing tactical plans; on the other, they often engage in independent skirmishes due to their positions, which are typically at some distance from the main force. This dual role places them as essential links in the strategic chain, thus requiring a focused discussion as an addition to the prior chapter.

When an army isn't fully battle-ready, it needs an advanced guard to detect an enemy's approach and gather preliminary intelligence about their strength before they appear within visual range, which typically extends only slightly beyond firearm range. An army without advanced scouts would be like a person who can't see beyond their own reach. As we mentioned before, these outposts serve as the army's eyes. However, the extent to which outposts are needed can vary. Factors like the size of the army, the amount of terrain it occupies, timing, location, specific mission objectives, and even the unpredictable nature of war all play a role. Therefore, military history doesn't provide a single, clear model for advanced guard and outpost use but instead offers a vast array of examples, each suited to unique situations.

In some cases, we see that an army's security is managed by a formally assigned corps acting as the advanced guard; at other times, a spread of isolated outposts fulfills this role. Occasionally, both approaches are combined, while sometimes neither one is employed. Sometimes an entire force is protected by a single advanced guard; in other instances, each column of troops has its own. Our goal here is to clarify what these roles entail and to see if we can establish some principles that apply broadly.

When troops are on the move, an advanced detachment of varying strength will serve as the vanguard, or advanced guard, and if the army reverses course, this same group will act as the rearguard. When troops are halted, whether in camp or quartered across a region, a broader line of light defenses becomes the vanguard, namely the outposts. This division reflects the natural logic of warfare—when the army is stationary, it needs to monitor a wider area than when it's on the march. So, in one case, a stretched chain of posts becomes appropriate; in the other, a more compact corps arrangement arises.

The specific size and composition of both advanced guards and outposts can vary widely. They may range from a sizable corps with an organized mix of infantry, cavalry, and artillery to a single regiment of light cavalry like hussars. The defenses they set up might range from a fortified line with elements from each military arm to simpler pickets scattered outside a camp, supported by soldiers from the main force. The missions of such forces also vary—some are only there to observe, while others are tasked with actively resisting the enemy. Resistance might serve merely to buy time for the main army to prepare, or it could be aimed at forcing the enemy to reveal their plans, thus giving the observation greater strategic significance.

The strength of an advanced guard or outpost depends on how much time needs to be secured and the degree of opposition expected. This opposition may be tailored to counter specific enemy movements, so the size of the guard must align with the expected resistance.

Frederick the Great, a general always battle-ready and often directing his forces in combat with quick verbal commands, rarely needed strong outposts. He frequently camped within sight of the enemy, relying instead on smaller, agile units—a regiment of hussars here, a battalion of light troops there, or perhaps just pickets and support detachments from the camp itself. On the march, he typically used a few thousand cavalry, taken from the flanks of his leading line, as his advanced guard, which would rejoin the main body once the march was completed. Rarely did he maintain a permanent corps as an advanced guard.

Frederick's approach showcases how an efficient leader could operate with minimal outposts, trusting instead in agility, readiness, and well-chosen small forces to provide the necessary protection and reconnaissance. This style, however, was uniquely suited to his own highly adaptable command style, allowing him to make effective use of the smallest detachments to safeguard his forces while advancing toward larger tactical or strategic goals.

If these corps are to withdraw and merge with the main body without prompting a retreat from the entire army, it logically follows that they shouldn't be positioned directly in line with the main force. Instead, they should be set slightly forward, so that if they do need to fall back, even without engaging in a major skirmish, they don't withdraw straight into the main army's position. This placement provides a kind of buffer, ensuring that their retreat won't compromise the security or stability of the main formation.

From these strategic needs, which stem from the internal structure and function of an army, we find a natural framework emerging for the deployment and arrangement of forces. This framework typically consists of four or five primary sections, depending on whether the reserve is held with the main body or assigned separately. Such a division is beneficial not only for operational clarity but also for flexibility in response to changing battlefield demands.

Just as the need for food, supplies, and shelter influences the overall choice of a position, it also shapes the way the army is divided into separate sections. These practical considerations, alongside the strategic factors discussed above, often drive commanders to find a balance that accommodates both needs. In most scenarios, an army split into five sections, each functioning independently but capable of supporting the others, can handle logistical and quartering challenges effectively without requiring major adjustments afterward.

Now, regarding how far these individual sections should be placed from each other, it's essential to balance the ability to provide mutual support with the need to consolidate quickly for battle. Previous chapters on the duration and decisiveness of combat have shown that there's no single fixed distance that's always ideal. Instead, factors like the relative strength of the units, terrain, and the overall strategy come into play, influencing what distances are practical.

Positioning the advanced guard is straightforward because it retreats back toward the main force, which allows it to maintain a distance of a long day's march without risking isolation or needing to engage independently. However, it's also crucial not to place it too far forward, as a lengthy retreat would wear down the troops and expose them to unnecessary risk.

For flank corps, we've seen that an average division of around 8,000 to 10,000 troops can typically sustain a half-day skirmish before the outcome is decisive. With this in mind, placing a division a few leagues or miles away should be manageable. Similarly, larger corps comprising three or four divisions could be stationed at a distance of a day's march or three to four miles, allowing them to support each other effectively.

This naturally leads to a general arrangement where the main body is organized into four or five sections at practical distances. Such a structure has given rise to a kind of default setup that's often used when there aren't specific circumstances calling for a different approach.

Even though each part of the army may be capable of handling an independent skirmish if needed, this division isn't meant to promote separate engagements by these parts. Rather, it's a practical way of adapting to the conditions imposed by time and movement. Once the enemy nears and a full engagement seems likely, the strategic phase of positioning ends, and everything converges on the single goal of preparing for the battle itself. As combat begins, logistical concerns such as quarters and supplies are set aside. The forward elements that monitored the enemy's approach and flanks have fulfilled their role by delaying or revealing the enemy's plans. Now, all elements are called back to form a cohesive whole, preparing for the one decisive event—the battle.

True skill in deploying an army is shown when the arrangement reflects not merely an intention to divide forces but rather an understanding of these divisions as necessary conditions. The end goal remains unification in battle, with the placement of troops supporting that aim. The arrangement, then, should be seen not as fragmentation for separate fights but as a preparation for concentrated action, ensuring the whole army can act as one when the decisive moment arrives.

1. Primarily, this is because the central section of the army typically contains the largest concentration of troops. The main body or "center" often comprises a substantial mass of soldiers, making it a pivotal point both in terms of manpower and strategic weight.

2. Secondly, the central point along the line of an army's front—stretching across the terrain—naturally holds more importance than either wing. This is due to the fact that the success of most strategic plans revolves around the central point, where coordination across the entire campaign is most easily managed. As a result, battles and major confrontations tend to unfold closer to the center than to the flanks, given that the center anchors the army's broader positioning and serves as the nexus of command.

3. Lastly, although a central corps positioned as an advanced guard may not directly cover the wings, it still indirectly provides them with a significant layer of security. This forward-placed corps prevents the enemy from approaching the wings without caution. For example, an enemy would be reluctant to move past this central guard without maintaining a safe distance, knowing that doing so would expose them to possible attacks from the side or even from behind. While this indirect protection might not offer the wings absolute security, it alleviates much of the potential risk, especially in situations where the enemy would otherwise attempt a maneuver against the flanks.

When the center's vanguard is notably stronger than the one on either wing—such as when it functions as a dedicated advanced corps—it serves beyond the basic duty of a mere forward guard against sudden attacks. In a larger strategic sense, this central vanguard takes on the role of an advanced corps, adding both a layer of direct security and an active, forward-reaching component that exerts influence across the entire battlefield.

1. Primarily, this is because the central section of the army typically contains the largest concentration of troops. The main body or "center" often comprises a substantial mass of soldiers, making it a pivotal point both in terms of manpower and strategic weight.

2. Secondly, the central point along the line of an army's front—stretching across the terrain—naturally holds more importance than either wing. This is due to the fact that the success of most strategic plans revolves around the central point, where coordination across the entire campaign is most easily managed. As a result, battles and major confrontations tend to unfold closer to the center than to the flanks, given that the center anchors the army's broader positioning and serves as the nexus of command.

3. Lastly, although a central corps positioned as an advanced guard may not directly cover the wings, it still indirectly provides them with a significant layer of security. This forward-placed corps prevents the enemy from approaching the wings without caution. For example, an enemy would be reluctant to move past this central guard without maintaining a safe distance, knowing that doing so would expose them to possible attacks from the side or even from behind. While this indirect protection might not offer the wings absolute security, it alleviates much of the potential risk, especially in situations where the enemy would otherwise attempt a maneuver against the flanks.

When the center's vanguard is notably stronger than the one on either wing—such as when it functions as a dedicated advanced corps—it serves beyond the basic duty of a mere forward guard against sudden attacks. In a larger strategic sense, this central vanguard takes on the role of an advanced corps, adding both a layer of direct security and an active, forward-reaching component that exerts influence across the entire battlefield.

The following are the main purposes that guide the use of a central corps, as well as the specific duties it undertakes in practice:

1. Strengthening Resistance and Slowing Enemy Advance: This corps is positioned to ensure a more robust defense, compelling the enemy to move forward with increased caution. When our plans require additional time to fully implement, this corps acts as an expanded version of a vanguard, holding off the enemy for as long as necessary to support our preparations.

2. Maintaining Distance for Large Army Masses: If the central section of our army consists of a particularly large number of troops, the corps allows us to keep this sizable and cumbersome force at a safe distance from the enemy. Meanwhile, we can stay in close proximity to the opponent with a more agile unit, which allows for quicker maneuverability without exposing the main body of the army.

3. Maintaining Close Observation of the Enemy: A well-positioned central corps serves as an effective observation unit near the enemy, especially if other strategic considerations require the main body of our forces to remain further away. While smaller posts or partisan corps might serve as sentries, they would be insufficient for substantial observation, given that a weak unit could be easily dispersed and

lacks the capacity to gather comprehensive intelligence compared to a larger, more capable corps.

4. Enhanced Pursuit Capabilities: During an enemy retreat, an advanced corps—especially one with the majority of the cavalry—can move faster and with more flexibility than the main body of the army. This unit can set up camp later in the day and break it earlier in the morning, thereby sustaining a quicker pursuit, keeping the pressure on the retreating enemy.

5. Rear Guard in a Retreat: In retreat, the central corps serves as the rearguard, particularly valuable for defending key natural barriers along the way. The center, in this role, is crucially important. At first glance, it might seem vulnerable to the enemy flanking it, but even if the opponent partially overlaps our lines, they would still have to cover a significant distance to reach the central mass. This buffer enables the rear guard of the center to hold its ground longer and to mount a steady, organized retreat.

Thus, whenever one of these scenarios is present, a dedicated corps should ideally be positioned forward as an advanced guard. This advanced guard concept becomes less relevant if the center of the army is no stronger than its wings. For example, when Macdonald advanced against Blücher in Silesia in 1813, or when Blücher moved toward the Elbe, both used three equal-strength corps moving in columns across separate roads, with each column advancing in parallel. In these cases, there was no mention of advanced guards.

However, this arrangement of an army into three equally strong columns is not typically recommended, partly due to the lack of a specialized advanced guard and partly because dividing an army into three large parts often makes it difficult to command, as discussed earlier. If an army is arranged with a center flanked by two wings—which, as noted in the previous chapter, is generally the most balanced setup unless specific conditions require something different—the advanced guard should logically be positioned in front of the center, extending beyond the line of the wings. However, as units stationed on the flanks also serve to protect the sides, they are often positioned in line with the advanced guard or even further forward, depending on the circumstances.

In terms of the advanced guard's size, there's little specific guidance, as current practice wisely assigns at least one major unit from the first class of the army to fulfill this role, often reinforced by a section of cavalry. Thus, the advanced guard may be composed of an entire corps in corps-based armies or a division if the structure is in divisions. Having more units at higher organizational levels generally benefits this setup, making it more adaptable.

How far the advanced guard should be placed in front of the main body is entirely situation dependent. In some scenarios, it might be positioned more than a day's march ahead; in others, it may need to remain immediately in front of the main body. The typical distance falls between one and three miles, as experience has shown this range to be most practical in many situations. Yet, this distance should not be taken as a rigid rule but rather as a flexible guide, adaptable to the specific requirements of each case.

In discussing advanced guards, we've thus far set aside the topic of outposts, so let us now address it. Initially, we noted that the relationship between outposts and stationary troops resembles that between advanced guards and troops on the move. This comparison was meant to emphasize the origins of these concepts and maintain clear distinctions moving forward. However, taken literally, this distinction can feel overly technical.

When an army pauses for the night, intending to resume its march the next day, the advanced guard naturally halts as well and sets up the necessary outpost arrangements to secure both itself and the main body. This does not mean it ceases to be an advanced guard in favor of becoming a mere line of outposts. To genuinely fulfill the function of outposts, the advanced guard would need to disperse into smaller posts, each with minimal troops or none in a massed formation, leaning more heavily toward a distributed defense.

The duration of the army's halt also affects the thoroughness of its covering. When the halt is brief, the need for complete security is lower since the enemy has little time to detect uncovered areas. However, when a prolonged halt is expected, observation and protection over every approach must be thorough. Typically, the longer the halt, the more the vanguard extends into a line of posts. Whether this shift results in a fully dispersed line or retains a concentrated corps depends on two key factors: proximity between opposing armies and terrain.

When armies are close relative to the breadth of their fronts, it may become unfeasible to position a vanguard between them, requiring instead a chain of outposts to monitor and secure the area.

A corps positioned in concentrated formation, while offering strategic strength in mass, tends to protect the approaches to the army in a less direct manner. This arrangement means it generally needs more time and room to operate effectively. Therefore, if the army stretches across a broad front, such as when stationed in extensive cantonments, and a single, compact corps is expected to secure all entry routes, it's often necessary to maintain a substantial distance from the enemy. This is why, in cases like winter quarters, a line or "cordon" of outposts is typically used to provide comprehensive coverage and security across a larger area.

The terrain also plays a significant role in determining the setup. For instance, if a substantial natural obstacle—such as a river, ridge, or dense forest—presents a strong defensive barrier, a thin line of posts can be positioned effectively with fewer troops, maximizing security and coverage while conserving resources. In such cases, taking advantage of the landscape can offer a substantial tactical benefit and help offset the need for larger numbers of troops.

Additionally, the severity of winter conditions can justify breaking up an advanced guard into a line of outposts, as dispersing the posts allows for more efficient and practical sheltering of the troops. In harsh weather, smaller units can be stationed in sheltered areas or villages rather than keeping a larger mass exposed, thus making the outpost line more sustainable.

An exemplary use of reinforced outposts, achieved with precision and tactical acumen, was demonstrated by the Anglo-Dutch army during the campaign of 1794–95 in the Netherlands. Here, the defense line was effectively formed by brigades comprised of all arms, each stationed at individual posts and backed by a reserve force. Scharnhorst, who observed this arrangement while serving with that army, later introduced this system to the Prussian army along the Passarge River in 1807. Elsewhere, however, this method has seen limited application in modern campaigns, primarily due to the fast-paced nature of more recent conflicts, which has favored continuous movement over fixed outpost lines. Nevertheless, even in situations where a reinforced line of outposts would have been advantageous, it has sometimes been overlooked. A notable example is Murat's engagement at Tarutino, where a more extended defensive line might have helped prevent the loss of thirty artillery pieces during an outpost skirmish.

It is evident that under certain conditions, the reinforced outpost system can provide substantial strategic and tactical advantages. Recognizing these circumstances and implementing such a system thoughtfully could offer enhanced security and flexibility to an army. We aim to revisit this concept in more detail on a future occasion.

Chapter VIII. Mode of Action of Advanced Corps

We have observed how an army's security relies, in part, on the effect an advanced guard and flank corps can have on a forward-moving enemy. Such units, however, are generally too weak to confront the full strength of the enemy's main body and thus require a specialized approach to achieve their objectives without risking substantial losses due to this imbalance in strength.

The primary role of this type of corps is twofold: to observe the enemy closely and to slow his advance. For observation alone, a small unit would be insufficient—it would be too easily pushed back and would lack the resources to effectively monitor enemy movement over any significant distance. Therefore, this corps must be large enough to compel the enemy to deploy his full force before it, revealing both his numbers and possibly his strategic intentions in the process.

Merely by holding its ground, this corps can observe the enemy's maneuvers as he tries to dislodge it, and it could then simply begin its retreat as soon as the enemy's plans become apparent. However, to effectively delay the enemy, the corps must also provide some degree of resistance rather than only observe.

How, then, can this corps resist the enemy's approach to the last moment without risking severe losses? Primarily, this is possible because the advancing enemy is generally led by his own advanced guard, meaning he won't immediately engage with his full force. Even if the enemy's advanced guard is intentionally stronger than our forward corps and his main body is closer to its own advanced guard than ours is to ours, our forward corps initially faces only the enemy's advance guard—a force not vastly superior in size. This setup buys valuable time by allowing us to observe the enemy's movements without risking immediate retreat.

Moreover, a well-positioned forward corps can offer resistance without necessarily facing the severe disadvantages usually posed by a larger enemy force. In a typical engagement with a more powerful enemy, the chief risk is often being outflanked, thus trapping our position in a vulnerable state. Here, however, the enemy is uncertain how close he may be to our main body, which could encircle his forces. This possibility forces the enemy to move forward with caution, keeping his columns in line and attempting a flanking maneuver only after he has thoroughly assessed our position. This hesitancy allows our forward corps ample time to retreat before any real threat materializes.

The duration of the resistance offered by this corps—whether facing a direct assault or the beginning of a flanking attempt—will depend on both the terrain and the enemy's proximity to his own support forces. Extending this resistance beyond a reasonable limit, either due to miscalculation or in order to buy time for the main body's preparation, inevitably results in significant losses.

It is only in rare circumstances, such as when local terrain provides a strong defensive advantage, that the resistance put up by such a corps becomes critical on its own. Usually, the duration of engagement from a small unit would not, by itself, buy the time needed. Instead, time is gained through a combination of factors inherent to this type of engagement, which operates on three key levels:

1. Through the enemy's more cautious and thus slower advance, which naturally buys more time as he attempts to assess and approach the position with care.
2. Through the duration of the direct resistance provided by the corps, allowing every moment of opposition to delay the enemy further.
3. Through the retreat itself, the corps falls back strategically, maintaining a controlled pace to keep the enemy from advancing too swiftly.

This retreat must be conducted at the slowest feasible pace that ensures safety, with the objective of delaying the enemy's progress as much as possible. Should the terrain present suitable defensive positions, these should be strategically utilized. Each position forces the enemy to halt, reassess, and prepare fresh attacks or maneuvers to outflank the retreating force. Such pauses demand time, offering the advancing corps crucial moments to regroup and reposition. In some cases, these favorable positions may even allow for a substantive engagement, which, although brief, can further impede the enemy.

The retreat and the resistance through combat are therefore intricately intertwined, with each short engagement supplementing the slower withdrawal by forcing frequent interruptions in the enemy's progress. This strategy is essential in maximizing delay, even though each individual battle may be brief. Consequently, the effectiveness of this type of resistance depends not only on the retreat itself but on how often these combative delays can be repeated along the way.

The level of impact achieved by such a retreat depends largely on the size of the corps and the configuration of the terrain. A stronger, well-prepared corps can delay an enemy far longer than a smaller force, even when each side has similar resources. The reason lies in the dynamics of larger forces, which naturally require more time to reorganize and fully execute their maneuvers. Additionally, a mountainous or rugged landscape slows the advancing army's movement, extends the time for each defensive stand, and allows each position to be more defensible, minimizing the risks associated with each delay.

The further the advanced corps is positioned from the main body of the army, the longer the retreat it must make, thus amplifying the total time gained by its resistance. However, this increased distance also means the corps has less immediate support from the main body and a reduced ability to resist for extended periods. Therefore, the retreat may need to be conducted at a quicker pace the further the advanced guard is from the primary force, balancing the need for time with the necessity of avoiding overextension and potential encirclement.

The support and fallback options available to an advanced corps naturally affect how long it can sustain its resistance. Every minute required for the safe withdrawal of the corps is time removed from its ability to actively delay the enemy, diminishing the total effectiveness of the resistance. The presence of strong backup, however, can help the advanced guard maintain a slower, more controlled retreat, preserving its strength and capacity to resist further as the enemy advances.

Another critical factor is the time of day at which the enemy appears. When an enemy arrives after midday, the advancing corps gains the advantage of nightfall, which typically halts any further advance. This break effectively grants the retreating corps additional time to regroup or reposition overnight. For instance, in 1815, on the short stretch from Charleroi to Ligny, the Prussian forces under General Ziethen, numbering around 30,000, managed to delay Napoleon's 120,000-strong army by nearly a full day. Ziethen's corps engaged in action from nine in the morning on June 15 until two in the afternoon on June 16, allowing the Prussian army to concentrate for the impending battle. This delay was achieved, albeit with a significant sacrifice of five to six thousand casualties.

Based on historical experience, we can draw some general guidelines for estimating the time gained through such maneuvers. A division of around ten to twelve thousand soldiers, accompanied by cavalry, positioned a day's march—about three to four miles—ahead of the main force in standard terrain (neither strongly advantageous nor disadvantageous) would typically be able to delay the enemy by about half as much time as it would ordinarily take them to march that distance. If the division is stationed only a mile ahead, then this same force should be able to extend the enemy's advance by two or even three times as long as it would normally take them to cover the distance in a straightforward march. This multiplier effect on time can provide a significant strategic advantage, allowing the main body crucial additional hours to prepare for engagement.

So, considering a situation where the distance from the advanced guard to the main body is about a four-mile march, which would typically take around ten hours to traverse, we can estimate that once the enemy's full force appears before our advanced guard, it would be roughly fifteen hours before they could position themselves to launch an attack on our main force. This estimate includes the time the enemy will spend in organizing and advancing, plus the time added by the resistance of our advanced guard as it falls back.

Alternatively, if the advanced guard is stationed only a mile ahead of the main body, the time gained before the main force might face an attack could still extend beyond three or four hours, and may even double, depending on the level of resistance and the enemy's cautious initial maneuvers. This proximity allows the advanced guard to mount a stronger initial defense before being forced to retreat, leveraging the close positioning to impede the enemy's progress more effectively. In such cases, the enemy would need to successfully push our advanced guard back within the first half of the day if they wish to mount a broader attack on our primary force by the afternoon.

In the first scenario of a longer distance, nightfall becomes an additional advantage, as it often halts any further movements and gives the main body further time to prepare or reposition. This dynamic demonstrates the strategic benefit of placing an advanced guard further forward when circumstances allow, offering the main army a full day or more to ready itself if the enemy begins an engagement with the forward troops.

When it comes to side corps, which are positioned to safeguard the flanks of the main body, their role and actions are often shaped by more specific, situational factors. Typically, these flanking corps act similarly to advanced guards but stationed on the peripheries. They are positioned forward on the flanks, with their retreat path angled toward the main body, ready to fall back if pressured. Since these flanking corps are not directly in front of the main army, they lack immediate support in comparison to a central advanced guard, putting them at slightly higher risk. However, this risk is mitigated by the reality that an enemy's offensive power is generally weaker toward the edges of their formation. If circumstances become critical, the flanking corps still have sufficient room to withdraw at an angle without bringing the enemy into direct confrontation with the main body of the army.

The best way to reinforce an advanced guard, whether positioned at the front or flanks, is usually through a strong cavalry contingent. Consequently, when an advanced corps is stationed at a significant distance from the main body, the reserve cavalry is often placed between the main force and the advanced guard. This way, the reserve cavalry can provide timely support, adding flexibility and mobility to our defensive arrangements as the advanced corps moves back.

From these observations, we conclude that an advanced corps operates as much by the influence of its presence as by any combat it undertakes. The potential of these troops to engage holds as much value as actual engagements. This strategic presence should not aim to halt the enemy's progress entirely but instead function as a moderating force. Like a pendulum, it serves to regulate and control the pace of the enemy's approach, making each step in their advance deliberate and allowing us to anticipate and plan accordingly.

Chapter IX. Camps

When examining the strategic conditions of an army in three key situations—marches, camps, and quarters—outside of active combat, we focus on factors of place, time, and troop numbers. Everything related to organizing the battle itself, as well as the transition into combat, pertains to tactics. The strategic layout of camps, which includes all forms of army encampment whether in tents, huts, or bivouac, aligns completely with the strategic plan for any potential battle. However, tactically speaking, a camp's position may not always correspond directly with the planned battlefield location, as there can be valid reasons to select a camping site that differs from the battlefield itself.

Historically, before armies swelled to their modern size and before wars became extended affairs with multiple connected operations fitting into an overarching strategy, armies almost universally used tents. This practice, standard up until the wars of the French Revolution, defined the "normal" state of a military encampment. Armies would leave their quarters with the onset of spring and only return to their quarters as winter approached. Winter quarters at that time were almost like a temporary halt in the war, where forces remained essentially inactive. Military operations, therefore, followed this seasonal rhythm, with "refreshment" quarters used during a campaign acting as short-lived transition points to rest troops until proper winter quarters could be secured. These transitional encampments allowed limited military actions, but the primary purpose was rest and logistical reorganization, especially for campaigns requiring extended operational planning.

It's not our purpose here to question how such regular interruptions in warfare could align with the fundamental nature and aims of war itself, though we'll delve into that later. For now, it suffices to note that it was simply the norm.

With the onset of the French Revolutionary wars, armies began to abandon tents due to the logistical burdens they imposed. For an army numbering 100,000, instead of dedicating thousands of horses to haul tents—up to 6,000 horses in some cases—the choice was made to convert that logistical capacity to combat support, such as adding 5,000 cavalry or hundreds of additional artillery pieces. Not only was this found to increase offensive and defensive strength, but tents also became cumbersome in rapid maneuvers. Armies focused on mobility to capitalize on swift advances or retreats, and the weight and volume of tents only added an unnecessary hindrance, with limited strategic benefit.

This shift, however, came with two significant drawbacks: an increased rate of casualties among troops, and a greater strain on the countryside to supply shelter and food for the soldiers.

The protective qualities of even the simplest tents might seem minimal—they are far from impermeable to cold or rain and provide only modest shelter from wind—but over time, these minor benefits accumulate. Although the difference may feel negligible in a single day, enduring such conditions without tents repeatedly throughout a campaign can weigh heavily on troop health. When soldiers lack any form of regular overhead shelter, it naturally results in a higher incidence of illness over time. Moreover, foraging or requisitioning additional food and shelter from the local region as a substitute for tents leaves an obvious toll on the countryside, increasing the likelihood of wastage and diminishing local resources.

One might assume that these negative effects—the strain on troop health and the intensified impact on the land—would have diminished the pace and energy of military campaigns. It would seem reasonable to expect that without tents, troops would need to stay in quarters longer, and some strategic positions might be neglected simply because they lacked necessary accommodations. However, in practice, this did not cause a significant reduction in the tempo or reach of campaigns, as armies adapted by pressing forward under alternative arrangements and simply enduring harsher conditions. The resulting wear on soldiers and the countryside became an accepted, if lamentable, reality of wartime.

Thus, while abandoning tents has brought real costs, armies have continued to manage sustained operations without them, even if this choice demands greater endurance from soldiers and inflicts heavier burdens on the land through which they march.

This shift would indeed have taken a toll on the effectiveness and endurance of armies if it hadn't coincided with a broader and monumental transformation in warfare—a transformation so comprehensive that it absorbed all these smaller, secondary concerns. The very essence of war had intensified to such a degree, its driving energy and sheer force had become so relentless, that the traditional, predictable periods of rest simply vanished. Every power involved in a campaign now pressed forward with unyielding force, relentlessly advancing toward the ultimate, decisive engagements. This intensity of focus on reaching conclusive battles, a topic we'll examine in greater detail in the ninth book, effectively overshadowed any questions about the minor impacts of no longer having tents available for shelter in the field.

In this context, armies adapted, making do with whatever the conditions demanded—whether it meant setting up makeshift huts, establishing temporary shelters, or bivouacking under the open sky. These decisions were no longer influenced by the time of year, the terrain, or even the prevailing weather; rather, the location and type of encampment were entirely dictated by the overarching goals and requirements of the campaign. The strategy and objectives of warfare had become the ultimate guiding factors, with the welfare of the troops now a secondary consideration to achieving the larger aims.

Looking forward, one might question whether warfare will continue to exhibit this constant, driving energy, indifferent to conditions and limitations. Could the pressure of perpetual movement and combat ease, allowing for a slower, steadier pace and a return to familiar methods of encampment, including tents? This is a question we'll address further along, considering both the durability of this relentless approach and the potential for changes in the demands placed upon armies. In cases where this level of intensity might diminish, a lack of tents might indeed exert a certain influence, potentially impacting how campaigns are conducted.

However, it seems unlikely that this influence would be strong enough to bring back the widespread use of tents. The field of war has been stretched far beyond its previous limits; it has expanded to accommodate far greater forces and broader operations. With this expanded scope, it's difficult to imagine warfare reverting to its previous, more confined approach for any extended period. Should the need for a more tempered pace arise in specific cases, the use of tents could return temporarily. But such returns would likely be fleeting, brief pauses that give way once more to the intense, all-encompassing nature of modern warfare, which defines itself by pushing boundaries and pressing forward. Therefore, any lasting preparations or accommodations for an army must align with this more intense and expansive nature of warfare, which seems here to stay, shaping the future of military operations and planning.

Chapter X. Marches

Marches represent the straightforward movement from one position to another, yet they hinge upon two vital principles that determine their success. The first principle is the careful preservation of the troops' energy and resources; no force should be wasted when it can instead be put to practical use in the future. The second principle is ensuring exactness in timing and coordination, so that all units move in harmony with each other and arrive as a cohesive body. If we were to attempt moving an immense force, say 100,000 men, along a single road in one continuous column without any structured intervals, the distance would stretch so long that the tail end of the force would arrive far later than the leading edge. This would force the entire column either to move painfully slow, which could expose them to unnecessary delays and risks, or would result in a long, dispersed line—almost like a thin stream of water breaking up into droplets. In such a disorganized state, those at the rear would struggle to keep pace with those at the front, and the entire movement would eventually dissolve into disorder, rendering the march ineffective and exhausting the troops.

At the other end of the spectrum, we find that the smaller and more manageable the force within each marching unit, the more smoothly and precisely the march proceeds. This leads to the necessity of dividing the force into segments, even when not required by strategic positioning but purely to make the movement itself feasible. Thus, although dividing an army into marching columns often stems from the broader strategy at play, it doesn't always do so for the same reasons. A large force that needs to assemble swiftly at a single destination must be broken down into separate groups to make this march efficient. However, there are cases where the disposition of forces isn't designed with combat in mind but rather focuses on logistical or practical movement requirements.

For instance, if the purpose of a disposition is merely for resting the troops in expectation of no immediate battle, then logistical aspects of the march, such as selecting well-maintained and frequented roads, become the priority. Here, the choice of route is influenced by considerations of comfort and convenience for the troops' quarters or camping. On the other hand, if the march is undertaken with the imminent expectation of battle and urgency in reaching a designated location with the full strength of the army, even difficult or lesser-known routes will be taken without hesitation. In such cases, arriving with haste at a strategic point outweighs all other concerns, and roads and quarters become secondary.

The nature of each march, whether purely logistical or strategically oriented, affects the way the army is organized. Whenever the possibility of combat exists, which is common in any region under the shadow of active warfare, a critical rule of modern military practice comes into play: columns must be organized so that each can engage independently in combat if required. This self-sufficiency is achieved by integrating the three main arms—infantry, cavalry, and artillery—into each unit, thereby ensuring that every marching division is essentially a complete, smaller army. This structure includes designated commanders for each segment, allowing each to operate with autonomy if separated from the main force.

Ultimately, the demand for organized marches has led to the establishment of a new approach to structuring armies in readiness for combat. By dividing forces into mobile and capable subdivisions, we allow the maximum benefit from this organized approach. It eliminates the past reliance on unyielding cohesion, where armies often waited until the entire force was united before engaging. Today's structure allows for partial engagement if necessary, knowing the remaining units can join and reinforce as needed, allowing each unit to fulfill its role in the broader objective without needing to pause for alignment. This more flexible and efficient mode of marching thus becomes a key advantage in warfare, contributing to an army's overall readiness and effectiveness.

In the middle of the last century, particularly in the theaters of war where Frederick II was active, generals began to understand movement not merely as a means of positioning but as a decisive factor in battle itself. They increasingly recognized that surprise maneuvers could shift the course of engagements, turning mobility into a tool for achieving victory. However, the lack of a structured and organized battle order complicated matters considerably, making these maneuvers on the march elaborate, cumbersome, and exhausting. Whenever armies moved close to the enemy, they had to be prepared to fight at any moment, yet in that period, they weren't considered combat-ready unless the entire army was present and united as one mass. Unlike today, where segments or divisions can act independently if needed, back then, nothing short of the complete assembled force was regarded as a fully functioning entity.

During flank marches, when the army aimed to move along the enemy's side, the forces had to maintain strict, pre-set distances. The second line needed to stay about a quarter mile from the first line, which required tremendous effort and a thorough understanding of the landscape. This often meant marching up and down varied terrains, with units straining to maintain order across the ever-changing landscape. Given the rare availability of two suitable roads running parallel within such a short distance, the soldiers had to press through rough terrain, demanding substantial exertion and an extensive familiarity with the territory. This was especially challenging for the cavalry stationed on the wings, who faced similar difficulties when moving directly toward the front line.

The artillery encountered further issues. Requiring its own dedicated road and needing protection from accompanying infantry, the artillery's inclusion expanded the army's line of march, complicating the overall arrangement and often disrupting the precise distances set for all other units. Reading through the descriptions of march dispositions in Tempelhof's History of the Seven Years' War, one sees clearly how the constraints of marching disrupted war operations and added severe limitations to what could be achieved in combat due to the complex logistics involved.

With the progression of military organization, however, the art of war evolved. Modern techniques led to a regular subdivision of armies, ensuring that each main segment formed a complete, self-sufficient unit. While each part was relatively small, it was equipped to operate in combat independently, much like the full army would, though for a shorter period. This transformation has proven revolutionary, as it allows forces intended to join in a larger battle to march without needing to maintain an overly tight formation. Instead, these segments can engage the enemy individually as required, gradually concentrating their force as the battle unfolds.

Smaller units are inherently easier to maneuver, making them less reliant on subdivisions purely for logistical reasons. For instance, a smaller force can often march along a single road and, if it needs to advance in separate formations, can typically find suitable roads in close proximity that are adequate for its needs. Larger masses, however, present a greater challenge. As the force grows, so does the necessity to break it into separate columns, each potentially requiring a distinct road. Consequently, the spacing between columns widens, underscoring the importance of finding suitable, sometimes major, roads. Thus, the challenge of spacing and separation increases as the army grows, making effective coordination critical.

This subdivision of forces introduces a delicate balance of risk and necessity, measured almost mathematically: the smaller the units, the easier it is for them to support each other. Conversely, larger units can afford greater independence and thus can be spread out more confidently. As discussed in the previous book, this dynamic reveal that in well-developed countries, parallel roads often lie within a few miles of a main road, typically in workable proximity. With these alternate paths, coordinating an advance that balances speed and precision with the necessary concentration of forces is feasible.

In mountainous regions, however, these parallel routes are rare, and the challenges of connecting them are considerable. Yet the terrain itself compensates to some degree by providing natural defensive advantages. A single column moving through mountains may not advance as quickly, but its defensive strength is significantly enhanced by the rugged landscape, lending it an increased ability to withstand attacks and maintain security. The strategic use of smaller, well-positioned columns on difficult terrain thus reflects an adaptable system that, while preserving mobility and cohesion, also accommodates the challenges posed by varying landscapes and logistical constraints.

To make these ideas more accessible, let's examine them through a concrete example.

Take a division of 8,000 soldiers, along with artillery and additional equipment. In a typical scenario, this division would occupy about one league of road space during a march. If two divisions were to follow each other along the same road, the second division would arrive at the destination an hour after the first. Now, based on observations in earlier chapters, we know a division of this size could hold its ground for several hours, even against a stronger force. So, in the event of an attack on the first division, the second would still arrive in time to support it. Furthermore, within one league on either side of the main road, especially in the cultivated regions of Central Europe, there are often side roads that can be used for marching, reducing the need for soldiers to trek directly across fields, as was frequently required during campaigns like the Seven Years' War.

Experience also shows that a column containing four divisions and a cavalry reserve, even on rough roads, can complete a three-mile march in approximately eight hours. If we allocate one league of depth for each division, as well as for the reserve cavalry and artillery, the full march takes about thirteen hours—quite reasonable when we consider that in this case, about 40,000 troops are moving along a single road. With so many soldiers on the march, using nearby side roads, even those at a greater distance, can help reduce the time it takes to reach the destination. When a larger number of troops than this is advancing, the arrival of all troops on the same day is less critical, as large armies seldom engage in battle immediately upon encountering the enemy. More often, they prepare for the next day.

By presenting these concrete examples, the aim is to clarify that, with today's military organization, marches no longer present the same difficulties they once did. Rapid and coordinated marches now require neither the specialized skills nor the detailed local knowledge that were essential for Frederick's exacting marches in the Seven Years' War. Due to improved army structures, marches now proceed almost autonomously, with little need for intricate planning. In the past, conducting battles relied on orders given on the spot, but marches had to follow detailed plans. Today, battle orders require detailed planning, while simpler commands often suffice for a march.

It's also well known that all marches are either perpendicular (directly forward or backward) or parallel (flanking). Parallel marches, or flank marches, alter the alignment of divisions in terms of geometry. Parts that were originally side by side in a line now follow one another, or vice versa. Even if a march line does not run exactly perpendicular or parallel to the front, the order of the march always falls into one of these basic categories.

A thorough tactical reorganization of a march could only be achieved by what's called a file-march, which isn't feasible with large numbers of troops. And in the realm of strategy, such complete geometric realignment is even less achievable. In the older battle formations, only the central and flanking units would adjust their positioning. In the current formation, adjustments happen at the level of the army corps, divisions, or brigades, based on the military structure. The principles guiding the new battle formations influence marches as well. Since it is no longer essential for the entire army to be assembled in advance of the battle, more attention is paid to keeping marching units together as self-contained groups. For instance, if two divisions are positioned with one as the reserve for the other and are ordered to move forward along separate roads, no one would split each division between both roads. Instead, each division would be given its own route, marching in parallel with the division next to it. Each division leader could then organize a reserve within his command in case of combat. Maintaining unity in command is far more valuable than adhering strictly to the original geometric arrangement of the formation, as the divisions can return to their original setup if they arrive without engaging in combat.

This same principle applies if two divisions, originally positioned together, make a flank march on two separate roads. Instead of assigning the second line or reserve of each division to the rear road, each division would be assigned one road for itself, considering one division as the reserve for the other during the march. For an army of four divisions, with three forming the front line and the fourth acting as a reserve, it makes sense to assign one road to each division in the front line and have the reserve follow the central road. If three roads aren't available, marching on two roads is a viable option without significant issues.

The same logic applies to a flank march in the opposite direction.

Another consideration is whether to start the march with columns moving from the right or the left flank. For parallel marches, or marches directed to one side, the choice is straightforward—no one would start from the right to march left, or vice versa. For marches moving directly forward or back, the chosen march order should ideally align with the orientation of the roads in relation to the planned deployment line. This approach is sometimes feasible in tactics because it involves a smaller area where spatial relationships can be assessed more easily. However, applying this method in strategy is nearly impossible, and while some have tried to impose such tactical analogies onto strategy, these efforts usually fall short.

Another important aspect to consider is how columns march off from the right flank or left flank. In the case of parallel marches, which are also referred to as flank marches, the concept is straightforward. No one would initiate a march from the right flank if the intention is to move to the left. When it comes to marches directed straight ahead or backward, the order of march should ideally be determined by the layout of the roads in relation to where the army plans to deploy. This principle can often be applied in tactics since the areas involved are smaller, making it easier to assess the geometric relationships of the terrain. However, in strategy, achieving such precision becomes nearly impossible. Although we sometimes see attempts to apply tactical analogies to strategic situations, such efforts are generally superficial and lack practical value.

Historically, the entire order of march was a tactical consideration because the army on the move was regarded as a single, indivisible unit focused solely on the prospect of engaging in battle as a whole. For instance, during his maneuver near Brandeis on May 5, Schwerin was unable to determine whether the future battlefield would be on his right or left side, which necessitated his famous countermarch to adapt to the situation.

When an army in the old formation moved against an enemy, it typically advanced in four columns. In this setup, the cavalry was positioned in the first and second lines on each wing, forming the two outer columns, while the infantry lines composed the central columns. Each of these columns could march off from the right or the left, and one wing could even move from the right while the other moved from the left, a maneuver known as a "double column from the center." Despite the expectation that these formations should align with future deployment strategies, in practice, they often had little significance in that regard.

For example, when Frederick the Great entered the battle of Leuthen, his forces had been organized into four columns and marched off from the right wing. The transition to a battle-ready formation was seamless because the king aimed to attack the left flank of the Austrians. However, had he intended to engage their right flank instead, he would have needed to countermarch his entire army, similar to his actions at Prague.

The fact that these formations were ineffective in their time raises questions about their relevance today. We still do not know the exact positioning of future battlefields concerning our chosen routes, and any slight delays caused by marching in reverse order are far less critical than they used to be. The modern order of battle has introduced significant advantages; it is now inconsequential which division reaches the battlefield first or which brigade is the first to engage the enemy.

Under these current circumstances, whether an army begins its march from the right or the left flank is of little consequence. The primary concern is that alternating these movements helps to distribute the fatigue experienced by the troops. This objective is indeed important, justifying the practice of both marching methods when large formations are involved.

Advancing from the center as a defined maneuver has largely become obsolete due to the aforementioned factors. Such an advance is now considered impractical in strategy, as it implies a dual road system, which simply does not exist in most scenarios.

Furthermore, the order of march is primarily a tactical consideration rather than a strategic one. It involves dividing a whole into smaller parts, which must then reassemble into a single unit after the march is completed.

In modern warfare, the need to maintain a strict connection between these parts during a march has diminished significantly. Instead, the units can become more autonomous, allowing for the possibility of independent engagements. These engagements must be treated as complete battles in their own right, which is why we've emphasized this point so thoroughly.

Additionally, the concept of an order of battle divided into three distinct parts, as we noted earlier, is the most natural configuration when there isn't a specific objective that requires alteration. This also informs us that marching in three columns is the most practical arrangement.

Finally, it is important to clarify that the term "column" in a strategic context does not solely refer to a single body of troops on a particular marching route. It can also describe groups of troops that march on the same road but on different days. The division into columns primarily aims to streamline and facilitate movement, as smaller groups can navigate and march more efficiently than larger formations. This efficiency can be achieved not only by utilizing different roads but also by organizing the troops to march on different days.

Chapter XI. Marches (Continued)

Regarding the length of a march and the time it requires, we naturally rely on the general results of experience gained over time. For modern armies, it has long been established that a typical day's march should cover a distance of approximately three miles. This distance can serve as a reasonable average, particularly when considering longer journeys that may average out to about two miles per day, allowing for necessary rest days and time for various repairs that might be required along the way.

In flat terrain with decent roads, a division comprising 8,000 men will typically take between eight to ten hours to complete such a march. Conversely, if the march occurs in hilly terrain, this duration can extend to ten to twelve hours. If multiple divisions are united in a single column, the overall march will likely take a couple of hours longer, not accounting for the necessary intervals that must occur between the departures of the first and subsequent divisions.

Consequently, we can see that a significant portion of the day is consumed by such a march. The fatigue experienced by a soldier carrying his pack for ten or twelve hours cannot simply be equated with that of an average person who might walk three miles on flat ground in about five hours. The demands on a soldier's endurance are vastly different, given the added weight and the extended duration of their movement.

In exceptional cases, the longest marches recorded are about five or, at most, six miles in a day; however, for a sustained period, four miles is more realistic. A march of five miles necessitates a halt lasting several hours, and even on a good road, a division of 8,000 men will not complete it in less than sixteen hours. If the march extends to six miles, and if multiple divisions are in the column, we can anticipate that it will take at least twenty hours to complete.

It is important to clarify that we are discussing the movement of entire divisions from one encampment to another, as this is the standard method for marches conducted in a theater of war. When several divisions are required to march in a single column, the first division to depart is gathered and sent off earlier than the others, thus arriving at its designated camping area sooner. Nonetheless, this difference in arrival time never fully accounts for the entire duration associated with the depth of a division along the line of march, a concept elegantly captured in the French term découlement, referring to the time required for the troops to flow down the column.

Consequently, the soldier benefits very little in terms of reduced fatigue through this method. Each march significantly lengthens in duration as the number of troops being moved increases. Coordinating the assembly and departure of various brigades within a division at staggered times is often impractical, which is why the division itself is typically considered the fundamental unit for planning these movements.

When covering long distances, if troops move from one cantonment to another and travel in smaller groups without specific assembly points, it is certainly possible to increase the distance covered each day. This is especially true when accounting for necessary detours required to reach their quarters. However, marches that require troops to assemble daily into divisions or corps and then make an additional effort to settle into quarters consume the most time. Such practices are only advisable in regions where resources are plentiful. In these cases, the advantages of easier access to provisions and the shelter offered to the troops justify the fatigue incurred from a longer march.

Reflecting on historical events, we see that the Prussian army made a critical error during their retreat in 1806 by insisting on establishing quarters for the troops each night in order to secure sustenance. They could have procured the necessary provisions while in bivouacs, which would have allowed the army to avoid spending an arduous fourteen days covering just fifty miles—a feat they achieved only through extreme exertion.

When considering the impact of poor road conditions or hilly terrain, all previously mentioned calculations regarding time and distance must undergo significant adjustments, making it challenging to accurately estimate the required duration for a march in any specific instance. Consequently, it is difficult to establish a universal theory that applies to every scenario. What theory can do is draw attention to the potential for error inherent in such calculations. To mitigate these risks, meticulous planning and an ample buffer for unforeseen delays are essential. Additionally, factors like weather conditions and the overall state of the troops must also be taken into account.

Since the abolishment of tents and the adoption of a system where troops are sustained through compulsory requisition of local provisions, the baggage carried by an army has noticeably decreased. As a natural and critical consequence, we initially anticipate that this will result in an acceleration of troop movements, leading to an increase in the length of daily marches. However, achieving this acceleration is contingent upon specific circumstances and conditions on the ground.

Marches within the theater of war have not seen a significant increase in speed due to the reduction of baggage. For many years, it has been standard practice that when operations require unusually long marches, armies leave their baggage behind or send it ahead, ensuring it is kept separate from the troops during these movements. As soon as the baggage is out of the way and no longer poses a direct hindrance, it typically receives little attention, regardless of the potential damage it might sustain during the journey. Historical examples from the Seven Years' War illustrate this point, particularly Lascy's impressive march in 1760, where he moved his corps of 15,000 men over a distance of 225 miles from Schweidnitz to Berlin through Lusatia in just ten days. This averages out to an extraordinary twenty-two miles per day, a feat that remains remarkable even by today's standards.

However, while the method of supplying troops has evolved, it has introduced new challenges that can slow down movements. When troops are partially responsible for procuring their own supplies, which is often the case, they require more time for supply operations than would be necessary if they were merely receiving rations from provision wagons. Additionally, during extended marches, it becomes impractical for large numbers of troops to camp at the same location. Divisions must be spread out to facilitate better management and coordination. Moreover, it is usually necessary to place part of the army—especially the cavalry—into quarters, which further contributes to delays. For example, during the pursuit of the Prussians in 1806, Buonaparte aimed to cut off their retreat, yet managed only thirty miles in ten days. Similarly, Blücher in 1815, while chasing the French with the same objective, achieved comparable results, demonstrating a notable reduction in pace compared to the rapid movements accomplished by Frederick the Great during his marches from Saxony to Silesia and back, despite the logistical challenges he faced.

At the same time, the mobility and agility of both large and small units within an army have improved significantly due to the reduction in baggage. This improvement occurs partly because the number of horses needed for transport remains the same while the overall number of animals decreases, resulting in reduced forage requirements. Furthermore, without the burden of a lengthy supply train, armies are less tethered to a specific position, allowing for greater operational flexibility. Frederick the Great's experience after lifting the siege of Olmütz in 1758, where he had to manage 4,000 carriages requiring half of his army's manpower, is no longer feasible even against a less aggressive opponent.

On long marches, such as those extending from the Tagus to the Niemen, the benefits of a lighter army become even more pronounced. Although the standard daily marching distance remains consistent due to the number of remaining carriages, in situations requiring urgency, forces can exceed this typical distance with comparatively less strain. Overall, while the reduction of baggage tends to save resources and power, it does not necessarily result in an acceleration of movement. Instead, it fosters a more efficient and responsive military posture, enabling armies to adapt and maneuver effectively in the face of changing conditions and demands on the battlefield.

Chapter XII. Marches (continued)

We now turn our attention to the destructive effects that marches exert on an army, which can be so significant that they must be regarded as an active principle of destruction, comparable to that of actual combat. While a single moderate march may not significantly wear down an army, the cumulative effect of a series of even moderate marches inevitably takes its toll. If an army undertakes a succession of severe marches, the detrimental impact on its effectiveness and readiness is exacerbated.

At the frontline of conflict, the challenges of inadequate food and shelter, poorly maintained and broken roads, combined with the constant need to remain ready for battle, create an excessive strain on the army's resources. This strain does not only affect soldiers but also extends to the horses, transport carriages, and all types of equipment, ultimately leading to their deterioration and wear.

It is often suggested that prolonged periods of rest are detrimental to the physical health of an army, with a greater incidence of sickness occurring during these times than during periods of moderate activity. While it is true that illness can arise when soldiers are confined too closely together, the same would occur if they were in temporary quarters taken during a march. The lack of fresh air and exercise cannot be attributed solely to the conditions of rest, as soldiers can easily be given opportunities for both during their exercises.

Consider the stark difference between the state of a soldier's health when he falls ill in the comfort of a proper shelter versus when he becomes sick while trudging through mud in the open, weighed down by a heavy knapsack and exposed to the elements. In a camp, a soldier can quickly be sent to the nearest village for assistance, while during a march, he may find himself stranded for hours, forced to continue moving alone, often turning minor ailments into serious health issues and potentially life-threatening conditions.

Take, for instance, the scenario of an ordinary march under the scorching sun of summer, where the soldier faces excessive heat and unbearable thirst. In such desperation, he may rush towards a seemingly refreshing spring of water, only to return suffering from illness or even death due to the sudden change in temperature and hydration.

These reflections are not intended to advocate for less activity in warfare; after all, the military instrument exists for the purpose of being utilized. If the toll of use leads to the wear of the instrument, that is simply the natural order of things. What we aim to highlight is the need for perspective, particularly against the backdrop of theoretical discussions that suggest rapid movements and incessant activity come without consequence, painting them as boundless resources that a general might be neglecting.

Similar to how one might overlook the extensive labor involved in mining for gold and silver, where the focus tends to be solely on the rewards, the complexities and costs associated with sustained military activity are often ignored.

During long marches outside the immediate theater of war, conditions are typically easier, and daily losses tend to be smaller. However, even in these circumstances, troops suffering from minor ailments can become temporarily lost to the army as they struggle to catch up. In the cavalry, there is a noticeable increase in the number of horses that become lame or suffer from sore backs, and many transport carriages may break down or require repairs along the way. Thus, by the end of a march covering one hundred miles or more, an army often arrives significantly weakened, particularly regarding its cavalry and logistical support.

When such extensive marches are necessary in the theater of war, particularly under the scrutiny of the enemy, these disadvantages compound, leading to substantial losses, especially when large bodies of troops are involved and the circumstances are unfavorable.

To illustrate this point, we can look at some historical examples. When Buonaparte crossed the Niemen on June 24, 1812, he began with an enormous center of his army, numbering 301,000 men, and by the time he reached Smolensk on August 15, he had detached 13,500, leaving approximately 287,500. However, the actual strength of his army at that date had dwindled to only 182,000, indicating a staggering loss of 105,000 men. Notably, up to that point, only two significant engagements had taken place, resulting in a maximum of around 10,000 casualties. Thus, the losses due to illness and straggling during fifty-two days of marching—approximately seventy miles directly toward the enemy—accounted for an astonishing 95,000 men, or roughly one-third of the entire force.

Three weeks later, during the battle of Borodino, the losses totaled 144,000, including casualties from that battle. Just eight days after, at Moscow, the number further increased to 198,000. The daily losses experienced by this army at the outset of the campaign averaged at a rate of 1 in 150, which later increased to 1 in 120, and eventually rose to an alarming rate of 1 in 19 of the original strength by the campaign's end.

The movement of Napoleon from the passage of the Niemen to Moscow can certainly be characterized as persistent; however, it is essential to note that this endeavor stretched over eighty-two days, covering only 120 miles. During this period, the French army made two significant halts—one in Wilna for approximately fourteen days and another in Witebsk for about eleven days—providing time for many stragglers to rejoin the ranks. Remarkably, this fourteen-week advance occurred in the summer months and along roads that were primarily sandy. The considerable mass of troops concentrated on a single road, coupled with insufficient provisions and an enemy that was retreating but not fleeing, contributed significantly to the adverse conditions faced by the army.

We will refrain from discussing the retreat of the French army from Moscow to the Niemen, but it is worth noting that the Russian army left Kaluga with 120,000 troops and reached Wilna with only 30,000 remaining. Many are aware that the losses sustained during that period were minimal in actual combat.

Lastly, we can examine Blücher's campaign of 1813 in Silesia and Saxony, which, while not characterized by extensive marches, was notable for the significant amount of back-and-forth movement. York's corps, initially around 40,000 strong when the campaign began on August 16, was reduced to just 12,000 by the time of the battle of Leipzig on October 19. The main battles fought by this corps—at Goldberg, Lowenberg, Katsbach, Wartenburg, and Mockern (Leipzig)—resulted in losses estimated at around 12,000 men. This indicates that their losses due to various other factors over eight weeks amounted to an alarming 16,000, accounting for two-fifths of their total strength.

In light of these examples, we must come to terms with the significant wear and tear on our forces if we intend to conduct a war rich in movements. This necessitates careful planning and the appropriate allocation of reinforcements to support our troops during extended campaigns.

Chapter XIII. Cantonments

In the modern system of war cantonments have become again indispensable, because neither tents nor a complete military train make an army independent of them. Huts and open-air camps (bivouacs as they are called), however far such arrangements may be carried, can still never become the usual way of locating troops without sickness gaining the upper hand, and prematurely exhausting their strength, sooner or later, according to the state of the weather or climate. The campaign in Russia in 1812 is one of the few in which, in a very severe climate, the troops, during the six months that it lasted hardly ever lay in cantonments. But what was the consequence of this extreme effort, which should be called an extravagance, if that term was not much more applicable to the political conception of the enterprise!

Two things interfere with the occupation of cantonments the proximity of the enemy, and the rapidity of movement. For these reasons they are quitted as soon as the decision approaches, and cannot be again taken up until the decision is over.

In modern wars, that's, in all campaigns during the last twenty-five years which occur to us at this moment, the military element has acted with full energy. Nearly all that was possible has generally been done in them, as far as regards activity and the utmost effort of force; but all these campaigns have been of short duration, they have seldom exceeded half a year; in most of them a few months sufficed to bring matters to a crisis, that is, to a point where the vanquished enemy saw himself compelled to sue for an armistice or at once for peace, or to a point where, on the conqueror's part, the impetus of victory had exhausted itself. During this period of extreme effort there could be little question of cantonments, for even in the victorious march of the pursuer, if there was no longer any danger, the rapidity of movement made that kind of relief impossible.

But when from any cause the course of events is less impetuous, when a more even oscillation and balancing of forces takes place, then the housing of troops must again become a foremost subject for attention. This want has some influence even on the conduct of war itself, partly in this way, that we seek to gain more time and security by a stronger system of outposts, by a more considerable advanced guard thrown further forward; and partly in this way, that our measures are governed more by the richness and fertility of the country than by the tactical advantages which the ground affords in the geometrical relations of lines and points. A commercial town of twenty or thirty thousand inhabitants, a road thickly studded with large villages or flourishing towns give such facilities for the assembling in one position large bodies of troops, and this concentration gives such a freedom and such a latitude for movement as fully compensate for the advantages which the better situation of some point may otherwise present.

On the form to be followed in arranging cantonments we have only a few observations to make, as this subject belongs for the most part to tactics.

The housing of troops comes under two heads, inasmuch as it can either be the main point or only a secondary consideration. If the disposition of the troops in the course of a campaign is regulated by grounds purely tactical and strategical, and if, as is done more especially with cavalry, they are directed for their comfort to occupy the quarters available in the vicinity of the point of concentration of the army, then the quarters are subordinate considerations and substitutes for camps; they must, therefore, be chosen within such a radius that the troops can reach the point of assembly in good time. But if an army takes up quarters to rest and refresh, then the housing of the troops is the main point, and other measures, consequently also the selection of the particular point of assembly, will be influenced by that object.

The first question for examination here is as to the general form of the cantonments as a whole. The usual form is that of a very long oval, a mere widening as it were of the tactical order of battle. The point of assembly for the army is in front, the head-quarters in rear. Now these three arrangements are, in point of fact, adverse, indeed almost opposed, to the safe assembly of the army on the approach of the enemy.

The more the cantonments form a square, or rather a circle, the quicker the troops can concentrate at one point, that is the centre. The further the place of assembly is placed in rear, the longer the enemy will be in reaching it, and, therefore, the more time is left us to assemble. A point of assembly in rear of the cantonments can never be in danger. And, on the other hand, the farther the head-quarters are in advance, so much the sooner reports arrive, therefore so much the better is the commander informed of everything. At the same time, the first named arrangements are not devoid of points which deserve some attention.

By the extension of cantonments in width, we have in view the protection of the country which would otherwise be laid under contributions by the enemy. But this motive is neither thoroughly sound, nor is it very important. It is only sound as far as regards the country on the extremity of the wings, but does not apply at all to intermediate spaces existing between separate divisions of the army, if the quarters of those divisions are drawn closer round their point of assembly, for no enemy will then venture into those intervals of space. And it is not very important, because there are simpler means of shielding the districts in our vicinity from the enemy's requisitions than scattering the army itself.

The placing of the point of assembly in front is with a view to covering the quarters, for the following reasons: In the first place, a body of troops, suddenly called to arms, always leaves behind it in cantonments a tail of stragglers sick, baggage, provisions, etc., etc. which may easily fall into the enemy's hands if the point of assembly is placed in rear. In the second place, we have to apprehend that if the enemy with some bodies of cavalry passes by the advanced guard, or if it is defeated in any way, he may fall upon scattered regiments or battalions. If he encounters a force drawn up in good order, although it is weak, and in the end must be overpowered, still he is brought to a stop, and in that way time is gained.

As respects the position of the head-quarters, it is generally supposed that it cannot be made too secure.

According to these different considerations, we may conclude that the best arrangement for districts of cantonments is where they take an oblong form, approaching the square or circle, have the point of assembly in the centre, and the head-quarters placed on the front line, well protected by considerable masses of troops.

What we have said as to covering of the wings in treating of the disposition of the army in general, applies here also; therefore corps detached from the main body, right and left, although intended to fight in conjunction with the rest, will have particular points of assembly of their own in the same line with the main body.

Now, if we reflect that the nature of a country, on the one hand, by favourable features in the ground determines the most natural point of assembly, and on the other hand, by the positions of towns and villages determines the most suitable situation for cantonments, then we must perceive how very rarely any geometrical form can be decisive in our present subject. But yet it was necessary to direct attention to it, because, like all general laws, it affects the generality of cases in a greater or less degree.

What now remains to be said as to an advantageous position for cantonments is that they should be taken up behind some natural obstacle of ground affording cover, whilst the sides next the enemy can be watched by small but numerous detached parties; or they may be taken up behind fortresses, which, when circumstances prevent any estimate being formed of the strength of their garrisons, impose upon the enemy a greater feeling of respect and and caution.

We reserve the subject of winter quarters, covered by defensive works for a separate article.

The quarters taken up by troops on a march differ from those called standing cantonments in this way, that, in order to save the troops from unnecessary marching, cantonments on a march are taken up as much as possible along the lines of march, and are not at any considerable distance on either side of these roads; if their extension in this sense does not exceed a short day's march, the arrangement is not one at all unfavourable to the quick concentration of the army.

In all cases in presence of the enemy, according to the technical phrase in use, that is in all cases where there is no considerable interval between the advance guards of the two armies respectively, the extent of the cantonments and the time required to assemble the army determine the strength and position of the advanced guard and outposts; but when these must be suited to the enemy and circumstances, then, on the contrary, the extent of the cantonments must depend on the time which we can count upon by the resistance of the advance guard.

In the third(*) chapter of this book, we have stated how this resistance, in the case of an advanced corps, may be estimated. From the time of that resistance we must deduct the time required for transmission of reports and getting the men under arms, and the remainder only is the time available for assembling at the point of concentration.

(*) 8th Chapter.—Tr.

We shall conclude here also by establishing our ideas in the form of a result, such as is usual under ordinary circumstances. If the distance at which the advanced guard is detached is the same as the radius of the cantonments, and the point of assembly is fixed in the centre of the cantonments, the time which is gained by checking the enemy's advance would be available for the transmission of intelligence and getting under arms, and would in most cases be sufficient, even although the communication is not made by means of signals, cannon-shots, etc., but simply by relays of orderlies, the only really sure method.

With an advanced guard pushed forward three miles in front, our cantonments might therefore cover a space of thirty square miles. In a moderately-peopled country there would be 10,000 houses in this space, which for an army of 50,000, after deducting the advanced guard, would be four men to a billet, therefore very comfortable quarters; and for an army of twice the strength nine men to a billet, therefore still not very close quarters. On the other hand, if the advanced guard is only one mile in front, we could only occupy a space of four square miles; for although the time gained does not diminish exactly in proportion as the distance of the advanced guard diminishes, and even with a distance of one mile we may still calculate on a gain of six hours, yet the necessity for caution increases when the enemy is so close. But in such a space an army of 50,000 men could only find partial accommodation, even in a very thickly populated country.

From all this we see what an important part is played here by great or at least considerable towns, which afford convenience for sheltering 10,000 or even 20,000 men almost at one point.

From this result it follows that, if we are not very close to the enemy, and have a suitable advanced guard we might remain in cantonments, even if the enemy is concentrated, as Frederick the Great did at Breslau in the beginning of the year 1762, and Buonaparte at Witebsk in 1812. But although by preserving a right distance and by suitable arrangements we have no reason to fear not being able to assemble in time, even opposite an enemy who is concentrated, yet we must not forget that an army engaged in assembling itself in all haste can do nothing else in that time; that it is therefore, for a time at least, not in a condition to avail itself in an instant of fortuitous opportunities, which deprives it of the greater part of its really efficient power. The consequence of this is, that an army should only break itself up completely in cantonments under some one or other of the three following cases:

1. If the enemy does the same: When the opposing force chooses to break their own army into cantonments, it often indicates a mutual recognition of the need for rest or a temporary pause in hostilities. In such cases, if both sides are engaged in establishing cantonments, it allows for a period of reduced tension, enabling armies to recuperate while remaining vigilant. This strategic decision can lead to a more favorable situation for both parties, as it creates a temporary stalemate that might provide opportunities for reinforcements or logistical improvements.

2. If the condition of the troops makes it unavoidable: The physical and mental state of the troops plays a crucial role in determining whether an army can continue active operations or needs to rest. If the soldiers are fatigued, suffering from sickness, or have experienced significant wear and tear from prolonged engagements or marches, it becomes essential to establish cantonments. Acknowledging the necessity of recovery not only preserves the effectiveness of the army but also ensures that it can operate at full capacity in future confrontations. Ignoring these conditions could lead to a decrease in morale, increased attrition, and ultimately, a compromised operational readiness.

3. If the more immediate object with the army is completely limited to the maintenance of a strong position: In situations where the primary objective shifts to securing and maintaining a fortified position, the focus should be on concentrating troops effectively at that designated point. The act of breaking into cantonments, in this case, is strategically advantageous, as it allows for the bolstering of defenses and provides a secure environment for regrouping and resupplying. Ensuring that troops are assembled in a timely manner becomes paramount, as the strength of the position relies heavily on the rapid mobilization of forces to counter any potential threats or to exploit any tactical advantages that may arise during the course of operations.

4. The campaign of 1815 provides a striking example of how an army can assemble effectively from its cantonments. General Ziethen, commanding Blücher's advanced guard of 30,000 men, was stationed at Charleroi, which was only two miles away from Sombreff, the designated assembly point for the army. The furthest cantonments of the troops were about eight miles from Sombreff, positioned beyond Ciney on one side and near Liège on the other. Despite this distance, the troops stationed around Ciney were able to gather at Ligny several hours before the battle commenced. Those near Liège, known as Bulow's Corps, would have similarly reached the assembly point in time if not for unforeseen circumstances and poor communication regarding orders and intelligence.

It is evident that proper precautions for the security of the Prussian army were not adequately taken. However, it's important to note that the arrangements were initially made when the French army was still dispersed across a broad area of cantonments. The real failure lay in not adjusting the plans promptly upon receiving the first reports indicating that the enemy forces were mobilizing and that Buonaparte had reunited his troops.

Nevertheless, it remains remarkable that the Prussian army managed to concentrate at Sombreff before the enemy launched their attack. On the night of the 14th, twelve hours prior to the assault on Ziethen, Blücher had received intelligence about the enemy's advance and began to assemble his army. However, by the morning of the 15th at nine o'clock, Ziethen was already heavily engaged with the enemy. It was not until that same moment that General Thielman, stationed at Ciney, received orders to march to Namur. He then had to organize his divisions and cover a distance of six and a half miles to reach Sombreff, completing this in 24 hours. General Bulow would have been able to arrive around the same time if the orders had been relayed to him as they should have been.

Interestingly, Buonaparte did not decide to launch his attack on Ligny until two in the afternoon of the 16th. The anxiety of facing Wellington on one flank and Blücher on the other, along with the imbalance in relative forces, contributed to this delay in action. This illustrates how even the most determined commander can be hindered by the cautious instincts that arise in complex situations where many factors are at play.

While some of the considerations discussed here are more tactical than strategic, we chose to explore them in detail rather than risk lacking clarity in our analysis.

Chapter XIV. Subsistence

This subject has gained significant importance in modern warfare due to two primary factors. Firstly, the size of armies today is considerably larger than those seen during the Middle Ages and even in the ancient world. Although there have been instances in history where armies matched or even exceeded the size of modern forces, such occurrences were rare and temporary. In contrast, modern military history, especially since the time of Louis XIV, has consistently seen the mobilization of very large armies.

The second factor is even more crucial and pertains specifically to contemporary warfare. It is the much closer internal connection that exists within modern wars, characterized by a constant state of readiness for battle among the warring parties. Historically, many wars were comprised of single, disconnected campaigns separated by intervals during which the conflict was either entirely dormant, existing only in a political sense, or where the armies were stationed far apart from each other. During these lulls, each army would focus on its own needs, rather than concern itself with its adversary.

In contrast, modern wars, especially those that have occurred since the Peace of Westphalia, have taken on a more systematic and interconnected form due to the efforts of the respective governments involved. The military objective tends to dominate every aspect of these conflicts, leading to a demand for adequate arrangements for the sustenance of the troops. While there were indeed lengthy periods of inactivity in the wars of the seventeenth and eighteenth centuries—often approaching a complete halt in hostilities—these periods were generally subordinate to military aims. They were caused primarily by harsh seasonal conditions rather than any genuine necessity related to troop subsistence. As these inactive periods regularly concluded with the arrival of summer, it can be stated that uninterrupted action was the rule of warfare during favorable weather conditions.

The shift from one method of operation to another occurs gradually, and this was also true in our context. For instance, during the wars against Louis XIV, the allies would send their troops into winter cantonments in distant provinces to facilitate their subsistence. However, this practice had changed by the time of the Silesian War, when such cantonments were no longer utilized.

This systematic and interconnected approach to warfare became viable only after states transitioned from relying on feudal armies to maintaining regular standing troops. The obligation to provide military service under feudal law was replaced with a monetary contribution, leading to a decline in personal service. Enlistment became the norm, and the nobility often regarded the obligation to supply a quota of men as a form of tribute or tax. Consequently, armies transformed into tools of the state, with their foundation resting primarily on the treasury and revenues of the government.

Similar transformations occurred in the methods used for the sustenance of these troops. With the privileged classes freed from the obligation of personal service by paying a monetary contribution, imposing the burden of sustenance on them became increasingly difficult. Therefore, the government and treasury assumed responsibility for providing for the army's needs, ensuring that it was not maintained at the expense of the local populace. Administrations were thus compelled to treat the sustenance of the army as a matter of official responsibility. This arrangement made subsistence more challenging in two significant ways: first, because it was now a government affair, and second, because the forces required to be permanently stationed had to be sufficient to confront those maintained by other states.

As a result, a distinct military class emerged within the population, complete with an independent organization dedicated to its subsistence, which was refined to the highest possible standard. This evolution not only redefined the relationship between the military and the state but also altered the very nature of warfare itself, ensuring that armies could be mobilized and sustained with greater efficiency and effectiveness than ever before.

Not only were provisions collected through purchases or deliveries from landed estates, known as Dominiallieferungen, from distant locations, but these supplies were also stored in magazines. They were then transported using specialized wagons and baked in temporary ovens set up near the troops' quarters. Ultimately, the provisions were carried away by the soldiers through a transport system that was integrated with the army itself. This logistics system is significant not only as a characteristic of military arrangements at the time but also because it embodies a structure that cannot be entirely eliminated; elements of it will always resurface in military operations.

As a result, military organization consistently aimed to become more self-sufficient and less dependent on civilian populations and local resources. This shift contributed to making warfare a more systematic and organized endeavor, allowing it to align closely with military and political objectives. However, this newfound independence also restricted operational mobility and significantly diminished the army's overall energy. As a consequence, armies became increasingly tied to their supply depots, limited by the capacities of their transportation services. This situation naturally led to a focus on conserving the troops' sustenance. Soldiers often subsisted on a meager diet of bread, moving about like shadows, with little hope for improvement in their circumstances, which compounded their suffering.

Those who trivialize the consequences of inadequate soldier rations and point to the effectiveness of Frederick the Great's troops, who were sustained under similar conditions, are adopting a limited perspective. While the ability to endure hardship is indeed a commendable virtue for soldiers, it must be recognized that such endurance should be temporary and dictated by necessity rather than a result of a poorly conceived system that prioritizes minimal rations for mere survival. When soldiers are forced into this level of deprivation as a standard practice, both their physical and moral resilience inevitably deteriorate. Frederick the Great's success with his troops cannot serve as a standard for modern armies, partly because he faced adversaries who employed similar strategies and partly because we cannot ascertain how much more he could have accomplished had his soldiers enjoyed a quality of life akin to that of Buonaparte's troops when circumstances permitted.

The artificial feeding of horses poses another challenge that has not been effectively addressed, primarily due to the logistical difficulties associated with providing forage, which is bulkier than human rations. A single ration for a horse weighs about ten times more than a soldier's ration, and the number of horses in an army typically exceeds one-tenth of the total number of soldiers; presently, it ranges from one-fourth to one-third, while historically, it was often one-third to one-half. Consequently, the total weight of forage required can be three, four, or even five times greater than that of the soldiers' rations for the same duration. This necessity prompted armies to rely on the most immediate and direct solutions, leading to foraging expeditions. However, these expeditions caused significant complications in military operations, primarily by necessitating that forces remain engaged in enemy territory. Additionally, they limited the duration that armies could remain in any given area.

During the Silesian War, foraging missions became less common as they resulted in considerable resource depletion and waste compared to securing supplies through requisitions and taxation. When the French Revolution reintroduced the concept of a national army onto the battlefield, it quickly became clear that the resources available to governments were insufficient. The entire framework of warfare, which had developed in response to these limited resources, collapsed, and this collapse included the subsistence system under discussion. Revolutionary leaders, unconcerned with maintaining supply depots or the elaborate organizational structures necessary for effective transport logistics, sent their soldiers into combat, compelled their generals to engage, and sustained their armies through a combination of exaction and plunder.

In this context, the wars conducted under Buonaparte, as well as those fought against him, found a middle ground. These campaigns selectively utilized the most effective means available from all options at their disposal, a practice that is likely to continue in the future.

The modern approach to subsisting troops—essentially seizing resources available in the country without regard for ownership—can be implemented in four different ways: subsisting directly from the inhabitants, contributions secured by the troops themselves, general contributions, and utilizing magazines. Typically, all four methods are employed together, with one method usually prevailing over the others; however, there are occasions when only one method is used exclusively.

1. Living On the Inhabitants, Or on the Community, Which Is the Same Thing.

If we consider that, even within the most populous urban centers, which are inhabited solely by consumers rather than producers, there must always be enough provisions stored for several days, it becomes clear that densely populated areas can support an army roughly equivalent in size to the number of their inhabitants, at least for a day, without requiring extensive prior preparations. In towns of significant size, this capacity yields highly favorable results, allowing a large military force to gather supplies and quarters at a single location with relative ease. However, in smaller towns or rural villages, the resources available would be far from adequate. For example, a population of 3,000 or 4,000 people per square mile, considered dense in a rural context, would only sustain an equal number of soldiers. If a larger force were to attempt to subsist in such an area, it would need to spread over an impractically large extent of land, which could undermine essential objectives and impose logistical challenges.

In flat, cultivated regions and even in modest towns, however, the availability of key provisions for military needs is generally greater. Farmers often keep a stock of bread or grains sufficient to feed their families for an extended period, sometimes lasting from eight to fourteen days. Daily access to meat is typically feasible, and a supply of fresh vegetables is often sufficient to bridge the gap until the next harvest. Therefore, when troops occupy unvisited quarters, it is possible to sustain a force three or four times the size of the local population for several days. This translates to a valuable degree of logistical flexibility. For a region where the population density averages around 2,000 to 3,000 per square mile, and if no large town is nearby, a 30,000-strong column could sustain itself across roughly four square miles, translating to an effective frontage of two miles. For a larger army of 90,000 combatants, approximately 75,000 of whom are active fighters, spread across three columns traveling in close proximity, a frontage of six miles would suffice if three suitable roads could be located within that span.

Should multiple columns advance into these regions in successive waves, the local authorities can make additional provisions to sustain them for a day or two more. Thus, even if the initial 90,000-strong force is trailed by another contingent of equal size the following day, both waves would likely find adequate sustenance, bringing the total force supported to about 150,000 combatants.

The provisioning of forage for horses poses even fewer challenges, as it does not require processing or preparation. The countryside generally maintains a stock of forage sufficient to feed local horses until the next harvest, meaning shortages are unlikely. Deliveries of forage, however, are best coordinated through communal arrangements rather than imposed on individual residents. It is generally understood that strategic planning will account for the characteristics of the countryside, so that cavalry, for instance, are not sent to areas dominated by commerce or manufacturing where forage may be scarce.

From this assessment, we conclude that in a country with moderate population density—approximately 2,000 to 3,000 inhabitants per square mile—an army of 150,000 combatants can sustain itself for one to two days without the need for extensive preparations or magazines, within a limited area that allows for strategic concentration. This observation suggests that such a force can continue marching while being sustained by local resources alone.

This principle underpinned the extensive campaigns of the French Revolutionary and Napoleonic armies. These forces advanced from the Adige River to the Lower Danube, and from the Rhine to the Vistula, with only minimal reliance on pre-prepared supplies, instead subsisting largely on local provisions and seldom experiencing scarcity. Their movements, underpinned by both morale and a distinct operational advantage, proceeded without significant delays due to indecision or hesitancy, translating into a relentless march of victory.

Where conditions are less favorable, where the population density is lower, where more residents are artisans than farmers, where the land is less productive, or where the area has already been heavily traversed, results may naturally fall short of this ideal. Nevertheless, by extending the column's front from two to three miles, the area covered more than doubles, from four square miles to nine. Such a span still allows adequate concentration for action in most scenarios, demonstrating that even under more challenging circumstances, this method of supply enables a continuous march.

If, however, the army is required to halt for several days, considerable distress will quickly arise unless certain preparations have been made beforehand to address such an event. These preparations are essential for the survival of a large force, even today, and are typically structured in two key ways. The first involves equipping troops with a wagon train dedicated to carrying essential provisions, particularly bread or flour, which are crucial for sustaining the soldiers. This system allows for a supply that can last for three to four days. If soldiers are also equipped with three or four days' worth of rations on their person, then the most vital provisions for an eight-day period are effectively secured.

The second measure is establishing a commissariat—a regular system of supply logistics that, whenever there is even a brief halt, can collect and transport food from more distant regions. This setup provides the army with the flexibility to shift from a system relying on local provisioning in cantonments to one that draws upon resources organized and managed by the commissariat.

Subisting while in cantonments offers substantial benefits, primarily because it minimizes the need for transportation, making it a much faster process. This system, however, presumes that sufficient cantonment accommodations are available for the entire army—a condition that may not always be met.

When it comes to subsistence through exactions enforced by the troops themselves, a smaller unit, such as a battalion, can theoretically occupy a camp near a few villages, notifying them to furnish provisions. In such a scenario, this method would not differ significantly from quartering in cantonments. But if the encamped forces are larger, then gathering supplies in this way becomes complex and problematic. In such cases, supplies would have to be amassed from the broader area, pooling enough resources for a brigade or division, and then distributing these collected supplies among the soldiers.

A closer look reveals the inherent challenges of supporting a large army through forced collections alone. For example, if a large group of soldiers attempted to gather provisions from a set area, they would yield far less than if they were individually quartered across the same area, because small groups of soldiers can be thorough, accessing even the last reserves in each household. In contrast, an officer with a small group sent out to requisition supplies has limited time, resources, and logistical support to locate all the provisions in a household, not to mention the challenges of transporting what he finds. Consequently, only a fraction of available supplies can actually be secured.

Additionally, in larger camps, troops are stationed closely together, meaning the area from which they can efficiently requisition supplies is far too limited to meet the needs of the entire force. In practice, an area of just three or four square miles could scarcely provide for a force of 30,000 soldiers. Even within this radius, some villages may be occupied by other small military detachments, who would likely prevent resources from being taken elsewhere. Moreover, this approach leads to considerable waste, as some troops inevitably receive more than they need, while a significant portion of the collected provisions is either lost or remains unused.

Thus, the forced requisition of provisions by the troops is feasible only for smaller groups, ideally not exceeding 8,000 to 10,000 men, and even then, it should be viewed as a last resort, to be employed only when absolutely necessary. This approach, though expedient under certain conditions, remains inefficient and challenging when applied to larger bodies of troops, highlighting the ongoing need for structured, systematic methods of provisioning that support the army without compromising its operational strength and cohesion.

It cannot in general be avoided in the case of troops directly in front of the enemy, such as advanced guards and outposts, when the army is advancing, because these bodies must arrive at points where no preparations could have been made, and they are usually too far from the stores collected for the rest of the army; further, in the case of moveable columns acting independently; and lastly, in all cases where by chance there is neither time nor means to procure subsistence in any other way.

The more troops are accustomed to live by regular requisitions, the more time and circumstances permit the adoption of that way of subsisting, then the more satisfactory will be the result. But time is generally wanting, for what the troops get for themselves directly is got much quicker.

3. By Regular Requisitions.

This system of subsistence, founded on contributions and requisitions within the areas of operation, is without a doubt one of the most direct and effective ways of sustaining an army. In fact, it has become a foundational approach in modern warfare. This method is distinctly different from the approach of forced collection: rather than seizing supplies directly and immediately from their sources, provisions are requested with the organized involvement of local authorities. In this way, the burden of supplying the army is equitably distributed across the population, which only the established officials of a region can effectively oversee and enforce.

The efficiency of this system, however, relies heavily on the time available. With sufficient time, the burden can be more evenly spread, minimizing strain on individuals and producing a more consistent and reliable supply. Moreover, given adequate time, the process can include purchases made directly with cash, which would make it even more akin to a system based on magazines or established supply depots. Within their own territories, armies can generally depend on structured requisitioning without issue, and this is often also the case during organized retreats. However, when advancing into enemy territories, time is often limited. In such instances, the army's advance guard typically has no more than a single day's lead to organize these requisitions, placing significant strain on the resources of the immediate vicinity.

The commissariat plays a crucial role here by carefully managing and distributing supplies to ensure troops with the most pressing needs receive what is available. As the army progresses, the situation typically becomes less strained, since each day's advance allows requisitioning from a broader area. For instance, if the first day's supplies cover a four-square-mile area, by the next day, the range might expand to sixteen square miles, and on the third, to thirty-six—illustrating how the radius for requisition can increase rapidly. While this growth model is idealized and subject to factors like regional supply variations, the general principle holds that with each additional day, the area and resources available increase significantly. Additionally, sometimes the requisition radius can expand even faster than anticipated, depending on the terrain and transportation options, possibly encompassing three or four miles daily or even more.

The enforcement of requisitions relies partly on military detachments and partly on the local population's fear of penalties, both of which encourage compliance. Though this is a high-level overview, the principle remains that, in general, even a large army with only a few days' worth of initial provisions can manage well enough through such organized contributions. Initially, these requisitions affect only the areas near the advancing forces, but with time, the system extends over larger distances with increasingly formal authority.

The primary constraint on this method is the eventual depletion and exhaustion of local resources, especially if the army remains in place for an extended period. When this happens, higher administrative officials may be appointed to organize requisitions, aiming to distribute the burden as fairly as possible and, at times, supplementing requisitions with purchases to ease the strain. Even an occupying army often moderates its demands as a prolonged presence necessitates a more sustainable approach. Over time, this requisition-based approach naturally begins to resemble a more organized magazine system, although it never entirely loses the dynamic impact it has on the conduct of the campaign. This is markedly different from an eighteenth-century army relying solely on self-supplied resources, where the host country was generally unaffected in terms of subsistence.

Two critical advantages come from this modern requisition system: the use of local transport resources and the local infrastructure, such as bakeries. This approach significantly reduces the reliance on an extensive military transport system, which, while essential, often hinders rather than aids army movement. Although military supplies like transport wagons are still necessary, the scale is much reduced, allowing troops to carry only minimal surplus supplies, generally no more than a day's worth of provisions.

Exceptional situations, like Napoleon's 1812 campaign in Russia, might force armies to carry vast supplies and even mobile field ovens, but these cases are rare. Such a scenario—an army of 300,000 men advancing over 130 miles on one primary route through sparsely populated and agrarian areas—is almost unique. In such cases, additional supply measures are a backup rather than the main supply line, with requisition from the country still serving as the primary basis for provision.

From the revolutionary wars onward, requisitions became central to French military strategy, which in turn compelled their adversaries to adopt similar measures. The benefits of this system—flexibility, simplicity, and reduced logistical strain—make it unlikely that it will ever be entirely abandoned. Through requisitioning, armies have achieved remarkable operational freedom, as long as they have some provisions initially and can later supplement these with magazines. Thus, logistical concerns rarely obstruct operations except in extreme situations, though the ease of requisitioning can still influence initial campaign planning.

One significant exception to this general rule is when an army is retreating through hostile territory. In such situations, logistical challenges increase dramatically. A retreat is typically a continuous, fast-moving operation with few pauses, leaving little time for proper requisitioning. The hostile environment and lack of friendly supply lines require the troops to remain compact, limiting the army's ability to spread out for foraging or requisitioning. Local resistance and hostility further complicate supply efforts, making it challenging to gather provisions without substantial military backing. As a result, armies in retreat often need to depend strictly on established supply lines and transportation routes prepared in advance.

Napoleon's retreat from Moscow in 1812 provides a case study of this difficulty. Constrained by the need to rely on his initial supply lines, he had no viable alternative but to retrace his path, as any other route would likely have resulted in faster depletion and greater losses. Criticisms that Napoleon should have chosen another path overlook the reality of these logistical constraints, underestimating the immense importance of reliable supply routes, especially in hostile territory.

4. Subsistence From Magazines.

To draw a general distinction between modern systems of army subsistence and the structured, centralized supply models of the late seventeenth and eighteenth centuries, we recognize that each approach aligns differently with the nature of warfare. An organized, magazine-based supply model could only feasibly return if armies were to remain in a single region for extended periods—seven, ten, or even twelve years, as once occurred in the Netherlands, the Rhine, Silesia, and Saxony. Few countries could sustain the ongoing burden of feeding large opposing forces indefinitely without risking complete exhaustion and ultimately becoming incapable of supporting either side's needs.

This leads us to an essential question: Should warfare adapt to the system of supply, or should the supply system adapt to the needs of warfare? The answer lies in a reciprocal influence: while subsistence methods indeed shape the form and pace of war, war itself will, in times of necessity, redefine and adapt its supply lines to meet operational demands. A campaign relying on requisitions and locally sourced supplies has undeniable advantages over one dependent solely on magazines. No state would dare field an army bound to the outdated, cumbersome magazine system against an enemy freely sourcing from the land. Even if a war minister attempted such a course, logistics would force the commander on the ground to adopt requisition-based supplies out of sheer practicality. The high costs of maintaining an extensive supply infrastructure would also limit a state's capacity to fund the actual fighting force, resulting in smaller armies and weaker combat strength—a trade-off unlikely to be accepted unless all parties agreed, which is a purely hypothetical notion.

Therefore, modern wars are expected to start with a requisition-based supply system. Supplementing it with an organized, centralized supply chain to ease strain on the home front may be desirable but would be limited to what is necessary, as strategic priorities will focus on immediate military needs rather than elaborate logistical arrangements. If a war's objectives are not as decisive or comprehensive, the requisition system can lead to the gradual depletion of local resources to the point where peace may become necessary. Alternatively, belligerents might implement supplementary methods to relieve local populations and avoid reliance solely on local provisions. This happened with Napoleon's forces in Spain, where local requisitions reached unsustainable levels, although such situations often drive governments to seek peace rather than continuing a prolonged conflict. Modern requisition systems thus tend to shorten wars by straining available resources, limiting prolonged conflict in most cases.

We cannot entirely dismiss the possibility of the old supply model reemerging under future circumstances where a prolonged conflict of attrition is anticipated, particularly if such methods serve both sides' strategic needs. However, such a system would remain abnormal, arising more from necessity than as a natural development in the art of war. This magazine-based system would not improve the humaneness of war—war itself is inherently destructive—and logistical systems only serve to sustain its course.

In practice, whatever method of subsistence is chosen, its implementation will vary according to the richness and population density of the theater of war. Population density has a dual impact on the availability of provisions. Larger populations not only create a greater demand, which tends to ensure consistent food stocks, but they also typically reflect areas of high productivity. Exceptions include manufacturing districts, especially those in mountainous regions with minimal agriculture, but generally, it is much easier to support armies in well-populated regions. An army of 100,000 cannot be sustained as effectively on 400 square miles with 400,000 people as it would be on the same area with 2,000,000 people, even assuming equal agricultural productivity.

Furthermore, richer countries typically have better infrastructure, which translates into more reliable and extensive roads, waterways, and transport options. These factors make it significantly easier to supply an army in a place like Flanders than in sparsely populated regions such as Poland. For this reason, war operations, seeking favorable conditions, tend to align along major roads, near large urban centers, in fertile river valleys, or along well-trafficked coastlines.

This preference underlines how subsistence concerns can shape the direction and scope of military operations, influencing the selection of a theater of war and the logistical paths along which armies move and sustain themselves.

The degree to which provisioning affects military operations depends largely on the nature and intended conduct of the campaign itself. If a war is to be fought with a relentless push toward engagement and decisive outcomes—where the core essence of warfare is a series of bold confrontations and maneuvers—then supply, while important, must remain a secondary concern. In contrast, if a state of equilibrium is intended, where armies linger and maneuver within the same theater over prolonged periods, then subsistence issues inevitably take precedence. In these scenarios, the logistics officer almost assumes the role of commander, and the war effort becomes dominated by a logistical machine focused on transportation, supply, and managing resources rather than on active combat.

History is replete with campaigns where the absence of decisive action was attributed to the complexities of supply, and this often became an excuse for prolonged inactivity. On the contrary, Napoleon's disregard for traditional supply limitations—famously declaring, "Let us not speak of provisions!"—stands in stark contrast. However, the Russian campaign demonstrated the dangers of this extreme approach. While the campaign's failure may not have been solely due to subsistence issues, the rapid attrition of Napoleon's forces on the advance, and their total collapse on retreat, are indisputably linked to a breakdown in supply.

Despite his gamble on logistics, Napoleon and the revolutionary generals who preceded him demonstrated that subsistence should not control the campaign but rather serve as one of its conditional elements. The hardships of warfare—be it supply shortages, physical exhaustion, or exposure to peril—are, within limits, factors that an iron-willed general can demand of his troops. The resilience of an army varies; some can endure privation for longer, buoyed by morale, loyalty to their commander, or patriotism. Nevertheless, enduring hardship in the field should ideally be followed by a period of relief, so that scarcity is only a transitional phase, eventually giving way to sufficient, or even ample, supply. The image of soldiers burdened by heavy packs, trudging through all manner of weather, constantly risking life and health, yet often without enough to eat, underlines the extreme demands of war on human endurance.

Leaders who demand sacrifice from their troops must recognize, if not out of empathy then at least for strategic prudence, that such sacrifices warrant compensation. For an army's morale and effectiveness, periods of hardship should be followed by relief whenever possible.

The question of supply also varies based on whether the campaign is offensive or defensive. The defender can draw from stockpiled provisions as long as they remain in control of the territory. Particularly in their homeland, but even in an enemy's territory, the defender is generally able to sustain themselves better. On the other hand, the attacker moves away from their base of supply, relying increasingly on resources from captured territory as they advance. This often entails significant challenges, especially during the initial phases of the advance and in the critical weeks before any decisive battle when supplies may lag behind or become insufficient just as troops prepare to engage.

Two critical points of scarcity for an advancing force typically arise: the first is in the preparatory stages before the decisive engagement, when the defender has accessible supply depots nearby, while the assailant may be forced to forego supplies for several days. This shortage, especially just before a decisive engagement, is far from ideal. The second critical moment occurs at the conclusion of a victorious advance, when supply lines may have grown perilously long. This situation worsens in sparsely populated or impoverished regions, particularly when local populations are hostile. A supply line stretching from Wilna to Moscow, where provisions and transport must be requisitioned by force, is incomparably more vulnerable than a line from

Cologne to Paris, where contracts and payments can reliably secure needed resources. Numerous victories have been dimmed by such logistical difficulties, compelling victorious forces to retreat and ultimately weakening them to the point of apparent defeat.

Forage, initially less problematic, can soon become scarce as a campaign progresses, since it is difficult to transport over long distances due to its bulk. Horses, far less resilient than men when deprived of sustenance, will show signs of weakness quickly under insufficient feeding. Therefore, having an excessively large cavalry or artillery contingent can become a liability rather than an asset, as the logistical burden of feeding and maintaining such forces can become unsustainable in resource-depleted areas.

Chapter XV. Base of Operations

When an army embarks on an expedition—whether to engage the enemy within their territory or to secure its own frontier—it must remain connected to the sources of its supplies and reinforcements, as these are critical to its operational viability and survival. This connection to supply lines grows in importance with the size of the force, as larger armies require greater resources. However, it's not always necessary for an army to maintain direct contact with the entirety of its homeland; connection to the immediate territory in its rear is generally sufficient. This area, protected by the army's position, becomes essential, hosting depots and infrastructure to supply the forward force with food, reinforcements, and essential materials. Thus, this supporting territory forms the foundation of the army's operations, creating a unified strategic entity where both territory and military effort are mutually reinforcing.

If provisions are stored in fortified positions for added security, this strengthens the concept of a "base," but such fortification is not always necessary, nor does the idea of a base rely upon it. In certain cases, the base itself may extend into occupied portions of the enemy's land. In these instances, an occupying force might source some of its needs locally, but this is only feasible when complete control over the area is established—meaning the local population respects or is subdued by garrisons and mobile patrols. Even under these conditions, the occupied territory rarely supplies all the necessities, especially given the limited geographic reach of small detachments. Consequently, even when partially relying on captured enemy territory, an army still depends heavily on its own land for sustained support, underscoring the continued strategic value of the immediate territory behind its position.

The needs of an army can be categorized broadly: those that any developed country can provide, like food, and those that require specialized resources unique to the army's homeland, like troops, weapons, and certain war munitions. While provisions might be sourced from enemy territory if sufficiently under control, replenishing troops and obtaining critical equipment usually necessitates continued access to the home country. Although there may be rare exceptions, this division remains significant, emphasizing the necessity of secure communications with friendly territory.

Supply depots, particularly for food and forage, are generally placed in accessible towns within both friendly and enemy lands. Limited fortifications necessitate flexibility, as consumables are in constant demand across various locations, and any losses in these depots are relatively easy to replace. In contrast, critical resources that "complete" an army—such as weapons, ammunition, and specialized equipment—are less expendable and thus seldom stored in unsecured areas near active theaters, and in enemy territory, they are kept exclusively within fortresses whenever possible. This distinction further highlights that a base is far more crucial for irreplaceable supplies than for food, which can often be obtained more locally.

The larger the supply reserves that are gathered in central depots before distribution, the more these stockpiles take on the role of the primary logistical foundation for the army, almost functioning as extensions of the home territory. However, even when supply depots become critical hubs, no single depot should be seen as the entirety of an army's base. When these depots are well-stocked, securely positioned, and in close proximity to the army with accessible routes, they allow for greater flexibility and mobility, enhancing the force's operational vitality. Efforts have been made to simplify the value of this arrangement by using the concept of a "base of operations" and reducing its complexity to geometric representations, such as the base's width and its angle relative to a hypothetical point of strategic importance. However, this geometrical simplification lacks practical application because it overlooks the real, nuanced dependencies and overlapping functions of different supply areas.

The base of operations for an army is best understood as a three-fold combination: the nearby country that offers resources, the designated depots, and the larger territory from which supplies are drawn. These elements, spread out over varying distances, cannot be fully represented by a single line or simplified model. Their contribution and function will differ significantly depending on the availability of local resources, the state of infrastructure, and the types of resources needed. For example, a surrounding countryside might provide ample food, reducing reliance on distant depots, whereas in other cases, even essentials like provisions must come from far away. Fortified areas might serve as substantial arsenals or just weak defensive outposts with little logistical value, varying from one location to another.

These complexities mean that any rule of thumb based solely on the dimensions or angles of a base fails in real-world application, leading instead to misunderstandings in theoretical studies. While the idea of a base is critical to strategy, it requires a comprehensive assessment rather than a reduction to abstract principles. Once a region is designated as a logistical base, sustaining an army's needs and allowing it to conduct operations in a specific direction, altering this base becomes labor-intensive and time-consuming, especially as supply chains lengthen. Even within the home country, an army cannot change its base at will; instead, it operates within the confines of pre-existing logistical networks. In an enemy's country, the entire border might theoretically serve as a base, but practically, only those areas with prior logistical preparation provide true support.

For instance, during the Russian retreat from Napoleon in 1812, the entire expanse of Russia could be viewed as the Russian army's base, offering abundant land for maneuver. However, at any given moment, the actual base was confined to the routes along which supplies and transport flowed. This limitation restricted the Russian forces from veering off to other routes, such as retreating toward Kaluga rather than Moscow, without extensive preparation beforehand.

The dependence on a base becomes more critical as the size of an army grows, much like a tree rooted in the earth. A smaller force can shift locations with ease, adapting to new surroundings; in contrast, a larger army cannot. Larger forces develop deep logistical "roots" in their supply lines, making them harder to move and increasingly reliant on the established base. When discussing the influence of the base, the size of the army must always be considered, as it determines the extent and impact of logistical needs on strategic choices.

It follows logically that while a reliable supply for immediate needs is vital, sustaining an army's overall capability over time depends more on access to reinforcements and resources for refitting and replenishing equipment. This ongoing maintenance and reinforcement demand is much harder to meet than daily provisions, as it requires specific supply lines and organized sources, unlike the basic subsistence that can often be procured locally. This focus underscores the fundamental role of a base in supporting an army's prolonged effectiveness, especially when logistics must align with strategic objectives across an extended period.

Nevertheless, although the base has a profound influence, it exerts its full effect only over time. This influence often unfolds gradually, impacting the overall campaign's outcome more as the duration extends. Consequently, when planning an operation, the immediate value of a base rarely dictates whether to pursue a particular objective right from the start. The practical obstacles presented by base limitations must be evaluated alongside other operational factors, including the army's readiness and the potential for decisive engagements that could shift the campaign dynamics entirely. In many cases, the obstacles posed by a challenging base of operations can be mitigated or even neutralized through a series of successful engagements that decisively influence the course of the campaign, ultimately allowing the army to operate effectively even in less than ideal logistical circumstances.

Chapter XVI. Lines of Communication

The routes connecting an army's position with its rear supply bases, reinforcements, and resources serve two crucial functions: they are both lines of communication for sustaining the army's operational needs and lines of retreat in cases of withdrawal. As previously noted, while modern armies often rely on resources from the areas they occupy, they still remain integrated with their bases. These connecting routes—vital lines of supply, communication, and support—are akin to an army's lifeblood, channeling everything from essential supplies and ammunition to administrative support, all of which hold immense value for an effective military presence.

The integrity and functionality of these routes are essential to an army's vitality; interruptions or excessive length can drain its strength over time, impacting operational efficiency. When these routes also double as potential retreat paths, they constitute the army's strategic rear, adding to their significance.

The value of these lines depends on various factors: length, number, general and specific direction relative to the army, quality of the roads, local terrain challenges, the attitude and loyalty of local populations, and the level of protection offered by fortresses or natural obstacles along the way. But not all roads leading back to the army's support base automatically serve as genuine communication lines. True lines of communication are specially prepared and secured: they include magazines, medical stations, designated posts for dispatches, and are managed by stationed commandants with garrisoned forces for protection.

Here, a stark contrast between operations in friendly and hostile territories becomes apparent—often underestimated in its impact. When operating in friendly terrain, an army is not strictly confined to its initially chosen supply lines; it can switch routes if necessary, as the army enjoys administrative support, access to resources, and favorable attitudes from local populations. Even if the alternative routes are less optimal, they remain viable options, particularly in cases where the army's direction must shift due to a strategic maneuver.

In contrast, an army operating within enemy territory usually relies solely on the routes along which it has advanced. Attempting to establish a new line of communication in hostile terrain introduces various complications. In enemy territory, the army imposes its logistical structure as it moves forward, leaving small garrisons to oversee these newly established lines and relying on the local population to cooperate. The presence of an enemy army often compels inhabitants to comply, seeing the arrangement as inevitable. However, creating new lines on alternate roads where the army's presence is less visible typically stirs resistance from the local population, who may view this as an imposed burden rather than a necessity.

If new routes are needed in hostile land, enforcing compliance requires strong garrisons to maintain order and suppress potential uprisings, making these routes vulnerable without substantial military support. The likelihood of rebellion against such measures is high unless previous decisive victories have already instilled a profound sense of caution among the inhabitants. Therefore, an army advancing into enemy land lacks the preexisting administrative mechanisms for maintaining compliance, which means that establishing effective logistical lines demands considerable effort, security measures, and time. Such operations often require significant sacrifices, making a change in the system of communications in enemy territory both difficult and costly. Consequently, an army in enemy land faces greater movement constraints and heightened vulnerability to any threats aimed at its communications, which limits its strategic flexibility compared to operations in familiar, friendly territory.

The selection and organization of an army's lines of communication from the outset are limited by multiple factors that shape their effectiveness. These lines must be solid, reliable main roads that are ideally wide and lead through densely populated, economically thriving towns with infrastructure capable of supporting the army's needs. The presence of strongholds or fortified locations along these routes offers protective advantages, while rivers, where available, provide essential water routes that complement and reinforce these lines. Bridges are also critical for crossing obstacles and ensuring the free movement of troops and supplies. Consequently, an army's choice of a communication line—and therefore the route chosen for initiating an offensive—remains only partially flexible, influenced heavily by the geographic layout and existing infrastructure.

Together, these factors determine the resilience or vulnerability of an army's communication with its base. When weighed against the enemy's communication structure, these factors help identify which side has the strategic advantage to disrupt the other's lines or potentially isolate them from retreat. This ability to "turn" the opponent hinges largely on the relative strength of each army's communications. Without this advantage, an adversary could counter quickly, nullifying any attempt to disrupt.

The objective behind turning the enemy can follow two general paths: either to compromise and weaken their communication lines so that they gradually diminish in strength, thereby compelling retreat, or to sever their retreat options entirely. For the first approach, a single, fleeting disruption seldom inflicts meaningful damage. Modern armies, sustained by various dispersed supply methods, are unlikely to be seriously impacted by the occasional loss of a single supply convoy. A lone attack on the enemy's flank would have proven critical in times when supplies were conveyed in large, organized convoys, but today, such an attempt would merely cause minor inconvenience unless the disruption were consistent and prolonged, especially on extensive, vulnerable lines exposed to insurgent attacks.

When attempting to cut off the enemy's retreat outright, expectations should be realistic; as recent conflicts have demonstrated, well-led and resilient troops are far more likely to break through an opposing force than to surrender when faced with a blocked retreat. This reflects the often-overlooked resilience of an organized force, even when escape routes are compromised.

There are few effective ways to manage the challenges of long communication lines, but several measures may mitigate their risks. Securing nearby fortresses or constructing temporary defensive positions along key points, cultivating a cooperative relationship with local populations, enforcing strict discipline on these routes, maintaining a well-functioning police presence, and improving the condition of roads are essential actions. Yet, while these measures can ease the burdens of lengthy communication lines, they cannot eliminate the challenges altogether.

The factors that apply to general logistics also extend specifically to lines of communication. The most advantageous lines of communication are those traversing prosperous towns and key provinces, even if they result in a longer route. Such routes, though lengthier, are preferable due to their stronger logistical support. They tend to exert a significant influence on where and how the army ultimately organizes and deploys itself for operations.

Chapter XVII. On Country and Ground

Beyond its influence on sustaining an army, the land itself—its topography, vegetation, and human-made features—plays an intrinsic and often decisive role in warfare, shaping battles both in terms of their immediate progress and their longer-term strategic outcomes. The French term terrain captures this broader concept, which we will now explore. Although much of this relates to tactics, as it encompasses the skillful use of the land during battle, the outcomes it produces are inherently strategic. A battle fought in mountainous terrain, for instance, differs drastically from one on flat plains in its conduct and potential consequences.

For a comprehensive understanding, however, we must first examine the broader differences between offensive and defensive warfare before analyzing how specific terrain features shape their effectiveness. For now, we'll consider the general characteristics of terrain that influence military actions. The land impacts warfare through three primary qualities: as an obstacle to movement, a hindrance to visibility, and as a source of cover against enemy fire. Every other effect stems from one of these three.

This triad of influence complicates warfare, introducing additional factors into military calculations, enriching its variety, and elevating its complexity. Truly open, flat land—void of any significant features—is exceedingly rare and, in practice, only temporarily relevant for small groups of troops or brief engagements. For larger forces or extended operations, the natural and human-modified landscape becomes an ever-present factor, influencing every aspect of the battle, particularly in moments of critical engagement.

The impact of terrain is thus inescapable, yet it varies in strength depending on the type of land. Broadly speaking, countries diverge from a perfectly level plain in three principal ways: by natural landforms, such as hills and valleys; by natural features, including woods, marshes, and lakes; and by modifications from human cultivation. Each introduces an added layer of complexity to military maneuvers and tactics. Following these categories to their extremes, we find mountainous regions, heavily forested or marshy areas, and regions highly shaped by agriculture. Each setting adds to the intricacy and the demands on military skill.

The degree to which agriculture impacts warfare varies by the cultivation style. In regions like Flanders or Holstein, for example, the landscape is heavily compartmentalized by ditches, hedges, dikes, walls, scattered homes, and patches of forest—conditions that pose distinct challenges to military operations. In contrast, an open, moderately cultivated plain presents fewer obstacles, creating more favorable conditions for the movement of troops, though this is a generalization that doesn't consider how defenders can exploit even slight terrain features to their advantage.

Each of these three types of terrain affects movement, visibility, and cover in unique ways.

In densely forested areas, the obstruction of sight is the dominant challenge. Thick woods make large portions of land nearly impassable for large-scale movements, and even when accessible, the limited visibility complicates efforts to clear paths effectively. This landscape has the effect of simplifying tactics for one side while amplifying operational challenges for the other. Although concentrating forces for a concerted action is challenging in such an environment, the fragmentation of forces is generally less pronounced than it would be in a mountainous region or a terrain heavily cut by rivers, canals, and other barriers. In this way, forests tend to impose a necessary separation of forces, but not to an extreme extent.

In contrast, mountainous terrain imposes movement obstacles in two critical ways: there are parts that are entirely impassable, and areas that are passable only with slowed and more strenuous efforts. This leads to significantly reduced movement speed and inserts a greater element of time into every operation. Another unique feature of mountains is that specific points of higher ground can command areas below, an attribute that we will examine further in the next chapter. This strategic characteristic elevates the significance of certain positions not only for their intrinsic worth but also for the influence they exert over surrounding areas. Such importance assigned to commanding points in mountainous regions results in a higher degree of force fragmentation, as individual positions become essential.

As noted earlier, each type of terrain, in proportion to its defining features, tends to limit the influence of centralized command and shift more responsibility onto subordinate leaders, down to the individual soldiers. This decentralization arises naturally as the level of fragmentation increases; the more divided the forces are, the less feasible it is to maintain undivided control, compelling subordinates to act independently. While this allows for greater initiative and responsiveness at lower command levels, it also requires a shift in the way outcomes are assessed. In warfare, it is ultimately the accumulation of individual results that carries weight, often more than the specific methods that connect these outcomes. If we imagine an entire army stretched into skirmishing lines, with each soldier effectively fighting his own miniature engagement, the collective success hinges on these individual victories rather than their coordination. Under these conditions, the courage, skill, and resolve of individual soldiers become critical factors in determining the outcome.

It is only when both sides have achieved a comparable level of quality in training, skill, and other military characteristics that the tactical acumen and decision-making ability of a commander once again become decisive. This implies that in challenging or fragmented terrain, forces with high individual morale, such as national armies or insurgent militias, may gain an advantage. Even if these forces lack superior training or organization, the nature of the terrain allows them to leverage their dispersed formations and local knowledge effectively. Such forces often rely on this dispersed strategy to maintain their position, as they usually lack the cohesion and discipline needed for coordinated large-scale actions.

The spectrum of military capability ranges between these extremes, and even regular standing armies, particularly those defending their homeland, can take on qualities similar to a national or local militia. This alignment with the local defense often grants them an added advantage in conducting a dispersed, decentralized form of warfare, which is naturally suited to the demands of a fragmented, obstacle-rich environment.

When an army lacks certain inherent qualities or advantages and faces an opponent possessing these strengths, the inclination to keep forces together in concentrated masses becomes even stronger, while the risks of operating in dispersed formations are increasingly avoided. This preference is particularly heightened in challenging terrains where fragmented positioning is risky. However, avoiding such difficult terrains isn't often a choice left to armies; unlike selecting from multiple options in a marketplace, an army typically must contend with the natural features of its theater of war. Armies that gain the upper hand in cohesive, concentrated formations may go to great lengths to adapt their strategies to preserve this structure, even when it conflicts with the landscape. The outcomes are other logistical and strategic hurdles: inadequate subsistence, challenging quarters, and vulnerability to attacks from various directions. Yet, the decision to forgo the advantages of concentrated force coordination would lead to even greater drawbacks.

These opposing strategies—the impulse toward concentrating forces versus the need for dispersion—are typically influenced by the specific nature of the forces involved, with each side adapting more toward one strategy or the other. However, no side can operate solely on either extreme. Even an army benefiting from concentrated formations may at times need to disperse, and forces oriented around a dispersed approach must occasionally gather for major engagements. For instance, the French in Spain had to partition their forces, even as the Spanish insurgents, defending their homeland, were at times compelled to meet the French in large-scale, open battles despite their preference for irregular resistance.

Beyond these general strategic inclinations shaped by the terrain, another critical factor is the composition of the three military arms: infantry, cavalry, and artillery. In terrains dense with obstacles like mountains, forests, or other impeding features, large cavalry forces lose much of their effectiveness due to limited maneuverability. Artillery faces similar limitations in wooded regions, where restricted space, limited transport paths, and scarce forage for horses make its deployment difficult. Highly cultivated regions are somewhat less obstructive to artillery, with mountainous terrain proving least restrictive. While both mountainous and cultivated regions offer some protection from artillery fire and can enable enemy infantry to endanger heavy artillery, they don't typically lack sufficient space for deploying artillery forces. In mountainous areas, artillery even has an advantage since the slowed pace of enemy movements enhances the impact of artillery fire.

Yet, despite these nuances, infantry retains a distinct edge over the other arms in rugged terrain, making it sensible to field larger numbers of infantry in such conditions. Where obstacles reduce cavalry's advantage and inhibit artillery deployment, infantry's flexibility and adaptability stand out, positioning it as the most strategically advantageous arm in challenging landscapes.

Chapter XVIII. Command of Ground

The term "command" holds a distinct allure in military strategy, capturing a significant part—arguably half—of the effect terrain has on troop deployment. Many revered principles of military knowledge are rooted in this idea: commanding positions, key locations, strategic maneuvers, and more. To clarify this concept without unnecessary detail, we will examine its core components, distinguishing between genuine tactical advantage and overstatement.

In any exertion of physical effort, an upward movement is inherently more challenging than a downward one, which also applies in battle for three clear reasons. First, any elevation creates an obstacle for those moving up toward it. Second, although shooting downward does not significantly extend one's range, geometry still favors those firing from above, enhancing accuracy slightly. Third, height provides a broader field of view. All these factors contribute to the tactical advantage gained from higher ground, combining to form what we regard as its primary strategic benefit.

However, the first and third of these advantages reappear directly within strategy itself since both marching and reconnaissance gain from a higher vantage. Thus, in a strategic context, a higher position is challenging for opponents to approach, which serves as the second advantage. The superior visibility from an elevated spot, allowing for broader reconnaissance, is the third strategic benefit.

These elements combined create the power to dominate, survey, and command. Standing atop a hill, looking down on the enemy, often produces a psychological edge: a sense of superiority and confidence, while those below may feel vulnerable. This impression can often surpass the actual tactical reality because the elevation advantage is immediate and visceral, while mitigating factors—such as terrain obstacles or strategic context—are less apparent. Here, imagination becomes an element, amplifying the perceived benefit of the height advantage.

It's also worth noting that the ease of movement on higher ground is not a constant benefit; it only serves the side defending from above, as they hold their position. If both sides prefer to fight on level ground, this advantage can disappear or even favor the lower position, as in the Battle of Hohenfriedberg. Furthermore, the advantage of visibility is not without its constraints; wooded valleys and the mountain's own structure can obscure sightlines. Many times, anticipated advantages of height seen on maps are difficult to realize on the ground, and elevated positions can unexpectedly turn into liabilities rather than assets.

Nonetheless, these constraints do not negate the intrinsic superiority that elevated ground grants both to defensive and offensive strategies. To sum up these strategic advantages of higher ground—greater tactical strength, a more challenging approach for the enemy, and improved visibility—the first two benefits are predominantly defensive, as they can only be exploited by holding a position. However, the third advantage—the command of view—is equally valuable for offensive movements as it allows for superior reconnaissance, benefiting both sides in a campaign.

From this, we understand that elevated ground holds notable significance for the defensive, and because such terrain can only be firmly held in mountainous regions, it might seem that the defensive would inherently gain an important advantage from mountain positions. However, as we will discuss further in the chapter on mountain defense, various factors influence why this advantage is not as straightforward in practice.

It's essential first to clarify whether we're considering elevated ground as a single, isolated position—such as an advantageous site for an army. In such cases, the strategic advantages largely condense into tactical benefits that favor the outcome of a single battle. But if we extend this idea across a broader landscape, such as a province sloping gradually like the descent of a watershed, then elevated ground takes on a much broader strategic value. This configuration allows forces to hold the upper ground over multiple marches, giving the defensive side an advantage not just for isolated encounters but in coordinating multiple engagements across a larger campaign.

For the offensive, elevated ground also provides some of the same strategic benefits, because strategic offensives unfold over a series of separate actions rather than a single, uninterrupted sequence like a machine in motion. With each pause, an attacking force temporarily assumes a defensive stance, making elevated ground advantageous for both sides as they prepare or consolidate between movements.

Additionally, the broader view provided by an elevated position benefits both the defensive and offensive by enabling more effective use of separated units. Each detachment can leverage the vantage point, becoming stronger as it gains better awareness and control of its immediate surroundings. This allows forces to establish positions with less risk, a subject to be addressed more fully in discussions on the use of dispersed units.

If elevated ground is further complemented by other geographic advantages, the strategic benefit increases. For example, if the enemy is already constrained in movement due to other factors—such as the presence of a major river nearby—these combined disadvantages can become critical, forcing the enemy into a position they must escape quickly. No army can effectively hold a valley if it lacks control of the surrounding high ground that defines it.

The control of elevated terrain may indeed hold substantial strategic significance, almost amounting to dominance, and there is a reality to this notion. However, terms like "commanding ground," "sheltering position," and "key of the country"—when solely based on the physical aspects of heights and slopes—are often superficial labels lacking true substance. These grand terms are commonly invoked to lend a sense of importance to basic military maneuvers; they've become favored topics for scholars of strategy and the celebrated touchstones of seasoned tacticians. Despite numerous examples in which experience has disproven the weight of such concepts, they persist in military literature and the minds of those who consume it, much like trying to fill a sieve with water.

In these cases, the conditions that facilitate success are mistaken for the essence of power itself; the terrain is viewed as if it inherently holds sway, like an active gesture or a powerful blow. However, the ground or position is more akin to a passive tool, lifeless without the force applied by the one who holds it. It serves as an addition or a subtracted influence but only takes on meaning when put into effect with decisive action, like a victorious battle. Such a victory is the true measure; it is the outcome that matters and the element that should always be the focus whether in the critique of theoretical works or in practical engagements on the field.

Thus, if the essence of war lies in the count and value of successful battles, it follows that the comparative strength of the armies involved and the skill of their commanders are the primary considerations. The influence of the terrain, however useful, can only ever play a supporting role in the hierarchy of war's determining factors.

Book VI. Defence

Chapter I. Offence and Defence

1. Conception of Defence.

What is the essence of defense? It is the act of warding off an attack. And what, then, is its defining characteristic? It is the state of readiness or expectation, awaiting the enemy's strike. This is the feature that distinguishes an action as defensive, setting it apart from offense. However, since pure defense would contradict the nature of war itself—implying only one side engages in battle—defense in war is inherently relative. Thus, this characteristic of expectation applies only to the overall concept, not to each specific action within a conflict.

A skirmish is defensive if we await the enemy's assault, a battle is defensive if we stand ready in our position, prepared for the enemy to approach and engage us within range, and a campaign is defensive if we wait for the enemy to enter our theater of operations. In all these scenarios, the principle of waiting and repelling the attack remains central, without clashing with the purpose of war. Waiting for the enemy to close in on our position, for example, may be to our advantage, providing a strategic edge. Yet, in order to actively participate in the conflict and avoid mere passivity, defense must incorporate a degree of offense, which is often done within the context of the chosen position or theater.

Thus, in a defensive campaign, we may still undertake offensive maneuvers; in a defensive battle, we may deploy certain divisions for offensive actions; and while we hold a position in anticipation of the enemy's assault, we still engage offensively by firing upon them as they approach. Defensive warfare, then, is not a static shield; it is a shield formed by strikes delivered with purpose and precision.

2. Advantages of The Defensive.

The goal of defense is to preserve. Preservation, by its nature, is less challenging than acquisition. This principle immediately implies that, assuming both sides have equal means, defense is inherently easier than offense. But what gives defense this comparative ease? Primarily, it's the fact that any time not actively used by the attacker works to the defender's advantage. The defender can benefit passively; every pause in the attacker's action—whether due to indecision, caution, or delay—tilts the balance in favor of the defense. This advantage notably saved Prussia from destruction multiple times in the Seven Years' War. It is a principle rooted in the fundamental nature of defense, much like in legal matters where the saying goes, Beati sunt possidentes—blessed are those who hold.

Additionally, defense benefits from a second advantage unique to warfare: the strategic use of terrain. Defense can leverage the ground to a degree that offense cannot easily match.

With these foundational ideas in mind, we can examine defense more closely. In tactics, a fight is deemed defensive if we cede the initiative to the enemy and await their approach. Once they advance, we can deploy offensive maneuvers without forfeiting the two core advantages of defense: the advantage of waiting and of controlling the ground. In strategy, the structure is broader: a campaign resembles a single battle, and the theater of war is akin to a defensive position. As campaigns continue, the entire war can be viewed in similar terms, with the defending territory itself becoming the defensive position. Across these different scopes, the essential character of defense remains the same.

The assertion that defense is easier than offense aligns with this broader perspective, but it's more precise to say that defense has a stronger form because it aims at preserving while offense seeks conquest. Conquest is inherently a positive goal and bolsters the attacker's resources and position; preservation, while critical, is more about maintaining the status quo. To put it plainly, the defensive form of war is inherently stronger than the offensive. This insight, while straightforward and supported by extensive experience, is often misunderstood—an example of how common opinions can stray under superficial interpretation.

Since defense is the stronger approach but focuses on preservation rather than gain, it follows naturally that it should be adopted only when weakness compels it and abandoned as soon as strength allows for an offensive turn. In the aftermath of victory, when defense has fortified the defender's position, a transition to offense is the logical progression. Thus, beginning with defense and shifting to offense is a natural flow in warfare. To assume defense as the ultimate goal of a conflict would be as contradictory to the nature of war as viewing defense as wholly passive. A war solely focused on repelling attacks without any intent to strike back would be as nonsensical as a battle fought entirely in passive defense without any active countermeasures.

Many instances might be cited that seem to challenge this general idea, examples where the defensive approach persisted to the end without any intent of shifting to the offensive. However, such objections miss the key point: we're discussing general principles (abstract ideas), and examples that appear contrary merely illustrate situations where the conditions for an offensive response had not yet matured.

Consider Frederick the Great in the final three years of the Seven Years' War. He did not actively seek to turn to offense; indeed, it seems that even when he did act offensively, it was primarily as a strategic means of securing his defensive position. His circumstances dictated this approach, as he naturally pursued strategies that best suited his current situation. Yet, one can hardly study this large-scale defensive strategy without sensing that the potential for a counter-offensive against Austria lingered behind his defensive measures, awaiting the right moment—a moment that ultimately never arrived before the war's conclusion. The peace settlement itself hints at this underlying potential. What likely pushed the Austrians to make peace was not the lack of a defensive option but rather the realization that without consistent external support, their strength alone could not balance Frederick's tactical skill. Their awareness that any weakening of their efforts might cost them dearly in lost territory made peace the sensible choice. And who can doubt that if Russia, Sweden, and the Imperial forces had ceased to collaborate against Frederick, he would have seized the opportunity to reclaim Austrian territory in Bohemia and Moravia?

With this understanding of defense clarified and its scope defined, we return to the point that defense is the stronger form of waging war. A closer comparison of offense and defense readily reveals this. For now, let's consider the inherent contradictions we'd face if we claimed otherwise. If offense were indeed the stronger form, there would be little need ever to adopt a defensive stance, as the defensive has only a negative goal. Under such a premise, everyone would default to attack, rendering defense almost nonsensical. However, pursuing the loftier objective often requires more substantial sacrifices. One who possesses sufficient strength may opt for the offensive to achieve greater gains, while one who seeks a more limited objective may choose the defensive for the added security it offers.

From experience, we never see a force fighting offensively on one front with its weaker contingent while committing its strongest resources to a purely defensive stance elsewhere. The opposite has been the norm, consistently indicating that while generals are often drawn to offensive tactics, they inherently view the defensive as the stronger form. In upcoming chapters, we'll examine further foundational aspects of this view.

Chapter II. The Relations of the Offensive and Defensive to Each Other in Tactics

To begin, let's examine the fundamental elements that lead to victory in battle. Setting aside factors such as the sheer number of troops, bravery, discipline, or the specific qualities of an army—considerations that don't directly fall under the art of war as we're treating it here, as they equally affect both offense and defense—we focus instead on three decisive elements: surprise, advantageous terrain, and the ability to attack from multiple directions.

Surprise, a powerful strategy, works by overwhelming the enemy at a particular point with significantly more forces than anticipated. This local superiority in numbers differs from general numerical superiority and represents one of the most impactful maneuvers in warfare. Advantageous terrain contributes to victory by offering both obstructive features, such as steep elevations, water obstacles, or thick hedges, and natural cover that can conceal troop movements. Furthermore, even seemingly unremarkable terrain can offer strategic assistance when navigated by those familiar with the landscape. The ability to strike from multiple directions, encompassing various tactical turning movements, enhances both firepower and the enemy's psychological fear of encirclement or having their retreat cut off.

Considering the offensive and defensive positions in relation to these elements, the situation becomes clear. In terms of victory, only parts of surprise and envelopment favor the offensive, while the bulk of these elements, especially terrain advantage, typically lie with the defensive side. The offense can only rely on a single overall surprise maneuver with its entire force, whereas the defense is better positioned to orchestrate continual surprises throughout the engagement by maneuvering in response to the attacker's movements.

While the offensive may possess an initial advantage in attempting to encircle or cut off the enemy, given that the defense is relatively fixed, this advantage mainly applies to movements against the whole opposing force. In the course of battle, however, the defensive position allows for smaller, more flexible envelopment maneuvers due to a stronger element of surprise and strategic responses. Additionally, terrain generally aids the defense, offering a chance to hide positions and strike at an opportune moment, an advantage the offensive rarely enjoys, as it must move along visible routes, often under observation.

Historically, reconnaissance missions were considered essential to gather intelligence on the enemy's position. However, with modern defensive techniques, reconnaissance has become less effective, as well-prepared defenses remain concealed until the decisive moment. This advancement reflects a broader shift away from the older concept of passive defense, where ground-based obstacles (steep slopes, etc.) dominated strategies. In earlier times, defensive lines, often spread thin and anchored between points of support, relied heavily on natural obstacles. This setup made flexible movement and surprise during the battle difficult, even unfeasible—a sharp contrast to modern defensive principles, which have incorporated increased adaptability and tactical surprise.

Historically, the ebb and flow of defensive strategies mirrored broader developments in military tactics. Early wars, such as the Thirty Years' War or the War of the Spanish Succession, prioritized the alignment of troops, giving an advantage to the defense. As troops' maneuverability improved, the offensive briefly gained the upper hand until the defense adapted by using challenging terrain for cover. Eventually, offensive forces, with improved mobility, learned to maneuver within such terrain, deploying columns to flank and weaken the defensive line. In response, the defense developed a new approach: concentrating forces in larger, concealed masses rather than thinly deployed lines, allowing for adaptability to the offensive's movements while still holding advantageous ground when possible.

This does not mean passive defense has vanished; ground-based defensive advantages are still essential, often invoked during campaigns. But in the modern context, a completely static defense of terrain is no longer the dominant approach.

Should the offensive one day uncover a novel advantage—a possibility, though unlikely given the refined simplicity of modern warfare—the defense would again need to adapt. For now, the defense benefits from the persistent advantages offered by terrain, giving it a natural strength, particularly as the varied properties of landscape have a greater than ever impact on warfare itself.

Chapter III. The Relations of the Offensive and Defensive to Each Other in Strategy

To understand the essence of strategic success, we must first clarify the unique circumstances that lead to successful outcomes in strategy. Unlike in tactics, strategy does not result in direct "victory" on the battlefield. Instead, strategic success manifests in two primary ways: first, as effective preparation that makes tactical victory more probable; the greater the strategic setup, the higher the likelihood of battlefield success. Second, strategic success lies in capitalizing on that tactical victory once achieved, amplifying the effects beyond the battle itself.

The measure of strategic success depends on how thoroughly the battle's outcome can be integrated into subsequent operations. In essence, it is about how effectively strategy can exploit a single victory to impact the larger campaign. This exploitation means converting the disarray and disruption wrought by a successful battle into lasting strategic gains. Strategy, in its optimal form, gathers what the effort of many hands has won on the battlefield, sweeping these gains into large, coherent results.

Key factors that drive such successful strategic outcomes, and the main principles that underlie effective strategic action, are as follows:

1. Effective use of terrain and natural advantages of ground.
2. The element of surprise, whether achieved through an unexpected attack or by suddenly concentrating large forces at critical points.
3. Coordinated attacks from multiple directions, enhancing pressure and disrupting the enemy's cohesion.
4. Strategic support from the theater of war, particularly through fortresses and their affiliated resources.
5. The backing and engagement of the local populace, offering logistical support and morale.

6. Harnessing significant moral forces, including the collective will, spirit, and determination of the forces involved.

Each of these elements, when skillfully applied, strengthens the strategic framework and amplifies the overall impact of military efforts.

The relative advantages of offensive and defensive positions depend on several factors. In terms of ground, the defensive side generally has the benefit, able to choose fortified or advantageous positions. Conversely, the offensive gains through strategic surprise, much as in tactics, though with a heightened impact in strategy. A strategic surprise, unlike tactical, often holds the power to end a conflict quickly. However, effective surprise in strategy also hinges on a significant, unusual error by the adversary, limiting its advantage as a standard tool for the offensive.

Positioning forces at key points offers another potential advantage, paralleling the tactical concentration of forces. If the defender must spread out along multiple entry routes to guard a region, the attacker can exploit this by striking heavily at a single point. Yet, modern defensive strategies have evolved to counter this. Unless defending vital assets like depots, fortifications, or even the capital, the defensive force is often free to await the attacker's approach. Additionally, should the attacker choose a different route, the defender can usually redirect their forces to meet the attacker on that chosen path.

In cases where the offensive force must spread due to supply demands, the defensive can often counter by concentrating against isolated segments of the attacking force. Strategic flanking or rear attacks — moves to threaten the edges or back lines of the enemy's theater of war — differ considerably from tactical flank or rear attacks, often bearing more sustained and impactful consequences for both the offensive and defensive.

1. In strategy, we cannot surround the enemy with concentrated fire across a wide theater of war; the spread of distance means that direct combat from multiple points is not possible in the way it is in tactics.

2. Concerns over losing a line of retreat are considerably reduced in strategy, as the larger scale of movement makes it far harder to block escape routes entirely, unlike the tighter spaces in tactical engagements.

3. Due to the expansive areas involved, shorter internal lines gain greater effectiveness in strategy, allowing forces to regroup or counterattack more efficiently against threats from multiple directions.

Another distinct principle in strategy is the heightened importance of secure lines of communication; disrupting these lines alone can produce significant effects by hampering supply, coordination, and mobility.

Due to the vast scale of strategy, the offensive generally holds the initiative and thus the potential to launch enveloping attacks or strikes from multiple directions. The defender, unlike in tactical situations, typically lacks the flexibility to counter-envelop, as positioning for strategic encirclement across expansive territory requires both depth of force and an element of surprise that are difficult to achieve defensively. However, even though the offensive can theoretically envelop, the benefits of doing so may not be as decisive as they are in tactical engagements. In large-scale operations, envelopment offers limited immediate payoff because the ability to disrupt the defender's lines of communication tends to emerge only gradually, often growing in impact as the campaign progresses and the offensive position stretches deeper into enemy territory.

At this point, as the offensive force becomes more reliant on extended supply lines, it begins to take on a more defensive posture to protect its communication networks. Then, the defender, if able to shift into an offensive role, can capitalize on this vulnerability by targeting the extended supply lines of the formerly advancing force. This delayed advantage underlines a peculiar feature of strategy: it is the originally defensive position that ultimately generates the conditions for potentially decisive encirclement and disruption as the attacker's resources become stretched.

Turning to the assistance of the theater of war—the fourth principle—this element is naturally inclined toward the defensive. An attacking force typically advances from its home territory and, as it does, loses immediate access to its strongholds and established logistical support, such as depots and supply centers. Every additional mile that an offensive force penetrates into hostile land requires both marches and garrisons, progressively reducing its available strength. Conversely, the defensive side remains close to its own fortified positions, continually benefiting from these strongholds and the proximity to logistical resources. This steady support grants the defender a distinct advantage in maintaining supplies, reinforcements, and overall operational coherence, enhancing the resilience of its campaign.

The fifth principle, the support of the population, is more context-dependent but remains largely favorable to the defensive. Although a defensive campaign can sometimes occur on foreign soil, in most cases it unfolds within one's own territory, where local support becomes a valuable asset. The influence of the population can manifest through general morale, logistical ease, and even the mobilization of last-resort reserves, such as local militias or, in some cases, a full-scale national mobilization. Such factors reduce logistical friction and expedite resource flows, often producing a steady, if indirect, strategic advantage. By tapping into these reserves, a defensive force can draw on both manpower and morale that an offensive force lacks, offering a powerful supplement to traditional military strength. This alignment of the defensive side with its population thus becomes a notable factor in enabling it to sustain operations and even mount counteractions more fluidly and robustly.

The campaign of 1812 offers a dramatic example of how the principles of attack from multiple quarters and support from the theater of war can decisively impact a campaign. Napoleon led an unprecedented force of 500,000 soldiers across the Niemen River, yet only 120,000 engaged in the climactic Battle of Borodino, and an even smaller fraction ultimately reached Moscow. The massive attrition suffered by the French in this campaign illustrates the cumulative effect of these principles. Even without Russia actively pursuing a counteroffensive after Borodino, the sheer logistical and strategic breakdown within Napoleon's ranks—exacerbated by the vastness of Russian territory and the scorched-earth tactics employed by the Russians—was enough to ensure that the French forces, depleted and far from supply lines, would not have the capacity to launch another invasion any time soon. While no other European country possesses the same vastness as Russia, the underlying principles remain valid universally, differing only in scale and intensity according to geography and context.

Moreover, when we consider that principles such as territorial support and population solidarity are typically stronger when the defensive force is operating on home soil, it becomes evident how these elements diminish in efficacy when the defense is conducted within foreign territory as part of an offensive operation. This introduces another inherent disadvantage for the offensive, akin to the limitations outlined regarding the principle of attacking from multiple quarters. An offensive campaign, while forward-moving, unavoidably incorporates some defensive elements because no strategic advance can be sustained without securing its rear and communications. Consequently, even the most aggressive offensive cannot function as a purely active strategy; it must include provisions for defense. Any offensive that fails to secure a conclusive peace settlement inevitably transitions into a defensive posture at some point, as the campaign's momentum slows and vulnerabilities are exposed.

When defensive elements—like securing lines of communication or establishing supply depots—are incorporated into an offensive campaign, they are inherently weakened by the nature of that offensive. This continuous shift in strategic posture is far from a trivial observation; it represents a core disadvantage of offensive campaigns. The moment the offensive loses momentum or is met with organized resistance, it finds itself grappling with defensive demands in unfamiliar or hostile terrain, further complicating the advance. Consequently, every strategic plan for an offensive must thoroughly account for these defensive responsibilities, as overlooking them would invite potential collapse. This strategic necessity becomes clearer when we examine campaign planning in depth.

The moral forces at play—such as fear, disorder, or breakdowns in cohesion—can become powerful allies for the commander who skillfully harnesses them. However, these moral forces can influence both offensive and defensive efforts alike. While some of these forces, like confusion within the enemy ranks, may seem naturally advantageous for the attacker, they rarely manifest until after a decisive blow has been dealt. Thus, while these forces may amplify the effects of a victory, they seldom serve as decisive factors leading up to it. For this reason, moral forces like troop morale, fear of capture, or chaos within the enemy's ranks do not inherently favor either the offensive or defensive side prior to a significant engagement, though they may affect the aftermath.

With these considerations, we can confidently affirm that the defensive remains the stronger form of war compared to the offensive. Yet there is one final element worth mentioning—the heightened morale and sense of purpose that typically accompanies an attacking force. This positive effect, rooted in the knowledge of being the advancing party, can indeed inspire an army. However, this motivational edge is often fleeting and soon becomes subsumed by broader forces such as victory or defeat, and ultimately the competence—or lack thereof—of the commanding general. While initiating an offensive may kindle a sense of momentum and determination, it cannot compensate for the systemic vulnerabilities inherent to an advancing force. The broader context of the campaign, including both strategic and moral elements, will always weigh more heavily on the overall outcome than any initial morale boost tied to the spirit of the attack.

Chapter IV. Convergence of Attack and Divergence of Defence

These two concepts—convergent and divergent actions—are so commonly encountered in both theory and practice that one might easily assume they are fundamental characteristics of offense and defense. However, a closer look reveals that they are not inherently tied to attack or defense, as even a moment's reflection will confirm. By examining these concepts now, we can clarify them from the outset, allowing us to consider offensive and defensive actions without repeatedly revisiting these impressions of apparent advantage or disadvantage that they might otherwise impose.

In both tactics and strategy, the defending side is seen as waiting and stationary, while the attacker is imagined in directed movement toward this static defender. Consequently, the attacker alone has the choice of employing a turning or enveloping movement—as long as the defender remains stationary. This flexibility in the mode of attack, with the option to proceed in a convergent or direct manner as deemed advantageous, can be seen as an inherent advantage of the offense, though this choice is unrestricted only in tactics.

In strategic contexts, the defender's flanks, often secured by natural barriers like seas or neutral borders, limit the attacker's options. When a defender's front stretches from one secure boundary to another, convergent attacks are not always feasible, narrowing the attacker's freedom. Furthermore, when an attacker must rely on converging lines of advance, like Russia or France converging on Germany, they cannot unite their forces easily. If we accept that convergent action, in most cases, presents an inherent structural weakness, the offensive's advantage in flexibility may be offset by the compulsion to operate within a weaker formation.

Examining the actual dynamics of these forms in tactics and strategy, one assumption about convergent force is its apparent advantage in driving forces from the outer limits inward, so that they close in on a single point as they advance. While this observation is technically accurate, the supposed benefit is illusory because convergence toward a central objective affects both sides equally, preserving the overall balance. The same applies to the dispersion of forces in divergent movements, where there is no imbalance created purely by spreading forces outwards.

A genuine advantage does arise, however, from convergent lines of action directing force toward a single point, while divergent lines do not. To understand the specific effects of these actions, we must distinguish between tactics and strategy. In tactics, the advantages of action on convergent lines come into sharper focus, but for clarity, we will limit our analysis to the primary benefits in tactical engagements.

1. The advantage of crossfire, or at least the enhancement of firepower, becomes significant as forces move within overlapping range, creating a compounded effect that intensifies pressure on the enemy from multiple angles.
2. Attacking a single point from multiple sides provides a powerful advantage, applying force in a way that disrupts and divides the enemy's defenses, weakening their ability to hold or reinforce that critical area effectively.

The potential to sever the enemy's line of retreat poses a critical threat, trapping the opposing force by blocking its escape routes, which can lead to encirclement or complete isolation, leaving the enemy with no viable means of withdrawal.

Strategically intercepting an enemy's retreat is undeniably more complex than it is tactically due to the sheer scale and open spaces involved. While in tactics, an army can create a blockade or cordon on a smaller scale, in strategy, the expansiveness of a theater of war makes complete encirclement challenging. The effect of attacking from multiple directions—while quite decisive when applied to smaller units, like battalions or divisions—is muted when dealing with large armies, as they have the flexibility to redistribute their forces over vast areas and defend from more than one front. Thus, while a tactical maneuver can strike from several directions effectively, the larger spaces and extended timelines in strategy diffuse this effect.

Another fundamental difference is in the realm of firepower. Tactics relies heavily on direct fire to create impact, whereas in strategy, this immediate influence of fire is replaced by the strategic pressure that builds when an enemy finds its supply lines or retreat paths compromised. The mere knowledge of a victorious enemy near these critical lifelines causes a weakening or "tottering" effect, casting doubt over the strength and security of one's position and adding a psychological pressure that can destabilize an army's stance or resolve.

This leads to a unique advantage in converging attacks within strategic operations: any force concentrated on one target indirectly impacts another—meaning that the effects against an opponent are cumulative. When forces converge on a single area, the impact is amplified not just at that location but also across the broader strategic theater. Consequently, the overall effect becomes greater than the sum of its individual parts; this amplified impact applies to both tactics and strategy, although in different ways depending on scale and context.

In counterbalance to this convergent advantage is the benefit provided by interior lines, where proximity allows for swifter coordination and reinforcement. This proximity is critical for the defensive side because it allows them to move forces efficiently between key points and provides them with a multiplier effect. While converging attacks offer a potentially swift breakthrough, the benefits of interior lines ensure a defensive force can respond rapidly and reinforce positions, particularly when movement can begin after the offensive's plans are revealed. As soon as a defensive force initiates movement, even though it may start behind the attacker, it can rapidly gain an advantage. Here, the combination of proximity and centralized positioning often outweighs the potential of a convergent attack unless the assailant holds a decisive numerical superiority.

However, it is crucial to recognize that a victory must first be achieved to exploit this strategic strength fully; the defensive side must succeed in one area before it can move to cut off the attacker's retreat. This balance between converging and interior lines in strategy mirrors the broader principles of offense and defense. Converging attacks promise bold, rapid outcomes but come with vulnerabilities, while interior lines provide secure, steady gains, reinforcing the defensive side. The former carries inherent risk but is driven by the lure of decisive action; the latter offers reliable strength through the defensive approach.

Considering these dynamics, we should not assume that converging lines alone grant an inherent superiority to the offensive. The defensive, too, can use converging lines, particularly as strategic demands shift; thus, the defensive side is not excluded from leveraging convergent forms. Once the defense takes initiative, converging lines may well come into play, mitigating the advantage of the offensive's movement freedom. This understanding liberates strategic planning from the misconception that the offensive always possesses an advantage due to convergence.

When moving to strategy specifically, there is a crucial point: the impact of interior lines becomes magnified as distances increase. In tactical situations, shorter distances (mere yards or less than a mile) offer minimal time advantages. However, in strategy, distances span many miles, often requiring several days to traverse. While this larger scale provides more time for positioning and response, these benefits still have limits. Strategic maneuvers rely on concealing movements from the opponent for days or even weeks, particularly when these maneuvers involve only segments or detachments of the larger force. This capacity for concealment grants the defensive side—typically the party with interior lines—a substantial advantage, as it allows them to conceal their repositioning, outmaneuvering the offensive side, which often relies on visible, predictable advances.

Thus, the strategic landscape's natural expanses and lines of communication give the defensive a latent power that can prove decisive over time. These factors combine to form a strategic reality where defensive forces are not just passively waiting but actively leveraging geography, lines, and timing to counter and control the aggressor's actions.

With this, we conclude our reflections on the convergent and divergent deployment of forces and the nuanced relationship these formations share with attack and defense. We intend to revisit this subject in further detail at a later point, allowing for a more comprehensive exploration as additional insights emerge.

Chapter V. Character of the Strategic Defensive

We have already examined the fundamental nature of the defensive, identifying it as a stronger approach to waging war, one that doesn't just resist an attack but seeks to turn the tide, capturing the opportunity to initiate an offensive response. This shift from defense to offense—the aim of all strategic defense—transforms the defensive posture into one of strength, giving it a unique advantage. Even when the purpose of war is simply to preserve an existing state, a purely reactive or passive defense would contradict the essence of warfare, which, by its nature, demands not merely endurance but active engagement. A well-executed defensive action, having repelled an opponent and gained momentum, should not hesitate to capitalize on its advantage; failing to strike back decisively risks future vulnerability and, ultimately, potential defeat. Common sense affirms that momentum must be seized, much like striking iron while it's hot; victory won through a defensive effort loses value if it is not used to forestall another assault.

This transition to a counteroffensive is intrinsic to a robust defense—it's not just a hopeful notion but an inherent aspect of successful defense. This capacity for shifting from defense to offense, this fierce turn to counterstrike, is what sets a powerful defense apart. Only when a leader includes this pivot to offense as an integral part of defensive strategy can the true strength of defensive warfare be grasped. A defense that remains entirely passive loses out on these powerful opportunities, failing to counter the gains of an attacking opponent. It's mistaken to equate defense with stagnation or resignation. Defense, when effectively managed, is not about simply tying the enemy up or enduring his attacks. Instead, it's about skillfully unwinding the offensive knots of the enemy and taking advantage of openings as they arise.

It's essential to dismantle the notion that the offensive alone is synonymous with sudden attack, surprise, and momentum, while defense is merely a reactive and cumbersome response. While it is true that an aggressor often decides upon war sooner and may set things in motion while the defender is less aware, this is more about external circumstances than an inherent quality of offense versus defense. The essence of war is more closely aligned with defense than offense, as wars often arise from the need to resist encroachment rather than the desire to invade. The instigator of conflict often sees himself as a peacemaker, eager to achieve his objectives with minimal resistance (as Napoleon frequently claimed). Thus, it is the defender who chooses war by preparing to resist and by arming himself against surprise attack, embodying a readiness that underlines the art of war itself.

Being the first to act on the battlefield does lend an advantage to the attacker, allowing him to gain initial momentum and potentially set the terms of engagement. Yet this advantage is not a foregone conclusion in every situation. Often, external factors determine who arrives first on the theater of war. A party who completes preparations before the other might adopt an offensive stance purely out of the expediency of readiness, rather than by a firm strategic choice. For the party that finishes preparations later, the defensive's strengths—especially its inherent advantages, such as familiar ground and fortified positions—can help mitigate this initial disadvantage.

The defensive, as it should ideally be conceived, is a position of prepared strength and readiness. It is the defensive that should embody full preparation, with an army well-trained, familiar with the rigors of combat, and led by a commander who faces the adversary with confidence and readiness, not from anxiety or indecision. This ideal defensive stance should include fortresses that do not shrink at the thought of siege, and a population that does not cower but instead stands as a source of support. When this kind of defensive position is established, it no longer appears as a weak stance but rather as a forceful one, capable of challenging the offensive's aggression. A well-prepared defense shatters the simplistic association of offense with courage and strength while viewing defense as mere resignation or fear. On the contrary, a fortified defensive posture, held by capable leaders and resilient soldiers, can rival or even surpass the vigor of an offensive.

In this light, we see that a strong defense does not represent passivity, helplessness, or timidity. Instead, it is the poised response, waiting for the right moment to launch its own decisive moves. The true strength of the defensive lies in its power to withstand and counterattack, converting the opponent's aggressions into opportunities for victory, and then seizing those opportunities with the readiness of an offensive stance, but only at the optimal moment. Thus, the defensive, properly executed and intelligently managed, stands not as a state of mere resistance but as a strategic stance with the inherent potential to swing into an effective and victorious offensive.

Chapter VI. Extent of the Means of Defence

We explained earlier in this book how defense naturally has some advantages when it comes to using certain elements that affect the results in both tactics and strategy, aside from just the sheer strength or quality of the fighting forces. These advantages include the benefits of the terrain, the ability to strike suddenly, the opportunity to attack from multiple directions (a converging attack), the support provided by the area where the battle is happening, the backing of the people, and the power of strong moral forces. Now, we find it helpful to take another look at the range of resources that are especially available to those on the defensive side, resources that can be seen as the essential pillars of the entire defensive structure.

1. Landwehr (Militia).

In recent times, this type of force has been used to fight the enemy on foreign soil, and it's clear that in some countries, like Prussia, its organization is almost as solid as the standing army. So, it can't be seen as something solely for defense. Still, it's worth noting that the extensive use of this force in 1813-14-15 was due to a defensive war. Also, very few places have it as well-organized as Prussia, and when it's not fully efficient, it tends to work better for defense than for offense. Besides, the very idea of a militia brings up the notion of a broad, often voluntary effort from the general population to support the war, both with their physical strength and with a willingness to sacrifice whatever they can. The more the organization of this force strays from this concept, the more it starts to resemble a standing army under a different name, gaining the strengths of such a force but also losing the unique qualities of a militia. One of these unique qualities is its flexibility, as it can expand easily by rallying the people's feelings and sense of patriotism. These qualities are the core of a militia, and its setup should allow for this broad support from the whole population; if we try to turn a militia into something more than this, we're only chasing an illusion.

But it's clear that this central nature of a militia system is closely tied to the concept of defense. In fact, a militia will always lean more toward defensive action than offensive, and it's in defense that a militia's strengths can truly shine, giving it an edge over the attack.

2. Fortresses.

Fortresses near the borders provide only limited support to the offensive, giving a weak advantage at best. In contrast, the defensive can rely on fortresses positioned much deeper within the country, allowing more of them to play a role, and their usefulness varies in intensity. A fortress that endures a formal siege and resists capture naturally has a far greater impact on the course of the war than one that, by sheer strength alone, deters the enemy from attacking. In this latter case, it neither engages nor drains any of the enemy's forces.

3. The People.

While the influence of an individual inhabitant within a theater of war might seem as negligible as a single drop in a river, the combined effect of the population in a country at war is far from insignificant, even when there is no mass uprising. In one's own country, everything proceeds more smoothly, so long as it isn't opposed by the general sentiment of the population. Every contribution, big or small, is only yielded to an occupying enemy through direct force, requiring the troops to enforce it, often at the cost of manpower and energy. By contrast, the defensive side obtains what it needs, if not always willingly or from enthusiastic devotion, then at least through established channels of state authority that citizens are used to following, a loyalty that becomes second nature, further reinforced by legal penalties—something the army itself does not have to manage. Yet, the genuine cooperation of the people, fueled by true loyalty, is crucial, especially as it flows naturally in areas that require no sacrifice.

One key area where this makes a difference is intelligence. It's not just about securing critical or high-level information from spies but about gaining insight into countless small matters that add up in the daily workings of an army. With a supportive population, the defending side is at a distinct advantage in gathering routine information and making logistical decisions that are often clouded by uncertainty. If we trace this beneficial influence from a steady, reliable undercurrent to instances where the population more directly supports the war, and then to the most extreme case—as in Spain—where the war itself becomes largely a people's fight, we see not just enhanced support but the rise of an entirely new force on the battlefield. Thus, the role of the people is not merely a boost to the defending side; it creates an additional power unto itself, transforming the very nature of the conflict.

4. The National Armament,

or general call to arms, may be considered as a particular means of defence.

5. Allies.

Lastly, we can count allies as a significant support for the defensive side. Here, we're not referring to general allies, which the attacker may also possess, but rather to those especially committed to upholding the country's stability. Looking at the various states that make up Europe today, we see—without presuming any precisely managed balance of power—that there is an intricate and ever-shifting web of connections among both large and small states, with each nation's interests and positions affecting those around it. Each of these intersections acts as a stabilizing knot, where one state's interests serve to counterbalance another's. Thus, these connections create a network that, as a whole, is more inclined to maintain stability than to provoke change. Any disruption to this equilibrium can partially unsettle the entire structure.

This complex network of intersecting interests among states functions as a natural balance of power, even if it's not a formal system. In this sense, such a balance will always emerge naturally whenever interconnected, civilised nations exist, helping to support stability within the whole.

How effective this general tendency to maintain the current state of things really is remains an open question; nevertheless, we can recognize that certain shifts in the relations between individual states can either enhance this overall stability or hinder it. When shifts promote this stability, they work to strengthen the political balance, aligning with the collective interests of many states. Such cases are likely to be supported by the majority of these interests. However, there are also cases where certain states overreach, acting in a way that disrupts stability—like imbalances or disruptions within the system. This isn't surprising in a collection of states that lacks tight cohesion, just as we find disruptions even within the intricate balance of nature itself.

If history offers examples where single states made significant changes solely for their own gain, or where one state rose to a position of power nearly dictating the course of events for others, we should still not conclude that this tendency toward stability doesn't exist. Rather, such examples reveal that, at specific times, this balancing influence wasn't strong enough. Aiming toward balance is distinct from achieving balance immediately. Still, this tendency isn't without influence; we see this same kind of struggle for balance in the natural order of the universe.

When we talk about this general leaning toward maintaining stability, we assume that a balanced state existed beforehand. If balance has already been disrupted, creating tension, then equilibrium might indeed shift as a result. But any resulting change is likely to impact only a few specific states, not the majority. Thus, the collective interests of the majority still serve as a stabilizing force, providing security and support for most states. Any single state not in direct opposition to these collective interests will naturally find more allies than opposition.

Those who dismiss these observations as merely utopian fail to grasp philosophical truth. While these reflections reveal essential relationships among key factors, it would be imprudent to derive specific, rigid laws for each unique situation without accounting for unforeseen influences. However, when a person, as one great thinker put it, "never rises above anecdote," and constructs history solely on isolated events, beginning with specific turning points, focusing narrowly on single motives without understanding the broader foundations—such an opinion is only valid in a limited sense, restricted to individual cases. To such a person, the broad applicability of philosophical insights may seem like nothing more than a dream.

Without this fundamental drive for stability and for preserving the current order, it would be impossible for a group of civilised states to coexist peacefully for long; they would inevitably merge into a single entity. But Europe has endured in its current form for over a thousand years, which can only be attributed to this underlying collective tendency toward balance. If this overarching protection has sometimes failed to safeguard every individual state's independence, we can view these instances as irregularities within the overall structure—disruptions that haven't destroyed the collective but have ultimately been absorbed and balanced within it.

It would be unnecessary to list all the many instances in history where changes that might have disrupted the balance of power were prevented or reversed through the direct or indirect resistance of other states. A brief look at history will reveal these occurrences. However, there is one example that critics of the idea of a political balance often bring up—because it seems to stand out as a case where a defenseless state received no foreign help and eventually fell. This example is Poland. To many, the fact that a state with eight million people could be divided among three neighboring powers without any intervention from the other European states seems to indicate a failure of the political balance. They argue that if no collective action was taken to stop such an extreme case of partitioning, then the whole idea of a political balance might be nothing but an illusion.

But we would argue that even one such striking instance doesn't disprove the general trend, and we also believe Poland's collapse is not as inexplicable as it might initially appear. To ask whether Poland truly functioned as a European state—a member of the European community of nations—is to question its place among them. Unlike other European states, Poland had long operated more like a Tartar state, but situated not on Europe's borders but in its heart, along the Vistula River. We don't say this to demean Poland or justify its partition, but to view the situation realistically. For over a hundred years, Poland had lost any independent influence in European politics and had become a prize fought over by others. Maintaining the country's state and constitution unchanged was impossible under these conditions, and a shift away from this "Tartar" identity would likely have required half a century or more, even if the leading Polish figures had desired it. But these leaders, embodying the old ways, resisted change, their unstable political system and carelessness ultimately leading them toward ruin.

Well before the partition, Russian influence had already become deeply rooted in Poland, and the notion of Poland as an independent state with firm borders was already fading. If the partition had not taken place, Poland would still likely have become a Russian province. Had Poland been a state capable of defending itself, those powers who benefited from its continued independence—such as France, Sweden, and Turkey—would likely have acted more forcefully to keep it intact. But if a state's existence depends entirely on foreign support, it is asking too much to expect that other nations will constantly intervene.

Discussions of dividing Poland had circulated for a hundred years, during which time foreign armies repeatedly traversed its lands, as though it were an open thoroughfare rather than a sovereign state. Should other states have been expected to intervene endlessly, sword in hand, to protect Poland's borders? Such an expectation would have been unrealistic. By that point, Poland had become politically little more than a vacant steppe; just as it's unrealistic to expect unprotected borderlands to remain untouched indefinitely, so too was it impractical to preserve Poland's "integrity" under those conditions. In light of these realities, Poland's gradual fall was no more surprising than the silent conquest of the Crimean Tartars. Even the Turks, who had a vested interest in the Tartars' survival, eventually acknowledged that safeguarding an unprotected region would have been futile.

Returning to our main subject, we believe we have demonstrated that the defensive, as a general rule, has stronger prospects for receiving foreign assistance than the offensive. A defender can more confidently rely on such support if their survival is seen as vital to others. The stronger and more stable a state is politically and militarily, the more likely others are to see value in defending it.

Of course, not every defensive position will benefit from each of the factors mentioned here. Some may lack one or more, depending on the situation, but these elements all form part of the broader concept of a defensive strategy.

Chapter VII. Mutual Action and Reaction of Attack and Defence

We will now look closely at attack and defense as individual elements, to the extent that they can be considered apart from each other. We start with the defensive for several reasons. While it may seem logical to define the rules of defense based on those of offense and vice versa, one of these two strategies must have an independent foundation if we're to have a starting point to understand war as a whole. The primary question is about finding this starting point.

When we consider the philosophical origin of war, the concept of war doesn't actually start with the idea of attacking. The core of the offensive approach is not inherently about fighting but about seizing or possessing something. The essence of war truly begins with the defensive, because defense is directly about battle itself. To defend is to confront and engage, while the purpose of offense is centered on capturing or acquiring, not necessarily on opposing. The defender, by necessity, prepares for combat to ward off an attack, which automatically introduces the confrontation of war. By contrast, the attacker's goal lies elsewhere—in taking something, not necessarily in facing resistance. Thus, logically, the side that first embodies the essence of war, creating the conditions of opposition, is the defender. Here, we aren't talking about any particular instance but are thinking broadly about war as a concept, as a framework that helps establish the principles of military strategy.

From this, we can determine the foundational point outside the cycle of attack and defense, and that point is the defensive stance. If this follows logically, it means that even before any knowledge of the enemy's plans, the defensive side already has its own reasons to act, based on its core objectives, which are essential to the structure of its forces and resources. Conversely, if the attacker remains unaware of the defender's preparations, they have no direct motive to organize their resources around combat; they can only proceed with their preparations for taking possession. So, while the attacker may bring their military force forward in anticipation of combat, carrying it with them does not itself constitute an act of war. However, the defensive side not only gathers its military apparatus but arranges it with battle in mind, marking the true beginning of wartime action.

The second question is: What are the theoretical motivations that the defender might have even before there is any consideration of an actual attack? Quite simply, these motives arise from the advancing force that intends to occupy or control, which we can imagine as a precursor to war. This advance becomes the basis of the initial defense measures, which inherently link the defender to the land, giving rise to general defensive measures. Once these defensive measures are in place, they form the foundation for offensive strategies, which in turn lead to further refinements in defensive principles. Here, we find a reciprocal process of action and counteraction, which we can analyze step by step as long as new outcomes continue to emerge that deepen our understanding of the strategic interaction.

This breakdown may seem detailed, but it's necessary to bring greater clarity and structure to the principles that follow. It's not meant as a guide for the battlefield or future generals; rather, it's for theorists, who often approach this complex subject too lightly. This analysis helps provide a structured view that can support a deeper, more nuanced understanding of war.

Chapter VIII. Methods of Resistance

The concept of defense centers on the idea of "warding off" or resisting an attack. This resistance comes with a state of "expectancy" or readiness, and it is this anticipatory stance that gives defense its main characteristic and its core advantage. However, since the nature of war doesn't allow for a purely passive approach, this expectation is relative, not absolute. Defense may apply this expectation to various scales, whether across a country, a theater of war, or a specific position. It also unfolds over time, whether across a single battle, a campaign, or an entire war. Though these elements blend together and are not rigidly separated, they are distinct enough in real-world application that they can anchor our understanding of defense.

A defense meant to protect a country awaits an attack on that country; a defense focused on a theater of war anticipates an attack within that theater; and a defense at a specific position stands ready to repel attacks on that position. Any subsequent positive action by the defensive side, involving some measure of offense, does not contradict its original defensive stance because the advantage of waiting, a defining feature of defense, has already been realized.

The defense, therefore, consists of two different phases: the phase of waiting, and the phase of action. By linking the waiting phase to a specific subject, such as a position or a theater, and establishing it before the action phase, we can see these two phases as a connected whole. However, a defensive operation, especially a large one such as a full campaign or a war, does not divide neatly into two distinct halves, one for waiting and one for action. Instead, it alternates between these two states, with waiting woven continuously through the act of defense as a stabilizing factor.

This state of expectancy holds such significance because it aligns with the natural essence of defensive action. Previous war theories have often overlooked this concept as an independent element, yet it has silently shaped strategy and guided decisions, serving as a central part of defensive tactics. This expectancy is so fundamental to warfare that separating it from the broader action seems almost impossible. As a result, we will revisit this concept frequently, examining how it influences the active, dynamic forces engaged in defense.

For now, let's look at how this principle of expectation integrates into the stages of a defensive operation. To simplify our discussion, we'll save the topic of defending a whole country—subject to numerous political influences—for the section dedicated to the planning of war. Likewise, since defensive operations involving specific positions or battles fall into the realm of tactics and serve as starting points for broader strategy, we will focus here on defending a theater of war. This example best illustrates the principles unique to defense.

We've noted that defense includes both the phase of waiting and the phase of action, with action taking the form of a counterstrike, a reaction to an attack. Without the waiting phase, there would be no defensive structure; without the action phase, there would be no war. This perspective leads us to the concept of defense as a stronger form of warfare, designed to secure victory and ultimately transition into offense, which is the active pursuit of war's objectives. This concept of transitioning from defense to offense is crucial; it sustains the dynamic balance needed between opposing forces in war.

If we attempt to separate the act of counteraction from the waiting state, focusing solely on repelling the enemy or holding ground, while dismissing the idea of further counterattacks or strategic offensives as irrelevant, we would contradict this understanding of defense. True defense has an element of "returning the blow" or retaliation embedded in its strategy. Without this underlying goal of eventual counterattack, even a well-executed defense that successfully wards off an enemy would fall short, failing to balance the energy between attack and defense.

Thus, defense is the stronger approach to warfare because it is designed to make overcoming the enemy easier. The extent of the response—whether it stops at holding the initial position or pushes further to regain lost ground or even advance—depends on the circumstances of the conflict.

However, because the defensive inherently includes waiting, its objective—defeating the enemy—exists only if an attack actually takes place. If no attack materializes, the defensive strategy is satisfied with simply holding its ground. This preservation of control over its position or assets is, therefore, its primary aim during the waiting phase. This goal of maintenance aligns defense with the advantages of a stronger, more stable form of warfare.

Let us imagine an army set up to defend a specific theater of war. There are several possible ways to organize this defense.

1. By engaging the enemy as soon as he crosses into the theater of war, as seen in examples like Mollwitz and Hohenfriedberg. This approach involves meeting the enemy at the outset and confronting him immediately. It's a proactive form of defense, aiming to disrupt the enemy's plans right from his initial advance.
2. By positioning the army close to the frontier and waiting until the enemy shows an intent to attack, then launching an attack, as demonstrated in examples like Czaslau, Soor, and Rosbach. This method embodies a bit more patience and anticipation. Here, the defending army remains prepared, but instead of rushing to meet the enemy, it waits until the enemy commits to an approach or maneuver, only then deciding to engage. Though this delay may add little time compared to an outright initial engagement, there's a tactical benefit: the defending force has a better opportunity to observe the enemy's movements, and the enemy may hesitate or reconsider the attack if the position appears daunting.
3. By waiting in position, not only to see the enemy's intent but to withstand an actual assault, as seen in the example of Bunzelwitz. This represents a traditional defensive stance. The army fortifies itself, preparing to resist the enemy's direct assault while retaining the flexibility to counterattack using parts

of the force. In this mode, time gained through patience becomes less significant than testing the enemy's resolve. Some attackers, seeing the defender's strong setup, may advance with initial aggression but then halt or withdraw once they see the defensive position's strength.

By transferring the defense deeper into the country's interior. Here, the defensive army retreats deliberately, aiming to draw the enemy further away from his own base of support. This approach weakens the enemy by forcing him to stretch his supply lines and exhaust his resources as he ventures deeper into hostile territory. The goal is to let attrition take its toll on the advancing force, leading to a halt or, at the least, to prepare for a stronger defensive stand when the enemy's momentum has significantly weakened.

This approach becomes especially clear when the defensive can strategically leave one or more fortresses behind him, forcing the attacking side to pause for a siege or blockade. This tactic is effective because the offensive must now commit resources to occupy or secure these fortifications, which drains its strength. The attacker's forces are thus spread thinner, creating a valuable opportunity for the defensive to strike a vulnerable point with a stronger force. This diversion weakens the offensive's cohesion, often providing the defender with a critical advantage in manpower and positioning for a counterattack.

Even when fortresses aren't available, a retreat deeper into the country can gradually provide the defender with the balance—or even the upper hand—that was lacking on the frontier. Each advance in the strategic attack reduces the offensive's strength, partly due to the direct toll of the campaign and partly from the necessary division of forces to maintain control of captured points. We can anticipate this principle here, as history provides ample examples of its truth across numerous wars.

In this fourth situation, the time gained is essential. If the offensive lays siege to a fortress, the defensive gains time until the fortress potentially falls—a delay that could extend for weeks or even months. But when the offensive weakens merely by advancing and spreading forces to garrison and secure various positions along their route, then the time available to the defensive tends to be even greater, as it is less bound to a fixed timetable and instead hinges on the pace of the offensive's progress.

By the time the offensive reaches the interior, there is a notable shift in power between attacker and defender, with the defensive benefitting more from its waiting position. Even if the attacker hasn't lost enough strength to prevent an attempt to strike at the defensive's main forces where they are positioned, their resolve may still waver. The further they are from the frontier, the more hesitant they may be to initiate a decisive assault. With their forces no longer fresh and their overall strength diminished, the risks of attacking seem heightened. Additionally, an indecisive leader may deem the acquisition of territory already achieved as sufficient, using it as a rationale for halting further battles. As a result, the offensive may shy away from battle, providing the defensive with a meaningful extension of time, even if it doesn't yield the same immediate advantages as a decisive confrontation would.

In all four outlined approaches, the defensive not only utilizes the advantages of familiar ground but also leverages fortresses and the local population to assist in weakening the enemy. The benefits from these tactics become even more pronounced as the defensive strategy moves from one phase to the next, particularly in the final stages, where the enemy's resources and resolve are likely most worn down. Similarly, the benefits of the "waiting" state also increase, suggesting that these stages collectively form a natural intensification of the defensive position. The further the defensive diverges from an offensive stance, the stronger it grows.

However, this shouldn't be mistaken as advocacy for complete passivity; rather, the strength of resistance grows with each progressive stage, not by weakening the response but by effectively delaying it.

The logic that a stronger resistance can be mounted from a well-chosen and fortified position—and that, when the offensive exhausts its strength on such a position, a potent counterstrike can be made—remains entirely valid. Without a strong position, Daun would not have succeeded at Kollin, and with greater persistence in pursuing Frederick's diminished forces (of only 18,000), that victory might have achieved historical renown as one of the most remarkable.

Thus, we assert that with each successive stage of the defensive approach, the balance—or rather, the counterbalance—tilts increasingly in favor of the defender, further enhancing their strength for a decisive counterstroke.

Do these increasing advantages of a defensive stance come without a price? Not at all; in fact, the cost grows alongside the benefits.

When we choose to wait for the enemy within our own territory—no matter how close to the border this confrontation might be—we allow the enemy to enter our theater of war, which brings a certain level of sacrifice. Had we taken the offensive approach, this burden would fall on the enemy instead. The further we hold back from engaging, the more we risk losing, as the enemy will advance, covering more ground and taking more time to reach our position. If we hold off on attacking and let the enemy decide when to engage, they might hold onto captured areas for some time, which means that the time we gain from their hesitation is effectively "purchased" with the price of lost territory. This cost rises even further if we must retreat deeper into our own land.

However, these sacrifices for the defensive are often felt more as a loss of potential power than an immediate reduction in military strength. In other words, while they may indirectly weaken the defender's forces later on, they usually don't have an immediate impact. The defensive, in essence, is strengthening its position in the present by borrowing against the future, similar to how someone might incur debt to manage a difficult situation.

To understand the full effect of these different defensive approaches, we must consider the aim of the aggressor, which is usually to take control of our theater of war, or at least a significant portion of it. We interpret "theater of war" broadly here, meaning the aggressor's goal is not simply to capture a narrow strip of land but a sizable region. As long as the aggressor doesn't secure this primary area—whether because our forces deter them, prevent them from reaching our main positions, or force them to decline our offers for direct combat—the defender's strategy has been effective. While this outcome doesn't immediately enable a counterattack, it has still achieved a partial victory by denying the enemy's objectives.

This result, though indirect, can lead toward a more favorable position for the defender. As time passes, the offensive side suffers setbacks because every delay takes a toll and gradually weakens them. In the first three phases of the defensive—particularly when defenses are focused at the frontier—even achieving non-decision is a positive outcome for the defensive side.

However, the situation shifts when we enter into the fourth phase.

If the enemy lays siege to one of our fortresses, it becomes crucial to relieve it in time, which necessitates taking decisive action on our terms. The same holds if the enemy pushes deep into the country without besieging any fortified points along the way. In such a case, we may have more time on our side to allow the enemy's forces to weaken gradually, but even so, at some point, we must move forward and take action to conclude the engagement. While the enemy might temporarily hold large parts of the territory he sought to conquer, his claim is not permanent; he occupies it conditionally, on loan, as the full resolution of the conflict remains outstanding. As long as we are growing stronger while the invading forces weaken, each day that passes is in our favor. However, this trend has a peak—an inevitable moment when the progressive advantage reaches its maximum, largely due to the cumulative losses and fatigue the offensive incurs simply by sustaining its position. At this critical point, the defender must act to bring about a decisive turn. Until that moment, the advantage gained from delaying direct confrontation works entirely in our favor, but once it's reached, the advantage of further delay has been fully realized, and the time has come to initiate a counter.

Determining the exact point at which this pivotal moment arrives cannot be reduced to a fixed rule, as it varies depending on the circumstances at play. However, the winter season often serves as a natural marker in most cases. Should the enemy manage to establish winter quarters within the territory he's seized, this often signals a significant loss for the defender, who may have to consider the territory surrendered, at least temporarily. However, this is not a hard-and-fast rule, as exceptions, like those illustrated by the campaign at Torres Vedras, demonstrate that the defender can still recover control under certain conditions.

How does this final, decisive turn typically manifest? Up to this point, we have discussed it as though it would inevitably take the form of a decisive battle. Yet, in practice, a large-scale battle is not always necessary to achieve resolution. A combination of strategic movements and smaller engagements may still shift the balance significantly. These actions may involve substantial segments of our army or sometimes only isolated corps, but whether through direct engagement or by compelling the enemy to anticipate such actions, they may force him to retreat. These maneuvers can be enough to tip the scales and change the strategic landscape without requiring an outright confrontation.

However, on the strategic level, it is clear that there is ultimately only one way to achieve resolution within the theater of war—by holding the adversary in check, through sustained, visible pressure. Even when an opponent withdraws due to supply shortages, it's ultimately the strategic presence of our army—our persistent "sword"—that drives the decision to retreat. If our forces were absent, the enemy would likely find ways to sustain his position and continue his campaign with renewed strength.

Therefore, even at the farthest extent of the enemy's advance, when hunger, sickness, and the demands of maintaining garrisons and detachments have eroded his strength, it is ultimately the influence of our forces that compels him to turn back, making it possible to restore a sense of stability. Nonetheless, there remains a significant distinction between securing such a resolution deep within our own territory and achieving it while still holding the frontier.

When we hold the frontier, our forces alone confront the enemy to keep him at bay or even break his ranks. However, when the enemy reaches the end of his aggressive advance, his own exhausting efforts have already caused significant damage to his forces, which now makes our military strength far more effective. This shift means that while our army is the final instrument of victory, it is not the only one that brought about the resolution. The gradual weakening of the enemy's force throughout his advance lays the groundwork for this outcome, so much so that the mere prospect of a counteraction from us can be enough to compel his retreat and turn the tide of events. In these cases, we may attribute the result to the adversary's own overextension and depletion rather than purely to our force.

In reality, it is rare to find instances where the defender's force hasn't contributed at all. Yet for strategic purposes, it's essential to identify which of these principles—active resistance or the enemy's self-destruction—primarily led to the outcome. This leads us to recognize a dual nature in defensive strategies, with two types of reactions that drive a successful defense. One is based on direct military confrontation, where the defender's force decisively counters the enemy, while the other relies on the enemy's own overextension and exhaustion.

In general, the first type of solution, where we achieve success through active resistance, is more common in the earlier stages of defense, while the latter, based on the enemy's self-inflicted losses, becomes significant mainly when the defensive strategy has drawn the enemy deep into the country. Only when these self-destructive conditions can be achieved does such a retreat make sense, despite the considerable sacrifices involved.

Military history offers instances that clearly illustrate both types of defensive solutions in their pure forms. For example, when Frederick the Great struck at the Austrians descending from the Silesian mountains at Hohenfriedberg, the Austrian forces had not yet been worn down by fatigue or detachments, so Frederick's direct assault was the primary force behind his success. By contrast, Wellington's strategy at Torres Vedras differed fundamentally. Wellington held his entrenched camp and waited as hunger and severe weather wore down Masséna's army to the point of retreat. Here, Wellington's defensive forces played almost no role in actively weakening the enemy; the hardships of the march did the work instead.

More often, however, these two approaches merge to varying extents, with one principle usually dominating. The 1812 campaign is an exceptional example of this combined effect. In that campaign, multiple bloody confrontations occurred—any one of which could have led to a decisive victory had circumstances been different. Yet this campaign distinctly shows how an advancing force may collapse under the weight of its own efforts. Of Napoleon's initial force of 300,000 French troops in the central advance, only about 90,000 reached Moscow. Of those lost, fewer than a third fell in battle; most perished from the strain and attrition of the march.

Campaigns noted for a "temporizing" approach—such as those of Fabius Cunctator—have often relied heavily on the principle of letting the enemy exhaust himself rather than engaging directly. This approach has been central to many defensive campaigns, even if historians rarely highlight it explicitly. Looking past conventional analyses to examine events objectively often reveals that this principle of the enemy's self-destruction is indeed the underlying cause of many a successful defense.

We believe we have clarified the foundational ideas behind defensive strategy, illustrating the two major forms of defense and how the principle of "waiting for" runs through the entire approach, connecting it to eventual action. This shows that while defense involves an initial stance of expectation, it inevitably transitions to a point where action becomes necessary, marking the culmination of the waiting advantage. We have thus covered the key elements in the domain of defense.

Additionally, some topics hold distinct importance and warrant individual discussion, including the use of fortifications, entrenched camps, mountain and river defenses, and flank maneuvers. We will explore these in later sections, but they remain firmly tied to the overarching sequence of defensive ideas we've established. This framework originates from the concept of defense and its relationship to offense; by rooting it in practical realities, we gain a firm basis for returning to these foundational ideas without being forced to rely on vague, unsupported assumptions that would otherwise collapse under scrutiny.

Still, the application of resistance through arms can appear to change in character depending on how battles are orchestrated, especially when these engagements don't materialize into full combat but exert influence through the mere potential for confrontation. This complexity might suggest that an additional underlying force exists, akin to how astronomers deduce the presence of other planets by observing gaps between known ones.

Consider situations where the enemy finds us in a formidable position that seems impossible to assault directly or behind a large river that's difficult to cross, or simply in a place where sustaining his army becomes impractical. In such cases, it's our potential military response—the sword of the defender—that makes the attacker hesitate, whether through fear of losing a major engagement or even of facing fierce resistance at specific key points. Yet the aggressor might be unwilling to acknowledge this directly or might attribute his decision to logistical concerns rather than to the force presented by the defender.

Even if it's granted that victories sometimes arise without bloodshed and that the decisive factor is an unaccepted challenge rather than an actual battle, many might argue that the real power lies in the strategic arrangement of potential battles rather than in the expected outcomes of those engagements. This argument suggests that strategy operates independently of battlefield outcomes. While we agree that strategic combinations are valuable, we also stress that they are grounded fundamentally in the anticipated tactical outcomes of combat. There's always the risk that an aggressive force will prioritize success in battle to nullify strategic defenses, so these strategies can never be viewed as entirely independent solutions. Strategic planning only holds true value when we can reasonably trust the anticipated outcome of the engagement, either due to the opponent's weaknesses, the relative strengths of the forces involved, or our own calculated superiority.

To make this clear, recall that commanders like Napoleon moved decisively through complex webs of their opponents' strategies, confidently pursuing decisive battle because they had no doubts about their own advantage. When strategy did not focus entirely on ensuring a battlefield advantage against such a leader, its intricacies dissolved quickly. A cautious commander like Daun, on the other hand, could be stalled by these strategic tactics, and so, what worked against Daun's slower-moving army in the Seven Years' War would be utterly insufficient against Napoleon. The difference lay in Napoleon's awareness that tactical victory was the core determinant, a belief Daun did not share as strongly.

Thus, it's essential to recognize that all strategic maneuvers ultimately rely on tactical success—both the direct clashes and the indirect pressures created by the threat of battle. Only if we have no significant reason to worry about that outcome—be it because of the enemy's limitations, comparable strength between forces, or a measurable advantage on our side—can we rely on strategic maneuvering alone to achieve objectives without a fight.

Military history is filled with campaigns where attackers abandoned their advances without a single battle, where strategic arrangements seemed decisive by themselves. This may give the impression that these combinations possess their own intrinsic power and could independently dictate outcomes in cases without overwhelming tactical dominance by the enemy. However, if we're speaking of factors that arise within the theater of war and are part of the war itself, this idea is incorrect. We'd go further to argue that the primary reason most offensive efforts falter lies in broader political considerations rather than in purely military calculations.

The underlying dynamics that fuel a war—and which naturally shape its entire character—stem from broad political and social factors. These factors often mold conflicts into half-hearted struggles where real animosity is tangled within a web of conflicting interests, resulting in only a faint echo of true hostility. We'll explore this in more detail when discussing the overarching strategies behind war planning. For now, it's important to recognize that the same diffuse energy that drives many wars shows up most prominently on the offensive side, which relies on decisiveness and positive action. It should hardly surprise us, then, if such a hesitant attack falters at the slightest resistance. A flimsy resolution, so entangled in competing considerations that it barely exists as true intent, can be deterred by the faintest display of defense.

When offense is weakened by its internal lack of resolve, it's often enough for defense to merely project a shadow of resistance. True, a defensive stance may benefit from geographical fortifications, mountainous barriers, or rivers that help blunt attacks. It may also draw on strategic arrangements and battle plans designed to immobilize the enemy's advance. Yet, none of these alone explain the many bloodless victories won by the defensive. Instead, the deeper reason for these successes lies in the lack of will that prevents the assailant from taking resolute action.

While it's useful to consider these structural advantages to defense, we must be careful to attribute their true influence correctly. Otherwise, we risk confusing symptoms for causes. If we're not precise, military history can easily mislead us by overemphasizing tactical maneuvers or strategic layouts while failing to account for the reality of weak offensive resolve.

Let's examine some typical offensive campaigns that stalled without bloodshed. Often, the attacker penetrates the enemy's territory, displaces the defending forces to a limited extent, yet hesitates when it comes to forcing a conclusive battle. The assailant may settle into a defensive posture within the seized territory, attempting to frame his campaign as a success. His government, army, and even he himself might be led to believe the operation is complete, awaiting only the enemy's willingness to engage. Yet the true reason behind this stasis is that the defender's position is too strong to challenge outright.

This situation differs from cases where the attacker, having reached a certain point of success, cannot push forward simply because he lacks the resources or will to advance further. Instead, we are examining cases where the offensive loses momentum halfway toward its goal, bogged down by hesitation.

In such scenarios, the attacker holds out, hoping for favorable developments to justify further action. Often, these "favorable circumstances" are mere illusions. If other, simultaneous operations are underway, the failure is often passed off as a lack of support or inadequate coordination. Rationalizations emerge, framing the attacker's stalled advance as the fault of insurmountable obstacles or unsatisfactory collaboration.

In truth, these justifications typically cloud the actual reason behind the delay: an apprehension toward facing the defender's full might.

As the attacker's forces stagnate in partial engagements without real purpose, the defender gains the advantage of time—a powerful asset. Weather turns, logistical strains mount, and soon the offense finds itself retreating to winter quarters without having achieved its original aims.

Thus, a string of half-truths and fabricated motives enter the historical record, masking the core truth: a fundamental fear of decisive engagement. When historians review these campaigns, they often become mired in a labyrinth of motives and counter-motives. Ultimately, these explanations evaporate, never reaching the underlying truth. The real source of an offensive's failure often lies in the complex motivations and political maneuvering between states—factors that remain hidden from the public, the soldiers, and sometimes even the commanding general. Few are willing to openly admit their concerns about the risks of advancing, whether they fear inadequate forces, the provocation of new enemies, or a shift in power among allies. These concerns are suppressed, but a presentable narrative is still needed, compelling leaders to construct intricate, though largely fictitious, explanations.

This consistent pattern of deceptive justifications has seeped into military theory itself, creating frameworks that misrepresent reality. A genuine understanding of strategy cannot emerge from elaborate theoretical structures built on these obscured motives. Instead, theory must trace the simple, direct path of cause and effect—an approach we have tried to maintain throughout.

When we examine military history with a critical eye, much of the elaborate terminology and philosophical arguments about offense and defense lose their weight, leaving only the clear, straightforward concepts we've discussed. By focusing on this simpler, more grounded understanding, we believe we can apply it effectively across the entire realm of defensive strategy, enabling a clearer interpretation of events and allowing us to make more accurate judgments.

Our next task is to explore how these different forms of defense might best be employed in practice. Each form, as we've noted, represents a degree of intensity in defensive strategy, and each demands an increasing sacrifice to achieve its particular advantages. Ideally, this understanding alone would guide a commander in choosing the right form based on what degree of defensive power his forces require to maintain an effective position—without expending unnecessary resources or strength.

However, practical considerations often limit a general's freedom of choice among these defensive forms, as various factors inevitably push one form to the forefront. For instance, executing a retreat into the interior requires a significant expanse of territory. In unique scenarios like Portugal in 1810, where allied support came from England behind them and the wide territory of Spain on one flank, the defensive forces could drain the enemy's advancing power. In other cases, the location of fortresses—whether closer to the frontier or deeper within—may make retreat to the interior more or less feasible. Furthermore, the natural terrain and ground conditions, along with the population's character, habits, and morale, can also heavily influence the choice.

Additionally, the decision to fight either an offensive or defensive battle may hinge on the enemy's overall strategy or even on the unique strengths of each army and the qualities of their generals. The presence or absence of a strong defensive position or defensive line can be decisive as well. When considering all these elements, it becomes evident that practical limitations often determine the form of defense more than a straightforward comparison of relative army strength.

As we explore these factors in greater detail, particularly the most significant ones touched upon here, their influence on strategic choice will become even clearer. Ultimately, these elements will come together in a structured approach in the section dedicated to the planning of wars and campaigns, helping to methodically shape strategy based on the realities of each situation.

However, this influence will typically only be decisive when the disparity in the strength of the opposing armies is relatively minor; if there is a substantial difference in force (as is often the case), then the sheer numerical strength of one side generally proves determinative. Military history provides countless examples where the side with superior numbers prevails, confirming this principle even without a detailed logical analysis—more as an instinctive outcome, much like many events in war, which often unfold with an intuitive sense of judgment. Consider that the same general, commanding the same army on the same battlefield, engaged in both offensive and defensive approaches as circumstances demanded: Frederick the Great led his forces at Hohenfriedberg in a bold offensive, but in other instances, like the camp at Bunzelwitz, even he was compelled by significant disadvantages in numbers to adopt a genuinely defensive posture.

Napoleon, too, typically unrestrained and aggressive—often attacking his enemies with the fierce determination of a cornered boar—found himself in 1813, as the tide of force turned against him, maneuvering cautiously. During August and September of that year, he moved back and forth, appearing hemmed in rather than lunging aggressively at any single opponent. By October, when this imbalance of power reached its peak, he sought refuge at Leipzig, positioning himself within the protection of the rivers Parth, Elster, and Pleisse, standing defensively, almost as if he were waiting for the enemy with his back pressed against the wall of a fortress.

It is essential to recognize that this chapter, perhaps more than any other in this study, reveals our purpose: not to introduce novel theories or revolutionary tactics for warfare, but to delve into and clarify what has long existed at the core of military conduct, reducing complex practices to their most basic, foundational elements. Here, we seek to explain the underlying mechanics, providing a structured understanding rather than creating new doctrines.

Chapter IX. Defensive Battle

In the preceding chapter, we discussed that when on the defensive, a defender might use a battle with offensive characteristics by moving against and attacking the enemy as soon as they enter the defender's territory. Alternatively, the defender may wait until the enemy appears within range and then proceed to launch an offensive; in such a case, the battle would again be offensive, though with a slightly different approach. Lastly, the defender might wait for the enemy to attack their fortified position directly, allowing the defender to combine both holding a specific area and launching offensives with parts of their force. In this approach, there can be various levels of emphasis on defensive versus offensive actions, with each stage moving further from a counterattack and leaning more toward defending a fixed point. We won't delve here into how far this balance should go or the most advantageous mix of offensive and defensive tactics to secure a decisive victory. Still, we maintain that to achieve a significant victory, the offensive aspect should not be entirely absent. We believe that a decisive victory's outcomes can and must stem from the offensive component of any defensive battle, just as they would in an outright offensive battle.

Strategically, just as a battlefield is merely a point in the broader campaign, the span of a battle is only a moment, and what matters strategically is the outcome, not the unfolding events of the battle itself.

If a complete victory can result from the offensive aspects inherent in a defensive battle, then, strategically, there is no essential difference between offensive and defensive battles in terms of overarching military planning. We are indeed convinced this is the case, though it may appear otherwise. To clarify this point and illustrate our perspective, let's outline what we imagine as an ideal defensive battle.

In this envisioned scenario, the defender awaits the attack in a fortified position chosen carefully for its strategic qualities. The defender has utilized the terrain to its full advantage, gaining a thorough knowledge of the landscape, constructing sturdy fortifications at key points, establishing clear lines of movement, setting up batteries, reinforcing villages, and selecting areas where the defender's forces can assemble out of sight. As forces on both sides clash at various contact points, the defender's fortified front line and obstacles like parallel trenches or commanding heights allow them to inflict heavy casualties on the enemy with relatively smaller forces, keeping the enemy engaged all the way into the heart of the position. Well-chosen flanking supports prevent sudden multi-directional assaults, while the defender's use of concealed spaces makes the enemy approach more cautiously. This cover not only offers security but also allows the defender to counter with effective, smaller offensives that slow down any retreating movement as the battle narrows and intensifies.

The defender, therefore, can maintain some control over the engagement's progress as the battle rages in front of them, recognizing, however, that their defenses will not hold indefinitely. They are aware their flanks are not invincible, and they don't rely solely on a single, heroic charge by a few battalions to alter the battle's entire trajectory. Instead, their defensive formation is layered and deep, with reserves for contingencies spread from divisions down to battalions, each prepared for renewing combat. Simultaneously, the defender keeps a significant portion of their forces—about a fifth to a quarter—well behind the front lines, stationed far enough back to avoid enemy fire and positioned beyond the range of any wide flanking maneuver. This reserve corps is there to reinforce flanks, provide a buffer against unexpected threats, and, crucially, to mount an offensive at the right moment.

In the later stages of the battle, when the attacker's plan is fully visible, and most of their forces are committed, this reserve will be directed at a concentrated section of the enemy's lines, transforming that area into a smaller offensive theater. Here, the defender unleashes all offensive tactics: sudden charges, surprise maneuvers, encircling movements, and pressure precisely where the battle is most intensely centered. This calculated pressure will force the enemy's forces to recoil, turning their earlier momentum against them, and potentially deciding the battle in favor of the defender.

This is the standard conception of a defensive battle based on modern tactical principles. In such a battle, the assailant typically attempts a wide turning maneuver to bolster their attack and increase the victory's impact. The defender, in response, counteracts this with a partial turning maneuver, specifically targeting the part of the enemy's forces that are attempting to encircle. This counteraction is usually sufficient to neutralize the enemy's attempt to encircle, though it does not lead to a complete encirclement of the assailant's forces. Therefore, a distinction in the outcome remains: the side fighting an offensive battle will tend to surround the enemy, directing their efforts toward the center, while the defending side, fighting a defensive battle, will often act outward, from the center toward the perimeter, in a radiating pattern.

On the battlefield itself and in the initial stages of pursuit, the encircling form is often the most effective. This is not just due to its form alone but because, if carried to its fullest extent, it can significantly limit the enemy's retreat options during the battle. Yet, it is precisely this extreme point of envelopment that the defender's counter-efforts are aimed at resisting. In many cases, even if the defender's efforts aren't sufficient to secure a victory, they can at least prevent such a constriction of retreat, which is the most dangerous threat in defensive battles. If the defender cannot prevent this constriction, the impact on the battle itself and the early retreat stages could be highly advantageous for the attacker.

However, this danger typically does not persist beyond the initial retreat stage, usually lasting only until nightfall. By the next day, the encircling effect generally dissolves, restoring both sides to a more balanced position regarding retreat options. The defender may still face the disadvantage of losing a primary line of retreat, leaving them in a weaker strategic position for future operations. However, the assailant's turning maneuver is often designed specifically for the battlefield and may not have broader application beyond it.

But what occurs if the defender is victorious? Typically, a division of the defeated force ensues. This initial split might seem to ease the retreat for the attacker, yet by the following day, a regrouping of all divisions becomes essential. Should the defender's victory be particularly decisive, and if they pursue the assailant with determination, this regrouping may become impossible. The consequences of this separation can be catastrophic, leading progressively toward a complete disintegration of the attacking force. For instance, if Napoleon had triumphed at Leipzig, the Allied forces would have been split, severely undermining their strategic stance. In the battle of Dresden, while not a purely defensive engagement, Napoleon's attack took on a similar central-outward form. The Allies suffered greatly due to the division of their forces, a predicament from which they were only saved by the victory at the Katzbach, prompting Napoleon to redirect the Imperial Guard back to Dresden.

The battle at the Katzbach offers a similar example: there, the defender shifted to an offensive stance at the last moment, which allowed them to operate along divergent lines. This maneuver effectively fragmented the French forces, and in the aftermath, several days later, Puthod's division fell to the Allies as a prize of victory.

From this, we can conclude that while an assailant, through their natural concentric approach, can amplify the scope of a victory, a defender, by leveraging their natural divergent form, can also achieve extended success. When the defender's divergent actions are executed skillfully, they can magnify the victory's consequences in ways similar to, if not equal to, the assailant's concentric advantage. Thus, both methods provide substantial means for each side to expand the results of their respective victories.

If, in military history, we seldom see defensive battles achieve the kind of overwhelming victories often associated with offensive ones, this does not disprove the assertion that both forms of battle are equally capable of yielding decisive victories. The root of this discrepancy lies in the typical circumstances surrounding the defender. The defensive army is often at a disadvantage, not only in terms of troop strength but also in other critical factors. This army usually finds itself unable, or perceives itself unable, to pursue victory to its fullest potential, often focusing instead on fending off immediate threats and maintaining its honor without pressing for a complete, decisive outcome.

We do not dispute that a defender may indeed be constrained by lesser numbers or other unfavorable conditions; these limitations can restrict the defender's ability to capitalize on victory fully. However, this pragmatic reality has frequently been misinterpreted as an intrinsic characteristic of the defensive role itself. Consequently, an inaccurate view has taken hold: one suggesting that defensive battles should only aim to repel the enemy's assaults rather than focus on decisively defeating them. We believe this view is a damaging misconception, one that substitutes the defensive form of war for its essence.

In the form of warfare we call defense, a successful battle may not only be as likely to achieve a victory as an offensive one but can also yield victories of equal magnitude and consequence. This is true not only in the aggregate outcomes of multiple engagements across a campaign but also in any single battle, provided the defensive army possesses the necessary strength and resolve. Thus, the defensive form of war is capable of producing results every bit as decisive and impactful as the offensive, so long as the defender's resources and intent are focused on achieving not just survival, but total victory.

Chapter X. Fortresses

In earlier times, up until the establishment of large standing armies, fortresses—whether castles or fortified towns—were built mainly to protect the people who lived within them. A baron, finding himself surrounded by enemies, would retreat into his castle, hoping to buy time and wait for a more favorable moment, while towns fortified themselves with walls to shield against the temporary storm of passing conflicts. This straightforward purpose of fortresses, rooted in protection and defense, didn't remain their only function for long. As the presence of a fortified place began to affect control over the surrounding territory and even influence the movement and success of armies across the land, fortresses gained a broader strategic value. Their significance began to extend beyond just the walls they encompassed; they played an essential role in the overall success or failure of military campaigns, becoming vital to the cohesion and strategy of war itself.

Over time, fortresses became so strategically important that they began to dictate the main objectives of military campaigns. In fact, capturing one or more of these fortresses often took precedence over directly defeating the enemy's army in open battle. Strategists returned to the idea of fortresses as integral points that influenced a broader area, affecting both territory and armies. They began to meticulously plan which points to fortify, often delving into detailed, almost philosophical reasoning about where these fortresses should be situated. This approach, however, eventually led to the original purpose of fortifications—protecting people and communities—being nearly forgotten. Planners started envisioning fortresses as purely military installations, disconnected from towns or inhabitants.

Meanwhile, the days when simply walling off a town could effectively shield it from widespread invasions had also come to an end. Such protection had once been viable due to factors like the fragmented nature of nations into smaller states and the seasonal nature of past invasions. These incursions were often brief, aligning with feudal obligations or mercenary contracts that expired with the seasons. But with the advent of large, standing armies equipped with powerful artillery, walls alone could no longer stand up to sustained assaults. Cities and towns, now aware that resistance would only lead to inevitable defeat and harsher treatment afterward, were less inclined to invest in fortifications. Similarly, armies could no longer afford to divide their forces into scattered garrisons. Such a strategy might temporarily slow an enemy's progress but would eventually lead to these garrisons' capture, weakening the overall defensive force.

To effectively counter an invading army, a defending force needs to maintain enough strength to match its opponent in open battle, unless it can count on an ally to reinforce or relieve these strongholds. This shift led to a reduction in the number of fortresses, which in turn led to a change in the purpose of these structures. The role of fortresses shifted away from providing direct protection to specific towns and toward a more indirect defense of the country. Rather than protecting people directly, fortresses became strategic anchors that held together the broader structure of military defense.

This evolution in thinking played out not only in theory but also in practice, though, as often happens, the ideas took on even greater complexity and abstraction in military literature. While this shift toward strategic importance was logical, these ideas were sometimes taken to excessive lengths, with theoretical notions overshadowing the practical need for fortifications. In looking to address these real, straightforward needs, we will consider the main objectives and essential functions of fortresses, starting with the simpler aspects and progressing to more complex considerations. In the next chapter, we will explore what these conclusions mean for determining both the placement and number of fortresses.

The effectiveness of a fortress comes from two main aspects: its passive and active capabilities. Passively, a fortress serves as a secure shelter for everything within its walls, offering protection to people, supplies, and strategic assets. Actively, it exerts an influence over the surrounding area, often extending beyond the range of its artillery. This active influence arises from the attacks or sorties that the garrison—troops stationed inside the fortress—may launch against any enemy forces that approach within a certain radius.

The size of the garrison plays a role in the range and impact of these actions. With a larger garrison, more troops can be deployed on these expeditions, allowing for a broader scope of operations. Consequently, a larger fortress can project its influence farther into the surrounding area, not just in terms of strength but also across a greater expanse. This active element, however, divides into two kinds: first, the direct sorties and operations undertaken by the fortress's own garrison, and second, the support of outside military units that, while not part of the garrison, can rely on the fortress for temporary safety and assistance.

For example, smaller corps that might not be strong enough to withstand an enemy on their own could operate near a fortress, using it as a fallback if the situation turns against them. This can allow them to control or at least influence the surrounding territory. However, the scope of operations a garrison can undertake is generally limited. Even in large fortresses with strong garrisons, these troops can only conduct operations on a small scale compared to the main field armies, with their range often limited to a few days' travel from the fortress. In smaller fortresses, any detachments sent out are usually minimal and restricted to the immediate vicinity, perhaps just the closest villages.

Yet troops not permanently assigned to the fortress—those who don't need to return to its safety each time—have much greater freedom of movement. Through their presence, the area of influence of a fortress can expand significantly, provided conditions are favorable. Thus, when we consider the active influence of fortresses in general, the actions of these external forces play a crucial role in shaping that influence.

Even the smallest active effort by a garrison remains vital to fulfilling the various purposes a fortress serves. Strictly speaking, even the most passive function of a fortress—resisting a direct assault—relies to some degree on this active element. That said, at different times and under different circumstances, a fortress may lean more heavily on its passive or active strengths, depending on its immediate role. Sometimes a fortress serves a straightforward purpose with a direct effect; at other times, its role may be more complex, with a more indirect impact. We will look at these purposes separately, starting with the simpler cases. However, it is important to note that a fortress may be intended to serve multiple purposes simultaneously or to shift its role over the course of a campaign.

In conclusion, fortresses are essential, powerful assets for the defense, providing stability, strategic support, and flexibility to defensive operations.

1. Fortresses as secure depots for supplies of all kinds While an attacking army typically depends on finding provisions as it moves forward, a defending army must prepare well in advance, stockpiling food, ammunition, medical supplies, and other necessities. This enables the defender to limit the strain on the local population and resources within the occupied territory. For the defensive side, therefore, secure depots are a critical need. Unlike the supplies of an advancing aggressor, which are safe in the rear and outside immediate danger, the defensive side's stockpiles are situated within the active theater of war, making them more vulnerable.

If these essential resources are not protected within fortified locations, it creates a dangerous liability. In such cases, the defending forces may need to disperse their positions across a wider area to protect these depots, stretching their line and potentially weakening their front. This dispersion can force the defensive into unfavorable or stretched-out positions simply to safeguard their supplies. Thus, for an army without the protection of fortresses, the risks increase significantly, much like a vulnerable body exposed without armor. The defensive, without these fortified storehouses, is left with multiple points of vulnerability, each one susceptible to attack and disruption.

2. As a safeguard for major and prosperous towns. This role of fortresses is closely linked to their use as secure depots, as large, prosperous cities—especially those that are commercial centers—naturally serve as reservoirs of supplies and resources for an army. The possession or loss of such towns directly impacts the army's ability to sustain itself. Additionally, beyond their logistical significance, preserving these wealthier areas is valuable as part of the national assets. These cities contribute essential resources to the war effort and, when peace negotiations come into play, controlling a prominent city provides the defending nation with substantial leverage.

In modern times, this protective function of fortifications has not always been prioritized, even though it remains one of the most effective and reliable purposes for which fortresses can be used. Imagining a country where all significant cities, wealthy commercial hubs, and even moderately populated areas were fortified and defended by their citizens and neighboring communities, the speed and ease of any military invasion would be dramatically hindered. In such a scenario, the defending population could exert its full influence, making any enemy general's strategic talents and willpower far less effective against a widespread, robust line of fortified resistance.

This ideal vision of fortification underscores the importance of direct protection provided by fortresses, preventing them from being overlooked. However, this concept will not preoccupy our further analysis, as it's understood that some fortresses need to be fortified more robustly than others to serve as key strongholds and genuine supports for an active army's movements and operations.

For the purposes outlined in points 1 and 2, fortresses primarily fulfill a passive defensive function by providing secure storage and protection for both supplies and critical urban centers.

3. As true barriers, they block main roads and, in many cases, rivers where they are strategically positioned. Fortresses serve not just as defensive strongholds but as actual obstructions to movement, effectively closing off key routes and waterways from the enemy. The challenge of bypassing a fortress is often far more complex than it may initially seem. It is not merely a matter of finding an alternative path around the fortress; any detour must stay beyond the fortress's artillery range and sufficiently far to avoid surprise attacks from the garrison. This requires a sizable deviation, which complicates the enemy's progress significantly.

In areas with rugged terrain or dense features, even the smallest road deviations can create time-consuming obstacles. A forced detour may result in the delay of an entire day's march, or, if it affects a main thoroughfare, it could create logistical bottlenecks that have larger implications for the movement of troops and supplies.

When a fortress controls a river's course, its influence extends even further, restricting navigation and thus disrupting essential supply lines or strategic movements by water. This ability to control or even close navigation routes is one of the most direct ways a fortress can exert strategic power over the surrounding area and block the enemy's advance.

As tactical points of support. Due to the considerable range covered by the fire of even modest fortifications—often extending several miles—fortresses serve as highly effective anchor points for the flanks of a defensive position. While natural barriers such as a lake stretching for several miles can be a strong support for an army's flank, a moderately fortified fortress provides an even better safeguard. Unlike with a natural barrier, the defensive line does not need to connect directly to the fortress. The enemy, concerned with maintaining a secure path for retreat, will generally avoid positioning themselves between our flank and a fortified stronghold, reducing the risk of flanking maneuvers and adding security to our defensive stance.

5. As a station or waypoint. When fortresses lie along the defensive side's communication lines, as is often the case, they act as stopping points for all traffic moving up and down these routes. The greatest threats to these lines typically come from irregular or mobile enemy units that cause disruptive "shock" attacks. However, if a valuable convoy or small troop detachment encounters such a threat, reaching a nearby fortress by quick maneuvering can provide shelter until the danger passes. In addition, troops marching to or from the main army can rest and regroup briefly at a fortress, strengthening their readiness for the remainder of their march. A halt in the midst of a march is particularly vulnerable to surprise attacks, but a fortress positioned halfway along a 30-mile communication line can essentially "shorten" that line by half, offering safe intervals of rest and cover.

6. As a refuge for weakened or retreating forces. A fortress of modest size can offer protection for retreating or weakened corps, shielding them from enemy pursuit even if no fortified camp is prepared. Though a corps may need to halt its retreat temporarily, this is often a minor compromise, especially in situations where further retreat might lead to complete annihilation. In certain cases, a fortress allows a battered corps to regroup and hold ground for a few days without necessitating full retreat. This is especially

helpful for slightly injured soldiers and scattered stragglers who precede a retreating force; they can find refuge in the fortress and await the chance to rejoin their units.

For example, in 1806, if the Prussian retreat had passed through Magdeburg and not been compromised at Auerstadt, the army could have paused there for three or four days, allowing it time to rally and reorganize. Even as events unfolded, Magdeburg still became a vital gathering place for remnants of Hohenlohe's corps, helping it regain some semblance of an organized force. The reassuring presence of fortresses becomes especially clear during times of crisis in war: they offer ammunition, supplies, forage, shelter for the sick, safety for the healthy, and a place for soldiers in panic to regain their composure. In this way, they serve as an "oasis" in the middle of a chaotic battlefield landscape.

In these last four purposes, fortresses take on a more active role, showing their dynamic utility in providing strategic and tactical advantages.

7. As a shield against the enemy's advance. Fortresses left ahead of the main defensive lines create significant obstacles for the enemy, acting like ice floes that slow or disrupt the forward current of an attack. These fortifications at least force the enemy to set up an encircling siege, which, if the fortress is well-manned with courageous and proactive defenders, could require the enemy to commit twice as many troops. Furthermore, these garrisons are often made up of soldiers who may not be fit for combat in open field, such as partially trained militia, invalids, recovering soldiers, armed civilians, or local defense forces. This setup means that the enemy may end up devoting up to four times the manpower compared to the forces required on the defensive side.

The primary and most significant advantage of a fortress under siege is the marked drain it imposes on the enemy's strength, as they must dedicate a large portion of their forces to encircle and besiege it. However, this is only the beginning of the advantages a fortress offers through its resistance. Once an enemy breaches our line of fortresses, they face increasingly restricted maneuverability. Their potential routes for retreat are narrowed, and they must continually monitor and shield the positions where they have committed to sieges, effectively slowing their advance and creating opportunities for the defensive side to exploit any weak points in their lines.

In this way, fortresses serve as a powerful ally to the defensive strategy, supporting the overall defense in a substantial and impactful way. This particular role of fortresses—acting as a force that disrupts, restricts, and forces adjustments in the enemy's strategy—can be seen as their most critical function. Although we might not frequently encounter this strategic use of fortresses in military history, this is due more to the nature of most wars than to the inherent value of this strategy. In fact, the role of fortresses in such a context may be seen as overly decisive or too conclusive a factor for the majority of campaigns, a complexity we will explore further at a later point.

This specific use of fortresses mainly draws on their offensive capabilities, particularly the ability of their garrison to launch sorties and disrupt enemy operations. If a fortress merely acted as an inaccessible point that couldn't be taken, it would certainly inconvenience the attacker but likely not enough to force a siege. However, leaving behind several thousand defenders with the capacity to conduct raids and harass supply lines creates an intolerable risk for the invader. Consequently, they are forced either to encircle the fortress with a large force or, if they wish to commit fewer troops to the task, to invest in a full siege and aim to capture it definitively. Once the siege is underway, the passive qualities of the fortress—its walls, defenses, and fortifications—become essential in prolonging its resistance and imposing further strain on the besieging force.

All of the purposes fortresses serve, as discussed so far, are achieved straightforwardly, often through immediate or direct effects. The next two roles, however, involve a more nuanced form of influence that operates indirectly.

8. As a shield for extended cantonments. A moderately-sized fortress naturally obstructs access to cantonments positioned directly behind it for a stretch of around three to four miles. But in military history, we often find examples where such a fortress is said to secure a line of cantonments stretching fifteen or even twenty miles. To understand this phenomenon, we must explore when this effect genuinely occurs and clarify instances where it may be more of a perceived than a real influence.

Several factors help clarify how this broader protection might arise:

(1.) The fortress, by nature, blocks a principal road, creating an obstruction across a few miles of territory. This naturally provides a buffer zone, making it harder for the enemy to approach any cantonments directly behind this zone.

(2.) The fortress often serves as an unusually robust outpost. Its location enhances the ability to monitor surrounding areas, both strategically and through local intelligence sources. For example, the fortress, being located within a larger town with thousands of residents, maintains closer connections with the surrounding districts, making it easier to gather information and observe enemy movements than a typical outpost stationed in a small village might be able to.

(3.) Small corps stationed near the fortress gain security from its protective cover, allowing them to push forward periodically for reconnaissance or intelligence-gathering. If the enemy attempts to bypass or encircle the fortress, these corps can launch small attacks against the enemy's rear. Thus, while a fortress is stationary, it can project influence similar to that of an active, advanced corps by guarding the areas around it and making enemy approaches more challenging.

(4.) When the defender gathers his forces near the fortress, he can position them just behind it. Any enemy advance toward this position would risk exposure to attacks from the fortress at their rear, effectively creating a natural defense that discourages direct encroachment.

In this way, a fortress can provide a broad area of protection to cantonments and support a defensive strategy, even across larger distances than it may seem capable of at first glance.

Certainly, any attack aimed at a line of cantonments, as we're discussing here, must be understood in the context of a surprise assault, or at least a sudden, unexpected action. It's evident that a surprise attack tends to achieve its effects far more quickly than a planned, regular offensive across a theatre of war. Consequently, while in a regular campaign a fortress positioned in the enemy's path would need to be encircled and neutralized to maintain the advance, this is not as strictly necessary in the case of a swift, surprise raid on scattered cantonments. Thus, the fortress itself may present a less formidable obstacle in such situations. That said, for cantonments situated within six to eight miles of the fortress, it's clear that direct security won't be provided by the fortress alone.

However, the real purpose of a surprise attack on cantonments isn't solely to capture a few isolated quarters. Without delving too deeply—since more details on this will come in the discussion on offensive tactics—it's worth noting that the primary aim of such an attack is generally achieved by engaging scattered units who are more concerned with regrouping than with preparing for combat. This sort of attack will likely drive forward toward the center of the enemy's cantonments, where any major fortress positioned before the center of these quarters will inevitably serve as a notable hindrance to the aggressor.

Taking into account all four points mentioned, it becomes clear that a strategically placed fortress offers a degree of protection to a far larger stretch of cantonments than might initially seem apparent. This "protection," however, should be understood as a layer of deterrence rather than an impregnable shield. The existence of the fortress makes any potential enemy approach more challenging and forces a more serious calculation of risks. The added complications may decrease the likelihood of a sudden assault but do not make it impossible. Direct security for each cantonment must still rely on well-organized outposts and the careful positioning of the quarters themselves.

Thus, while attributing the ability to cover an extensive line of cantonments to a fortress does carry some truth, it's equally necessary to acknowledge that in both campaign plans and historical accounts, one can often encounter exaggerated or vague interpretations of this defensive role. This indirect protection relies on the alignment of various factors; when conditions deviate—particularly under an especially bold or determined enemy—such a protective influence may prove less effective or even illusory. Therefore, in practical warfare, the defensive commander should refrain from assuming the effectiveness of a fortress without closely examining how it fits into the specific circumstances and vulnerabilities of each unique case.

9. As a defense for an unoccupied province. If a province, during wartime, is either left unoccupied or only lightly guarded, and is thus vulnerable to raids or incursions by small, mobile enemy forces, then a fortress of significant size can serve as a form of protection or, at the very least, a safeguard for that province. At the very least, it provides a measure of security since the enemy would have to capture the fortress before truly controlling the area, which buys time for reinforcements to be sent to defend it. The actual "covering" effect, however, is quite indirect. The fortress alone cannot effectively block enemy incursions; instead, its influence is mostly limited to how actively it can deter small enemy groups from advancing freely.

If this opposition is strictly left to what the garrison can achieve on its own, the impact will generally be minor. Typically, garrisons in these places are relatively small, often made up of infantry units, and these are not always the highest-quality troops. The concept of protection becomes slightly more substantial if small columns or detachments are stationed nearby, able to use the fortress as a secure base of operations and to retreat there for refuge if necessary. In such cases, the fortress acts as a stabilizing point, allowing these mobile units to venture into the province to monitor and check enemy advances, albeit in a limited capacity. This indirect protection can help mitigate the risks of enemy raids by creating a certain degree of security and flexibility for defensive operations within the vulnerable province.

10. As a rallying center for a national uprising. In a People's War, supplies of provisions, arms, and ammunition are rarely managed in a structured way. Instead, the very essence of such a war is to make use of

whatever resources can be gathered from diverse, often unconventional sources. In this way, countless small contributions for resistance emerge that otherwise might have remained unused, and a well-fortified, spacious fortress serves as a central stockpile for these resources. This strengthens the defense significantly, providing the entire effort with greater unity, effectiveness, and impact.

Moreover, a fortress becomes a haven for the wounded, a seat for civil authorities, a secure location for state funds, and a rallying point for planning and executing larger maneuvers. It serves as a resilient focal point for the defensive effort, allowing these dispersed efforts to gain greater coordination. During a siege, the fortress also demands a considerable portion of the enemy's attention and resources, thus creating a strategic advantage by weakening the aggressor's hold and making it easier for local militias and national levies to mount coordinated attacks in support. In this way, the fortress not only preserves the immediate resources of war but also magnifies the potential of widespread resistance, bringing cohesion and support to the defenders.

11. For defending rivers and mountain regions. A fortress placed on a major river serves numerous crucial functions, acting almost as a multi-purpose stronghold. Such a fortress not only secures a crossing point on the river for friendly forces, enabling safe passage whenever needed, but also restricts the enemy's access to crossing for several miles along both banks. Additionally, it controls the river for trade and transport, shelters vessels within its secure walls, blocks key bridges and roadways, and supports an indirect defense by holding positions on the enemy's side of the river. Through this extensive influence over river access and control, a fortress in such a location becomes a fundamental asset for the broader river defense strategy.

Similarly, fortresses positioned in mountainous regions hold immense strategic value. Situated at critical junctions of road networks that begin and end at their location, these fortresses command the entire region covered by these pathways, making it difficult for an enemy to penetrate without facing substantial resistance. Effectively, they become the cornerstone for defending the mountainous terrain, functioning as the structural supports, or "buttresses," of the whole defensive setup in these challenging environments. In both river and mountain defenses, the fortress's role is to bind the broader defensive network together, securing vital points and strengthening the integrity of the entire defense system.

Chapter XI. Fortresses (Continued)

We have now discussed the purpose of fortresses, so let's turn to where they should be situated. Initially, this seems complex, especially given the range of objectives and how local features might influence each one. But if we focus on the core essentials and avoid unnecessary complexities, the matter simplifies.

It's clear that all these requirements can largely be met by fortifying the largest and wealthiest towns within any war-impacted regions—especially those on major highways that connect the two countries in conflict. This approach should prioritize towns near harbors, bays, large rivers, or mountainous terrain. Typically, significant towns align naturally with major highways, which, in turn, often connect with important waterways and coastal areas. These four elements—key towns, main roads, rivers, and the coast—harmonize well, creating a cohesive structure without contradictions. Mountains, however, are an exception, as large towns rarely appear in such rugged locations. When a mountain range serves as a strong defensive line, its roads and passes should be secured with smaller, specialized forts built at minimal cost, reserving major fortification efforts for key military hubs in flatter areas.

We haven't yet addressed considerations like the country's borders, the geometric arrangement of the entire fortress network, or specific geographic points tied to fortress locations. We focus here on these primary factors as they often suffice, especially for smaller states. However, in certain cases, additional considerations may be necessary, particularly in larger countries. In more expansive regions, there may be either a surplus of crucial towns and roads or, conversely, very few; some countries may already possess numerous fortifications but need more, while others are resource-constrained and require only a minimal number to serve their needs. Essentially, if the number of fortresses doesn't align with the available significant towns and roads—whether due to surplus or scarcity—further adjustments are essential.

Now, let's consider the nature of these additional factors. The main questions that remain concern

1. Selecting the most strategic main roads, especially when there are multiple routes connecting the two countries, is crucial if we can't afford to fortify every single one. This requires identifying which roads are most essential to the defense strategy, typically those that could either enhance the defender's mobility or most disrupt the enemy's advance.

2. Deciding whether fortresses should be positioned solely along the frontier or distributed more evenly throughout the interior is another key consideration. Placing fortresses exclusively on the frontier can create a strong initial defense, forming a barrier at the country's edge; however, spacing them across the country allows for a more layered defense, providing fallbacks and logistical support points as the enemy advances deeper.

3. Determining if fortresses should be distributed evenly or clustered in groups is also important. A uniform spread may help defend broader areas but grouping them strategically can establish strongholds that are difficult for the enemy to bypass or isolate, creating points of concentrated resistance.

4. Lastly, geographic conditions unique to the region must also be taken into account. Natural barriers like mountains, rivers, or even dense forests can enhance the defensive value of fortresses, potentially reducing the need for extensive fortifications while still providing formidable defense points.

There are a few additional considerations regarding the optimal arrangement of a line of fortifications, including whether these defenses should be positioned in a single line or multiple, layered lines—that is, determining if a staggered formation, with fortresses positioned one behind another, is more effective than a side-by-side arrangement along a straight line. Additionally, there is the option to place them in a checkerboard pattern or in a layout resembling a fortified line with strategic salients and re-entering angles. However, we view these decisions as largely inconsequential compared to more significant strategic choices. In many military texts, these subtleties receive undue attention, yet in the context of larger defensive objectives, they hold limited practical value. We mention them here only because of the attention they receive, even if they contribute little to the broader strategic picture.

For clarity, consider the example of southern Germany's strategic relationship with France, specifically along the upper Rhine. If we imagine southern Germany as a unified territory—disregarding the separate states within it—numerous high-quality roads extend from the Rhine into the interior regions of Franconia, Bavaria, and Austria. While many towns of varying significance populate this area, several are especially prominent, such as Nuremberg, Würzburg, Ulm, Augsburg, and Munich. Yet, if only a select few locations can be fortified, choosing becomes crucial. Even if we prioritize the wealthiest and largest towns, there are still strategic implications based on each town's position. For example, the distance between Nuremberg and Munich suggests that Nuremberg has a different strategic role than Munich. Therefore, we might consider fortifying a nearby area closer to Munich, even if that place itself is of lesser inherent importance.

To address such questions, we can turn to principles outlined in previous discussions on defense planning and the choice of key points for attack. Ideally, defensive preparations should align with the likely points of enemy aggression. Thus, when faced with multiple significant roads leading from the enemy's territory into ours, we should first fortify the one leading most directly to our nation's heartland or one that provides the enemy with logistical advantages, such as access to fertile provinces or parallel routes along navigable rivers. By fortifying such roads, we force the assailant into a direct confrontation with these defenses. If they choose to bypass them, it may expose their flanks, creating a strategic vulnerability we can exploit.

Using the example of Vienna as the focal point of southern Germany, Munich or Augsburg would hold greater value as principal fortresses against a French advance compared to Nuremberg or Würzburg. This importance is heightened when considering access routes from Italy through Switzerland and the Tyrol, making Munich and Augsburg critical, whereas Würzburg and Nuremberg hold much less strategic significance by comparison.

Turning to the second question—whether fortresses should concentrate on the frontier or be spread throughout the country—this becomes largely irrelevant for smaller states, where the entire territory often aligns closely with what could be termed the "strategic frontier." For larger states, however, this consideration becomes more pressing.

The initial response is to place fortresses along the frontier, as they are designed to protect the state, which, in theory, remains secure as long as its borders hold. Yet, while this logic holds in the abstract, practical considerations introduce many nuances that require modification of this approach.

Any defensive strategy relying heavily on outside assistance places considerable emphasis on the value of time. It's less about delivering a forceful counterattack than about sustaining a prolonged defense where the primary benefit comes from slowing down the enemy rather than directly reducing his forces. Naturally, it follows that, when all other factors are equal, fortresses spread out across a country and encompassing a large territory take longer to fall than those compressed into a concentrated line along the frontier. Additionally, in cases where an enemy can be weakened due to the length and difficulty of his supply lines, it's illogical to concentrate all defenses solely on the border.

Consider, for instance, that fortifying the capital is often essential; beyond this, the principal towns and economic centers within each province may also require fortification. Rivers, mountain ranges, and other geographic barriers offer opportunities for new defensive lines, and some towns, by virtue of their strong natural positions, lend themselves well to fortification. Certain vital military assets, such as armories and weapon factories, are safer when situated within the interior rather than near the border, and these often deserve the added protection of fortifications. With these factors in mind, even if a state possesses many fortresses along its frontier, it would be a serious oversight to neglect placing some in the interior. For example, we believe France may have erred by under-fortifying its interior regions.

In regions where border provinces lack significant towns, while these lie further inland—such as in South Germany, where Swabia has few large towns compared to Bavaria—a definitive answer on whether to place fortresses in the interior may not be necessary. Often, factors specific to a region's unique situation should guide these decisions rather than rigid general rules. However, it is worth noting the strategic importance of this balance.

Now to the third question: should fortresses be arranged in clusters, or more evenly dispersed? This issue is rarely pressing but is not without relevance. For example, a group of two to four fortresses located within a few days' march of a central point creates a fortified area with increased defensive power, which could serve as a stronghold for stationed armies. Such a grouping, where conditions permit, might tempt military planners to create a strategic bastion.

Finally, we should examine other geographic attributes when selecting sites for fortresses. While fortresses along coasts, rivers, and in mountainous areas have been previously noted for their strategic advantages, there remain numerous additional geographical factors that influence the effectiveness and placement of fortresses, all of which deserve careful attention.

If a fortress cannot be directly situated on a river, it's actually more strategic to place it further away—around ten to twelve miles distant—rather than close by. If positioned too near, the river divides and limits the effective range of the fortress's influence in all the important functions it serves. For instance, Philippsburg is a classic example of poor positioning; it was like a person standing so close to a wall that they could hardly see anything beyond it.

Mountains present a different case since they don't limit movement for large or small forces on specific points as a river does. However, fortresses placed on the enemy's side of a mountain range tend to be poorly positioned since they're harder to support and defend. When on our side, however, they are difficult for the enemy to lay siege to, as the mountain range cuts across his lines of communication. Olmütz, during the 1758 campaign, serves as an illustrative example.

The influence of forests and marshes, which are difficult to cross, can be similar to that of rivers when it comes to strategically positioning a fortress.

There's also been debate about the value of fortifying towns located in particularly challenging terrain. While these can indeed be blockaded more easily, their defense and fortification can often be accomplished at a lower cost. Fortresses in difficult landscapes can often be made stronger with the same resources and sometimes even impregnable. Since the role of a fortress is more often passive than active, this objection about blockading does not carry as much weight.

Now, if we take a step back to review this straightforward framework for national fortification, we see that it's built on enduring and substantial factors directly tied to the foundational needs of the state, rather than on temporary strategies or fashionable military theories. It avoids unnecessary strategic complexities or unique requirements, errors which might be disastrous when applied to structures intended to last for centuries. For instance, Silberberg in Silesia, built by Frederick the Great on one of the Sudetic ridges, has lost nearly all its original strategic value due to shifting circumstances. In contrast, Breslau, if fortified as a reliable stronghold, would have retained its significance in defense, serving well against potential threats from the French, Russians, Poles, and Austrians alike.

It's important to remember that these insights aren't intended as a blueprint for an entire country to undertake building new fortifications all at once, since such sweeping projects are exceedingly rare. Instead, they serve as guiding principles that can be applied whenever a single fortress is planned or constructed.

Chapter XII.
Defensive Position

Every position where we take a stand to fight, while also using the natural features of the land for protection, is a defensive position. This applies whether we fight more passively or actively. This follows the basic understanding of defense that we've explained.

We can also call it a defensive position if an army on the march toward the enemy would take up a fight if the enemy decided to attack. Most battles happen this way, and during the Middle Ages, it was nearly the only way battles were fought. But that is not quite the type of position we are describing here; most positions actually are like this, and calling a position "defensive" compared to a "camp taken up along a march" would be enough to explain the difference. So, for a position to be specifically called a defensive position, it must have certain defining characteristics.

In decisions made in an ordinary position, the element of time usually plays the biggest role; armies approach one another to engage in battle, and the location matters less as long as it's not a poor choice. But in a true defensive position, the significance of place is key; the battle is meant to be fought in that specific location, or rather, that particular spot will play a major role in deciding the battle's outcome. This is the only kind of position we mean here.

This connection with the place is twofold. First, the position of the defending force has an overall effect on the war. And second, the natural features of the area help strengthen the defending army by providing protection. In other words, it connects both strategically and tactically.

The idea of a defensive position technically originates from a tactical perspective, as its strategic purpose—where an army stationed at this spot helps defend the region—could also apply to an army that's attacking. We can only fully explain the strategic effects of a position later, when discussing defending a whole war zone; here, we'll consider it as much as possible by examining two ideas that are similar and sometimes confused: turning a position and bypassing it.

Turning a position involves its front lines and is done either by attacking the side of the position, striking its rear, or targeting its retreat and communication routes.

The first approach, attacking the flank or rear, is tactical in nature. With the high mobility of today's forces, most battle strategies include plans to turn or surround the enemy, so every position should be chosen to prepare for such tactics. For a position to be strong, it must allow good setups for fighting on its flanks and rear in case these are threatened, not just relying on the front lines. This way, a position doesn't become useless if the enemy moves to attack from the side or rear, since the choice of the position itself was made with such possible battles in mind, ensuring that the defender keeps all the advantages they expected.

If the enemy turns the position to target its retreat and communication routes, this becomes a strategic issue, and the question then is how long the position can be held, or if the defender can counter the enemy's plan with one of their own. Both questions depend on the location of the point strategically—that is, mainly on how the communication lines are situated for both sides. A good defensive position should offer the defending army an advantage on this point. In any case, the position will not become useless in this way, as it holds off the enemy when he is drawn in by it as we've described.

However, if the attacker ignores the defending army waiting in its defensive position and instead moves forward with his main forces along a different path to reach his target, then he effectively bypasses the position. If he can do so safely and actually succeeds, this would immediately force the defenders to abandon their position, thereby nullifying its purpose.

There are very few places in the world that cannot be bypassed in this straightforward sense; exceptions like the narrow isthmus of Perekop are so rare they're hardly worth considering. So, when we talk about a position being impossible to bypass, what we really mean is that the disadvantages for the attacker are significant if they try to bypass it. We'll discuss these disadvantages in greater detail in chapter twenty-seven; they range in severity but in all cases serve as a substitute for the tactical impact the position would have had if directly defended, and together, they form the purpose of the position itself.

From the above discussion, we can conclude that two strategic qualities emerge as essential for any defensive position:

1. That it cannot be easily bypassed.
2. That in the contest over control of communication lines, it provides advantages to the defender.

Additionally, we must consider two more strategic qualities:

3. That the alignment of communication lines may also positively shape the form of the battle itself; and
4. That the general characteristics of the surrounding terrain offer additional advantages.

The orientation of communication lines affects not only the feasibility of bypassing a position or disrupting the enemy's supplies, but also influences the entire battle's progression. For instance, an oblique line of retreat enables the attacker to outflank tactically while limiting our own tactical flexibility. Sometimes, this angled positioning with respect to communication lines isn't a tactical choice but results from a strategic flaw, such as when the road's direction shifts near the position (as at Borodino in 1812). In such a setup, the attacker can maneuver around our line without straying from his established alignment.

Furthermore, the attacker gains additional tactical flexibility if he has access to multiple roads for retreat while we are constrained to just one. In these situations, tactical skill on the defensive side is often insufficient to counter the negative impact from such strategic positioning.

As for the fourth point, certain terrain conditions can exert such a strong disadvantage that even the most strategically chosen position and careful tactical planning may not overcome them. Under these circumstances, key considerations include the following:

1. The defensive position should ideally offer clear visibility over the opponent, allowing for quick maneuvers within the defensive lines. Only when ease of oversight and the difficulties of approach combine does the terrain truly benefit the defender. Conversely, areas influenced by higher ground can disadvantage the defender; mountainous positions, in particular, tend to facilitate encirclement even while complicating a

straightforward bypass. Similarly, positions with one flank anchored to mountains are harder to bypass but easier to flank. Positions with a mountain immediately in front or generally corresponding to these unfavorable conditions are similarly problematic. Conversely, a position backed by a mountain provides multiple strategic benefits, making it one of the most advantageous settings for defense.

2. The nature of the terrain should align with the army's composition. An army with substantial cavalry, for instance, would benefit from an open area, while a lack of cavalry and artillery but a strong infantry force seasoned in the area would suggest using rough, enclosed terrain to its advantage.

We are not examining the specific tactical relationship between a defensive position's local features and the forces occupying it; rather, we are focusing on the overall strategic outcome, as it alone constitutes a strategic measure.

Certainly, any position where an army is set to face the full force of an enemy attack should provide the troops with a significant advantage from the ground itself, acting as a force multiplier. Where natural defenses aren't entirely sufficient, entrenchments and artificial fortifications can come into play, occasionally making some sections of the position impenetrable—or even the entire position itself. In this last scenario, however, the goal shifts: instead of seeking a battle with favorable conditions, where victory might decide the campaign, we aim for an outcome without needing a battle. By placing our forces in an unassailable position, we deny the enemy any opportunity for a direct battle, forcing them to seek alternative methods for resolution.

Thus, these two cases—the unassailable strong position and the defensive position intended for battle—must be distinctly separated. We'll discuss the unassailable position in the following chapter, under the concept of a strong position. Here, however, we are considering a defensive position that is effectively just a battlefield with additional favorable elements for the defender. To ensure it becomes a battlefield, though, these advantages should not be overly strong.

The strength a defensive position can hold depends on how committed the enemy is to launching an attack, which in turn hinges on the specific situation. For instance, against a commander with the audacity of Napoleon, we would likely retreat behind more formidable defenses than we might need if facing a less aggressive leader, like Daun or Schwarzenberg.

If parts of a defensive position are entirely unattackable—say, the front—then that becomes a specific advantage, as troops that would otherwise defend this front can be redeployed elsewhere. However, it's worth noting that if the enemy is completely denied access to certain areas, their approach will adapt, taking on an altered strategy, and we need to assess if this shift is ultimately favorable for us.

For example, some armies have positioned themselves immediately behind a large river, using it to block their front. This strategy effectively anchors the army's right or left flank on the river since the enemy must move to either side to cross and approach, often needing to shift its orientation in doing so. Therefore, the key question is what strengths or weaknesses this adjustment in the enemy's approach brings to our position.

In our view, a defensive position approaches its ideal when its true strength is not obvious to the enemy and where the terrain allows for tactical surprises in battle. Just as we would try to hide the size and intent of our forces from the enemy, we should also seek to conceal the tactical advantages we hope to gain from the land itself. Though difficult to achieve entirely, this approach is worth considering, even if it requires unconventional methods.

Proximity to a substantial fortress, regardless of its specific location, provides any defensive position with a significant strategic benefit, giving added mobility and support to forces in the vicinity. Artificial field-works can compensate for natural weaknesses, allowing us to prepare the battlefield's major features ahead of time. By combining these constructed defenses with natural obstacles that obstruct enemy movements without entirely blocking them, we can capitalize on our knowledge of the terrain, particularly if it enables us to move with less detection than the enemy. A position designed with these principles in mind creates a decisive influence over the enemy, causing them to fail without necessarily understanding the reasons for their defeat. This is our concept of a defensive position, and we regard it as one of the key strengths of defensive warfare.

Generally, an undulating countryside that's neither overly cultivated nor too bare is most likely to provide this type of favorable defensive ground.

Chapter XIII. Strong Positions and Entrenched Camps

In the previous chapter, we discussed that a position so fortified by natural features, supplemented by human engineering, to the point of being unassailable belongs to a unique category. Such positions don't qualify as merely advantageous battlefields but occupy a special status, which we shall refer to as strong positions due to their similarity to fortified areas. These positions typically can't be created solely through entrenchments unless they rest on nearby fortresses as entrenched camps, nor are they often found naturally complete without some support from artifice. In practice, natural defenses are usually supplemented with fieldworks, which is why they are sometimes termed entrenched camps or fortified positions. However, this term can apply broadly to any fortified site, even if its strategic purpose differs from the strong positions we're considering here.

The aim of a strong position is to render any stationed forces practically immune to attack. This either protects the area directly or enables those forces to secure a space by positioning themselves effectively, thus protecting the country indirectly. Historically, the first method underpinned the design of defensive lines, such as those along the French frontier, which shielded a specific stretch of land from enemy advances. The second method pertains more to entrenched camps situated near fortresses, designed to hold the front in multiple directions to ensure flexible defense.

To illustrate, if a defensive position has a front so robust with barriers and natural obstructions that direct attack is infeasible, the opponent would have no choice but to attempt an approach from a side or rear flank. To counter this risk, defensible points, or points d'appui, are sought along these lines, such as a river or mountain range that can secure one or both flanks, much like the Rhine and Vosges Mountains did for the lines in Alsace. The longer the fortified line, the harder it is for the attacker to circumvent it, since any attempt to do so increases the risks to the force making the maneuver, especially if this requires significant deviation from their primary path of advance. Thus, a long, well-secured front with solid flanks offers strong direct protection for a substantial area, safeguarding it against invasion. This principle guided the construction of defensive works like those in Alsace, with the right anchored by the Rhine and the left by the Vosges, as well as the Flanders lines, which extended fifteen miles and rested their flanks on the Scheldt River and the fortress of Tournay on one end, and the sea on the other.

However, in cases where such extensive, protected fronts and strong flank supports are absent, and the terrain must be defended by an entrenched force, that position must be fortified to withstand flanking or encirclement, displaying a strong front on all sides. Here, the concept of a wholly covered region fades away since this type of position functions more as a single strategic point, safeguarding the troops within and enabling them to remain in the field—to maintain a foothold in the area, if not to prevent every incursion into the surrounding territory. Unlike a line that resists flanking due to its span, an entrenched camp with fronts in all directions cannot be flanked because it has no single front; however, it can still be bypassed since its area is limited, making circumvention easier than with an extended defensive line.

Entrenched camps associated with fortresses fall into this latter category. Their primary role is to safeguard the troops gathered within, offering them protection and a strategic point of strength. However, these fortified camps also carry a broader strategic significance, as they protect not only the troops stationed within but also serve as a staging ground, supporting other strategic objectives that rely on these sheltered forces for maintaining a presence in the contested area and applying pressure on the enemy.

With this background on the development of these three distinct defensive approaches, we can now examine the effectiveness of each individually. We will look in detail at strong lines, strong positions, and entrenched camps supported by fortresses, analyzing the unique advantages and strategic significance each one holds.

1. Lines — These represent the least effective form of defensive strategy, often referred to as cordon war, where lines of defense are set up to obstruct an advancing enemy. Such lines offer no real resistance unless heavily reinforced by active firepower; otherwise, they are essentially useless. A line without substantial support from troops, positioned to fire, lacks the strength to serve as a true deterrent. The defensive coverage an army can provide is generally limited, meaning these lines must either cover a small area or spread too thin to be effectively manned at each point. This inherent limitation led to the idea of not fully occupying every part of the line but instead watching key points and defending them with powerful reserves, similar to how one might guard a small river. However, this approach contradicts the very nature of entrenched lines, which are intended for fixed, localized defense.

If the terrain itself offers substantial natural barriers, then these entrenchments become unnecessary or, worse, liabilities. Terrain that can be guarded through flexible defense does not need the rigidity of entrenchments, which suit only local defenses. On the other hand, if the entrenchments alone are expected to serve as the primary barrier, their effectiveness is limited. An empty trench, even if fortified with ditches and ramparts, provides little resistance to an organized assault unless defended. In short, if a line is short and sufficiently manned, it can be circumvented, while an extensive line that is thinly defended can be taken head-on with minimal resistance.

Lines are not only vulnerable but also impose a rigid structure, tying down troops in fixed positions and stripping them of flexibility. Against a determined enemy, such lines quickly prove inadequate. Despite these clear drawbacks, lines were often used in past wars, particularly where the general conduct of warfare was more cautious or static. In these cases, even minor obstacles could sometimes achieve results on par with genuine ones. Lines were primarily reserved for guarding against minor incursions rather than full assaults; when deployed for this purpose, they were somewhat useful, though they still occupied troops that might have served more effectively elsewhere. In recent wars, such defensive lines have largely fallen out of favor, and it is uncertain if they will ever be widely used again.

2. Positions — The defense of a region continues as long as the designated defending force remains in place; it only ends when that force leaves or relinquishes the territory. When a defending force needs to maintain its ground against a significantly stronger enemy, creating a position that is unassailable becomes essential. Such a position, as discussed previously, must be capable of presenting a front in all directions. For practical purposes, especially with a smaller defending force (which would likely be the case here), this setup would cover a limited area. However, this compact layout, even if reinforced with fortifications, faces many tactical disadvantages that could hinder a successful defense.

To hold a fortified position that can face attacks from all directions, the extent of the defensive lines would need to be quite large. For this, the position must rely on natural terrain obstacles, making certain areas impassable or difficult for the enemy to approach. Achieving the required strength for such an extensive line isn't feasible with man-made defenses alone; natural barriers like steep hills, rivers, or rugged terrain must form the foundation of the position. In cases where such terrain isn't available, field fortifications alone won't provide the necessary protection. These considerations are primarily tactical, aiming to establish the possibility of such a defensive setup. Examples that illustrate this strategic approach include locations like Pirna, Bunzelwitz, Colberg, Torres Vedras, and Drissa.

From a strategic perspective, the first condition for a position like this is ensuring that the defending force can be supplied for as long as the position is needed. This condition can only be met if the position is backed by a port, as seen in Colberg and Torres Vedras, connected to a fortress like Bunzelwitz and Pirna, or holds large depots within or close to it, as at Drissa. With a port, supplies can be guaranteed for an extended period, making this the most stable scenario. However, if supplies are dependent on depots or nearby fortresses, the ability to sustain the position is time-limited, introducing a vulnerability. Therefore, the logistical demands of such a position reduce the number of suitable locations and make strong, well-supported positions scarce.

To assess the suitability of a defensive position like this, one must consider both its strengths and weaknesses, especially in light of potential enemy actions. A critical question is: What can the aggressor do to challenge or compromise this position?

a. The assailant might bypass a strong position, continue with his objectives, and keep the defensive force at bay with a greater or lesser contingent.

We must differentiate between situations where the primary defensive force holds this position and those where a smaller force alone occupies it.

If the main defending force holds the position, bypassing it only benefits the attacker if there is another significant target nearby that he can seize to gain an advantage—such as a fortress, a capital, or another critical asset. Even if such a target exists, the attacker can only pursue it confidently if his own supply lines and strategic foundation are robust enough to prevent the defending force from threatening his flanks as he advances.

From this, we understand that a strong position is only advisable for the defender's main force under specific conditions. First, the defending force should have a clear opportunity to threaten or strike at the attacker's strategic flank with enough force to halt his advance or, at the very least, restrict his ability to carry out his primary objective. Alternatively, if no important target is within reach of the attacker, then holding a fortified position is advantageous, as it allows the defender to dictate the field without risk. However, if such an objective exists, and the defender cannot effectively threaten the attacker's flank, holding the position becomes inadvisable. In this case, a strategic position might only serve as a temporary feint to distract the attacker, though this brings the risk of being too late to intercept the true point of threat if the feint fails.

When only a smaller force defends the position, the attacker almost always retains another viable target, namely, the defender's main army itself. Here, the true value of the fortified position lies solely in its potential to threaten the attacker's flanks, as any direct opposition would be of limited strategic value without that advantage.

b. If the attacker hesitates to bypass a strong defensive position, he might try to surround it and starve out the defending force. But this approach relies on two key conditions: first, that the defensive position doesn't have an open retreat route at the rear, and second, that the attacker has sufficient numbers to carry out a full encirclement. If both conditions are met, the attacker can indeed neutralize the defensive force by containing it in the strong position; however, this also costs the defensive side its freedom of action and reduces its force's overall strength.

From this, we understand that using a strong position for the main force should only be done when:

(aa) The rear of the position is completely secure, as was the case at Torres Vedras, allowing the defenders to maintain their stronghold without risk of complete encirclement.

(bb) The defending force is aware that the attacker's numbers are insufficient to maintain a successful siege. If the attacker attempts it regardless, the defending force has an advantage, as it can break out of the position to attack sections of the enemy's lines piecemeal, gaining ground and potentially defeating the attackers in segments.

(cc) The defending force is confident of eventual relief, as the Saxons were at Pirna in 1756 or as Prince Charles was at Prague. In these cases, the stronghold serves as a fortified camp where the defenders can wait for reinforcement or rescue. Prince Charles, for example, would not have allowed himself to be surrounded if he hadn't expected relief from the Moravian army.

Thus, at least one of these three conditions must hold for the main body of an army to justifiably occupy a strong position; however, the latter two conditions carry significant risks for the defender, as the gamble of being outmatched or delayed in receiving relief could lead to severe consequences.

If the strong position is instead held by a smaller force that may need to sacrifice itself to benefit the whole, these requirements change, and the focus becomes whether the potential sacrifice of this corps prevents a greater loss elsewhere. While rare, this tactic is feasible; for instance, the entrenched camp at Pirna in 1756 effectively stopped Frederick the Great from advancing into Bohemia. At that time, Austria was underprepared, and losing Bohemia would likely have resulted in far more casualties than the 17,000 allied troops who eventually surrendered at Pirna.

c. If neither of the scenarios described in points a and b provide a viable option for the attacker—meaning that the defensive side's conditions have been effectively met—then the attacker has little choice but to halt in front of the position, much like a hunting dog pointing towards hidden game. In this case, the attacker may disperse smaller detachments to occupy nearby areas or secure minor, less impactful gains but must ultimately accept that the decisive question of who controls the region remains unresolved for now. In this situation, the strong defensive position has achieved its purpose.

3. Entrenched camps near fortresses: These camps are essentially a type of fortified position, created not to defend a particular area of land but to shield a military force from direct attack. What makes them distinct is that they are designed as an integral part of a nearby fortress, which adds significant strength to their defense.

a. Entrenched camps can serve the specific purpose of making the siege of the fortress either impractical or highly challenging. Such an aim might justify a significant commitment of troops, especially if the fortress includes an open port that cannot be effectively blockaded. However, if the fortress is one that could fall quickly to starvation tactics, the sacrifice of troops may not be warranted.

b. Camps of this type allow for smaller troop contingents than those required in open-field encampments. Under the protection of a fortress, four or five thousand men could hold their ground, whereas they might not last in an unfortified position in open terrain.

c. These fortified camps can also be used as bases for assembling and training forces, particularly when those forces are not yet ready to face the enemy in open conflict. Such troops might include new recruits, local militias, and national levies, who benefit from the protective buffer of the fortress walls.

While these camps offer a range of strategic advantages, they come with a considerable downside: if the entrenched camp is abandoned or cannot be defended, it can compromise the fortress itself. Keeping a fortress permanently garrisoned with enough troops to defend both the camp and the fortress can be an overwhelming logistical burden. For this reason, these camps are generally more practical along coastlines where naval support may alleviate some defensive pressure; elsewhere, their disadvantages often outweigh the benefits.

To summarize, strong and entrenched positions are:

1. Most necessary in smaller countries with limited space for retreat.
2. Less risky if relief can be anticipated from external sources, whether through reinforcements, seasonal changes, national uprisings, or other factors that weaken the enemy's position.
3. More effective against an adversary whose attacking force lacks resilience or momentum.

Chapter XIV. Flank Positions

We've dedicated a separate chapter to this common concept in military theory for easy reference, but we don't consider the term to signify something distinct or independent on its own. Any position intended to be held—even when the enemy bypasses it—functions as a flank position. The moment an enemy decides to pass it by, the position's value shifts entirely to its impact on the enemy's strategic flank. Thus, all strong positions inherently act as flank positions as well; since they cannot be directly attacked, the enemy is forced to bypass them, making their primary significance lie in their influence over the enemy's strategic flank. The specific alignment of the strong position, whether it runs parallel to the enemy's strategic flank (as with Colberg) or perpendicular to it (as with Bunzelwitz and Drissa), is irrelevant, because a strong position is inherently capable of facing attacks from any direction.

Additionally, there may be times when it's advantageous to hold a position that isn't entirely unassailable, even if the enemy bypasses it. This would be the case if the location provided such a significant advantage in terms of retreat routes and supply lines that we could not only effectively threaten the advancing enemy's strategic flank but also prevent the enemy from fully controlling our line of retreat. However, if this last condition is not met, a non-unassailable position could leave us at risk of being forced to engage without secure retreat options.

An illustrative example from 1806 sheds light on this concept. If the Prussian army had taken a position along the right bank of the Saal River, facing Buonaparte's advance from Hof, it could have functioned as a flank position with respect to Buonaparte's line of approach. Suppose the Prussian forces had positioned themselves parallel to the Saal, maintaining this stance to observe the enemy's movements. With a less overwhelming imbalance of physical and psychological strength between the forces, and had someone like Daun commanded the French, the Prussian position could potentially have resulted in a brilliant outcome. Bypassing it would have been nearly impossible—something even Buonaparte acknowledged when he resolved to attack directly. And while Buonaparte attempted to cut off their retreat, he didn't fully succeed. Had the balance of forces and morale been slightly more equal, a complete encirclement would have been just as unachievable as bypassing the position, given that the Prussian army faced far less risk of having its left wing overpowered than the French would from a defeat of their own left.

Even with the imbalance in physical and morale conditions at the time, a decisive and skilled use of command could have provided hope for victory. Nothing prevented the Duke of Brunswick from organizing his forces on the 13th so that by daybreak on the 14th, he could have massed 80,000 troops against the 60,000 Buonaparte had crossed the Saal with at Jena and Dornburg. If even this numerical superiority, combined with the natural barrier of the steep Saal valley, failed to deliver a decisive victory, it would have indicated that this region could not yield a successful resolution. A tactical retreat would then have been advisable to secure reinforcements and weaken the enemy's position.

Thus, while the Prussian position on the Saal was assailable, it could still be considered a flank position relative to the major route through Hof. However, as with any position that is not completely unassailable, this flank characteristic would only apply if the enemy chose not to engage.

Calling a position a "flank position" merely because the defender aims to attack the enemy's side after they've bypassed it does not accurately capture what makes a flank position effective. In such cases, the flank attack is not a natural result of the position's characteristics or its strategic impact on the enemy's advance. It's simply an attempt to exploit a vulnerable angle, without the position itself contributing significantly to the maneuver's success.

From this, it's clear that there's no additional quality or unique feature that defines a flank position beyond what we've already discussed. However, it's worth mentioning the character of this tactic briefly, excluding truly unassailable positions, which we've covered in detail elsewhere.

A flank position that is genuinely unassailable can be an extremely powerful tool, yet precisely for that reason, it's also risky. If the position stops the enemy's advance, it delivers a great strategic advantage with minimal force—it's like using a lever to apply pressure with little effort. But if the position fails to stop the attacker, the defender's retreat may be compromised. They would then be forced to retreat quickly and possibly take a roundabout path, both of which are less than ideal. Worse still, the defender could find themselves with no open escape route, compelled to fight under poor conditions. Against a bold opponent with a moral and strategic upper hand, one who seeks a decisive outcome, this tactic is exceedingly risky and inappropriate, as illustrated by the 1806 example previously mentioned.

Conversely, against a cautious adversary in a less intense conflict, a flank position can be one of the best tools available to a defender. Examples include the Duke of Ferdinand's defense along the Weser from the left bank and the well-known positions at Schmotseifen and Landshut. However, it's important to note that in 1760, Fouqué's corps faced disastrous consequences at Landshut, which demonstrates the danger of misapplying this strategy.

Chapter XV. Defence of Mountains

The impact of mountains on warfare is substantial, making it a crucial topic in military theory. Since mountainous terrain introduces a slowing effect on movement and operations, it generally favors the defensive side, so we will explore it here more broadly than just as "mountain defense." Our analysis has revealed some conclusions that differ from common beliefs on this topic, so a detailed examination is necessary.

To start, we'll look at the tactical aspects to understand how mountains connect with strategic planning. The significant difficulty large columns face when navigating narrow mountain roads, combined with the substantial defensive power a small post gains from a steep slope or ravines on its flanks, are the main reasons mountains are widely regarded as strong defensive assets. Only certain historical changes in weaponry and tactics have prevented armies from fully utilizing mountains as defensive barriers.

Imagine a column moving slowly, snaking up a steep mountain pass, artillery and drivers struggling with rough, narrow roads, cursing over broken wagons blocking the way and delaying everyone behind. In such moments, anyone would think, "If the enemy attacked with just a few hundred troops, they could disrupt this entire force." This has led historians to describe narrow passes as places where "a small force could hold off an entire army." However, any soldier with field experience knows that moving troops through mountain terrain is not the same as attacking it. Assuming that the difficulty of marching through mountains translates to an equally challenging assault is a flawed perspective.

It's understandable for a newcomer to draw this conclusion, and even the military itself fell into this misconception for a time. This idea was fairly new to experienced soldiers as well as laypeople up until the Thirty Years' War. Before then, armies typically fought in tightly packed formations with numerous cavalry units and rudimentary firearms, making it almost impractical for regular forces to defend mountains. Only when infantry and their weapons evolved to be the backbone of armies did the strategic potential of highlands and valleys become apparent. But it was not until the mid-1700s that this concept was fully appreciated.

Another factor that inflated the perceived strength of mountain defenses was the defensive potential a small post could achieve when situated in difficult terrain. This led to the belief that a simple multiplication of fortified posts could somehow transform a single battalion into an effective army and a single mountain into a fortress chain.

It's true that a small post gains considerable strength when positioned well in the mountains. A small detachment that would be quickly overrun on flat land by a couple of cavalry squadrons—and would consider itself fortunate to avoid capture—can stand firmly against an entire army in the mountains. It could demand the "military honor" of a proper attack with flanking maneuvers and so on. This defensive power stems from obstacles that hinder enemy approach, natural supports for the flanks, and fallback positions that the terrain naturally provides. While the exact mechanisms are tactical matters, we can accept this defensive advantage as established fact.

It seemed logical to think that lining up a series of strong posts along a mountainous area would create a highly formidable, nearly unbreakable line of defense. The idea was to extend this line far enough in each direction until it either met natural barriers on the flanks, or became long enough on its own to guard against being outflanked. Mountainous regions are especially suited to such tactics, offering a series of seemingly ideal defensive points, each one looking more secure than the last, making it hard to decide where to stop. As a result, this defensive approach often turned into a widespread setup, with numerous individual posts spaced ten or fifteen miles apart covering various entry points. Each post seemed as though it could resist an enemy's attempt to bypass it. With these strongholds linked by difficult terrain, often impassable except on established roads, defenders assumed they had created a near-impenetrable "wall of brass." To further ensure stability, reserves of a few battalions, horse artillery, and several cavalry squadrons were often held back to respond if any point in the line appeared compromised.

This mindset has appeared throughout history, and it's uncertain if modern strategy has fully shaken off these misconceptions. The gradual evolution of tactics since the Middle Ages, along with increasingly large armies, also helped bring mountain defense tactics into more common use. Defensive warfare in mountainous terrain is characterized by its almost complete passivity. Before armies achieved the maneuverability they possess today, defending mountain ranges seemed sensible. As armies grew and their weaponry improved, battle lines became thinner and longer, stretching out and requiring significant effort to mobilize. Establishing a battle formation could take hours, and once set up, the arrangement left little room for adjustments. As attackers often set their positions last, they could arrange their formations based on the defender's setup, forcing defenders to adapt late in the game. This gave the offensive side an upper hand, and defenders had little recourse but to anchor their forces within protective terrain features, for which mountains offered the best shield. The army and the mountain essentially worked together, with the soldiers defending the terrain and the terrain bolstering the soldiers' efforts. The drawback was reduced maneuverability, but at the time, this wasn't fully understood or utilized.

In any strategic face-off, weaknesses on one side attract attacks from the other. When a defending force is locked down into a series of strongholds that are inherently resilient but static, the offensive side gains confidence in using flanking maneuvers since they needn't worry about exposing their own sides. This is exactly what happened: turning maneuvers became common practice. To counteract these moves, defenders extended their lines further, only to weaken their overall strength and invite concentrated attacks in the center. Eventually, offensive tactics gained the upper hand again, this time by exploiting the increased mobility of troops, which the mountainous terrain inherently limited, leading the defensive theories around mountain warfare to suffer setbacks. The inability to move freely in rugged terrain made mountain defenses vulnerable, and historical outcomes, especially during the Revolutionary Wars, show that many defensive efforts in mountainous regions were ultimately overwhelmed.

However, it would be an error to dismiss the strengths of mountain defenses altogether, as their effectiveness varies based on the defensive goals. It is crucial to understand whether the defense aims to offer temporary resistance or achieve a complete victory. For a relative, time-bound defense, mountains provide a significant advantage. However, for absolute, conclusive resistance leading to a decisive victory, mountains are generally less suitable, with rare exceptions.

Mountain terrain slows movement, making every step harder and more costly in terms of both time and troops. This delay impacts both sides but more heavily affects the attacker, giving the defender a valuable edge in terms of endurance. As long as the defending side can maintain its position, it holds the upper hand. But once the defender needs to move and adapt, this advantage diminishes. Since a limited or relative resistance can rely more on passive tactics than a defense seeking a decisive outcome, mountainous terrain—with its natural obstacles—perfectly suits this type of stationary defense.

It's been established that a small post can gain considerable strength in rugged terrain. This is widely accepted, though we should clarify the concept of relative versus absolute size. A post that is small relative to the overall army, detached to defend a specific position, might still face attacks from the full force of the enemy, meaning it's in a relatively weaker position. In such cases, only relative defense is achievable, and this applies more the smaller the detachment is compared to the main body. Conversely, a genuinely small post—one not facing a superior force—might still hope to achieve absolute defense or even outright victory, especially in mountains, where it can exploit terrain to an advantage that a larger army cannot as effectively use.

Thus, it's clear that small outposts in mountainous regions possess exceptional defensive strength. This defensive capability is especially decisive in situations requiring only a relative, limited defense. But the question remains: can these advantages also translate into absolute, decisive resistance by an entire army? This is the point we now aim to explore.

First, we need to ask ourselves whether a defensive line, made up of several individual posts, retains the same collective strength as each post would if it were evaluated independently. It's clear that the answer is no, and to think otherwise would lead to two main kinds of errors in judgment.

In the first scenario, there's often confusion between terrain that simply lacks good roads and terrain that is truly impassable. Where the main column, artillery, and cavalry may struggle to maneuver, infantry might still be able to pass through, and artillery can sometimes be moved over such terrain with intense, short bursts of effort not comparable to regular marches. Therefore, the belief that there is a secure connection between each defensive post within the line is often based on an illusion, and in reality, this leaves the flanks exposed to the enemy.

The second error assumes that a line of smaller posts, which may be strong in their frontal positions, would also maintain equal strength along their flanks simply because they're supported by natural obstacles like cliffs, ravines, or other steep terrain. But these features don't make it impossible to turn or bypass the posts; rather, they add time and effort to the enemy's attack, requiring a greater commitment of force, which provides an opportunity for defenders to act effectively. When an enemy chooses to maneuver around such a post—despite the challenging terrain—due to the post's impenetrable front, this could require the attacker to take up to half a day and still result in losses. If that individual post can be reinforced in time, or if it only needs to hold for a short while to delay the enemy, or if it's strong enough to match the advancing force on its own, then these natural flank supports will have done their job, lending strength to both the post's front and flanks. In the case of a continuous line of posts forming an extended defensive position, however, none of these factors are guaranteed. If the enemy concentrates his forces against one weaker point with minimal support in the rear and absolute resistance expected, then the presumed advantage of flank support diminishes greatly.

Typically, the enemy's main attack will focus on these weak points, applying intense pressure with concentrated forces where he perceives vulnerability. Such an attack may indeed encounter fierce resistance at the specific point, yet it may still have little impact on the overall defense line's integrity. But if this weak point falls, the line is breached, and the enemy achieves a decisive breakthrough.

From these observations, we can conclude that the relative effectiveness of defense in mountain warfare is generally higher than on flat terrain and reaches its peak effectiveness in smaller, isolated posts. However, this defensive advantage doesn't grow proportionally as the defender's forces increase.

Now let's consider the primary purpose of large battles: to attain a decisive victory, which may also be the aim of mountain defense. When the entire defensive force, or at least the majority, is devoted to this goal, mountain defense effectively transitions from a simple holding action into a comprehensive defensive battle in the mountains. Here, the aim shifts from merely maintaining positions to actively engaging with all available strength to overcome the enemy. In this context, mountain defense no longer serves as the main objective but becomes a tactical tool within a larger battle plan. With this new purpose in mind, we must consider how effectively mountainous terrain can help secure such an outcome.

The nature of a defensive battle in mountainous terrain involves holding ground with a mostly passive front-line reaction, paired with increased tactical activity in the rear. However, mountain landscapes inherently hinder this kind of flexible action for two primary reasons. First, the scarcity of roads limits rapid troop movements between rear and front lines, and the irregular, steep terrain disrupts any attempts at sudden, swift attacks. Second, the obstructed visibility prevents defenders from easily observing the broader landscape and monitoring enemy maneuvers. This same terrain that offers defensive advantages in front ultimately limits our responsiveness and mutes much of the defensive strength in a significant confrontation.

A third, even more concerning factor is the risk of being surrounded or cut off. While mountainous regions are often favorable for orderly retreats under broad, steady pressure along the front, and while the terrain can slow an enemy's flanking maneuvers, these benefits apply best to cases of relative defense, where the intent is to delay rather than decisively resist. In a pitched, final battle, these mountain advantages wane. The battle can only continue until the enemy's flanking columns secure positions that either obstruct or fully cut off the defenders' retreat. When that happens, breaking through becomes nearly impossible. No rear assault will dislodge the enemy from these critical positions threatening our retreat. If we attempt a desperate counterattack with our remaining forces, it will likely fail to clear the blocked path.

Some may see this as contradictory, assuming that defenders would have similar advantages when breaking through the lines as attackers do during initial maneuvers. Yet, this overlooks critical differences in circumstance. The forces obstructing the escape only need to delay the defender for a short period; they are not engaged in a prolonged, absolute defense. These troops are like small posts with temporary objectives.

Moreover, the defenders, after a prolonged struggle, are usually depleted, disorganized, and often short on ammunition. As a result, the chances of cutting through are slim, creating a risk that looms over the entire defensive action, impacting the morale and efficacy of the defense. A pervasive unease spreads along the flanks as the defenders anxiously monitor any enemy detachment positioning itself on high ground to the rear, sensing a new threat with every move, each one a lever toward the attackers' victory.

However, many of these limitations diminish when defensive operations occur on a larger, accessible mountain plateau. Here, one could envision a fortified front line with formidable, nearly inaccessible flanks and ample room for maneuvering both behind and within the defensive position. Such a setup would be one of the most formidable defensive arrangements. But in reality, this scenario is rare. While mountains are indeed easier to traverse along their ridgelines than on steep inclines, most plateaus are simply not large or flat enough to accommodate a concentrated army position. The term "plateau" is often applied to mountainous regions more in geological terms than with regard to practical military requirements.

Smaller forces encounter fewer issues when defending mountain positions, as we've noted. This stems from their reduced need for space and fewer logistical demands, like supply routes and escape paths. A single, well-positioned hill may provide all the advantages of mountain terrain without the pitfalls of an extended mountain range. The smaller the force, the easier it is to secure a ridge or prominent peak without becoming lost in a web of steep, interlocking valleys. Thus, while large armies face numerous challenges in mountainous defense, smaller, nimble units can capitalize on the terrain's natural strengths.

Chapter XVI. Defence of Mountains (Continued)

We now proceed to the strategic use of the Now, we'll look at how to strategically apply the tactical outcomes explored in the last chapter, distinguishing between several main points:

How to use a mountainous area as a battlefield.

The broader impact of controlling mountains on other areas of the country.

How mountains serve as natural strategic barriers.

The unique requirements mountains impose regarding troop supplies.

The first, and most critical, of these points—mountainous terrain as a battlefield—needs further breakdown:

a. Using mountainous terrain in a large-scale battle.

b. Managing smaller, localized skirmishes in the mountains.

1. A mountain system as a battle-field.

In the prior chapter, we discussed the significant limitations of mountain terrain for defensive operations in a large, decisive battle while highlighting how it can, in contrast, advantage an attacker. This view may contradict common beliefs, yet it's clear how often general opinion overlooks important distinctions between very different aspects of warfare. The remarkable resistance that small, agile forces can put up in mountain terrain has led to the widespread idea that all mountain defenses are inherently strong. People are often surprised when it's suggested that this perceived strength does not extend to full-scale defensive battles in mountainous regions. Then, when a defensive position is lost in mountain warfare, conventional opinion quickly attributes it to the supposed folly of "cordon warfare"—a setup where defensive positions are stretched along a long line, as if guarding a fence—without considering that some level of this structure is nearly inevitable in mountainous combat.

We willingly counter this popular view. In fact, our perspective is supported by a highly credible authority: Archduke Charles, whose own experience in the campaigns of 1796 and 1797, as documented in his analysis, offers invaluable historical and tactical insights. As a seasoned general, historian, and critic, Archduke Charles emphasized how mountainous terrain can mislead military judgment. His observations directly echo our analysis, suggesting that a more nuanced understanding of mountain warfare, especially regarding large battles, is crucial.

When a weaker defending force has, with intense effort, gathered all available troops to demonstrate its resolve and defend its homeland, and chooses to meet the opponent in mountainous terrain, the situation is often fraught with challenges. Positioned amid dense, rugged mountains, and restricted in movement by difficult terrain, the defending general stands vulnerable to countless possible attacks that his powerful adversary may launch. The only advantage left lies in creatively using natural obstacles, yet this strategy risks descending into the "cordon defense," a scattered and vulnerable setup that should be avoided whenever possible. Far from offering a safe haven for the defender in a decisive battle, mountainous terrain actually makes such a battle unwise. In cases where a decisive engagement must occur, a level field is preferable for better mobility and coordination. However, if a mountain battle is unavoidable, it will require a very different approach from one in flatlands.

Troops must usually be spread out far more—often doubling or even tripling the deployment's typical length. Resistance will inherently become more passive, while counterattacks lose their punch. These are unavoidable effects of mountain warfare, and despite the challenging nature of fighting on such ground, the defender must avoid transforming the battle into a series of disconnected mountain defenses. Instead, the ideal strategy is to set up a well-coordinated, concentrated order of battle within the mountains, with unified control under a single commander and sufficient reserves on hand to ensure the defensive plan isn't merely about holding ground but also about making a decisive impact. This structured setup is difficult to achieve in practice, and there's always a natural tendency to slip into purely defensive mountain warfare, but theory insists on a firm warning against falling into this ineffective approach.

This approach primarily concerns the main body of the army and a major defensive action. But when dealing with minor skirmishes or smaller, less crucial conflicts, mountainous terrain may actually serve as an advantage. In these cases, the goal isn't absolute defense, and decisive outcomes are not expected. Let's clarify by examining the purposes such engagements serve:

a. To gain time. This is a common objective, appearing in any defensive line set up for observation or when awaiting reinforcements.

b. To repel small-scale enemy incursions. If mountains shield a province defended by limited forces, these troops can often repel minor raids or plundering parties. Without the mountains, a thinly stretched defense would fail to offer protection.

c. To make defensive demonstrations. While popular opinion still holds mountains as highly defensible, some opponents may hesitate to engage when confronted with mountain defenses. In less aggressive campaigns, mountain defense can thus serve as a deterrent, provided the defender does not plan to engage in a large-scale battle on this terrain and can avoid being forced into one.

d. To hold positions without seeking a decisive battle. Mountainous terrain is suitable for defending positions where a major confrontation is undesirable. Here, isolated units can function more effectively, while the combined force may be weaker. Such positioning also reduces the likelihood of being caught off-guard in a decisive battle.

e. For popular uprisings. Mountains are well-suited for the defensive tactics of a civilian army. While these movements benefit from the support of small regular units, placing a large force near an uprising may actually dampen its impact. Thus, the presence of a full army rarely justifies moving into the mountains solely to support a local revolt.

These points summarize the conditions under which mountainous terrain may enhance defensive positions suitable for battle.

The effect of mountains on the control and influence over other areas of the country is notably stronger than in flatter, more open terrain. In mountainous regions, a small contingent of forces, even if relatively weak, can secure a vast area due to natural defenses that offer support which would be unavailable in open country. In accessible land, the enemy can advance quickly, often compelling any forces in his path to retreat or give up the territory. But in mountains, even a small force can mount a formidable resistance, making the pace of advance much slower and securing possession in a way that is far more enduring than in the plains, where control may shift day by day.

When it comes to seizing mountainous territory, if the mountains aren't the focal point of primary operations in a war, their control isn't necessarily guaranteed by successes in other, flatter areas of the country. Unlike flatlands where success in one region might ripple out to influence others, the defensive advantages and isolated strongholds in mountains make them more autonomous and resilient to change. In such cases, operations in mountains require dedicated, specialized forces and maneuvers specifically designed for that terrain, often consuming both time and resources to establish solid control.

Adding to the advantage of a mountainous district is the natural high ground it provides. From mountain crests, defenders have broad visibility over surrounding open land, while remaining hidden and secure within the rugged terrain themselves. This makes mountains a valuable asset, even if the main force doesn't occupy them directly, because enemy forces can use them as both a refuge and a base from which to launch attacks. Mountains thus become a "laboratory of hostile forces," providing a nearly invisible yet impactful threat to the surrounding areas. When the enemy occupies the mountain terrain, the challenges multiply: smaller, agile forces or partisans can use the hills as cover, retreating easily when pursued only to reappear somewhere else unexpectedly. Larger enemy formations can also remain concealed until they're close enough for an attack, making it essential for defenders to maintain a safe distance to avoid getting drawn into disadvantageous skirmishes or unexpected assaults.

Mountain ranges, therefore, exert a substantial influence over adjacent flatlands within a certain range. Whether this influence shows up in immediate impacts like battles (as it did at Maltsch on the Rhine in 1796) or in a more gradual effect on supply and communication lines, it depends on the situation. In some instances, a critical event in the open land may override the mountain's influence entirely. For example, when Napoleon advanced on Vienna in 1805 and 1809, he wasn't significantly hindered by the Tyrol region. In contrast, Moreau in 1796 had to abandon Swabia largely due to the demands of keeping troops posted in the nearby higher elevations to monitor enemy movement.

During campaigns marked by balanced, back-and-forth engagements, it's risky to allow the enemy to maintain control over nearby mountains, as this can lead to constant setbacks for forces stationed in the open country. Under such circumstances, commanders often focus on seizing key segments of the mountains needed to support the primary lines of their attack, resulting in smaller skirmishes and contests for specific areas of high ground on both sides. Yet, while mountain chains can be highly significant, they shouldn't always be treated as decisive or as "keys" to the entire campaign. Ultimately, if a decisive victory is within reach in the open field, that should remain the primary aim, as seizing victory allows for reorganization and solidifying control over mountain areas afterward.

The role of mountains as a strategic barrier is best analyzed by breaking it down into two major aspects.

First, let's consider mountains as a potential stage for a decisive battle. Mountains, like rivers, create natural barriers that restrict movement and offer defined points of passage. This setup can be advantageous to the defender, who may take advantage of the terrain to weaken the assailant. When advancing through a mountain range, an invading force cannot rely on a single path or march in a single column without exposing itself to serious risks; any surprise encounter could trap the force in a battle with just one line of retreat, placing it in a vulnerable situation. Instead, the assailant will generally divide into several columns, often dispersed along different routes, to avoid being entirely bottlenecked. This dispersion creates opportunities for defenders who are concentrated on the far side of the mountains to launch attacks on isolated portions of the invader's forces. Therefore, from a defensive standpoint, concentrating forces behind a mountain barrier, where the enemy has to split up to make headway, can be a highly favorable approach.

However, using mountains in this way is complicated by a few key limitations. For one, the structure and layout of the mountain terrain vary widely; some mountain chains have many crossings, while others are almost impassable. The defensive advantage here relies heavily on the terrain's specific attributes, including the number of passage points and the practicality of staging an effective battle with limited retreat routes. Additionally, even if the defenders succeed in dealing a powerful blow to part of the advancing enemy, two difficulties arise. The first is that the defeated enemy has easy access to the mountainous region for shelter and reorganization; the terrain itself serves as a shield that can facilitate a swift retreat and regrouping. Second, the mountains often give the assailant higher ground as they advance, which, while not always a decisive advantage, can still place the pursuers in a challenging position should they try to follow.

Historical examples of such strategies in action are rare. The closest might be Alvinzi's engagement in 1796, though it only partially fits this scenario. A clearer instance of the mountain barrier strategy could have been realized during Napoleon's crossing of the Alps in 1800. During this campaign, the Austrian general Melas had a chance to intercept Napoleon before his scattered columns could merge, potentially disrupting the French forces before they consolidated their power.

The second way mountains act as a strategic barrier relates to their impact on lines of communication, especially when mountain ranges intersect these routes. During a campaign, the difficulties inherent to mountainous terrain can seriously hamper supply lines and reinforcements. Beyond the direct obstacles of steep paths and narrow passes, seasonal changes can transform mountain roads into treacherous routes that exhaust the invading force, draining its resources and morale. Entire campaigns have been forced into retreat after facing the unrelenting physical toll of mountain marches. When conditions are extreme, mountains themselves can sap the strength of an army before it ever engages with the enemy, effectively bleeding it dry.

This barrier effect is intensified if the defending side bolsters its mountain positions with strongholds or smaller forts at key passes, making access even more arduous for the assailant. Furthermore, if local populations are hostile and mobilize against the invader, or if small partisan groups start to harass the enemy's supply lines and flanks, the invader's situation becomes extremely precarious. Under such conditions, the invading force may be compelled to fragment its troops into numerous small detachments, each tasked with securing specific sections of the mountainous area. Over time, this strategy forces the attacker into a defensive stance, as maintaining control over even a few key mountain passes becomes a costly endeavor, with troops spread thin and constantly vulnerable to ambush or sabotage.

In cases where a rising or partisan campaign escalates, these scattered posts can turn into a serious liability, trapping the attacker in a defensive posture even as they continue their offensive operations. The invading force, hamstrung by natural obstacles and reliant on fragmented supply lines, will likely experience one of the least favorable scenarios for any offensive campaign, forced to engage in an exhausting series of defensive actions while trying to push forward in enemy territory.

Mountains, therefore, serve as a powerful strategic barrier that can both restrict enemy movement and create insurmountable logistical challenges. Whether the goal is to set up for a decisive battle by taking advantage of limited enemy routes or to disrupt their advances by forcing them into exhausting efforts on mountain roads, the defender's knowledge and utilization of mountain terrain can be a decisive element in the larger campaign.

Considering mountains as a supply base for an army presents a straightforward yet essential aspect of military strategy. Their utility in provisioning troops shines especially when the enemy is compelled to operate within mountainous terrain or has stationed forces close by, leaving supply lines vulnerable. A defender who controls the mountainous region can leverage this natural advantage, making it difficult for the enemy to maintain supply lines and access resources. When the assailant is forced to keep their provisions and reinforcements close, any movement becomes precarious, as difficult mountain paths increase the likelihood of disruptions.

The strategic complexity of mountain warfare may initially seem disconnected from broader campaigns, as the choice of battlefield and region often depends on various uncontrollable factors. However, these considerations become critically relevant in major operations where the main body of an army can be repositioned by several marches to avoid the mountains and fight on level ground instead. When an army positions itself wisely and concentrates its main forces in a nearby plain, the advantage of a mountain barrier can be effectively neutralized. By bypassing the constraints of rugged terrain, the defender can keep a position of strategic strength while maintaining a more favorable vantage.

After analyzing the tactical and strategic aspects, we can conclude that mountains are generally less advantageous to the defensive side, especially when it comes to achieving decisive victories that determine control over a country. Mountains tend to restrict visibility and make movement more challenging, which can lead to a passive and fragmented approach where every path must be guarded, creating a situation similar to the flawed "cordon" style of defense. As a result, it's often better to station the primary force on one side of the mountains, using them as a buffer or choosing to keep them ahead or behind.

However, mountains do offer substantial benefits for smaller-scale operations, especially when the defender's aim isn't a conclusive victory but rather delaying or diverting the enemy. Such terrain may not be ideal for large armies due to the restrictions imposed by rugged geography, yet it offers a solid defense for smaller forces. A mountainous region, then, becomes a refuge for those who cannot risk direct confrontation. While minor troops may find mountains a haven for resistance, large forces often find the opposite; despite the challenges they pose to the enemy, mountains rarely allow a full military body to execute coordinated maneuvers effectively.

The very sight of mountainous terrain can induce a psychological reaction—a natural dread for inexperienced leaders or those accustomed to conventional tactics. This sentiment may lead to excessive fear of the mountainous landscape's obstacles and its potential to disrupt an advancing army. Even military historians of the last century, influenced by the slow-moving nature of wars waged with more limited tactics, might view mountain defenses as stronger than they are, leading them to favor mountainous defenses for certain nations, like Austria on the Italian frontier. Yet, leaders with experience and practiced judgment, such as those trained under Napoleon, may readily recognize that a well-prepared army can confront mountain terrain without undue concern, focusing instead on the broader context of their military objectives.

It's important to clarify that the preference for open plains over mountains does not imply that countries like Spain or Italy would be more defensible without the Pyrenees or the Alps. For instance, while Spain's defense would benefit from the Pyrenees' natural barrier, a concentrated defense on the plains beyond, near the Ebro River, may prove more advantageous than dispersing troops across multiple mountain passes. Similarly, an Italian force fighting in the plains of Turin would stand a better chance than one spread thin across the high Alps, where each isolated outpost could be overwhelmed by a determined adversary. This doesn't mean, however, that a military aggressor would find it easy to cross or leave behind a mountainous obstacle like the Alps.

Choosing to engage in a battle in the plains does not exclude preliminary mountain defenses. A layered approach, where smaller, secondary forces hold mountain passes while the main army waits in a favorable lowland position, can be a practical strategy. The assailant's ultimate success in mountainous areas often hinges on achieving a single decisive victory to subdue the defender entirely. Without this, mountains become increasingly disadvantageous for an occupying force as the campaign progresses, especially if enemy reinforcements, allied forces, or local resistance emerge. In such cases, the burden of maintaining control over mountainous areas can swiftly turn against the attacker, draining resources and morale.

In optics, as in strategy, clarity intensifies up to a focal point; beyond that, perspective distorts. The same principle applies here: while mountains present a challenging environment, their full impact must be viewed in context. If mountains prove a liability for the defensive, it doesn't necessarily suggest that an attacker should always prefer a mountainous route of advance. Other factors—such as the logistical burden of supplying troops, the limited availability of roads, and the uncertainty of whether the defender will even accept a battle in the mountains—can outweigh the potential advantages. As such, mountains as a strategic asset present nuanced benefits, both limiting and enhancing the defender's power, depending on how they are approached and used.

Chapter XVII. Defence of Mountains (continued)

In chapters fifteen and sixteen, we discussed the nature of battles in mountainous regions and how to incorporate mountains strategically. In doing so, we often encountered the concept of mountain defense without closely examining its structure and specific tactics. Now, we turn to a more detailed exploration of this approach.

Mountain ranges often span long distances like ribbons across the land, serving as natural boundaries between watersheds. These ranges direct rivers toward various basins and divide entire water systems. This broad, elongated form is repeated in the mountain's internal structure, where individual ridges branch off from the main spine, creating more localized separations between smaller rivers and streams. Thus, the notion of a mountain defense system developed naturally from the perception of mountains as barriers—long and narrow formations functioning as significant obstacles to movement. This concept has led strategists to visualize mountain ranges as ramparts, with valleys acting as natural "gates" through these barriers.

Geologists may continue to debate the origins of mountains and the forces that shaped them, but whether water actively carved these landscapes (as some propose) or simply followed pre-existing forms, river courses reliably reveal the general layout and elevation of any mountain system. Consequently, when designing a mountain defense system, it's been natural to use watercourses as guides. Valleys created by streams and rivers, after all, provide the clearest paths to higher ground, smoothing the mountain's natural slopes and shaping accessible paths to summits.

Following this model, a mountain defense strategy would position forces along a main mountain chain roughly parallel to the defense front, treating it like a vast natural wall. The primary defense would occur at the crest of this wall, while cross-valleys leading into the mountains would function as choke points. When the main ridge forms an angle with the defense front, a secondary ridge might instead serve as the primary line, parallel to one of the main valleys and extending to the main ridge, effectively blocking access from that direction.

This geological approach to mountain defense, however, relies heavily on theoretical assumptions that do not hold up well in real-world conditions. The concept of organizing defenses strictly by following natural topography, such as rivers and mountain ridges, eventually led to what some termed a "ground theory" for mountain defense. In this theory, principles of geological and hydrological structure became intertwined with tactical and strategic decisions in warfare.

Yet this approach is filled with misconceptions. When these are stripped away, very little remains that can serve as a reliable foundation for a mountain defense system. Real mountain ridges, even primary ones, are often too challenging and inhospitable for stationing large troop formations. Adjacent ridges often share these limitations; they can be too brief, irregular, or steep to provide substantial tactical advantages. Plateaus, though occasionally present on mountain ridges, are often narrow and ill-suited for mass deployments. Furthermore, uninterrupted ridges or slopes that might serve as usable terraces are rare. Instead, the main ridge often twists, forks, and breaks into substantial offshoots that extend in arcs toward the surrounding lowlands, sometimes ending in higher peaks than the main ridge itself. Such formations branch into peninsulas that surround deep valleys in irregular patterns, rather than conforming to a neat, linear organization.

In areas where multiple mountain ranges intersect or branch outward, the concept of a singular "belt" or linear defensive chain loses all coherence, transforming instead into a complex network of watercourses and mountain ridges radiating outward like spokes from a central point.

Anyone familiar with mountains as they appear on the ground will immediately recognize that applying any rigid system of organization to mountain defenses is impractical. Relying on these natural features as the guiding structure for defensive measures is a flawed approach, as the landscape's irregularity makes systematic planning nearly impossible.

One final point remains to be addressed—a consideration of great significance for practical deployment in mountain warfare.

In examining the tactical aspects of mountain warfare, we can identify two primary defensive approaches: defending steep slopes and defending narrow valleys. This latter approach—defending valleys—is generally favorable for the defender. However, it often conflicts with a strict occupation of the main ridgeline, as the most effective valley defense often requires control over the valley itself, particularly at its outer edges closest to open country, rather than at the valley's upper end where slopes tend to be steeper. In fact, defending the valleys can allow an effective defense of mountainous terrain even if the main ridge does not provide suitable positions. This role becomes increasingly significant when the mountains are higher and more difficult to access.

Thus, based on these observations, the idea of maintaining a continuous, defensible line along a main geological ridge is impractical. Instead, we must treat a mountain range as a highly varied surface full of irregularities and obstacles. Our task is to leverage the natural features as best we can under the circumstances, recognizing that while understanding the mountain's geological structure is useful for grasping the overall layout, it has limited application in organizing effective defenses.

A historical survey of the War of the Austrian Succession, the Seven Years' War, and the French Revolutionary Wars reveals no evidence of attempts to create a defensive system covering an entire mountain range. Armies rarely took up positions solely on the main ridges or consistently stationed troops along the slopes. Positions varied in altitude and orientation—sometimes positioned at higher or lower points, sometimes oriented parallel or perpendicular to the watercourses, and sometimes facing against them. In more formidable mountain ranges like the Alps, forces often positioned themselves along the valleys, while in less dramatic ranges, such as the Sudetes, armies sometimes occupied slopes that faced the oncoming enemy with the principal ridges positioned in front of their camps. A notable example of this occurred in 1762 when Frederick the Great defended the siege of Schweidnitz with the Hohe Eule ridge in front of his encampment.

Famous positions, like those at Schmotseifen and Landshut during the Seven Years' War, primarily occupied the lower parts of the valleys. This approach also applied to positions like Feldkirch in the Vorarlberg region. During the campaigns of 1799 and 1800, both the French and Austrian forces regularly stationed their main positions deep in the valleys. They did not just block valley entrances but also extended their positions along the valleys. The ridges themselves were often left unoccupied or only lightly manned by scattered posts.

This historical pattern underscores the adaptability required for mountain defense, as rigid alignment along geological features is generally less effective than a flexible approach that makes practical use of varied terrain.

The highest ridges of the Alps, due to their extreme inaccessibility and limited space, cannot practically accommodate large numbers of troops. Therefore, if armies are required to secure control over such mountainous regions, they must be stationed in the valleys. While initially this may seem counterintuitive—since conventional theory suggests that higher positions dominate lower ones—the reality is different. Mountain ridges are usually accessible only by narrow paths, fit mainly for infantry, whereas the main roads for movement and supply follow the valleys. Thus, an enemy can only approach through certain mountain paths with limited forces. The significant distances within these mountain ranges further lessen any real threat from such piecemeal advances, making a defensive position in the valleys safer than it might appear.

However, valley defense has its own vulnerability: the risk of being cut off. Although an enemy can only descend slowly and in limited numbers at specific points, meaning that surprise attacks are unlikely, none of the valley positions effectively control the exits of those mountain paths into the valley itself. This allows an enemy to bring down larger forces gradually, who can then spread out and break through the thin, vulnerable line of defense—often defended by nothing more than the rocky bed of a shallow mountain stream. When a retreat is attempted under these circumstances, it becomes chaotic and fragmented along the valley line, as each segment of the line must withdraw independently until they can finally escape from the mountain area. This inability to retreat cohesively resulted in substantial losses for the Austrian forces in Switzerland, where they often lost a third to half of their troops as prisoners.

Now, as to the customary organization of troops in such a mountainous defense: each secondary position typically relates back to a primary position held by the main force, usually situated centrally on the main road of approach. From this central stronghold, detachments are sent out to occupy critical points along the approaches to the left and right. This setup extends in a line, creating a series of three, four, or even six defensive posts. The extent to which the line is stretched depends on the particular strategic needs of the area. A defensive line spanning six to eight miles is considered modest, while more extensive lines may cover as much as twenty or thirty miles.

Between these main posts, typically one to two leagues apart, there are likely additional, less significant approaches that require attention. To strengthen the line, smaller posts accommodating a few battalions are established between the primary positions, creating cohesion across the defensive front. This approach to troop distribution can become quite granular, eventually resulting in posts manned by single companies or squadrons. There is, therefore, no definitive limit to the degree of division possible in this type of defense.

1. The more rugged and inaccessible the mountains are, the more necessary it becomes to divide the defending force across multiple positions—both for practical reasons and for effective coverage. When a mountainous region is so impassable that moving troops swiftly between points is unfeasible, each section must secure itself independently. In areas like the Alps, where the terrain is exceptionally challenging, this separation of forces naturally resembles a cordon system, where each point acts as its own stronghold. This approach contrasts with defending lower ranges like the Vosges or the Giant Mountains, where positioning can rely more on troop mobility and mutual support.

2. Historically, mountain defenses have generally been organized with a series of main posts, each typically manned by a single line of infantry, with cavalry units positioned in a second line as support. Often, only the central stronghold along the defensive line has had additional depth, possibly with several battalions positioned behind the primary line. This structure has meant that each post maintains a straightforward composition, focusing on concentrated lines rather than layers of reinforcements, and aiming to make each post resilient yet simple.

3. Maintaining a strategic reserve behind the main line for reinforcing threatened points has rarely been practical in mountain defense due to the extensive front that a defensive line in such terrain demands. The stretched-out nature of these positions often leaves every segment feeling vulnerable, unable to spare forces for a strategic reserve without weakening its own post. When an enemy attacks a particular location, support typically comes from nearby positions along the line rather than from a more distant reserve force, which can lead to stretched and precarious defenses.

Even when the mountain defense setup involves a reasonable division of forces, with each post given a solid complement of troops, the defense tends to rely heavily on localized resistance at each point. This means that if the enemy captures a post, it's often impossible to reclaim it, even if reinforcements later arrive. Mountain posts, once lost, rarely regain their effectiveness within the broader defense, as each post is structured to function independently rather than as part of an adaptable and reactive network. This lack of recoverability underscores the static nature of a mountain defense, where each position serves as a strong but singularly vulnerable point.

The effectiveness of mountain defense, the circumstances under which it should be applied, and the acceptable extent of force dispersion and segmentation are all matters that ultimately depend on the judgment and adaptability of the commanding general. Theory can only guide by clarifying the nature and potential of these defensive strategies and by indicating the role they may play within broader military operations.

It is ultimately up to the skill of the general to decide how to employ these strategies effectively. However, any commander who allows themselves to be defeated while holding an extended mountain position—a position inherently designed to provide a formidable defensive advantage—would be rightly subject to the harshest scrutiny and perhaps even a court martial for failing to utilize such a naturally strong defensive asset effectively.

Chapter XVIII. Defence of Streams and Rivers

Streams and large rivers, when considered for their defensive potential, are much like mountains in that they serve as strategic barriers. However, rivers differ from mountains in two key ways—one concerning their relative defense and the other their absolute defense.

Like mountains, rivers support relative defense, but they do so with a particular nature: they act like rigid barriers that either completely hold against an assault or shatter under pressure, at which point their defensive value is entirely lost. When a river is exceptionally large and other conditions align in favor of defense, crossing it might be entirely out of the question for an attacking force. But if an enemy breaks through at any one point, the defense is irreparably compromised, and the advantage the river once provided is quickly nullified. This contrasts with mountain defenses, where even after one section is breached, resistance can still continue across the rugged terrain, unless the river itself is bounded by mountains.

Another distinguishing feature of rivers in warfare is that, in some cases, they offer more effective, even optimal, opportunities for structuring a decisive battle compared to mountains.

Yet, both rivers and mountains share a similar danger in warfare: they can be deceptively alluring and have frequently led to strategic missteps, placing commanders in difficult predicaments. We'll observe these outcomes in greater detail when examining river defense tactics specifically.

While historical records do not abound with successful cases of river defenses, casting doubt on their reputation as formidable barriers once strongly upheld by advocates of absolute defensive strategies, rivers undeniably influence both the outcome of battles and the defense of a region.

To approach this topic in a structured way, we should separately examine the direct strategic impacts that arise from defending rivers and streams and the broader influence they exert on the defense of a country, even when no specific defensive measures are put in place along their course

The defense of a river can generally be approached in three distinct ways:

1. Absolute Defense with the Main Army: Here, the main force is concentrated to hold the line of the river and prevent the enemy from crossing at any point.
2. Demonstrative Resistance: This approach involves a show of force along the river to suggest a full defense without actually committing significant forces. It can serve to delay or deter the enemy without engaging in a major battle.
3. Relative Resistance by Secondary Troops: In this case, the river is defended by smaller, subordinate groups, such as outposts, covering detachments, or flanking corps, which aim to slow down the enemy's advance rather than entirely prevent a crossing.

Additionally, within each of these approaches, we can identify three levels or styles of defense:

1. Direct Defense at the River Line: This involves actively confronting the enemy's attempts to cross, deploying troops directly at key crossing points to oppose the passage.
2. Indirect Defense Using the River and Valley for Strategic Advantage: Here, the river itself is not defended as an impenetrable line but is instead utilized as part of a broader strategic setup, using the terrain to create favorable conditions for a larger engagement nearby.
3. Holding a Secure Position on the Enemy's Side of the River: This approach is the most direct of all, as it places defensive forces in a fortified position beyond the river, aiming to create an unassailable foothold on the opposing side to disrupt the enemy's plans and control access to the river crossings.

We'll divide our analysis based on the three levels of defense and, after exploring each in relation to the primary form—direct defense, aimed at stopping the enemy's crossing—we'll apply the same principles to the other two levels. We begin with direct defense, intended to physically prevent the passage of the enemy's main forces across the river. This kind of defense is practical only when dealing with large rivers—formidable bodies of water where an opposing force cannot easily establish a crossing.

The complex interplay of space, time, and available forces involved in planning such a defense introduces layers of complexity. Grasping this interplay requires a breakdown of these factors to find a starting point. After thorough consideration, the following principles emerge.

The first element is time—specifically, the time it takes for the enemy to construct a bridge. This time requirement sets the distance between defensive corps stationed along the riverbank, as it determines how quickly the defender can counter the enemy's efforts. If we divide the riverfront by the effective distance each defensive corps can cover, we obtain the number of corps needed for defense. Dividing the total number of troops by the number of corps tells us the size of each defensive unit. Then, comparing the strength of each unit to the number of enemy troops that could be brought across in the time it takes to construct a bridge provides insight into the defender's capacity to resist.

For a crossing to be deemed unfeasible, the defender must be able to confront the enemy forces coming over the river with significant numerical superiority, ideally double, before the bridge construction is complete. A brief example illustrates this principle.

If an enemy needs twenty-four hours to construct a bridge and can move only 20,000 men across in that time, while the defender can reach any point along the river within twelve hours with an equivalent 20,000 men, then the enemy's crossing is unfeasible. The defender would reach the site when only half of the enemy's troops—10,000 men—have crossed, ensuring the defender a significant advantage. As twelve hours allow a march of about four miles, defensive forces stationed every eight miles with 20,000 men each could effectively cover twenty-four miles of river. With 60,000 troops, the defender could respond to crossings at two points simultaneously or concentrate double the enemy's force at one crossing point.

Thus, three primary factors decisively affect a river's defense: (1) the river's width, (2) available crossing methods, as these determine both the bridge construction time and the number of troops that can cross during that time, and (3) the defender's available forces. At this point, the enemy's overall strength isn't the key focus. According to this reasoning, there exists a threshold beyond which an attempted crossing becomes impossible, rendering any numerical advantage on the enemy's part insufficient to force a passage.

This outlines the straightforward theory of directly defending a river to prevent the enemy from completing a bridge and crossing over; for now, we'll ignore enemy feints or distractions. Let's move to the specifics and the steps necessary for this type of defense.

First, disregarding unique geographic aspects, we note that the defending corps, based on this theory, must be stationed close to the river and kept concentrated. Staying close to the river is essential because positioning further back would unnecessarily increase the distance to any threatened point, wasting precious response time. The river itself acts as a natural buffer, eliminating the need for reserves in the rear, unlike a typical defense line without a river in front. Additionally, roads running parallel to the river are generally more reliable and direct than those approaching from farther inland. Furthermore, placing forces close to the river enhances surveillance far more effectively than a dispersed chain of posts; it keeps commanders immediately ready to respond.

Each corps also needs to remain concentrated because dispersing troops for defense would undermine the time calculations critical for an effective response. Concentration within each position maximizes the defensive advantage, especially considering the significant time lost when attempting to rally and concentrate dispersed forces. While it may initially seem appealing to post guards along the entire riverbank to prevent the enemy from crossing, particularly with boats, this is usually impractical and counterproductive. Unless certain points are especially suitable for crossing, stationing scattered posts primarily serves to push the enemy to choose another crossing location. If resources allow treating the river as if it were a fortress moat—guarding it with a dense line of troops—different principles apply, as this method falls outside typical river defense tactics. Hence, attempting to guard the riverbank directly may lead to an inefficient and ultimately unsuccessful defense unless one has abundant resources.

In addition to these general positioning principles, three other factors require close attention: first, understanding the specific characteristics of the river; second, removing any means the enemy could use to cross; and third, leveraging any fortresses along the river.

To act as a strong defense line, the river must ideally have solid "anchors" at both ends, such as the sea or a neutral region. Otherwise, natural or logistical barriers that make it impossible for the enemy to bypass the river at its ends are needed. However, such flanking supports or obstacles are typically far apart, meaning a river defense will generally involve a large section of the river. Therefore, the notion of stationing a concentrated body of troops along a relatively short stretch of the river becomes impractical. By a "relatively short length," we refer to a segment not much longer than a line troops would usually occupy on solid ground without a river. Situations where such a setup is feasible are rare; direct river defenses naturally lead to a more extended cordon of forces, creating inherent risks. If the enemy can bypass the defended river's ends, relying on a direct river defense, while effective in other respects, becomes extremely risky.

Now, regarding the length of the river between its endpoints, it's understood that certain sections will naturally be better suited for crossing than others. This can be theorized to some extent in general terms but can rarely be predicted definitively, as the smallest geographic features often outweigh theoretical guidelines. Since the river itself and local insights will usually reveal suitable crossing points, there's no pressing need to rely on rulebooks or formal instructions.

In examining the finer aspects of river defense, we see that certain conditions make some points along a river more favorable for crossing. Key factors include access roads that lead directly to the riverbank, tributaries or smaller rivers feeding into the main river, large towns situated along the river, and, perhaps most crucially, any islands within the river itself. Each of these features can simplify the logistics of crossing for the enemy. However, in contrast to common theoretical discussions, elements like higher ground on one side of the river or a sharp bend at a particular crossing point—while frequently emphasized in military texts—often have limited practical impact. This is because these advantages rest on an outdated assumption of a rigid, bank-side defense of the river itself, which is rare for larger rivers.

No matter what specific characteristics make some points more advantageous for crossing, these elements inevitably shape the placement of defending forces and compel adjustments to the overall strategic alignment of the defense. However, it's critical to avoid deviating excessively from the established defense plan based on the challenges that particular crossing points might present. If defending forces concentrate only on naturally challenging crossing points, the enemy would likely target precisely those points, knowing these spots are less defended or easier to exploit. This underscores the need for balanced distribution along the river to avoid inadvertently providing the enemy with an unguarded passage.

Occupying river islands as fully as possible is a strategic measure with significant benefits. If the enemy commits considerable forces to attack one of these islands, it often reveals their intended crossing point, serving as an advance warning of their broader operational plans. Thus, river islands act as early indicators, adding to the defender's ability to anticipate enemy movements effectively.

Because troops stationed along the river must be able to quickly shift up or down the river as circumstances change, securing efficient movement along the riverbank becomes paramount. When a main road doesn't run directly parallel to the river, establishing such a road is one of the most critical preparatory actions. Existing minor roads that run close to the riverbank should be improved to ensure they can support rapid troop movements, and, where needed, new connections between critical points along the river must be constructed. In this way, the defenders maintain their mobility, an advantage that's essential for a responsive and flexible defense.

The second focal point in effective river defense is removing all materials that could aid the enemy in crossing. Clearing the main body of the river of boats, barges, or any equipment that could assist in a makeshift crossing is a considerable undertaking, as it requires ample time and preparation. The situation becomes even more challenging when it comes to the smaller tributaries flowing into the river, particularly those on the enemy's side, since these are often under the opponent's control. Fortifying the mouths of these tributaries is, therefore, a strategic imperative. Securing these points helps prevent the enemy from using these secondary channels as potential crossing sites and limits their operational options.

The equipment that an invading force brings with them, like pontoons and other bridge-building materials, typically has limited capacity and isn't always sufficient for crossing large rivers. Consequently, much of the defense depends on restricting the enemy's access to resources they might find along the river itself. This includes securing boats and other watercraft, controlling materials available in nearby towns, and managing timber from surrounding forests, which could otherwise be used by the enemy to construct temporary crossings like rafts or floating bridges. In some instances, such limitations can make crossing the river nearly impossible for the enemy, significantly strengthening the defender's position.

Fortresses located along the river play a critical role in this defensive arrangement, particularly those situated on both sides of the river or even solely on the enemy's side. These strongholds serve multiple functions: they create a physical block against crossing attempts at nearby points, they help close off the mouths of tributaries, and they provide a secure location to gather and store any seized rivercraft or crossing materials taken from the enemy. By doing so, these fortresses increase the defender's ability to control river access and hinder the enemy's progress.

These principles outline the main components of a direct river defense, assuming the river is a significant waterway. If the river is flanked by steep valleys or bordered by marshy banks, these natural features enhance the difficulty of crossing and further strengthen the defense. However, the sheer volume of water remains essential for a robust river defense, as steep valleys or marshes alone cannot replicate the defensive advantage of a substantial water barrier. In essence, these additional obstacles may complicate the enemy's crossing attempts, but only the river's inherent separation of terrain can create the level of difficulty required for a truly effective, comprehensive defense strategy.

When we consider what role a direct river defense can occupy in a broader strategic campaign, it becomes clear that, while it may not lead to a decisive, game-changing victory, it does serve critical purposes. A river defense is inherently limited in delivering an outright victory because its primary aim is to block the enemy's passage across or, failing that, to overwhelm and neutralize any initial groups that manage to cross. Furthermore, the river itself acts as a barrier that prevents the defender from launching an immediate and overwhelming counterattack that could capitalize on any initial advantage.

However, a river defense can achieve a highly valuable outcome in the form of a substantial delay in the enemy's advance—a factor often crucial to the defensive side. The process of gathering sufficient crossing materials and engineering a bridge can consume significant time, and should any initial attempts to cross be thwarted, the resulting setbacks accumulate further delays for the enemy. If the river forces the enemy to change their approach or redirect their forces significantly, even more time can be gained. Moreover, when the opposing side is not fully committed to an aggressive push forward, the river's very presence may slow them down, offering a degree of sustained security for the defending territory.

Thus, when the defending force is substantial, the river wide, and additional circumstances favorable, a direct river defense can be a highly effective defensive tactic. This strategy may yield outcomes that, though often overlooked by modern commanders—likely due to a focus on past failed attempts at river defenses caused by inadequate resources—deserve closer consideration. If we envision a well-prepared defense stretching across a significant river like the Rhine or Danube, it's feasible for 60,000 troops to effectively secure a 24-mile length of river against a much larger enemy force. Such an achievement would undeniably represent a significant strategic advantage.

It is crucial here to emphasize the point regarding facing a numerically superior enemy. According to the principles we've discussed, the success of a river defense largely depends on the availability and control over crossing materials rather than the sheer size of the enemy force (as long as that force is at least equal to the defending troops). This notion may seem counterintuitive, yet it holds true: if the enemy lacks the means to cross effectively, their numerical advantage is moot. However, it's equally essential to recognize that few river defenses offer absolute strongpoints, meaning they're generally vulnerable to being outflanked. Such flanking maneuvers become considerably easier when the enemy possesses substantial numerical superiority.

Finally, even if a river defense is eventually breached, this outcome should not be viewed in the same way as a failed or devastating battlefield defeat. A broken river defense does not equate to a total collapse; rather, only a portion of the defending forces would have been actively involved. And because the enemy will be preoccupied with the slow and cumbersome task of transporting their troops across a single bridge, they are unlikely to be able to immediately pursue the defenders and press their advantage. This limitation means that the defenders retain their overall cohesion and avoid the worst repercussions of a rout, making a well-prepared river defense an option worth serious consideration.

In all practical matters, finding the exact right approach is crucial; this is particularly true in the defense of a river, where success often depends on accurately assessing one's situation in all its dimensions. Small details—those that might initially seem insignificant—can profoundly alter the outcome, transforming a strategy that would be wise in one scenario into a disastrous mistake in another. Judging the circumstances accurately and avoiding a simplistic view, such as assuming "a river is a river" under all conditions, is perhaps more challenging here than in other military contexts. Misjudgments and overgeneralizations in river defense are common pitfalls. However, once these risks are recognized, we are confident in asserting that it's also wise to disregard those who, driven by vague instincts or superficial understandings, advocate for attack and aggressive movement above all else, thinking that the essence of warfare lies solely in dramatic action, like a cavalryman charging forward, sword raised high.

Such aggressive, headstrong approaches, though they may sometimes achieve impressive results, often fail when complex situations arise. The weight of multiple interconnected factors will often cause these initial flashes of energy to fade, leaving a commander vulnerable just when judgment and resilience are most needed. Historical examples, like the unfortunate case of the dictator Wedel at Züllichau in 1759, show that impulsive aggression without balanced strategy often crumbles under the real demands of complex, multi-dimensional warfare.

Therefore, we believe a direct defense of a river by large forces under favorable conditions can indeed succeed if the goals remain reasonable and focused. Yet, this logic doesn't apply when smaller forces are involved. While an army of 60,000 troops might successfully prevent a larger force of 100,000 or more from crossing at a designated stretch, a smaller corps of just 10,000 troops would struggle to prevent a similar-sized opposing force—10,000 troops—from crossing that same section. In fact, they may not even be able to resist a group half that size if the enemy is willing to take the risk of engaging on the same bank of the river with a numerically superior force. The principle is straightforward: the logistical requirements for crossing don't change just because the size of the defending force changes.

We have touched only briefly on feints or mock crossing attempts, as these tactics don't play a central role in the direct defense of a river. A direct river defense is not generally about massing the army at a single point; instead, each corps or unit typically defends its own segment of the river. Additionally, these feigned maneuvers are often impractical under the conditions we've discussed. For instance, if the assailant's crossing equipment is limited, meaning they don't have as many resources for multiple crossing points as they might wish, they are less likely to dedicate a portion of these resources to mere show. If they do attempt it, then the main body of troops that they can pass over at the real crossing point will be reduced, thus allowing the defender additional time to organize and respond effectively to the actual crossing.

This approach to river defense seems particularly well-suited to large rivers and generally in the lower, broader parts of their courses. The second type of defense, however, is more applicable to smaller rivers with steep, enclosing valleys and even to minor streams. Here, the defending force takes up a position farther back from the river at a distance that will allow them to strike the enemy in detail if they attempt to cross at multiple points. Alternatively, if the enemy attempts to cross with the full force at a single point, the defenders will be close enough to press the enemy army back against the river or narrow valley and confine them to a single bridge and road. Such a position leaves an army backed up against a river or deep valley with limited options for retreat—a highly disadvantageous situation for any battle. Skillfully leveraging this kind of positioning against the enemy makes this approach especially effective when defending against smaller rivers with constraining valleys.

The arrangement of an army in large corps positioned close to a river, which we regard as optimal in a direct defense scenario, rests on the assumption that the enemy cannot cross the river suddenly or in significant strength. If they could, maintaining such a layout would risk our forces being overwhelmed individually. Therefore, if conditions do not sufficiently favor the defense—if the enemy has ample means for crossing, if the river has many islands or fords, if it isn't wide enough, if our forces are too limited, and so forth—then this strategy must be reconsidered. In such cases, to ensure stronger interconnectivity between our forces, they should be drawn back somewhat from the river. The goal then shifts to concentrating our forces quickly at whichever point the enemy attempts a crossing so that we can strike before they secure enough territory to control multiple access routes. Here, a chain of outposts can monitor and partially guard the river and valley, while the main force is arranged in several corps, positioned at suitable points a few leagues back from the river.

The most challenging aspect lies in navigating the narrow terrain created by the river and its valley. Now, it's not just the river's water volume we're dealing with, but the entire constricted area, which often forms a difficult passage. Generally, a deep rocky valley can be a more formidable barrier than a broad river. The march of a large troop column through an extended defile poses significant challenges that may not be immediately obvious. The time involved in such a movement is considerable, and there's always the concern that the enemy might take control of the surrounding heights during this maneuver. If the forward troops press too far, they risk engaging the enemy prematurely and potentially being overpowered; yet if they remain closer to the crossing point, they face the disadvantage of fighting in poor terrain. Thus, crossing such a geographical obstacle with the aim of challenging the enemy head-on is an audacious endeavor, one that requires either superior numbers or great confidence in leadership.

This type of defensive line shouldn't be extended as far as in a direct defense along a large river, since here, the goal is to consolidate the whole force in a single engagement. Additionally, the passages are less challenging to manage than those across a broad river, so it becomes easier for the enemy to flank us. However, such a flanking maneuver would divert them from their intended path (since we are assuming that the valley intersects their route roughly at right angles). This diversion won't immediately relieve the disadvantages associated with a constrained line of retreat; these constraints will persist, at least partially, allowing the defender to retain some advantage over the advancing enemy. Even if the enemy executes a detour, gaining slightly more space to maneuver, they are still not fully freed from the restrictive nature of their line of advance.

It's worth clarifying that when we discuss rivers in this context, we aren't solely referring to bodies of water but also to deep valleys or channels created by the surrounding terrain. This does not mean a regular mountain gorge, as that would fall under mountain warfare principles. Many lowland regions, however, contain deeply incised channels carved by even small streams, with steep banks that can be quite challenging to cross. Additionally, rivers with swampy banks or banks that are otherwise difficult to approach fall into this category as well.

Under such circumstances, a defensive position for an army stationed behind a wide river or a deep, steep-sided valley is an excellent strategic choice. This method of river defense ranks as a superior strategic measure, offering many advantages to the defender. However, it comes with a potential flaw—the tendency to overextend the defensive forces. This temptation arises naturally, as there is an inclination to defend too many points of passage, losing sight of the optimal point at which to halt. Should we fail to engage with our entire army consolidated, we lose the strategic advantage we sought. The outcome could be a defeat, the need for an immediate retreat, confusion across multiple areas, and significant losses, potentially reducing our army to a vulnerable state—even if we hadn't been completely overpowered in the engagement.

In emphasizing that the defensive force, given these conditions, should not be overly spread out and must be able to consolidate entirely by the evening of the day the enemy initiates a crossing, we underscore a critical principle. This single guideline encapsulates what might otherwise require complex calculations of timing, force, and space, elements that, in this scenario, must adapt to numerous local conditions.

The battle shaped by these specific conditions must be marked by extreme urgency and determination on the defender's part. The deceptive crossings that the enemy will employ will keep the defender uncertain for some time, making it unlikely for him to identify the real crossing point in advance. The unique advantage for the defender lies in the disadvantageous position of the enemy corps that he faces directly. If other enemy corps, having crossed at different points, begin to threaten his flank, he cannot easily counter such movements with strong maneuvers from the rear, as might be possible in a regular defensive battle. Doing so would forfeit the main advantage of his position. Therefore, he must confront the enemy in front with maximum speed and strength, aiming to resolve the conflict before these other enemy forces can close in from the flanks, thus ensuring a swift and decisive outcome through the defeat of the enemy immediately before him.

However, the goal of this form of river defense is not to repel a vastly superior force, as might be feasible in the direct defense of a large river. In this context, the defender is generally facing the main strength of the enemy's army. While he does so under advantageous circumstances, it's evident that if the disparity in force is too great, this will quickly become apparent in the struggle.

This type of river defense, suited to medium-sized rivers in steep valleys, is relevant when the bulk of the armies are involved. For major forces, the isolated resistance that could be achieved along the ridges or embankments of a valley cannot outweigh the problems posed by a scattered formation. For them, a decisive victory is essential. But if the goal is only to strengthen a secondary line of defense meant to hold temporarily and rely on subsequent reinforcements, then a direct defense along the valley ridges or even the riverbanks may be appropriate. Though it doesn't offer the same advantages as mountain terrain, such a defense would nonetheless hold out longer than on open ground. Only one factor would make this approach very risky, if not impractical: when the river meanders significantly, creating sharp turns—common with rivers running through deep valleys, as with the Mosel River. In such a defense scenario, corps positioned on the outward bends would face near-certain capture if a retreat became necessary.

A larger river can indeed support similar defensive methods as are best suited to moderate rivers when an army's main force is involved, though here the conditions are typically even more favorable. This approach becomes especially relevant when the defender's goal is to achieve a decisive victory, as seen in engagements like the Battle of Aspern.

On a tactical level, the situation where an army aligns itself with its front positioned tightly against a river, stream, or steep valley to create a barrier to the enemy's approach, or to strengthen its front, is another matter entirely. Analyzing such positioning belongs more to the field of tactics. It's worth noting here that the effectiveness of such a stance is often illusory. If the gap or valley is exceptionally wide or deep, then the front of the position does indeed become unassailable. However, given that the enemy can bypass this front as easily as any other position, the effect is often no different than if the defender had voluntarily removed himself from the enemy's path—a result hardly in line with the intended purpose of taking up such a position. Thus, this type of positioning can only be recommended when, due to its location, it directly threatens the assailant's lines of communication, such that any diversion from the main route would have severe enough consequences for the enemy to render this risk unacceptable.

In this second form of river defense, the danger of feigned crossings by the assailant increases significantly, as they can be executed with greater ease, while the defender's task remains to concentrate his forces at the correct point of real threat. However, the defender here enjoys slightly more time because his advantageous positioning remains effective until the assailant manages to assemble his forces fully and establish control over several crossing points. Also, the impact of a simulated attack is not as critical here as in the defense of a broad cordon, where every point along the line must be held. In that scenario, deploying reserves is not only about discerning the main strength of the enemy but also involves the complex challenge of determining which specific crossing the enemy will target first.

For both forms of river defense—whether it is a large or a small river—it's important to note that if these defenses are implemented hastily, amidst the confusion of a retreat, without the necessary preparation, including removing any accessible means of crossing, or without a thorough knowledge of the terrain, they cannot realistically achieve the intended objectives. In such cases, the conditions needed for a successful defense are absent, and therefore any plan of extended positions over a wide area would be a grave mistake for an army.

Just as in any military operation, success in river defense depends on clear, deliberate planning, supported by strong determination and unity of purpose. A river defense will generally falter if it is chosen merely because the defender lacks the courage to engage the enemy in open battle and instead hopes that the expanse of water or a steep valley will serve as a natural barrier. In such circumstances, the defender's lack of confidence in their position typically results in feelings of foreboding among both the commander and the troops—fears which are all too likely to become a reality. An effective battle does not rely on a perfectly even match of forces, like a duel; rather, the defender must actively work to create advantages, whether through the specific characteristics of the defensive stance, swift and calculated movements, familiarity with the terrain, or freedom of maneuver. Without these elements, success is elusive, and neither a river nor a deep valley will provide a guaranteed safeguard.

The third approach to river defense—involving a strong position taken up on the enemy's side of the river—derives its effectiveness from the danger it imposes on the enemy, specifically the threat of cutting off their supply lines and limiting their access to certain bridges for retreat or reinforcement. Naturally, we are considering only major rivers with a significant volume of water here, as only these can create the types of conditions that make this defensive approach effective. Rivers that are simply contained within deep valleys or ravines often provide numerous crossing points, which reduces the risks associated with cutting off access to supply lines.

For this type of defensive stance to be effective, the defender's position must be very strong, ideally close to unassailable. Otherwise, the defender would only expose himself to unnecessary risk by moving halfway toward the enemy and, in doing so, lose the natural advantages of his position. But if the defender's position is indeed formidable enough to deter the enemy from attempting a direct attack, it may effectively keep the enemy on the same bank, unable to cross without serious risk. Should the assailant decide to cross the river despite this risk, he endangers his own supply routes; yet, by the same move, he also presents a threat to the defender's communications. As in all scenarios where one army bypasses another, the crucial issue becomes whose supply lines and strategic connections are more secure, whose positions are better protected, and which side stands to lose more should the enemy threaten these lines. Additionally, a critical factor is which side retains greater confidence in their ability to prevail if forced into a decisive encounter.

In this situation, the river's influence acts as a double-edged sword, intensifying the risks associated with movement for both armies since both rely heavily on limited crossing points and bridges. Given the usual strategic conditions, the defender often has a logistical advantage, as his own crossing points and supply depots are frequently reinforced by fortresses. This defensive strategy, therefore, becomes viable and may serve as a valuable alternative to direct river defense, especially when conditions for a straightforward defense are unfavorable. Here, the river isn't directly defended by the army, nor is the army defended solely by the river; rather, the defense relies on the strategic connection between them, ensuring that the larger objective—the protection of the country—is achieved.

If we consider this third mode of river defense carefully, it becomes clear that while it holds potential, it lacks the power to fully halt a determined and forceful enemy. Much like two electrical charges in close proximity without directly engaging, this form of defense creates a tension, offering no decisive clash. It can be an effective choice against an enemy superior in numbers, especially if led by a cautious commander hesitant to advance aggressively. Similarly, this approach may be viable if both sides are evenly matched in strength and neither expects to gain any overwhelming advantage. However, when facing a force led by a bold, decisive leader commanding greater resources, the defensive position risks becoming precarious, bordering on peril. Such a defense style appears daring and calculated, almost scientific in its strategy, to the point that it might be termed "elegant." Yet, just as elegance can slip into folly when carried to excess, in warfare, it is much less forgiving; thus, we find few examples in history where this sophisticated defensive style was successfully executed.

An additional strategic option emerging from this third defense model involves retaining control of a bridge and establishing a tête du pont, or bridgehead, to continually threaten a counter-crossing. In doing so, the defender creates a persistent potential for offensive action that disrupts the enemy's confidence in holding the river boundary.

Each of the three methods of river defense, whether absolute with the main force or not, also lends itself to a feigned defense—a deliberate show of resistance intended not as a serious obstacle but as a strategic delay. Such a display of readiness to defend involves a series of measures typically taken for a more genuine defense but without the commitment to sustain them if seriously challenged. The feigned defense of a significant river, therefore, evolves into a full-fledged stratagem, where actions mimic those of an earnest defense but ultimately serve to postpone the enemy's advance. Given the importance an adversary places on planning a river crossing—an endeavor requiring time, caution, and ideally favorable conditions—this delay can prove particularly effective.

For a feigned defense to succeed, it typically involves deploying the main forces along the river in a way that mimics the setup for actual defense. However, since this setup is fundamentally an illusion and does not entail a fully equipped position capable of withstanding a committed enemy assault, it risks spreading the defending troops too thinly across multiple points. If, at any point, the opposing force escalates their efforts, even temporarily, and the defenders find themselves forced into genuine combat, they face the potential danger of significant losses and scattered forces—a classic case of a half-measure defense. To mitigate this risk, the defenders must have a designated fallback point where the army can quickly concentrate, positioned perhaps several days' march to the rear. This fallback distance enables the defense to disengage as necessary while maintaining enough flexibility to avoid extended engagements at individual crossings.

The importance of a well-planned defensive demonstration becomes clearer when looking at historical examples, such as the end of the 1813 campaign. Following his losses, Napoleon withdrew with a reduced force of around forty or fifty thousand men, crossing back over the Rhine. Attempting to defend the river across its extensive length, from Manheim to Nijmegen—where Allied forces could have crossed with relative ease—would have been a fruitless endeavor with such a limited force. Napoleon's practical objective was to position his forces effectively further inland, where he could regroup and reinforce his army, likely along the French Meuse. Yet, had he fallen back to this defensive line immediately, the Allies would almost certainly have pressed on his heels, likely entering French territory without delay. Similarly, had he dispersed his troops behind the Rhine for recuperation, the Allied forces would have viewed this as a signal of French weakness, likely sending Cossacks and light forces across immediately, with additional forces following once these initial incursions were successful. Napoleon's forces had no alternative but to establish a serious-looking defense along the Rhine.

Aware that any serious Allied attempt to cross the river would render the defense moot, Napoleon essentially intended this as a strategic display to buy time. He was correct in judging that, even though this defensive line was not designed to halt a determined advance, it could still delay the Allies. By presenting a formidable defense along the Rhine, Napoleon compelled the Allies to delay their crossing, waiting instead for reinforcements. This postponement lasted a full six weeks, during which the Allies refrained from advancing further, allowing Napoleon critical time to reorganize and consolidate his forces. These six weeks, bought by a mere demonstration of defense, proved invaluable; without this strategic stalling at the Rhine, Paris might have been the Allies' immediate objective following their victory at Leipzig, and Napoleon's forces would have been deprived of an opportunity to engage the enemy before they reached the capital.

In a second-class river defense—those defenses concerned with smaller rivers—demonstrative actions may be employed as well, but they generally prove less effective since minor rivers are easier to cross. In these cases, the psychological barrier of the river does not hold for long; the enemy may quickly test and break through with minimal effort. Hence, the impact of mere demonstrations here is comparatively short-lived.

In the third type of river defense, where smaller or temporary positions are held on the enemy's side to strategically contain or observe their movements, a demonstration would likely have even less influence. It might serve as nothing more than the effect of any temporary setup, without producing a strategic halt or forcing a redirection in the enemy's plans. Here, the presence of a river offers limited value, as it does not impose a substantial enough barrier to instill caution or delay the enemy's movement in any lasting way.

However, both the first and second forms of river defense are well-suited to augment and solidify a chain of outposts, any extended defensive line, or even an observational corps focused on secondary objectives. The natural barrier of a river lends itself well to increasing the defensive capacity of these forces by affording them a fortified front, enhancing their deterrent effect. In these cases, the purpose is not an absolute halt but a relative resistance, achieved by the inherent difficulty the river presents to enemy movement. This relative resistance is bolstered by the physical presence of the river, which forces the enemy to approach with increased caution.

Moreover, we should not underestimate the influence of a river's presence on the mindset of the attacking force. A river introduces many strategic uncertainties, making it a powerful psychological barrier that often leads the enemy to hesitate or abandon plans unless compelled by a pressing necessity. This hesitation, which adds an element of unpredictability to the enemy's actions, often provides defenders with a valuable window of time or even compels the aggressor to shift tactics. Such benefits may not be easily quantifiable, but they have a tangible impact on the enemy's planning and movement, potentially averting a confrontation altogether in most cases.

Chapter XIX. Defence of Streams and Rivers (continued)

To expand on the influence rivers and streams exert on a country's defense, even when they are not directly defended, it is important to understand that any major river—together with its main valley and surrounding smaller valleys—presents a formidable natural barrier within a region. This factor inherently strengthens a defense, though its specific impact depends greatly on the direction in which the river flows relative to the primary front line or the border of the defending country. We must thus examine whether the river flows in a parallel direction, at an oblique angle, or perpendicular to the strategic front line, and how its placement affects both defensive and offensive maneuvers.

In cases where a significant river runs parallel to the border or defensive front line, its strategic importance shifts depending on which side of the river the defending or advancing army occupies, as well as the river's proximity to the active forces. For instance, if a defending army has a large river directly behind it but within reach—ideally no more than a day's march away—and with multiple secure crossings available, this river offers considerable strategic security. Such a positioning greatly enhances the stability of the defender's communications and supply routes. Even though some freedom of maneuver is sacrificed due to the need to guard crossings, the trade-off is generally positive, as the defender's rear remains strategically safeguarded, providing a fallback point if necessary.

However, this scenario changes if the defensive posture is in enemy territory. Even with the enemy before them, a defending army would need to guard against surprise attacks from across the river, where narrow and difficult passages may complicate an already vulnerable supply and retreat line. In such cases, the river's benefits can turn into liabilities, imposing logistical bottlenecks that become challenging under pressure. As the river lies farther from the defending forces, its influence wanes, ultimately having little to no strategic impact if positioned too far in the rear.

On the contrary, if an advancing army has to leave a river at its rear, this setup introduces a potential vulnerability, constraining its communications to just a few accessible crossings. The historical march of Prince Henry against the Russians on the right bank of the Oder near Breslau exemplifies this: here, the Oder provided him with a reliable point of support within reach of a single day's march, giving him a stable defensive fallback. Conversely, the Russians under Czernitscheff later found themselves at a disadvantage after crossing the Oder. Restricted to only one crossing point, they faced a real risk of losing their line of retreat—a stark reminder of how a river at one's back can be a double-edged sword, especially if contingencies for crossing are limited.

When a river runs at a right angle or oblique to the primary front line, the advantage tilts again towards the defender. Such rivers provide multiple defensible positions that lean on the river's natural barrier, while also offering protection from smaller cross-valleys that feed into the primary river valley. This scenario can force an attacker to either leave one side of the river unoccupied or split their forces. For example, during the Seven Years' War, the rivers Oder and Elbe significantly bolstered Frederick the Great's efforts to defend his core territories of Silesia, Saxony, and the Mark, despite him not establishing a rigid defense along these rivers. Positioned at various angles to the advancing Austrian and Russian forces, these rivers posed a consistent obstacle to enemy forces, protecting the lands under Frederick's control without requiring a direct river defense.

The role of rivers for an advancing army, however, can be somewhat advantageous if the river flows perpendicularly or obliquely to the campaign's direction. In these cases, the river can serve as a natural conduit for transport, aiding the attacker by easing the logistical strain of supply movements along elongated lines. For instance, as attackers typically have longer supply lines, rivers can be a valuable aid in ferrying supplies, relieving them of some transport burdens, and enabling smoother operations. Defenders, however, can limit the utility of river transport within their territory by establishing fortresses at critical points along the river to interrupt the navigation and disrupt the enemy's plans. Even with these limitations, an attacker could still use the river up to the defender's border, if advantageous.

Nonetheless, the logistical advantage rivers provide is not always as critical as might be inferred. Practical considerations such as the navigability of a river, its seasonal limitations, the lengthening effects of its winding course, and the fact that armies increasingly source provisions locally rather than relying on distant supply lines, diminish a river's impact. Today, roads are often more vital for an army's movements and resupply than rivers. Given these modern logistics, the impact of a river on campaign outcomes is often overstated and may have a relatively minor, sometimes indirect, influence on the overall progression of a campaign.

Chapter XX.

A. Defence of Swamps

For truly extensive, difficult-to-navigate swamps—like the Bourtang Moor in North Germany—these landscapes are so rare that a detailed examination might seem unnecessary. However, it's important to recognize that smaller marshlands and low-lying riverbanks are more common and can serve as considerable defensive barriers, often posing greater resistance than large rivers in some situations. While defense tactics here share similarities with river defense, they come with distinctive challenges worth noting.

First, unlike rivers where bridges provide primary crossing points, a swamp can be even harder to traverse, especially for infantry, and any accessible causeway presents a significant bottleneck. Building a makeshift crossing or causeway through marshy terrain requires far more time than constructing a bridge over water, as there is often no way to send troops ahead to secure the construction. Unlike the ease of moving an initial guard across a river with boats, swamps offer no such flexibility, making it nearly impossible to advance and secure positions without substantial preparation. When additional obstacles, such as a river running through the marsh, are involved, the difficulty multiplies. While individual soldiers might manage to cross using boards or planks, transporting the heavier equipment needed to construct a bridge is another matter entirely. In such cases, the logistical demands of securing and crossing a swamp may become nearly insurmountable.

Second, the tools used for crossing marshes cannot be removed or destroyed with the same effectiveness as river bridges. While a bridge can be dismantled to hinder a river crossing, it's much harder to eliminate access across a swamp's causeways or dykes entirely. A dyke may be damaged but rarely to the extent of permanently blocking passage. Although a bridge over a river within the swamp can be removed, this action rarely has the full effect of disabling access as it would on a larger, single river. As a result, the remaining causeways must be defended with considerable force to maintain any defensive advantage offered by the swamp.

Because marshland defense relies heavily on holding specific, narrow access points, it becomes more localized and static compared to river defense. This requires a stronger defensive force in proportion to the line of defense than a river crossing would, demanding that the defensive line itself remain relatively short. In well-developed regions, where numerous crossings may already exist, this limitation becomes especially pronounced, as multiple entry points can dilute the effectiveness of a focused defense.

In this way, swamps offer both advantages and drawbacks compared to large rivers. On one hand, their breadth can exceed even the widest European rivers, allowing defensive posts to be safe from enemy fire from across the expanse. Additionally, when an enemy force attempts to cross a narrow dyke, they are exposed to prolonged defensive fire, as these crossings often require more time to navigate than a simple bridge. These factors can make lowlands and marshlands, when the number of viable crossing points is low, some of the strongest natural defense lines available.

For an indirect defense similar to that used for rivers—where natural barriers are utilized to set up a major engagement in favorable terrain—swamps are also highly suitable. By positioning defensive forces with the swamp as a buffer, commanders can maneuver the enemy into a challenging position, delaying or complicating their movements until a better opportunity arises to engage them on more advantageous terms.

The third type of river defense—establishing a position on the enemy's side—becomes extremely risky with marshes, due to the physically demanding nature of the crossing. Attempting to secure such a position across a swamp or marsh would mean overcoming not only the difficulties of crossing but also the vulnerability of extended supply and reinforcement lines across unstable ground.

Defending a line across open, softer bogs, wet meadows, or similarly unstable terrain beyond established dykes is generally very risky. These areas may allow some foot traffic, but a single crossing point discovered by the enemy could penetrate the entire defensive line, leaving the defender highly exposed and at risk of significant losses if serious resistance is needed. In such settings, a defensive position can quickly become a liability if any unforeseen weaknesses in the swamp's impenetrability are exploited by the advancing force. Thus, marshes, though valuable as natural barriers, require a disciplined and measured defensive approach to avoid the risks inherent in relying too heavily on uncertain terrain for security.

B. Inundations

Now, let us turn to the subject of inundations. As defensive measures and natural phenomena, inundations closely resemble swamps, though they present some distinct characteristics. While not typically widespread, inundations are significant in areas like Holland, where they have historically been utilized with notable success. Specifically, the campaigns of 1672 and 1787 showcase how Dutch flood controls shaped the defense of the country, which holds strategic importance as a buffer zone between France and Germany. Given this historical context, it is worth examining the unique features of inundations and their impact on defense.

The nature of Dutch inundations differs from that of typical marshy or waterlogged lowlands in a few key ways.

1. The terrain itself in these inundated areas generally consists of dry meadows or cultivated fields when not flooded, offering solid ground under normal conditions.
2. The land is crisscrossed by numerous small ditches of various depths and widths, created primarily for irrigation and drainage. These ditches tend to run in parallel lines, forming a grid that is visible and systematic.
3. Larger canals also weave through the region in multiple directions. These canals, lined by dykes, serve purposes beyond just irrigation and drainage—they facilitate the movement of vessels. Due to their substantial width and depth, crossing these canals is only feasible at specific bridge points.
4. A notable feature of this area is that the entire district vulnerable to inundation lies significantly below sea level and, consequently, below the water level of the canals. This geographical setup makes it possible to create intentional flooding as a defensive measure.
5. When the dykes are breached or the sluices manipulated, the entire region can be rapidly flooded, with water levels rising to cover most roads. Only the dyke tops remain accessible, while all other paths become either submerged or heavily waterlogged, rendering them unusable. Even a moderate inundation of three or four feet deep could potentially be crossed by wading in theory, but the presence of the numerous hidden smaller ditches (mentioned in point 2) makes this impractical. These ditches are submerged and invisible, turning what might have been shallow areas into risky, unpredictable passages. Only in rare cases where a route aligns precisely between two parallel ditches can movement continue without crossing them—such exceptions, however, are extremely limited in scope, and only allow for specific tactical maneuvers under very narrow conditions.

From these observations, we can conclude the following:

1. The attacker's movement options are confined to a limited number of narrow, viable paths that typically run along slender dykes. These dykes often have wet ditches or flooded terrain on either side, effectively creating elongated defiles that restrict lateral movement and make it difficult for forces to maneuver freely.
2. Any defensive position established on these narrow dykes can be fortified easily, often to the extent that they become almost unbreachable. The confined nature of the terrain allows the defender to concentrate their efforts, turning each position into a strongpoint of significant resistance.
3. However, due to this constricted environment, the defender is also forced into a primarily passive role at each individual point. The lack of room to maneuver necessitates reliance on static defenses, where the primary strategy becomes holding ground rather than conducting offensive or mobile operations.

4. In such a setting, defense is not based on a single, continuous line but rather on a flexible, modular system. Since obstacles to movement exist in all directions, each position enjoys natural flank protection. This setup allows the defender to create new posts continuously, compensating for any section of the defense that may be lost. In this way, the area operates less as a line and more as a grid or network, where the loss of one point does not compromise the entire system. The potential for defensive configurations, much like the endless possibilities on a chessboard, is vast.

5. Given that such defensive landscapes are typically found in regions of advanced agriculture and high population density, the number of viable crossing points will be significant. As a result, more defensive posts and personnel are needed to secure these points effectively. Consequently, the total length of such a defensive line must be kept relatively short, as a longer line would require an unsustainable level of resources and manpower.

The main defensive line in Holland, running from Naarden on the Zuyder Zee to Gorcum on the Waal and largely positioned behind the Vecht, spans approximately eight miles, extending ultimately to the Biesbosch. In the historical campaigns of 1672 and again in 1787, forces of about 25,000 to 30,000 men were stationed along this line to secure it. If such a line could be defended effectively and consistently, it would serve as a substantial shield, protecting the provinces of Holland situated behind it.

In the 1672 campaign, the defensive line indeed held up against considerably larger forces led by two experienced generals—Condé and Luxembourg—who commanded a combined force of 40,000 to 50,000 troops. These generals, despite their numerical advantage, did not attempt a direct assault on the line, opting instead to wait for winter in the hope that severe weather conditions might work in their favor. However, the winter proved to be milder than anticipated, and their strategy of waiting ultimately came to little effect. This period highlighted the effectiveness of the Dutch defensive measures when backed by strong leadership and preparation. On the other hand, in 1787, the line's defense was ultimately unsuccessful, as the Dutch forces stationed there failed to repel the Prussian advance. Even a secondary defensive line, which was considerably shorter and located between the Zuyder Zee and Lake Haarlem, only delayed the Prussian forces briefly. The Duke of Brunswick, leveraging an astute tactical plan adapted to the Dutch terrain, managed to break through in a single day with a force roughly equivalent in size to that defending the lines.

The starkly different outcomes between these two defenses underscore the critical importance of strong and unified command in mounting an effective resistance. In 1672, when Louis XIV's forces first launched their invasion, the Dutch were taken by surprise and found themselves largely unprepared, with their military system still on peacetime footing. As a result, many fortresses lacked the necessary supplies, equipment, and adequate garrisons. Additionally, these fortifications were often manned by poorly trained soldiers or unreliable foreign mercenaries. The French took advantage of this situation, capturing many Dutch and Brandenburg fortresses along the Rhine with minimal resistance. It was only after these fortresses had been taken that the French could concentrate their efforts on the primary Dutch defensive line, having largely neutralized much of the surrounding defense structure.

However, in August 1672, with the murder of the De Witt brothers, Prince William of Orange assumed command, bringing with him a much-needed sense of purpose and coherence to the Dutch defensive strategy. His leadership unified the military efforts and reinforced the main defensive line, making it formidable enough that neither Condé nor Luxembourg dared attempt a direct assault. Their hesitation to attack underscored the effectiveness of a well-coordinated defense, even against a numerically superior force.

In contrast, the situation in 1787 was markedly different. This time, it was not the collective effort of the United Provinces but primarily the province of Holland standing alone in resistance. Consequently, the Prussian objective was not the capture of various fortresses, as it had been in 1672, but rather the challenge of breaking through the singular defensive line itself. Moreover, the Prussian army of 1787 consisted of only around 25,000 men, a far cry from the 150,000 troops deployed by Louis XIV. Yet, despite the relatively small Prussian force, the conditions in 1787 should have favored the Dutch, especially given the prevailing spirit of republicanism that had taken hold in Holland. However, a critical deficiency undermined the defense: the lack of centralized command. Unlike in 1672, when Prince William of Orange's unified leadership enabled a cohesive response to the French threat, in 1787 the defense was managed by a commission of officials. While this commission included capable men, it was ill-suited to the complex demands of wartime coordination and could not inspire the level of confidence required to effectively mobilize and direct the defense. Consequently, the defensive effort suffered from fragmentation and lack of decisive action.

This comparison between the two campaigns demonstrates how essential unified leadership is in defending a strategic line. The tactical deployment of defenses along the line may be crucial, but without clear command and a cohesive approach, even the best-laid plans may falter. This historical example from 1787 also illustrates how a defensive strategy along a dyke or a similar confined line can be supplemented by limited offensive maneuvers. Although each position along a defensive line must naturally maintain a largely passive stance, there may still be opportunities for effective counterattacks from select points if the situation allows. Such offensive actions are particularly viable if the attacker is not overwhelmingly superior. Despite the constraints imposed by the narrowness of the dykes, which limit maneuverability and the force of any attack, the offensive side typically cannot occupy every road and dyke that remains unused. Therefore, defenders with intimate knowledge of the local terrain and control over strategic points could exploit unoccupied dykes to launch flanking attacks or cut off enemy supply lines.

In such scenarios, where the attacking army is restricted to narrow pathways and heavily reliant on secure supply lines, even minor counterattacks can have a significant psychological impact, potentially deterring further advances. A single, well-executed offensive maneuver—such as a sally from Utrecht, for instance—might have created enough disruption to prevent the Duke of Brunswick from advancing further toward Amsterdam. This case illustrates how even a modestly scaled offensive action can serve as a potent deterrent, particularly if it aligns strategically with the overall defensive objectives.

Chapter XXI. Defence of Forests

First and foremost, it's essential to distinguish between dense, tangled, and largely impassable forests and expansive wooded areas that have undergone some degree of cultivation, which are often partially clear and intersected by multiple roads. When considering a defensive strategy, the latter type of forested terrain should generally be avoided or kept to the rear of the defensive line whenever feasible. The defender, often at a disadvantage compared to the attacker, needs clear visibility to make effective decisions. The defender also tends to be more reactive, basing strategies on the assailant's moves rather than on a preemptive offense, making visibility and a solid understanding of surroundings crucial. If a defender positions a tangled or obscured wooded area in front of their forces, they effectively handicap themselves, engaging in a blind struggle against an opponent who may have greater visibility or positional advantage. Should the defender position themselves within the wooded area, both sides become "blind" to some extent, leveling the visual playing field. Yet, this mutual blindness does not satisfy the inherent strategic needs of the defender, who depends on clarity to leverage any advantageous terrain features or anticipate the assailant's moves effectively.

In such scenarios, a forested region best serves the defender if it is positioned behind their forces, where it can act as a natural screen to conceal troop movements, reinforcements, or other strategic preparations from the enemy's sight. A forest to the rear also provides a secure cover, aiding in withdrawal or retreat if needed, and creates a buffer that can help shield forces regrouping or recovering from an attack. Here, it's necessary to emphasize that these remarks specifically concern forests situated within relatively flat terrain; when mountains enter the equation, the topographical and strategic influence of the high ground typically supersedes that of any forested areas within the same region, a topic that has been explored separately under mountain warfare.

Impenetrable forests, or those traversable only along specific roads or paths, present different strategic benefits. In the context of an indirect defense, they offer opportunities similar to mountainous regions for staging battles under more controlled conditions. If positioned to the rear, such forests allow the defending army to concentrate and hold back, then strike as soon as the assailant exits the forest's roadways or narrow passages. Here, a dense forest resembles the role of a mountain more than that of a river. Like mountains, an impenetrable forest offers both the cover and restrictive approach paths that slow the assailant's advance and create favorable conditions for the defender. Furthermore, the defender retains a strategic advantage in retreat within or behind these forests, where the enemy's movement is slowed by terrain and limited sightlines.

Attempting a direct defense within any forest, even a dense and challenging one, is risky, particularly if relying solely on thin outpost lines or basic barricades like abatis. Such barriers, while potentially slowing an enemy, often prove to be only temporary obstacles. No forest is so utterly impenetrable that determined small units cannot infiltrate at multiple points. These infiltrations are analogous to the first few drops of water leaking through a weakened roof—what starts as a trickle can quickly become a deluge, eventually overwhelming the line of defense. Thus, while a forest can serve as a substantial barrier and concealment feature, holding it directly with thin defensive positions usually proves ineffective and precarious.

However, forests—particularly extensive, largely untouched ones—offer significant defensive advantages when employed in the arming and mobilizing of local or national militia forces. In this setting, forests are exceptionally well-suited to the needs and strategies of irregular forces, especially when large-scale levies and less formal troop formations are mobilized. If the defender can strategically integrate these expansive forests within a broader defense plan, especially so that enemy supply and communication lines must pass through them, these natural barriers become potent assets. They not only facilitate guerrilla or partisan tactics that harass and weaken enemy forces along their lines of communication but also enable a continuous, stealthy form of resistance that leverages both the landscape and the unique advantages of local knowledge.

Chapter XX. The Cordon

The term cordon refers to a defensive strategy where a line of connected posts is specifically organized to directly protect an entire district or region. This direct protection distinguishes it from a situation where various corps of a large army, though aligned, do not form a cordon because their defense is achieved through combined movements and strategic maneuvers rather than through a continuous line of posts. A cordon's purpose is to establish an immediate physical barrier, directly covering the area rather than relying on the broader effects of mobile forces.

At first glance, it's apparent that a long defensive line tasked with covering an extensive region lacks the robustness needed for sustained resistance, especially when considering a formidable attack. Even if sizable forces were positioned along the line, they would be vulnerable if the attacker approached with a similarly substantial force. Thus, the practical goal of a cordon is limited to opposing a relatively minor offensive—whether due to a weak or minimally committed adversary or simply the modest scale of the attack itself.

Historically, large-scale structures like the Great Wall of China were created as cordons to deter raids from Tartar groups. This example illustrates the principle of a cordon system designed to resist relatively low-intensity incursions. Similarly, many European states bordering Asia and Turkey established defensive lines to help curtail cross-border incursions. In this context, the cordon isn't seen as inadequate; it fulfills its purpose by making incursions more challenging, thus reducing their frequency. This distinction matters in settings with neighboring populations inclined toward small-scale raids or whose martial customs are embedded in frequent skirmishes.

A second example of cordons is the lines established during European wars, like the French defensive lines along the Rhine and in the Netherlands. These were created to guard territories against raids and minor incursions, often aimed at plundering or imposing taxes on the local populace. In these instances, cordons were not intended to withstand a full-scale assault by an enemy's main force but to serve as a hindrance to lesser operations, with the expectation that smaller forces would man the posts. However, should the main body of the enemy's army decide to engage with these lines, the defender would inevitably need to mobilize more substantial forces for defense—an outcome far from ideal for efficient military planning. The more concentrated and aggressive a campaign's objectives, the more counterproductive such lines become; they tie up troops in static positions that are more costly to maintain than they are valuable in strategic terms. Today, such formations are generally regarded as ineffective, with the belief that they often squander resources without offering proportional security.

Finally, extensive lines of outposts established to guard an army's encampment also qualify as cordons. These lines provide an initial deterrent against raids or small-scale incursions targeting specific cantonments. However, against an advancing enemy army, they offer only a temporary check. The primary objective here is to delay the enemy's approach for as long as possible, though the amount of time gained is generally minimal. In such cases, the outposts serve a limited purpose; if the army's first knowledge of the enemy's movement comes from these outposts, it implies a significant breakdown in intelligence and preparedness. Thus, even these lines are set up primarily to oppose smaller threats, and the defensive aim is aligned with the limited strength such formations provide.

The notion of an army defending a country by dispersing itself across a long defensive line, stretching out in a continuous cordon against the enemy, seems irrational. It is therefore essential to understand the conditions and motivations that might compel a military force to adopt such a seemingly ineffective approach. The effectiveness of a cordon, where each post is strategically connected and collectively acts as a defensive network, can only be rationalized under specific circumstances that constrain more flexible and dynamic defense methods. Understanding these conditions is key to assessing whether a cordon system has legitimate strategic merit or if it is merely a defensive measure born out of necessity rather than tactical soundness.

In mountainous regions, any defensive position taken by an army — even when fully assembled for a decisive engagement — is bound to be more spread out compared to a position in level terrain. This necessity stems partly from the natural fortifications provided by mountainous ground, which bolster defensive strength. Additionally, a wider retreat path is essential in mountains, as outlined in the discussion on mountain defenses. When there's no immediate likelihood of battle, and the enemy is positioned opposite with no intention to advance unless given a strategic opportunity, it's not uncommon for an army to expand its control beyond essential positions to occupy territory along the flanks. By securing more ground left or right, within the army's safe operational reach, various strategic advantages can be gained, as we'll discuss.

In flat, open terrain with an abundance of navigable routes, armies can usually achieve this broader control through mobility alone, reducing the need to disperse forces across an extended line. Moreover, such dispersal would be more dangerous in open ground, where the resistance of each separated unit is relatively low, and the value of a coordinated defense is much higher.

In contrast, a mountain position tends naturally toward a defensive layout where posts are more fixed to specific locations due to the reliance on local defenses. Relief forces cannot be sent quickly to any threatened point, and should an enemy gain control of a location, it's often challenging to reclaim it unless a significantly stronger force is deployed. These constraints mean that a defensive position in mountains, even if not strictly a "cordon" line of connected posts, still ends up resembling one — a distributed system of defensive outposts that closely resemble cordon arrangements. Such a setup inevitably invites comparisons to a formal cordon structure, and once generals start extending their positions by small degrees to protect additional ground, they often find themselves on a slippery slope toward creating a true cordon without intending to do so.

As a campaign unfolds, commanders frequently extend their lines to cover more territory, moving from controlling immediate territory to securing the flanks of individual posts. Each outpost's commander considers defensive points extending to their left and right, aiming to strengthen their position. Over time, this tendency can evolve from covering essential ground to safeguarding the army itself through distributed posts, progressing gradually from defensive posts to a cordon-like structure.

A cordon defense, therefore, when implemented by a main force, is typically not a deliberate strategy aimed at blocking every potential advance by the enemy but rather a structure that emerges as the army seeks to control as much ground as possible without engaging in decisive battle. Such an arrangement can be regarded as a tactical error when the broader strategic intention is misunderstood, leading commanders to authorize one small post after another in an attempt to maintain comprehensive control over a territory without consolidating their forces effectively. The cordon, in this context, is sometimes mistakenly viewed as a defensive "system." However, this so-called "system" can seem acceptable or even commendable when it achieves its objectives without severe consequences.

For instance, campaigns led by Prince Henry during the Seven Years' War are often celebrated as exemplars of precision, particularly since they received the king's endorsement, even though they also included networks of posts extended so broadly that they could be seen as classic cordon formations. Prince Henry's success in such campaigns illustrates that a cordon can be suitable if the commander understands the opponent well — in this case, recognizing that no large-scale offensive was imminent. His objective was to occupy and control territory to the maximum extent permitted by local conditions, rather than to engage in a full defensive cordon intended to withstand decisive attacks. If he had experienced significant losses with this dispersed approach, it would not necessarily have reflected poor strategy but rather an isolated misjudgment of the specific circumstances.

While a cordon approach for a primary army force within a theater of war can be viable, history offers cautionary examples where the cordon structure was misapplied or misunderstood. In some instances, leaders or their advisors overestimated the cordon's ability to withstand any form of attack, treating its utility as a general defensive approach when, in reality, it can be overwhelmed by a well-coordinated offensive. Such misapplications, including those seen in the Austrian and Prussian defense of the Vosges in 1793 and 1794, demonstrate that a cordon — even if occasionally effective — should be used with full awareness of its inherent vulnerabilities and should not be mistaken for a foolproof defensive configuration. In these cases, the issue wasn't an incorrect application of the cordon principle for a temporary, low-intensity defensive purpose, but rather a fundamental misconception that it could serve as a comprehensive defense against large-scale offensives.

Chapter XXIII. Key to the Country

In the art of war, few theoretical ideas have been as widely used and yet as poorly defined as the notion we are now examining. This concept has served as the go-to critique for countless battles and campaigns, becoming the favored analytical tool in military discussions. Often, it provides critics with a semblance of learned authority, a fragment of supposed military science that can be paraded for its weight. Yet, despite its prominence, the concept has rarely, if ever, been rigorously defined or practically explained.

Our purpose here is to uncover the idea's true meaning and assess its real-world value. This discussion finds its place here because foundational defensive considerations—mountains, rivers, entrenched camps, and other strong defensive positions—must be understood before the term we examine can be properly contextualized.

Historically, this term has been used in a vague, almost mythical sense, sometimes referring to the most vulnerable point in a country, at other times the most fortified. If we describe a location without which an advancing force cannot effectively enter an enemy's territory, calling that point the "key" of the country makes straightforward sense. This usage is easy to comprehend because it aligns with basic logic: controlling such a point might be necessary to secure access to the broader region.

But theorists have expanded this simple idea into something grander, envisioning a key location that dictates the fate of an entire country. For example, when Russian forces advanced into the Crimean Peninsula, they needed control over the Perekop isthmus—not solely to gain entry, as Lascy demonstrated by bypassing it twice (in 1737 and 1738), but to ensure a secure foothold within the Crimea. This example is clear-cut, and the term "key-point" here doesn't add much beyond its straightforward meaning. However, if one were to argue that whoever controls Langres effectively "controls all of France as far as Paris," implying that this location's capture automatically leads to the occupation of the rest of the country, this would be a vastly different claim, suggesting something bordering on the mystical.

The first type of thinking is grounded: it states that the country's occupation hinges on controlling this particular point—a clear notion easily grasped. But the second interpretation is almost magical, suggesting that merely controlling this "key-point" ensures the possession of the entire country by some inevitable consequence. Common sense is insufficient to support this view, requiring instead a mystical leap, as if invoking ancient, hidden knowledge. This interpretation began to surface in writings published roughly fifty years ago and peaked towards the end of the previous century. Despite the straightforward clarity and effectiveness with which Napoleon conducted warfare, this mystique of key-points persists, clinging to relevance in military literature.

Now, stepping away from mystical interpretations, it's evident that every country has strategically valuable locations—points where multiple roads converge, where supplies can be efficiently amassed, or that are centrally positioned relative to other critical areas. Control over such a point might naturally offer various strategic advantages, helping secure broader objectives. If military leaders occasionally refer to these points as the "key of the land" to emphasize their importance, it would be pedantic to critique this metaphor. In fact, it's a vivid and fitting way to underscore the site's significance.

The issue arises when this metaphorical language is inflated into an elaborate and rigid system, where the simple expression becomes a foundation for convoluted theoretical structures. At this point, reason intervenes, cautioning against reading too much into the phrase and advising instead that we confine the term to its plain, practical value.

To create a structured theory from the notion of a "key position," military thinkers needed to rely on something more definitive and absolute than the often vague and flexible meaning generals gave it when describing campaigns. Out of its various potential interpretations, the concept of "high ground" was eventually selected as the foundation.

When a road crosses a mountain ridge, we breathe a sigh of relief at reaching the summit, knowing the difficult ascent is over and the descent lies ahead. This sense of completion, so natural to an individual traveler, becomes even more pronounced for an army. The feeling of conquering the climb brings a psychological advantage, as it often simplifies the descent and grants a clear view over the land, allowing one to anticipate and command the terrain below. Thus, any highest point on a road over a mountain naturally appears decisive and has genuine strategic importance in many situations—though not universally. These high points are commonly referenced in generals' reports and termed "key-points," albeit usually with a more limited sense than theoretical writings would later propose.

This notion eventually served as the origin of a flawed theory, which we may attribute in part to Lloyd's writings. From here, elevated points from which several routes descend into surrounding territory came to be regarded as strategic "keys" to entire countries—points that were thought to "command" the nation. This perspective dovetailed naturally with the idea of systematically defending mountain ranges, and thus, strategic theory drifted further into speculative, abstracted thinking. Soon, elements of mountain defense tactics began influencing this notion, so that instead of focusing on the highest road points, theorists turned to the absolute highest peaks of a mountain system—the watershed, as it were—as the ultimate "key" to controlling a country.

At that time, in the late 1700s, scientific understanding of geological forms shaped by water erosion gained traction, bringing natural science to the service of military theory. This geological approach dissolved the barriers of practical thinking and allowed speculation to flourish, as strategic reasoning was tied to the analogies of natural geology. Consequently, by the end of the 18th century, military discourse became filled with references to the "sources of the Rhine and Danube," with theorists assigning them an almost magical power over military outcomes. This trend mainly occupied theoretical writings, as the more fantastical ideas of books rarely translate into practice; the more absurd the theory, the less it tends to impact actual war. Yet, this particular theory did lead to some practical missteps in Germany, which we can confirm with historical examples.

The first example comes from the scientifically complex campaigns of the Prussian army in 1793 and 1794 in the Vosges, where theoretical justifications relied heavily on the works of Gravert and Massenbach. A second example occurred in 1814 when an army of 200,000 soldiers was drawn through Switzerland towards the Langres plateau, following similar theoretical principles.

The simple truth is that a high point in a land from which its waters spring remains merely a high point. All the inflated ideas written at the close of the 18th and start of the 19th centuries about its supposed military significance were based on mere imagination. Even if all of Germany's rivers shared a common source atop a single mountain, this would not render the mountain any more militarily valuable than a convenient spot for a surveyor's marker. It might make a fine location for a signal tower but offers no real utility for strategic purposes like a commanding view for a watchman, let alone for an entire army.

Thus, looking for a "key position" at the supposed "key" of a country—where mountain ranges converge or waters begin to flow—is a purely theoretical concept found only in books. Nature itself defies this idealization because ridges and valleys are not typically arranged in smooth, easily traversable paths as theorists of the "ground theory" imagined. Instead, they are chaotic, with peaks and valleys arranged in irregular ways, often placing the lowest watercourses amid the highest mountain masses. If one examines military history, it quickly becomes apparent that the dominant geological features of a landscape have minimal and irregular influence on military campaigns. More often than not, other factors and needs overshadow their significance, allowing armies to position themselves close to these features without being inherently attracted to them.

We have addressed this flawed idea at length because it spawned an entire system that, though elaborate, was ultimately misguided. Moving past this misconception, we return to a more practical interpretation.

If the term "key position" is to have an independent, strategic meaning, it should represent a location that is essential for an army intending to enter enemy territory. Yet if we label any strategically useful or conveniently situated location a "key position," we strip the term of any meaningful distinction and reduce it to a simple rhetorical flourish.

Such positions, if taken seriously, are rare indeed. Generally, the best "key" to a country lies within the strength of its defending army; only under particular conditions—such as exceptional geographic advantages—does the idea of a key position gain validity. According to our view, such conditions are marked by two primary outcomes: first, the location should enable the defending force to leverage the terrain for a strong tactical advantage; and second, it should provide a position from which the defender can threaten the enemy's lines of communication more effectively than the enemy can threaten their own.

Chapter XXIV. Operating Against a Flank

It is worth noting that we are discussing the strategic flank—essentially a side of the larger theatre of war. This should not be confused with the tactical concept of an attack from one side in battle or a move against an enemy's flank on the battlefield. Even in cases where a strategic flanking operation culminates in a tactical engagement, these two remain distinct and are easily separable because one does not inevitably follow from the other.

The concept of flanking movements and the positions related to them often appears in military theory but is far less common in actual war. This is not because the approach is ineffective or illusory; rather, both sides typically take precautions to prevent their opponent from executing such maneuvers. Situations where these precautions are impossible are rare, but in those unusual instances, flanking operations can indeed prove highly effective. For this reason, and due to the constant vigilance they demand, it is valuable to provide a theoretical explanation of these maneuvers.

Although strategic flanking operations can be conceived by either offensive or defensive forces, they naturally align more with the defensive and thus fit well within the scope of defensive strategies. Before delving deeper into the subject, we should establish a simple principle that is essential to remember: troops allocated to target an enemy's rear or flank are not available to engage the front. Therefore, whether tactically or strategically, considering an action solely aimed at an enemy's rear as an inherent advantage is misguided. By itself, a flanking maneuver holds no intrinsic benefit; rather, it becomes advantageous or disadvantageous based on its alignment with other elements, the specifics of which warrant closer examination.

In addressing strategic flanking maneuvers, we can distinguish between two principal objectives: targeting the enemy's lines of communication and threatening the line of retreat, which may simultaneously affect the lines of communication. These distinctions are critical as they highlight differing aims and impacts of flanking operations.

For example, in 1758, when Daun detached forces to capture supply convoys heading to the siege of Olmütz, his intention was clearly not to cut off Frederick the Great's retreat back to Silesia. Quite the opposite—Daun sought to force Frederick's withdrawal and would have willingly left a retreat path open. In contrast, during the 1812 campaign, Russian forces dispatched in September and October aimed solely to sever French lines of communication rather than prevent Napoleon's retreat. However, the intent of the Russian Moldavian army under Tschitschagof, advancing toward the Beresina, and General Wittgenstein's actions against French positions on the Dwina, was explicitly to block the retreat path and trap Napoleon's forces.

These examples serve to clarify the purpose and distinctions in flanking actions. Attacking an enemy's communications focuses on disrupting convoys, intercepting smaller units trailing the main army, capturing couriers, seizing supplies, and obstructing smaller depots. Such efforts are aimed at depriving the enemy of essential resources needed to keep their army well-supplied and functional, weakening the enemy's logistical support and ultimately compelling them to retreat.

The objective in attacking an enemy's line of retreat is to sever their army from that path, effectively trapping them. However, this outcome hinges on the enemy's actual decision to retreat; simply cutting off the route alone doesn't guarantee the result. Yet, by positioning forces to threaten their line of retreat, the defender can compel the enemy to consider withdrawal, creating the same impact as attacking their communications. This is primarily because the psychological pressure and logistical concerns act as a powerful demonstration, pushing the enemy into defensive thinking. But none of these results stem merely from the maneuver itself or the geometric positioning of troops. Instead, they emerge from certain tactical and strategic conditions that maximize the maneuver's impact.

To examine these conditions more precisely, we can break down the two forms of flanking actions, starting with the action directed specifically at the enemy's communication lines. In this type of operation, two primary conditions must be present to make the tactic feasible.

The first condition is that the forces deployed to attack the enemy's communications must be limited enough that their absence from the main battlefront goes unnoticed. If too many troops are removed, the enemy could capitalize on the defender's weakened front. Thus, this action requires a small yet effective force capable of moving independently without undermining the main defensive line.

The second condition applies to situations where the enemy's advance has effectively reached its limit—when their army, even with a victory, lacks the capacity to pursue further or exploit the defender's vulnerabilities fully. This scenario is far more common than might initially be assumed, as armies often reach logistical or operational limits where they must consolidate before continuing. Setting aside this scenario for now, let's examine the auxiliary conditions needed for the first approach: operating with a small, mobile force against the enemy's communications.

For this tactic to succeed, the enemy's lines of communication must extend over a significant distance and lack protective strongholds. If a few fortified posts could adequately secure the line, the enemy would not be vulnerable to the disruption caused by smaller attacking detachments. Additionally, the enemy's line must be situated in such a way that it is within reach of the attacking force and accessible for effective disruption.

The vulnerability of a communication line can stem from two main factors: its orientation relative to the defending army and whether it crosses into the defender's own territory. First, if the line runs at an angle rather than perpendicularly to the strategic front of the enemy's main force, it becomes more challenging for the enemy to guard all entry points. Second, when the line passes through the defender's territory, the attacking forces gain the advantage of operating on familiar ground. When both conditions are met, the line becomes even more exposed and difficult for the enemy to defend effectively. Let's explore these two vulnerabilities more closely.

At first glance, one might assume that whether the army's position forms a right angle or an oblique angle in relation to a communication line that extends forty or fifty miles is largely irrelevant. Compared to the length of the line, the breadth of the army's position is relatively minor. Yet this angle is far more critical than it appears. When an army occupies a position perpendicular to its communications, even a significant numerical superiority on the defender's part does not easily threaten the enemy's lines with interruption by detached forces or partisan groups.

Thinking theoretically, one might assume that covering such an expanse from intrusion is nearly impossible for the occupying army; it would seem that even a modest force of light troops or partisans could easily break through at various points. However, this simplistic view ignores the inherent fog of war. If both sides were as aware of each other's positions as on a map, it might indeed be challenging to protect an extended rear effectively. But in actual warfare, where intelligence is sparse, delayed, and often unreliable, both armies operate in a state of limited visibility, effectively "groping in the dark." In this environment, small detached units aiming to reach the rear of an army entrenched in a perpendicular position are essentially navigating blind, like one person in a crowded, pitch-black room. Inevitably, these units will find themselves isolated and surrounded, cut off from their support, and vulnerable to the enemy's counteractions.

Such partisan groups moving around the flank of an army in a perpendicular position expose themselves to multiple risks. Not only can these units easily lose strength and effectiveness due to attrition, but their very presence can trigger a chain reaction of timidity and hesitation among other units attempting the same maneuver. If even a single detachment meets with misfortune, fear will permeate the ranks, curtailing the initial boldness and turning what began as a plan for aggressive raids and disruptive movements into a retreating operation, marked by hesitation and avoidance.

The attrition effect is not solely physical; it impacts morale, strategy, and coordination. What was once an effective tool for harassment becomes a weakened initiative, unable to sustain its momentum or achieve its purpose. Instead of maintaining offensive pressure, these forces shift into defensive postures or outright withdrawals, thereby nullifying the intended strategic disruption and allowing the enemy to restore order along their lines. Thus, in cases where the defending army holds a perpendicular position, its communication lines are inherently more secure, diminishing the effectiveness of detached harassment and flanking efforts.

This inherent challenge means that an army adopting a perpendicular alignment to its lines of communication offers a natural shield to its most crucial segments, especially within a range of two to three marches, depending on its size and maneuverability. This protective coverage is particularly vital for those sections closest to the enemy, as they are often the most susceptible to attacks or disruptions. By positioning perpendicularly, the army provides a strategic buffer zone, minimizing the enemy's ability to impact or sever communications at these sensitive points.

However, with an oblique stance, this protective advantage disappears entirely. The communication line is left vulnerable without coverage, making it susceptible to even minor assaults or skirmishes. A small enemy force, or even a minor attempt at pressure, could immediately expose a weak point in the communication line, leading to vulnerabilities that could escalate quickly if not addressed.

This leads us to a fundamental question: if the position's front isn't determined by a perpendicular orientation to the communication line, then what defines it? Primarily, it is the enemy's front, yet this alignment also tends to depend on our own chosen front, creating a mutual dependency. This reciprocal dynamic requires us to examine its root causes and underlying strategies, as each side's orientation can compel or influence the other's positioning.

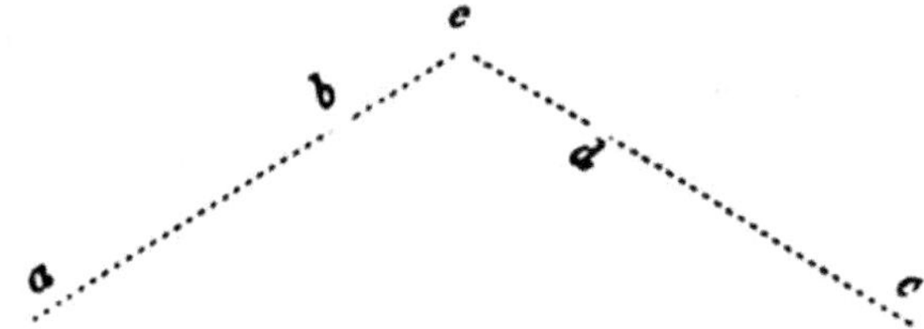

When we consider the positioning of communication lines, say the attacker's line labeled as a b and the defender's as c d, creating an intersecting angle, a significant strategic dilemma emerges. If the defender seeks to hold a position at e, the intersection point, this geometric alignment allows the attacker to easily force the defender into a frontward stance by approaching from b. In doing so, the defender is compelled to expose his communication lines. However, if the defender instead positions himself at a point on his side of the intersection, say around d, the roles are reversed. Now the attacker must orient towards the defender, potentially placing his own lines at risk—assuming, of course, that his operational path cannot simply be reoriented, as if adjusting from a d. Although this situation might seem to give the defender an edge by exploiting this intersection arrangement, practical conditions—geographical, logistical, and other specific constraints—typically weigh much more heavily than the mere geometric relation.

While this simplified illustration clarifies the potential exposures for both sides, it falls short of reflecting the actual complexity of such decisions, which cannot depend solely on geometric factors. Rather, the defender's local position and strategic context are often shaped by myriad unique conditions, meaning that neither side can universally secure a consistent advantage. For instance, if both communication lines run parallel, an oblique stance by either party would likely force a similar response from the opponent, equalizing any tactical outcomes for both.

Now, considering the situation in which only one party's communication line remains exposed, we find a host of additional concerns when that line traverses enemy territory. Should local inhabitants have mobilized against the advancing force, this hostile environment effectively multiplies the risks along the line, as if a scattered yet pervasive defensive force were in place throughout. Though such resistance lacks consolidated strength, its cumulative effect across numerous vulnerable points is enough to compromise even the most well-organized line. This type of disruption requires little explanation—any lengthy communication line through hostile territory is intrinsically compromised.

Even when the local population is not overtly hostile, or if the region lacks organized militia, the mere fact of their allegiance to the defending power subtly undermines the intruding force's communication stability. Expeditionary forces or partisan groups operating in such territory enjoy critical advantages: better intelligence, intuitive geographic knowledge, reliable access to informants, and the implicit backing of local officials. These assets, effortlessly available to defenders, can pose significant hurdles for the opposing side. Moreover, within a given proximity, there will almost always be natural refuges like fortresses, rivers, and mountainous areas, which inherently favor the defending side unless the intruding force has formally secured and occupied these locations.

In situations where an army's lines of communication are at a considerable length, follow an oblique direction relative to the army's position, and run through hostile territory, particularly favorable conditions emerge for disrupting these lines. Under these specific conditions, smaller, nimble enemy detachments can act effectively against the communications without needing to regroup directly with the main defending force. This is particularly feasible when the hostile forces operate within their own territory, where they can evade capture more easily by relying on local knowledge, terrain, and civilian support.

Thus, we identify several key conditions that increase the likelihood of successful disruption:

1. Extended Line Length: The greater the communication line's distance, the more opportunities for the enemy to exploit weak points, particularly where protection may be thinly stretched.
2. Oblique Line Direction: If the communication lines do not run perpendicular to the main position but are at an angle, it creates more areas where they are vulnerable to attack.
3. Enemy Territory: When these lines traverse through hostile land, local knowledge and support from civilians increase the likelihood of sustained partisan activities, minor skirmishes, and other tactics that can disrupt communication without the need for substantial military force.

In addition to these three conditions, a fourth element—sufficient time—is essential for such disruptions to yield lasting effects. Without this temporal factor, the disruptions may only cause brief disturbances that the enemy can quickly recover from. However, given adequate time, the effects of interrupting supply lines, isolating detachments, and delaying communications can progressively erode the operational integrity of even a well-organized force.

But these four conditions are only the chief This brings us to a deeper understanding of how smaller local and situational factors can wield influence just as decisive—if not more so—than the primary strategic conditions. These additional circumstances, which encompass the state of the roads, terrain characteristics, natural barriers like rivers and mountains, seasonal factors, weather, and the presence of essential supplies or specialized convoys (such as siege equipment), all shape the outcome of any attempt to disrupt an opponent's lines of communication. Other factors include the availability and use of light or mobile troops, which are especially suited for swift, targeted actions against these supply routes. Each of these variables plays into the overall capacity a general has to impact the enemy's movement and logistics effectively. By evaluating how all these conditions align, we can determine which side holds the advantage in controlling and pressuring the opponent's supply and retreat routes, ultimately deciding which general can afford to take greater risks.

Though this overview may seem detailed, in practice, seasoned military judgment quickly synthesizes these factors into a tactical decision. Experienced commanders, having mentally mapped such scenarios, avoid the simplistic logic often seen in military critiques that assume "turning" or "acting on a flank" alone explains the situation, without any further context or rationale.

We then turn to a second main condition that makes a strategic flank attack viable: if an enemy is unable to advance due to factors other than direct opposition from our forces. Whether from logistical issues, geographical constraints, or political reasons, any limitation restricting the enemy's forward momentum grants the defending side the freedom to dispatch forces to pressure and harass the opponent's flanks. In this scenario, should the enemy attempt to counter these actions with an attack, our army can simply fall back, avoiding a major confrontation. The Russian army at Moscow in 1812 exemplifies this approach—when the

French were stymied not by direct Russian opposition but by logistical and environmental obstacles. Although a similarly extreme case may not often repeat, smaller examples abound in military history, such as Frederick the Great's positioning on the frontiers of Bohemia and Moravia during the Silesian Wars, where he used such tactics to his advantage.

When an enemy is hindered from advancing, the defending force can afford to take more risks in dividing its resources, dispatching troops to pressure the opponent's communications. In such cases, it's less critical to maintain a superior positioning of our own supply lines, as the opponent's inability to capitalize on our retreat reduces the risk of retaliatory strikes. With the enemy focused on securing his own line of retreat, this strategic situation often allows the defending force to achieve advantageous results through tactics less dramatic and less risky than direct battle victories. Under these conditions, positioning forces along a flank becomes more feasible, as the enemy is forced to orient his front at an angle to protect his communications.

When this positioning aligns with favorable local conditions and other positive factors, the likelihood of success in these maneuvers increases. But when fewer favorable circumstances are present, the chances of success depend heavily on superior skill in devising strategies, executing movements quickly, and timing them with precision.

Historically, such circumstances provide the perfect setting for strategic maneuvers, like those frequently observed in the Seven Years' War, particularly in the Silesian and Saxon theaters during the campaigns of 1760 and 1762. Such maneuvers often emerge when direct, forceful confrontation is minimized due to either genuine constraints or, as sometimes occurred, the cautious tendencies of commanders who might avoid decisive actions due to fear of the risks and responsibilities involved. Marshal Daun, who often displayed caution in such scenarios, serves as a fitting illustration of how strategic maneuvering can sometimes substitute for a more enterprising, resolute approach.

Summing up our exploration of flanking strategies, it becomes clear that targeting an enemy's flank proves most impactful under a specific set of conditions. These conditions are as follows:

1. In Defensive Operations: Flanking actions are particularly potent when employed in defense. This is because defensive positioning often allows for leveraging terrain and established lines of retreat, enabling the defender to strike at the enemy's communications or logistics without compromising their own structural integrity. In defense, the defender can channel the enemy into unfavorable positions, making it easier to target their flanks and supply lines without risking a major engagement. This type of flanking action is often more controlled and minimizes exposure, making it a safer choice when protecting one's own resources and personnel.
2. Toward the End of a Campaign: Flanking maneuvers become increasingly advantageous as a campaign progresses toward its later stages. By this point, an enemy force is likely to be stretched thin in terms of supplies, morale, and manpower, particularly if it has been operating on foreign or hostile ground. At this juncture, flanking actions can disrupt exhausted forces more effectively, magnifying any logistical strains or gaps in discipline that have emerged over the campaign's duration. Furthermore, the defender, being closer to home and more familiar with the terrain, can execute flanking strikes that exploit any disarray or overextension within the enemy ranks. As such, flanking attacks during this phase can force an exhausted opponent into retreat or prevent them from

advancing further into defensible territory.

3. During a Retreat into the Heart of One's Country: When retreating deeper into one's own territory, a defensive force finds the opportunity to make powerful flanking strikes. Such a retreat usually results in the enemy extending its supply lines, making it particularly vulnerable to disruptions. As the defending force retreats into areas with better logistical support, local familiarity, and fortified fallback positions, it can focus resources on selective strikes against the enemy's flank without stretching its own lines too thin. The retreating force can also rely on established infrastructure and reinforcements from local militias, which become increasingly accessible the deeper they move into familiar territory. This approach turns a retreat from a mere fallback maneuver into a potent form of defense that depletes and demoralizes the advancing enemy.
4. In Concert with a General Arming of the Population: A flanking strategy gains unparalleled strength when combined with widespread civilian support, particularly in cases where the population takes up arms in defense of the homeland. With an armed populace supporting these flanking efforts, a defending force can vastly expand its capacity to strike at the enemy's extended lines. Local armed groups, familiar with the terrain and often highly motivated, can conduct guerrilla-style attacks on supply depots, convoys, and isolated enemy detachments. This broader civilian involvement not only disrupts the enemy's logistics but also forces them to spread their forces thin in an attempt to secure every segment of their supply routes, leaving gaps that the defending army can exploit further. Additionally, a well-armed population adds an unpredictable and resilient layer to the defense that complicates the invader's strategy, effectively turning every part of the occupied territory into a potential zone of resistance.

To effectively target the enemy's lines of communication or retreat, especially at the rear or flank, it is crucial that these operations are led by experienced and highly skilled detachment commanders. These leaders must manage small, nimble units capable of swift movements, launching rapid attacks on vulnerable points like isolated garrisons, supply trains, or smaller enemy detachments on the move. Such forces should also aim to bolster local militias (landsturm), not only to encourage resistance but to use their local knowledge to enhance the effectiveness of coordinated strikes. An optimal structure for these units involves a greater number of smaller, specialized detachments, allowing for flexibility and agility in carrying out sudden, impactful operations. These units should be organized with the capability to merge seamlessly for larger-scale engagements when needed, avoiding any conflicts over rank or command, which could hinder the fluidity and success of their coordinated efforts.

When it comes to cutting off the enemy's line of retreat, there is an inherent principle that must be considered: deploying forces to operate against the enemy's rear or flank diverts those resources from the main front. This reallocation is not an increase in overall strength but rather a focused application of force aimed at exploiting weaknesses, an approach that seeks to heighten potential outcomes but naturally raises the risks involved. Any form of opposition that relies on indirect actions—like targeting the enemy's retreat—introduces an element of unpredictability, elevating both the potential success and the inherent dangers. An operation that aims to sever the enemy's retreat route, if serious and not merely demonstrative, generally leads to a pivotal encounter, or at least the convergence of conditions for such an engagement, enhancing the possible outcome but also intensifying the risks.

In this approach, two main strategies emerge: one involves directing an entire force against the enemy's rear, either from a strategic position taken on the flank or by executing a deliberate turning maneuver; the other divides the force, so one portion holds the front while the other moves to encircle the enemy's rear. Each method aims to force the enemy into a critical position, potentially surrounding and capturing their forces or driving them into a difficult, extended retreat. The risk varies with each approach, but both intend to significantly disrupt the enemy's movement and supply.

If a commander chooses to turn entirely against the enemy's rear, the greatest risk lies in exposing the attacking force's own lines of retreat, and thus it requires carefully weighing the spatial and logistical relationships between both sides' lines. Just as disrupting the enemy's communications requires a consideration of their locations relative to those of the defender, turning an enemy in the rear is only as effective as the defender's own security along their retreat. A defender within their own territory generally enjoys an advantage over an assailant, having greater flexibility in their retreat routes and fewer logistical constraints.

However, while this territorial advantage often provides the defender with better maneuverability, it alone does not ensure success. Each case demands a comprehensive assessment of the specific conditions, as broader situational awareness and particular operational details ultimately guide strategic decisions. We might infer that conditions favoring such flanking actions are more frequently found in expansive operational theaters, where forces have room to maneuver, rather than in confined settings. Likewise, nations or coalitions with a solid internal infrastructure and independent military organization are better equipped to execute such operations than those whose survival depends on the backing of stronger allies, as such dependencies limit their ability to operate independently or risk detachment from supporting forces.

Flanking and rear attacks become most viable in the latter stages of a campaign, when the aggressor's initial drive may have lessened, potentially leaving them vulnerable to disruptions in their lines. This shift in momentum echoes the advantages observed in targeting the enemy's communications; as the offensive energy dissipates, a focused strike on their retreat line could lead to a decisive effect. The defender, capitalizing on the dwindling resources and fatigue of an invading force, may thus find strategic opportunities to turn the tide without engaging in direct battle.

In summary, targeting the enemy's rear or flanks—whether using the full force or by dividing and encircling—represents a high-stakes, calculated approach. It leverages a smaller force's potential impact through precision tactics and positioning, aiming to maximize disruption while remaining mindful of the inherent risk. This tactic, while powerful, requires exceptional judgment and adaptability, taking advantage of both favorable conditions and the nuanced dynamics of a campaign's progression.

A strategic flanking position, such as the one the Russians established along the road from Moscow to Kaluga, exemplifies a highly effective maneuver when timed correctly and executed under favorable conditions. At that stage, with Napoleon's aggressive advance exhausted and his forces strained, the Russian position proved invaluable. However, had they attempted a similar stance at the outset of the campaign—such as at the camp of Drissa—it likely would have backfired, leaving them overexposed and vulnerable. Recognizing this, the Russian command wisely adjusted their plan early on, adapting to the evolving pressures of the campaign.

The second approach to turning and intercepting an enemy—dividing one's forces to cut off their retreat—introduces a new set of challenges, mainly due to the inherent risks in separating forces. When one army splits to surround or intercept, the opposing force, if positioned on interior lines, retains the advantage of a concentrated formation. This united front allows them to respond with superior numbers against either of the divided forces, effectively weakening the divided attacker. This risk is inherent and inescapable; thus, it requires a highly justified basis to attempt such a maneuver.

Three main reasons can validate this risky strategy:

1. Pre-existing Division of Forces: If forces are already separated due to initial strategic choices, or if bringing them together would result in a significant delay, then the need for speed and coordination can make a division of forces the more practical option. This situation may arise when rapid deployment or immediate action is essential, and consolidating would come at too high a cost in terms of lost time.

2. Superiority in Numbers and Morale: A force that enjoys both moral and physical dominance can justifiably adopt bolder strategies, including dividing its forces for decisive, simultaneous attacks. Such superiority in both the physical number of troops and their psychological resilience equips the divided forces to withstand the heightened risk. This advantage allows each segment of the divided army to operate with confidence, knowing they possess the strength to handle local confrontations effectively.

3. Reduced Enemy Momentum: When the adversary has reached a peak in their campaign—what might be termed the "culminating point"—and their initial drive has lessened, the division of forces can become less dangerous. An opponent in this state is less likely to mount a vigorous counteraction, making it feasible to divide forces strategically without facing immediate, powerful retaliation.

When Frederick the Great invaded Bohemia in 1757 using converging lines, his objective was not primarily to launch a combined attack that struck the enemy both in front and on their strategic rear. Instead, his main focus was to preserve the element of surprise by keeping his forces dispersed until the invasion, thereby avoiding the loss of surprise that would come from consolidating his troops beforehand in Silesia or Saxony. Concentrating his forces too early would have signaled his intentions to the enemy, negating the advantage of catching them off guard—a key element in his strategy.

In the Allies' campaign of 1813, their significant numerical superiority allowed them to consider attacking Napoleon's right flank along the Elbe as part of a strategic shift from the Oder to the Elbe, aiming to bring their overwhelming strength to bear against a concentrated French force. The Allies had the resources to concentrate around 220,000 troops at Dresden against Napoleon's 130,000—a favorable ratio that, under better tactical and strategic alignment, could have led to success. Their failure at Dresden was not a flaw in the broader plan but rather due to specific shortcomings in executing both their strategic movements and their battle tactics. Despite the French having spread their forces relatively thin to defend their position along a single line, which led to disparate distributions (70,000 French against 90,000 Allies in Silesia and 70,000 against 110,000 in Brandenburg), Napoleon's position would still have been vulnerable on the Elbe without a significant abandonment of Silesia. Additionally, the Allies could have called on Wrede's forces positioned near the Maine to threaten Napoleon's retreat route to Mainz, further compounding the French difficulties.

In 1812, the Russian forces in Moldavia might have taken advantage of their strategic positioning by moving towards Volhynia and Lithuania, creating a threat against the French army's rear, as it was clear that Moscow marked the farthest practical point for the French advance. With no immediate threats to Russian territory beyond Moscow, the Russian main army did not need to worry about being overpowered if they diverted resources to threaten French communications. This approach was initially part of the defensive plan proposed by General Phul, which had Barclay's army holding at Drissa while Bagration's forces advanced against the French rear. However, the two scenarios held starkly different circumstances: in the earlier case, the French outnumbered the Russians by a significant margin, whereas, in the latter, the Russians held a numerical advantage. Furthermore, during the first approach, Napoleon's forces were propelled by a momentum that carried them well beyond Drissa, whereas by the second, their strength had depleted after reaching Moscow, making it impossible for them to extend further without significant strain. Finally, the distance to retreat to the Niemen was much shorter in the initial advance, about 30 miles, compared to a lengthy 112 miles upon their return from Moscow, illustrating why an interception of Napoleon's retreat in the second phase proved highly effective while attempting the same in the initial advance would have been catastrophic for the Russians.

When the goal is to threaten the enemy's line of retreat, such actions often act more as powerful demonstrations than as intentions to truly intercept. While it may seem straightforward that a demonstration should rest on the potential for real action, practical applications reveal differences between a display of power and an all-out attack, as we'll explore further in discussions on strategic demonstrations. This distinction underlines the nuance required in planning such maneuvers: they don't need to lead to full engagement to affect the enemy's decisions or contribute to overall strategic objectives.

Chapter XXV. Retreat into the Interior of the Country

In analyzing a voluntary retreat deeper into one's own territory as a specific type of indirect defense, we see that this approach seeks to weaken the enemy less by direct combat and more by the sheer drain of advancing deeper into hostile lands. This strategy does not hinge on winning a major battle but rather on the enemy becoming progressively depleted, so that any battle fought will occur once their strength has substantially waned.

As an advancing force pushes forward, its military capacity naturally decreases, a concept explored in detail in later discussions, but one that is well-supported by historical campaigns where prolonged advances led to heavy tolls on the offensive army. This attrition is even more pronounced if the defending force has not been decisively beaten. When the defender withdraws deliberately, maintaining an intact force and resisting the advance with steady, calculated skirmishes, the enemy faces constant, costly resistance, making each gained mile a hard-won prize rather than a swift pursuit.

Conversely, the losses for a defending army can be vastly magnified if retreat follows a decisive defeat. If the retreat begins after a major loss, daily clashes cannot be expected to unfold in an organized fashion because the defender is likely to be in disarray. Even the strongest army forced to pull back deeply into its own territory after a severe loss will inevitably face overwhelming casualties. If the enemy is significantly stronger and pushes forward with determination, as is typically the case in contemporary warfare, a devastating rout is highly probable, with the retreat devolving into disorganized flight. Historically, such pursuits often leave retreating armies on the brink of annihilation.

In a voluntary retreat, however, the defender can sustain losses more manageably by engaging in measured, controlled resistance each day. This controlled resistance means that each skirmish is fought with a tactical balance, disengaging and ceding ground at opportune moments to avoid defeat and maintain order. In these encounters, the advancing enemy will generally incur casualties equal to, if not greater than, the defender's. Though the defender inevitably loses some soldiers in retreats or as prisoners, these losses are largely counterbalanced by the enemy's casualties sustained from assaulting fortified or advantageous positions. Additionally, while the retreating force may forfeit its wounded who cannot move with the army, the advancing enemy also sustains non-combat losses from soldiers who must be left in local hospitals for months due to severe injuries.

Thus, as the two forces engage in repeated, drawn-out skirmishes, both armies tend to suffer attrition at comparable rates, each gradually eroding the other's strength. This pattern, though taxing, is strategic for the defender as it neutralizes the aggressor's initial advantage by wearing them down, ultimately leading to a near-equal rate of depletion on both sides.

The dynamic changes entirely when pursuing an army that has already suffered defeat. In such cases, the demoralization of the troops, the chaotic disorganization, the anxiety over securing a retreat, and the psychological blow to their courage make it difficult, if not impossible, for the retreating forces to muster significant resistance. Unlike an orderly, voluntary retreat, where the defender can control their withdrawals, the beaten army is typically too disordered to mount effective rear-guard actions. Here, the pursuing force advances with a confidence and determination born of recent victory, driving forward as though invincible, their progress empowered by the momentum of success and the intangible strength of morale.

Where a deliberate retreat by an intact force requires caution on the part of the assailant, who must advance carefully, almost blindly, feeling his way forward to avoid ambushes, a pursuit is altogether different. The victors press on assertively, taking advantage of the morale advantage and pushing hard to maintain the enemy's flight. Each step they advance intensifies the psychological pressure on the retreating army, pushing the defenders further into disarray. Pursuit is the ideal environment for the intangible moral factors to fully express their power—driving the flight of the defeated party and amplifying the ease of advance for the victor.

It becomes clear how vastly different the outcomes are depending on whether an assailant is dealing with an organized retreat or a defeated, disorganized retreat. The cumulative losses for both forces—sustained from continuous clashes and battlefield attrition—are just one part of the equation. As discussed more fully in later analysis, the advancing force also bears the compounded strain of continuous movement and supply-line difficulties, which heighten as they penetrate deeper into hostile territory.

At the same time, the defending army, falling back towards familiar ground, can often call upon reinforcements more easily, whether from fresh troops, mobilizations, or assistance from local allies. By moving away from their supply depots and into potentially hostile or barren regions, the attackers risk the depletion of critical resources, while the defenders, moving closer to their home front, enjoy more dependable lines of supply and reinforcements.

Further, the asymmetry in the availability of supplies becomes starkly apparent as the retreat progresses. For the retreating army, the resources of the land are theirs for the taking; advancing towards supply bases, they can gather sustenance with relative ease. In contrast, the pursuing army faces severe challenges in securing provisions. As they advance, they find villages stripped of supplies, fields stripped bare or damaged, and wells emptied or fouled. Scarcity becomes a constant burden, even with well-managed supply lines, especially in areas of difficult terrain or vast distance. The advancing army is often forced to rely on what it can carry, encountering deprivation from the outset. Rarely, if ever, can they hope to intercept significant supplies from the retreating force unless by an unusual lapse in the defender's strategy.

In vast territories, this imbalance between the defender's access to resources and the assailant's logistical difficulties can shift the odds significantly in favor of the defender. Such a protracted retreat deep into the heart of the country can dramatically improve the defender's prospects for a favorable outcome, compared to a scenario where they might have risked a direct, decisive battle on their borders. With the retreat allowing attrition to sap the attacker's strength, the likelihood of a successful counter-offensive or final stand grows. Not only does the chance of achieving victory increase as the defender draws the attacker deeper into difficult terrain, but any such victory promises far more significant outcomes.

The contrast between a defensive victory near one's own frontier and a similar victory deep within enemy territory cannot be overstated. For the assailant, a defeat near their own borders may be manageable; they have the option to retreat, regroup, and defend from a more favorable position. But a defeat far from home, deep within hostile territory, can spell disaster. Even a victory under such circumstances may ultimately force the attacker to fall back, as any remaining energy may be insufficient to capitalize on their win or to replenish lost strength adequately. Thus, there are occasions when the assailant, after an extended campaign, finds themselves so weakened that even a successful battle forces them into retreat, effectively nullifying their gains.

There is, consequently, a profound difference between striking a decisive blow at the beginning of a campaign and doing so after an extended advance into the heart of enemy territory. When executed at the campaign's onset, a decisive engagement may indeed set the tone, potentially stalling or even neutralizing the enemy's entire strategy. But if that decisive confrontation happens after the enemy has exhausted significant resources in their advance, its impact is magnified many times over. By then, the assailant is typically weakened by attrition, supply issues, and the extended reach of their operations, so any setback can be devastating. This mode of defense—drawing the enemy deeper before delivering a decisive blow—presents unique advantages, though it also involves substantial risks.

On the positive side, as the defender retreats deeper into their own territory, their army becomes more fortified. Moving towards secure supply bases, reinforcements, and familiar terrain can bolster both the morale and operational effectiveness of the defending force. In this retreat, the advancing enemy's lines of supply are stretched thinner, making resupply increasingly complex and risky. However, this form of defense does impose two primary costs: the potential material damage to one's own territory and the psychological impact on both the army and civilian population.

The material losses from allowing an enemy to advance within national borders, while not the primary concern, do affect the defender's resources, economy, and local support. While the ultimate objective is a lasting peace—secured through a favorable military outcome rather than short-term preservation—these losses still matter, especially when the enemy enters populous and economically vital regions. Here, the invader's presence not only disrupts local life but may also deplete military supplies that were either stored or in preparation in those areas. This loss, although indirect, still weakens the defending army's ability to maintain its operational tempo, especially if the enemy targets essential stockpiles or production centers.

The second and arguably more impactful drawback is the psychological effect of such a retreat on both the army and the nation. A well-planned withdrawal might be fully understood by military strategists, but the general populace and even the rank-and-file soldiers often lack insight into its tactical advantages. To the average soldier or citizen, a retreat may appear as a panicked fallback rather than a calculated maneuver. This perception can sap morale, as civilians see their homes and regions abandoned to the enemy, and troops face daily skirmishes that reinforce a sense of constant threat rather than strength. While some exceptional leaders manage to communicate the purpose of such a strategy effectively, rallying the nation and the army around it, this clarity of purpose is the exception rather than the rule. More often, uncertainty prevails, creating an atmosphere of fear and mistrust that weakens the defending force from within.

Indeed, such strategic retreats demand patience and trust, which can wane under the strain of retreat. The emotional toll is significant; a national identity that aligns with values of bravery and direct resistance may feel tarnished by tactics that rely on evasion and delaying action. There is a natural, almost visceral, national desire to meet an invader directly at the border, fighting to protect each inch of homeland soil. This approach appears nobler, more aligned with a people's spirit, and symbolically honors their collective identity. But strategy often requires flexibility, and the tactical withdrawal, though it may seem ignoble on the surface, can lead to far greater strength in the long run.

For such a defensive tactic to succeed, certain conditions are essential. A vast territory or, at the very least, a substantial distance available for retreat is fundamental. A short withdrawal, only a few days' march, won't significantly weaken the enemy; it may even embolden them. In 1812, Napoleon's army set out with over 250,000 men, a formidable force that diminished only slightly as it reached Smolensk, then dwindled further at Borodino. By then, the advancing force had shrunk to 130,000 men, leveling the field against the Russian defenders who could now muster a comparable force. By the time Napoleon's troops reached Moscow, they were weakened to such a degree that even their victory at Malo Jaroslavets could not counteract the strategic disadvantage of being so deep into Russian territory with limited resources and winter fast approaching.

No other state in Europe could offer Russia's vast distances and harsh winters, but most would not face an invading force with the initial strength of Napoleon's 1812 army, a force unmatched in its numerical superiority and morale. In other theaters, the defender might only need to withdraw a fraction of the distance, perhaps 30 to 50 miles, to achieve a comparable strategic effect. Nonetheless, a tactical retreat of this nature remains a gamble, requiring an intricate understanding of timing, terrain, and the psychological endurance of both army and nation.

The success of a strategic retreat into the heart of a country is influenced heavily by certain environmental, social, and seasonal factors. These elements work together to amplify the defensive advantage, allowing a withdrawing army to weaken the enemy over time rather than through immediate, direct confrontation. There are three primary conditions that greatly enhance the efficacy of this method of defense:

A Sparsely Cultivated Landscape: A country with little agricultural development or sparse infrastructure makes it inherently difficult for an invading force to rely on the land for supplies. When the countryside is rugged, barren, or not consistently cultivated, it offers few resources that an advancing enemy might seize to sustain themselves. Unlike in well-developed regions where foraging and local requisition can easily support an occupying force, a poorly cultivated area leaves an army vulnerable to supply shortages. This lack of available provisions increases the strain on the invader's already extended supply lines, forcing them to transport essential resources from afar, which can slow their advance, sap their morale, and create logistical bottlenecks. The landscape itself, therefore, becomes an ally to the defenders, functioning as an obstacle that wears down the enemy incrementally.

A Loyal and Warlike Population: The commitment and fighting spirit of the local population can serve as a powerful force multiplier in a defensive strategy that emphasizes attrition. A loyal and war-ready people provide not only moral support but also active resistance against the invading forces. They may form militias, act as guides for the defending army, or conduct guerrilla-style operations to harass the enemy's supply lines, ambush small units, and relay vital intelligence about enemy movements. When a populace is fiercely protective of its homeland and willing to take up arms, the retreating army gains a network of informal defenders who can disrupt the invader's operations and create an atmosphere of constant threat. Such a population is challenging for any foreign army to subdue, as their resistance not only slows the enemy's progress but also amplifies the costs of occupation, keeping the invader in a state of alert and insecurity.

An Inclement Season: The seasonal climate can be a decisive factor in a protracted defense, especially when harsh weather works against the invader's ability to sustain their campaign. Winter, with its severe cold, snow, and reduced daylight, presents enormous challenges to any advancing army. Troops are more susceptible to illness and frostbite, while rivers may freeze over, impeding mobility and further complicating supply efforts. Wet seasons, with heavy rains and flooding, can also bog down the enemy, making roads impassable, cutting off essential routes, and slowing the transport of provisions and reinforcements. By retreating during a season of inclement weather, a defending force can effectively turn the elements themselves into a defensive barrier, leveraging nature's obstacles to increase the enemy's hardship, while they themselves are better prepared to endure these conditions on familiar terrain.

Together, these circumstances—an undeveloped landscape, a fiercely loyal populace, and adverse seasonal conditions—create a setting where a strategic retreat into the interior becomes a slow and grinding ordeal for the enemy. Each step deeper into such a territory becomes progressively harder for the invader, increasing the likelihood of attrition and eventual exhaustion. This approach to defense is not only a matter of geographic withdrawal but a calculated retreat that aims to erode the enemy's strength and resolve, setting the stage for a more favorable final confrontation or forcing a costly and unsustainable occupation.

All these factors make it considerably harder for an advancing army to sustain itself as it pushes deeper into hostile territory. This situation necessitates large convoys for consistent supplies, numerous detachments to protect the lines, constant fatigue from challenging duties, and an increase in sickness within the ranks, all while making the army more vulnerable to attacks on its flanks by the defending forces.

Finally, we should address the sheer size of the armed force, as its absolute mass plays a significant role in the outcome of a campaign. The nature of large versus small forces suggests that, regardless of relative power, a smaller force exhausts itself more rapidly and is, consequently, more limited in both range and duration of its campaign. In effect, there is an intrinsic relationship between the size of an army and the extent of the territory it can effectively control. This relationship does not lend itself easily to quantification, as many factors influence it, but it remains a consistent principle. For example, advancing on a distant objective like Moscow might be feasible for a force of 500,000 soldiers but implausible for one of only 50,000, even if the smaller force enjoys a superior relative strength compared to the defenders.

Assuming this relationship between absolute size and spatial range applies in both scenarios, the effects of a defensive retreat into the interior of a country in weakening the attacker increase proportionately with the size of the advancing force. The following factors become more impactful as the invading force grows:

1. Supply and lodging challenges: The difficulty in supplying and housing troops intensifies with larger armies. Even if the area occupied expands in line with the army's size, local resources will never fully meet the needs of such large forces. Supplies must be transported over long distances, increasing the risk of loss and shortage. While only a fraction of the occupied area is necessary for housing troops, the logistical burden of moving and protecting the army's supply lines grows disproportionately with the size of the army, further complicating its advance.
2. Slower progress and accumulated losses: The larger the force, the slower its progress, extending the time required for its campaign and thus amplifying the daily attrition it suffers. For instance, if a force of 3,000 troops drives 2,000 defenders ahead of them across open ground, they may only move a mile or two per day, with occasional pauses. Catching up to, attacking, and forcing the smaller retreating force to withdraw can be accomplished in hours. In contrast, when both forces are multiplied by a factor of 100, the logistics become much more complex. Movements and engagements that might have taken hours now require days, sometimes multiple days, to complete. With each increase in scale, the attacker faces additional challenges, as it must stretch its forces more thinly than the defenders to secure supply lines, exposing its flanks and allowing the defenders to concentrate their forces more effectively, as seen in Russian maneuvers near Witepsk.
3. Increased fatigue and operational strain: As armies grow in size, the strain on each soldier intensifies. A force of 100,000 requires considerable time to assemble, march, and reposition, with prolonged pauses for basic functions like ration distribution, bivouac setup, and readiness checks. Even tasks that may seem routine, like mustering or cooking rations, demand more time and coordination than a smaller, more agile army would need. The logistical complexities grow exponentially with size; all movements take longer, and individual efforts required from soldiers multiply. Although these logistical strains affect both advancing and retreating forces, they place a greater burden on the attacker, who not only must manage the increased demands of daily operations but must also contend with more substantial logistical needs due to extended supply lines and greater exposure to attrition and sickness

Thus, as the scale of engagement grows, so does the difficulty for the advancing force, magnifying the strain on its troops, reducing its speed, and exposing it to more effective resistance from the defenders. These cumulative effects make large-scale invasions increasingly difficult to sustain, rendering a defensive strategy of gradual attrition, such as a calculated retreat, especially potent against a larger invading force. By forcing the attacker to extend itself over greater distances, endure prolonged hardship, and expend valuable resources, the defending force gains a strategic advantage, weakening the enemy more effectively and potentially even compelling a retreat.

1. First, the defender holds an advantage because his forces are greater in mass, owing to the relative superiority we assumed in his favor. This strength in numbers provides resilience and flexibility to absorb the strain of continuous movement and to maintain strategic positions when needed. The defender's capacity to manage the shifting dynamics of the retreat more effectively than the pursuer

also strengthens his position over time.

2. Second, by retreating and thereby yielding ground, the defender effectively purchases the strategic advantage of setting the terms of engagement. This choice to withdraw voluntarily enables the defender to control the pace and course of the action, effectively granting him the initiative. As the one who establishes the direction and timing of each movement, the defender can shape his strategies and follow them through with minimal need for alteration. Conversely, the aggressor must constantly adapt, reacting to the defender's actions and deciphering his intentions, which requires both time and resources. This fundamental difference between planning proactively and reactively generates a series of efficiencies for the defender that accumulate and translate into meaningful advantages in the long run.

It's essential to emphasize that this scenario refers to a defender who is retreating strategically rather than after a defeat or a lost battle. This distinction prevents confusion with prior discussions, specifically those in the twelfth chapter of the fourth book, which examined pursuits following an outright loss. Here, the retreat is a voluntary action, not a response to defeat, which changes the nature of the interaction significantly.

The ability to set the terms of engagement and force the opponent to react offers the defender meaningful savings in time and energy while granting him certain secondary benefits. Although these might seem minor in isolation, they accumulate over the course of a sustained retreat and can significantly impact the outcome.

3. Finally, the retreating force can use the very act of retreat to simplify its own movement and impede that of the pursuer. As the defender moves, he can facilitate his own retreat by improving the conditions of the route, repairing bridges, preparing convenient sites for rest or encampment, and ensuring supplies are more readily available along his line of retreat. Conversely, he can actively create obstacles to the advancing enemy. By destroying bridges, for instance, he forces the pursuer to expend time and resources rebuilding them; by moving quickly over poor roads, he can worsen their condition and delay the enemy. By occupying key locations for rest or supplies first, he deprives the pursuer of these benefits, heightening the difficulty of their advance and thus building further advantage.

Through a combination of resource management, tactical foresight, and the careful manipulation of terrain, the retreating defender, even in yielding ground, positions himself favorably by creating increasingly challenging conditions for the pursuer to overcome.Lastly, we must add still, as a specially favourable circumstance, the war made by the people. This does not require further examination here, as we shall allot a chapter to the subject itself.

Until now, we have discussed the benefits this kind of retreat offers, the sacrifices it demands, and the conditions required for success. Now, we turn to how such a retreat might best be carried out. The first matter to consider is the direction in which the retreat should be conducted.

Ideally, the retreat should head into the interior of the country, so the advancing enemy is increasingly surrounded by friendly territory on all sides. In doing so, the invader becomes vulnerable to the influence and resistance of the population, while we avoid the risk of separating ourselves from our main territory. For instance, had the Russians in 1812 retreated south rather than east, they risked losing connection with the heart of Russia. This consideration is inherent in the retreat's purpose. Deciding which point in the country to aim for—whether it aligns with protecting the capital or another important area or drawing the enemy away from them—will depend on specific circumstances.

If the Russian forces had carefully planned their 1812 retreat in advance, taking a more organized approach, they might have chosen the road to Kaluga as early as Smolensk, which they only later took after leaving Moscow. This strategic move might have saved Moscow entirely. To illustrate: at Borodino, the French had approximately 130,000 troops, and it's doubtful that their numbers would have been any higher if the battle had occurred halfway to Kaluga rather than closer to Moscow. Given this setup, how many of these troops could Buonaparte have risked sending to Moscow? Very few. An expedition fifty miles to a large and strategically important city like Moscow required more than a small detachment.

Consider the scenario: if Buonaparte, with 160,000 troops in Smolensk, had attempted to send a contingent to Moscow prior to a major battle and allocated 40,000 for that purpose, this would have left him with only 120,000 to face the main Russian force. Consequently, in battle, this force would have been reduced to 90,000 soldiers, effectively 40,000 fewer than what he brought to Borodino. With a resulting 30,000-man advantage, the Russians would have been positioned for a far more favorable engagement than they had at Borodino, possibly achieving a victory. But as it happened, the Russians didn't retreat with a carefully constructed plan; they fell back repeatedly simply because they didn't yet feel adequately reinforced to engage fully. With all supplies and reinforcements coming along the road from Moscow to Smolensk, it didn't occur to anyone at Smolensk to leave that vital route. Furthermore, even a decisive victory between Smolensk and Kaluga might not have justified abandoning Moscow, as it would have likely shocked and angered the Russian public.

In another example, Buonaparte could have shielded Paris more effectively from potential assault in 1813 by positioning his forces a little to the side, perhaps behind the Burgundy Canal, rather than directly in its path. With Paris defended by the National Guard and a few thousand regular troops, he could have kept 100,000 men at Auxerre. In this position, he would have forced the Allies to reconsider advancing on Paris, as they would be unlikely to send a 50,000- or 60,000-strong corps toward the capital while Buonaparte was positioned to intercept them with a superior force. However, if the roles had been reversed, and the Allies faced Buonaparte with Paris undefended, they would have been strongly advised against leaving their own capital exposed, as Buonaparte would not hesitate to march on an unprotected capital given the chance. Thus, the psychological influence of each side's unique situation impacts strategic choices significantly.

We'll delve further into this concept when examining war planning, but for now, it suffices to note that if a lateral defensive position is adopted, the capital or any other area the defense aims to secure should be capable of offering some resistance on its own. This resilience is necessary to prevent it from being easily overrun by minor forces or raiding detachments.

We must also examine a further strategic element in the choice of a retreat direction, specifically the benefit of a sudden change in the route. The Russians' retreat in 1812 offers a prime example. Initially, they withdrew directly toward Moscow, but after reaching the city, they shifted from the route toward Wladimir, turning instead along the road to Riazan. They then altered course once more, moving toward Kaluga. Had the Russians needed to extend their retreat, this new direction would have allowed them to head toward Kiev, a location much closer to the enemy's frontier. Even if the French maintained a numerical superiority over the Russian forces, it is clear they could not have relied on a stable line of communication through Moscow under such circumstances. The French would have likely abandoned both Moscow and, most likely, Smolensk, forfeiting their hard-won territories and conceding control of the campaign area east of the Beresina.

While it's true that by taking the Kiev route, the Russian army would risk separation from the core of their own territories, by this point, the disadvantage would be almost inconsequential. The situation facing the French would have been vastly different from a scenario in which they had advanced directly to Kiev without first detouring through Moscow. Thus, this type of abrupt change in retreat direction—a tactic made feasible in a vast country like Russia—offers substantial strategic benefits.

A sudden shift in the retreat direction disrupts the enemy's planning and can often force them to abandon crucial positions or supply lines. In a country with wide, open spaces, the defender's ability to veer unexpectedly and take a new direction can be used not only to confound the invader but also to maneuver closer to the enemy's borders, potentially pressuring their lines of communication or supply. This strategy limits the aggressor's gains and can effectively reframe the campaign's dynamics, positioning the defender in a place of greater leverage while forcing the attacker into difficult logistical decisions.

1. A sudden shift in the line of retreat effectively forces the enemy to abandon their established line of communication, which disrupts their logistical stability. Setting up a new line is inherently challenging, especially if it needs to be adapted in phases. This means that the advancing force will likely have to experiment with multiple lines before achieving a new, secure route, complicating their efforts and creating vulnerabilities.
2. If both forces subsequently move closer to the frontier, the advancing army's initial territorial gains lose strategic significance. The attacker's position no longer secures the conquered areas, and the attacker may find themselves compelled to relinquish these territories altogether. Russia, with its vast expanse, provides a unique environment for this kind of strategic maneuvering, allowing two armies to engage in a type of territorial "game," where they alternately draw each other deeper into unfavorable positions.

This kind of retreat is also feasible in smaller countries if specific conditions align favorably. Such factors depend on a variety of local and strategic details, each unique to the situation, and must be evaluated case by case. Once a chosen direction for retreat is decided, our primary army must follow this line, since only then can we draw the enemy along the intended path. If we diverged from this line with a significant portion of our force or tried to guide the enemy in a different direction, it would diminish our ability to control their movement and impose the conditions we aim to create.

As for whether to advance with our forces concentrated or dispersed along lateral routes to create a divergent (or eccentric) pattern in the retreat, this scattered form generally introduces more risks and complications and should, therefore, be avoided unless the situation specifically calls for it.

1. Dividing our forces weakens the advantage we gain by concentrating at a single point, which is one of the main challenges we impose on the enemy. By staying concentrated, we make it difficult for the enemy to predict and respond effectively to our movements.
2. When our forces are spread out, the enemy can exploit interior lines, allowing them to keep their forces more united than ours. This means they can mass more troops at any single location, creating a risk that they will overpower one of our detached units. While this might be less of a concern during

a retreat, where we continually give ground, the entire strategy depends on remaining a constant threat to the enemy. If the enemy perceives us as weaker or fragmented, they might seize the opportunity to defeat us piece by piece. Another key goal of this type of retreat is to gradually increase our strength relative to the enemy, allowing us to eventually deliver a decisive blow. Partitioning our forces would undermine this strategy and reduce our chances of achieving a conclusive victory.

3. Generally, a weaker force benefits more from maintaining a convergent or concentrated action rather than spreading out. In scattered formations, weaker forces lose the collective strength that comes from mutual support and coordination, making each part more vulnerable.

4. Many inherent weaknesses in an aggressive approach can be diminished if the defender's forces are scattered. Keeping our forces united preserves our ability to exploit any weaknesses in the enemy's strategy and minimizes the risks we would face if forced to rely on isolated units.The weakest features in a long advance on the part of the aggressor are for instance;—the length of the lines of communication, and the exposure of the strategic flanks. By the divergent form of retreat, the aggressor is compelled to cause a portion of his force to show a front to the flank, and this portion properly destined only to neutralise our force immediately in his front, now effects to a certain extent something else in addition, by covering a portion of the lines of communication.

For a purely strategic impact, a divergent retreat—where forces spread outward rather than moving directly back—is generally not ideal, as it weakens the core strength of the retreating army. However, it may serve as a preparatory maneuver if the intention is to ultimately strike at the enemy's line of retreat, discussed in prior strategies. A divergent retreat might be justified in cases where the defender can prevent the enemy from advancing into certain provinces that would otherwise be left vulnerable. Deciding where to place troops effectively to guard such territory, anticipating where the enemy may move, and identifying regions he might avoid altogether, demands keen strategic judgment.

In 1812, for example, the Russians left a significant force under General Tormassow in Volhynia to face the Austrians, who were anticipated to invade. Volhynia, with its complex terrain and obstacles, presented a viable setting where 30,000 Russian troops could reasonably hope to maintain their ground against an Austrian force of similar size, keeping important territories closer to Russian control. This was also a practical choice, as this contingent was unlikely to reach the main Russian army in time even if they attempted to regroup. By contrast, General Phul's initial proposal for the Russian campaign strategy was to have Barclay's main force retreat to Drissa, while Bagration's army would hold position on the French flank, poised to harass their rear. Such a strategy, though bold, was likely unsustainable, as Bagration's forces would have been vulnerable to overwhelming French numbers in South Lithuania, risking their quick destruction so close to the main French advance.

It's natural for the defender to seek to keep as much territory as possible from falling into enemy hands; the narrower the territory available for the invader's movements, the more challenging his advance. Yet these secondary objectives must not come at the cost of weakening the main defensive force too much, as it is this core army that will create the conditions forcing the enemy's eventual retreat, increasing his attrition and weakening both his physical resources and morale.

In general, the defender should retreat gradually, keeping his main force directly before the advancing enemy. A steady, controlled withdrawal, without divisions, and combined with frequent resistance, compels the aggressor to remain battle-ready, thus draining his resources through continuous tactical and strategic vigilance. Once the enemy has been forced deep enough into the defender's territory, the defender should ideally shift to an oblique position in relation to the enemy's line, taking any opportunity to strike at his rear.

The campaign of 1812 in Russia exemplifies this on a grand scale. Although the Russian retreat was not initially a deliberate strategy, its effects illustrate the impact such a retreat can achieve. Were the Russians to face an invasion today with similar circumstances, they would likely approach the defense in a similar systematic and voluntary manner, applying the lessons learned from 1812 to inflict greater damage on an invader. Nevertheless, it would be mistaken to assume that this approach is only feasible in vast territories like Russia; similar methods could be adapted and applied effectively in other regions under the right conditions.

When a strategic offensive falters solely due to the overwhelming challenges it encounters—without the decisive force of battle—the retreat that follows tends to reveal the core characteristics and impacts of indirect, defensive resistance. In such cases, the defender achieves substantial success by exhausting the enemy, ultimately forcing a retreat that often becomes disorderly and costly. Numerous campaigns illustrate this pattern. Frederick the Great's 1742 campaign in Moravia and his 1744 campaign in Bohemia, the French 1743 incursions into Austria and Bohemia, the Duke of Brunswick's 1792 campaign in France, and Massena's winter campaign of 1810–11 in Portugal all provide examples where the offensive effort deteriorated due to the compounding difficulties of advance and supply rather than through pitched battles. Although these instances reflect this defensive method in more limited scopes compared to larger campaigns, they nonetheless confirm the power of indirect attrition in deterring and demoralizing an aggressor. There are countless smaller examples as well, where only partial reliance on this principle is evident, but illustrating each would require detailed examination, taking us far afield.

In Russia and the other larger cases mentioned, the turning point of the campaign occurred without the definitive outcome of a major victory at the point of highest threat. Even when a decisive battle may not be entirely avoidable, the key in this defensive strategy is to shift the balance of forces toward the defender's advantage until victory becomes feasible. Securing this victory then acts as the initial push in a chain of disastrous consequences for the enemy, whose retreat often escalates into an increasingly unmanageable and self-perpetuating decline, as if following the inexorable pull of gravity on a falling object.

In this manner, strategic defense through indirect methods, attrition, and the cumulative exhaustion of the enemy remains not only an effective alternative to seeking immediate battle but a potent means of setting in motion a gradual unraveling of the offensive that accelerates once it has begun, often becoming irreversible and catastrophic for the invader.

Chapter XXVI. Arming the Nation

A people's war within civilized Europe emerged as a distinct feature of the nineteenth century, carrying both strong supporters and staunch critics. Some opponents view it as politically destabilizing, potentially unleashing anarchy by legitimizing mass resistance, posing risks akin to an external threat to the nation's order. Others criticize it from a military standpoint, suggesting the outcomes do not justify the toll it takes on the nation's resources. Here, however, our interest in a people's war lies solely in its strategic and military dimensions—as a means of defense against an enemy, rather than in its political implications.

Critics argue that a people's war requires disproportionate expenditure for questionable results. But it's essential to understand that this method, though resource-intensive, aligns with the broad expansion of modern warfare's scope and reach. Much as the requisitioning system, massive increases in army size, universal conscription, and mobilization of militias extended the boundaries of warfare beyond what was conceivable in earlier, limited military systems, so too does the people's war. These mechanisms are interconnected, evolving from a shared impulse to amplify the available military power. In this way, arming the general populace follows the same trajectory as these other military expansions. And, just as larger, more agile armies transformed the military landscape and compelled adversaries to adapt, nations that skillfully implement people's war stand to gain distinct advantages over those who dismiss it.

This evolution raises broader questions—such as whether this expansion of military potential, on the whole, serves humanity's interests or works against them. But such a question is as complex as asking whether war itself is ever in humanity's best interest. We leave that question to philosophical debate. However, some may argue that the resources poured into people's wars might be better allocated elsewhere in the military sphere. Yet a closer examination reveals that these resources, primarily the population's morale and commitment, are not readily deployable by alternative means. Their full potential is only activated when called upon specifically to resist occupation.

Thus, instead of asking about the cost to a nation of mobilizing its entire populace for defense, we should instead ask what effects this type of resistance can achieve, the conditions under which it proves effective, and the best ways to deploy it.

Due to its distributed and decentralized nature, a people's war isn't suited for delivering concentrated, decisive blows. Instead, it works through a more diffuse influence—similar to evaporation in nature—acting across a broad surface area. The greater the occupied territory or the wider the contact with the invading forces, the more effectively the people's war can undermine the enemy. Like a steady, sustained heat, it erodes the strength and morale of an occupying army. This erosion takes time, creating a period of tension where attrition slowly wears down the invader. The outcome may manifest gradually as certain regions resist less intensely while others continue their active resistance, or it may culminate in a decisive moment if the widespread resistance becomes an all-consuming threat to the invading army, forcing it to retreat to escape total annihilation.

For such an outcome to be achieved solely through people's war, the invaded country would need to be vast—on the scale of Russia—or else the invading force would need to be exceptionally undersized relative to the territory it aims to control, a disparity rarely seen in Europe. Therefore, a people's war should ideally operate in tandem with regular military forces under an integrated strategic plan that coordinates both types of defense across the theater of war.

The critical conditions for maximizing the effectiveness of a people's war are as follows—

1. The people's war should take place deep within the heartland of the nation. When the conflict unfolds far from the country's frontiers, the people feel directly threatened, motivating them to resist with greater intensity and a sense of defending their homes, families, and way of life. This central

positioning also complicates the enemy's logistics and lines of communication, heightening the impact of widespread, local resistance.

2. The conflict should not hinge on a single decisive event. If victory could be achieved through one major battle or swift conquest, the extensive mobilization of the populace would have limited impact. Instead, the people's war thrives when prolonged resistance can continually harass, disrupt, and gradually weaken the invading forces over time, rather than relying on a quick resolution.

3. The theater of war should cover a substantial expanse of territory. In a broader area, the enemy's forces must spread out to occupy, govern, and protect their interests, making it difficult for them to maintain a concentrated front. A larger area provides greater opportunities for localized resistance to emerge and continuously apply pressure, wearing down the invaders as they attempt to control vast, unfamiliar terrain.

4. The character and spirit of the population must be inclined towards resistance. The effectiveness of a people's war relies on the populace's willingness to take up arms, endure hardships, and engage in guerilla tactics. A strong national identity, a history of resilience, or cultural values that promote autonomy and defiance against foreign control significantly enhance the effectiveness of a people's war.

5. The country's geography should favor defensive actions, making occupation and control challenging. Terrain that is mountainous, forested, marshy, or otherwise difficult to navigate gives natural advantages to local forces, providing cover, concealment, and obstacles for the enemy. Regions where land cultivation is dispersed or uniquely arranged further complicate the invaders' ability to navigate, sustain their troops, and control the population. These geographic features create a natural ally for resistance efforts, allowing smaller, less organized forces to stand against better-equipped armies.

The density of the population matters less in a people's war than one might expect, as the primary concern is rarely a lack of manpower. Whether the inhabitants are relatively wealthy or impoverished does not hold decisive importance either, although it is often observed that a population accustomed to hard labor and privation proves to be more resilient and better adapted to the rigors of sustained conflict.

A particular feature of the land that greatly aids the success of a people's war is the dispersion of rural homesteads, commonly seen in areas of Germany. This layout creates a landscape that is both more segmented and well-covered, with numerous yet poorly maintained roads complicating movement. This dispersed setting presents significant logistical challenges for occupying troops, as accommodations become scattered and difficult to organize.

In such a landscape, the people's resistance operates with the elusive quality characteristic of large-scale people's war but applied on a micro level: resistance is present everywhere but lacks a centralized, tangible form. Where the population is concentrated in villages, occupying forces may find it easier to impose control by billeting troops, plundering as punishment, or, in extreme cases, setting fire to dwellings. Such punitive measures, however, become far less effective in areas with dispersed farmsteads and isolated homes, like the rural regions of Westphalia. In these areas, the decentralized nature of settlements frustrates attempts to apply collective retribution, as there is no single hub of resistance or identifiable group to target effectively.

National levies and armed peasants should never directly engage the enemy's main forces or even substantial detachments; they are not suited for cracking the tough "nut" of a concentrated army. Instead, they are best employed at the edges, gnawing away at the outer layers of control the aggressor hopes to maintain. They should rise up within regions at the fringes of the primary battleground—territories where the enemy presence is weak or nonexistent. This enables these provinces to fully escape the enemy's grasp and influence. Without a powerful enemy immediately in sight, courage and the will to resist flourish, drawing in nearby populations who, inspired by their neighbors, begin to take action themselves. This spark of resistance spreads like wildfire across the land, slowly reaching the crucial supply and communication lines that sustain the invader's operations.

Although it's an exaggeration to view a people's war as an invincible force that an army cannot subdue—like weather beyond human control—we must acknowledge the tenacity and resilience of armed peasants. Unlike trained soldiers who march as a cohesive unit, these local forces scatter when dispersed, slipping away rather than standing in rigid formations. In mountainous, wooded, or broken terrain, this resilience makes every enemy movement hazardous. Even if these peasants appear to have been pushed out by the head of an advancing column, they may easily reappear in its rear, striking unexpectedly. If roads are to be blocked or narrow passes obstructed, the improvised efforts of a people's war can achieve results far more flexible and enduring than the calculated attempts of military outposts or detachments. Where the latter are limited by protocol and procedure, the locals operate with the natural adaptability of people who know the land intimately.

The enemy's only effective response is to thin out his forces by dispatching numerous small detachments to guard convoys, occupy key points, or secure routes. In the beginning, with resistance low, these detachments will be modest, as commanders are reluctant to spread forces too thin. But as scattered outposts are overpowered by swelling numbers of peasant fighters, morale rises among the defenders, escalating the struggle. In this gradual buildup, courage and combativeness intensify until a critical threshold is reached, setting the stage for larger confrontations.

The essence of a people's war, however, lies in its ability to remain fluid and elusive, like a drifting mist, never solidifying into a structured front. Should it harden into a single organized force, the enemy would send in a well-equipped detachment to crush it, capturing large numbers and dampening the spirit of resistance. People would believe that the main struggle had ended, their efforts futile, and their weapons would fall from their hands. Yet, while avoiding such consolidation, it's equally essential that this resistance gathers enough strength at certain points to pose a real threat. Like storm clouds massing, it should sporadically unleash "lightning strikes"—sudden, concentrated attacks that leave the enemy wary of an unpredictable threat.

These focal points for resistance should be situated on the flanks of the enemy's operational area. Here, the people's forces should be organized into larger, more systematic units, supported by a minimal number of regular soldiers to give them a semblance of formal structure and a capacity for coordinated operations. These better-organized groups, trained and equipped to strike where the enemy is most vulnerable, serve dual purposes. They can target larger enemy garrisons left to hold captured territory, while also cultivating a persistent sense of dread within the occupying force. These organized clusters magnify the psychological impact of the people's war, ensuring that the enemy feels increasingly insecure, as if they are surrounded by a hostile land eager to expel them. Without this element, the entire strategy would lose its sharpness, failing to truly unsettle and wear down the invading force.

To bolster the effectiveness of a people's war, a general can spur civilian resistance by deploying small detachments from the main army into vulnerable territories. These regular troops provide a necessary spark—without them, the inhabitants often lack the confidence or initial motivation to take up arms. The larger the detachment, the more powerful its effect; a sizeable contingent has a magnetic pull, rallying more locals into an expanding force. However, this tactic has clear limits. Firstly, too many troops diverted for this secondary purpose risks dissolving the army's core strength, creating an overextended line of skirmishers and reducing both the formal army and the peasant levies to a fragile, scattered force vulnerable to serious setbacks. Secondly, when a district becomes too crowded with regular troops, the dynamism of a people's war tends to diminish. This happens partly because the enemy, perceiving a threat, increases their presence in the area, and partly because locals begin relying more on the professional soldiers for protection. Additionally, the large force places logistical strains on the people, burdening them with the need for quarters, provisions, and other contributions that dilute their enthusiasm for the resistance.

To counter any significant reaction from the enemy against this popular uprising, the primary strategy is to avoid committing the local levies to direct tactical defense. Popular forces generally exhibit a strong initial fervor but lack the tenacity needed for prolonged confrontations. While these forces may accept defeat and regroup, substantial losses in combatants or prisoners will quickly undermine their morale. Tactical defense requires disciplined, sustained resistance and readiness for risks that the levies cannot support; unlike a regular force, a peasant army thrives on unpredictability, not entrenched defense. Thus, when civilian militias are used to protect key terrain—such as mountain passes, dykes, or marshlands—they should prepare for a fluid form of defense. Once a position is breached, they should disperse to launch sporadic attacks rather than regroup in defensive lines that would only be cornered and crushed.

For a people's war to ignite, it must operate from regions away from the main thrust of conflict, where the resistance has room to breathe without being snuffed out by a single concentrated strike. Even in the most ideal circumstances, with a motivated populace, favorable terrain, and deep-seated animosity against the enemy, no uprising can sustain itself indefinitely in a zone too rife with danger. To foster a lasting insurgency, the resistance must spread across a wide field, where sporadic strikes accumulate into a larger impact rather than risking everything in one vulnerable location.

This analysis, though subjective, offers insight into a phenomenon that remains uncommon and underexplored. While experience with people's wars is limited, strategists must recognize that national resistance can be integrated into broader defensive plans in two primary ways: either as a final measure after a defeat or as a supporting force before any decisive engagement. The latter scenario generally presumes a gradual retreat into the country's interior, following the principles of indirect resistance outlined in prior discussions. Here, however, we consider the role of popular levies following a significant loss in battle.

No nation should ever hinge its survival solely on a single battle, regardless of its significance. Even in defeat, new strengths can be summoned, and the enemy's prolonged advance will inevitably drain its momentum over time. Assistance may also come from external allies. To despair and accept collapse prematurely is both unwise and unnecessary; when survival is at stake, a nation, like a person on the brink, should instinctively reach for any available means of defense, rallying whatever resources and willpower remain to avert disaster.

No matter how small or seemingly powerless a state may be in relation to its enemy, if it refrains from making one final, determined stand, it essentially abandons its own spirit. Choosing to negotiate peace through concessions may still offer a path to survival, but the active defense of the nation remains crucial. Efforts to defend, even after a severe defeat, will not make peace less attainable or add to its cost. Rather, a continued resistance will make any terms of peace more favorable and possibly more sustainable. Especially if allies are anticipated, those who share an interest in preserving the state's independence, these defensive efforts become indispensable. A government that, after a crushing defeat, thinks only of how to quickly submit and shows no courage to muster every available resource, undermines its own standing. It risks revealing a lack of resilience, signaling that it may have lacked the very will to achieve victory in the first place.

Thus, even in the face of what seems an overwhelming defeat, a state can still leverage a retreat, the strength of its fortifications, and a people's war to maintain resistance. When the strategic conditions allow for this—especially if the principal theater of war is bordered by mountainous regions or challenging terrain that naturally serve as defensive bastions—the state can use these natural barriers to slow the enemy's advance. These rugged flanks, like walls positioned to protect key areas, can strategically deter the enemy's forward movement and provide advantageous positions for counterattacks.

If the victorious enemy is drawn into sieges, leaving significant forces to secure supply lines and occupying troops to maintain control over conquered areas, he inevitably stretches his resources. As he becomes weaker with every siege, dispersed garrison, and skirmish, his active fighting force dwindles due to natural attrition, logistical exhaustion, and battle losses. This phase is precisely when the defending army should re-engage, waiting for the opportune moment to strike. By carefully timing a coordinated counterattack when the enemy is overextended, the defending forces can deliver a strategic blow, causing the aggressor to falter, and potentially turning the tide in the defender's favor.

Chapter XXVII. Defence of a Theatre of War

Having covered the essential elements of defense, we could theoretically save a discussion of how these elements relate to an overall defense strategy until we explore the Plan of a War, where we would look at how major attack and defense strategies unfold and shape the broader conflict. In many scenarios, the plan for an entire war can be largely characterized by the defense or attack plan for the primary theater of war. However, we didn't start with a full-scale view of war, since in warfare—more than in any other human activity—the parts are defined by the overall strategy, each segment taking on the character and purpose of the whole. Instead, we've begun by dissecting each individual component. Without advancing step-by-step from simpler ideas to more complex concepts, we would face a chaotic mix of poorly defined ideas, where the diverse phases of counteraction constantly obscure our understanding. So, we'll proceed in stages, considering each key facet of defense on its own and finding the links between the topics covered and their influence on defending a specific theater of operations.

From our perspective, defense is essentially a more robust form of combat. Its goal is to protect our forces and eliminate the enemy's, ultimately securing victory, yet even this outcome is not the final goal. The ultimate objective is to safeguard our political existence and undermine that of the enemy, culminating in the peace we desire, for it's only through peace that the conflict is resolved and a shared outcome emerges.

In relation to war, the concept of the enemy's state is paramount. Above all else, its military strength and its territory stand out. Still, many other factors can take on heightened importance due to specific conditions, such as foreign and domestic political alliances, which at times carry more weight than all other elements. However, while military strength and territory do not represent the enemy's full state, they overwhelmingly dominate its relevance to the war effort, often dwarfing all other factors in significance. The military's purpose is to defend the territory of the state or seize that of an enemy, while the territory itself continuously replenishes and sustains the military. Thus, military power and territorial control are interdependent, each strengthening and complementing the other in importance.

Despite this interdependence, there is a subtle difference in how these elements influence each other. If the military is destroyed, rendering it unable to resist further, the loss of territory is inevitable. Conversely, territorial conquest does not necessarily entail the destruction of the enemy's military, as they may choose to abandon their lands to regroup and retake them later with a strengthened force. Not only does a complete defeat of the enemy's forces determine the fate of a nation, but even a substantial weakening of the military will usually lead to territorial loss. Yet, while the loss of land will gradually impact military strength, it may not immediately weaken the army to the same degree within the timeframe in which a war unfolds.

The preservation of our military power, alongside reducing or destroying that of the enemy, must always outweigh the mere occupation of territory and should be a commander's primary objective. Territory itself only becomes a pressing concern if reducing the enemy's military strength has not effectively secured it. If all the enemy's power were concentrated into a single army, and the entirety of the war reduced to one conclusive battle, then the conquest of territory would hinge directly on the outcome of that single clash. Destroying the enemy's forces, occupying his territory, and securing our own would all flow from that decisive moment.

But what circumstances might lead the defender to diverge from this straightforward strategy and distribute forces across space? The answer lies in the potential limits of victory when achieved by a unified force. Every victory has a particular reach or influence. If a single, unified victory could affect all parts of the enemy's state, including both his military and territory, then dividing our forces would be unwarranted. However, if certain parts of the enemy's territory or forces remain outside the reach of our victory, we must turn our attention to those areas. Since territory cannot be gathered in one place like military forces, dividing our own forces may become necessary to protect or contest these areas.

In smaller, more compact states, unity of military forces is feasible, and success often depends solely on defeating that unified force. Such concentration becomes practically unfeasible with larger territories or when multiple allied states join forces against us, as these scenarios naturally demand divisions across various theaters of war. The effectiveness of a victory is inherently tied to its magnitude, especially when it decisively impacts the bulk of the enemy's forces. Consequently, the most significant blow should be directed at areas where the enemy has concentrated his largest forces, and the more we concentrate our own forces in that endeavor, the surer we become of our success.

A useful analogy here is the concept of a center of gravity in mechanics. Just as a physical center of gravity is located where the largest mass is concentrated, and as any impact directed toward this center yields the greatest effect, so too in war: the largest concentration of the enemy's forces represents a kind of "center of gravity." Effective action targeted at this military center can potentially influence all parts connected to it. However, just as in mechanics, the force exerted against this center must be precisely measured; excessive force can overshoot, leading to wasted effort.

The cohesion of an army under one leader is notably stronger than that of an allied army stretched across a wide theater or with forces originating from separate areas of the war front. In a unified force, coherence and decisiveness are at their peak, while with allied forces spread across vast distances or with different agendas, unity becomes tenuous. In such cases, political goals may serve as the only tenuous bond holding the coalition together, making it fragile and susceptible to dissolution. Thus, while concentrating power increases our strike's impact, over-concentration can waste resources and weaken efforts elsewhere.

The ability to identify these "centers of gravity" in the enemy's military strength and to understand their areas of influence is a crucial strategic skill. Commanders must continually assess how the movement—forward or backward—of any segment of forces might influence the remainder on both sides. Here, we are not suggesting any new approach; rather, we clarify the underlying rationale that has driven generals across history, aligning it with fundamental principles.

How this understanding of the enemy's center of gravity impacts a comprehensive war plan will be explored in the final sections devoted to strategic planning. This approach has helped us recognize the core motives that often drive the division of forces in warfare: the opposing pressures of securing territory and concentrating force against the enemy's From this concept of a strategic core, we see how specific theaters of war, or defined army regions, naturally come into being. These areas represent the essential boundaries within a country where its forces are allocated, and within which any decisive action by the main military power in that region will have a direct and immediate effect on the whole area, aligning the theater's outcome with the result of that decision. This influence extends directly to the region itself, yet also indirectly reaches neighboring theaters, impacting adjacent territories in ways that may accumulate or compound strategically.

While this seems intuitive, it is essential to stress that the definitions here focus on central ideas within hypothetical frameworks, and the boundaries of these theaters or regions are not precisely fixed—they shift with circumstances, and we cannot rigidly define them.

Thus, a theater of war, regardless of its size or the scale of its military force, can be envisioned as a unified structure with its own center of gravity. The primary objective in each theater must be to make a decisive move at this center of gravity, where victory would mean not only holding ground but securing the theater itself in the broadest sense, fundamentally shaping the direction of the conflict across that entire region.

Chapter XXVIII. Defence of a Theatre of War (continued)

Defense, as a concept, encompasses two primary elements: the moment of decision and the state of expectation. The strategic blend of these elements forms the focus of this discussion. First, it's important to recognize that the state of expectation doesn't represent the entirety of defense; rather, it serves as the phase in which defense aims to achieve its objective. As long as a military force maintains control over the territory it's meant to defend, a tension exists between the defensive and offensive forces. This tension holds until a decisive outcome is reached. A true decision, in this context, is only reached when either the attacker or defender exits the theater of war altogether.

So long as an armed force remains within its theater, it continues to defend that space, effectively making the defense of the theater synonymous with defense within the theater. Whether the attacker has momentarily seized parts of the territory is, in a sense, immaterial—the land is held provisionally until the decisive outcome is determined.

However, this framing, where the state of expectation works within an overall defensive strategy leading to a decisive outcome, is valid only when a decision is anticipated and considered inevitable by both parties. The true center of gravity for each force—and the boundaries of the theater determined by it—are only engaged when a conclusive solution is actively sought. When a decisive outcome is no longer the goal, these centers of gravity lose relevance, and the armed forces, to an extent, become neutralized. At this point, territorial possession, the second primary factor in the theater of war, becomes the immediate objective. In other words, the more a war moves away from pursuing a decisive victory and toward a strategic standoff, the more important territory itself becomes, prompting the defense to cover as much ground as possible and the offense to stretch its advance.

It's essential to acknowledge that many wars and campaigns align more with this observational stance rather than a life-or-death struggle where at least one side commits to total victory. Wars characterized by such definitive stakes are more a phenomenon of the nineteenth century, allowing a theoretical framework built on the expectation of absolute war. Yet, not every future war will carry this definitive character; it's more likely they'll lean back toward observational strategies. Therefore, a theory intended for practical use must account for this possibility.

With that in mind, let us begin by examining the scenario where the desire for a decisive outcome directs every move, embodying what we may call absolute war. We'll then explore, in a subsequent chapter, the modifications necessary for wars that align more closely with a state of observation.

In this first case, where one side—be it the attacker or defender—actively pursues a decisive result, the defender's objective must be to establish control over the theater in a way that offers an advantage in any potential decision. This decision could manifest as a major battle, a series of significant engagements, or even through the cumulative impact of military positioning—essentially the potential for combat.

If battle were not already proven to be the most decisive, frequent, and effective means of resolving conflict in war, as has been repeatedly demonstrated, even the fact that it is a primary means would still make the maximum concentration of forces a critical imperative in defense. In a major battle on a theater of war, one force meets another in a powerful clash—each side aiming to bring as many troops as possible to bear, as this maximizes the outcome's certainty and magnitude. Therefore, dividing forces without a justifiable reason—whether for a purpose that a victorious battle wouldn't secure, or for a necessity to secure victory itself—constitutes a strategic error.

However, concentration alone isn't the only factor; it's equally crucial that these forces are optimally positioned to enable a favorable battle outcome. The defensive approaches detailed in prior chapters align seamlessly with these core requirements. We can incorporate them based on specific circumstances, adapting them as needed. One challenge, however, stands out: pinpointing the enemy's center of gravity—the true focus of their strength. This central point of force requires careful analysis to meet effectively.

Typically, if a defender can identify early on the roads and approaches an attacker will use, especially those most likely to bear the main forces, they can intercept. This is the usual scenario; while defense has prior advantages in fortifying strongholds, establishing supply depots, and positioning forces, it also typically benefits from having the advantage of acting second, reacting as the enemy's intentions become clearer.

The scale of preparations required to move a large army into foreign territory is substantial and takes time—supplies, equipment, and provisions all need to be stockpiled. During this buildup, defenders have time to respond accordingly, an advantage since a defensive strategy typically requires less time to assemble than an offensive one. Nevertheless, exceptions exist where the defender may still remain unsure of the enemy's precise line of advance. This uncertainty is especially likely in cases where defensive maneuvers themselves demand considerable time, such as fortifying a strong position.

Furthermore, even when the defender aligns their forces on the anticipated path of attack, if they are not prepared to take an active stance against the attacker, the assailant can shift direction slightly to bypass the defended line. In Europe, for instance, developed regions often provide roads to the right or left, enabling an aggressor to sidestep an entrenched defensive line with relative ease. In such situations, the defender cannot simply wait in one spot with the expectation of engaging in battle.

To address this, we must examine the specific nature and likelihood of scenarios where a defender, even with the advantages of a fortified position, may still face ambiguity regarding the enemy's path of attack. By understanding these factors, we can then explore the effective means a defender might employ in response.

In every state, and within every theater of war—our primary focus here—there are strategic targets and locations where an attack is likely to yield the most significant impact. We'll delve further into these specific targets when discussing the mechanics of an offensive strategy. For now, it's sufficient to note that if the assailant's decision is influenced by the most advantageous points for attack, this logic also impacts the defender's positioning. When the defender has limited information about the adversary's intentions, the expectation that the attacker will aim for such key points can serve as a guide. Should the attacker choose not to follow the most favorable route, they lose some of their potential advantage. Thus, if the defender positions themselves along this anticipated route, the attacker can't simply bypass them without paying a cost, which inevitably reduces their efficiency.

Consequently, for the defender, the risk of misjudging the enemy's route is generally lower than it might seem. Nor can the attacker easily circumvent the defender since, in most cases, a dominant motive exists favoring a specific direction of advance. If the defender has accurately positioned themselves, they can feel reasonably assured that the attacker will confront them. Yet, it remains possible that the defender, despite these preparations, might not encounter the advancing force. This raises the question: what should the defender do in such a case, and to what extent do they retain the initial advantages of their position?

When considering the options available if the attacker evades a defensive position, several key responses come into play:

1. Immediate division of forces: The defender may split their forces at once, ensuring contact with the advancing enemy using a portion of their army. This initial contingent then holds the enemy until reinforcements from the remaining forces arrive, thus maintaining pressure without weakening their overall position.

2. Rapid repositioning with united forces: By maintaining their forces as a unified body, the defender can reposition themselves quickly along the enemy's path by making a lateral movement to intercept. Due to time constraints, such a maneuver is often more practical when moving slightly to the rear rather than directly to the side.

3. Flank attack: With the full force intact, the defender can attempt a direct assault on the enemy's flank, exploiting any vulnerability created by the assailant's movement.

4. Targeting communications: The defender can choose to disrupt the enemy's line of communication, creating logistical and supply issues for the advancing force and forcing them into a less advantageous position.

5. Counter-attack on the enemy's theater: The defender can mirror the enemy's strategy by advancing onto the enemy's own theater of war, seizing the opportunity to place reciprocal pressure on the assailant by shifting the conflict closer to the enemy's support bases and resources.

The final defensive measure, involving a counterattack on the enemy's flank with a change of front, holds distinct advantages over other defensive tactics, though it may appear unorthodox at first. We include this option because there are situations in which it may yield a favorable outcome, though it deviates from the typical goals of defense. This approach would only be practical if the enemy had made a considerable error or if unusual conditions in the theater of war allowed it to succeed.

Operating against the enemy's communications relies on the assumption that the defender has superior or secure communication lines—an essential element of a strong defensive position. However, although this tactic could provide the defender with some degree of advantage, it rarely leads to decisive results. In most theaters of war, the scale is not large enough to place the enemy's communication lines at significant risk from lengthy, drawn-out attrition. Moreover, since a decisive outcome is usually the campaign's primary aim, targeting communication lines might not yield immediate or strategic impact. Even if such lines were at risk, the limited time the assailant needs to press their main attack generally outweighs the slower effects of actions aimed at disrupting communications.

Thus, targeting communication lines may prove ineffective against an adversary set on a conclusive battle, and it is unlikely to aid the defender in achieving that goal either. The remaining strategies—the division of forces, positioning in front of the enemy's route, or a direct flank attack—all seek a more immediate, force-on-force confrontation, the kind that better aligns with a decisive outcome. Among these options, the third—flanking the enemy with a positional shift—is generally the most advantageous and often the preferable defensive choice.

Dividing forces into multiple groups carries the inherent risk of a "war of posts," a prolonged engagement that, even if executed skillfully, often leads only to a large-scale defensive stance without a clear resolution. At best, this tactic results in a relative, not absolute, defense. Should the defender succeed in avoiding this kind of engagement, the fragmented initial resistance would still weaken the impact of the first strike, and the advanced corps might incur disproportionate losses. Additionally, any withdrawal by the forward units back toward the main body tends to erode morale, as it can be perceived as a setback or tactical misstep.

The second option, moving the main force to intercept the enemy along their march, has its own risks. A delayed response could lead to missing the enemy's route entirely and failing to position effectively, leaving the defender between two inadequate strategies. Additionally, a defensive battle requires calm preparation, detailed understanding of the terrain, and the ability to choose positions suited to holding the line; hurried lateral movements reduce the ability to assess these elements fully, making it harder to secure an ideal defensive position.

The third method, however—launching a flank attack with a realignment of front lines—presents distinct advantages. It allows the defender to turn the strategic tide by exploiting the attacker's inherent vulnerability along the flank and communication lines, including their retreat routes. This approach leverages the defender's natural advantages, particularly the inherent strength of a well-chosen defensive stance, to seize opportunities that can disrupt the enemy's structure and momentum significantly.

Secondly, and perhaps most critically, an assailant who attempts to bypass his opponent must balance two opposing priorities. On one hand, they are driven by the need to advance, pressing forward to achieve their objective. But on the other, the persistent risk of a flank attack forces them to stay in constant readiness for an unexpected blow from that side. This dual demand creates internal tensions and complicates decision-making significantly. Strategically, there are few positions more uncomfortable than this, as the assailant must grapple with the conflicting aims of progressing and protecting their flank simultaneously. If the assailant could foresee the exact moment of a potential flank attack, they could set up a deliberate defense; however, with no such knowledge and under pressure to keep moving forward, the likelihood is that they will be caught mid-preparation, hurried, and in a less-than-ideal stance for engaging the defender.

For a defender seeking the ideal moment to counterattack, it is precisely in situations like this, when the assailant's advance and protection are in conflict, that success is most attainable. Coupled with the defender's advantage of knowing the land and choosing the ground, they can time their movements effectively to enhance this strategic edge. With these factors combined, the defender possesses a clear strategic superiority.

A defender in a fortified, strategically chosen position, with unified forces, can often afford to wait for the enemy to pass. If the enemy doesn't attack directly, and if disrupting the enemy's lines of communication isn't viable, the defender still has the valuable option of a decisive flank attack. Although historical instances of this are rare, the reason lies in the defender's typical hesitancy to hold firm in these positions, often opting instead to split forces or make a hasty advance. Equally, few attackers are willing to risk advancing past a waiting enemy, and such maneuvers tend to stall under these conditions.

In such cases, the defender may have to abandon their defensive stance and engage offensively. While this means relinquishing the advantages of fortified positions or entrenchments, it may offer other benefits depending on the assailant's positioning. The attacker's choice to bypass the defender's stronghold in pursuit of progress suggests they sought to avoid those very advantages. Thus, while the defender might not enjoy the full protective benefits of their original setup, they can still find a certain compensation in taking the offensive under these terms. Contrary to the simplifications often introduced in historical theory, this complex balance is rarely a mere canceling of pros and cons.

This concept is not merely an academic exercise but a fundamental principle that shapes the nature of defensive war. It profoundly influences decisions and actions across the board, underscoring that defensive strategy, especially in warfare, is about more than passive waiting; it is a dynamic art that allows the defender, at critical moments, to impose structure and timing upon the attacker.

Only by firmly resolving to strike at the opponent with full force once the enemy has attempted to bypass his position does the defender successfully steer clear of two significant risks: dividing his forces and executing a hurried flank march to intercept the advancing enemy. Both strategies effectively submit to the attacker's terms, forcing the defender to rely on high-risk maneuvers that necessitate dangerous haste. In every case where a determined, aggressive adversary has encountered this kind of defense, it has been overwhelmed. However, if the defender has concentrated his forces at the right location for a decisive engagement and is steadfast in his intent to flank the enemy in a general action, he is on the proper course and fully benefits from the strategic advantages inherent to his defensive stance. His actions, in this case, are characterized by thorough preparation, calmness, confidence, unity, and simplicity.

A historical example illustrates the hazards of ignoring this principle. In October 1806, the Prussian army stationed in Thuringia awaited the advancing French under Napoleon. The Prussian forces were positioned between two major routes by which Napoleon might proceed: the road to Berlin via Erfurt and the route through Hof and Leipzig. Initial plans to move directly into Franconia through the Thuringian Forest were abandoned, leaving the Prussians uncertain about which route Napoleon would choose. This uncertainty led them to occupy an intermediate position, which, in practice, encouraged precisely the kind of defensive errors we've discussed—attempting a hasty, lateral move to intercept the enemy from the front.

If Napoleon had advanced via Erfurt, there were adequate roads available for such an interception maneuver. However, the notion of moving to intercept along the route through Hof was impractical, as the Prussian army was already two or three marches away from that road and would have had to contend with the formidable obstacle of the deep Saale Valley. Despite the impracticality, Prince Hohenlohe, influenced by Colonel Massenbach, persistently advocated this plan, trying to draw the Duke of Brunswick into an ill-advised course of action. But taking an offensive stance against Napoleon as he advanced—essentially a flanking strike from the left bank of the Saale—was even more unrealistic. The Saale River, which was already an obstacle for a last-minute interception, would have become an even greater barrier for an offensive engagement with the French, who would be at least partly established on the opposite bank.

The Duke of Brunswick ultimately resolved to wait defensively behind the Saale to observe the enemy's moves, though "resolve" might be too strong a term in light of the uncertainty and lack of coordination that plagued the Prussian high command. The practical result of this indecision was a defensive stance fraught with vulnerabilities, as the Prussian army's situation at this time of "expectation" revealed.

1. The Prussian forces could potentially engage the enemy if he attempted to cross the Saale to launch an attack against their position.
2. Should the enemy choose not to advance directly toward the Prussian army, they might initiate operations to disrupt his lines of communication.
3. If circumstances allowed and it proved advantageous, a swift flank march could enable an interception near Leipzig.

In the first scenario, the Prussian army held a significant strategic and tactical advantage due to the Saale's deep valley, which naturally fortified their defensive line and provided a formidable obstacle for any enemy force attempting to cross. This natural barrier would make it challenging for the French to execute an effective assault without risking considerable losses. In the second scenario, the strategic advantage was equally notable;

the French forces had a restricted base limited by the narrow region between the Prussian position and the neutral territory of Bohemia, whereas the Prussian base was much broader, offering greater flexibility for supply lines and maneuver. Even in the third scenario, where a rapid flank march might have allowed the Prussians to intercept near Leipzig, the Prussian army's position was still advantageous. The Saale continued to serve as a protective feature, helping prevent the French from easily encircling or flanking the Prussian forces.

These three potential courses of action, despite the disorganized and unclear thinking prevailing within the Prussian headquarters, were actively debated and considered. However, given the confusion and lack of decisiveness among the leadership, it is unsurprising that even a sound strategy struggled in execution due to the absence of unified resolve and clarity.

In both the first and second scenarios, the position on the left bank of the Saale can be viewed as a genuine flank position, and as such, it had substantial inherent advantages. Yet, realistically, against a vastly superior enemy, especially one led by a commander as formidable as Napoleon, adopting a flank position without a confident and assured strategy was an especially daring measure, one that would require both determination and coordination—qualities that were conspicuously lacking among the Prussian leadership at that time.

After extensive indecision, the Duke, on the 13th, finally chose the last of the proposed plans, but by then it was too late, as Buonaparte had already started crossing the Saale, making the battles of Jena and Auerstadt unavoidable. Due to this hesitation, the Duke found himself in a precarious middle ground; he left his initial position too late to preempt the enemy effectively, yet too early to set up a battle that would best align with his strategic objectives. Despite this, the inherent strength of the Saale position was evident; it enabled the Duke to strike a decisive blow against the enemy's right wing at Auerstadt, and Prince Hohenlohe, albeit with heavy losses, managed a retreat, barely extracting himself from a dire situation. However, at Auerstadt, there was an unfortunate lack of will to secure the victory that was within grasp, while at Jena, they optimistically counted on a victory that was simply out of reach. Buonaparte, recognizing the strategic significance of the Saale position, was cautious enough not to bypass it; instead, he committed to crossing the Saale under the watchful eye of the enemy. With this, we believe we have delineated the core strategic dynamics between defense and attack when decisive action is intended, showing the connections to which the various components of a defensive plan adhere, based on their specific context and relationship to one another. To delve into each possible variation in further detail would be beyond our present scope, as it would open a vast array of individual cases. However, when a general has determined a clear strategic objective, he must consider how it aligns with geographic, logistical, and political factors, as well as the particular strengths and conditions of both his own forces and those of the enemy, adapting his plans as necessary for practical execution. To solidify the connections among the various gradations of defense outlined in our discussion of defensive types, we will now outline what we consider the most universally significant elements of defensive strategy.

1. Reasons for advancing toward the enemy with the intention of engaging in an offensive battle can be considered under several circumstances:

(a) when we have reliable information that the enemy is advancing in a highly fragmented formation, meaning that his forces are significantly dispersed, and therefore, despite being generally outmatched in terms of overall strength, we may reasonably anticipate achieving victory due to this tactical advantage.

However, an advance based on the assumption that the enemy is moving forward with forces divided in a way that leaves them vulnerable is, by its very nature, unlikely. Unless we possess clear intelligence that confirms this with confidence, such a plan is precarious. Relying solely on hopeful assumptions without concrete evidence tends to result in significant risk. Typically, when reality does not align with our expectations, we're forced to abandon the initial plan for an offensive engagement, often finding ourselves unprepared for a shift to defensive positioning. This shift may then compel us to retreat unexpectedly, positioning us on the back foot and forcing us to leave much of the outcome to chance. The historical case of the defense undertaken by Dohna's army against the Russians in the 1759 campaign illustrates this danger, especially in how it concluded under General Wedel with the unfortunate battle of Züllichau.

In this case, the assumption that an enemy advance might be split in a way that left them exposed created an overly optimistic forecast, one which led to a strategic misstep. This type of plan is deceptively attractive to military planners due to its straightforward and potentially decisive nature. However, because of this simplicity, it often encourages quick adoption without the critical, in-depth assessment of the supporting assumptions required for successful execution. Thus, the appeal of such a tactic often lies in its perceived efficiency, prompting strategists to recommend it too readily and, at times, without a thorough and skeptical analysis of whether the foundational premise holds true in the field.

(b) If we possess adequate overall strength to engage the enemy in battle, and—

(c) If the opposing commander shows signs of confusion, hesitation, or poor decision-making, creating an opportune moment to launch an attack. When an adversary's mistakes or lack of resolve become evident, the potential impact of a well-executed surprise assault may outweigh any advantage provided by securing a strategically favorable position. Seizing on such psychological dynamics and taking advantage of an opponent's weak resolve, hesitation, or tactical blunders is central to effective leadership, as it brings the power of morale and psychological leverage into play. The true skill of generalship lies in harnessing these intangible but influential forces. However, theory must continually stress the importance of having a concrete basis for these suppositions. Without such a foundation, reliance on speculative notions of surprise or unconventional tactics to achieve superiority often leads to plans built on unstable assumptions. To discuss surprises and the supposed efficacy of atypical methods without clear, objective grounding risks basing decisions on little more than wishful thinking, rendering such approaches unreliable and unsound.

(d) When the nature and characteristics of our own forces make them particularly well-suited for offensive maneuvers. If the strengths of our army align more naturally with the demands of an aggressive strategy—whether due to its tactical agility, training, or combat experience—then an offensive stance may offer the best prospects for success. In cases where an army possesses exceptional capabilities for swift movement, sharp strikes, or morale-boosting confidence in attack, an offensive posture can be a rational choice that leverages these qualities. Each of these conditions justifies, to varying degrees, a proactive approach, provided they are rooted in tangible, validated factors rather than vague or unverified assumptions.

It was certainly neither an unrealistic nor misguided notion when Frederick the Great recognized that his agile and brave army, fully confident in him and accustomed to disciplined obedience, was ideally suited for offensive maneuvers under his bold leadership. This army was trained meticulously for rapid, precise movements and animated by a pride and high morale that enhanced its aggressive potential. The Prussian army's excellence in oblique attacks gave Frederick a unique advantage. In most situations, he found that harnessing these strengths in offense proved more advantageous than relying on defensive positions fortified by entrenchments and natural barriers. In contrast, his adversaries lacked these qualities, offering him a significant edge.

Yet, such a blend of advantages remains rare. While a well-drilled army practiced in complex maneuvers might share some of these qualities, it may not possess them all in the same measure. Although Frederick famously claimed that the Prussian army was particularly adept at offensive action—an assertion that has been echoed persistently by military leaders since then—it is essential not to overly rely on perceived superiority. Often, armies and commanders alike feel a natural lift in morale and enthusiasm when operating offensively rather than defensively, a sentiment common across most military forces. Many generals have made similar claims about their armies, underscoring the importance of balancing perceived strengths with tangible, strategic advantages, rather than allowing the allure of offensive tactics to overshadow more concrete benefits available on the defensive.

Another very practical and compelling reason to pursue an offensive battle lies in the composition of the army's arms. For instance, an army with a significant proportion of cavalry and limited artillery would find offensive maneuvers more compatible with its strengths, as cavalry movements align well with the mobility and adaptability required in attack. In such cases, leveraging the tactical characteristics of the force may outweigh the advantages of a purely defensive approach. Here, we proceed with further reasons justifying an offensive stance.

(e) An offensive approach may be warranted if no suitable defensive positions are available. When the natural landscape fails to provide cover or advantage for a defensive stand, seeking out and engaging the enemy offensively can prevent being cornered in a disadvantageous location and afford greater control over the battlefield.

(f) An offensive decision may also be necessary if time is a critical factor. If circumstances demand a swift outcome—perhaps due to imminent reinforcements for the enemy, limited supplies, or pressing political objectives—hastening the decision through attack can serve strategic imperatives that cannot wait.

(g) Finally, any or all of these factors may collectively encourage an offensive stance, presenting a combination of incentives that collectively outweigh the benefits of remaining on the defensive. When such reasons align, the impetus to seize the initiative often becomes irresistible.

2. Waiting to strike the enemy in a specific location, as at Minden in 1759, typically arises from the following conditions:

(a) The balance of forces is relatively equal, meaning that we do not face such a marked disadvantage that would necessitate a fortified or highly defended position. In these cases, it is not essential to reinforce our position excessively, as we are confident in our army's ability to withstand a direct engagement.

(b) A particular locality has been chosen for its suitability to the intended tactics. Certain geographic features or strategic aspects of the area provide unique advantages, allowing a defensive force to remain poised for attack. This suitability hinges largely on tactical considerations: the terrain allows easy access for the defender and presents obstacles to the enemy, thus allowing a structured, controlled confrontation.

3. Taking a position specifically to await the enemy's attack and to engage in a defensive battle can be justified when:

(a) There is a substantial disparity in forces. If our army is at a marked disadvantage, defensive measures such as positioning behind natural obstacles or constructing field-works are critical to offset the opponent's numerical or material superiority.

(b) The terrain offers an exceptional position that aligns with our strategic intentions. When the landscape includes fortifiable points, natural defenses, or access to resources, occupying such a position can transform it into a stronghold against a superior force.

The approaches in points 2 and 3 become more relevant when a decisive outcome is less critical, and merely preventing the enemy from progressing might suffice. These methods are particularly suited to situations where we suspect the adversary is hesitant or uncertain and may ultimately abandon or fail in their plans due to delays or loss of momentum. Here, achieving a stalemate or forestalling the enemy's advance may indeed be the best path to a strategic advantage.

4. Establishing an entrenched, impregnable camp can only serve its strategic purpose effectively under specific conditions:

a. When it is positioned at a location of extreme strategic importance. The defining feature of such a camp is that it cannot be dislodged by the enemy, forcing them to either seek an alternative path or attempt to blockade and starve out the camp. If the enemy is unable to bypass or starve the forces within, then the position's strategic value is indeed significant. This type of fortified encampment represents not merely a tactical stronghold but a critical barrier that the enemy must navigate around or contend with directly, often at great cost or by severely compromising their campaign objectives.

b. When there is a reasonable expectation of reinforcements from allies or support from external forces. The Saxon army at Pirna serves as a historical example: although the decision to fortify there has been criticized due to the eventual unfavorable outcome, it was nonetheless a sound move under the circumstances. By establishing a strong defensive position, the Saxons effectively tied down 40,000 Prussian troops, a feat that 17,000 Saxons could not have achieved in an open engagement. The failure of the Austrian forces to capitalize on the advantage gained at Lowositz reflects more on the inefficiency of their overall strategy and military organization than on the validity of the fortified camp at Pirna. If, instead, the Saxons had retreated into Bohemia, it's likely Frederick the Great would have pursued both Saxons and Austrians beyond Prague, even taking the city within that same campaign. Limiting one's view only to the capture of the Saxon army misses the broader strategic impact of tying down Prussian forces, overlooking the longer-term implications and failing to recognize the utility of the entrenched position.

That said, these conditions—(a) positioning at a crucial strategic point, and (b) anticipation of aid from abroad—are rare. Entrenched camps, as a result, are measures that require careful deliberation and are rarely advisable in practice. The risk lies in expecting that such a camp will automatically induce caution or inactivity from the enemy; there is a real danger of becoming trapped with no means of retreat. Frederick the Great's use of a fortified camp at Bunzelwitz is often admired for its success in stalling his opponent, but his success was also due to his keen judgment of his adversary. Additionally, as a monarch, he had unique resources and autonomy that allowed him to maneuver his forces or devise escape routes if necessary, should the camp have been breached. Such high-stakes decisions carry inherent risk, and without the support of calculated options for fallback, they are seldom recommended as a general approach.

5. When there is one or several fortresses positioned near the frontier, a significant strategic question arises: should the defender engage the enemy in battle before reaching these fortifications, or wait to do so behind them? Engaging behind the fortresses has clear advantages:

a. The enemy's numerical superiority often necessitates weakening their forces before a decisive engagement, which positioning behind a fortress can facilitate.

b. The close proximity of these fortresses near the frontier can mean that any sacrifice of territory involved is limited, only extending as far as absolutely necessary.

c. The suitability of these fortresses for defense adds further justification to this strategy.

One of the primary purposes of fortresses, ideally, is to disrupt and sap the advancing strength of an invading force, leaving them significantly weakened for a more decisive engagement. While this strategic advantage of fortresses is not often utilized, it's primarily because few campaigns involve one side actively seeking a decisive battle. However, in cases where such a decision is indeed sought, this principle becomes both simple and powerful. When a defender has access to one or multiple fortresses nearby, he should ideally position them between himself and the approaching enemy, arranging for the decisive engagement to occur behind the line of fortifications.

It's true that losing a battle within the protective perimeter of these fortresses would likely mean a deeper retreat into the country than a defeat outside this line of defenses. This difference, though, is more a matter of perception than a tangible strategic disadvantage, as it's rooted in psychological effects rather than in concrete tactical or material conditions. Additionally, there is the possibility of selecting an optimal position outside the fortress line, where a defensive battle might be possible. In contrast, within the line of fortresses, there is often a need to take an offensive stance, especially if the enemy is besieging a fortress on the brink of falling. However, these nuanced distinctions pale in comparison to the substantial advantage of meeting the enemy after their forces have been diminished by as much as a fourth, a third, or potentially even half if multiple fortresses are effectively leveraged in the defense strategy.

We conclude, then, that in all cases where a decisive outcome is inevitable, whether pursued by the offensive or defensive side, and provided the defender cannot be relatively confident of victory or that the terrain does not present an overwhelmingly compelling reason to hold a more forward position—under these conditions, if a fortress nearby is defensible, the defender should ideally withdraw to a position behind it and let the crucial engagement unfold on this side, leveraging the fortress as an active element in the strategy. By positioning close enough to the fortress so that the enemy cannot initiate a siege or blockade without first confronting the defender, the situation effectively compels the attacker to engage the defender in his chosen position. Therefore, among all defensive strategies in a pressing situation, none appears as straightforward and effective as selecting a strong position near and behind a well-fortified stronghold.

However, this approach would appear differently if the fortress were located far back from the frontline, as this would mean relinquishing a substantial part of the theater of war—a sacrifice not to be undertaken lightly unless the circumstances are exceptionally dire. In such cases, this would more closely resemble a retreat further into the country's interior.

A further consideration is the suitability of the fortress itself for defense. It is well understood that certain fortifications, especially larger ones, may be unsuitable for direct engagement with an approaching army, either because they lack the defenses necessary to withstand a forceful initial assault or because their structure is compromised under the weight of an enemy's full force. Here, the defender's position should be close enough to provide necessary support to the fortress.

Finally, a strategic withdrawal into the country's interior becomes a natural resort under specific conditions, namely: a. When, due to either physical or moral limitations, the defender cannot reasonably expect to mount a successful resistance on or near the frontier. b. When time is of the essence and its extension becomes a primary goal. c. When certain geographic features favor such a retreat, as previously discussed in the twenty-fifth chapter.

This closes our discussion on defending a theater of war when a decisive outcome is sought by one side or the other. It must be remembered, however, that war rarely presents itself in such clean, theoretical terms. Consequently, when applying these principles to real-world scenarios, it is critical to also consider the insights of the thirtieth chapter. In most situations, a general is positioned between opposing strategic impulses, moving more strongly in one direction or the other, depending on specific circumstances.

Chapter XXIX. Defence of a Theatre of War (continued)

Successive Resistance.

As established in chapters twelve and thirteen, strategy is fundamentally incompatible with a piecemeal resistance; rather, all available forces should be deployed concurrently. This principle is self-evident for mobile forces, but when we factor in the fixed elements of the battlefield itself—such as fortresses, natural divisions of terrain, and the sheer expanse of territory—these immovable elements can only be introduced gradually or by positioning far enough back so that all defensive resources are at the front. In this configuration, every resource that can weaken the advancing enemy is immediately engaged. This includes the assailant's need to blockade fortresses, establish garrisons to maintain control over the territory, undertake long marches, and rely on distant supply lines. These factors exert a strain on the enemy whether they advance before or after a decisive engagement, though their influence is slightly more pronounced in the latter case. Thus, if the defender opts to delay the decisive battle by retreating further into the interior, they harness the full strength of these static defensive elements at once.

Conversely, this postponement doesn't alter the impact of an eventual victory won by the attacker. We'll delve deeper into this in discussing offensive tactics, but here it suffices to say that a victory's influence extends only as far as the attacker's initial advantage—determined by both physical and psychological factors. This initial superiority is gradually eroded by the demands on forces across the theater of war and the attrition of combat. Whether the battles occur early or late, at the frontier or deeper within the country, this depletion remains constant. For instance, a victory for Napoleon at Wilna in 1812 would have likely taken him no farther than his win at Borodino—both hypothetically stopping him at Moscow. In fact, a frontier victory might have yielded even greater outcomes, potentially extending the range of influence. Thus, relocating the decisive point further back is not necessarily a requirement for a robust defense.

In examining the spectrum of resistance methods, one extreme—retreating into the interior to wear down the attacker rather than seeking outright battlefield destruction—is a distinct strategy. Only when such attrition becomes the dominant goal can postponing the decisive clash be seen as a distinct method of defense. Otherwise, varying degrees of this strategy may be interwoven with all other defensive tactics. The gradual engagement of immovable defenses on the battlefield, therefore, is not a standalone approach but rather a flexible choice, allowing these static resources to be incorporated according to situational demands.

If the defender believes they do not need to draw on these immovable defenses for the immediate decision or considers the associated sacrifices too great, these resources remain in reserve, forming a tiered reinforcement structure. This approach could allow the defender to sustain a favorable position following an initial positive outcome or even a second or third favorable outcome, thus enabling a phased deployment of their forces over time. For instance, if the defender suffers a setback at the frontier but is not entirely defeated, they might regroup behind the nearest fortress and potentially reengage the enemy successfully. With an adversary lacking resolve, even a substantial natural barrier could serve as a sufficient check.

Therefore, strategy calls for the economical use of the theater of war, as in any other facet of military planning; using only as much force as needed is wise, but economizing without endangering the outcome is paramount. This cautionary approach parallels sound financial strategy, where thrift must be balanced against the necessity for adequate resources.

To avoid any misunderstanding, we are not discussing the extent of an army's resistance or the operations it might pursue after losing a battle but rather the anticipated efficacy of such secondary resistance as part of the initial plan. The main consideration for the defender here is the character and position of their adversary. A hesitant or constrained opponent, lacking confidence and high ambition, may settle for modest gains and hesitate at any fresh challenge presented by the defender. In such cases, the defender may expect to make effective use of all successive resistance means within their theater, through a series of minor engagements that cumulatively increase the prospect of an ultimate favorable resolution.

This gradual deployment approach, however, veers toward campaigns of limited decisiveness, characterized by a protracted use of successive forces. This type of campaign, which relies on continuous incremental engagements, will be addressed in the following chapter.

Chapter XXX. Defence of a Theatre of War (continued)

When no Decision is Sought for.

The question of whether a war can truly exist where neither side pursues an offensive, where neither party actively aims for a positive outcome, will be further discussed in the final book. Here, we set aside that apparent contradiction, as we can envision circumstances on a single theater of war where both sides might adopt a defensive stance based on their respective connections to a larger whole. Alongside examples from history of specific campaigns that lacked a clear imperative for resolution, we also find numerous cases where, despite an aggressor's presence and thus a positive will on one side, this will was so weak that it failed to pursue the objective decisively. Instead, the aggressor settled for circumstantial gains that arose almost by chance, or alternatively, set no distinct goal, letting the unfolding of circumstances determine the course while harvesting whatever opportunities happened to present themselves.

This type of offense, which departs significantly from a strict, logical progression toward the objective—resembling almost a leisurely approach to campaigning, drifting right and left to seize whatever incidental benefits arise—closely aligns with a defensive approach that allows the general to capitalize on available gains. While a deeper philosophical examination of this form of warfare will be left to the section on the attack, here we may conclude that in such campaigns, neither the attacker nor the defender seeks to settle matters decisively through a major battle. Consequently, a great battle ceases to be the central pillar of strategy that organizes and directs the strategic structure. Campaigns of this nature (as evidenced across different eras and regions) are not only plentiful but constitute the vast majority, leaving campaigns that seek decisive battles as rare exceptions. Even if this ratio changes in future conflicts, there will undoubtedly still be many campaigns of this kind. Therefore, in studying the theory of defending a theater of war, such campaigns merit careful consideration, and we will attempt to outline the distinctive traits that characterize them.

In actual practice, wars often fall somewhere between these two extremes—sometimes leaning closer to one end, sometimes to the other. Thus, we can only observe the practical effects of these characteristics in how they modify the absolute nature of war through their opposing tendencies. As noted earlier in this book, particularly in chapter three, the state of expectation is one of the most significant advantages the defensive enjoys over the offensive. In life generally, and especially in warfare, things seldom unfold exactly as expected. Human limitations, fear of adverse outcomes, and unpredictable events that disrupt the implementation of plans are all factors that often prevent actions that circumstances might otherwise suggest. In war, where knowledge gaps, the risk of catastrophic failure, and random chance weigh far more heavily than in any other area of human activity, the frequency of these "shortcomings," so to speak, is proportionately higher.

This creates a fertile ground where the defensive reaps benefits that arise almost naturally. Adding to this the intrinsic value of territorial control in war, the old maxim beati sunt possidentes (blessed are those who possess) applies here as strongly as in times of peace. This principle essentially stands in place of a decisive outcome, the central focus in wars oriented toward mutual destruction. It is immensely productive, not in terms of actions it spurs but rather in its justification for avoiding action, motivating decisions that favor maintaining the status quo. When a decisive outcome is neither sought nor anticipated, there is no incentive to relinquish any ground, for doing so would only be justified by some advantage in achieving resolution. As a result, the defender retains as much as possible—whatever they can reasonably cover—while the aggressor seizes as much as they can without risking decisive engagement, extending their reach laterally wherever possible. For our purposes here, we are primarily concerned with this defensive aspect.

Wherever the defender's military forces are absent, the assailant is free to take possession of that area, thereby gaining the advantage of the state of expectation himself. This dynamic leads the defender to attempt to cover as much of the territory as possible directly, risking that the assailant might engage the scattered defensive forces positioned across the area.

Before delving into the specific characteristics of this form of defense, it is helpful to pull from the discussion on the attack to identify the objectives typically pursued by the assailant when a conclusive battle is not the primary goal. These objectives are as follows:

1. Gaining control over a substantial stretch of territory, as long as it can be done without forcing a decisive conflict.
2. Seizing an essential supply depot or magazine under the same condition, avoiding a direct and potentially costly engagement.
3. Capturing a fortress that lacks defensive coverage. While a siege can demand significant resources and effort, it doesn't inherently risk a catastrophic defeat; if circumstances turn unfavorable, the siege can be lifted without a major loss.
4. Engaging in a strategically modest yet noteworthy skirmish—one that carries minimal risk and does not seek substantial gain but serves instead to secure morale or achieve a symbolic victory. Such engagements are not pursued at any cost; instead, they rely on waiting for favorable conditions or creating a setting where the engagement can proceed with minimal risk.

These four objectives of the attacker lead to corresponding defensive actions:

1. Protecting fortresses by positioning them within the defensive line, keeping them secure behind the main forces.
2. Shielding the territory by deploying troops across its expanse, ensuring broad coverage.
3. When such distribution is insufficient, quickly maneuvering the army into a position that intercepts the enemy through a rapid lateral movement.
4. Avoiding engagements that could result in unfavorable outcomes, thus minimizing the risk of unintended losses in combat.

The purpose of the first three defensive measures is to compel the enemy into making the first move, allowing the defender to capitalize on a state of anticipation. This goal is so integral to the nature of defensive strategy that it would be a mistake to disregard it outright. It assumes even greater importance when a decisive engagement is unlikely and serves as the main principle in such campaigns, often resulting in minor yet active skirmishes without significant outcomes. Both Hannibal and Fabius, as well as Frederick the Great and Daun, adhered to this principle whenever they neither pursued nor expected a decisive battle. The fourth measure, meanwhile, functions as a necessary counterbalance to the other three, acting as their essential condition.

Now, let's delve into these topics more closely. At first glance, it seems counterintuitive to protect a fortress by stationing an army before it, as fortifications are inherently designed to withstand attacks. Yet, this tactic has been used countless times in military history. Despite the seeming contradiction, its frequent use suggests it must be based on a profound strategic rationale. This rationale stems from the natural inclination toward caution and defensive inertia. When an army positions itself in front of a fortress, the enemy is unable to assault the stronghold without first defeating the forces guarding it; however, a battle itself implies a decision. If the enemy is not seeking a decisive confrontation, no battle will occur, and the defender will hold the fortress without engaging. Thus, whenever there is doubt that the enemy will press for a battle, it's advantageous to rely on the likelihood that they won't. The defender can still retreat behind the fortress if the enemy unexpectedly advances; positioning before the fortress, therefore, entails little risk while offering a solid chance to maintain the current situation without a single sacrifice.

If the defender positions his forces behind a fortress, he essentially presents the attacker with an objective that perfectly aligns with the attacker's circumstances. If the fortress isn't particularly strong, and the attacker is reasonably prepared, a siege is likely to begin. To prevent this from ending in the fortress's capture, the defender will then be compelled to advance to its relief. The defender thus assumes the role of taking the offensive, while the attacker, advancing toward his goal through the siege, is positioned as the occupier. History repeatedly demonstrates that such situations naturally unfold in this way. A siege doesn't inherently lead to a major catastrophe, even if led by a cautious or passive commander with no particular drive for battle. Such a leader may still begin a siege with only basic artillery if he can approach the fortress safely. In the worst case, he can abandon the siege without suffering any significant losses. Additionally, the vulnerability of most fortresses to direct assault or irregular capture is a factor the defender must consider when assessing likely outcomes.

When weighing the possibilities, it's reasonable for the defender to prioritize the chance of avoiding combat entirely, even if they could potentially win under favorable battle conditions. This perspective sheds light on the common practice of positioning a defensive force in the field directly before its fortress. Frederick the Great, for example, often employed this tactic at locations like Glogau against the Russians and at Schweidnitz, Neisse, and Dresden against the Austrians. However, this approach didn't work in favor of the Duke of Bevern at Breslau; had he stayed behind Breslau, he wouldn't have been attacked, and the Austrian advantage in Frederick's absence would have been neutralized by Frederick's advancing presence. A position behind Breslau might have allowed the Duke to delay battle until Frederick arrived. Nevertheless, the Duke likely opted for an exposed position to avoid subjecting Breslau to bombardment, which he knew Frederick, who was particularly averse to such damage, would have strongly disapproved of.

While the Duke's attempt to protect Breslau by establishing an entrenched position might seem questionable, it's defensible. Given that Charles of Lorraine, who had just captured Schweidnitz and faced Frederick's approach, might have halted his advance if he'd encountered resistance from the entrenched position, the Duke's choice could have been reasonable. In hindsight, the Duke's best move would have been to decline battle entirely, retreating through Breslau just as the Austrians advanced. By doing so, he could have leveraged the benefits of holding a defensive stance without the risk of a full-scale confrontation.

If we have traced the justification for positioning an army before a fortress to reasons rooted in strategic principles of a superior and absolute order, thus defending its tactical merit, it is also worth noting a secondary, albeit practical, reason that often contributes to this decision. This reason, although of a more immediate nature and readily apparent, is nonetheless insufficient on its own and lacks the absolute authority that might make it a decisive factor. This secondary consideration is the use of a nearby fortress as a central depot for provisions, munitions, and other essential supplies. The convenience offered by such proximity to resources is substantial, providing numerous logistical benefits that make it difficult for a commander to consider obtaining supplies from more remote areas or risking storage in open, less secure towns. Consequently, if a fortress functions as the army's primary supply center, then a position in front of it becomes not just strategically sound but sometimes an operational necessity, providing a natural alignment between the army's location and its supply line. However, despite the clarity and immediacy of this motive, which might seem paramount to those who prefer practical considerations over strategic foresight, it does not entirely account for every instance of this defensive measure. The circumstances connected with supply logistics, while undeniably significant, do not offer a fully sufficient rationale to settle the choice of position in all cases.

Moreover, the capture of one or more fortresses without engaging in a decisive battle presents such an obvious strategic goal in campaigns where the attacker does not seek an outright military decision, that thwarting this intent becomes one of the defender's primary objectives. Consequently, on warfronts with multiple fortresses, these strongholds often become focal points of nearly all maneuvers. The attacker tries to surprise or approach a fortress under a feint, and the defender promptly counters with well-planned movements to foil such attempts. This characteristic tactic dominated nearly all of Louis XIV's campaigns in the Netherlands up to Marshal Saxe's era. Thus, covering and protecting fortresses is central to the defense.

When it comes to covering broader territory, this requires an extended positioning of forces and is only feasible in regions with significant natural obstacles. Large and small posts established to cover territory must derive their defensive strength largely from strategic locations, often enhanced by field fortifications, to offer credible resistance. However, the defensive power of any individual post is always relative (as discussed in the chapter on the significance of the combat) and should not be viewed as absolute. Certainly, a single post may, at times, withstand every attack, achieving a level of stability that resembles absolute resistance. Yet, any given post, when seen within the larger structure, remains vulnerable to attack by superior enemy forces; thus, relying entirely on the steadfast defense of a single position would be unwise. In such an extended configuration, the defensive capacity is based only on relative, not permanent, resistance.

This relative resistance, however, is sufficient for the purpose of a well-considered defensive strategy, particularly in campaigns where no major decision is anticipated or where the attacker lacks the overwhelming drive needed to subdue all opposition completely. Engaging in post-to-post defense entails limited risk, even if one post is eventually lost, as the effects of a small victory for the attacker don't generally alter the campaign's overall direction. Usually, the loss amounts to that single post and a few trophies; the victory does not reverberate across the broader structure, destabilizing foundations or creating a cascade of consequential losses. In the worst-case scenario, if the fall of a single post disrupts the entire defensive layout, the defender can still gather his dispersed forces and regroup for a concentrated effort. In such cases, the defender might gather his troops for a decisive battle that, according to our assumptions, the attacker does not particularly seek. Typically, once the defender consolidates, the campaign pauses, halting further advances by the attacker. The defender's casualties may include a limited stretch of land, some troops, and a handful of artillery—losses that the attacker is generally content with.

Facing this level of risk is reasonable for the defender, especially if there's a likelihood—indeed, a probability—that the overly cautious attacker may hesitate and halt before engaging these fortified posts. In a scenario where the attacker avoids decisive action, even a modest but strongly fortified post may suffice to deter him. Although such a post could be taken with effort, the attacker must weigh the costs of capturing it against its strategic worth. Here, the question arises: is the expenditure in resources, time, and men worth the gain? For an attacker unwilling to gamble on decisive outcomes, the answer may very well be no.

In this manner, we can observe how the strong relative resistance offered by a well-distributed defensive arrangement, made up of several strategically positioned posts, can yield a positive outcome in the defender's overall campaign strategy. When considering historical military campaigns through this lens, it's essential to note that such extended defensive positions are often adopted later in a campaign, as the defender gains clearer insights into the enemy's intentions, strategies, and current situation. By this stage, the initial vigor and offensive energy the attacker brought to the field often wanes, and the defender's strategic position strengthens accordingly.

In a defensive stance designed to protect the countryside, secure supply lines, and safeguard fortresses, natural geographic features—such as rivers, streams, mountains, forests, and swamps—inevitably play a significant role and assume major strategic value. In managing these elements, a nuanced understanding of terrain is crucial, bringing to the forefront the expertise and actions that are traditionally the domain of the army's general staff. The skill and knowledge required for coordinating operations in line with such complex geographical features are often attributed to the general staff, who are tasked with managing the intricacies of topographical challenges. As a result, their records and analyses of these military operations often become prominent in historical accounts, offering detailed documentation of how natural barriers were utilized.

Yet, this focus on topography by the general staff can inadvertently lead to an inclination to generalize specific historical outcomes into universal principles, assuming that a single case's solution could apply to all subsequent situations. This drive toward systematization is appealing but ultimately misguided; each defensive campaign involving natural barriers is unique, with conditions that vary significantly from one case to the next, requiring a tailored approach each time. Consequently, the best critical and analytical writings on these campaigns may offer valuable insights into individual events, but they should not be mistaken for universally applicable doctrines.

While this concentrated effort from the general staff can be commendable, it occasionally leads to an overreach, which may inadvertently constrain the campaign's broader strategy. The expertise held by the most informed leaders of this branch can give them an outsized influence over military thinking, including the mindset of the general in command. This influence often gives rise to a rigid set of ideas, resulting in a form of cognitive bias where the general might become overly focused on geographical features like mountains and passes. This perspective shift can turn a flexible, adaptive strategy into a rigid pattern—a sort of ingrained routine.

A case in point is found in the campaigns of 1793 and 1794, when Colonel Grawert of the Prussian army, known for his strict adherence to mountain and pass strategy, convinced two very different generals—the Duke of Brunswick and General Mollendorf—to adopt an almost identical, location-bound approach to warfare. Both generals, despite their contrasting personalities, were persuaded to follow Grawert's geography-focused methodology. Here, the focus on specific terrain features became so dominant that it shaped the conduct of war, showcasing how an otherwise versatile plan can be reduced to formulaic responses under the influence of a single-minded approach.

A defensive line running parallel to a significant natural obstacle can easily lead to a "cordon war," where troops are lined up across the area to block the enemy. This kind of setup often happens if the entire area could actually be covered directly by such a line. But most battle areas are so large that the usual way troops are positioned for defense can't fully cover it. Meanwhile, the attacker has to stick to certain main routes and roads because straying from them—even if they aren't facing an active defender—would create major difficulties and disadvantages. So, the defender usually only needs to protect areas a few miles or so to the left and right of the attacker's main routes. To do this, defensive posts are set up along the main roads and approaches, while smaller posts keep an eye on the areas in between.

As a result, the attacker could find ways to move troops between these posts and launch attacks from different directions at the same time. To prepare for this, defensive posts are set up with flank supports on their sides, defensive angles (called crochets), and the ability to get help from reserves stationed behind them or from nearby posts. In this way, the number of posts needed is kept low, so an army on the defensive usually ends up spread across four or five main posts.

For important routes farther away that are at some risk, additional central points are set up that serve as smaller defense zones within the main one. During the Seven Years' War, for instance, the Austrians typically divided their main army into four or five posts in the mountains of Lower Silesia, while a smaller, somewhat independent group created a similar defense system in Upper Silesia.

The more a defense plan moves away from covering areas directly, the more it has to rely on mobility (an active defense) and sometimes even offensive moves. Some units are considered reserves; in addition, one post might send help to another, using as many troops as it can spare. This help might mean rushing forward from the rear to reinforce the defense, attacking the enemy from the side, or even threatening the enemy's retreat path. If the attacker threatens a post from the side without attacking directly but by setting up a position that disrupts its supply routes, then the defender must either launch a strong attack on that new position or try to disrupt the enemy's supply routes in return.

Although this kind of defense may seem passive in its main approach, it includes many active strategies and can be set up to handle complex situations. Typically, defenses that make the most use of active or offensive strategies are thought to be the best, but this also depends on the land, the type of troops, and the general's skill. Sometimes, though, we tend to put too much faith in movement and active strategies while underestimating the power of local defenses behind a strong natural barrier. We believe this explains the meaning of an extended defense line, so now we'll look at the third kind of supportive measure: positioning ourselves in front of the enemy with a quick side march.

This method becomes a crucial part of the defensive approach that we're discussing. To start with, even when the defender spreads his forces as widely as possible, he often cannot cover all the paths that might be vulnerable to enemy attack. Additionally, there are situations in which he will need to move the main portion of his forces to support a specific post if the enemy seems prepared to concentrate their strength there. Without such readiness, that particular post might quickly fall. Lastly, for a general who doesn't favor keeping his army tied to passive defense in a wide, spread-out position, the aim of protecting the country must instead rely on swift, carefully timed, and skillfully coordinated maneuvers. The greater the area left exposed, the more skillfully the general must plan his movements to ensure his forces can arrive at the right place exactly when needed.

By aiming to do this, the defender often ends up looking for and establishing strategic positions throughout the region. These are spots where, as soon as a part of the army arrives, they can immediately discourage the enemy from attacking. By securing these positions, the defender can create natural deterrents that require only a portion of his force to hold the line. Over time, as these locations are repeatedly occupied and relied upon, they become central to the entire strategy, almost like the focal points of the whole defensive plan. For this reason, this type of approach is often described as a war of posts, since the defender depends on these various locations, strategically moving from one post to another rather than expecting any single decisive engagement.

An extended defensive position and the use of relative resistance in campaigns without decisive battles are, therefore, not as risky as they may initially seem. Similarly, blocking the enemy's advance by marching to a position from the side is not as dangerous as it might be if a major confrontation were expected. Trying at the last possible moment to slip an army in front of a strong, determined opponent—especially one fully prepared to deliver powerful attacks without concern for conserving his forces—would be setting the defender up for disaster. Such a hurried lateral movement would likely be overwhelmed by the enemy's full-force blow. But against an adversary who moves more tentatively, who doesn't leverage the openings that would allow a greater victory, and who seeks only minor gains at little cost, this approach can work effectively.

As a natural result, this method is also more common in the later part of a campaign rather than at its start, when commanders have a better sense of the enemy's movements and intentions.

In this scenario, the general staff has an opportunity to showcase their command of local geography by crafting a network of coordinated actions tied to choosing and preparing positions, as well as identifying the best roads to quickly access these points when necessary.

When one side's main objective is to ultimately reach a certain goal, while the other side's purpose is to prevent this, both forces often find themselves moving directly in each other's view. Because of this close proximity, each movement must be conducted with a high degree of caution and precision, far more than if the forces were further apart. In earlier times, when armies were organized as unified masses rather than in separate, independent divisions, their movements demanded even more formal coordination and complex tactics. While individual brigades sometimes had to break away from the main army line to secure strategic points and act independently until reinforcements arrived, these were considered exceptions. The general goal of an army's march back then was to move as a single whole, keeping its formations intact and limiting any such deviations whenever possible.

Today, however, the main body of an army is broken down into independent units, each capable of holding its own against a significant force of the enemy as long as the other divisions are close enough to support and complete the engagement. This setup makes flanking maneuvers more feasible, even within the enemy's line of sight. What once required an intricate setup and careful alignment during a march can now be managed by sending out certain divisions earlier, speeding up others' marches, and employing the army's overall freedom and adaptability in its positioning.

Using these defensive strategies, the defender can prevent the assailant from seizing a fortress, occupying any strategically valuable area, or capturing supply depots. The attacker will face resistance in every direction if the defender can continuously present battles that appear risky or likely to end poorly for the attacker, or if there is simply too high a price to pay in resources or risk involved.

If the defender succeeds in achieving this level of mastery and skill, and if the attacker, everywhere he looks, sees only well-prepared obstacles blocking his aims, he may then abandon his original goals and turn instead to the idea of achieving honor on the battlefield. Winning even a single notable engagement could lend prestige to his army, satisfy the pride of his general, leaders, and people, and help fulfill the expectations that come with an offensive effort.

Thus, the last hope of the assailant might become a strategically advantageous combat for the sake of victory and the glory it brings. This goal can appeal to a sense of superiority, helping to calm the ambitions of the army and its supporters back home. It's essential to understand, however, that this doesn't contradict our initial claim that a capable defender can prevent an attacker from reaching specific objectives through combat. Securing any lasting success in such engagements depends on two things: achieving a favorable result in the engagement and, secondly, having that result directly lead to one of the attacker's broader goals.

The first outcome can easily happen without the second, so the defender's separate corps or posts are often in more danger of losing a skirmish if the attacker is merely chasing battlefield honor, compared to when the attacker is aiming for a greater strategic goal.

If we consider the perspective of Daun, a cautious commander, his decision to attempt a surprise attack at Hochkirch seems consistent with his nature as long as he only sought battlefield honors and day-to-day success. But the notion of an overwhelming victory with far-reaching consequences, which might force the king to surrender Dresden and Neisse, presents a vastly different challenge—one that Daun likely wouldn't have felt ready to confront.

It's important not to think of these distinctions as trivial or unimportant; in fact, we're now dealing with one of the most fundamental principles in warfare. The significance of a battle is its core in strategy, and we must emphasize repeatedly that, in strategy, major events always stem from the ultimate goals of both sides, almost like a conclusion drawn from all their combined ideas. This explains why, strategically, one battle can differ so vastly from another that they hardly seem like the same tactic at all.

Even if a fruitless victory doesn't deal any direct damage to the defense, the defender won't freely concede even this small gain to the attacker. Unpredictable elements can always emerge in battle, so the defender must vigilantly monitor the status of each of his forces and posts. It's true that much depends on the leaders of these individual groups making the right decisions on the ground, but any one of them might still end up in an unavoidable disaster due to poorly chosen orders from the commanding general. We're reminded here of Fouqué's corps at Landshut and Fink's corps at Maxen.

In both cases, Frederick the Great relied too much on familiar concepts. He couldn't realistically expect that 10,000 men would hold their ground against 30,000 at Landshut, or that Fink would withstand a larger force closing in on him from all sides. However, he assumed that the fortifications at Landshut would function as usual, like a check already accepted, and that Daun would see the movement against his flank as reason enough to abandon his uncomfortable position in Saxony for a safer one in Bohemia. Frederick misjudged both Laudon and Daun in these instances, and this led to flawed decisions in these actions.

But beyond these specific miscalculations—mistakes that even less proud, bold, or stubborn generals than Frederick might make—there's an inherent challenge here: the general-in-chief cannot always count on the intelligence, dedication, bravery, and resolve of his corps commanders. He can't simply rely on their judgment for everything. Therefore, he often has to lay out guidelines on various matters, limiting their responses in ways that may sometimes conflict with the actual situation on the ground. This is an unavoidable drawback. Without a strong and determined command presence that affects every level of the army, it's impossible to conduct a campaign effectively. A commander who constantly relies on getting the best from his subordinates would actually be poorly suited for overall leadership.

Consequently, the positions and conditions of each group and outpost need to be constantly reviewed to ensure that none are unexpectedly pulled into disastrous situations. The entire purpose of these efforts is to maintain the existing conditions, or status quo. The more effectively these efforts are carried out, the longer the campaign remains centered at the same location. But, as time stretches on, securing sufficient provisions becomes a bigger challenge.

Instead of relying on supplies and contributions from the countryside, a structured system of subsisting troops from stored provisions quickly comes into play, or does so in a short time. Rather than gathering local wagons as needed, a more formal transport system is developed, using either local carriages or those belonging to the army. Essentially, there begins a shift towards the organized supply chain from magazines, which we discussed earlier in the fourteenth chapter on subsistence.

However, this shift to magazine supplies doesn't significantly change the approach to this type of warfare. Because this form of warfare is inherently limited to a confined area by its purpose and nature, the question of provisions might still influence its actions—and often will—without fundamentally altering its character. What does become increasingly important in such a campaign, however, is the security of both sides' communication lines. This is due to two reasons: first, in these kinds of campaigns, where larger, more sweeping strategies are absent, generals must put their focus on smaller, less critical operations; and second, in these circumstances, there's enough time to wait for these methods to produce effects. For the defender, securing the communication lines becomes crucial, because while disrupting them may not directly impact enemy operations, it could nonetheless force a retreat, opening other targets for attack.

Every measure taken to protect the operational area of the theater of war also serves to safeguard the communication lines, so their security is partially assured through these efforts. It's important to note, though, that protecting these lines is a key factor in selecting defensive positions.

An additional means of securing these lines lies in escorting convoys with troops of various sizes. First, the far-reaching positions held by troops aren't always enough to guarantee the safety of communication lines. And second, escorts become particularly necessary when the general wishes to avoid overly extended positions. Tempelhof's History of the Seven Years' War is filled with examples of Frederick the Great ordering his food and flour wagons to be guarded by individual regiments of infantry or cavalry, and sometimes even by entire brigades. Meanwhile, there's little mention of such escorts on the Austrian side, which could be partly due to the absence of a detailed historian recording their actions. But it's also likely that the Austrians took up much more extended positions, which lessened their need for escorts.

Having now covered the four foundational elements of a defensive approach that doesn't aim at decisive action—and which are mostly free of offensive components overall—we'll now discuss the offensive tactics that can be added to these defenses, in a sense giving them a more dynamic quality. These offensive means primarily include:

1. Actions directed at disrupting the enemy's communication lines, which also encompass efforts to target their supply points.

2. Conducting diversions and raids within the enemy's territory.

3. Launching assaults on enemy corps and outposts, or even on the main force when conditions are favorable, or simply threatening to do so.

The first of these measures is constantly at work in nearly all campaigns of this nature, though often in a subtle way that doesn't necessarily draw attention. A significant portion of the effectiveness of any strategic position chosen by the defender stems from the unease it creates in the assailant about the security of their communication lines. Since, as we previously mentioned, supply and subsistence are crucial in this type of warfare and impact the assailant just as much, this constant worry about potential offensive moves arising from the defender's strategic positioning often shapes a large part of the campaign's overall framework. We'll revisit this idea when discussing the offensive.

Not only does this indirect influence—the choice of advantageous positions that generate a silent yet tangible pressure, similar to unseen forces in mechanics—play a role, but direct offensive maneuvers with a portion of the army aimed at the enemy's communication lines also fall within the scope of this type of defense. However, for such actions to be effective, the defender's position relative to these lines, the nature of the landscape, and the qualities of the troops available must be especially suited to the undertaking.

Raids into the enemy's territory, meant for either retaliation or the collection of contributions, are primarily offensive moves. Yet, when paired with the aim of creating a diversion to weaken the enemy force facing us, they can align with defensive goals. However, because these tactics could equally be applied by an attacker and serve more as offensive strategies in nature, we'll save a deeper examination for the next section. For now, we only acknowledge it here to complete the list of minor offensive tactics available to the defender on a theatre of war, noting that such raids can sometimes grow so influential in scale and scope that they lend the entire campaign a sense of offensive action, along with the perceived honor of an attack.

Frederick the Great's maneuvers into Poland, Bohemia, and Franconia before the 1759 campaign offer good examples of this approach. Although his campaign itself was purely defensive, these incursions into enemy territory gave it a look and feel of aggression, adding to its strategic value, perhaps especially due to the added moral impact this appearance provided.

An attack on one of the enemy's corps or on their main army should always be regarded as a key component of a defensive strategy, especially if the attacker becomes overconfident and leaves specific points poorly guarded. This underlying, unspoken objective runs through all defensive actions. Here, too, the defender can venture further into offensive territory, much like the attacker might, by seizing opportunities for a decisive strike. For such an approach to succeed, the defender must either be significantly stronger than the attacker—a scenario somewhat inconsistent with a defensive posture, but not impossible—or else possess the method and skill to keep his forces tightly coordinated, compensating for the risks inherent in such actions with agility and mobility.

In the Seven Years' War, Daun represented the former approach, while Frederick the Great embodied the latter. Nevertheless, Daun's offensives rarely surfaced except when Frederick's overboldness and disdain for him created an opening, as seen at Hochkirch, Maxen, and Landshut. Conversely, Frederick the Great was nearly always maneuvering, aiming to catch one or another of Daun's forces with his main army. True, he rarely achieved outright success, and the rewards of his efforts were often modest. Daun's sheer numerical advantage, along with his remarkable caution, tempered Frederick's ambitions. Yet, we should not conclude that the king's efforts were in vain. On the contrary, these attempts amounted to a substantial form of resistance; the vigilance and exertion Daun was forced to expend in sidestepping disadvantageous fights effectively neutralized forces that would otherwise have driven forward his offensive strategy. We need only look back at the campaign of 1760 in Silesia, where Daun and the Russians, fearing an attack from Frederick, were so hampered by the need to protect against such moves that they struggled to make any progress at all.

We believe that, with this, we have thoroughly reviewed the main concepts, objectives, and foundational strategies that support a defensive approach to managing a theatre of war where neither side seeks outright victory. Our primary goal in assembling these points is to illustrate the strategic structure of the entire defensive effort at a glance; the specific tactics that bring these ideas to life, such as marches, positions, and other maneuvers, have already been explored in detail.

By stepping back to view the whole, it becomes evident that, with only a weak inclination toward offense, minimal drive for outright victory, few compelling motivations, and numerous internal constraints, the line between attack and defense inevitably begins to blur. Though a campaign might start with one side moving into the other's territory, thereby adopting the appearance of an offensive, it frequently transpires that they must soon devote all their resources to defending their position on foreign ground. In such cases, the two forces essentially find themselves in a mutual standoff, each intent on avoiding losses and perhaps equally determined to secure even a minor advantage. Indeed, a defender, like Frederick the Great, might sometimes even pursue greater ambitions than the nominal attacker.

The less the attacker actively seeks progress, the less the defender feels pressured to assume a purely defensive stance, motivated solely by safety concerns. This dynamic fosters a balance in their relations, where both sides seek opportunities to gain advantages and guard against setbacks. This creates a scenario of genuine strategic maneuvering, where both are focused on outmaneuvering the other while managing risk. Ultimately, this mutual maneuvering defines the essence of most campaigns, particularly when the circumstances of the combatants or political factors prevent any decisive outcome.

If we delve into this notion of strategic maneuvering and see it through the lens of balanced forces, we realize it has often been given an outsized importance, particularly in defensive warfare, where it is sometimes viewed as the pinnacle of a general's skill. In this scenario, both forces remain in a state of equilibrium, neither side moving forward to a great offensive action or retreat. Instead, they remain on relatively even footing, watching and reacting to each other. This can occur when neither force has a compelling reason to launch a full assault. As a result, rather than pressing toward a clear objective, they instead focus on maneuvering around one another, cautiously moving to avoid disadvantage and seek opportunities to gain small, incremental advantages.

In the absence of a larger goal, this balanced standoff creates a situation where lesser, secondary objectives naturally come to the forefront. With no pressing danger or urgency, these objectives can develop and be pursued freely, without the restrictions that would normally be imposed by the need to concentrate on a larger, more decisive engagement. What might have been high stakes actions become, in a sense, smaller moves on a strategic chessboard, as the main action of the war fragments into a series of more minor exchanges. In this way, strategic maneuvering is somewhat of a contest of skill between the generals involved. However, given the unpredictable nature of war, even these smaller-scale actions are not exempt from chance or the element of luck, which inevitably turns the whole affair into a form of game in which calculated risks and adaptations are constantly required.

This style of warfare gives rise to a couple of important questions. First, does the reduced scope for decisive actions mean that luck and unpredictability play a smaller role than they would in an all-encompassing battle? Second, does it place an even greater premium on intelligence and meticulous calculation? For the first question, we can cautiously say that it does. As the overall strategic landscape becomes more defined and stable, individual moves and actions become easier to plan and execute precisely. In this environment, calculated thought takes on an increasingly influential role, reducing the random and unpredictable elements slightly, though never fully. As for the second question, we can say with some confidence that a heightened level of careful planning and consideration does indeed allow superior intellect to shine more clearly here, since there is less distraction from large-scale, chaotic clashes and more room for fine-tuned tactical choices. However, it's important to keep in mind that sheer intellect and reason are not the only defining attributes of a strong military leader. Other qualities, such as courage, determination, and quick thinking, also play a crucial role, especially when there is a single, make-or-break decision to be made. In these moments, when everything is on the line, a strong, bold decision can often be the difference between victory and defeat.

This interplay of qualities means that in moments of great decision, luck can still be tempered by a leader's bravery and quick thinking, lessening its potential impact. So, rather than asserting that balanced warfare completely minimizes the role of chance, we might instead say that it opens up more room for skill in calculated judgment to steer events while reducing the importance of some of the qualities needed for the intensity of direct conflict.

This leads to a subtle, but crucial distinction. A skilled commander who excels at using calm, methodical calculation to gain minor advantages may be a genius in strategic maneuvering, but this alone does not encompass all the qualities of a truly great general. War, by nature, requires moments of decisive courage and instinct that go beyond meticulous planning. If we focus only on the art of maneuvering and forget that war demands a balance between careful thought and the ability to make bold, sometimes risky decisions, we overlook a vital aspect of military genius.

Over time, some theorists and strategists have placed too much weight on maneuvering, seeing it as the end-all-be-all of a commander's skill. But this has often led to misconceptions, particularly in campaigns where the real underlying reason for indecisive warfare lies not in the generals' abilities to outmaneuver each other, but in broader political or strategic limitations that turn the war into a series of cautious moves rather than decisive engagements. In the end, it's not enough for a commander to simply maneuver skillfully; they must also recognize when to break from maneuvering and commit to a decisive action, understanding that war ultimately demands both skill in calculation and the courage to act boldly when the moment calls for it.

Because most wars between civilized states have generally focused more on monitoring the enemy than on outright destruction, it's unsurprising that many campaigns took on the nature of strategic maneuvering. Campaigns without any notable generals faded into obscurity; however, when a celebrated commander led one side, or two legendary leaders clashed—like Turenne and Montecuculi—the whole art of maneuvering seemed to reach new heights under their guidance. The brilliance of these commanders left a lasting impression on this approach, stamping it with an air of prestige and excellence. Consequently, this style of warfare became revered as the pinnacle of military art, the epitome of war's mastery, and the very foundation upon which the art of warfare should be studied.

Before the French Revolutionary Wars, this perspective largely dominated military theory. However, the arrival of these wars shattered previous norms, presenting a radically different set of wartime phenomena that were initially wild and chaotic but later organized under Napoleon into a comprehensive, large-scale system that produced results both thrilling and unprecedented. This upheaval led many to abandon the old models entirely, attributing the era's changes to new principles, grand ideas, and evolving societal conditions. The consensus emerged that the older ways would never return nor hold relevance again. Yet, as is common in shifts of opinion, a faction clung to the old standards, dismissing the new developments as little more than brute strength and a deterioration of military finesse. They argued that true mastery lay in the balance and sophistication of non-decisive, maneuver-focused war, holding this even-handed game of war as the purest expression of military perfection.

The argument supporting the old view lacks philosophical and logical grounding, muddling ideas in a way that can only be described as a deeply flawed interpretation. Nevertheless, the contrary opinion, that nothing from the past will ever resurface, is equally misguided. Few of the new tactics observed during the era came from novel discoveries or groundbreaking ideas; rather, they mostly stemmed from social transformations and the era's pressing circumstances. Since these changes occurred in a turbulent, revolutionary period, they can't be taken as the standard for all future warfare. Therefore, we should expect to see many aspects of former wartime practices resurface. Although this isn't the place to delve deeply into those changes, it's enough here to note that by examining how this balanced play of forces fits into broader war conduct—its significance and ties to other objectives—we see that such a method arises when both sides face constraints and lack substantial military power.

In this type of maneuver-focused campaign, a general with greater skill may outmaneuver his opponent. If his army is of equal size, he could gain several advantages, or, if his forces are smaller, he might use his talents to level the playing field. However, it is contradictory to regard this style of warfare as the highest form of military honor and glory. Campaigns dominated by maneuver are typically indicators that neither general is displaying great talent, or that one of them is constrained by circumstances, hindering any bold decisions. And when this occurs, there is little room for a general to demonstrate the full breadth of military genius.

So far, we have focused on the overall nature of strategic maneuvering. Now we must address a particular influence it has on warfare: namely, that it often leads combatants away from main roads and significant places, directing them instead toward remote or relatively unimportant locations. When minor, short-lived interests take precedence, the main geographical features of a region have less sway over how the war unfolds. As a result, we frequently find troops moving to unexpected points that, from the perspective of the broader aims of the war, might seem out of place. This also means that the variation and unpredictability in the smaller details of the conflict grow, especially compared to wars that revolve around major, decisive outcomes. Looking at the last five campaigns of the Seven Years' War, we see how each campaign took a different form despite the general relationships remaining unchanged. Examining these campaigns closely, we find that not a single measure appears twice, and yet, the offensive tendency on the part of the allied army is far more pronounced here than in most earlier conflicts.

In this discussion of defending a theatre of war without a decisive outcome as its goal, we have highlighted the tendencies, combinations, and relationships that shape its character, along with its connections. The specific measures that make up this strategy have already been described in detail in earlier parts of our work.

Now, the question arises: is it possible to establish any broad, all-encompassing principles, rules, or methods for these various tendencies of action? Our answer is that, based on history, no firm conclusions have been reached that follow recurring patterns. And for a subject as varied and shifting in nature, any theoretical rule could only be valid if it is grounded in actual experience. Warfare aimed at decisive outcomes is not only simpler but also more in line with natural law; it is less riddled with contradictions, more grounded in objective reality, and guided by an intrinsic necessity. Thus, the mind can create forms and laws for it. However, in warfare without a decisive end, establishing such laws appears far more challenging.

Even the two fundamental principles of the earliest theories of strategy in recent times—Breadth of the Base as described by Bülow, and Position on Interior Lines as outlined by Jomini—have shown no absolute or consistent effectiveness when applied to defending a theatre of war. As these concepts are structural forms, they ought to prove particularly effective in such a context, as structure often gains an advantage over other factors as the scope of action broadens over time and space. Yet, these concepts have proven to be just individual aspects of the broader subject and not decisive strengths in themselves. The unique nature of resources and circumstances significantly hinders the application of universal principles. What Daun achieved through broad, well-chosen positions, Frederick accomplished by keeping his army concentrated, staying close to the enemy, and remaining ready to improvise with his entire force. Each general's method reflected both the type of army under their command and the unique circumstances surrounding them. Improvising maneuvers, for instance, is always easier for a king than for a commander who bears direct accountability.

We must point out that critics should not view these differing methods and styles as mere steps on a scale of improvement, with one superior to the other. Each method deserves equal respect and should be evaluated based on its suitability to the specific situation at hand. Our goal here is not to list all the varying styles that might emerge due to the specific characteristics of an army, a country, or a set of conditions; instead, we have already acknowledged the general impact of these factors.

In this chapter, we recognize that we are unable to establish specific maxims, rules, or methods because history simply doesn't provide the necessary basis. Instead, historical records frequently reveal unique circumstances that are often inexplicable and occasionally surprising in their singularity. However, this does not mean that studying history lacks value on this subject. Where there is neither a formal system nor a strict doctrine, there may still be valuable truths to be discovered, and these insights are usually accessible only to a well-practiced judgment and the subtle understanding that grows with experience. So, even though history does not supply us with a set formula, we can be sure that studying it sharpens the judgment—here, as in any other aspect of warfare.

We will present one overarching principle, or rather, we will bring forward a foundational presumption underlying everything we have discussed so far. All the methods discussed here possess only relative value; they operate within limitations that apply equally to both sides, and beyond this restricted scope lies a different order of strategies and a completely distinct set of conditions. A general must remember this and avoid mistaking the smaller arena in which they are operating for one where actions have absolute certainty. They should not view the methods they employ as indispensable or irreplaceable and certainly not cling to them if they already feel apprehensive about their adequacy.

Though it may seem almost impossible to make such a mistake from the perspective we're taking, in reality, these distinctions can be much less clear. To emphasize clarity and provide a solid foundation for understanding, we have framed this discussion in terms of stark opposites, treating only the two extremes of the question. In real-world warfare, however, situations typically fall somewhere in between, influenced by each extreme according to how close they come to one or the other.

Consequently, the general's first task is to determine whether their adversary has the will and means to adopt bolder, more decisive measures. As soon as the general sees signs of this, they must abandon small, defensive maneuvers intended merely to counter minor setbacks. Instead, they should look to place themselves in a stronger position through a deliberate sacrifice if needed, positioning themselves to withstand a greater, more decisive action. In simpler terms, it is crucial that the general sets the right scale for their strategy from the outset.

To illustrate these ideas further with real-world examples, we'll consider several instances where, in our view, a general used an incorrect measure of judgment—specifically, where they greatly underestimated the level of decisive action intended by their adversary. We'll start with the 1757 campaign, where Austrian commanders, judging by their troop deployments, clearly hadn't anticipated such a bold offensive from Frederick the Great. Similarly, when Piccolomini's corps hesitated at the Silesian frontier, despite Duke Charles of Lorraine facing near-certain surrender, it showed a serious underestimation of the situation's gravity.

In 1758, the French misjudged twice: first regarding the effects of the Kloster Seeven Convention (though this is tangential to our point here), and again, two months later, when they were unprepared for what their opponent might attempt, ultimately losing the territory between the Weser and the Rhine. Frederick the Great also miscalculated the resolve of his opponents in 1759 at Maxen and again in 1760 at Landshut, as noted earlier.

But perhaps one of the greatest misjudgments recorded in history came in 1792. The assumption was that a moderate-sized auxiliary army could quell a national uprising—a miscalculation that quickly drew the full might of the French populace, roused to extreme action by revolutionary zeal. We label this error as significant because of its profound consequences, not because it was necessarily easy to foresee. In military terms, the seeds of the struggles that followed were planted in the 1794 campaign. During that campaign, the Allied forces failed to recognize the strength of the French attack, relying instead on a feeble system of extended lines and strategic maneuvering. Additionally, the political rift between Prussia and Austria and the hasty abandonment of Belgium and the Netherlands revealed how little the rulers of that era anticipated the immense force unleashed by the Revolution. In 1796, the Austrians' initial responses to Napoleon's actions at Montenotte, Lodi, and elsewhere showed just how deeply they misjudged the new reality that a general like Bonaparte represented.

In 1800, it wasn't merely the surprise that led to Melas's downfall but his misinterpretation of its potential consequences. By 1805, at Ulm, we find the culmination of a loose web of technically sound but fundamentally weak strategic plans. Such plans may have sufficed to restrain generals like Daun or Lascy, but they were no match for Napoleon, the Emperor of the Revolution.

The indecision and confusion of the Prussians in 1806 arose from a blend of outdated, ineffective tactics mixed with a few insightful ideas and a genuine recognition of the gravity of the moment. Had they fully understood and appreciated the situation in which their nation was placed, would they have left 30,000 troops in Prussia, entertained the idea of opening a separate theater of war in Westphalia, or anticipated any meaningful results from a minor offensive, as planned for the corps under Ruchel and the Weimar forces? How could they have even considered the danger to magazines or the potential loss of small areas of land during their final moments of planning?

Even in 1812, that grand campaign also saw its share of missteps resulting from a failure to properly assess the situation. At Wilna's headquarters, a faction of distinguished figures insisted on a battle at the frontier, determined that no invader would step onto Russian soil unpunished. They were prepared to admit that the battle might be lost, or even would be lost. Although they did not know they'd be facing 300,000 French against their own 80,000 Russian troops, they knew the French held a clear advantage in numbers. The key error lay in the weight they gave to this battle; they assumed it would be like many lost battles before. Yet, with certainty, we can say that if this major battle had occurred on the frontier, it would have set in motion an entirely different chain of events from those that actually unfolded. Similarly, the camp at Drissa rested on a wholly misguided assumption about the enemy's potential. Had the Russian army been forced to stay at Drissa, they would have been completely isolated, cut off from any support, leaving the French army with numerous options to force the Russians into surrender. The architect behind the Drissa camp had never considered power or will on such a scale.

But even Napoleon sometimes fell prey to a poor reading of the situation. After the 1813 armistice, he thought he could control the Allies' secondary armies under Blücher and the Crown Prince of Sweden with forces that, while not strong enough for an effective stand, might intimidate cautious leaders into holding back, as had happened in previous wars. He underestimated the fierce determination of Blücher and Bulow, as well as the serious danger surrounding both leaders. Generally speaking, he failed to recognize Blücher's relentless fighting spirit. At Leipzig, it was Blücher who wrested victory from him. At Laon, Blücher had the chance to completely devastate him; he didn't, but only because of factors far beyond Napoleon's calculations. Finally, at Waterloo (Belle Alliance), this repeated misjudgment struck Napoleon with the force of a lightning bolt.

Book VII. The Attack

Chapter I. The Attack in Relation to the Defence

If two ideas are in exact logical opposition to each other, meaning that each completes the other, then, in reality, each concept implies the other. Even when our minds are too limited to fully grasp both concepts at once, and we fail to see the entire picture in one unified view, this opposition still allows one idea to cast a strong and often adequate light upon the other. Thus, we believe the first chapter on defense sheds enough light on the related aspects of attack that it covers. However, this isn't universally true for all points; the reasoning process cannot always be fully extended in a single direction. Naturally, in areas where the opposition of ideas isn't foundational, everything that can be said about the attack doesn't necessarily emerge directly from the discussion on defense. When we change our perspective, we bring ourselves closer to the subject, allowing us to observe details that might have been missed from our previous standpoint. What we then perceive adds to our earlier line of reasoning, and it will often happen that examining the attack will bring fresh insights to our understanding of the defense.

While discussing the attack, we will frequently revisit topics that were central in discussing defense. However, it is neither our aim nor consistent with the nature of the subject to take the conventional approach found in engineering texts, where each point on the attack is aimed at neutralizing or overturning every strength identified in the defense. The defense has areas of strength and areas of vulnerability; even if those strengths are not completely invulnerable, they can only be overcome at a disproportionately high cost, and that principle should remain constant no matter how we approach the topic, or else we risk inconsistency. Additionally, we do not intend to exhaustively examine the back-and-forth interactions of defensive and offensive methods; each defensive measure naturally suggests an offensive countermeasure. Yet, this is often so apparent that it doesn't always require shifting our focus from defense to attack in order to understand it—the two are naturally connected.

Our aim, rather, is to focus on the unique aspects of the attack in each situation, specifically those that do not emerge directly from the defense. This approach will inevitably lead us to cover many topics specific to attack, which may not have corresponding discussions in the context of defense.

Chapter II. Nature of the Strategical Attack

We have observed that the defensive in warfare—especially in strategic terms—is not an absolute state of waiting and repelling, nor is it completely passive. Rather, it is a relative state that incorporates some offensive elements to various extents. Similarly, the offensive isn't a singular approach but is constantly intertwined with defensive actions. However, a key difference exists: a defensive strategy without some form of counterattack is unthinkable; this counteraction is an essential aspect of any defensive approach. By contrast, in an offensive operation, the initial strike or action is, in itself, a complete concept. The defensive is not inherently a component of the offensive, but due to the inevitable constraints of time and space, defensive actions become an unavoidable necessity in offensive operations. First, the offensive cannot proceed nonstop to its ultimate goal but must take breaks, and during these pauses, when forward movement is stalled, a defensive stance naturally comes into play. Second, as an advancing military force leaves behind critical territory vital to its sustenance, this area cannot always be protected by the advancing force and must often be guarded separately.

Thus, the act of attack in warfare—particularly in strategy—becomes a continual interchange between attack and defense. Yet, defense within this framework doesn't serve as a purposeful preparation to enhance the attack; rather, it's a necessary burden, like a weight that slows the momentum of the offensive. This defensive aspect does not strengthen the attack but actually diminishes its effectiveness by consuming time, thereby acting as a "retarding weight" on the advance. But might this embedded defensive element actually exert a negative influence over the entire offensive? If we consider the defense as the stronger form of warfare and the attack as the weaker, it would seem that defense cannot inherently weaken attack; for if there's enough strength to undertake the weaker form, that strength should suffice for the stronger as well. In general terms, this holds true, which we'll explore in more detail when discussing the "culminating point of victory." Still, it's important to remember that the superiority of strategic defense partly arises because an attack cannot unfold without incorporating weaker forms of defense. These weaker elements of defense that accompany an attacking force are its weakest links. So, while the offensive's overall purpose holds, these defensive aspects can, in some cases, act as a weakening factor.

It is during these vulnerable defensive moments within the offensive that the defensive side's offensive actions should ideally come into play. Take, for instance, the twelve-hour rest following a day's advance. The defender rests in a well-prepared, familiar position, while the assailant finds himself bivouacked in a new, often hastily chosen spot, having reached it blindly. Or consider a more extended period of rest needed for resupply and reinforcements: here, the defender is close to fortified locations and supply routes, while the attacker's position remains tenuous, almost like a bird perched on a branch. Every offensive eventually shifts into a defensive stance; the outcome of that defensive stance will depend on prevailing circumstances. These circumstances could be highly favorable if the attacker has successfully weakened the enemy forces. However, if that is not the case, they could be decidedly disadvantageous. Although this defensive element isn't intrinsic to the attack itself, its nature and potential impact will undoubtedly influence the attack's overall success, becoming a crucial factor in assessing the offensive's ultimate value.

From this perspective, it follows that with every attack, it is crucial to consider the defensive aspects that naturally accompany it. Doing so enables one to recognize and prepare for the specific drawbacks inherent in the defensive component of an offensive operation. However, while the attack maintains a consistent, active nature, the defensive approach, rooted in waiting and observation, varies as it nears its objective. This shift in defensive emphasis produces different forms, as outlined in the chapter on defense types.

Unlike defense, attack is characterized by direct, active engagement, with any defensive actions taken along the way merely adding weight to the operation. Though the force and speed of an attack can vary greatly, resulting in differences in intensity, they do not create differences in form. It's possible, for example, to envision an attacker adopting a defensive posture temporarily—like choosing a fortified position to bait the enemy into attacking—but such cases are so uncommon that they don't need to be included in our overall practical framework. Therefore, we can conclude that the attack doesn't display the same variety of structural types found in the defense.

Finally, in most cases, the scope of resources available for attack consists solely of the attacking force. Nearby fortresses can certainly aid the attack by influencing the battle space, but this effect lessens as the offensive progresses. Unlike in defense, where fortresses often take on central significance, they play only a secondary role in attack. Similarly, while an attacker might benefit from support by the local populace—especially if they favor the invading force over their own—such cooperation is rare and usually circumstantial, not an intrinsic part of offensive strategy. Allied forces, too, can sometimes bolster an attack, yet this type of support stems from specific alliances and circumstances rather than from the inherent nature of offensive warfare. So, while we consider fortresses, popular uprisings, and allies essential to a robust defense, they hold no such inherent place in attack; they are more exceptional and incidental rather than fundamental aspects of an offensive campaign.

Chapter III. Of the Objects of Strategical Attack

In war, the ultimate aim is to overthrow the opponent, and the key method for both attack and defense is the dismantling of the enemy's armed forces. This destruction of the enemy's forces propels the defender into a position from which they can launch an offensive, while for the attacker, it leads to gaining territory. Securing territory is, therefore, the main objective of the attack, but this objective doesn't always have to involve seizing an entire nation. The goal might be the capture of a smaller area, a specific province, a strategic strip of land, or even a fortress. Each of these holds value, either for its political significance or its worth in peace negotiations, whether the attacker intends to keep it or potentially exchange it later.

The goals of a strategic attack can thus vary greatly—from the ambition of conquering an entire country to capturing a single minor location. Once this intended objective is achieved and the active phase of the attack is concluded, a defensive phase naturally follows. In this way, we might visualize the strategic attack as a clearly defined, contained act. However, this view is somewhat idealized and doesn't fully reflect the realities of war, where practical situations often create a more fluid boundary between attack and defense. In real-world conditions, the intentions and actions of the attack may shift as seamlessly into defensive operations as a defense might slide toward offensive measures.

Frequently, a commander won't precisely predetermine the extent of territory they plan to conquer, instead letting circumstances on the battlefield dictate how far to press. An attack might progress further than initially intended, with the attacker gaining renewed momentum after a pause for rest or reinforcements, without needing to classify each new advance as a separate act. Conversely, an attack might stall sooner than expected, yet without fully shifting into a defensive stance or abandoning its aims. So, just as a successful defense can subtly transform into an offensive maneuver, an attack might also transition gradually into a defensive posture under certain conditions.

Keeping these fluid transitions in mind is essential to avoid misinterpreting the principles of an attack in a rigid, overly literal way. Recognizing these gradations allows a more flexible understanding of the dynamics at play in real-world military strategy.

Chapter IV. Decreasing Force of the Attack

This is one of the core elements of strategic planning: how accurately we evaluate it in a specific situation largely determines our ability to assess what actions are feasible. The gradual weakening of an army's absolute power during an attack occurs for several reasons:

Advancement into Enemy Territory: When the attacking force occupies portions of the enemy's territory, it starts right after the first major success. However, this advancement doesn't mean the attack stops after that initial victory.

Securing Rear Areas: As the army advances, it must secure the regions it leaves behind. Maintaining control over these areas is essential to protect its lines of communication and ensure a steady flow of supplies.

Casualties and Illness: With each encounter and from the strains of the campaign, the attacking force suffers losses, not just in combat but also from illness, which together reduce its strength over time.

Distance from Supply and Reinforcement Bases: The further an army moves from its depots and sources of reinforcement, the harder it becomes to sustain its supply lines, impacting both its material and manpower reserves.

Fortress Sieges and Blockades: Capturing fortified positions or laying siege to strongholds is time-consuming and often requires detaching forces, which dilutes the strength of the main attack force.

Diminished Momentum: As time passes, the vigor and motivation of the troops may begin to wane, leading to a drop in the overall effort and energy behind the campaign.

Loss of Allied Support: Allies may withdraw or cease their cooperation for various reasons, leaving the attacking army to rely more heavily on its own resources.

However, despite these factors that tend to weaken the attacking force, there are often opposing factors that may actually reinforce the attack. It's clear, therefore, that we can only reach a balanced assessment by weighing these different elements against each other; for instance, the diminishing power of the attacker could be partially or fully offset, or even exceeded, by the diminishing strength of the defending force. This scenario, where the defender is weakened more significantly than the attacker, is uncommon, and usually, we can only compare the forces directly engaging each other or those positioned at decisive points—not all forces available on either side in the entire field.

Different historical instances illustrate this concept: consider the French campaigns in Austria and Prussia, their invasion of Russia, the Allies' advance into France, or the French occupation of Spain. Each of these campaigns reflects unique balances of weakening and reinforcing factors, showing how crucial it is to weigh both sides to understand the true momentum of the attack.

Chapter V. Culminating Point of the Attack

The success of an attack comes from having a current superiority in force, encompassing both moral and physical strength. In the previous chapter, we discussed how the power behind an attack gradually diminishes; although there may be instances where this superiority increases, it generally decreases over time. The attacker is, in essence, investing upfront in advantages meant to be leveraged later in peace negotiations, but these come at the expense of a certain amount of military force immediately. If the attacker's advantage, although steadily declining, can be maintained until peace is reached, then the goal has been achieved. Some strategic attacks do lead directly to peace, but such cases are rare; more commonly, the attack reaches a stage where the remaining forces are just enough to sustain a defensive position and wait for negotiations. Beyond this point, the balance tips in the defender's favor, sparking a reaction—often one that strikes back with greater intensity than the original advance. This stage is what we term the culminating point of the attack.

Since the aim of the attack is to gain possession of enemy territory, the advance must continue until this superiority wanes; this drive toward the objective thus often urges the attacker forward, sometimes past the optimal point. When we consider the many variables that make up the balance of power in these engagements, it becomes apparent how challenging it is, in many cases, to judge accurately which side holds the upper hand. Often, everything depends on a delicate thread of perception and morale.

Thus, recognizing the culminating point relies heavily on a refined sense of judgment. This brings us to an apparent contradiction: the defense is considered the stronger form of warfare compared to the attack. Therefore, one might assume that an attack could never go too far, as long as the weaker form of engagement (the attack) is still viable, the stronger form (the defense) should theoretically be even more so.

Chapter VI. Destruction of the Enemy's Armies

The destruction of the enemy's armed forces is the method to achieve the ultimate goal in warfare. But what does this entail, and at what cost? There are several perspectives on this matter:

1. Destroy only as many of the enemy's forces as the specific objective of the attack demands.
2. Aim to eliminate as many of the enemy's forces as possible overall.

3. Prioritize sparing one's own forces above all else.
4. Take a minimal approach to engaging the enemy's forces, intervening only when a highly favorable opportunity presents itself—a perspective that might also apply to the attack's objective, as discussed earlier in the third chapter.

The principal method of destroying the enemy's forces is through combat, though this can be achieved in two main ways: directly through engagement or indirectly through a series of coordinated battles. While battle is the primary method, it isn't the sole option. The capture of a fortress or control over a piece of territory effectively reduces the enemy's power and may even lead to greater destruction indirectly. Therefore, occupying an undefended area holds value not only in serving as a direct accomplishment of the campaign's objective but also in its potential to weaken the enemy's strength indirectly.

When maneuvering forces to drive the enemy from an occupied region, this action should be seen from the same perspective—not as a direct victory, but rather as a strategic move. However, these methods are often overvalued and rarely match the decisive impact of an actual battle. Additionally, there is always a risk that the unfavorable position resulting from such maneuvers will be overlooked; they tend to appeal because of their relatively low immediate cost.

These indirect means should always be viewed as small investments, likely to yield only modest returns and most appropriate for scenarios involving limited State ambitions and low-stakes motives. In such cases, they are certainly preferable to battles fought without a clear purpose or to victories that cannot be fully capitalized upon.

Chapter VII. The Offensive Battle

What we discussed regarding the defensive battle also sheds significant insight on the offensive. Previously, we focused on that specific category of defensive battles where its nature is most fully realized to highlight its character. However, only a minority of battles truly fit this strict defensive mold; most are more like half-encounters, where the defensive aspect largely fades away. This stands in contrast to the offensive battle, which consistently retains its character and can assert it more confidently, as the defender is already somewhat out of their intended element. Consequently, even in mixed or encounter battles, where neither side is purely defensive or offensive, some differences in battle character between the two sides remain noticeable.

The primary feature of an offensive battle is the attempt to turn or encircle the opponent, which inherently involves the initiative. Conducting a line of combat designed to envelop offers inherent advantages, though this belongs more to tactical concerns. The attacker should not abandon these advantages merely because the defense has countermeasures; after all, the offensive cannot employ these countermeasures, as they are highly specific to the defensive stance. To effectively counter an opponent who seeks to turn our line, the defender needs a carefully selected, well-prepared position. Yet, what holds greater importance is that the defense often cannot capitalize on its inherent strengths; in reality, most defensive setups are weak improvisations. A large portion of defenders find themselves in highly strained and precarious circumstances, often bracing for the worst and attempting to meet the attacker halfway.

Thus, battles involving enveloping lines, or even with an angled front, which ideally emerge from advantageous conditions in terms of communication lines, typically arise due to both moral and physical superiority (as seen at Marengo, Austerlitz, and Jena). In the opening battle, the attacker's base, if not more secure than the defender's, generally has a broader scope, due to the close proximity to the frontier, allowing for greater risk-taking. Moreover, a flank attack—essentially a battle with an oblique front—often proves more effective than the fully enveloping form. The notion that such an enveloping maneuver should be accompanied by a corresponding strategic advance from the start, as seen at Prague, is a misconception. This strategy seldom aligns with an enveloping battle form and tends to be highly risky—a topic we'll explore further in the context of attacking a theater of war.

In a defensive battle, the commander's goal is typically to delay a final outcome as long as possible, aiming to buy time, since a defensive battle that remains undecided by nightfall is often considered a success. Therefore, in an offensive battle, the commander's objective is to accelerate the decision. However, this push for speed carries significant risk, as excessive haste can lead to unnecessary expenditure of forces. One unique aspect of offensive battles is the frequent uncertainty surrounding the exact position of the enemy; it often involves navigating through unknowns (as seen in battles like Austerlitz, Wagram, Hohenlinden, Jena, and Katzbach). The greater this uncertainty, the more critical it becomes to concentrate forces and favor a flank attack over attempting a complete encirclement.

We've already noted in the twelfth chapter of the fourth book that the main gains from a victory are usually achieved in the pursuit phase. By its very nature, the pursuit is more tightly integrated with the entire offensive operation than it is in a defensive battle.

Chapter VIII. Passage of Rivers

1. A large river crossing the line of an advancing army creates significant difficulties for the attacker. Once they cross it, their movement is usually restricted to a single crossing point, meaning that unless they stay close to the river, their flexibility becomes severely limited. Whether they intend to initiate a decisive battle after crossing or expect the enemy to attack them, the risk involved is substantial. Thus, without a clear advantage in both morale and physical strength, a general would be cautious about positioning their forces in such a vulnerable setup.

2. This inherent disadvantage of having a river behind an army often makes rivers easier to defend than they might otherwise be. If the defense doesn't rely solely on the river but allows for a fallback position nearby, then the attacker must consider not only the resistance they may encounter at the river itself but also the additional benefits that the defender has, as discussed in the first point. Together, these factors usually lead generals to approach rivers with considerable caution when a defense is in place.

3. As we noted in the previous book, under certain conditions, a dedicated river defense can yield very effective results. Historical experience even shows that such defenses succeed more often than theoretical calculations might suggest, because in practice, attackers often perceive obstacles as more challenging than they are in reality, which then hinders their actions. For instance, if an attack is not meant to end in a major victory or lacks determined force, countless small setbacks and complications will emerge, making the defender's position stronger than theory alone might account for, as the attacking force is the one constantly confronting these obstacles first. Consider how often even small rivers in Lombardy have been defended with success! Conversely, historical cases where river

defenses fell short of expectations generally involved unrealistic hopes placed on this method—expectations not aligned with the actual tactical advantages of the river but rather on a generalized belief in its power, as if it had no limitations.

4. The defense of a river may actually favor the attacker if the defender makes the error of relying entirely on it. In cases where the river is breached, the defender can end up in severe difficulties or even face a catastrophic outcome. For, while forcing a river crossing poses challenges, it is often easier to accomplish than winning a conventional battle.

5. From the previous points, it follows that defending a river can be highly valuable when a decisive outcome is not the goal. However, when faced with an opponent who has superior numbers or greater momentum, relying too much on this method may actually work to the attacker's benefit if it is misapplied.

6. Very few river defenses are impossible to bypass, either along the whole length or at specific points. An assailant with greater numbers and serious intent to deliver powerful blows has the advantage of demonstrating force at one crossing and, while diverting the defender's attention, crossing elsewhere. Once across, they can push forward to overcome any setbacks from initial encounters through sheer superiority. This strategy rarely involves directly overpowering the defender's main post by force alone, as "forcing a passage" typically refers to strategic maneuvers. It means that the attacker, by crossing at an undefended or weakly defended location within the defender's line, defies the dangers that the defender had hoped would make crossing untenable. The worst tactic for an assailant, however, is to attempt crossings at multiple, widely separated points unless these points are close enough to allow quick support across all crossing forces. When forces are split, the assailant risks losing their advantage by scattering resources. This occurred at the Battle of the Mincio in 1814, where the Austrians, divided by the spread of their crossing points, lost to the French who maintained a more unified approach.

7. If the defender remains on the river's near side, there are two strategic ways to gain an advantage: the attacker can either cross at a point away from the defender's position, using the river itself as a tactical element, or engage directly in battle. In the first approach, the choice of crossing point is influenced by the locations of bases and communication lines, although specific situational factors may weigh more heavily than overall positioning. The side that can better select advantageous ground, organize more effectively, maintain troop readiness, and respond quickly often succeeds in maneuvering over basic geographic conditions. The second approach, involving a direct battle, requires that the attacker is prepared and willing to engage in combat. However, defenders will rarely risk defending a river with direct confrontation if they expect the attacker to force a battle.

8. In conclusion, while river crossings rarely present extreme difficulties, they come with numerous potential complications and uncertainties that can slow an assailant's progress, making it likely they will either remain on the far side of the river or, if crossing, stay close to the riverbank. Rarely do two armies stand on opposite sides of a river for extended periods. In cases where major decisions or breakthroughs are needed, a river can still be strategically significant—it complicates and weakens an attacker's movements. In the best-case scenario for the attacker, a river may tempt the defender into treating it as a defensive barrier, making the river itself the focal point of their resistance. This strategy

can open opportunities for the attacker to deal a decisive, though initially limited, blow. Instead of achieving a complete defeat, this series of advantageous skirmishes creates an unfavorable shift in overall positions for the defender, as seen with the Austrians along the Lower Rhine in 1796.

Chapter IX. Attack on Defensive Positions

In the book on defense, we've already examined how certain defensive positions can force an assailant either to confront them or abandon their advance. Only those positions with the power to create this dilemma serve our purpose, as they can exhaust or partially neutralize the attacking forces, providing a strategic advantage that the offensive lacks the tools to counter. However, not all defensive positions are this effective. If the attacker can pursue their goal without directly engaging a position, then initiating an attack would be a mistake. If the position does obstruct their objective, the question then becomes whether the attacker can maneuver to threaten the defender's flank, potentially forcing them out of position. If these efforts fail, only then might a commander resolve to attack a well-fortified position, and, generally, an attack on a single side is the least challenging approach. The choice of which side to attack should consider the alignment and direction of both armies' lines of retreat, weighing the risk of compromising the defender's retreat against protecting our own. A balance between these priorities may emerge, where targeting the defender's retreat takes precedence, being offensive in nature and more aligned with the overall goal of an attack, whereas securing one's own retreat is more defensive.

That said, it's essential to recognize the critical nature of attacking a battle-hardened enemy in a strong position. There are, of course, instances of such attacks being successful—such as the battles of Torgau and Wagram (though Dresden is less definitive, as the opposing forces there were not as seasoned)—but these are outliers when compared to the many cases where even the most determined leaders have decided against attacking formidable positions (e.g., Torres Vedras). We should also avoid confusing these situations with standard battles, which are often "encounters" where one side occupies a position, though not one that has been carefully prepared.

Chapter X. Attack on an Entrenched Camp

For a while, it was fashionable to dismiss the usefulness of entrenchments. Incidents like the breaches in the French frontier's cordon lines, the loss at the entrenched camp in Breslau where the Duke of Bevern was defeated, and battles such as Torgau all contributed to a diminished view of their value. Moreover, Frederick the Great's victories, achieved through decisive movement and offensive tactics, cast a shadow over defensive strategies, especially those relying on fixed positions and entrenchments, furthering this dismissive attitude. Of course, when a few thousand troops are expected to hold down several miles of territory with basic, hastily dug defenses, these entrenchments may offer little security and can even become a dangerous illusion of safety. But to extend this skepticism to the general concept of field fortification is not only inconsistent but, in a sense, absurd. What would be the purpose of entrenchments if not to strengthen the defense? Reason, supported by countless examples, confirms that a well-designed, sufficiently manned, and properly defended entrenchment is typically an impregnable point, one that the attacking force respects and approaches with caution. Given the reliability of a single strong entrenchment, it's reasonable to conclude that assaulting an entrenched camp is a highly challenging endeavor and, in most cases, unlikely to succeed.

The nature of an entrenched camp usually involves a modest garrison. However, with good natural defenses and well-prepared fortifications, even a smaller force can hold firm against a much larger one. Frederick the Great, for example, judged an attack on the camp at Pirna to be impractical, despite his forces being twice as numerous as the garrison's. Later, some argued that the camp could have been taken, but the reasoning relied largely on the poor condition of the Saxon troops there—an argument that doesn't weaken the intrinsic value of solid entrenchments. It's also debatable whether those advocating the attack's feasibility and ease would have been willing to execute it themselves at the time.

Thus, we consider that attacking an entrenched camp falls into the realm of exceptional measures for the offensive side. An attack on an entrenched camp is generally advisable only if the defenses have been hastily erected, left incomplete, lack sufficient obstacles to prevent close approach, or if, as is often the case, the entire camp is only a faint outline of what it was intended to be—a half-finished shell. In such cases, an assault may indeed lead to an easier victory over the defending force.

Chapter XI. Attack on a Mountain

The strategic considerations of mountains in warfare, discussed in the fifth and subsequent chapters of the sixth book, lay out both defensive and offensive viewpoints on these natural barriers. In that analysis, we clarified how mountains can serve as a line of defense, setting the groundwork for understanding how an attacker should approach them. This has left us with only a few additional points to cover on this topic. Our key takeaway was that a defender must approach the situation by choosing between two distinct objectives: either fighting smaller, secondary skirmishes or preparing for a decisive general battle. In the case of secondary engagements, attacking mountainous terrain becomes an unavoidable but inherently disadvantageous task. However, if the goal is a larger-scale engagement, the attacker can actually gain an upper hand in the mountains, as long as the appropriate resources and intent are brought to bear.

Thus, when an attacking force is ready and resolved to engage in a major battle, it can benefit from meeting the enemy in the mountains. However, it is important to note that this conclusion often meets resistance, as it may appear counterintuitive and seems to run counter to historical experience. Historically, attacking armies have often viewed unoccupied mountain ranges as a fortunate situation, typically racing to secure these areas before the enemy could entrench. It's worth clarifying that this proactive seizing of unoccupied mountain terrain does not conflict with the attacker's objectives; rather, it supports them in specific contexts, which we need to clarify.

When an army advancing toward an enemy with the aim of a decisive battle finds an unoccupied mountain range in its path, it risks the possibility that the enemy might, at the last minute, block key passes that are critical to the planned route. In this case, the attacker would lose some advantages usually associated with battling the enemy in mountains since the defender would not be in an overly extended position nor uncertain about the attacker's approach. Here, the attacking army has not been able to strategically select its path based on the defender's position, making a potential mountain battle more difficult. Such conditions might leave the defender occupying a seemingly impregnable stance. Consequently, while it is theoretically possible for a defender to leverage the mountain terrain for a significant advantage in battle, the practicality of securing a favorable position under time constraints—and if the mountains were previously unoccupied—is limited. Therefore, while such a scenario is rare, it remains natural for the attacker to harbor this concern, since war often gives rise to plausible concerns that may ultimately prove unnecessary.

Another scenario for which the attacker must prepare is a preliminary defense by the defender, consisting of an advance guard or a network of outposts in the mountains. Although this approach may not always align with the defender's best interests, the attacker cannot predict its likelihood, so preparations for such a challenge are essential.

Our perspective does not discount the potential for a position to be unassailable due to the mountainous terrain itself. There are indeed locations, not necessarily within mountains, that are exceptionally well-suited to defense for precisely this reason, such as Pirna, Schmotseifen, Meissen, and Feldkirch. Notably, these sites are defensible due to their natural features rather than a specific mountain setting. It's also conceivable that a few advantageous defensive positions exist within mountain ranges—such as on high plateaus—where defenders can avoid the typical drawbacks of mountainous engagements, but these are not the norm and do not represent the majority of cases.

Military history demonstrates that mountain positions rarely serve well in large, decisive defensive battles. Prominent generals throughout history have favored positioning on plains for significant confrontations, highlighting the unsuitability of mountain terrain for such engagements. Aside from the Revolutionary Wars, history offers few examples of major battles fought successfully in mountains. In those exceptions, mountains were used based on a flawed analogy, where a decisive battle was required in difficult terrain, as seen in the Vosges during 1793-1794 and in Italy from 1795 to 1797. General Melas was frequently criticized for not securing the Alpine passes in 1800, but this critique appears simplistic. In reality, Buonaparte, placed in Melas's position, would likely have made the same decision to bypass those passes rather than defend them directly.

The general strategy for attacking mountainous defenses involves tactical planning, but there are essential aspects of the outline that overlap with strategic considerations:

1. In mountains, movement options are limited compared to open areas. The forces cannot easily split into multiple columns or create lateral movement on demand. More often, troops are restricted to narrow, elongated defiles, so advancing on multiple routes—or a wider front—is generally advisable.
2. When facing an extensive mountain line of defense, the attacking strategy should be to concentrate forces for a focused breakthrough rather than attempting an encirclement. If a meaningful outcome is to be achieved, success should focus on breaking through the enemy's line, splitting his forces, rather than surrounding him entirely. The primary goal should be a rapid and sustained drive toward the main line of the defender's retreat.

However, if the defender's position is more compact, flanking maneuvers become a necessary component of the attack plan. These flanking moves should primarily aim to sever the enemy's retreat rather than attempt to flank them in a tactical sense, as rear attacks in mountainous terrain are less effective when sufficient defensive forces are present. Victory is more likely if the defender feels an imminent threat of losing their retreat path, which induces anxiety sooner in mountainous regions due to the difficulty of maneuvering freely. Thus, in these scenarios, the attacker should focus less on mere demonstrations and more on physically blocking the defender's line of escape.

Chapter XII. Attack on Cordon Lines

If a crucial outcome hinges on the defense or attack of these entrenched lines, then the advantage clearly shifts to the assailant, as such defensive lines, due to their broad spread, counter the essential requirements for a decisive battle even more than direct defenses on rivers or mountain ranges. The lines of Denain in 1712, held by Eugene, serve as a pertinent example. The loss of these defenses was nearly equivalent to a complete defeat, though Villars would have struggled to claim such a victory if Eugene had instead held a more concentrated, unified position. However, when the attacking force lacks the resources necessary for a decisive engagement, even entrenched lines are approached with caution, particularly if held by the main body of the enemy's army. For instance, the Stollhofen lines, commanded by Louis of Baden in 1703, were respected by Villars, who understood that his forces were not positioned for an overwhelming attack.

In cases where defensive lines are only manned by a secondary force rather than a central, unified army, the attack becomes merely a matter of determining the strength of the forces that can be spared to breach them. In such scenarios, the resistance encountered is rarely formidable, though the rewards of victory are often equally modest. Essentially, these victories bring limited strategic benefits because breaking a secondary defensive line typically does not lead to a significant advancement of military aims.

A particular variety of defensive lines—the circumvallation lines constructed by besieging forces—holds unique strategic implications, which will be addressed more fully in the discussion of theater-wide attacks in warfare.

Positions that fall under the broader classification of cordon defenses, such as entrenched lines of outposts, generally share one main characteristic: they are relatively easy to breach. However, unless an assault on such lines is carried out with the intent to press forward and push toward a significant result, the gains from attacking them often prove minimal. In most cases, the limited strategic value of capturing these lines scarcely justifies the effort and resources required for the assault.

Chapter XIII. Manœuvring

1. We've already briefly discussed this topic in the thirtieth chapter of the sixth book, as it concerns both defense and offense in warfare. However, it inherently leans more towards an offensive nature, so here we will delve into it in greater depth.
2. Manœuvring contrasts not only with the offensive executed by sheer force through major battles, but also with any approach that directly employs offensive strategies—whether targeting the enemy's communication lines, cutting off retreat paths, or engaging in diversions.
3. Commonly, manœuvring involves creating an advantage seemingly out of a neutral or balanced situation, often by capitalizing on mistakes the enemy is led to make. This is somewhat akin to the initial moves in a chess game, where evenly-matched powers seek to gain from a favorable opportunity and exploit any advantage.
4. The core factors that serve as the objectives and guiding pivots in manœuvring include:

(a) Disrupting or hindering the enemy's access to supplies.

(b) Securing or impeding the junction with other friendly forces.

(c) Threatening other lines of communication within the country or with other forces.

(d) Compromising the enemy's retreat path.

(e) Engaging isolated enemy positions with superior force.

These interests can manifest in minute details within any given scenario, turning something as specific as a bridge, road, or defensive position into a key focal point around which events unfold. It is only the relationship of these features to one of the primary goals above that gives them true significance.

(f) For the side initiating a maneuver—or even for the defending side if taking an active stance—a successful maneuver can yield strategic assets like control over new territory, supplies, or advantageous positioning.

(g) In strategic manœuvring, two complementary tactics emerge that can be mistakenly viewed as separate techniques, leading to misapplied principles and rules. These two opposing concepts each have four aspects but should actually be seen as essential components of the same tactic. The first pairing is encircling the enemy versus operating along interior lines; the second is concentrating forces versus distributing them across several positions.

(h) Regarding the first pairing, no universal advantage exists between encircling the enemy and using interior lines. One approach naturally provokes the other, each serving as a counterbalance. Enveloping, or encircling, aligns with the offensive; interior lines are more consistent with defense. Consequently, the offensive typically favors an encircling approach, while the defensive finds strength in interior lines. Whichever side applies its method with the highest skill will likely hold the upper hand.

(i.) The branches of the other antithesis can just as little be classed the one above the other. The stronger force has the choice of extending itself over several posts; by that means he will obtain for himself a convenient strategic situation, and liberty of action in many respects, and spare the physical powers of his troops. The weaker, on the other hand, must keep himself more concentrated, and seek by rapidity of movement to counteract the disadvantage of his inferior numbers. This greater mobility supposes greater readiness in marching. The weaker must therefore put a greater strain on his physical and moral forces,—a final result which we must naturally come upon everywhere if we would always be consistent, and which, therefore, we regard, to a certain extent, as the logical test of the reasoning. The campaigns of Frederick the Great against Daun, in the years 1759 and 1760, and against Laudon, 1761, and Montecuculis against Turenne in 1673, 1675, have always been reckoned the most scientific combinations of this kind, and from them we have chiefly derived our view.

(j.) Just as the four parts of the two antitheses above supposed must not be abused by being made the foundation of false maxims and rules, so we must also give a caution against attaching to other general relations, such as base, ground, etc., an importance and a decisive influence which they do not in reality possess. The smaller the interests at stake, so much the more important the details of time and place become, so much the more that which is general and great falls into the background, having, in a certain measure no place in small calculations. Is there to be found, viewed generally, a more absurd situation than that of Turenne in 1675, when he stood with his back close to the Rhine, his army along a line of three miles in extent, and with his bridge of retreat at the extremity of his right wing? But his measures answered their object, and it is not without reason that they are acknowledged to show a high degree of skill and intelligence. We can only understand this result and this skill when we look more closely into details, and judge of them according to the value which they must have had in this particular case.

We are convinced that there are no rules of any kind for strategic manœuvring; that no method, no general principle can determine the mode of action; but that superior energy, precision, order, obedience, intrepidity in the most special and trifling circumstances may find means to obtain for themselves signal advantages, and that, therefore, chiefly on those qualities will depend the victory in this sort of contest.

Chapter XIV. Attack on Morasses, Inundations, Woods

Impassable swamps, or morasses, crossed only by limited embankments, create distinctive challenges for an attacking force, as we previously discussed in relation to the defense. Their considerable width generally prevents artillery from effectively driving the enemy away from the opposite bank and constructing a direct roadway across the swamp becomes almost impossible. Strategically, this often forces the assailant to seek ways around these obstacles rather than attempt a direct assault. In cases where marshland areas have been developed extensively, as seen in many densely populated lowlands, numerous routes may exist through the swamp. Although these routes still offer the defender a solid resistance, their ability to contribute to a decisive, absolute defense is significantly reduced, making them unsuitable for blocking major advances. However, if these lowlands are fortified with controlled flooding, as in the case of Holland, the defensive strength can become absolute, capable of thwarting nearly any attack.

Historical examples highlight this resilience. In 1672, Holland effectively blocked a French invasion led first by Condé and later by Luxemburg. Despite occupying all external fortresses around the perimeter of the flood zone, 50,000 French soldiers could not breach the line of inundation, which was defended by only around 20,000 Dutch troops. In stark contrast, during the Prussian campaign of 1787, under the Duke of Brunswick, these very lines were overcome with minimal force and loss. This success, however, stemmed from political turmoil and leadership discord among the Dutch, not from the inherent weakness of the flooded defenses. The Prussian breakthrough ultimately hinged on a single, highly precarious decision—the Dutch had failed to guard the Sea of Haarlem, allowing the Duke to circumvent the flood line and approach Amsterdam from the rear, bypassing the heavily fortified position at Amselvoen. If the Dutch had stationed just a few armed vessels on the Sea of Haarlem, the Duke would have been completely halted and unable to advance on Amsterdam. Although the broader impact of this hypothetical barrier on peace negotiations lies beyond our current discussion, it is clear that such a misstep nearly sealed the campaign's outcome, underscoring that these flooded defenses were indeed formidable when properly executed.

Severe winters pose a natural challenge to flood-based defenses, as demonstrated by the French campaigns of 1794 and 1795 when harsh winter conditions froze the waterways and allowed passage. Nevertheless, it must be an exceptionally harsh winter to compromise these defenses entirely.

Dense forests, which are challenging to traverse, also offer significant advantages to defenders. If a forested area lacks considerable depth, an attacker might force their way through by utilizing several nearby roads to reach more manageable terrain, since no single forested point offers substantial tactical strength compared to an impassable river or morass. But in territories like Russia and Poland, where vast stretches of forest cover the landscape and offer no clear way around, the attacking force may face an extremely challenging situation. In such deep, continuous woodlands, logistical obstacles multiply—feeding an army in a thick forest becomes a constant struggle, while the attacker's numerical advantage diminishes in effectiveness as they can scarcely apply concentrated force or bring the full weight of their troops to bear on their elusive opponent.

In summary, these natural defenses—morasses, flood zones, and deep forests—pose unique obstacles for an attacking force. They often require the assailant to adapt their approach or, in some cases, reconsider the feasibility of their objectives altogether.

Chapter XV. Attack on a Theatre of War With the View to a Decision

Much of what we've discussed regarding an enclosed theater of war has already been introduced in the sixth book, offering a preliminary view of these concepts as they relate to defense, while also indirectly shedding light on their impact on the attack. In fact, the very idea of an enclosed theater of war is more closely aligned with defensive strategies than offensive ones. Many of the main aspects, such as the purpose behind an attack and the scope of actions following a victory, have already been explored, laying the groundwork for understanding the essential nature of the attack itself. However, the most pivotal elements of the attack's character—those that define its true direction and aims—only fully come to life when we consider the overall war strategy.

Nonetheless, there are still points left to address, particularly as we turn our attention to campaigns where a decisive outcome is specifically sought. We will continue our examination by beginning with such a campaign—one in which a major, deliberate decision is intended from the outset. Here, we'll delve further into how an attack strategy unfolds within these conditions, exploring the unique challenges and opportunities it presents in an enclosed theater. In doing so, we aim to deepen our understanding of how the plan of war shapes and influences the course of an attack, guiding it toward its end objectives.

1. The primary objective of an attack is to secure victory. While the defender enjoys advantages inherent to a defensive stance, the attacker must counterbalance these with superior numbers and, perhaps, a slight edge derived from the morale boost that often accompanies advancing. However, the influence of this morale boost is often overestimated; it tends to diminish quickly in the face of real obstacles. This assumes, of course, that the defender is just as capable and prudent as the attacker. The purpose of this discussion is to dispel misconceptions around sudden assaults and surprise attacks, which many assume to be core tactics for attackers. In reality, these elements rarely occur without specific, favorable conditions, and true strategic surprise has already been discussed in other sections. Thus, if an attack lacks sufficient physical power, it must compensate with moral strength to overcome the intrinsic disadvantages of an offensive posture. If neither physical nor moral superiority exists, the basis for launching an attack is weak, and success becomes unlikely.

2. Just as prudence and cautious foresight characterize a defender's best qualities, boldness and self-assurance are essential traits for an attacker. This doesn't imply that the attacker should lack prudence or that the defender should have no boldness; rather, each quality aligns naturally with its respective role. These traits are necessary because war strategy relies not only on calculations but also on active decision-making in conditions that are, if not entirely obscure, at least dimly illuminated, requiring a leader with both judgment and confidence in their aim. The more the defender shows hesitation or lacks resolve, the bolder the attacker can afford to be.

3. To achieve victory, it's crucial to engage the enemy's main force directly. This necessity is generally more pronounced in the attack than in the defense, as the attacker seeks out the defender in their prepared position. However, we've argued (in the discussion of defense) that the attacker should avoid engaging the defender if the defender has set up in a strategically weak position. In such cases, the defender is likely to come out and engage, allowing the attacker the benefit of fighting on ground less prepared by the defender. The importance of this approach hinges on the specific routes and directions that bear the most strategic weight, a topic reserved for this chapter and one which was only briefly mentioned when discussing the defense. Here, we'll examine these crucial strategic considerations in greater detail.

4. We have previously discussed the objectives an attack should prioritize, especially those that serve as the goals of victory. If these objectives lie within the theater of war and within the potential reach of a victory, then the route to them naturally becomes the best path for the attacking force to pursue. However, it's important to remember that such objectives generally gain their full value only once victory is secured; thus, every objective must be approached with victory as the ultimate end. For the attacker, then, it's not simply about reaching the objective but about reaching it victoriously. Consequently, the direction of attack should not aim solely at the objective itself but should instead focus on intercepting the route the enemy must take to defend it. This route becomes the immediate focus of the attack. The goal is to confront the enemy before they can establish a defense, cut off their access to the objective, and defeat them along that line, thereby achieving a more decisive victory.

For instance, if the capital city is the intended target, and the defender has not stationed themselves between the city and the advancing force, then it would be unwise for the attacker to march directly toward the capital. Instead, the attacker should concentrate on the line that connects the defender's army to the capital, securing victory there to then claim the capital itself.

In cases where no major target falls within the scope of a potential victory, the most critical point for the attacker becomes the enemy's line of communication to the nearest significant objective. Every attacker, therefore, should ask, *What is the first advantage I'll gain if I win this battle?* The answer to this question reveals the logical direction of the attack. If the defender has already positioned themselves along that route, they have made a wise choice, and the attacker should meet them there. Should the defender's position prove too formidable, the attacker must attempt to outflank it—turning a strategic challenge into an opportunity. However, if the defender has not stationed themselves in this ideal position, the attacker should take that route and, upon aligning with the defender's position, angle toward the defender's line of retreat and aim to engage them there. If the defender remains fixed in place, the attacker should adjust to strike them from the rear.

Among the available routes, the main roads used for trade and commerce are usually the most effective and logical choices for the assailant. But to avoid unnecessary diversions, it's sometimes preferable to opt for smaller, more direct routes, as a retreat that strays too far from a straight line can be risky.

5. When the attacker begins an operation aimed at achieving a major strategic decision, they rarely have valid reasons to divide their forces. If they do split up despite this, it often signals a lack of strategic clarity. Thus, the attacker should only spread their columns across a front wide enough to ensure that all forces can engage together when battle begins. If the enemy has already divided their own forces, this plays to the advantage of the assailant, who can capitalize on the situation by using small, calculated demonstrations to

distract or apply pressure on those isolated enemy corps. Such maneuvers—strategic feints, or *fausses attaques*—are then justified, allowing the attacker to retain a unified main force while keeping the enemy's scattered elements in check.

Any necessary division into multiple columns should serve the purpose of forming a tactical attack in an enveloping configuration, a natural approach in offense that shouldn't be disregarded without sound reasoning. However, this envelopment should remain strictly tactical; using a strategic envelopment during a decisive engagement tends to dilute the attacker's strength, resulting in wasted effort. Such a tactic only makes sense if the assailant has overwhelming superiority, where the outcome is virtually certain in their favor.

6. Prudence remains essential in any attack, as the assailant also has a rear to protect and lines of communication that must remain secure. Ideally, the attacking force itself, through its advance and formation, serves as its own rear guard, reducing the need to split off forces for protection. Should circumstances necessitate a dedicated detachment for safeguarding lines of communication, any division of forces like this will inevitably weaken the core attacking strength. Large armies generally advance with a frontage of at least a day's march, so if the line of retreat and supply routes don't deviate significantly from a perpendicular alignment, the forward presence of the army itself often provides sufficient cover for these rear connections.

The risks posed to the rear of an advancing force depend largely on the disposition and mindset of the defender. When a critical decision in the campaign looms near, defenders rarely have the freedom to engage in significant disruptions of the attacker's rear. As such, the attacker generally faces minimal threats in typical conditions. However, as the initial phase of advance winds down and the assailant begins to assume a more defensive posture, the need to secure the rear intensifies, becoming of utmost priority. In these later stages, the attacker's rear is often more vulnerable than the defender's; hence, even as the defender retreats or cedes ground, they may already be mounting operations aimed at disrupting the assailant's supply lines and communications, long before initiating a full counteroffensive.

Chapter XVI. Attack on a Theatre of War without the View to a Great Decision

Attack on a Theatre of War without the Aim of a Major Decision

1. Even without the determination or strength for a major strategic decision, an attack may still have a clear, if secondary, strategic objective. In these cases, success is defined by reaching this secondary goal rather than forcing a decisive shift in the campaign. If the objective is reached, the campaign tends to settle into a renewed state of balance or rest. However, if substantial difficulties arise before this objective is achieved, the attack often loses momentum, halting its primary advance. In its place, the campaign shifts to more sporadic offensive actions or a state of strategic maneuvering. This characterizes the majority of historical campaigns.

2. The specific goals that may guide such a limited offensive typically include

(a) A Strip of Territory – Securing a slice of land can serve various purposes: gaining new resources, levying contributions, sparing one's own territory from devastation, or providing leverage in peace negotiations. Often, the reputation of the army may be tied to holding this land, a sentiment frequently seen in the French Marshals' campaigns during the reign of Louis XIV. It's crucial to consider whether this portion of territory can be retained beyond the campaign. Generally, lasting occupation is only feasible when the land borders the army's established theater of war and naturally extends it. Territories that fulfill this role may serve as negotiation chips for peace talks; other regions tend to be temporarily occupied during the campaign season, only to be relinquished when winter approaches

(b) Capture of a Key Enemy Magazine – Seizing one of the enemy's primary supply depots can deal a significant blow. However, if the magazine lacks substantial importance, it generally doesn't justify a prolonged or full-scale campaign. While capturing such a depot undeniably harms the defender and aids the attacker, the true strategic benefit lies in forcing the defender to withdraw further and relinquish territory they would otherwise have protected. Thus, the capture of a magazine is better understood as a tactical means rather than an ultimate goal. Nonetheless, until it's secured, this target can serve as a central focus of the campaign, guiding immediate operations toward its capture.

(c) The capture of a fortress. We have dedicated a separate chapter to the siege of fortresses, which readers may consult for more in-depth insights. As outlined there, fortresses often become the central objectives in those offensive campaigns where the attacker's goals do not aim for the complete destruction of the enemy or for the conquest of a significant territory. Particularly in regions like the Low Countries, where fortified places are plentiful, the possession of individual fortresses frequently becomes the primary focus. Here, the conquest of a single stronghold often held more significance than control over broader areas, with campaigns revolving around the feasibility of besieging these fortresses rather than their intrinsic value alone.

However, attacking a key fortress is always a formidable endeavor due to the substantial resources required. In conflicts where not everything is risked at once, these resource demands are critical considerations. Thus, a siege ranks among the most substantial objectives of a strategic offensive. Conversely, when a place of lesser importance is besieged or when the siege itself lacks conviction, preparation is minimal. Such actions are often conducted "en passant" or incidentally, fitting campaigns where smaller forces are at play or where the goals are modest. In these cases, the entire operation can take on a symbolic character, often intended to add a sense of completion to a campaign and uphold the attacker's honor, especially when the situation demands some form of offensive display.

(d) A successful encounter or battle undertaken purely for trophies, the honor of arms, or even the ambition of commanders. The historical record is filled with instances where battles were fought with these aims rather than solely strategic considerations. In Louis XIV's era, for instance, French campaigns were frequently marked by such offensive battles. Beyond being vanity exercises, these actions hold genuine strategic value. While seemingly superficial, they influence peace talks by reinforcing the moral authority, reputation, and military confidence of the victorious army and its general. These intangible advantages, while subtle, exert a lasting impact across the broader campaign.

Such combats are naturally undertaken with the understanding that (a) the likelihood of victory is considerable, and (b) the stakes are not prohibitively high. Engaging in a battle with limited objectives or within constrained circumstances should not, of course, be mistaken for a wasted victory resulting from a failure of resolve to capitalize on success. Instead, these engagements may serve a strategic end by enhancing morale, demonstrating readiness, and strengthening one's bargaining position in the long term.

3. In general, all of these goals (except for the last one) can be reached without a big fight, and most of the time, the offense can achieve them pretty easily. The attacker has certain ways to make progress without

needing a decisive battle. These tactics come from the interests the defender has to protect in their area of conflict. For instance, the offense can threaten the defender's supply routes, which might include things like storage centers, rich farmlands, water routes, or other critical areas. Additionally, the offense might try to capture important locations like bridges or mountain passes, or even set up bases in strong spots near the defender, making it hard for them to drive the offense out. Other tactics might include taking over important towns, fertile lands, or areas that could be stirred up to rebel. They could also threaten the defender's weaker allies. If these moves succeed in cutting off the defender's supplies, especially if it would take a lot of effort for them to restore these lines, the defender may be forced to move their position back or shift to the side to protect their resources, even if it means leaving behind less important items. As a result, some territory may become exposed; supply stores or a fortress might be left unprotected, which means the offense could seize them or surround them. Battles, either large or small, might arise from these situations, but in these cases, fighting isn't the main goal of the war, just an unavoidable consequence, and these battles are usually kept within a certain limit of size and importance.

4. When the defender takes action against the attacker's supply routes, it's a form of counterattack that, in wars focused on achieving big outcomes, usually happens only if the attacker's routes are very long. However, this kind of counterattack is more likely in wars that don't have a major outcome as their main goal. In these cases, the attacker's supply routes are usually not very long, and the main point isn't to cause major losses, but rather to disrupt and cut off the attacker's supplies. Sometimes, just slowing down the attacker's supplies is enough to have an effect, and what the routes lack in length can be made up for by the amount of time that can be used up in this kind of struggle. For this reason, protecting their strategic flanks becomes a big priority for the attacker. If this kind of back-and-forth does take place between the attacker and defender, then the attacker needs to rely on greater numbers to make up for their natural disadvantages. If the attacker still has enough strength and determination to attempt a decisive attack on one of the defender's groups, or on the defender's main force itself, the threat of this powerful move becomes their best way to protect themselves.

5. In summary, there is another major advantage that the attacker typically has over the defender in wars like this: the attacker can usually get a better sense of the defender's plans and strength than the defender can of the attacker's. It is much harder to figure out how daring and aggressive the attacker is than to sense when the defender has something important planned. In practical terms, simply choosing to defend often signals that the defender doesn't intend to take bold actions. On top of that, the preparations needed for a big counterattack are usually quite different from the typical defenses, whereas the preparations for a major offensive are not as different from those for smaller attacks. Finally, the defender usually has to act first, which gives the attacker the advantage of making the last move.

Chapter XVII. Attack on Fortresses

The topic of attacking fortresses is not covered here in terms of fortification techniques or military engineering; instead, we need to look at it first for its strategic importance, then for how to choose between different fortresses, and finally, how to properly secure a siege. When a fortress is lost, it weakens the defense, especially if that fortress plays a critical role in the defense. Capturing a fortress provides many benefits to the attacker, as they can use it as a storage center or depot and use it to protect nearby areas and encampments. Additionally, if the attacker eventually has to switch from offense to defense, a fortress becomes an excellent stronghold for that defense. All these roles that fortresses play in a war, as the conflict unfolds, make their value clear, as discussed in the section on defense, which sheds light on how fortresses relate to offensive strategies.

When it comes to capturing strongholds, there's also a big difference between campaigns aiming for a major victory and those with lesser goals. In the former, capturing such strongholds is always seen as an unavoidable challenge. Until the outcome of the conflict is clear, only absolutely necessary sieges are undertaken. Once the outcome has been decided—the peak of strength has passed, some time has elapsed, and there is a pause in the fighting—then taking control of strongholds helps secure the victories already won. In these situations, sieges can usually be accomplished, if not without some effort and resources, then at least without significant risk. However, during the peak of conflict, a siege increases the intensity of the crisis to the attacker's disadvantage; it is obvious that nothing weakens the attacker's power more than a siege, which is bound to tip the balance against them, at least temporarily. Yet, there are times when capturing a particular fortress is absolutely necessary if the attack is to continue. In these cases, a siege is seen as a more intense step in the offensive, with the crisis growing greater the less has been resolved beforehand. Any further details on this subject are covered in the section on war planning.

In campaigns with limited objectives, a fortress is usually not a means to an end but the end itself; it's treated as a smaller, standalone victory and has the following benefits over other conquests:

1. A fortress is a small, clearly defined conquest that doesn't require additional force to maintain, so there's no need to worry about a counterattack.
2. In peace negotiations, a fortress can serve as a valuable bargaining chip.
3. A siege is a real advancement for the offensive, or at least appears to be, without continuously wearing down the attacking force like other advances.
4. A siege is an operation without the risk of a sudden disaster.

The outcome of these considerations is that capturing one or more of the enemy's strongholds often becomes the goal for strategic attacks that aren't aimed at a larger victory. When it's unclear which fortress to target, the choice is typically influenced by the following factors:

(a) The fortress should be one that can be easily held, making it valuable as a bargaining tool in peace negotiations.

(b) The resources needed to capture it should be readily available. Smaller resources are only enough to capture smaller strongholds, but it's better to take a small one than to fail before a larger, more fortified one.

(c) The fortress's engineering strength, which isn't always equal to its overall importance. It would be wasteful to focus efforts on a highly fortified but insignificant place if a weaker but more strategic location is available.

(d) The strength of the fortress's weapons and garrison. A fortress that is poorly armed and lightly guarded is naturally easier to capture. However, the strength of the garrison and armament adds to the place's overall importance because these are direct parts of the enemy's military force, unlike fortification structures. Therefore, capturing a fortress with a strong garrison is often more worth the effort than one with powerful defenses alone.

(e) The ease of transporting the siege equipment. Many sieges fail due to a lack of resources, usually because transporting them is too difficult. The siege of Landreci by Eugene in 1712 and Frederick the Great's siege of Olmütz in 1758 are notable examples.

(f) Lastly, the ease of securing the siege is another factor to consider.

There are two main ways to secure a siege: by fortifying the besieging force with a surrounding line of fortifications or by setting up observation lines. The first method has fallen out of favor, though it has the advantage of not dividing the attacker's forces, which is a common weakness in sieges. However, this method does cause a significant weakening in other respects because—

1. The position around the fortress is generally too large for the strength of the army to fully defend.
2. The garrison, whose strength combined with that of any relieving army equals the force we originally faced, becomes like an enemy force positioned in the center of our camp. Protected by the fortress walls, it is invulnerable or at least beyond our ability to overpower, making its power considerably greater.
3. Defending a line of circumvallation forces the army into a purely defensive stance, as the outward-facing circular formation is the weakest and least advantageous battle arrangement, especially unsuited for launching any effective counter-attacks. In such cases, the only choice is to hold the entrenchments to the very end. This situation may drain more than a third of the army's strength, whereas forming an observation army might not cause such losses. Since Frederick the Great's time, there's been a preference for what's called "the offensive" (though it isn't always truly offensive) and for maneuvers and movements over entrenchments, which explains why lines of circumvallation have fallen out of favor. This weakening of tactical defense is just one disadvantage; additional concerns about circumvallation lines have influenced judgments against them, as they are closely related to these weaknesses.

A line of circumvallation only protects the area it encloses; all other areas are largely left open to the enemy unless special detachments are used to cover them, which defeats the purpose by dividing forces. As a result, the besieging army is constantly anxious about the supply convoys it needs, and protecting them with circumvallation lines is impossible if the siege demands large forces or supplies, and if the enemy is actively in the field. The only exception is in regions like the Netherlands, where a network of closely placed fortresses and connecting lines helps cover the rest of the battle area and reduces the transport distances.

During Louis XIV's time, the concept of a theater of war hadn't yet connected closely with the position of the army itself. Especially in the Thirty Years' War, armies often roamed from one fortress to another without an enemy force nearby, laying siege for as long as their supplies lasted until an opposing army arrived to relieve the fortress. In those situations, circumvallation lines were more suited to the nature of warfare at the time.

In the future, it's unlikely that lines of circumvallation will be used often, unless the enemy's field forces are very weak, or the concept of a war theater shifts entirely to focus on the siege itself. In those cases, concentrating all forces on the siege would naturally make the siege much stronger.

During the reign of Louis XIV, the circumvallation lines at Cambray and Valenciennes didn't prove very effective, as Turenne stormed the lines against Condé at Cambray, and Condé did the same against Turenne at Valenciennes. However, we shouldn't overlook the countless other situations in which these lines were respected, even when there was an urgent need to relieve the fortress. For example, in 1708, despite being a bold commander, Villars didn't dare to attack the allied lines at Lille. Frederick the Great at Olmütz in 1758 and at Dresden in 1760 didn't use strict circumvallation lines but had a system similar in all essential ways. He relied on the same army for both the siege and as a covering force. At Olmütz, the distance of the Austrian army led him to this approach, though he regretted it after losing his convoy at Domstädtel. At Dresden in 1760, he chose this method due to his disregard for the German States' imperial army and his desire to capture Dresden swiftly.

One final drawback of circumvallation lines is that if the siege fails, it becomes harder to save the siege equipment. If a defeat happens a day or more away from the besieged location, the siege may be lifted before the enemy arrives, giving the heavy equipment a chance to retreat by about a day's march.

When positioning an observation army, a key question is the distance it should keep from the besieged site. This is usually determined by the landscape or the location of other allied armies or units with which the besiegers need to stay in touch. Otherwise, it's clear that a greater distance better covers the siege, but a closer distance, within just a few miles, allows both armies to provide each other with stronger mutual support.

Chapter XVIII. Attack on Convoys

The tactics involved in the attack and defense of a convoy may seem straightforward on the surface, but they are layered with strategic considerations that make such operations highly complex. Examining these complexities from both offensive and defensive perspectives reveals a range of factors that influence whether a convoy can successfully reach its destination or fall into enemy hands. To truly grasp the issues at play, we need to go beyond simple tactical maneuvers and consider the broader strategic conditions that make defending or assaulting a convoy possible. Although the defensive aspect could have been discussed earlier, it is crucial to cover both offensive and defensive approaches here, as the principles apply similarly to both situations, with a stronger emphasis generally placed on the offensive.

A convoy, even one of moderate size containing only three or four hundred wagons, presents a unique challenge. Stretching over half a mile, this formation demands significant resources and coordination, and larger convoys can span multiple miles, complicating matters even further. Given the length and vulnerability of such convoys, the few troops typically assigned to defend them may seem grossly inadequate for the task. Additionally, convoys are often cumbersome and slow-moving due to the sheer volume and weight of the wagons, which limits their ability to maneuver or accelerate, making them particularly prone to confusion and delay if disrupted. This immobility compounds the vulnerability of each section of the convoy, as any single point of attack can halt the entire column and create widespread disorder. With these challenges in mind, one might reasonably wonder how a convoy's defense can be effectively managed. Why, in light of these issues, aren't all convoys attacked as soon as they come within reach of enemy forces? And why do convoys that require escorts frequently succeed in reaching their destination despite these vulnerabilities?

Various tactical adjustments have been proposed to address these issues. Templehof, for instance, suggested a method of frequently halting and reassembling the convoy at intervals, though this approach has limited practicality and may only mitigate rather than solve the core problems. Scharnhorst's more feasible approach recommended breaking up the convoy into separate columns to improve maneuverability and reduce vulnerability. Although this tactic may offer some advantages, it still does not entirely eliminate the fundamental challenges inherent in protecting a convoy over a long distance.

The key to understanding why most convoys are able to move safely through hostile territory lies in recognizing that their security often comes less from their immediate defenses and more from the larger strategic situation. Most convoys move at a safe distance behind their own army or, at the very least, far enough away from the enemy's main position that only small enemy detachments can be sent to intercept them. These enemy forces, in turn, must protect themselves with strong reserves, as they risk retaliation if they overextend themselves. Furthermore, the bulkiness of the wagons and equipment makes them difficult for the enemy to quickly seize and remove. Instead, attackers are usually limited to sabotaging the convoy by cutting the traces, taking the horses, or blowing up powder wagons. While such actions can cause disruption and delays, they do not typically result in the complete capture of the convoy. In this sense, the convoy's safety is more a product of its strategic placement than the strength of its escort.

Additionally, the presence of the convoy's escort, though it may be insufficient to fend off a full assault, can still disrupt the enemy's plans and create enough resistance to deter an attack. Even if the escort cannot fully shield the convoy by taking an offensive stance, it can still interfere with the enemy's movements and hinder their approach, adding an additional layer of security. This combination of factors—strategic positioning, the logistical challenges for the enemy, and the escort's defensive maneuvers—shifts the perception of convoy attacks from being simple and straightforward operations to complex, uncertain endeavors with unpredictable outcomes.

Another crucial factor affecting the feasibility of a convoy attack is the potential threat of retaliation from the main army or a nearby corps. The fear of a counterattack can discourage enemy forces from pursuing a convoy, even when it appears vulnerable. This unseen threat often explains why convoys are left unmolested; the enemy is cautious about initiating an attack that could provoke a strong response. For instance, during Frederick the Great's well-known retreat through Bohemia after the siege of Olmütz in 1758, he divided his army to cover a convoy of 4,000 wagons, forming a long and vulnerable line. Marshal Daun, who observed this massive yet exposed formation, refrained from attacking, wary that Frederick could counter with his remaining forces and force Daun into an unwanted battle. Similarly, General Laudon, who was shadowing the convoy, also held back, fearing a strong reprisal from Frederick. Although Laudon approached closely at Zischbowitz, he was cautious not to overextend himself, aware that he was separated from his main army and vulnerable to an attack if Frederick decided to concentrate his forces against him.

Convoys only face real danger when an army's strategic positioning requires it to stay connected to the convoy along its flanks or from the front. In such situations, the convoy becomes an exposed target that the enemy can exploit, especially if they have forces available to launch an attack. The 1758 campaign provides a notable example in the capture of the convoy at Domstädtel. Here, the road to Neiss lay along the left flank of Frederick's position, and his forces were already stretched thin by the siege and by monitoring Daun's corps, allowing the raiders to attack the convoy without fear of reprisal. This example illustrates the vulnerability created when an army's strategic position forces it to rely on a convoy's proximity, which can make an assault both feasible and advantageous for the enemy.

A similar situation arose during Eugene's siege of Landrecy in 1712, where his supplies had to be transported from Bouchain via Denain, effectively relying on a route positioned along the front of his strategic position. This dependency created logistical challenges, forcing Eugene to devote substantial resources to protect his convoys, which ultimately led to considerable setbacks and a complete shift in the strategic landscape.

In summary, while attacking a convoy may appear to be a straightforward and tactically advantageous move, the strategic realities are often far more complex. A convoy's safety is more dependent on the broader strategic conditions than on the strength of its escort, and successful attacks on convoys are rare unless the convoy's route is unusually exposed. Thus, while convoys may seem like easy targets in theory, in practice, only specific situations—where an army's strategic position forces it into close connection with the convoy—create the conditions where an assault promises significant results.

Chapter XIX. Attack on the Enemy's Army in its Cantonments

In the section on defense, we didn't address attacks on an army in cantonments, since cantonments aren't really a defensive measure; instead, they represent a stage where the army is in a relaxed position with minimal readiness for battle. In terms of readiness, we touched on this topic only briefly in the 13th chapter of the 5th book, considering the army's state in such conditions. However, when discussing offensive tactics, it becomes crucial to view an enemy's army in cantonments as a specific target of strategic importance.

An attack on an army in cantonments differs considerably from other types of assaults, both in its nature and in its potential as a highly effective strategic move. Here, we're not concerned with a simple raid on a single cantonment or on a small group of troops scattered among a few nearby villages. That sort of engagement is tactical and involves localized maneuvers. Instead, we're considering an attack on a full army, spread across multiple cantonments over a broad area. The aim of this attack is not merely to surprise a particular cantonment but to prevent the army from forming up into a unified fighting force.

Thus, an attack on an army in cantonments is essentially a surprise assault on an unassembled army. If this surprise is successful, it prevents the enemy from reaching their designated rallying point, forcing them to select a fallback position further to the rear. This shift in position is not trivial; given the chaos of an unplanned retreat, it usually requires at least a day, and often several days, to regroup further back. This forced retreat results in a substantial loss of ground, which is the first significant advantage gained by the attacker.

In addition, while this kind of surprise is primarily strategic, it can also involve an immediate tactical element. As the assault begins, some of the enemy's isolated cantonments might indeed be attacked, though not all, nor even most, of them. Attempting to attack all cantonments would require spreading the attacking forces too thinly, which is rarely advisable. Instead, only the most forward positions, those directly in the path of the advancing columns, are likely to be targeted. Even then, only a limited number will be truly caught off guard, as it's challenging for large forces to approach undetected.

However, even though this aspect of the attack may be limited, it still holds value. Catching some of the enemy's outlying cantonments off guard adds to the overall impact of the assault and creates further disruption. This immediate, localized surprise can lead to smaller skirmishes, confusion, and possibly even minor captures, which together form a secondary advantage in the larger operation.

A third advantage of attacking an enemy's army in cantonments is the opportunity to engage in numerous minor skirmishes, which can inflict significant losses on the enemy. When a large force gathers, it doesn't typically converge at the designated assembly point battalion by battalion; instead, it usually first consolidates into brigades, divisions, or even corps before proceeding as a unified army. These larger formations can't just rush to the rendezvous at full speed; if they encounter an enemy column along their path, they are forced into combat. Even if they manage to win such encounters—particularly if the attacking column lacks sufficient strength—they still lose valuable time. More importantly, since they're already under pressure to retreat toward a safer rear position, any victory they achieve is unlikely to yield further advantages.

In many cases, however, these isolated units face a high likelihood of defeat because they are unable to prepare a solid defense quickly. A well-planned and executed surprise attack on an army in cantonments can thus lead to numerous smaller victories for the attacker, resulting in a collection of enemy prisoners, weapons, and supplies—trophies that contribute to the overall success of the campaign.

The fourth advantage, which is also the ultimate outcome of such a maneuver, is the momentary disorganization and demoralization of the enemy. When the enemy's forces finally do assemble, they are often not immediately ready for battle due to the disorder caused by the surprise and the series of minor engagements. This disruption frequently compels the defending army to yield even more ground to the attacker and may force adjustments to their overall plan of operations. This breakdown in organization and morale is the crowning achievement of a successful surprise on an army in cantonments, preventing the enemy from assembling at their designated location without incurring losses.

However, success in these types of operations can vary widely in scale. A well-executed surprise attack might yield extensive results, while a less effective attempt may hardly be noteworthy. Even in the best-case scenario, the outcomes from such an operation generally don't match those of a decisive large-scale battle. There are two main reasons for this. First, the tangible rewards, or trophies, from an attack on cantonments are rarely as substantial as those from a significant battle. Second, the psychological impact of these engagements doesn't penetrate as deeply or resonate as strongly as that of a large victory on the battlefield.

This distinction is crucial to keep in mind to avoid overestimating what can be gained from an operation of this type. While some view it as the pinnacle of offensive action, both historical analysis and military history suggest that it is not necessarily the ultimate form of attack.

One of the most remarkable examples of a surprise attack on cantonments is the Duke of Lorraine's 1643 assault on the French forces under General Ranzan at Duttlingen. The French army, consisting of 16,000 troops, suffered a severe defeat, losing their commanding general and 7,000 men. The lack of outposts to secure the cantonments played a major role in this disaster, illustrating the critical importance of preparedness even when an army is in a supposedly secure position.

The surprise attack on Turenne at Mergentheim in 1644 (known as Mariendal in French accounts) had effects comparable to a full defeat. Turenne's forces, numbering 8,000, suffered a significant loss of 3,000 men. However, this outcome was primarily due to Turenne's decision to make an ill-timed stand after gathering his troops. This error in judgment led to heavy losses, though Turenne could have avoided the encounter altogether by withdrawing and regrouping his forces with those stationed in more distant locations. Thus, the heavy losses stemmed less from the initial surprise and more from Turenne's choice to engage under unfavorable conditions.

Another notable example of surprise occurred in 1674 when Turenne attacked the Allied forces led by the Great Elector, Imperial General Bournonville, and the Duke of Lorraine in Alsace. While the immediate losses for the Allies were relatively small, amounting to around 2,000 to 3,000 men, this was insufficient to decisively impact their overall force of 50,000 troops. Nonetheless, the psychological and strategic implications were substantial. The Allies, feeling they couldn't risk further engagement in Alsace, withdrew across the Rhine. This retreat aligned with Turenne's objective, although it wasn't solely the surprise attack that compelled their retreat. More than the surprise itself, Turenne's tactical foresight disrupted the Allies' strategic plans, exacerbated by disagreements among the Allied generals and the Rhine's proximity, both of which facilitated their retreat. This event deserves careful analysis, as it is often misinterpreted as solely a result of surprise when strategic missteps and divided leadership among the Allies played key roles.

In 1741, another attempt at a surprise occurred when Neipperg attacked Frederick the Great in his quarters. The main result here was that Frederick, caught off guard, had to engage in the Battle of Mollwitz before he had fully assembled his forces and had to adjust his positioning mid-battle. This case exemplifies a surprise attack's potential to disrupt an opponent's preparation and timing, though it did not decisively impact the campaign beyond forcing Frederick's premature engagement.

In 1745, Frederick the Great successfully surprised the Duke of Lorraine's forces in cantonments across Lusatia. One of the more significant results of this action was the unexpected capture of the important cantonment at Hennersdorf, where the Austrians lost around 2,000 men. Strategically, this surprise compelled the Duke of Lorraine to retreat into Bohemia through Upper Lusatia. However, this withdrawal didn't prevent him from later re-entering Saxony by moving along the left bank of the Elbe. Consequently, without the subsequent victory at the Battle of Kesselsdorf, the surprise attack on its own wouldn't have produced a major shift in the campaign's outcome.

In 1758, the Duke Ferdinand achieved a surprise on the French quarters. This led to immediate losses for the French, with several thousand men lost and a forced retreat to a position behind the Aller River. The surprise likely had an even more impactful psychological effect, contributing to the French decision to evacuate Westphalia later. While this was a tactical success, the primary value lay in the morale shift rather than in any decisive strategic gains.

If we examine these examples collectively to assess the effectiveness of surprise attacks on forces in cantonments, only the first two—the surprises at Mergentheim and Alsace—can be compared to the strategic impact of winning a full battle. However, in those instances, the forces involved were relatively small, and the lack of defensive outposts, typical in that era's warfare, made such operations particularly effective.

The other four examples, although successful in their immediate objectives, fall short of the impact of a fully decisive battle. The outcomes depended significantly on the enemy's lack of resolve and leadership strength, which ultimately determined the extent of success. In cases like the 1741 incident, where Frederick the Great was forced into the Battle of Mollwitz, the surprise did not lead to a lasting strategic advantage, highlighting that an opponent with strong resolve and character can minimize the effects of a surprise, making it less consequential in the larger scope of the campaign.

The most effective organization for such an attack involves several key principles:

1. Attack the front broadly. The first requirement is to strike the enemy's quarters along a broad front. This approach maximizes the likelihood of catching multiple cantonments by surprise, potentially isolating some and disrupting the overall coordination of the enemy army. The exact number of attacking columns and the intervals between them depend on specific circumstances, but the principle remains to engage along a wide area to destabilize the enemy's defenses.

2. Converging columns. Each column must advance with the goal of converging at a specific point, where they can regroup to consolidate their strength. This point of convergence should ideally be near the enemy's designated assembly location or along their line of retreat. The best locations for this meeting point are those where the enemy's retreat path crosses a significant geographical feature, such as a river or mountain pass, which can hinder their escape and amplify the pressure on them.

3. Aggressive engagement. When each column encounters enemy forces, it should attack decisively and with boldness. Given the general advantages that favor the attackers in such a maneuver, commanders should be granted autonomy to act with initiative and authority. This freedom allows them to respond dynamically to conditions on the ground and to press the attack vigorously, which can further disrupt the enemy's response.

4. Focus on flanks. The tactical approach for engaging any enemy corps that attempts to form a defensive line should prioritize turning one of their flanks. By doing so, the attackers can cut off and isolate enemy forces, which typically results in the most substantial outcomes. This focus on flanking maneuvers increases the chances of capturing or scattering parts of the enemy's forces, adding to the general disorganization.

5. Balanced columns with all arms. Each attacking column should include units from all branches of the military—infantry, artillery, and cavalry—to ensure adaptability and effectiveness in diverse combat situations. Cavalry, in particular, should not be overly centralized in reserves; instead, it may be beneficial to assign all reserve cavalry among the columns, as the terrain and tactical needs of this kind of attack rarely allow for large-scale cavalry maneuvers. Even small obstacles, such as a village or narrow bridge, can halt massed cavalry, so dispersing them among the columns increases their usefulness in local engagements.

6. Push advanced guards forward after initial contact. Although the nature of a surprise attack usually requires the main force to maintain a close formation during the initial approach, this caution only applies up until the attack commences. Once fighting has begun within the enemy's quarters and the element of surprise has been achieved, advanced guards—including cavalry, infantry, and artillery—should push as far forward as possible. This rapid movement can deepen the confusion among enemy forces by capturing supplies, artillery, support personnel, and any non-combat units that are still retreating. These advanced guards are instrumental in flanking and cutting off retreating enemy forces, adding to the chaos and maximizing the impact of the surprise.

7. Plan for retreat if needed. Finally, a contingency plan for retreat must be established in advance. In the event of a failed attack, it's essential to have a designated rallying point where the scattered forces can regroup. This measure ensures that an unsuccessful assault does not devolve into a disorderly retreat, preserving as much cohesion and strength as possible.

These principles outline an ideal structure for executing an effective attack on an army in cantonments, balancing strategic objectives with tactical realities. By understanding both the potential and the limitations of such a maneuver, military leaders can better gauge when and how to employ this strategy, minimizing the risk of overestimating its effectiveness and avoiding unnecessary losses.

Chapter XX. Diversion

In general usage, a diversion refers to an operation where a force enters the enemy's territory with the aim of drawing away part of their troops from a more critical location. A diversion only qualifies as a distinct type of operation when its main objective is to pull the enemy's forces away from their primary front, rather than to capture or gain control of the chosen target itself. If the operation's aim includes holding the objective or capturing it, it simply becomes an ordinary attack rather than a diversion.

Nonetheless, a diversion still requires a clear target, as this target's perceived value will prompt the enemy to respond by sending troops to protect it. Should the diversion fail to divert enemy forces, the target's intrinsic value serves as compensation for the resources spent in the attempt. Suitable targets for diversions might include fortresses, critical supply depots, wealthy cities—particularly capital cities—or even the prospect of collecting financial contributions. Additionally, a diversion may support any internal unrest among the enemy's population by exploiting these discontented groups to cause further strain on their forces.

While diversions can indeed be useful, they are not inherently advantageous and can sometimes prove counterproductive. For a diversion to be effective, it must draw more of the enemy's forces away from the primary front than the number of troops committed to the diversion itself. If the diversion only succeeds in drawing an equal number of enemy troops, its purpose as a true diversion fails, effectively turning it into a mere secondary attack. In cases where the aim is to achieve a significant outcome with minimal force, like capturing a key fortress with ease, or if an additional attack supports the main assault, this still doesn't qualify as a diversion. For instance, if two states are at war and a third one attacks one of them, this might be informally called a diversion; however, this is merely a standard attack in another direction and does not need a separate term. In theory, unique terminology should be reserved for operations that are fundamentally distinct in nature.

For a smaller force to effectively draw away a larger one, there must be a compelling reason for the enemy to respond. This means that sending a few troops to an unoccupied point alone isn't sufficient for creating an effective diversion. For example, if an attacker sends a small force of around 1,000 men to move through one of the enemy's provinces that lies outside the main theater of war, imposing financial demands and disruptions, it's clear that the defender cannot simply counter by sending an equal force of 1,000 troops. Instead, if they wish to protect that province from invasion, they'll need to send a significantly larger force to ensure security.

However, one might ask whether the defender could instead retaliate by sending a comparable detachment to plunder one of the attacker's provinces. For this reason, before committing to such a diversion, the attacker must first confirm that there's a greater potential gain—or a larger threat—posed to the enemy's province than their own. If this condition holds, a small diversion can indeed tie up more enemy troops than it originally involved. Conversely, the larger the diversionary force, the more the effectiveness decreases, as a sizeable force (like 50,000 troops) can protect a moderate-sized province against not only an equal but even a slightly larger opposing force.

Large-scale diversions, therefore, are generally less advantageous, and as they increase in size, the operation requires far stronger supporting conditions to be successful. The larger the diversion, the more crucial it becomes to have favorable strategic factors to ensure that the resources committed to the diversion yield a beneficial outcome.

The effectiveness of a diversion depends on several key conditions:

a. Forces that the attacker can allocate to the diversion without significantly weakening their main army. For a diversion to work, the attacker must be able to commit these troops without undermining the strength of their primary force, ensuring they still maintain enough power at the main front to resist any counteraction from the enemy.

b. Critical points within the defender's territory that hold essential value to them and can be effectively threatened by a diversion. These targets must be of such importance that the defender feels compelled to divert forces to protect them, thereby fulfilling the diversion's purpose.

c. A population within the enemy's territory that is discontented with their own government. Such internal unrest can be an asset to the diversion, as the assailant may exploit these grievances to amplify pressure on the enemy, encouraging local resistance that ties down even more of the defender's forces.

d. A wealthy province capable of providing substantial resources, particularly supplies or munitions for war. If the diversion reaches such an area, it not only pressures the enemy to protect this valuable region but also offers the assailant the chance to gain supplies and bolster their own resources, giving the diversion a dual advantage in both weakening the defender and strengthening the attacker.

If only those diversions are undertaken that, when evaluated against these various criteria, appear likely to yield tangible results, it becomes clear that opportunities for effective diversions are relatively rare.

There is also another critical consideration. Every diversion introduces conflict into an area that would otherwise remain unaffected by the war. This inevitably triggers the mobilization of local military resources that might have stayed inactive under other circumstances. This effect becomes particularly significant if the enemy has an organized militia or any system for arming the population. History and experience show that when a region is suddenly threatened, and no preemptive defense has been set up, local officials will often take immediate, extraordinary measures to resist the intruding force. This response can generate new sources of resistance, similar to the onset of a popular uprising or a people's war, and may even lead to one.

It's essential to keep this potential backlash in mind with any diversion to avoid unwittingly escalating resistance that could ultimately backfire.

The British expeditions to North Holland in 1799 and to Walcheren in 1809 serve as examples. As diversions, they were only justifiable because the British troops lacked alternative deployment options. Yet these operations likely increased the overall resistance capacity of the French forces, with each landing on the

French coast serving to stimulate and strengthen local defense measures. While threatening the French coast can neutralize significant enemy forces by keeping them occupied with coastal defense, a large-scale landing can only be justified if there is reasonable certainty of support from a local population hostile to the government.

The fewer decisive outcomes expected from a war, the more permissible diversions become; however, the benefits derived from them also decrease accordingly. In such cases, diversions act primarily as a method for stirring otherwise inactive forces into action.

Execution.

1. A diversion can involve an actual attack as part of its operations. In such cases, the nature of the execution is not unique, aside from requiring boldness and speed to maintain the element of surprise and momentum.
2. A diversion might also aim to appear more substantial than it truly is, thereby serving as a demonstration to mislead the enemy. For this type of diversion, success relies on a keen understanding of human psychology and the current conditions, allowing a skilled commander to manipulate perceptions effectively. The nature of this approach often requires forces to be divided into smaller units to maximize the appearance of a widespread threat.
3. If the forces employed in a diversion are of moderate size and the retreat is limited to certain fallback points, it becomes essential to have a reserve unit in place. This reserve provides a point for regrouping, ensuring that the diversionary force can withdraw safely if needed, consolidating strength for future operations.

Chapter XXI. Invasion

Almost everything that needs to be said on this topic lies in clarifying the term itself. Modern authors frequently use the expression, and they often imply that it represents something unique. The term guerre d'invasion appears repeatedly in French military writings, used to describe any attack that penetrates deeply into the enemy's territory. Occasionally, it seems they mean it to stand as the opposite of a more methodical attack, one that merely tests or "nibbles" at the frontier. However, this usage introduces a rather unhelpful and imprecise distinction.

Whether an attack should be limited to the frontier or press forward into the heart of the country, and whether the main focus should be on capturing the enemy's strongholds or directly targeting the center of their power, is ultimately dictated by the specific circumstances of the war rather than by any overarching system or principle. In some situations, advancing further into the enemy's land may actually prove to be the more methodical and cautious approach, rather than lingering on the frontier. But more often, it simply reflects the successful outcome of a strong, determined attack. Therefore, it doesn't inherently differ from a conventional offensive in any essential way.

Chapter XXII. On the Culminating Point of Victory (*)

A conqueror in war isn't always able to completely overpower their adversary. In fact, in nearly every case, there exists a "culminating point of victory." History provides ample evidence of this concept, but due to its critical role in war theory and its central influence on campaign planning, it deserves closer scrutiny. Additionally, this topic often presents what seem like contradictions, shifting and elusive, which makes it even more essential to analyze deeply and identify its core causes.

Victory typically arises from an overall advantage in both physical and moral strength. This advantage undeniably grows with each victory—if it didn't, victory wouldn't be so eagerly pursued or come at such high costs. While victory itself contributes to this growing advantage, so do its aftereffects; however, these benefits seldom increase endlessly. More commonly, they build only to a certain point. Sometimes, this point is so close at hand that the rewards of a winning battle may extend only to an enhanced moral advantage. Understanding how this dynamic unfolds is key to grasping the nature of victory's limits.

In the course of warfare, each side's strength continually interacts with factors that either reinforce or diminish it. Thus, superiority in combat becomes a relative matter, shifting in response to these influences. Since any loss on one side effectively strengthens the other, this dual process of gain and loss persists, whether an army is advancing or retreating.

To fully understand this, one must identify the primary causes of this shifting balance of power. In the case of advancing forces, the main factors that enhance the strength of the attacker are:

1. The enemy's army typically incurs more significant losses than the advancing force, giving the attacker an edge as the enemy's numbers dwindle faster.
2. The defender loses various static military assets—such as supply depots, storage facilities, and bridges—that the attacker does not have to forfeit, gradually eroding the defender's logistical base.
3. Once the attacker penetrates enemy territory, the defending force also loses control of entire regions, along with their potential to supply fresh military resources, manpower, and support.
4. The advancing army benefits by tapping into these conquered areas, gaining resources from the enemy's land, effectively reducing its reliance on its own supplies.
5. The defender's internal systems and routines—everything from military organization to civil operations—begin to break down, disrupting the coordination and regular function of their defense efforts.
6. Allies of the defending side may withdraw their support, while others might even join forces with the attacker, shifting the balance of alliances in favor of the advancing army.
7. Finally, the morale of the defending army declines, sapping their will to fight and leading them to a state of discouragement where they may lose their grip on their weapons and resolve.

The factors that weaken an advancing army's strength are as follows:

1. The advancing army often finds itself obligated to besiege, blockade, or keep watch over enemy fortresses. Meanwhile, the retreating enemy, who previously had to allocate troops to these tasks, can now consolidate these forces into their main army, strengthening their position.
2. Upon entering enemy territory, the advancing army finds that the nature of the war theater shifts—it becomes hostile ground. Unlike in friendly territory, every area beyond what is directly occupied cannot be considered secure, and this resistance within the terrain adds complications, slowing and

weakening the overall momentum of the advancing force.

3. The advancing army moves further away from its own resources, creating delays in replenishing its strength, while the retreating enemy draws closer to their supply lines, enabling quicker reinforcement and resupply.

4. The threat posed by an advancing army often prompts other powers to come to the defense of the invaded state, which may shift the balance of power against the attacker.

5. Finally, as the danger to the defender increases, the adversary typically makes greater efforts to protect their homeland, while the victorious state may begin to ease its own efforts, feeling prematurely secure in its advantage.

These advantages and disadvantages can occur simultaneously, counterbalancing each other to varying degrees, moving in opposite directions but impacting the outcome in their respective ways. However, the last point—where the defeated may either be stunned into retreat or driven to heightened exertion—serves as a true opposition between attacker and defender and cannot coexist as one cancels out the other. This alone illustrates how the outcome of a victory can vary immensely depending on whether it demoralizes the defeated or spurs them to greater resistance.

Now, let's examine each of these points in brief detail.

1. The losses suffered by a defeated enemy may be at their highest immediately after the defeat, then gradually decline until balance with the advancing force is regained. However, these losses could also intensify daily in an increasing pattern, depending on the circumstances. Typically, with a well-organized and high-spirited army, the former situation occurs, whereas with a less capable force, losses are more likely to continue escalating. Apart from the spirit within the army, the determination of the government plays a crucial role here. In warfare, it is essential to distinguish between these scenarios so as not to halt an advance at the very point where pursuing it with vigor is crucial—and vice versa.

2. The enemy's loss in terms of inert military resources, like depots and supplies, can similarly rise and fall, largely determined by the position and nature of the supply depots they rely upon. However, in today's warfare, this factor generally holds less weight compared to other considerations.

3. The third advantage—territorial gain—naturally grows as the advancing army pushes forward. In fact, it becomes relevant only once the advancing force has penetrated significantly into enemy territory, leaving about a third or a quarter of the country behind them. Additionally, the strategic value of each province, in terms of its role in supporting the war effort, also plays an important role here.

4. Similarly, the fourth advantage, which involves gaining access to the enemy's resources, increases with the advance. However, it is worth noting that these last two benefits do not typically have an immediate effect on the actively engaged combat forces. Their impact is more indirect and gradual, so it's wise not to over-rely on them or place oneself in overly risky positions expecting these benefits to compensate.

5. The fifth advantage—weakening the enemy's internal organization and breaking up their territorial unity—only becomes relevant after a substantial advance. It's particularly effective when the

geography of the enemy's territory allows for parts of it to be isolated, as provinces cut off from the main body tend to "wither" over time, like limbs deprived of circulation.

6. and 7. For the sixth and seventh advantages—loss of alliances and diminished morale on the enemy's side—it's reasonable to assume that they also increase as the advancing force pushes forward. Further discussion on these will follow later.

Now, let's consider the factors that contribute to weakening an advancing army.

1. The tasks of besieging, blockading, and investing fortresses typically grow as an army advances. This alone has a powerful weakening effect on the advancing force's condition and can quickly outweigh the benefits gained. While modern tactics allow for blockading with fewer troops or keeping watch over fortresses with minimal forces, the enemy must still maintain garrisons in these strongholds. Despite these adjustments, fortresses remain vital for security. Often, garrisons comprise many soldiers who haven't previously engaged in combat, yet before those strongholds situated near critical communication lines, the assailant is forced to leave a force at least double the garrison's size. To formally besiege or starve out even one major fortress, a substantial force is needed, often amounting to a small army.

2. The second factor, the need to establish a theater of war within enemy territory, necessarily increases with each advance. Although this might not weaken the combatant force immediately, it invariably impacts them over time. Only those areas of the enemy's territory where small detachments or strong garrisons are stationed in key towns or along major routes can be considered secure. Even though these garrisons may be relatively small, their allocation still diminishes the combat force's strength. But this is only the beginning of the challenge.

Each advancing army has what are called strategic flanks: the regions bordering both sides of its supply and communication lines. As long as the enemy's lines of communication face similar vulnerabilities, the advancing army's weakness on these flanks isn't acutely felt. However, once the army moves into enemy territory, this vulnerability becomes increasingly apparent. Even the smallest enemy operation directed at a long, weakly defended line can create issues, and such attacks can come from any direction in enemy territory.

With each forward step, these flanks grow longer, and the risk posed by them rises sharply. Not only does securing them become more challenging, but the extended lines also inspire the enemy to launch more ambitious attacks. The potential consequences of losing these communication lines—especially in case of a retreat—become a serious concern. All of this adds a burden on the advancing army, limiting its flexibility and weakening its momentum, eventually leaving it in a state of heightened caution and uncertainty.

3. The third weakening factor is the increasing distance from the main supply sources, which makes it harder to replace the advancing force's continuous losses. In this way, a conquering army resembles a lamp: the further the oil that fuels it recedes from the flame, the dimmer the light grows, until eventually it is extinguished altogether.

The wealth of the conquered provinces can certainly alleviate many of the logistical strains on an advancing army; however, it can never fully eliminate the challenges of operating far from home. There will always be essential resources that can only be reliably obtained from the army's own country, and foremost among these are manpower and reinforcements. Even when local resources are accessible, they are rarely available as quickly or reliably as those from home. The conquered territory might not supply funds, provisions, or logistical support promptly, and the uncertainty of relying on an occupied region's resources introduces a degree of instability.

In addition, unforeseen needs or emergencies cannot be met with the same speed and efficiency as they could in home territory. When unexpected requirements arise, securing additional supplies, equipment, or troops becomes a slower process, often hindered by unfamiliar procedures or local resistance. Communication barriers, misunderstandings, and administrative errors are more common, and detecting and correcting these issues in a foreign land is far more challenging. Any of these factors can hinder the momentum of an advancing army, further complicating the benefits of relying on conquered resources.

When a ruler is not personally leading the army, as has often become customary in recent wars, another substantial challenge arises—namely, the delays caused by the need for communication between the army in the field and the ruler back in the capital or elsewhere. Even when the army's commander is granted significant authority, the sheer scope of military operations inevitably brings situations that require higher-level decisions. Communications must be relayed back and forth, which consumes precious time and often leads to delays in vital decisions, adjustments, and reinforcements. Thus, even the most capable general, if distanced from the primary decision-maker, is limited by the slow process of obtaining necessary orders or approvals.

4. Another significant factor in the strength or vulnerability of an advancing army is the shifting nature of political alliances. Any changes in alliances, whether beneficial or detrimental to the advancing power, tend to correlate directly with the progress of their campaign. The nature of these shifts depends on existing political interests, regional alliances, cultural affinities, and the inclinations of influential leaders, ministers, and statesmen. Generally speaking, when a powerful state with numerous minor allies is defeated, these allies are likely to break off their alliance quickly, strengthening the victor with each successive triumph. However, if the defeated state is small, especially if its very survival appears at risk, nearby powers may be inclined to come to its aid. Even states that initially contributed to its weakened position might step in to prevent its complete downfall, fearing a major shift in the regional balance of power.

5. The increased resistance from the enemy that is provoked by an advancing attack is another significant factor. Sometimes, the shock of defeat paralyzes the enemy, leaving them demoralized and prone to drop their weapons in despair. At other times, the effect is quite the opposite: a surge of nationalistic fervor and determination drives them to rally with renewed intensity, making their resistance stronger after the initial defeat than it was before. Predicting whether a population will respond with submission or renewed energy depends on several factors, including the character of the people, the resilience of their government, the country's geographical nature, and its political alliances.

The influence of these last two points alone—the potential for either increased resistance or demoralization—creates vastly different paths in planning military campaigns. Some commanders, overly cautious and obsessed with method, can squander their advantage by advancing too conservatively, while others, impulsively pushing forward without careful thought, risk disaster by overextending.

Moreover, there is often a tendency among the victorious forces to relax once the immediate threat has passed. This is precisely when sustained effort is needed to secure and expand the initial success. Reviewing these opposing dynamics, the likely conclusion is that an advancing army, as it progresses deeper into enemy territory, gradually erodes the initial advantage it brought into the campaign or gained through victory.

This naturally raises a crucial question: if advancing tends to reduce the initial advantage, why does a conqueror continue to push forward after a victory? Is pressing the offensive genuinely an extension of the initial victory, or would it be wiser to consolidate gains before they diminish?

The answer lies in understanding that military superiority is a means, not the ultimate goal. The real objective is to subdue the enemy or to capture enough of their territory to force advantageous peace terms. Even if complete conquest is the goal, each advance may diminish the advantage, but that doesn't imply the advantage will disappear before the enemy is defeated. The enemy might collapse while there is still some advantage left, and if the conqueror's superiority must be spent down to its last reserves to achieve this, then it would be a mistake to hold back.

Thus, the advantage we hold or gain in war is the means to an end, and it must be used to achieve that end. However, it's essential to gauge the limits of this advantage to avoid overextending and turning potential gains into ruinous losses.

It's unnecessary to provide specific historical examples to demonstrate how strategic advantage often depletes during an extended offensive. Instead, the sheer number of examples in military history prompted the need to examine these causes. Only since Napoleon has it been possible to observe campaigns between civilized nations where uninterrupted advantage led to an opponent's total defeat. Previously, campaigns typically ended with the victorious army seeking a point where it could maintain equilibrium, ceasing its advance to hold its position, or in some cases even retreating. This "culminating point of victory" will likely reappear in future wars where total enemy overthrow isn't the aim, as most wars will still fall into this category. The practical goal in planning any single campaign is identifying the point where the offensive must shift to the defensive.

Overstepping this point doesn't merely waste resources without further gains; it becomes a self-destructive move that triggers a reaction. Such reactions, based on universal experience, yield disproportionately negative results. This principle is so well-documented and straightforward that we needn't delve into its causes in depth. Fundamentally, the inability to secure control over newly conquered territories and the devastating impact of a serious loss—when a fresh victory was anticipated—are key factors. Psychological forces then come into play, with the advancing army's courage sometimes verging on recklessness, while the defeated side experiences extreme morale collapse. Losses during retreat are intensified by these dynamics, leaving the formerly successful army grateful if it can retreat with only a loss of its gains and not any of its own territory.

At this point, we need to address an apparent contradiction.

It's commonly assumed that as long as the offensive push continues, the attacker must still hold the advantage. Further, it is believed that once the offensive naturally transitions into the defensive—considered a stronger form of warfare—the risk of becoming unexpectedly weaker should diminish. Yet historical examples show that the point of greatest vulnerability often coincides precisely with the moment when the offense ceases and turns into defense. The cause of this lies in understanding the inherent strengths of the defensive form of war.

The superiority of the defensive typically arises from four main factors:

1. The effective use of terrain,
2. The advantage of a prepared war theater,
3. The support of the local population, and
4. The benefit of the state of expectancy.

However, these factors are not consistently present or equally effective in every defensive situation, which means one defense may differ greatly from another. This inconsistency is especially apparent when defense follows an exhausting offensive campaign, where the defender's theater of war is often located at the peak of an advancing triangle thrust deep into enemy territory. Under such conditions, of the four defensive strengths, only the use of terrain remains relatively intact. The other factors are significantly weakened: the advantage of a prepared war theater generally disappears, popular support becomes unreliable or even turns against the defender, and the benefit of expectancy is greatly diminished.

A closer look at the last factor, the state of expectancy, provides additional insight. Often, in warfare, a delicate balance or "equilibrium" can develop where both sides hesitate to take the initiative, leading to prolonged standoffs. This hesitation often favors the defender, who gains from waiting, as it slows the opponent's progress and minimizes risks. However, when the defender has already made an offensive push that disrupts this balance, inflicts damage on the enemy, and stirs them into action, the chances of the enemy remaining passive are reduced. A defensive stance in conquered territory can feel more provocative than one on home soil, as it implies the potential for further attacks. In this way, an offensive element is embedded within the defensive stance, weakening its effect. For instance, the stillness that Marshal Daun allowed Frederick II in Silesia and Saxony is something he would likely never have permitted had Frederick entered Bohemia.

From this, it becomes clear that a defensive position taken after an offensive thrust loses much of the defensive's natural advantage. It lacks the core principles that typically give the defender the upper hand, and thus it can no longer provide the same level of superiority over the attacker.

No campaign is purely offensive or defensive. Even in a primarily defensive campaign, there are occasional offensive maneuvers; similarly, in an offensive campaign, there are intervals where both armies adopt a defensive posture. Additionally, any offensive that doesn't conclude with a peace settlement will eventually require a defensive stance to hold the ground gained.

This paradoxically means that the defensive posture itself contributes to the decline of the offensive's strength. Far from being an abstract notion, this is a central disadvantage of an offensive campaign, as it ultimately reduces the attacking force to a vulnerable defensive position once the offensive momentum subsides.

This perspective clarifies how the initial advantage between the offensive and defensive gradually decreases until it can vanish entirely—and, for a short time, may even turn into a disadvantage for the attacker.

To make this clearer, let's consider an analogy from nature: every force in the physical world requires a certain amount of time to exert its effect. A force that can stop a moving body when applied gradually may be overcome if there's not enough time to apply it fully. This principle from the physical world offers a useful analogy for human behavior and decision-making. Once our thoughts and intentions are set in a certain direction, not every influence—no matter how strong—is enough to halt or change that direction immediately. Instead, time, calm, and lasting sensory impressions are often needed to bring about a shift in perspective.

The same principle applies in war. When an army's focus is fixed on a specific objective, or its attention has turned toward a point of retreat, the natural tendencies to restrain in one scenario and to pursue in another don't immediately exert their full force. As events continue to unfold, an army may find itself pushed forward by momentum, surpassing the equilibrium point or the "culminating point of victory" without realizing it. The exhaustion of resources might even become secondary to the sheer will to press on; much like a horse struggling up a hill, the advancing force can find it harder to halt than to keep moving forward. Thus, an attacker can unknowingly cross the point where stopping would have allowed them to consolidate their gains and maintain a balance, reaching instead a vulnerable position beyond it.

Identifying this crucial point is essential when planning a campaign, both for the attacker, to avoid overextending (or "overdrawing" their resources, as it were), and for the defender, to recognize when the attacker has made this error and to capitalize on it.

When we consider all the variables a commander must weigh, the challenge becomes evident. The commander can only assess the tendencies and impact of each crucial factor by analyzing a host of other interrelated and distant influences, often relying on educated guesses. They must, to some extent, "guess" whether the enemy's army, after an initial defeat, will rally and grow stronger or, like a fragile glass, shatter with further pressure. They must estimate how deeply the disruption of resources or the interruption of communication will affect the enemy's strength. They must also judge whether the shock of a significant blow will leave the enemy paralyzed or, like a wounded bull, provoke them to a fierce counterattack. Finally, the commander must speculate on how outside powers might respond—whether they'll be cowed into submission or stirred to action, and which alliances might dissolve or form as a result. With all these uncertainties and more, the commander's judgment must be as precise as a marksman's aim. It's an immense mental task, requiring clarity and insight.

It's no wonder that most generals prefer to hold back rather than risk pressing too far. Conversely, those driven by boldness and a strong sense of initiative often surpass this critical point and fail to achieve their goals. True success, however, lies in accomplishing great feats with limited resources, in balancing risk with opportunity, and in skillfully gauging the moment to press forward or to hold back. Only then can a general be said to have truly hit the mark.

Book VIII. Plan Of War

Chapter I. Introduction

In the chapter on the essence and objectives of war, we began with an overarching view of its fundamental concept, examining its broader context and interconnections. This allowed us to establish a solid foundation, offering an initial understanding of war's purpose and dynamics. In that discussion, we also acknowledged the multitude of challenges that arise in comprehending war, while deferring a more detailed exploration of those challenges. Ultimately, we concluded that the primary aim of warfare is the defeat of the enemy—specifically, the dismantling of their combat strength. This conclusion enabled us to assert in the following chapter that combat itself is the exclusive means through which war pursues its goals. With this, we believe we achieved an accurate initial perspective on the nature of war.

Having now examined in detail each significant aspect and form of military activity that lies outside of direct combat, we have sought to assess their value, drawing insights both from the intrinsic nature of warfare and the vast lessons of military history. This process has allowed us to eliminate ambiguous and misleading notions that often accompany discussions on warfare. Our aim has been to highlight the ultimate goal of military action—the destruction of the enemy's combat force—as the essential, universal objective of war. Now, as we shift focus back to war in its entirety to discuss the Plan of War and campaign strategy, we find it necessary to revisit the foundational ideas introduced in the first book.

In these upcoming chapters, which address the entirety of war, we will cover the essence of strategy in its most comprehensive and consequential forms. We now enter the core of strategic thought, where all facets converge, but we approach this with a sense of trepidation, fully aware of the task's complexity.

On the one hand, the conduct of war can appear deceptively simple. We read accounts and hear the great generals speak of it in remarkably straightforward, succinct terms. Despite commanding immense armies with tens or even hundreds of thousands of soldiers, they describe managing the machinery of war as if it were an extension of themselves, so that the monumental undertaking of war resembles, in their words, a duel on a grand scale. Their decisions often seem based on a few clear ideas or momentary insights, and their approach seems light, assured, and seemingly effortless.

Yet, on the other hand, the reality of war presents a vast and complex array of elements for consideration. There are innumerable factors to evaluate, threads of influence that extend indefinitely, and countless possible combinations of actions. When we contemplate the theory's responsibility to organize this complexity systematically—with clarity, depth, and a consistent logic—it becomes daunting. We fear that, in attempting to encapsulate the full scope of warfare, we may end up trapped in a maze of pedantic dogma, caught in the depths of overly detailed and abstract concepts. Such an approach could risk losing the essential, intuitive grasp that defines the truly exceptional military leaders, those with a natural "coup d'œil"—that ability to grasp the entirety of a situation with simplicity and ease.

If theoretical work were to fall into such an overly rigid, dogmatic approach, it would ultimately alienate those it aims to serve—the strategic geniuses—and would fade into obscurity. Yet this coup d'œil, this intuitive way of seeing and understanding the whole structure of war, is itself the heart of effective command. It embodies the freedom of thought that enables a commander to master circumstances rather than be mastered by them. This freedom of mind is essential for truly commanding events, and without it, strategic theory would lose relevance.

Thus, we proceed with some caution, following the method we originally set out for ourselves. Theory's role is to illuminate the intricate landscape of war, making it easier for the mind to navigate. Theory must weed out the errors that have taken root, clarify the interrelationships among elements, and distinguish what is truly significant from what is trivial. When ideas crystallize naturally into principles, and when they align into clear guidelines, it is theory's task to highlight these, not to impose them artificially.

In sum, theory should aim to reveal the structure of war without confining it, illuminating the principles that naturally arise from the subject itself. This way, theory can aid the strategist, preserving that essential freedom of thought that is the hallmark of great commanders.

Whatever insights the mind gains from delving into the core ideas and fundamental concepts of warfare, it is these sparks of understanding that Theory offers as its true benefit. Theory does not provide formulas that yield definite solutions, nor does it attempt to limit the mind's journey along a narrow path bounded by rigid Principles. Instead, it encourages the mind to observe the full spectrum of elements and their relationships, giving it the freedom to rise to the higher realms of action. Here, the strategist acts not by rigid calculation alone but by drawing on the full measure of their inner resources, fusing all these energies into one powerful and intuitive grasp of truth.

In this way, Theory seeks to prepare the mind to perceive the True and the Right as a singular, vivid realization—a realization that emerges under the combined force of all these insights. This clear understanding feels almost more like an instinctive feeling than a product of rational thought, as if it were an innate sense rather than a logical conclusion. Theory, then, does not dictate or restrict; it illuminates and liberates, helping the mind to see the broader picture and enabling it to respond with the depth and unity of insight that only an unfettered vision can provide.

Chapter II. Absolute and Real War

The Plan of War encompasses the entire Military Act, binding its actions into a unified whole with a single, definitive objective. In this unity, all specific aims and operations must be subsumed under one overarching purpose. Ideally, no war should begin—nor would one be launched by rational actors—without first clarifying the intended outcome and the means to achieve it. The first question to ask is what final result is to be secured, and the second is what interim goals will guide the way. This primary purpose not only shapes the entire trajectory of the war but also dictates the scale of resources and intensity of efforts required. Its impact reverberates down to the smallest action.

We previously noted that the ultimate aim of war is the defeat of the enemy, a goal that lies at the core of warfare's philosophical essence. From a theoretical standpoint, this must be true for both belligerents, which implies that there is no true cessation in military action until one side is decisively subdued and peace achieved only upon one party's defeat.

In our discussion on the suspension of hostilities, we explained that while the principle of absolute enmity might suggest continuous combat, the practicalities and complexities of war introduce pauses and variations in intensity. War, as manifested through human motives and circumstances, is affected by numerous influences that temper its absolute nature. This results in a reality far removed from the purely philosophical idea of total annihilation.

In practice, wars often resemble a tense standoff rather than a full-scale collision of mutually destructive forces. Instead of relentless battle aimed at obliteration, each side may be primarily focused on self-preservation, intimidating the other, and striking only when the opportunity arises. Thus, wars often resemble two highly charged entities separated by insulating forces, occasionally releasing energy in limited encounters.

But what is this "insulating medium" that prevents an all-encompassing clash? Why doesn't war adhere to its idealized form? This barrier is the multitude of interests, forces, and variables intertwined with the life of the state itself—each with complex links and consequences for the war. Unlike a clear logical progression, war becomes entangled in a web of political, economic, social, and military considerations. In this maze, the straightforward logic of pure warfare falters, and human decisions, influenced more by impulse and perception than strict reasoning, introduce inconsistencies and ambivalence.

Even if those who declare war could maintain an unwavering focus on their objectives, the many other actors involved in the state often struggle to do the same. This divergence creates resistance and inertia, requiring a strong force to overcome. Yet such force—unity of purpose, motivation, resources—is rarely fully available. This inconsistency may emerge in one camp or in both, leading to a war that diverges significantly from its theoretical ideal, resulting in a half-formed endeavor lacking internal coherence and singularity of purpose.

In this way, wars often unfold as imperfect, partial expressions of the pure concept, a blend of competing aims and fragmented resolve, rarely achieving the unity suggested by their philosophical origins.

This, indeed, is how we find the nature of war almost universally; and we might question whether our notion of war's absolute character truly has a basis in reality if we had not seen this concept of war in its fullest, most uncompromising form emerge in recent history. The French Revolution laid the groundwork, and soon Buonaparte drove war to its extreme—conducted without a moment's pause until the enemy was utterly defeated, with counterattacks following with equally relentless force. Isn't it inevitable, then, that this modern example would lead us back to viewing war as it was originally conceived, with all its uncompromising conclusions?

But this raises a fundamental question: should we now be satisfied with this view and judge all wars by it, regardless of how much they may differ from it? Should we develop all theoretical principles based on this idealized notion alone?

We must answer this question clearly, for we can't offer reliable insights on the Plan of War until we decide whether war must always take this pure, absolute form, or whether it can legitimately vary. If we conclude that war should always align with this extreme model, our Theory will be simpler, more necessary, and more consistent. However, such a stance would require us to dismiss the reality of almost all historical wars, from Alexander's campaigns to those just before Buonaparte, with the possible exception of a few Roman campaigns. Rejecting this broad swath of history seems unreasonable and even presumptuous. Furthermore, we would have to acknowledge the possibility that a very different kind of war could emerge within the next decade—one that diverges from this rigorous Theory due to specific circumstances.

Thus, we are compelled to recognize war as it truly is, shaped not purely by its ideal form but by the mixture of factors that influence it: the inertia and friction inherent in all its parts, the inconsistency, indecision, and human apprehension. We must acknowledge that the form war takes is influenced not by a perfectly calculated alignment of all its relations, but rather by the dominant ideas, feelings, and circumstances of the time. Even Buonaparte's campaigns, though they approached the absolute model of war, were molded by these surrounding forces.

If we accept that war's character and direction emerge from the dominance of certain factors over others, rather than a logical synthesis of all its influences, then we see that war inevitably involves a play of possibilities and probabilities, good and bad fortune, where strict logical reasoning often falls short. This means that war can vary in intensity—being more or less "war" depending on the circumstances.

Theory must acknowledge this variability, yet its role remains to give precedence to the absolute form of war. This ideal should serve as the guiding point, so that anyone seeking guidance from theory becomes accustomed to keeping this uncompromising form in view. It serves as the benchmark against which to measure expectations and caution, allowing the strategist to approach it where feasible or required.

Just as a fundamental idea underpins our thoughts and actions, imbuing them with a particular tone or character even when the immediate details come from entirely different considerations, so too does this guiding principle color the strategist's understanding of war. This principle shapes the strategist's view, much like a painter chooses a color tone for the background of a painting, imparting a unified depth and character to the whole.

Theory owes a great debt to the most recent wars for its newfound effectiveness. Without these vivid examples of the unleashed destructive potential of absolute war, theoretical discourse alone might have fallen on deaf ears; no amount of reasoning would have convinced people of the reality that we have now all witnessed firsthand.

Would Prussia, for example, have dared to push into France in 1798 with a force of 70,000 if it had foreseen that a failure could provoke such a powerful reaction that it would shatter the long-standing balance of power across Europe? Or would Prussia, in 1806, have committed 100,000 troops against France if it had anticipated that a single shot could ignite a spark deep within the powder keg, setting off an explosion that would engulf and consume it?

These questions reflect the humbling lessons learned from the overwhelming consequences of such actions, where miscalculations unleashed forces far beyond those expected, forces that transformed not only the war itself but also the political and social landscape of Europe. Theory, now informed by these catastrophic examples, can guide us more effectively, grounded in the harsh reality that what once seemed implausible is now undeniable.

Chapter III.

Depending on whether we consider the absolute form of war or a more realistic variant, our understanding of its outcomes shifts accordingly. In the absolute form, where each event is driven by its natural, necessary cause, events unfold in rapid succession without pause; there is, metaphorically, no neutral ground. Due to the chain of reactions inherent in war and the interconnectedness of each combat, the entire sequence of engagements forms a continuous line. Each victory has its culminating point, beyond which losses and setbacks begin to arise. In this absolute view, all of these natural dynamics in warfare converge to produce a singular outcome—the final result. Until this ultimate outcome is achieved, nothing is definitively decided, gained, or lost. Here, the proverb holds true: "the end crowns the work." In this sense, war is an indivisible whole; each individual outcome (or subordinate result) holds value only in its contribution to this larger aim.

Take, for instance, Napoleon's conquest of Moscow and a substantial portion of Russia in 1812. These successes held no intrinsic value for him unless they secured the peace he sought. These gains were merely parts of his larger campaign plan; one critical element remained: the complete destruction of the Russian army. Had this final element been achieved alongside his other successes, peace would have been nearly assured. However, Napoleon missed the opportunity to destroy the Russian army at the decisive moment, and he was never able to regain that chance, rendering his initial victories not only meaningless but ultimately disastrous for his campaign.

In this perspective, war's outcomes are interconnected to the extreme, forming an inseparable chain where each part relies on and enhances the next. This view contrasts sharply with another, which considers war as a series of isolated outcomes, where each result stands alone without bearing on what follows—much like a sequence of independent games. In this view, each result is like a separate counter, collected one after another, with the total sum alone determining the overall outcome. Here, previous victories or losses have no impact on the battles that follow, reducing war to a series of individual, self-contained engagements.

Just as the first perspective on war—the idea of an absolute and interconnected process—draws its validity from the inherent nature of war, we also find support for the second view in history. Countless instances show that minor or moderate victories could be gained without committing to an overwhelming or unmanageable series of consequences. As the context of war becomes increasingly complex and moderated, these types of limited gains become more common. Yet, just as no war fully embodies the absolute, interconnected model, no war completely aligns with the view of isolated engagements, where each result stands alone without bearing on future actions. In practice, both perspectives coexist, each offering useful insights in different scenarios.

If we adhere to the first perspective, we must recognize the necessity of approaching every war as a unified whole from the outset. Each decision and move should ultimately align toward a single overarching objective. A commander who adopts this view must always keep this end goal in sight, ensuring that every action aligns with the final purpose.

However, if we consider the second perspective, pursuing smaller, more immediate gains without strictly linking them to the broader campaign is an option, leaving future developments open to adaptation as the situation evolves.

Neither of these views is without merit, and theory cannot dismiss either one entirely. Theory should, however, prioritize the first view as a foundational principle, using the second perspective as a conditional adjustment justified by the situation.

For example, when Frederick the Great launched offensives from Silesia and Saxony into Austria in 1742, 1744, 1757, and 1758, he did so not with the goal of permanently conquering Austria but rather to gain time and bolster his own strength. His objectives were smaller, allowing him to pursue them without risking Prussia's survival. Conversely, if Prussia in 1806 or Austria in 1805 and 1809 had sought to drive the French back across the Rhine without first considering the potential series of events their initial moves could trigger—whether leading to success or setback—they would have failed to approach the campaign sensibly. In these cases, it was essential for them to visualize the chain of events that might unfold to ensure they could pursue victory without jeopardizing their position, or, in the event of defeat, understand where they could effectively counter the enemy's advances.

Frederick's 1757 campaign provides further context. Had he won the Battle of Kolin and captured the main Austrian army and its two field marshals at Prague, he might then have considered advancing on Vienna itself to compel the Austrian court to seek peace. Such a decisive victory would have been extraordinary for the time, similar in scale and impact to some modern achievements, and particularly striking given the disparity between Prussia and Austria. But this outcome was beyond Frederick's original expectations. His initial offensive strategy aimed to secure limited gains, not an outright victory over Austria. Encircling and capturing the Austrian army in Prague was an outcome beyond his initial calculations, made possible only by the Austrian army's strategic missteps near Prague. This extraordinary turn of events, though, does not contradict his broader approach, which focused on realistic, manageable gains rather than attempting to dismantle Austria entirely.

A careful examination of history reveals the key differences between these two forms of warfare. During the Silesian Wars in the eighteenth century, war was still largely an affair managed by state cabinets, where the general populace participated only as passive instruments. By contrast, at the beginning of the nineteenth century, the people on both sides played an active and significant role. The generals opposing Frederick the Great acted under strict orders and were largely characterized by caution, while Napoleon, leading the French forces against Austria and Prussia, embodied the very spirit of war itself, driving his campaigns with unparalleled aggression and innovation.

These contrasting circumstances naturally called for very different strategic considerations. In 1805, 1806, and 1809, the possibility of catastrophic defeat was not merely a distant concern but a very real, immediate likelihood, requiring strategies beyond the modest goal of seizing a few fortresses or a minor province. Austria and Prussia did sense the gathering storm, as evidenced by their substantial military preparations. However, they failed to fully grasp the scale of the impending conflict or to align their strategies with the transformative forces shaping this new, more intense form of warfare. This was largely because the dynamics of total war were still in the process of unfolding and weren't yet clearly understood. Indeed, it was precisely the campaigns of 1805, 1806, and 1809, and the events that followed, that crystallized for posterity the concept of modern, all-encompassing war with its sheer destructive power.

Theory thus requires that the character and overall design of each war be defined at its outset, based on an assessment of political conditions and likely developments. As the nature of a war increasingly approaches the model of total, absolute warfare, involving the full resources and population of the states in conflict, the interconnectedness of events grows stronger. In such cases, taking the initial steps without a clear understanding of how the war might conclude becomes ever more perilous. The more the probability points toward absolute war, the more necessary it is for the war's strategy to account for its likely scope and intensity. This foresight ensures that each step aligns with the end goal, making it essential to consider the ultimate outcome from the very first move.

B. On the Magnitude of the Object of the War, and the Efforts to be Made.

The degree of force we must apply to compel the enemy depends on the balance of political objectives between the two sides. When these aims are clearly understood by both, they help determine the level of effort each side will exert. However, these objectives are not always perfectly clear, which can be the first source of divergence in the strategies each side adopts.

Further complicating this calculation, the specific circumstances of each state—its position, alliances, and resources—are not identical. This discrepancy can serve as a second source of variation in approach. Additionally, the resolve, character, and capability of each government differ significantly, creating a third source of unpredictability.

These three factors introduce an element of uncertainty in estimating the likely resistance of the enemy and, consequently, in determining the amount of force to be applied and the goals to be set. Since insufficient effort in war can lead not only to failure but even to tangible harm, both sides naturally strive to outdo one another, creating a reciprocal escalation.

Such a race could drive both sides to the utmost limits of their capacities—if such an endpoint could be defined. However, at such extremes, the original political goals may become obscured, and the resources committed may become disproportionate to those goals. In most cases, such an all-out approach collapses under its own weight, as internal limitations on each side check the potential for complete escalation.

Thus, those who embark on war are drawn back toward a more moderate path, one that aligns with the principle of applying only as much force and setting only such aims as are necessary to achieve the political objective. To make this approach workable, the strategist must forgo an absolute insistence on specific outcomes and avoid factoring in remote, unpredictable contingencies.

At this point, the nature of decision-making moves beyond strict science—beyond pure logic or mathematics—and becomes an art. It requires the skill to discern, through a refined sense of judgment, the most essential and influential factors within an overwhelming field of variables. This skill in judgment relies, to a large extent, on an intuitive comparison of factors, enabling the strategist to quickly disregard distant, less relevant issues and to focus on those elements that are immediate and impactful. This intuitive sorting process allows for quicker and more effective decisions than could be achieved through strict logical reasoning alone.

To determine the full scale of resources required for war, we must carefully analyze not only our own political objectives but also those of the enemy. This involves assessing the power, position, and character of both states, the capabilities of their governments and people, and the diplomatic landscape of other states that may be influenced by the conflict. The complex web of these diverse elements and their interconnections forms a tremendous challenge—one that requires flashes of intuitive genius to untangle and make strategic sense of, something that would defy purely methodical study.

Napoleon rightly compared this complexity to an algebraic problem that even a mind as brilliant as Newton's might find bewildering. The immense diversity of variables and the challenge of measuring them accurately make finding the right answer extraordinarily difficult. Although the critical importance of war doesn't directly increase the complexity of the problem, it certainly raises the value of a successful solution. While the weight of responsibility can overwhelm most minds, in those rare individuals with exceptional resilience and insight, it actually sharpens their judgment. Such individuals must indeed possess an extraordinary strength of character.

Thus, an accurate judgment regarding an impending war—the objectives it should pursue and the means required—demands a comprehensive understanding of all relevant factors, including specific nuances of the current moment. Furthermore, these decisions, like all in the military realm, are influenced by the mental and moral qualities of those leading the effort, whether in one person or shared among princes, statesmen, and generals.

To understand the nature of war more broadly, it is useful to examine the varying historical circumstances and motivations of states across different periods. In this respect, a brief survey of history reveals how different cultures and political structures have waged war in unique ways, with different means and objectives.

For instance, the semi-nomadic Tartars pursued war for entirely different reasons. They set out as whole nations with their families in search of new lands, making their armies enormous by sheer numbers. Their goal was either to subjugate or completely displace their enemies. This approach made them a formidable force, one that would have overpowered all before them if it had been possible to blend this nomadic lifestyle with a high degree of civilization.

The wars of the ancient republics—aside from Rome—were smaller in scope. These republics were typically limited in size, and so were their armies, as they often excluded much of the population from military service. The close proximity and number of these small republics created a natural balance that prevented extensive campaigns; their wars focused on ravaging open land or capturing towns to secure future influence, rather than full-scale conquest.

Rome presents a significant exception, particularly in its later years. Initially, it engaged in the same limited warfare with neighboring states, focused on raiding and forming alliances. Its strength grew gradually, not through outright conquests, but through alliances that assimilated nearby peoples into a single entity. Only after establishing control over southern Italy did Rome expand as a conquering power, eventually defeating Carthage, conquering Spain and Gaul, subjugating Greece, and extending its influence to Egypt and Asia. At this point, Rome's military power became immense, supported by its wealth, setting it apart from the smaller republics and even its own earlier model of warfare.

Equally distinctive were the campaigns of Alexander the Great. With a relatively small but highly efficient army, he dismantled the fragile structure of the Asiatic states. Driven by relentless ambition and disregard for the usual risks, he crossed vast expanses, advancing through Asia to reach India. This was something no republic could have achieved. Only a monarch who wielded power with the authority of a self-made commander, akin to a condottiere, could accomplish such feats so quickly and decisively.

The monarchies of the Middle Ages, both large and small, conducted their wars using feudal armies. These forces operated under strict time limitations—what could not be accomplished within a short campaign was deemed unfeasible. Feudal armies were organized around a system of vassal obligations, combining legal duties with voluntary agreements, creating what was, in effect, a loose confederation of forces. The structure of feudal armies, as well as their combat tactics, reflected a culture of individual prowess and single combat, which did not lend itself well to coordinated large-scale maneuvers. In this period, political unity among states was fragile, and individual citizens enjoyed considerable autonomy. Consequently, wars tended to be brief and focused on punitive actions rather than conquests. Armies would raid an enemy's lands, capture livestock, burn towns, and then return home without seeking permanent control.

In this same era, the rise of wealthy commercial cities and small republics led to the employment of condottieri—mercenary leaders who commanded professional soldiers. While effective for some purposes, these mercenary forces were limited in size due to their high cost and often lacked intensity on the battlefield, resulting in staged or ceremonial battles rather than genuine combat. As warfare became a transaction rather than a passion, it lost much of its original danger and intensity, transforming into a formalized service rather than a genuine clash of enmities.

Over time, the feudal system evolved, shifting towards a more defined territorial sovereignty. The bonds uniting states became stronger, and feudal duties increasingly turned into financial obligations. Gold replaced personal service as a means of securing loyalty, and feudal levies gradually gave way to paid soldiers. During this transition, condottieri became the bridge, temporarily serving as tools for emerging powers until the idea of limited-term soldiers was replaced by the concept of standing armies, funded by state treasuries.

This progression unfolded slowly, creating a patchwork of military systems. For instance, under Henry IV, feudal levies, mercenary condottieri, and a nascent standing army coexisted. Traces of the condottieri even lingered through the Thirty Years' War and into the eighteenth century.

The political landscape of Europe during these periods was as complex as its military systems. Europe had fragmented into countless small states—some republics mired in internal strife, others small monarchies with limited, often unstable authority. In such a fragmented environment, no state functioned as a unified entity; rather, each was a collection of loosely connected forces, lacking a cohesive strategic identity or an intelligence capable of acting with consistency and foresight.

Understanding the foreign policy and wars of the Middle Ages requires this context. Consider, for instance, the repeated campaigns of the German Emperors into Italy over five centuries. These expeditions rarely led to substantial territorial gains, nor did they aim for enduring conquest. While such campaigns might seem misguided by today's standards, they arose from the complex realities of the time. It's more accurate to view them as the product of a hundred significant influences, which we can only partially grasp, though their full urgency and vitality were known intimately by those who lived them.

As the larger states began to emerge from this fragmented political landscape, they required time to consolidate their power and establish internal organization. Consequently, their focus was inward, directed toward achieving stability and cohesion. The few wars they did engage in during this transitional period reflected the incomplete unity within these states, bearing the marks of a political identity still in the process of forming.

The wars between France and England mark the early stages of recognizable state conflict, though France at that time was still a loose assembly of duchies and counties rather than a unified monarchy. England, though presenting a somewhat more cohesive front, still fought with a feudal structure and was encumbered by serious internal strife.

France took a major step toward centralization under Louis XI, and by the time of Charles VIII, it entered Italy with ambitions of conquest. By the era of Louis XIV, France had achieved significant internal unity and developed its standing army and state apparatus to a level of high sophistication.

Spain, meanwhile, achieved unity under Ferdinand the Catholic, and through strategic marriage alliances under Charles V, rose suddenly to immense power. This Spanish empire unified Spain, Burgundy, Germany, and Italy into a vast realm, though its political cohesion was far from complete. What Spain lacked in unity, it compensated for with wealth, particularly gold, which enabled its powerful standing army to engage in notable conflicts, including clashes with France's own organized forces. Upon Charles V's abdication, the empire split, giving rise to two great powers: Spain and Austria. Austria, further fortified by the acquisitions of Bohemia and Hungary, became a dominant state, towing along the German Confederation like a smaller vessel.

By the end of the seventeenth century, the time of Louis XIV, standing armies reached a peak that defined much of eighteenth-century military power. These forces were primarily sustained through enlistment and wealth. States had evolved into unified entities, with governments centralizing authority by converting citizens' personal obligations into monetary contributions, amassing significant power in their treasuries. Social advancements and more enlightened governance increased this power considerably, allowing France, for instance, to field a standing army of hundreds of thousands, with other powers maintaining proportionally similar forces.

International relations among European states had also evolved. Europe was now composed of roughly a dozen kingdoms and two republics, making it possible for two states to engage in war without necessarily involving the entire continent—a significant change from the more entangled dynamics of previous centuries. Political alliances and conflicts became more manageable and could be assessed based on prevailing probabilities.

Internally, most states had settled into a clear monarchical structure. The influence of privileged estates and assemblies had largely faded, while cabinets unified in purpose represented the entire state in external affairs. This consolidation of power, combined with efficient military resources and an authoritative will, allowed for a form of warfare closer to its theoretical ideal.

During this period, three military leaders emerged—Gustavus Adolphus, Charles XII, and Frederick the Great—who wielded compact but highly trained armies to elevate small states to the ranks of great powers, unhesitatingly challenging any who stood in their path. Had they faced only Asiatic states, their feats would likely have mirrored those of Alexander the Great even more closely. As it was, they foreshadowed Napoleon in their audacity, pushing the limits of what could be risked and achieved in war.

Yet, while these developments brought greater force and organization to war on one side, there was an inevitable counterbalance: as warfare became more structured, it also faced limitations from the very states and resources that fueled it.

Armies during this period were funded directly from the treasury, which the sovereign often viewed as a private reserve or, at minimum, a government resource separate from the people. International relations, except in a few trade-related cases, largely concerned the treasury's interests or those of the ruling government rather than the public's. The ruling cabinets saw themselves as landlords of vast estates, always eager to expand their holdings but without involving the common people, who showed little interest in these expansions. In earlier times, such as during the Tartar invasions, the people were central to war efforts; similarly, in the ancient republics and the Middle Ages, citizens (at least those with civic rights) played vital roles. However, by the eighteenth century, the people had no direct part in war, their influence only indirectly felt through their collective qualities and characteristics.

As governments distanced themselves from the public and viewed themselves as the embodiment of the state, war increasingly became a government affair. It was conducted with funds from the treasury and with recruits from the ranks of the idle and displaced, drawn both from within and beyond the country's borders. This shift placed practical limits on the resources a government could marshal for war, making those resources somewhat predictable in both size and duration. With these defined constraints, the most dangerous aspect of war—the drive to extreme measures and the unpredictable possibilities associated with them—was effectively neutralized.

Governments could generally estimate their opponents' financial means, treasury contents, and credit standing, as well as the size of their military forces. There was little room for a dramatic increase in these resources at the onset of war, which allowed states to gauge the bounds of their own and their adversaries' capabilities. With this knowledge, states felt relatively safe from total conquest, which, in turn, limited the aims of their campaigns. Shielded from extreme risks, they had no need to pursue extreme strategies. Since there was no pressing necessity to push boundaries, only ambition or courage could drive a ruler to greater risks. Yet these motivations were often tempered by political realities. Even monarchs in command of armies had to treat war as a delicate tool, to be wielded with caution. If an army was lost, there was no easy way to replace it, and without an army, there was nothing to rely on. This necessity for prudence shaped every decision, and commanders engaged only when a clear advantage seemed attainable. Crafting such opportunities was a general's art, but until such a moment arose, the situation often seemed suspended in a kind of vacuum—there was no clear directive, and all strategies remained in abeyance. The original motives of the aggressor faded in the face of caution.

As a result, war became more like a structured game where Time and Chance dealt the cards. War was, in effect, diplomacy taken to a higher level—a form of negotiation with intensified stakes, where battles and sieges replaced diplomatic notes. The primary aim, even for the most ambitious leaders, was to secure some moderate advantage to strengthen their position in peace negotiations.

This limited, constrained form of warfare arose from the narrow foundation on which it was based. Even exemplary generals and rulers like Gustavus Adolphus, Charles XII, and Frederick the Great, commanding equally distinguished armies, found themselves restricted to modest outcomes. This restraint can be attributed largely to the balance of power in Europe. As states grew in size and their capitals moved further from one another, diplomatic efforts intensified, evolving into a highly refined system of alliances, influences, and deterrents. What once had been managed through personal connections, familial ties, and close proximity now required intricate diplomatic engagement. The result was that a single cannon shot in Europe reverberated through the entire continent, drawing every cabinet into the fray.

Thus, a would-be conqueror in this era had to wield a diplomatic pen as skillfully as a sword. Louis XIV, who aimed to disrupt this European balance of power, had built the largest and wealthiest army on the continent but still conducted war in the conventional manner. While his ambitions disregarded the hostility of other states, his approach to warfare reflected the norm. The wars he waged, despite his army's size, followed traditional patterns.

By this time, pillaging and devastation—the hallmarks of Tartar invasions, ancient conflicts, and even medieval warfare—no longer aligned with contemporary values. Such tactics were rightly viewed as unnecessary cruelty that harmed the enemy's people more than their government and risked provoking equal retaliation. It was seen as backward, a form of violence that set back a nation's progress in arts and civilization. Consequently, warfare became more and more contained, focused solely on the armed forces and fortified positions. Armies, along with their bases and fortified encampments, became entities unto themselves—a "state within a state"—where warfare's intensity played out largely in isolation.

Europe, as a whole, welcomed this change, seeing it as an inevitable outcome of progress. Although this view had its flaws—progress does not lead to absurdities nor make contradictions of simple truths—this shift had some positive effects for civilians. However, it also further entrenched war as a matter of state policy, increasingly separated from public interests. Offensive war strategies generally centered on capturing one or more of the enemy's provinces, while defensive plans focused on preventing such losses. Campaign plans were often limited to the capture or defense of individual fortresses, and battles were only fought when absolutely necessary for these objectives. Generals who fought purely for victory's sake were viewed as overly audacious.

Typically, campaigns featured one major siege, or perhaps two in especially active years, before both armies retired to winter quarters—a practice considered essential. During these breaks, each side's strategic missteps were rarely exploited, and relations between opposing forces came to a halt. Winter quarters marked a clear boundary for the campaign's activity, effectively pausing hostilities and dividing the campaign season into distinct, separate phases.

IWhen the opposing forces in a campaign were fairly balanced, or when the attacking side was significantly weaker, large-scale battles and sieges were often avoided. Instead, the campaign would revolve around holding certain strategic positions, maintaining supply depots, and systematically drawing resources from local regions. This approach allowed the weaker side to maintain its footing without committing to a decisive confrontation.

In a period where war followed this restrained model, with its natural limits clearly defined, these practices were seen as entirely rational. Nothing seemed absurd about this approach to warfare, and it was widely accepted as the norm. Criticism of military conduct, which began to emerge in the eighteenth century as people turned their attention to the art of war, mainly focused on the finer details, leaving larger questions of strategy and purpose relatively untouched. There was a sense of prestige and refinement in this style of warfare, and generals were praised for skill within this restrained framework. Even Field Marshal Daun, who played a central role in preventing Maria Theresa from achieving her goals while helping Frederick the Great to secure his own, could still be celebrated as a great general. Occasionally, however, sharper judgments arose, and pragmatic voices pointed out that a force with superior numbers ought to achieve something concrete or risk being accused of poor leadership, no matter the skill demonstrated in minor tactics.

This status quo remained until the outbreak of the French Revolution. Initially, Austria and Prussia attempted to wage war through the typical diplomatic maneuvers and limited military commitments, but these methods quickly proved inadequate. The situation changed dramatically in 1793, as France unleashed an unprecedented force. War once again became an affair of the people, but now on a massive scale: a nation of thirty million people, each of whom identified as an active citizen of the state, was mobilized for the struggle.

The involvement of the French people transformed warfare fundamentally. Where once only the cabinets and armies of nations had been engaged, now an entire nation contributed its full, natural weight to the conflict. This infusion of popular energy meant that the available resources and efforts could no longer be easily quantified or limited. The energy driving the war became virtually unrestrained, erasing the traditional checks and balances and raising the stakes to the utmost level for opposing forces.

Despite these profound changes, the full impact of this "people's war" wasn't immediately felt across Europe. The generals of the Revolution, while formidable, did not consistently press their advantage to its extreme potential. They did not pursue a strategy of total conquest to topple Europe's monarchies. Furthermore, German armies occasionally managed to hold their ground and halt the surge of French victories, delaying the spread of revolutionary success. The explanation for these temporary checks lies in the technical and structural limitations within the French military forces. Initially, these limitations surfaced among the common soldiers, who often lacked the training and discipline of traditional armies. The challenges extended to the generals, who were navigating uncharted territory in leading such vast, ideologically driven forces. Finally, by the time of the Directory, these deficiencies had reached the government level, where administrative issues and internal discord weakened France's ability to sustain continuous, decisive advances.

In this way, the revolutionary forces, despite the new intensity they brought to war, were not yet able to maximize their potential for sweeping success across the continent. It was this technical incompleteness within the revolutionary war machine that allowed opposing monarchies a reprieve, giving them critical moments to regroup and resist amid the changing face of warfare.

After Napoleon perfected the method of mobilizing military power by harnessing the strength of an entire nation, his forces swept across Europe, achieving rapid and decisive victories against conventional armies. The old-style forces, still reliant on limited, structured methods, were no match for Napoleon's all-encompassing, national war machine, and the outcomes of battles were often decided almost immediately in his favor. However, in time, resistance against him mounted in the form of a widespread reaction.

In Spain, warfare began to evolve naturally into a national affair, as local forces mobilized to resist the French occupation. In Austria, by 1809, the government initiated unprecedented efforts to increase its military capacity, using Reserves and the Landwehr, marking a notable shift toward a larger mobilization of the population, achieving a degree of commitment that surpassed anything the state had previously managed. When war reached Russia in 1812, the Russians followed the examples of Spain and Austria, using their country's vastness to their advantage. Despite beginning their preparations later than ideal, the size of the Russian territory allowed these efforts to have a significant impact. This strategy ultimately succeeded, producing a powerful resistance. In Germany, Prussia took the lead, transforming the conflict into a cause for the whole nation. Even with limited financial resources and a severely reduced population, Prussia managed to field an army that was twice the size of what it had mustered in 1806. Gradually, other German states followed Prussia's example, and even Austria, though less vigorous than it had been in 1809, re-entered the war with renewed strength. Ultimately, the combined forces of Germany and Russia, along with other allies, rose up against France, amassing close to a million troops by 1813 and 1814.

This vast mobilization brought a new level of energy and commitment to the war effort. Although the coalition forces did not entirely match the French in terms of intensity, and although certain hesitations remained, the general conduct of these campaigns exhibited a new, bolder approach that had departed from the older, cautious methods. Within eight months, the war's focal point moved from the Oder River all the way to the Seine, and Paris, the proud heart of France, was forced into submission for the first time. Napoleon himself was ultimately defeated and lay figuratively bound, his campaigns and ambitions halted.

Following Napoleon, warfare took on a profoundly altered nature as entire nations became involved. With each side now mobilizing its full power, war drew closer to its fundamental essence, approaching what could be called "absolute perfection." The resources tapped for war seemed limitless, as the enthusiasm and determination of both governments and their citizens knew few bounds. The magnitude of the forces in play, the wide array of potential outcomes, and the intense emotions driving each conflict raised the energy and stakes to unprecedented levels. Victory could only be achieved by fully defeating the enemy, making complete subjugation of the opponent the only acceptable endpoint of such conflicts.

In this way, warfare shed many of its past constraints and emerged in its natural, unrestrained state. This transformation was largely due to the people's involvement in these critical matters of state, a change brought about by both the influence of the French Revolution on domestic politics and the aggressive stance that France adopted toward other nations.

Whether future wars in Europe will maintain this character—where states fight with their entire national power over issues that deeply affect their people—is an open question. It's possible that a separation between the interests of governments and the interests of their citizens might emerge again over time. However, once such limits are breached, they are rarely restored with ease, and it's likely that, whenever high stakes are involved, conflicts will again take on this total nature.

Here, we conclude our historical overview, as the aim has not been to rapidly outline the principles guiding warfare in each era but to demonstrate how different periods had unique approaches to war, influenced by their own constraints and prevailing mindsets. Each period therefore held its own corresponding theory of war, influenced by the context of its time. To understand past events accurately, one must look beyond mere facts and immerse oneself in the spirit of each era. Only those who can do so—who can understand the period in a comprehensive way—are fully equipped to evaluate and appreciate the generals and strategies of each historical period.

Despite the unique nature of warfare in each age, shaped by specific political relationships and military resources, there remains a core of universally applicable principles, and these are what theory seeks to understand. The most recent era, where warfare reached its peak intensity, contains many lessons of general significance. However, while wars in the future might not all take on this grand scale, it's equally unlikely that the vast scope of modern warfare will ever again be completely restricted. Theory that focuses solely on the concept of absolute war would overlook the variety of factors that can shape conflict, dismissing any deviation as incorrect. Instead, theory should aim to be a study of war under real circumstances rather than purely ideal conditions. By carefully examining, distinguishing, and organizing key ideas, theory should always remain open to the diverse causes that can influence warfare and outline broad principles that can adapt to the demands of different times and contexts.

Ultimately, every person or state engaging in war will set their objectives and select their means based on the specifics of their unique circumstances. These choices will naturally bear the imprint of their time and context, but they will also remain subject to the fundamental conclusions that emerge from the nature of war itself.

Chapter IV. Ends in War More Precisely Defined

Overthrow of the Enemy

The aim of war, in its core conception, must always be to achieve the overthrow of the enemy. This fundamental idea forms the basis of all military objectives. But what exactly does this overthrow entail? It does not necessarily require the total occupation of the enemy's country. For instance, if the German forces had reached Paris in 1792, they likely would have ended the war with the Revolutionary government, at least temporarily, without needing to defeat all of the French armies in advance. At that early stage, those armies were not yet strong enough individually to be considered a significant threat. Contrast this with 1814: capturing Paris alone would not have been enough if Napoleon still commanded a sizable army. However, by that time, his forces had dwindled to the point where Paris's capture was decisive in both 1814 and 1815.

Consider another example from 1812. If Napoleon had managed to decisively defeat the Russian army of 120,000 troops stationed on the Kaluga road—either before or after taking Moscow—this victory would likely have secured peace, even though vast Russian territories remained unconquered. In 1805, the decisive factor was the battle of Austerlitz; thus, capturing Vienna and much of the Austrian territories before that battle did not bring about peace. But once the victory at Austerlitz was achieved, even though Hungary was still untouched, the peace negotiations proceeded unhindered.

During the Russian campaign, the full defeat of the Russian army was essential. Without another strong army nearby, a Russian defeat would have made peace inevitable. Had the Russian army joined the Austrians along the Danube and then suffered defeat, the capture of Vienna would not have been required, and peace might have been agreed upon at Linz instead.

In other situations, capturing a nation's entire territory did not guarantee victory, as shown in Prussia in 1807. There, the initial engagement at Eylau, which ended inconclusively, failed to decide matters. Only the clear victory at Friedland, comparable to Austerlitz, achieved the decisive result Napoleon needed.

From these cases, we see that outcomes cannot be anticipated based solely on general principles; each situation is shaped by specific factors that often remain unknown to all but those directly involved. Moreover, many intangible elements—often moral in nature, or even small events and minor incidents that may only be remembered as anecdotes—can play critical roles in determining the outcome. Given this, theory can only advise the following: the essential task is to remain focused on the dominant relationships and power dynamics of both sides. Within these dynamics, a "center of gravity" will emerge—a focal point of power and influence on which everything hinges. The concentrated force of the entire army must then be directed against this center of gravity in the enemy's structure.

The smaller goals always depend on the larger ones; the less significant relies on the important, and chance events are governed by core essentials. This understanding should guide strategic perspective and planning in war.

Alexander the Great, Gustavus Adolphus, Charles XII, and Frederick the Great each had their "center of gravity" in their armies; if their armies had been destroyed, their campaigns would have ended swiftly. In states afflicted by internal conflict, this center of gravity is often the capital. For smaller states reliant on more powerful allies, it usually resides in the allies' armies. In a coalition of states, unity of interests serves as the focal point, while in a national uprising, it rests with the chief leader and the public's opinion. Any strategic blow should aim directly at these pivotal points. If such a blow disrupts the enemy's balance, immediate follow-up attacks are essential to prevent recovery. The conqueror must continue targeting the central mass of the enemy's power, rather than dispersing efforts on minor targets. It's not by seizing a single province with minimal opposition that true victory is achieved, but by pursuing the core of the enemy's strength, staking everything to achieve the decisive outcome. Only this unyielding focus on dismantling the heart of the adversary can effectively bring them down.

No matter what focal point of power our efforts are directed toward, beginning with the enemy's army is the surest approach and, in almost every case, the most essential action. From this, we conclude that several critical factors contribute to the enemy's ultimate collapse.

1. The dispersal of the enemy's army, particularly if it serves as a significant force and central support, can critically weaken his capacity to sustain the conflict.
2. The capture of the enemy's capital, especially when it functions as the central hub of state power and political activity, can disrupt command, control, and morale, impacting both the government and its people.
3. Delivering a decisive blow against a primary ally of the enemy, particularly if this ally surpasses the enemy in strength, can severely limit the enemy's overall resources, support, and resolve to continue the fight.

We have thus far considered the enemy in war as a single entity, which is reasonable for broad, overarching strategies. However, if our goal is the complete subjugation of the enemy by targeting their center of gravity, we must sometimes depart from this assumption and account for cases where multiple adversaries are involved.

When two or more states unite against a third, they form a coalition that may constitute, in political terms, a single war. But the unity within such a coalition varies in degree. The question arises: does each state in this alliance have a separate interest and an independent capability to conduct the war, or is there a single dominant power within the coalition upon which the others depend? The closer the coalition resembles a singular force under a dominant leader, the more feasible it becomes to treat the opposing alliance as one enemy. This simplification allows us to focus our efforts on a single decisive blow. And whenever this approach is feasible, it is the most effective and thorough path to success.

Thus, we can establish a guiding principle: if we can defeat all our enemies by defeating just one, then this single opponent should become the primary objective of the war. In targeting that one, we strike at the shared center of gravity for the entire coalition.

Few situations exist in which we cannot apply this approach by condensing multiple centers of gravity into a single one. In rare cases where such consolidation is impossible, we have no choice but to view the conflict as multiple, separate wars, each with its own aim. Such scenarios typically imply that each enemy possesses substantive independence and the coalition as a whole holds a significant advantage in power, making outright overthrow unlikely or impractical.

Now, let us examine more closely when such an objective is both possible and advisable. The first consideration, naturally, is that our forces must be sufficiently strong for this approach.

1. Achieve a decisive victory over the enemy's forces, aiming to dismantle their primary resistance and destabilize their overall position.
2. Exert the necessary force to follow up on this victory, pushing it to a point where the enemy cannot recover their footing or re-establish their strength.

Additionally, we must be certain that our political circumstances won't lead to new enemies arising in response to our success, forcing us to relinquish our gains in order to fend off fresh threats. France in 1806, for example, was able to conquer Prussia fully, despite this action drawing Russia's full military strength against it, because France was capable of continuing the struggle with Russia in Prussia's territory. Likewise, France might have achieved a similar outcome in Spain in 1808 despite British opposition, yet it faced a different situation with Austria. In 1809, France was compelled to dilute its strength in Spain significantly and might have had to abandon the campaign there altogether had it not maintained a substantial physical and moral advantage over Austria. These examples underscore the necessity of thoroughly analyzing such circumstances to avoid losing what we have already gained, risking a complete reversal of fortunes.

When estimating the strength of our forces and their potential, one might be tempted to view time through a dynamic analogy, as if it functions as a multiplier of force. This assumption would imply that smaller, incremental efforts over two years could accomplish what a concentrated force could achieve in a single year. Such a notion, often the underlying basis of military strategies—sometimes explicitly stated, other times merely implied—is fundamentally flawed.

Every operation in war, like any other endeavor, requires a certain amount of time; there are limits to how quickly one can march, plan, and execute. But in warfare, there is no dynamic interaction between time and force similar to what is found in physics. Rather, the effective use of time in warfare depends on who, given the circumstances, stands to gain the most from its passage. Generally speaking, the vanquished stands to benefit more from time than the conqueror, although this advantage is governed not by physical laws but by psychological and political forces.

The sympathy and favor of the vanquished may attract new allies, while internal tensions, jealousy, or sheer weariness can weaken alliances against them. With time, these dynamics frequently work in favor of the defeated, giving them more chance to regroup or find support. On the other hand, the victor, if aiming to capitalize on an initial victory, must sustain a heavy outlay of resources; this is not a one-time expense but an ongoing commitment, akin to maintaining a vast estate. The forces sufficient to seize control of a region may not suffice to cover the cost of sustaining that hold, which will only escalate as time wears on. Eventually, the demands may outstrip the conqueror's resources altogether, and time alone may reverse the advantage.

Could the contributions Napoleon extracted from the Russians and Poles in 1812—whether in money or resources—have ever matched the scale of manpower he would have needed to deploy to Moscow simply to hold his ground there? Not even close. The sheer scale of forces he'd require, hundreds of thousands more soldiers, could not be supported by resources collected locally. Yet, if the conquered regions are critical enough to the wellbeing of the enemy's unconquered territories—like a cancer that eats its way further in despite external treatment—then the conqueror might stand to gain more over time, even if no additional efforts are exerted. In such cases, if the enemy does not receive aid from elsewhere, then time itself could eventually complete the work of conquest; the remaining portions of territory, left vulnerable and isolated, may collapse without further offensive actions. In these instances, time could indeed act as a force multiplier—but only if the conquered party is rendered incapable of resistance, and any chance of reversal is out of the question.

Our aim here is to clarify that no conquest can be completed too swiftly; rather, spreading the effort across an unnecessarily long period actually complicates and obstructs it. If this assertion holds, it also implies that if we are strong enough to secure a certain conquest, we should be capable of doing so in a single, decisive advance without prolonged pauses or intermediary stops. To be clear, this doesn't mean avoiding short halts to reassemble forces or address immediate logistical needs, but it does mean avoiding an overextended, leisurely pace that risks delay and reversal.

By emphasizing that offensive warfare is best conducted with speed and consistent pressure, moving decisively toward a goal, we believe this undermines the basis of the so-called "methodical offensive." This traditional approach, one that replaces relentless pursuit with a slow, stepwise advance, is often viewed as more cautious and reliable. However, this notion, which seems logical on the surface, contradicts both strategic effectiveness and the historical lessons of rapid, decisive warfare. Still, even for those who understand the benefits of a sustained offensive, the idea of dispensing with the methodical approach may feel counterintuitive. This view, reinforced by tradition and countless writings, is so entrenched that it can initially seem paradoxical to abandon it. This is why a closer examination of the fundamental logic behind the arguments supporting a "methodical" approach is necessary.

Certainly, an objective close at hand is easier to reach than one farther away; but if the nearest objective doesn't suit our aims, assuming an arbitrary halfway halt on the path doesn't make the rest of the journey any easier. It's similar to a wide jump—a short jump is obviously simpler than a long one, but to cross a broad ditch, no one would think to try leaping only halfway.

On examining the foundation of the so-called "methodical offensive war," we find it generally rests on the following key points:

1. Securing enemy fortresses encountered along the way. These strongholds, by their strategic position and potential as supply centers, serve to reinforce our position and deny the enemy valuable points of support. Capturing these fortifications is typically viewed as essential, since each conquered fortress theoretically strengthens our advance and weakens the enemy's ability to resist.
2. Stockpiling essential provisions and equipment. Ensuring a reliable chain of supplies for the advancing forces is critical to sustaining momentum. Without a well-organized supply system, an advancing army risks collapse from shortages. Therefore, the accumulation and proper distribution of supplies form the backbone of this methodical approach, intended to maintain the army's strength over time.
3. Fortifying key positions, such as supply depots, bridges, and advantageous points. By securing these critical locations, we aim to create a series of defensible positions that can serve as fallback points if the advance encounters significant resistance. This process also helps protect vital communication and transportation lines, ensuring that supplies can reach the front without obstruction.

4. Providing troops with periods of rest, whether in winter quarters or during other intervals, to recover strength, health, and morale. These pauses allow the army to rebuild its resilience, ensuring it can continue the campaign with renewed vigor. The colder months, in particular, tend to halt operations, giving armies a natural opportunity to recuperate, even if this extended downtime risks allowing the enemy to regroup.

5. Awaiting reinforcements from the next campaigning season. Fresh recruits and supplies from home bases often arrive annually, especially in wars stretching across years. This injection of strength is seen as essential for replenishing forces depleted by combat and hardship, enabling a renewed offensive with greater strength and morale.

When we divide the course of an offensive campaign by setting intentional pauses, the assumption is that we gain a fresh foundation and renewed strength, almost as though the state itself were advancing closely behind the army to sustain it with constant support. The idea is that each pause recharges the campaign, preparing the army with new vigor for each upcoming phase. While these concepts may lend a sense of security to offensive action, they do not necessarily ensure success. More often, they serve to disguise inner hesitations — whether from the general's personal caution or indecision at higher levels of command. Let us break down these assumptions and look at them critically.

1. The expectation of reinforcements favors the enemy equally, if not more so. Generally, a state can put almost as many troops in the field in a single year as it might over two, making reinforcements in later campaigns a relatively minor increase in strength. In many cases, these pauses afford the enemy time to reinforce and reorganize, leveling the balance of power or even tilting it in their favor as they recuperate from earlier losses.

2. Just as we benefit from resting our forces, the enemy does too. A pause can give the opposing side an opportunity to regroup, recuperate, and reinforce — undermining the cumulative gains made in the earlier stages of the campaign.

3. Constructing fortifications for captured positions or establishing secure supply points does not involve the bulk of the army. These logistical tasks, while essential for secure advances, should not significantly delay the forward push of main forces. Typically, separate logistical teams or smaller detachments can handle these tasks without halting the momentum of the advance.

4. Contrary to common assumptions, supply needs tend to be greater while the army is in quarters rather than advancing. An advancing force often captures enemy supply depots, thereby reducing its own reliance on previously prepared supply lines. So, as long as the advance is sustained, a reliance on fixed supply sources is minimized; only when the forward momentum stalls do logistical needs grow.

5. Seizing the enemy's fortifications is not a real pause but rather a part of the intensified offensive itself. Whether through siege, blockade, or observation, the capture or neutralization of these strongholds is, in effect, a sustained offensive move. The seeming pause is therefore not a strategic lull, but a tactical adjustment within the overall assault, and does not indicate a suspension of the main campaign. The decision between a full siege, a looser blockade, or simply monitoring enemy fortifications depends on specific conditions, particularly on whether a deeper advance would be

riskier if these strongholds were left behind as potential threats. If conditions allow, leaving a stronghold under mere observation until the campaign's conclusion may often be wiser, keeping the focus on the essential goal of weakening the enemy's primary power.

The core aim is thus to avoid letting a fixation on securing minor gains interfere with the broader objective of defeating the enemy. By analyzing and questioning each of these strategic elements, we ensure that necessary measures to fortify and supply the army do not inadvertently slow down the offensive or diminish its impact.

There is a natural hesitation in advancing too boldly in an offensive war, as it seems to risk all previous gains, casting them into potential jeopardy. However, in principle, we maintain that any division of action, any pause, or establishment of intermediate positions runs contrary to the essence of an offensive campaign. These interruptions do not increase the certainty of success; instead, they introduce a level of unpredictability and risk. When compelled by limitations, whether in strength or circumstances, to halt before achieving the primary objective, we contend that resuming the advance with the same momentum is generally impractical. If a second attempt does become possible, then the initial pause may have been unnecessary, indicating that the target was never truly within reach from the outset.

This view emphasizes that time, in and of itself, does not inherently benefit the assailant. Nonetheless, political dynamics evolve year by year, which may introduce exceptions to this general perspective. Changing alliances, shifting state resources, and diplomatic developments can offer new opportunities or demands that weren't present at the campaign's start.

While our analysis here might seem exclusively focused on the offensive strategy, it in fact applies broadly. A commander aiming for a decisive overthrow of the enemy typically does not resort to a defensive stance unless compelled by circumstance. The defensive, if it lacks any proactive intent, becomes a contradiction within strategic and tactical frameworks alike. Every effective defensive approach seeks at some point to switch to the attack after gaining whatever advantage the defensive position affords. Thus, regardless of how large or small the scale of the defensive stance, there remains the underlying intention to turn the tables on the enemy, bringing the campaign towards a decisive conclusion. The defensive strategy, therefore, includes a potential shift to the offensive, with the ultimate goal still being to achieve a powerful outcome against the adversary.

To illustrate, consider the Russian campaign of 1812. Tsar Alexander, at the outset, may not have had the complete annihilation of Napoleon's forces as his explicit goal. But, as events unfolded, this outcome became not only possible but strategically realized. Was it unrealistic, even in the early stages, to contemplate such a result? Hardly. Indeed, beginning the campaign with a defensive posture did not exclude the possibility of achieving a decisive victory; rather, it allowed Russia to absorb the initial blows, bide its time, and marshal its strengths, ultimately turning the tables in a historic manner. In this context, the defensive strategy was simply a phase within a larger design aimed at eventual conquest. Thus, using the defensive at the onset does not inherently conflict with a grand objective; rather, it may lay the groundwork for the eventual offensive and ultimate victory.

Chapter V. Ends in War
More Precisely Defined (continued)

Limited Object

In the previous chapter, we discussed that the "overthrow of the enemy" represents the ultimate aim of the act of war in its absolute form. Now, we will explore what course remains when conditions needed to achieve this aim are not present. These conditions often require either a significant physical or moral superiority or a pronounced willingness to undertake extreme risks. When these elements are absent, the purpose of war shifts to one of two objectives: either to capture a small or moderate part of the enemy's territory or to defend one's own until circumstances become more favorable. The latter is typically the objective in a defensive war.

Determining which of these aims is appropriate hinges on assessing the likelihood of a more advantageous future. This "waiting for better times" implies that there is reason to anticipate improved conditions eventually, and the decision to conduct a defensive war is grounded in that expectation. Conversely, an offensive war, which capitalizes on current circumstances, is more pressing if the future looks more favorable not for ourselves but for the enemy.

A third, common situation arises when neither side has a clear advantage to gain from waiting for the future. Here, the future does not serve as a motivator for decisive action. In this scenario, it becomes clear that offensive action is required by the party who has assumed the role of the political aggressor, the one who has taken up arms for a specific goal. For this side, any delay without a clear rationale is a squandered opportunity, as time works against their initial momentum and aim.

Thus, we see decisions for offensive or defensive war can, at times, be guided by factors unrelated to the relative military strength of the combatants. Although it might seem that the choice between offense and defense should be based primarily on comparative military strength, we argue that following this assumption alone would stray from a strategic path rooted in context. The logic behind this argument, though simple, is robust, and we will now examine whether applying it to actual scenarios leads us in a productive direction.

Imagine a small state confronted by an impending conflict with a far more powerful adversary, and one that anticipates its position will only worsen over time. In such a case, if war becomes unavoidable, shouldn't this smaller state capitalize on the moment when its situation, though precarious, is at its best relative to the future? This would mean launching an attack—not because an offensive provides any inherent advantages, which it often does not, especially against a stronger enemy, but because the state faces a stark necessity. It must either force a conclusive outcome before circumstances deteriorate further or at least secure some gains that could provide leverage in the future. This approach doesn't appear unreasonable; rather, it aligns with practical reasoning. However, if the smaller state is confident that the enemy will soon launch an attack against it, then taking a defensive stance to seek an initial advantage becomes a viable option. In such a scenario, the danger of wasting time is minimal, as the onus of initiating hostilities falls on the opponent.

Now, let's suppose a small state engaged in hostilities with a larger one, where both sides are relatively unaffected by future considerations. Even in this case, if the smaller state has politically assumed the role of aggressor, it should also be expected to advance toward its objectives. If it has taken the bold step of setting a definite objective despite the overwhelming strength of its opponent, then it must follow through with action—that is, engage in an offensive unless the adversary preempts it. To simply wait under these circumstances would be irrational unless the state has re-evaluated its political aims and, at the moment of execution, shifted its stance. This scenario is not uncommon and, in fact, often contributes to the lack of a clear purpose in many conflicts.

These reflections on limited objectives apply equally to both offensive and defensive warfare. For a clearer analysis, we will examine these two forms of war in individual chapters, turning first to yet another aspect of strategic objectives. So far, we have considered modifications to war objectives solely based on internal factors, such as timing and immediate advantages. The fundamental nature of the political aim itself has only come into focus as it pertains to whether the objective is definite and specific. Beyond this, other elements in the political design—such as the scope of demands or the nature of the relationship with the enemy—remain external to the act of war. However, as we observed in the second chapter of the first book, "End and Means in War," the nature of the political objective, the scale of demands on either side, and the overarching political relationship have undeniable and profound impacts on the conduct of war. We will therefore examine these factors in greater detail in the following chapter, devoting focused attention to how these considerations shape the broader approach to conflict.

Chapter VI.

A. Influence of The Political Object on the Military Object

A state rarely, if ever, commits itself with the same intensity to an ally's cause as it would to its own. Instead, it often sends a moderate-sized auxiliary force; should this prove unsuccessful, the ally typically sees it as an indication to withdraw, seeking a resolution that minimizes its losses. In European diplomacy, alliances typically involve pledges of mutual support, both offensive and defensive, but not to the extent of fully sharing each other's conflicts or ambitions. Instead, each state promises to contribute a set force—often modest—without regard for the scale of the primary conflict or its ultimate objectives. In such alliances, an ally might not even consider itself truly at war with the opponent, seeing no need for formal declarations of war or peace settlements in cases where its contingent does not fundamentally engage the enemy.

In an ideal structure, an ally's contingent might be handed over entirely to the primary state, becoming a subsidized force that serves the greater campaign. Yet, the reality is usually more complex. Frequently, the auxiliary troops retain their own command structure, reporting to their own government, which may assign them objectives tailored to its own careful, often hesitant, approach to the conflict. Moreover, even when two allied states join forces against a third, they rarely view the common adversary as one they must confront directly or decisively. Instead, the effort is often treated like a commercial agreement: each state calculates its risk or gain, assigning a force proportional to its level of involvement, typically 30,000 or 40,000 men, and operating as though no more is at stake than the resources committed.

This approach prevails not only in cases where a state intervenes on behalf of an ally with whom it has limited connection but also in cases where both parties share a genuine, substantial interest in the war's outcome. Here, diplomatic discretion reigns, with each party contributing only a stipulated portion of its forces, reserving the remainder for other objectives dictated by its broader political interests.

Historically, this fragmented approach to allied warfare was the norm. It only yielded to a more unified, "natural" form of war in recent times when existential threats—such as those posed by Napoleon—forced nations to embrace a more complete and committed approach to alliances, driven by survival and necessity. During these exceptional conflicts, the shared danger united states into cohesive forces, casting aside diplomatic hesitation. Yet such instances were anomalies, exceptional conditions imposed by unprecedented threats and unmatched power. Indeed, the typical restrained form of alliance-based warfare wasn't a mere diplomatic convenience but a reflection of humanity's inherent limitations and vulnerabilities.

Finally, even in wars without allies, the political motivations behind a conflict heavily influence its conduct. When one state's demands on the other are modest, it generally scales down its military efforts accordingly, seeking an outcome that matches its objectives with only moderate investment. The opponent, reasoning similarly, often responds in kind. If, however, either side misjudges the balance of power, finding itself weaker than anticipated, then practical challenges often prevent greater mobilization. Financial resources may be limited, and moral resolve to escalate may be lacking. In such cases, each side merely strives to do "the best it can," pinning hopes on future opportunities without any concrete basis for optimism. The war thus proceeds in a lackluster manner, languishing like an ailing body struggling to keep itself moving.

In situations like these, the dynamic interaction, competition, and intense force of war gradually give way to a state of near stagnation, fueled by weak and diluted motives. Both parties become constrained, moving cautiously within narrow bounds and with a relative sense of security. This leads to a form of warfare that lacks the defining qualities of direct confrontation. If the political objective takes precedence and restrains the engagement, the conflict may devolve to mere posturing or prolonged negotiations, in which any active attempt at domination becomes secondary to caution.

This shift presents a unique challenge to the theoretical study of war as a philosophical field. The core characteristics of war—its intrinsic violence, decisive movements, and intense struggles—seem to dissipate, leaving theory with less substance to examine or analyze. However, a natural resolution becomes evident: as external factors or diluted motivations begin to dominate the nature of war, it naturally trends toward passive resistance rather than offensive action. The more this passive resistance becomes the prevailing mode, the fewer significant events will punctuate the course of the war, and the less it will require guiding principles or elaborate strategies.

In such a scenario, the essence of military art itself transforms into an exercise in careful prudence, where the primary aim shifts from achieving decisive victories to simply maintaining equilibrium. Here, the focus lies on carefully managing resources and moves to avoid tipping the delicate balance toward a complete and decisive conflict. The main concern is to keep the war in its subdued form, preventing it from escalating into a full-scale engagement that would demand far greater efforts and expose each side to considerable risks.

B. War as an Instrument of Policy

Having thoroughly examined the inherent opposition between the nature of war and the various human interests, both individual and societal, it's now essential to seek the unity into which these conflicting elements merge in real life. This antagonism, rooted deeply in human nature, remains unresolvable by any philosophy.

However, in practice, these opposing forces partially neutralize each other, coalescing into a unified concept: the understanding that war is merely a continuation of political interaction, not an independent entity.

While it's commonly understood that war arises from the political interactions of governments and nations, it is also widely assumed that war breaks off such interaction, establishing a radically different state of affairs subject to its own unique laws. On the contrary, we assert that war is simply a continuation of political discourse through alternative means. By describing it as "mixed with other means," we emphasize that political discourse persists throughout the conflict, rather than transforming into something completely distinct. Indeed, the underlying political dynamics and the primary objectives guiding the events of war remain intact, continuously influencing the course of action until peace is achieved.

It is difficult to imagine otherwise. Does the absence of formal diplomatic communications sever political relations between nations and governments? Rather, war is simply a different form of expression for political intentions—one with a unique grammar, though the underlying logic remains rooted in political thought. Consequently, war can never be isolated from political interaction. Any attempt to examine war apart from its political context is to strip it of purpose and direction, leaving a hollow, senseless form.

This perspective would be essential even if war embodied the pure, unbridled hostility suggested by its abstract definition. After all, the fundamental elements on which war rests—our own power, the enemy's power, potential allies, and the specific characteristics of the people and governments involved—are all political in nature. These elements are so intertwined with broader political interaction that they cannot be separated. But recognizing this connection is even more critical given that real war is rarely a pure, single-minded push to extremes. Rather, it exists as a complex and often contradictory phenomenon. War, by its very nature, is an extension of policy and can only be fully understood as a component of this broader framework.

Policy, when employing war as a tool, disregards the harsh finalities inherent in war's nature, opting instead to focus on probable, immediate outcomes rather than ultimate possibilities. This shift from the absolute to the probable introduces uncertainty, rendering war a sort of strategic game. Each state, confident in its own political prowess, trusts that its skill in navigating this game will outmaneuver rivals.

Through this lens, policy transforms the overwhelming power of war from a weapon demanding a decisive and all-encompassing effort into a more adaptable instrument. The massive, double-handed sword, intended for a single, ultimate strike, is refashioned into a lighter weapon, occasionally even a dueling rapier for parrying and sparring. In this way, policy softens the inherent conflicts war imposes on a naturally cautious humanity, offering a kind of resolution by accommodating war's violent nature to serve as a flexible tool rather than a relentless pursuit of destruction.

When we accept that war is an extension of policy, we see that war's character is inherently shaped by the policies directing it. If the policy is ambitious and powerful, the war it produces will mirror those traits, potentially driving conflict toward its most extreme, absolute form. Thus, this view allows us not to dismiss the pure, absolute concept of war but to keep it always in our perspective as a guiding ideal or endpoint. With this framework, war regains its unity. We can then classify all wars as variations of a single phenomenon and build, evaluate, and modify strategies with consistency. From this vantage, we gain the clarity and solid foundation necessary for constructing sound and comprehensive war plans.

The political element, however, does not penetrate the minutiae of war's execution; for instance, routine tasks like setting up sentry posts or dispatching patrols are not dictated by policy. Yet, its influence becomes paramount in broader strategic planning—whether for an entire war, a campaign, or even a specific battle. Therefore, while policy might seem remote from the immediate actions of soldiers on the ground, it profoundly shapes the overall plan and direction.

This perspective—allowing for the political basis of war without forcing it into all tactical details—was unnecessary to introduce at the outset. For practical purposes, a focus on immediate tasks would have benefited little from this abstract layer of understanding and could have even diverted attention from critical technical details. In the grander scope, however, such as planning a war or campaign, this strategic vision becomes indispensable.

Finding and adhering to the correct vantage point for observing and assessing events is perhaps life's most crucial skill. From a singular, consistent standpoint, we can understand the collective weight of events and retain a consistent perspective that prevents contradictory actions. In planning a war, shifting between multiple perspectives—the views of a soldier, an administrator, a politician—leads to inconsistency and confusion. Thus, the central question arises: if one viewpoint must govern, should policy necessarily stand as the supreme directive to which all else is subordinate?

This question remains at the heart of determining war's true nature and the degree to which it should remain an instrument of policy or embrace an independent identity in the strategic and tactical decisions shaping its course.

It is assumed that policy naturally encompasses and reconciles all interests of domestic administration, even considerations of humanity and other rational matters, since policy itself is nothing more than the outward representative of all these interests in relation to other states. While it's possible for policy to take a misguided direction, perhaps serving only the ambition, personal motives, or vanity of leaders, this issue is outside our scope here; the art of war cannot act as a corrective to policy's missteps. In this context, we view policy simply as the representative of the collective interests of the community as a whole.

The real question, then, is this: when devising war plans, should the military point of view take absolute precedence over the political one—if we can even separate such a point purely—meaning should policy fade away entirely or at least become secondary? Or should policy remain the primary viewpoint, with military objectives supporting it?

For the political perspective to completely disappear once war begins would be conceivable only in cases of wars driven purely by hatred, battles fought for the sake of total annihilation. But, as we have noted earlier, wars are generally expressions or extensions of policy. Therefore, subordinating the political perspective to the military would contradict common sense because it is policy that has initiated the war; policy is the guiding intelligence, and war is merely its instrument. Consequently, only the subordination of the military viewpoint to policy is feasible.

If we reflect on the nature of actual war and consider what has been established earlier—that every war should be evaluated in light of the character and main features deduced from its political origins and purposes—and if we consider that modern wars are almost invariably an organic whole where individual actions cannot be separated from the main body, then it becomes evident that the highest standpoint for conducting a war must be that of policy. War today is rarely an isolated series of actions; instead, it represents a unified effort where each element contributes to and originates from the whole, with each individual engagement tied to the greater purpose. Therefore, the overarching guidance for any major military action must be policy itself.

With this perspective, the plans seem to come from a unified mold, making them easier to understand and assess. Our judgments about them gain clarity, our motivations feel more coherent, and, in turn, our understanding of historical events becomes more transparent and well-grounded. In aligning with policy as the primary guide for military conduct, we achieve a more consistent and comprehensive approach, where the reasons behind decisions are clear and aligned with a broader vision.

From this standpoint, there is no inherent or unavoidable conflict between political and military interests; any apparent discord should be understood as a reflection of incomplete understanding or limited insight. For policy to demand outcomes from war that it cannot practically achieve would contradict the foundational assumption that policy is aware of the instrument it intends to employ. If policy truly grasps the nature of military operations, then determining which events and which directions of military action will best serve the overall objectives of the war is inherently its responsibility.

In essence, the highest view of the art of war is nothing other than policy itself—though policy here does not merely craft written agreements but instead operates through military engagements. Given this perspective, delegating a substantial military enterprise or plan solely to military judgment without political oversight is not only impractical but harmful. Consulting professional soldiers purely for their military opinion on what the cabinet ought to decide in war planning, without considering the wider political context, is an incomplete approach. Equally flawed is the assumption by theorists that a general, once informed of available resources, could devise an entirely "military" plan for war or a campaign in isolation from political input.

Experience demonstrates that, despite the highly technical and specialized branches of military knowledge today, it is still political leadership—the cabinet—that ultimately shapes the general outlines of war strategy. This is not an accident but a natural outcome of the way political considerations are woven into military planning. Political objectives inherently demand insight into alliances, relationships, and motives that purely military perspectives do not capture. When critics argue about the negative impact of policy on war execution, they often confuse the effect with its source. It is not the influence of policy that is flawed but rather a mistaken or misdirected policy itself. When policy is aligned correctly with its goals, it enhances the conduct of war.

Policy becomes a problem in military operations only when it misunderstands the true impact of military actions or expects results inconsistent with the realities of warfare. Just as someone unfamiliar with a language might say something unintended, so too may policy, aiming for the right objectives, mistakenly issue directives that conflict with its own aims. History offers many examples of policy missteps due to an incomplete understanding of military necessities, which underscores that any political engagement with war requires some grasp of war's nature.

It's critical, however, not to misinterpret this as suggesting that a minister of war, entangled in bureaucratic duties, or a highly trained engineer, or even a veteran soldier, would necessarily make an ideal statesman. The qualities essential to effective political leadership—mental acuity, strategic vision, strength of character—are primary. Familiarity with military affairs can be acquired in various ways, but without a balanced and discerning perspective, even experienced soldiers may falter as political advisors. France's unfortunate decisions under the guidance of the Belleisle brothers and the Duke of Choiseul, all skilled soldiers yet lacking political acumen, illustrate this perfectly. Therefore, while knowledge of military affairs is essential, it must be paired with the capacity to exercise high-level judgment and clear political vision to truly align the interests of policy and war.

If war is to fully align with political aims and to be conducted within the limits of the resources available, an effective arrangement is necessary when the roles of statesman and soldier are separate. The ideal recommendation in such cases is to ensure that the chief military commander is a member of the cabinet. This integration allows the commander to actively participate in the key decisions and deliberations of government, bringing military insight directly into political strategy. However, for this approach to be efficient, the government itself, or at least its primary decision-makers, should be located close to the theater of war to minimize delays in communication and decision-making.

Historical examples validate this arrangement. The Emperor of Austria implemented this structure in 1809, and it was similarly adopted by the allied sovereigns during the campaigns of 1813, 1814, and 1815, yielding highly successful results. On the contrary, involving any military officer other than the General-in-Chief in cabinet decisions is fraught with risk, as it often leads to fragmented strategies and diluted action. France's experience during the Revolutionary Wars, where Carnot oversaw military operations from Paris, serves as a cautionary tale. This setup only functioned under the extreme measures of a revolutionary government and should not be viewed as a sustainable model under more conventional circumstances.

Reflecting on historical patterns further enriches this perspective. In the last decade of the 18th century, Europe witnessed a transformative shift in the art of war—a shift so profound that traditional armies suddenly found many of their methods obsolete. The magnitude of this change caught all of Europe off guard, sparking a reassessment of the art of war itself. The surprise felt was not solely due to failures in military methods but to an unpreparedness for a new environment, one shaped by changing forces that lay beyond the old strategic paradigm.

Some thinkers of the time attributed this shock to the restrictive influence policy had exerted over the art of war, diminishing its effectiveness and, at times, reducing warfare to a series of superficial maneuvers. While they were correct in observing this decline, they misattributed it to something incidental—something that, in theory, could have been avoided. Others claimed the explanation lay in the policies of individual states—Austria, Prussia, and England—each looking out for its own interests. But this interpretation overlooked the fundamental issue: the surprise and confusion extended beyond military tactics to the core of policy itself.

The transformative influence of the French Revolution provides a clear example. Its effects on the rest of Europe were less due to innovative military tactics than to a radical shift in governance, civil administration, and societal structure. The revolution upended traditional political and social systems, creating forces that overwhelmed conventional state policies. Instead of recognizing and adapting to these new forces, other governments clung to outdated methods, mistakenly believing their usual measures would suffice against this unprecedented challenge. Consequently, their failure was rooted more in policy missteps than in any military oversight.

In essence, it was a policy failure—a failure to grasp the broader changes in governance, public spirit, and civil organization introduced by the French Revolution—that left other European powers struggling. Their policies were ill-prepared for the seismic shift in both society and the nature of the state, and thus they found themselves attempting to counter transformative forces with tools that were no longer adequate for the task at hand.

Could this error have been identified and corrected by formulating a strategy purely from a military standpoint? The answer is decidedly no. Even if, hypothetically, there had been a strategist so philosophically insightful as to foresee all the implications of the new French forces and to predict even the most distant potential outcomes, it would have been nearly impossible to translate that knowledge into practical action. Policy, had it fully recognized the immense shift in France's internal dynamics and its impact on Europe's political landscape, might have anticipated the scale and scope of the war, along with the magnitude of resources required and the optimal application of those resources. Only through such a far-sighted policy could a comprehensive and correct strategy for countering revolutionary France have emerged.

In truth, the sweeping victories of revolutionary France over two decades can be largely attributed to the political miscalculations of the governments opposing it. The errors first became apparent in the course of the war itself, as the military events shattered the expectations held by policymakers. Yet, this breakdown did not result from a failure to consult military experts. The art of war as understood by the era's politicians—that is, the practical application of military strategy as it then existed, harmonized with the politics of the time—was itself limited by the prevailing policy framework. This established form of warfare, the familiar tool of policymakers, was naturally part of the broader misjudgment, unable to offer insight beyond the limitations set by policy's own view of the conflict.

While warfare indeed evolved during this period, taking on characteristics more aligned with what one might call "absolute" war, these changes didn't result from the French government distancing itself from political influence over the military. Rather, they emerged from a radically different policy, transformed by the French Revolution, not only within France but across Europe as a whole. This revolutionary policy spurred new means and capabilities that allowed war to be conducted with an intensity previously unimaginable.

Therefore, the true alterations in the art of war stemmed directly from shifts in policy; they don't suggest a separation between military and political spheres. Instead, they highlight the essential connection between them. Thus, once again: war is fundamentally an instrument of policy, one that inevitably reflects policy's objectives and methods. It must align with policy's scale and scope, and so, in its primary elements, war is essentially policy itself—an extension of it, wielding the sword instead of the pen but always adhering to the same foundational principles and logical structures.

Chapter VII. Limited Object — Offensive War

Even if the complete overthrow of the enemy cannot be the objective, a positive aim is still possible, and in such cases, that aim is typically the conquest of a part of the enemy's territory. The strategic value of occupying enemy provinces lies in weakening the enemy's resources overall, which in turn reduces their military power while simultaneously bolstering our own. Additionally, by conducting the war partly at the enemy's expense, we gain leverage in peace negotiations, where these territorial acquisitions may be considered a net gain that can be retained or traded for other strategic advantages.

This concept of territorial conquest seems straightforward and would generally be without issue if it weren't for the vulnerabilities that often arise when shifting to a defensive posture after an offensive campaign. In our discussion on the "culminating point of victory," we covered how an offensive action can strain and weaken our forces, potentially leaving us in a precarious position once we assume a defensive stance.

The degree to which our forces are weakened by such territorial gains largely depends on the geographic characteristics of the occupied region. The closer and more connected the acquired territory is to our own, or if it lies within or near the path of our main force, it imposes far less strain. For example, during the Seven Years' War, Saxony was effectively integrated into Prussia's theater of operations, and Frederick the Great's forces were strengthened by holding it, as its proximity to Silesia and its natural alignment with Prussia's defense made it an asset rather than a liability. Similarly, in 1740–1741, Frederick's hold on Silesia didn't overstretch his forces because the region's layout and position meant it only presented a limited point of contact with Austrian forces, especially while Saxony remained under his control. This small contact point also lay in the line of the main operations, further reinforcing his position.

Conversely, if the conquered territory is irregularly shaped, stretching into enemy territory or positioned unfavorably, it can weaken our forces to the point that even a successful battle becomes significantly easier for the enemy or sometimes unnecessary. Historical campaigns provide numerous examples of this. The Austrians, for instance, were often compelled to abandon Provence without a fight when advancing from Italy. In 1744, the French considered themselves fortunate to withdraw from Bohemia without incurring defeat. In 1758, Frederick the Great's hold on Bohemia and Moravia proved unsustainable due to the dispersal of his forces—a situation that sharply contrasted with the successes he achieved with the same army in Silesia and Saxony the previous year. Instances where armies could not retain control of conquered areas solely because of the resulting strain on their forces are frequent enough in military history that additional examples are scarcely needed.

Thus, the decision to aim for such objectives depends on our ability to realistically hold the territory or whether a temporary occupation (invasion or diversion) is worth the cost in manpower and resources. It's also crucial to consider whether a vigorous counterattack might follow, one capable of shifting the balance of power entirely. The feasibility of sustaining such a conquest without risking a devastating counterstroke is always a central consideration, and this critical balance is a key element discussed in the chapter on the culmination point of victory.

There is one further aspect that merits attention. An offensive campaign aimed at a limited objective may not always balance the losses incurred on other fronts. While we are occupied with capturing a part of the enemy's territory, the enemy might simultaneously succeed in taking parts of ours. If our objective does not far outweigh these counteractions in strategic value, our efforts may fail to compel the enemy to abandon their advances, leaving us with a situation where what we gain does not cover what we lose.

Even in a scenario where both sides capture provinces of equal value, we often feel the loss of our own territory more acutely than we appreciate what we have gained. The reason is that when defending our own land, the forces committed to protecting it become an essential, non-negotiable investment. Although this is also true for the enemy, the impact is often more significant on our side, as the loss of familiar ground strikes deeper, both strategically and psychologically. To offset this imbalance, the gains from our conquest must offer a much higher return, or "yield a high percentage" — meaning, the captured territory must deliver substantially more in terms of resources or strategic advantage than what is lost.

This leads to another strategic consequence: an attack with limited objectives requires extra measures to protect areas not directly covered by the campaign, compared to an attack focused on the enemy's core strength. Therefore, a limited-objective offensive cannot achieve the same concentration of forces in terms of time and space as a direct, central offensive might. To attempt some level of concentration in timing, such an offensive requires simultaneous, synchronized advances from as many points as possible. This necessity, however, removes the flexibility to maintain a defensive posture at specific points, which is often an advantage of concentrating forces around a primary target.

In aiming at a more modest objective, the entire war effort becomes more dispersed, with each part requiring support and protection, reducing the operation's ability to focus intensely on a single outcome. This dispersion increases "friction" — the natural resistance in operations caused by distance, delays, and logistical complexity — and introduces more opportunities for chance events to sway the course of action unpredictably.

This decentralized nature of a limited-objective offensive weighs heavily on commanders. Those with a clear sense of their abilities and the resources at their disposal will often feel constrained by these dispersed operations. Commanders may look for ways to escape this inherent diffusion of effort by giving one operation or one point a decisive, preponderating focus, even if that requires taking on greater risks. By doing so, they aim to bring unity and momentum back to their campaign, trying to shape events around one decisive outcome rather than allow the campaign to drift among smaller, scattered successes.

Chapter VIII. Limited Object — Defence

The ultimate aim of defensive war cannot be reduced to mere negation or a passive stance of avoiding defeat, as we have previously noted. Even the weakest defender must possess some point of pressure—a way to make the adversary feel the costs of their campaign and to create a threat against their operations. While it might seem that the defensive side could focus solely on wearing down the attacker, this approach has its limits. If we assume that the attacker seeks a positive gain and that every unsuccessful blow they deal depletes their resources, we might say these failed attempts retroactively benefit the defender. But this perspective assumes an eventual exhaustion that isn't a given in reality. The offensive side is not guaranteed to wear out and cease attacks simply through a series of failed blows.

Indeed, while the attacker grows weaker over time, their position does not automatically deteriorate in proportion to each failed assault. Often, the defensive side is the more vulnerable, having fewer resources and being potentially less capable of sustaining long-term attrition. Even if losses on both sides are comparable, the defender's loss is proportionally larger, given their typically smaller starting position. Furthermore, the defender often loses territory and valuable resources along with every setback. Therefore, without a proactive counterbalance, mere passive endurance—fending off attacks while doing nothing to shift the tide—offers the defender little reassurance that the enemy's advance will ever end. Ultimately, a strategy that relies solely on the attacker's exhaustion risks eventual failure.

Although history provides examples where peace was achieved as a result of the stronger side's gradual weakening, such outcomes often hinge on indecisive engagements rather than calculated plans. This phenomenon cannot serve as a dependable, universal objective for defensive war in a philosophical or strategic sense. Instead, the defender's position must include the concept of "waiting for"—a fundamental component of defensive strategy. This idea assumes an eventual shift in the situation, an improvement in circumstances or a new element in the broader context that favors the defender. If this improvement cannot arise from internal actions alone, then the hope rests on external support—whether through new alliances forming in the defender's favor or through the disintegration of those aligned with the attacker.

This anticipation of change forms the foundation of the defender's strategy when their strength does not allow for a direct counterstrike. But not every defensive war is limited to this passive model; defensive operations can take various forms, as we have defined. Defensive war, by nature, can often be a powerful approach that enables both endurance and, when possible, a significant counterattack. These two approaches—the purely passive defense and the defensive strategy that aims to strike back at a decisive moment—should be recognized as distinct from the start, as each influences the conduct of the defense differently.

In the purely passive defense, the defender's primary goal is to retain as much of their own territory as possible for as long as they can, using time as a strategic asset. Buying time may allow new alliances to form, opponents of the aggressor to emerge, or other factors to tip the scales in the defender's favor. In this approach, the defensive goal centers on stalling the aggressor and preventing decisive breakthroughs. While this can provide advantages at specific points—such as repelling a particular assault or briefly gaining superiority in localized skirmishes—these limited victories typically serve only to delay the attacker's overall progress. Should the defender find themselves hard-pressed on all sides, these small, localized advantages may simply provide temporary relief, delaying but not reversing the aggressor's course. In such cases, the positive objective of affecting peace negotiations may be included in the broader strategy but often remains beyond reach until some tangible change, either political or material, alters the balance in favor of the defender.

When the defender is not excessively weak, small-scale offensive moves can still have a role within a defensive framework without changing its essential nature. These operations, which may involve limited invasions, diversions, or targeting a single fortress, are not aimed at permanent territorial control but rather at achieving temporary gains to offset any subsequent losses. By creating opportunities for tactical advantage, these actions provide a buffer against the attritional costs of purely defensive maneuvers.

However, when the defensive strategy incorporates a distinct positive objective, the nature of defense becomes more dynamic. Here, the defensive approach increasingly takes on offensive characteristics proportional to the scale of the counterstroke it intends to deliver. Essentially, the more deliberate the choice to assume a defensive stance in order to prepare a decisive blow, the more latitude the defender has to set elaborate traps for the adversary. Among these, a strategic retreat deeper into home territory is the boldest tactic, and when successful, it can be immensely effective. This tactic also represents the most pronounced divergence from a passive defensive system.

To illustrate, we might compare Frederick the Great's situation during the Seven Years' War with Russia's approach in 1812. When Frederick entered the war, his preemptive preparations granted him a temporary superiority. This advantage enabled him to capture Saxony, which served as a natural extension of his operational area, thus bolstering rather than depleting his forces. At the start of the 1757 campaign, Frederick sought to press the attack further, a move that remained feasible as long as the Russians and French had yet to join the war theater in Silesia, the Mark, and Saxony. However, when the offensive faltered, Frederick was forced to revert to a defensive stance, ultimately relinquishing Bohemia. From that point on, he focused on reclaiming and defending his own strategic zones, which he managed by pivoting his forces to successively confront the French and Austrians. This maneuver succeeded largely due to the defensive approach he adopted.

By 1758, as the enemy forces closed in more tightly and Frederick's resources waned, he resorted to a limited offensive operation in Moravia. His objective was not to retain control over Moravia or use it as a launchpad for further advances but rather to capture Olmütz and thereby compel the Austrians to expend time and resources recapturing it. The idea was that Olmütz would serve as a forward position, forcing the Austrians into a prolonged effort to reclaim it, thereby buying time. Nevertheless, this attempt also failed, leading Frederick to abandon true offensive action, recognizing that it only exacerbated the mismatch between his diminishing forces and those of his adversaries.

As a result, Frederick's strategy shifted to holding a fortified position within the core of his territory in Saxony and Silesia. He adopted a compact formation and used short, interlocking lines of communication to reinforce any threatened area swiftly. Where combat was unavoidable, he engaged in decisive battles, but more frequently, he conducted minor incursions and patiently conserved his strength in anticipation of more favorable conditions. Over time, his approach grew increasingly conservative, even embracing a "cordon" strategy in which he prioritized defense over risk-taking. His positions, as exemplified by Prince Henry's in Saxony and Frederick's in the Silesian mountains, were configured to hold ground tenaciously, relying on quick reinforcement and defensive strength rather than aggressive engagement. In his correspondence with the Marquis d'Argens, Frederick often expressed his impatience to reach winter quarters and his satisfaction in settling there without having suffered significant losses, illustrating how defensive strategy became a way to preserve his forces over time.

Critics who accuse Frederick of faltering in spirit when he adopted a more defensive strategy during the Seven Years' War lack a thorough understanding of the context and strategy of his time. While tactics like the entrenched camp at Bunzelwitz or the positions established by Prince Henry in Saxony and Frederick in the Silesian mountains may not appeal to modern sensibilities and might seem weak or overly cautious by today's standards—particularly under a figure like Napoleon, who would have swiftly cut through such defenses—it's crucial to recognize the era-specific nature of warfare and the unique circumstances Frederick faced. At that time, war lacked the rapid mobilization and relentless pace seen later under leaders like Napoleon, and methods that seem outdated today were often sound strategies suited to their period. Additionally, one must consider the opponent: against the armies of the German States and commanders like Daun and Butturlin, employing defensive tactics may have been a highly prudent approach. While Frederick would have dismissed such tactics if used against him, in this context they proved highly effective.

The outcomes reinforced Frederick's strategic prudence: by maintaining a stance of cautious expectation, he successfully navigated obstacles that might otherwise have shattered his forces against stronger enemies. His approach preserved Prussia's position without the need for reckless offensives that could have left him vulnerable.

Similarly, in 1812, the Russian army faced an even more challenging numerical disparity against Napoleon's forces than Frederick had against his enemies. However, the Russians anticipated reinforcements throughout the campaign, and Napoleon was at the height of his power, struggling to maintain control in Spain while managing a continent increasingly hostile to his rule. The vast expanses of Russian territory provided the opportunity to exhaust French resources through a prolonged retreat. In a situation of this magnitude, Russia could realistically expect a massive counterstroke if Napoleon's offensive failed—a counterstroke with the potential to utterly dismantle the French forces, especially if peace negotiations or uprisings in France's territories could be avoided. This approach, though unplanned initially, evolved into a masterstroke, perfectly suited to Russia's circumstances and strengths.

While such a strategy may have seemed outrageous at the time, historical hindsight proves its effectiveness. To truly learn from history, we must regard these successful strategies as lessons applicable in future contexts and recognize the chain of significant events that unfolded from Napoleon's march on Moscow as more than a series of coincidences. If Russia had made a strong effort to defend its borders more traditionally, it is likely that French power would have eventually waned, and a reversal of fortunes might have occurred. But such a cautious approach would not have yielded the same dramatic results. Russia's strategy, which involved tremendous sacrifice and suffering (levels which few other nations could or would have endured), was ultimately the catalyst for one of the most monumental shifts in European power dynamics.

This illustrates a fundamental truth of war: achieving a decisive and positive outcome, even in a defensive war, demands bold, deliberate action and a willingness to risk greatly. True gains do not come from mere passivity or cautious waiting — they arise from calculated decisions and decisive moves aimed at clear objectives. Even on the defensive, success on a grand scale can only be secured by an equally grand commitment to decisive, impactful measures.

Chapter IX. Plan of War when the Destruction of the Enemy is the Object

With a clear understanding of the different possible objectives in war, we can now consider the organization of warfare in alignment with each of these objectives, addressing the three distinct gradations these aims may represent.

Guiding the planning of any military campaign are two overarching principles that shape all subsequent decisions.

The first principle dictates that efforts should focus on reducing the power of the enemy to as few key points as possible, ideally concentrating it into a single "center of gravity." This applies to every aspect of the attack: concentrate on these central forces with as few primary initiatives as possible, preferably just one, while keeping all secondary operations in a clearly subordinate role. In essence, this principle calls for maximizing concentration of force wherever possible.

The second principle emphasizes the need for speed in action. Delays and deviations should be avoided unless there is a strong justification; the swifter the maneuver, the more forceful its impact on the enemy.

Centralizing the enemy's power around a single focal point is influenced by several factors:

The Nature of Political Alliances and Connections: If the enemy's forces consist of a single unified power, concentration is straightforward. If the enemy comprises allied forces where one ally has a limited, perhaps auxiliary, role, then centralization of force is still manageable. However, in a coalition where each ally has its own interests, effective concentration may be challenging and depends greatly on the unity and shared commitment of the coalition members, which has been discussed previously.

Geographical Distribution of the Theatre of War: The location and arrangement of the theatre impact how different enemy forces can be encountered and contained, influencing the feasibility and effectiveness of concentrating attacks on primary objectives.

When the enemy's forces are gathered in one main army within a single theatre of war, they form a unified front, eliminating the need for further analysis of their interdependence. However, if these forces are organized as separate armies within the same theatre, yet controlled by distinct powers, the situation changes. Although not a perfect unity, these separate forces remain sufficiently connected so that a decisive blow against one would likely impact the other due to the forces' close proximity and shared objectives.

If the enemy's forces are positioned in adjacent theatres of war without significant geographical obstacles separating them, there will still be a clear interconnection; the outcome on one front is likely to influence the other. However, if these theatres are distant, with neutral territories, vast mountain ranges, or other barriers in between, this interdependence weakens. When forces are stationed on opposite sides of the targeted state, where operations would naturally diverge, nearly all strategic unity between these forces disappears.

For example, if France and Russia were to simultaneously attack Prussia, these conflicts would resemble two distinct wars in terms of military strategy, though diplomatic negotiations would likely still treat them as one. In contrast, during the Seven Years' War, Saxony and Austria operated as a single strategic force against Frederick the Great, largely because their theatres of war aligned and Saxony lacked political independence, making their struggles interlinked.

In 1813, Napoleon faced many enemies across Germany, yet their alignment against him, along with the interconnected battlefields, created a situation where actions in one theatre greatly influenced others. Had Napoleon managed to concentrate his power and defeat the main Bohemian army decisively, the ripple effects would likely have affected the entire front. For instance, if he had routed the Bohemian army and advanced on Vienna via Prague, Prussian General Blücher, though determined, would have been pressured to shift his focus to Bohemia. The Crown Prince of Sweden, likewise, might have reconsidered his position, likely retreating from the Mark to avoid being isolated.

By contrast, Austria, fighting France on both the Rhine and Italian fronts, faces challenges in decisively influencing one front through successes on the other. Switzerland's mountainous terrain acts as a natural barrier, complicating attempts at convergence, while the roadways themselves tend to lead in opposing directions. Conversely, for France, the situation is somewhat more favorable. Victory on either front could impact Vienna, the heart of the Austrian Empire, due to the geographical layout. Notably, success in Italy is more likely to affect the Rhine theatre than a success on the Rhine would impact Italy. This is because an Italian victory hits closer to Vienna, the empire's center, whereas a win along the Rhine would only affect Austria's flank.

This example illustrates that the extent to which an enemy's forces act in unison or remain independent can vary. Each specific case thus requires an analysis of how one theatre may influence another. Once this inter-theatre influence is understood, a commander can then determine how much the opposing forces might be consolidated into a single, decisive center of power.

The guiding principle of focusing all efforts on the center of gravity of the enemy's power has only one true exception: when secondary expeditions present exceptionally promising advantages. However, even in such cases, this approach is only justifiable if we possess enough decisive superiority to undertake these side operations without risking the core objective, which remains our primary focus.

An illustration of this principle occurred in 1814 when General Bülow's advance into Holland with a corps of thirty thousand men not only neutralized an equivalent force of French troops but also provided a strategic opening for English and Dutch forces to mobilize effectively—forces that might otherwise have remained inactive. This action achieved a considerable secondary benefit without diverting essential resources from the primary campaign against Napoleon in France.

Thus, when forming a comprehensive war plan, the first priority is identifying the centers of gravity within the enemy's power structure, with the aim of consolidating these into a single target whenever feasible. Once these critical points are determined, the second priority becomes organizing our forces to concentrate as much as possible on achieving a single decisive action against this focal point of enemy strength.

However, certain considerations may arise that lead us to consider dividing our forces. These may include:

1. The initial positioning of military forces and the geographic distribution of allied States involved in the offensive play a significant role in determining the feasibility of concentrating forces. If concentrating forces involves substantial detours and delays that reduce the effectiveness and speed of the first strike, proceeding with a dispersed advance along separate lines may be advisable—provided the risks associated with this dispersion are manageable. Particularly when an element of surprise is part of the strategy, the freshness and momentum of the initial attack are critical, and any delay could detract from its effectiveness.

This issue becomes even more complex when multiple allied States are engaged in the offensive from different directions. For instance, if Prussia and Austria jointly launched an offensive against France, it would likely be counterproductive to have both armies start from the same location. Prussia's natural approach would be from the Lower Rhine, while Austria's logical line of advance would be from the Upper Rhine. Forcing a concentration at a single point might waste precious time and resources. In cases like these, the fundamental question becomes: is the strategic necessity for concentration substantial enough to justify these potential sacrifices in time and effort?

2. Advancing along separate lines can sometimes promise greater results. Here, we refer specifically to advancing on converging lines toward a single strategic center. Unlike advances along parallel or eccentric lines, which fall under the category of ancillary operations, converging lines aim to unite separate forces toward one decisive target. This type of approach can sometimes offer enhanced strategic flexibility and create opportunities to encircle or decisively strike the enemy from multiple angles, concentrating effects without necessarily unifying forces in one location initially.

In strategy, a convergent attack—just like in tactics—offers the potential for substantial gains, for if it succeeds, it can lead to more than just a simple defeat. It can mean isolating the enemy by cutting them off, thereby delivering a blow with far-reaching effects. This approach inherently holds the promise of significant results, but, because it necessitates separating the force into distinct parts and spreading across a larger battlefield, it also introduces greater risk. Similar to the relationship between attack and defense, here, too, the weaker method is the one that may yield the highest rewards.

Thus, the essential question is whether the attacker has the strength and confidence to pursue this ambitious outcome.

Frederick the Great's campaign into Bohemia in 1757 exemplifies this principle. He advanced with a split force from Saxony and Silesia, influenced by two main considerations. First, his troops were dispersed in winter quarters, and bringing them together at a single point would have forfeited the advantages of a surprise attack. Second, by advancing on separate but converging paths, he was able to threaten each of the two Austrian fronts in their flanks and rear, thereby increasing the pressure. The risk Frederick faced was that one of his two armies might fall to a superior Austrian force. However, should the Austrians fail to capitalize on this, they would either have to battle with their central forces alone or risk being cut off from their own lines of supply, leaving them exposed to a potentially devastating outcome. It was this significant potential reward that drove Frederick's decision to proceed with his concentric advance.

Ultimately, the Austrians chose to concentrate their defense around Prague, but their static position left them vulnerable to the converging Prussian forces, which allowed Frederick's plan to unfold fully. When the Austrians lost the subsequent battle, it culminated in disaster for them: nearly two-thirds of their army, along with their commander-in-chief, were forced to take shelter within the city of Prague itself. This swift and significant success at the campaign's outset showcased the rewards of a bold, concentric strike. Frederick, weighing the reliability of his own coordinated movements, the commitment of his generals, the morale of his troops, and the Austrians' characteristic sluggishness, likely saw these advantages as sufficient assurance for his approach. We cannot discount these qualitative factors in the campaign's success, nor can we attribute it solely to the geometric structure of the attack.

By comparison, Buonaparte's campaign in Italy in 1796 offers a notable counterexample, illustrating the pitfalls of a poorly managed convergent attack. In this case, the Austrians attempted a convergent march, only to suffer significant setbacks at Buonaparte's hands. Despite having many of the same resources as Frederick in 1757 (with the exception of a comparable morale factor), the Austrian general could not match Buonaparte's effectiveness, even though he was not at a numerical disadvantage. This illustrates that when the form of attack allows the enemy to exploit interior lines to mitigate any imbalance in numbers, a convergent attack might not be the best choice.

In such scenarios, if a separate converging advance is unavoidable due to the layout of forces, it should be approached with caution and regarded as a strategic compromise rather than an ideal solution.

When we examine the 1814 invasion of France from this perspective, it's difficult to endorse the plan that was followed. The Russian, Austrian, and Prussian armies initially assembled near Frankfort on the Maine, positioned along the most direct and logical route to the core of France's power. However, these forces were then divided, with one group advancing from Mayence and the other from Switzerland. Given the reduced state of the French defenses, there was no longer any meaningful prospect for them to defend the frontier effectively. Consequently, the only potential benefit of this concentric advance was the opportunity for one army to capture Lorraine and Alsace while the other took Franche-Comté. This minor territorial gain hardly justified the extensive maneuver into Switzerland. Although other justifications for the march were offered, they were equally inadequate from a strategic standpoint, and here we focus solely on this operational consideration.

On the opposing side, Buonaparte demonstrated a profound understanding of the defensive measures necessary to counter a concentric attack. His adept campaign of 1796 had already showcased his skill in this area. Despite the Allies' considerable numerical advantage, Buonaparte's tactical superiority often offset this, earning recognition even from his adversaries. Although he joined his forces near Chalons a bit too late and at times underestimated his opponents, he came close to isolating each army in turn. By the time he confronted them at Brienne, Blücher's forces were reduced to 27,000 of an intended 65,000, while the main Allied army fielded only 100,000 of the expected 200,000 troops. This dispersion gave Buonaparte a significant opportunity, creating a situation that clearly illustrated the drawbacks of dividing Allied forces. From the very start of hostilities, the need to reunify forces was acutely felt.

Considering all these aspects, while a concentric attack can potentially yield high rewards, it is generally advisable only when it results from an already dispersed arrangement of the forces. There are indeed few instances where it is strategically sound to abandon the most direct route in favor of the added complexities of a concentric approach.

3. The wide expanse of a battlefield can sometimes make it necessary to launch attacks from different directions.

If an advancing army moves deep into the enemy's territory with success, it doesn't only control the specific route it travels. Instead, it gains a measure of control over an area around that route. However, how much of this area can be controlled largely depends on how unified and strong the enemy state is. If the enemy country is loosely organized and its people are not used to war, the army can secure a large portion of territory without much effort. But if the people are brave and loyal to their country, the space the invading army controls will be smaller, forming a narrower path behind it.

To avoid this issue, an attacking force should maintain a broad front as it advances. If the enemy's main forces are concentrated in one area, this wide formation may only be possible until the opposing armies come close enough to engage, at which point the advancing army would naturally tighten its front. This makes sense as a practical strategy.

However, if the enemy has spread out across a wide front, then it's reasonable for the advancing army to do the same. Here, we're referring to one main area of battle or to several that are close together. This approach is relevant when the primary operation is also expected to influence smaller, connected engagements.

But can we always take this risk? Is it wise to face the potential threat if the main operation fails to settle things on smaller fronts? Isn't it worth considering the need for a broad command over the battlefield?

It's true that there are endless possible scenarios, but with few exceptions, the outcome on the main battlefield will typically determine what happens on minor fronts. So, it's best to base our actions on this idea whenever the opposite is not clearly necessary.

When Buonaparte invaded Russia, he had good reason to believe that a decisive victory over the main Russian army would force their other forces stationed on the Upper Dvina to yield. Initially, he left only Oudinot's corps to deal with them. However, when Wittgenstein launched a counterattack, Buonaparte was compelled to send a sixth corps to reinforce that area.

At the same time, he had initially sent part of his forces against Bagration, but that general was drawn into retreat due to the movements of the central army. Buonaparte was then able to recall that part of his forces. If Wittgenstein hadn't been obligated to defend the second capital, he would likely have also followed the main Russian army under Barclay in its retreat.

In 1805 and 1809, Buonaparte's victories at Ulm and Ratisbon also decided matters in Italy and the Tyrol, even though those areas were somewhat distant and had their own challenges. Likewise, in 1806, his victories at Jena and Auerstadt resolved any attempts that could have been made against him in Westphalia, Hesse, or along the road to Frankfurt.

Among the many factors that can affect resistance at secondary locations, two stand out prominently.

The first is that in an expansive and relatively powerful country, such as Russia, the main strike against the central point of power doesn't have to happen immediately. There is room to wait, to plan, and not rush every move. The second factor is when a secondary area (like Silesia in 1806) has significant independent strength due to its many fortresses, making it a tough stronghold on its own. Despite this, Buonaparte barely gave Silesia a second thought; on his march to Warsaw, he left only 20,000 troops under his brother Jerome to handle it, even though it lay fully behind him.

If the main blow aimed at the capital point isn't likely to impact a strong secondary position, or has already failed to do so, and if the enemy still has forces there, it becomes necessary to oppose them with enough of our own forces. This is because no one can risk leaving their communication lines fully exposed from the start. But sometimes, prudence requires more than just covering these lines; it may demand that the advance on the primary target is slowed to match the progress at the secondary points, delaying the main push whenever these secondary areas hold out.

This idea doesn't directly contradict the principle of focusing all efforts into one main endeavor, but its approach is fundamentally opposed to the spirit of that principle. Following this cautious method would lead to careful, restrained movements, dampening the momentum and drive needed to push forward, giving too much opportunity for chance to interfere, and resulting in significant delays—all of which go against the nature of a determined offensive aimed at defeating the enemy.

The challenge becomes even more complex if forces stationed at these secondary locations are able to withdraw along divergent paths. What then becomes of the unity and focus of our main attack?

For this reason, we must firmly stand against making the main offensive dependent on these minor advances. An attack meant to destroy the enemy cannot afford to hold back; it must drive forward like an arrow, straight to the core of the enemy's strength, if it is to have any chance of success.

4. Lastly, there is also a fourth reason to consider advancing separately: it may make it easier to gather the supplies needed to sustain the army.

Marching with a smaller army through a wealthy region is certainly more comfortable than advancing with a larger force through a barren one, but with careful preparation and troops used to hardship, the latter can be managed. Thus, supply considerations should never influence a plan to the point of leading the army into serious danger.

We've now reviewed the reasons for dividing forces in a way that breaks the main operation into multiple efforts. If this kind of separation is undertaken with a clear understanding of the objectives and after weighing all benefits and risks, we have no grounds for criticism.

But if, as often happens, a plan is developed by a well-trained but formulaic staff, laying out separate theaters of war like squares on a chessboard, each needing its own force before anything even begins; if these forces are then assigned to complex, roundabout maneuvers and expected to reunite under risky circumstances in a matter of weeks, then we can only recoil. This departure from simple, practical thinking toward deliberate complexity leads to unnecessary confusion. Such strategies tend to arise when a general-in-chief isn't directing the war personally, as we emphasized in the first chapter, where we described the role as one of singular authority and judgment. Plans crafted in this manner typically reflect the ideas of several lesser-experienced strategists, rather than the focused vision of one capable leader.

Now, let's consider the third part of our initial principle: keeping secondary operations as secondary.

In focusing all efforts on a single goal and pursuing it through one main endeavor, we reduce the autonomy of other theaters and activities between opposing states. Ideally, if all forces could converge on one decisive action, then these secondary theaters would become inconsequential. However, this level of concentration is rarely possible. So instead, the goal is to limit these secondary fronts to prevent them from drawing too many resources away from the main effort.

Next, we assert that a war plan should focus as much as possible on centralizing the enemy's resistance to one main target. Even if circumstances require engaging in two almost separate wars at once, one must always be treated as the primary focus, where most of our forces and attention should be directed.

From this perspective, it's wise to go on the offensive only at that main target and to maintain a defensive stance on all other fronts, attacking secondary points only when exceptional circumstances demand it. The defensive actions at these secondary points should involve as few troops as possible, maximizing the natural advantages that defense offers.

This approach is even more effective on all battlefronts where the opposing forces belong to various allied powers that will still feel the impact when the central point is struck.

When the main attack is underway, there should be no defensive maneuvers on minor fronts against that primary opponent. The major offensive, along with any secondary attacks that support it, forms a unified force that makes additional defensive actions unnecessary on points not directly protected by it. Success in this main offensive will compensate for any losses elsewhere. If we have sufficient forces to pursue a decisive victory, then the possibility of failure should not push us toward overly defensive measures on other fronts, as this approach would make failure more likely, creating a contradiction in strategy.

This focus on the primary action over secondary ones should apply to every branch of the attack. While other factors may guide decisions about which forces to advance from different theaters of war toward the enemy's center of power, the primary goal should be to give the main action clear precedence. The more dominant this primary action becomes, the simpler and less vulnerable the strategy will be to random setbacks.

The second principle is about the swift use of forces.

Any wasted time or unnecessary detours weaken the attack and run counter to strategic principles. It's critical to remember that one of the offensive's main advantages is the element of surprise. Sudden, powerful advances are its greatest strengths, and when total defeat of the enemy is the goal, it rarely succeeds without them.

In line with this, strategy demands taking the most direct path to the goal, dismissing endless debate over minor adjustments in direction. Reflecting on our earlier discussions about strategic attacks and the importance of timing in war, it's clear that this principle has substantial influence.

Napoleon exemplified this approach, always taking the quickest, most direct routes—from army to army, or capital to capital.

What, then, will this primary action entail, which we have identified as the central focus and for which we demand a rapid, straightforward execution?

In the fourth chapter, we explored in general terms what it means to achieve a total defeat of the enemy, and there is no need to repeat those points here. Whatever specific factors may influence the outcome in each particular situation, the initial goal remains the same: the destruction of the enemy's fighting force, meaning a decisive victory that disperses and incapacitates his army. The earlier, and therefore closer to our own borders, that this victory is pursued, the easier it will be to achieve; conversely, the later, or deeper within enemy territory it is won, the more conclusive the victory will be. As with many aspects of war, ease of success and its impact often balance each other.

If our forces are not overwhelmingly superior, making victory inevitable, we should actively seek out the enemy's primary force, provided that this pursuit does not lead to excessive detours, misdirections, or wasted time, which could ultimately backfire. If the main enemy force does not lie directly along our route and other priorities prevent us from hunting it down, we can be certain that it will eventually position itself to block our path. When that time comes, as previously mentioned, we may face less favorable conditions, a reality we must accept. However, if we succeed in battle, our victory will be all the more decisive for having fought it under more challenging circumstances.

Thus, it would be an error to deliberately bypass the enemy's main force if it stands in our way, especially if we hope that doing so will make victory more attainable. Conversely, if we possess a clear superiority over this primary force, we might choose to bypass it intentionally, aiming to engage later under conditions that allow for an even more definitive victory.

Here, we refer not just to winning a battle but to achieving a full-scale defeat of the enemy. Such an outcome demands either an encircling maneuver or an attack with an oblique formation, as these strategies typically ensure a more decisive result. Therefore, it is crucial to include plans for such movements in the overall strategy, taking into account both the necessary concentration of forces and the intended direction of attack. We will address these considerations further in the chapter on campaign planning.

Although it's not impossible for battles with opposing forces arrayed directly against each other to result in total defeat, such occurrences are rare, and they will likely become even rarer as armies grow more evenly matched in discipline and tactical proficiency. The days when twenty battalions could be pinned down in a single village, as they were at Blenheim, are largely past.

Once the major victory is secured, the focus should not shift to resting, catching one's breath, reorganizing, or pausing for reflection. Instead, it must turn to pursuing further action as needed—whether that involves striking new blows, seizing the enemy's capital, engaging the forces of his allies, or attacking any other positions where the enemy might attempt to regroup.

If, as we advance with victory on our side, we come close to the enemy's fortresses, the decision to lay siege will depend on our resources. If we have a substantial advantage in strength, it would be inefficient to bypass these fortresses without capturing them quickly. However, if we're unsure about upcoming developments, it's wiser to hold these strongholds in check with a minimal force rather than divert our efforts to formal sieges. The moment when a fortress siege halts our strategic advance usually marks the peak of our momentum. Thus, we argue that the main force should push forward relentlessly, without pauses; we've already dismissed the idea of making further advances reliant on success in secondary actions. Consequently, in most cases, the primary army leaves only a narrow area of secured territory in its wake, marking the real boundaries of its operational reach. We have already discussed how this narrows the driving force at the front, creating vulnerabilities for an advancing force. Will this challenge—this natural limit—eventually halt the advance? Certainly, such a point may be reached. However, just as we previously argued against slowing down the advance early on to keep the theatre of war expansive and flexible, we now assert that the commander must continue pursuing his goal of decisively defeating the enemy as long as he has the strength. Though this may increase the risk, it also enhances the chance of a greater victory.

Once the commander reaches a point beyond which he cannot proceed without compromising his position, where he must widen his defenses on both sides to secure his rear, that's likely his turning point. His momentum may be spent, and if the enemy remains undefeated, he probably will stay so. Any continued action by the attacker—such as taking fortresses, securing mountain passes, or occupying provinces—is a slower form of progress but no longer as definitive as the initial advance. The enemy may no longer be in retreat; he may be regrouping for a counter-attack, so that while the attacker progresses, the defender's position improves daily. Ultimately, once an advance halts, it's rare to regain that momentum.

Theory dictates, therefore, that as long as the goal is to dismantle the enemy's forces, there should be no let-up in the forward movement. If the commander abandons this objective due to excessive risk, it makes sense to pause and solidify his position. Theory only objects if he stops with the belief that this will somehow make the enemy easier to defeat later.

It's not to say there are no examples of countries that have been brought down slowly, step by step. The principle discussed here is not an absolute truth but rather reflects the most likely outcomes. Further, it's essential to distinguish between cases where a state's collapse came through a prolonged process and those resolved in a single campaign. Our discussion pertains only to the latter, where a concentrated effort either topples the enemy's core or risks being overturned by it. If in the first year we gain a small success and add to it gradually, moving closer to our goal, the danger is spread out and less intense. But each interval brings new chances for the enemy to rally: the early victories have diminishing impact on subsequent outcomes, or sometimes even negative effects, as the enemy recovers, becomes more determined, or seeks allies. When all success flows from a single, continuous advance, each day's gain builds on the previous day, and one victory sparks the next. While it's true there have been instances where a state was defeated by successive blows, those are rare compared to the many cases where this cautious approach has doomed the attacker's plans. Consider, for example, the result of the Seven Years' War, where Austria's careful, measured approach missed its ultimate objective entirely.

From this perspective, we cannot agree with the idea that careful preparation of the war theater and the drive to push forward are equally important, or that the former should serve as a balance to the latter. Instead, any hardship that arises from moving forward should be seen as an unavoidable issue, only worthy of consideration when there is no longer any hope of progress ahead.

Napoleon's campaign in 1812 actually strengthens this view, rather than weakens it. His efforts failed not because he advanced too quickly or too far, as many assume, but because the necessary means for success weren't available. Russia is not a country that can be conquered in the conventional sense; it can't be held securely—at least not by the armies of Europe, nor by the 500,000 soldiers Napoleon brought with him. A nation of this scale and resilience could only be undermined from within, through internal weakness and disunity. To disrupt Russia's core stability, Napoleon's campaign needed to shake the government's resolve and test the loyalty of its people, reaching into the heart of Russian society. By marching on Moscow, he hoped to break the government's will and destabilize its citizens' resolve. Capturing Moscow wasn't just a prize; it was the only rational goal he could set for such a massive undertaking.

Thus, he led his main forces against the main Russian army, which fell back as he advanced. Napoleon bypassed the Russian camp at Drissa, pursued them through Smolensk, pulled along Bagration's forces, and finally won a major battle, taking Moscow itself. In this campaign, Napoleon acted as he always had; his strategy of relentless forward pressure was precisely what had made him Europe's dominant military leader in the past, and only by staying true to this approach could he hope to continue succeeding.

So, anyone who admires Napoleon's earlier campaigns as a testament to his genius cannot fairly criticize his decisions in this one. Evaluating events based solely on their outcome is fine—it's often the clearest form of critique. But claiming such an outcome alone shows "superior insight" is a mistake. If we want to critique a campaign fully, we must show that its causes for failure were evident from the start and should have been anticipated or avoided. Then, we can say we've surpassed the general's judgment.

However, labeling the 1812 campaign as a "blunder" only because of its disastrous end while calling it a "brilliant strategy" if it had succeeded shows a serious lack of critical understanding. If Napoleon had remained in Lithuania, as some of his critics believe he should have, securing fortresses (although, besides Riga, there were scarcely any substantial ones to claim), he would've been trapped in a grim defensive stance for the winter. The same critics would then have been the first to complain, "This isn't the Napoleon we know! Why hasn't he even reached a major battle yet? The old Napoleon sealed his conquests at the enemy's stronghold with victories like Austerlitz and Friedland. Has he lost his nerve that he won't even march on the defenseless Moscow, with its gates wide open? By hesitating, he's left an opportunity for the Russians to rally!"

Napoleon had the rare fortune to surprise this vast and seemingly invulnerable empire as easily as if he were invading a neighboring state—almost like Frederick the Great annexing the tiny Silesia at his doorstep.

Critics would surely have cried out against him if he'd held back, halfway through his advance, as if some ill fate had stopped him mid-victory. This is how the campaign would have been judged in hindsight, for this is often how critics tend to assess historical outcomes.

In response to these critiques, we argue that Napoleon's campaign in 1812 ultimately failed not because he advanced too far, but because the Russian government remained unwavering, and the Russian people stayed loyal and resilient. Given these conditions, success was not possible under any strategy. Although Napoleon may have miscalculated in even launching this campaign, as the outcome revealed flaws in his planning, we assert that if he was determined to pursue his goal, there was no other viable approach.

Rather than entangling himself in a drawn-out, expensive, defensive war in the east similar to the one he was already waging in the west, Napoleon chose the only method he saw to achieve victory: to shock the Russians into submission with one powerful stroke and extract peace from them. He risked the destruction of his army, knowing it was the price of high-stakes ambitions. If the loss of his army ended up being greater than necessary, that misfortune was not due to his deep incursion into Russia, which was essential to his strategy. Instead, the missteps lay in several tactical errors: the delayed start of the campaign, the cost in lives from his aggressive tactics, his lack of foresight in provisioning his army, poor maintenance of his supply lines, and finally, his prolonged stay in Moscow.

That the Russians reached the Beresina River before him, aiming to cut off his retreat, is often cited as evidence against his strategy, but this argument does not hold up under scrutiny. First, their failure to intercept him shows how challenging it is to truly cut off an army—even one in a position as vulnerable as Napoleon's, caught in unfavorable conditions, managed to break through. While this attempt did add to the overall disaster, it was not the primary cause. Second, it was the unique geography of the region that allowed the Russians to press the attack as they did; without the marshes of the Beresina, with their dense woods forming a nearly impassable barrier across the main road, their chances of blocking his escape would have been even slimmer. Third, there is no surefire way to prevent such an attempt at interception other than advancing with a wide front—a strategy we previously deemed ineffective. Relying on central advances while covering the wings with detached armies only works as long as those forces can hold; any check to these flanking forces would require the center to fall back, thus negating any gains made in the advance.

It is also incorrect to say Napoleon neglected his flanks. He left strong forces in place: a superior force opposed Wittgenstein in the north, a siege corps, though arguably unnecessary, stood before Riga, and in the south, Schwarzenberg commanded 50,000 men, making him stronger than Tormasoff and nearly as strong as Tschitschagow. Additionally, Victor's 30,000 troops protected the rear of Napoleon's main army. Even as late as November, when the Russian forces were reinforced and the French army had dwindled, the Russians did not possess overwhelming superiority in the rear of Napoleon's army. Wittgenstein, Tschitschagow, and Sacken combined had about 100,000 troops. Meanwhile, Schwarzenberg, Regnier, Victor, Oudinot, and St. Cyr collectively retained an effective force of 80,000. For any general advancing on an enemy, this allocation of resources to protect the flanks would be considered more than sufficient.

In conclusion, we view Napoleon's plan not as an error in the boldness of his advance but in the finer details of its execution. The campaign did not fail simply because he reached too deeply into Russia but because the circumstances on which he depended did not play out in his favor.

If, of the 600,000 men who crossed the Niemen in 1812, Napoleon had managed to bring back 250,000 instead of just the 50,000 who eventually returned with Schwarzenberg, Regnier, and Macdonald, the campaign would still have been deemed unfortunate. Yet, strategic principles would not have faulted it, as losing half of an army in such a context is hardly unusual. We are only inclined to see it as unusual here because of the massive scale of Napoleon's entire endeavor.

This observation speaks to the core approach Napoleon took with his main operation, the inherent risks that came with it, and the unavoidable sacrifices it entailed. When we shift our focus to the supporting operations, however, there must be a unifying objective across all such efforts. But this shared objective should be structured in a way that allows each force the flexibility to act independently rather than stalling progress. For example, if forces were advancing into France from the upper and middle Rhine and Holland with the intent to converge on Paris, it would be detrimental for each army to avoid risk and hold back until they all meet up. This approach leads to a harmful plan because it invites constant comparison of each front's progress, leading to delays, indecisiveness, and hesitation among all advancing forces. Instead, it is wiser to give each segment a specific mission and let the different advances naturally align at the decisive point without enforced synchronization.

When separate forces advance across different theatres of war, each army should be assigned a particular target to direct its force toward. Here, the key is for these advances to align in timing, with all forces making their attacks simultaneously. However, it's not crucial for each front to achieve proportional success. If one force encounters unexpected difficulties because the enemy shifted their resources differently, and if that force faces defeat, this setback should not impact the progress of the other forces. The alternative would be to compromise the entire strategy from the outset, transforming the likelihood of success into a risk of failure. Only when the majority of the operations or the primary offensive is unsuccessful should the outcome influence the actions of the remaining forces, as this would mean that the overall strategy has indeed faltered.

The same principle applies to armies that start on the defensive but, through successful engagements, turn to the offensive. In these cases, it may be beneficial to link such additional forces to the primary offensive effort, though this decision largely depends on the geographic relationships of the theatres involved.

This approach raises questions about what happens to the coherence and "geometry" of the broader attack plan, especially regarding the flanks and rear of various corps if neighboring units face setbacks. Here, we confront the main misunderstanding that strategic success hinges on a perfectly arranged, "geometrical" attack, where forces move in flawless harmony. To rely on such a rigid, geometrical setup is to fall into an illusion.

In the fifteenth chapter of the Third Book, we discussed how geometry matters less in strategy than in tactics. Reaffirming that concept here, we conclude that, especially in an offensive strategy, actual outcomes at various points should be the focus, not an abstract geometric structure that may or may not emerge based on varying battlefield results.

However, it remains certain that, given the vast scope with which strategy operates, any conclusions or decisions based on the geometric positioning of units should be left entirely to the general-in-chief. Subordinate commanders have no right to inquire into the actions or inactions of their peers. Instead, each one should be firmly instructed to focus solely on achieving their specific objective. If any significant misalignment arises, the supreme command can step in to correct it as needed. This approach addresses the primary risk associated with a separate, independent mode of action: that rather than responding to actual events, commanders may become overly influenced by imagined threats and assumptions, leading each mishap to impact not just the unit affected but the entire operation. Additionally, this approach reduces the likelihood that personal rivalries or weaknesses among commanders will disrupt the campaign's progress.

These ideas might seem unusual only to those who have not closely examined military history or who fail to distinguish critical elements from minor details. They also might overlook how human nature, with its inevitable flaws, affects warfare at all levels. If even in battlefield tactics, where experienced soldiers agree that coordinated attacks from separate columns are challenging due to the need for perfect alignment, then the challenges become even more daunting in strategic planning, where distances and separations are greater. If constant synchronization were truly essential for success, such a plan would be unrealistic for strategic operations. Yet, we cannot simply discard this approach, as circumstances might require it, and, even in tactics, exact alignment at all moments of an action isn't always essential. In strategy, it becomes even less critical, making it more important to ensure each part of the operation is given a clear, independent task.

One additional observation concerns the proper assignment of tasks. In 1793 and 1794, for instance, the main Austrian force was positioned in the Netherlands, while Prussian forces were on the Upper Rhine. The Austrians advanced from Vienna toward Condé and Valenciennes, which crossed paths with the Prussian route from Berlin to Landau. While Austria had an interest in defending its Belgian provinces and potentially expanding into French Flanders, this interest was ultimately deemed insufficient. After Prince Kaunitz's death, Minister Thugut pushed to abandon the Netherlands entirely to better concentrate Austrian forces. Austria was roughly twice as distant from Flanders as it was from Alsace, and, at a time when resources were scarce and every cost was paid directly, this geographic distance was a significant concern. Nonetheless, Thugut also had another objective in mind: he aimed to leverage the urgency of the threat to pressure Holland, England, and Prussia—nations invested in the defense of the Netherlands and the Lower Rhine—into stepping up their own efforts. Ultimately, his strategy failed as the Prussian cabinet was uncooperative, but the incident underscores how political motives can influence military decisions.

Prussia didn't have much to gain or defend in Alsace. Back in 1792, it marched through Lorraine into Champagne, driven more by a sense of honor than practical interest. But when that venture went nowhere due to unfavorable events, Prussia continued the war without much enthusiasm. If Prussian forces had been stationed in the Netherlands, however, they would have had a direct link to Holland—almost like an extension of their own territory, as they had conquered it back in 1787. This positioning would have secured the Lower Rhine and protected nearby Prussian territories. It also would have strengthened Prussia's alliance with England, bolstered by subsidies, and kept them aligned more closely, preventing Prussia from straying into the inconsistent policies it pursued at the time.

A better outcome could have been expected if Austria had deployed its main force on the Upper Rhine, leaving Prussia to take the Netherlands with its full strength, while Austria maintained only a supporting corps there. In 1814, for example, if the determined Blücher had led the grand army alongside Schwartzenberg, rather than commanding the Silesian army, which instead might have been headed by General Barclay, the entire campaign's outcome might have been different. Similarly, if the bold General Laudon had not been tied down in Silesia—the strongest part of Prussian territory—during the Seven Years' War, but rather was positioned with the army of the German states, the course of that war could have shifted significantly. To look deeper into these distinctions, we can examine the situations according to their main differences.

The first distinction is when a country is at war alongside other powers who are not only allies but have their own, separate interests at stake. The second is when an allied army is sent in direct support of one's own forces. The third distinction relates to the particular character and traits of the generals in command.

In the first two cases, a question arises: is it better to fully integrate troops from different powers into mixed units, as was done in the wars of 1813 and 1814, or to keep each nation's forces distinct, with their own independent command structure? Clearly, the first option is the more effective, but it requires a level of unity and shared interest that is rare. When armies fight side-by-side in this close cooperation, it's much harder for their respective governments to divide their aims, and any selfish ambitions of individual commanders are limited mainly to the tactical level. In this cooperative model, issues from personal agendas are more controlled, as there's less freedom for one commander to act solely in their own interest compared to when units are kept separate, where such attitudes can have a strategic impact.

However, this integrated approach depends on an unusually high degree of harmony among the participating governments. In 1813, the dire need of the moment pushed all governments towards this approach. The Russian Emperor deserves particular credit for his willingness to set aside pride, despite entering the field with the largest force and playing a major role in turning the war's fortunes. Rather than insisting on leading an independent Russian army, he allowed his troops to serve under Prussian and Austrian commanders.

If merging armies fully is not feasible, it's better to keep them completely separate rather than in a confusing middle-ground arrangement. The worst scenario is when two independent commanders from different countries find themselves leading separate armies in the same region, which frequently happened in the Seven Years' War with the forces from Russia, Austria, and the German States. When armies are completely separated, each commander only bears the burden of his own army and is more driven by necessity to act. But when they operate closely or in the same area, the situation changes. The hesitation of one commander can paralyze the other's actions, leaving both armies stalled and less effective.

In cases where separation is achievable, each country's natural interest usually guides how it uses its forces, making separation easier to accomplish. However, in situations where separation is not practical, the best approach is often to align fully with the auxiliary army's command if it is of comparable strength. For instance, the Austrians took this approach in the latter part of the 1815 campaign, and the Prussians followed suit during the 1807 campaign.

When considering the strengths of individual generals, it's essential to avoid the common mistake of putting cautious and prudent commanders in charge of secondary armies. Instead, the most daring and enterprising commanders should lead these independent forces. In operations where armies are separated, each one needs to maximize its potential, allowing any shortcomings in one area to be balanced out by successes in another. This level of proactive action typically comes from bold, energetic leaders who are naturally driven to push forward. Relying on a commander's rational understanding of the need for action rarely achieves the same intensity.

Additionally, whenever possible, it's wise to match the strengths of the troops and their leaders with the characteristics of the landscape. Well-trained, disciplined troops, numerous cavalry, and experienced, prudent commanders are best suited for open terrain. In contrast, militia, national levies, and young, daring leaders are better matched with rugged terrains, including forests, mountains, and narrow passes. Auxiliary armies work most effectively in wealthier areas where they can sustain themselves comfortably.

Our discussion on planning for war, especially those aimed at decisively defeating the enemy, seeks to underscore the primary objective and outline guiding principles for organizing forces and resources. We've focused on highlighting the essentials and universal elements, while also allowing space for unique circumstances and chance. However, we've tried to exclude anything arbitrary, trivial, unrealistic, or overly complex. If we have achieved this, we consider our purpose fulfilled.

Now, if anyone is looking for advice on tactical maneuvers like redirecting rivers, dominating mountains from above, avoiding strongholds, or locating the "keys" to a region, then they may have missed our central points and may still not grasp the broad nature of warfare as we see it.

In earlier books, we discussed these strategic aspects more broadly, concluding that their significance is generally overestimated. Consequently, they should not play a dominant role—particularly in shaping the overall war strategy when the goal is the enemy's total defeat.

Later, we'll dedicate a chapter to exploring the role of supreme command in detail; for now, let's wrap up with an example.

Suppose Austria, Prussia, the German Confederation, the Netherlands, and England decide to go to war with France, while Russia remains neutral—a scenario that has occurred multiple times over the last century and a half. Under such conditions, these countries would be capable of launching an offensive with the goal of completely subduing France. Despite its power and size, France could see more than half its territory invaded, its capital occupied, and its resources exhausted to the point of incapacity, with little hope of external support, except from Russia. Spain is too far removed and disadvantageously positioned, while the Italian states currently lack the cohesion and strength needed for effective assistance.

These allied nations, not counting their overseas territories, have a combined population of more than 75 million, compared to France's 30 million. Realistically, they could mobilize an army of considerable size and capability, one that would bring substantial force to a concerted war effort against France.

Austria: 250,000

Prussia: 200,000

The rest of Germany: 150,000

Netherlands: 75,000

England: 50,000

Total: 725,000

This chapter appears to have been written in 1828, during a period when the balance of military power across Europe was markedly different from what we see today. Should these allied armies be mobilized on a full wartime footing, they would almost certainly present a formidable force, exceeding what France could effectively oppose. Historically, even under Napoleon's leadership, France had never assembled an army of this potential scale. When we account for necessary deductions—such as forces committed to garrison fortresses, maintain supply depots, and secure the coastlines—it's clear that the allies would hold a significant advantage in the main theater of war. This advantage forms a crucial foundation for any plan focused on the comprehensive defeat of the enemy.

The central pillar of France's power lies within its military strength and the capital, Paris. For the allies, then, the primary objective must be to achieve multiple victories over French forces, advance on Paris, and drive any remaining French forces south of the Loire River. The heart of the French monarchy's power, its true center of gravity, lies between Paris and Brussels, where the frontier is merely thirty miles from the capital, an extraordinarily strategic position for any invading force. The allies have a natural assembly point here: England, the Netherlands, Prussia, and the northern German states, which all either border this zone or lie directly behind it in a line of reinforcements. For Austria and the southern German states, the more logical base of operations lies along the Upper Rhine, allowing a march toward Troyes, Paris, or even Orleans. Therefore, both offensives—from the Netherlands and the Upper Rhine—present not only efficient and strategically sensible routes but converge on the heart of French power. The entire allied invasion force should ideally be concentrated between these two crucial points, maximizing strength and coherence.

However, two notable factors complicate this otherwise straightforward plan. Austria, for instance, would be reluctant to leave its Italian territories unprotected and would prefer to maintain a solid position in that region to control events there. Understandably, Austria may hesitate to risk a major invasion of central France that would leave Italy covered only indirectly. Given the political context of the period, this collateral consideration cannot simply be dismissed. Nevertheless, it would be a strategic misstep to try a familiar yet flawed approach of mounting an invasion through Italy toward southern France. Such a move would draw too many resources away from the primary invasion, thereby violating the essential principle of a unified, concentrated strategy. To imagine conquering France by advancing up the Rhone Valley would be similar to attempting to lift a musket by its bayonet—it lacks the effectiveness needed for a successful outcome. Moreover, as an auxiliary maneuver, an attack on southern France should be avoided, as it would only ignite new resistance in the region that might otherwise remain dormant, thus diverting energy and resources from the main campaign. Only if Italy has an overabundance of forces needed to secure the region—forces that would be wasted if left idle—would there be any practical justification for initiating even a limited offensive in southern France.

By focusing their efforts where they can have the greatest impact and refraining from unnecessary distractions, the allies would be better positioned to achieve their strategic goals.

Thus, we reaffirm that the forces retained in Italy must be minimized as far as the situation allows. A force just large enough to prevent Austria from losing all of Italy within a single campaign should be sufficient. For the sake of example, let's assume this would require about 50,000 troops.

Another significant factor worth considering is France's relationship to its extensive coastline. Given that England commands the seas, France is inherently vulnerable along its entire Atlantic coast. This susceptibility necessitates the deployment of defensive garrisons along the shorelines to varying degrees. Regardless of how limited or effective this coastal defense might be, the existence of such a vast maritime frontier effectively triples France's borders, forcing it to allocate resources away from the main theater of war. The English, by preparing a landing force of 20,000 to 30,000 troops for potential operations against France's Atlantic coast, could compel the French to withdraw twice or even three times as many troops from their main forces to guard against such threats.

Furthermore, it isn't just troops that France must allocate. The defense of these coastal areas demands financial resources, artillery, coastal batteries, and ships—all critical for a robust defense. For illustrative purposes, let's assume the English could dedicate 25,000 troops to this objective. This deployment would require France to commit a considerable portion of its own resources in response, redirecting not only soldiers but also significant sums of money, armaments, and logistical support toward fortifying and securing its coastlines, thereby weakening its capacity to focus on the main front against allied forces.

Our plan of war would then consist simply in this:

1. That in the Netherlands:—

200,000 Prussians,

75,000 Netherlanders,

25,000 English,

50,000 North German Confederation,

Total: 350,000 be assembled,

of whom about 50,000 should be set aside to garrison frontier fortresses, and the remaining 300,000 should advance against Paris, and engage the French Army in a decisive battle.

2. Two hundred thousand Austrian troops, along with one hundred thousand troops from South Germany, should gather on the Upper Rhine. Their advance should be coordinated to move simultaneously with the army coming in from the Netherlands. The intended path for this combined force would lead toward the Upper Seine, followed by an advance toward the Loire, with the ultimate objective being a decisive, large-scale battle. It's possible that these two attacking forces would eventually merge into a single, unified assault on the Loire. This alignment of forces would enhance their overall effectiveness, combining their momentum in a significant strategic offensive designed to maximize impact and potentially lead to a swift and decisive outcome on French soil.

This determines the central focus of the plan. What follows primarily aims to dispel any misconceptions about its execution:

1. The primary objective is to engage in a major battle under conditions where the balance of numbers and circumstances promises a decisive victory. This should guide the commanders' actions above all else, and everything else should be secondary. Resources should be spared as much as possible from sieges, blockades, and garrison duties to focus on achieving this battle. If commanders, as Schwartzenberg did in 1814, spread their forces outward in wide, scattered directions as soon as they cross into enemy territory, it risks undermining the entire campaign. The Allies in 1814 escaped such an outcome only because France was weakened and unable to fully respond. An attack should press forward with the force and precision of a well-driven wedge, not dissipate like a bubble stretching itself thin until it bursts.

2. Switzerland should rely on its own defenses. If Switzerland stays neutral, it provides a strong support base along the Upper Rhine. Should France attempt to invade it, Switzerland is fully capable of mounting its own defense. Assigning Switzerland a significant geographic influence in warfare simply because it is Europe's highest terrain is an outdated notion. Such geographical advantages only matter in highly specific scenarios, which do not apply here. When the French are challenged at the core of their own territory, they lack the capacity to launch an offensive from Switzerland aimed at Italy or Swabia, and the country's altitude alone won't alter strategic outcomes. High ground primarily benefits defensive maneuvers, and only rarely does it hold strategic offensive value, perhaps in a single engagement. Anyone who thinks otherwise hasn't fully grasped the nature of this issue. Should any future military council include an overly cautious strategist who promotes this flawed view with misplaced conviction, it would be wise for a straightforward, practical voice to intervene and put an end to the discussion.

3. The gap between the two main attacks is of minimal concern. Imagine 600,000 troops assembled thirty or forty miles from Paris, poised to strike at the heart of France. In that scenario, should we worry about covering points along the middle Rhine, or far-off places like Berlin, Dresden, Vienna, and Munich? Such a strategy would be nonsensical. Are we trying to protect the supply lines? That has its importance, of course, but focusing too much on covering these lines could tempt us into treating this task as an additional front, leading us to advance on three lines instead of the two that the geopolitical landscape actually requires. This could soon spiral into advancing on five or seven lines, bringing us back to old, ineffective strategies.

Our two attacks each have clear objectives and a likely numerical advantage over the enemy. If both advance with strong momentum, their efforts will naturally reinforce one another. If one of the two faces setbacks because the enemy has concentrated more troops in one area, we can reasonably expect the other offensive to counterbalance that loss. This is the real interaction between the two attacks. Attempting to coordinate them in real time across a broad distance is unrealistic, and frankly, unnecessary; thus, a direct and constant connection between them holds no great advantage.

Furthermore, the enemy, pressed deep within their own territory, will likely lack the spare forces needed to disrupt the link between our advancing forces significantly. The only threat to that connection might come from local militia or partisan groups. To prevent this, a force of 10,000 to 15,000 men, heavily equipped with cavalry, should move from Trèves toward Rheims, sweeping away any small disruptive bands and staying aligned with the main force. This unit should avoid besieging or guarding fortresses and instead march freely between them, without being anchored to a specific base, and simply retreat in the face of any superior enemy force. Should an issue arise with this unit, it wouldn't constitute a serious setback for the entire operation. Under these conditions, this smaller force could serve as an effective link between the two main attacks.

4. The two secondary operations—the Austrian army stationed in Italy and the English forces prepared for coastal landings—should carry out their respective missions as strategically advantageous. So long as they remain active and avoid inactivity, they fulfill their role relative to the primary offensive. Under no circumstances should either of the two major attacks be contingent upon these secondary efforts.

We are thoroughly convinced that, by following this approach, France can be decisively subdued whenever it resumes the domineering posture it has held over Europe for a century and a half. Only beyond Paris, along the Loire, can we impose upon France the terms essential for Europe's stability. This approach will swiftly reveal the natural imbalance of 30 million people against a united force of 75 million, unlike the past 150 years where France has been surrounded from Dunkirk to Genoa by a fragmented array of armies. In such scattered undertakings, dozens of minor goals are pursued, each too weak to overcome the inertia, friction, and discordant influences inherent in coalition forces.

The flaws in the current structure of the German confederate forces become all too apparent in this context. The current system treats the federated parts of Germany as the core strength, thereby weakening Prussia and Austria, depriving them of their natural leadership role. Yet, in times of war, a federative power lacks unity, energy, coherent leadership, clear authority, and accountability—all essential elements for effectiveness.

Prussia and Austria are the true cores of German strength, the unifying fulcrum around which the might of the German empire should pivot. These are well-established, monarchical states accustomed to the demands of war, with clearly defined interests, independent resources, and dominant influence. The organizational structure should align with these natural focal points, rather than attempting an unrealistic unity which, in such a case, is unattainable. To disregard practical possibilities in favor of unrealistic ideals is misguided and unwise.

The Maxims of War

Napoleon Bonaparte

Introduction

The publisher has thoughtfully reissued this concise volume as a timely publication for the current moment. A compilation of maxims that guided the military maneuvers of one of the most distinguished commanders of the modern era is bound to be invaluable for young officers genuinely seeking to deepen their understanding of the art of war. Each maxim is accompanied by examples from the campaigns of Gustavus Adolphus, Turenne, Frederick, and Napoleon. These legendary leaders were all guided by consistent principles, and by examining their respective campaigns through this lens, every military professional can not only recognize the strategic wisdom behind these principles but also learn to apply them in ways best suited to their unique talents and insights in future endeavors.

NAPOLEON'S MAXIMS OF WAR

MAXIM I.

State frontiers are typically defined by significant natural barriers, such as vast rivers, mountain ranges, or expansive deserts. Among these natural obstacles, deserts present the greatest challenge to the movement of an army, posing unique difficulties in logistics, sustenance, and navigation. Mountains, while formidable with their rugged terrain and high altitudes, rank as the next most challenging. Broad rivers, though also obstructive, are comparatively easier to cross, especially with proper engineering and logistical support, making them the third in order of difficulty for an advancing military force.

NOTE.

Throughout his military campaigns, Napoleon faced and overcame nearly every conceivable obstacle typical of invasion warfare.

In Egypt, he led his forces across vast deserts, defeating the Mamelukes, renowned for their skill and bravery, adapting his strategies to the unique challenges of a far-off land with limited resources for his army.

In the conquest of Italy, he twice navigated the formidable Alps, choosing some of the most difficult passes and undertaking these crossings in seasons that made the feat even more daunting. Within three months, he crossed the Pyrenees, defeating and scattering four separate Spanish armies. From the banks of the Rhine to the distant reaches of the Borysthenes, no natural barrier could halt the swift advance of his triumphant forces.

MAXIM II.

When devising a campaign plan, it is essential to anticipate all potential actions the enemy might take and to be equipped with the appropriate strategies to counteract them effectively. Campaign plans can be modified endlessly based on numerous factors, including the unique talents of the commanding general, the specific qualities and morale of the troops, and the geographical layout of the area where the campaign unfolds.

NOTE.

At times, a risky campaign may succeed even when its plan defies established principles of warfare. Such outcomes, however, typically result from fortune's whims or the enemy's mistakes—factors that no general should ever rely upon. There are instances when a campaign plan, though well-grounded in sound military principles, may risk failure if the adversary, initially defensive, swiftly seizes the initiative and leverages highly skillful maneuvers to surprise the opposing forces. This was precisely the case in the campaign of 1796, directed by the Aulic Council under Marshal Wurmser. With his numerical advantage, Wurmser anticipated a decisive victory, aiming to destroy the French army by cutting off its retreat. His strategy relied on the assumption that the French, stationed along the Adige to protect both the siege of Mantua and broader Italian territories, would remain defensive.

Wurmser, expecting the French to be fixed near Mantua, split his army into three separate corps, each advancing independently toward Mantua with plans to unite there. However, Napoleon discerned Wurmser's plan, realizing the opportunity to exploit the Austrian army's division into three isolated units with no mutual communication. He promptly abandoned the Mantua siege, consolidated his forces, and thus gained a numerical advantage over the Austrians. He then decisively attacked and defeated the Austrian divisions one by one. Wurmser, who had anticipated an easy path to victory, found himself retreating into the Tyrol after a brief ten-day campaign, having lost twenty-five thousand men in casualties, fifteen thousand captured soldiers, nine regimental colors, and seventy cannons.

Thus, prescribing a strict course of action for a general to follow throughout a campaign proves extremely challenging. Success often hinges on unforeseen circumstances, and nothing stifles military genius more than imposing an external command over the leader of an army, whose autonomy and judgment are crucial to adapting to dynamic battle conditions.

MAXIM III.

An army setting out to conquer a territory typically anchors its two wings on either neutral lands or substantial natural barriers, like rivers or mountain ranges. Occasionally, only one wing finds this support, while in other cases, both wings are left exposed. In scenarios where both wings are protected, a commander's primary task is to safeguard the front line from enemy penetration. When only one wing has such support, the army should focus on leaning into this protected wing for stability. In situations where both wings are vulnerable, it's essential to adopt a central, cohesive formation, ensuring that no corps strays far from the main force. This is particularly critical because having two exposed flanks is challenging enough, but the difficulties multiply when multiple corps are positioned separately, potentially leaving four or six flanks exposed, depending on the number of divisions.

In the first scenario—where both wings are secured—the line of operations can extend either to the right or the left with little restriction. In the second scenario, where only one wing is supported, the operations should pivot toward that side for added defense. In the third, where both wings are exposed, the line of operations should run perpendicular to the army's central axis of advance, allowing the force to hold firm in the middle.

Regardless of the scenario, establishing strongholds along the operational line is crucial. Every five or six days' march, a secure post or fortified position should be constructed to stockpile supplies, manage convoys, and serve as a central movement base. This approach provides a fortified location that not only shortens the operational line of the army but also serves as a fallback defensive point, streamlining and securing the army's overall advance.

NOTE.

The foundational principles of warfare were largely disregarded or forgotten during the Middle Ages. The crusaders, in their campaigns to Palestine, seemed focused solely on the immediate objective of engaging in battle and achieving victory, often neglecting to consolidate their gains. As a result, vast armies were lost in Syria, obtaining little beyond the fleeting satisfaction of winning through sheer numbers.

This same disregard for strategic continuity led Charles XII of Sweden to abandon his essential line of operations and sever ties with Sweden as he plunged into the Ukrainian heartland. During a harsh winter campaign in a barren region with minimal resources, he lost most of his forces. Following his defeat at the Battle of Poltava, Charles XII, with his forces reduced to little more than a thousand men, had no choice but to flee across the Dnieper River and seek refuge in Turkey.

In contrast, Gustavus Adolphus revived the art of warfare by adhering to these key principles. His military campaigns in Germany were marked by boldness, rapid movement, and precise execution. Unlike his predecessors, Gustavus capitalized on each success to ensure long-term security, securing his line of operations and safeguarding his communications with Sweden. His approach to war defined a new era, marking a resurgence of strategic discipline and foresight in military operations.

MAXIM IV.

When the conquest of a region involves two or three separate armies, each with its own line of operation, converging toward a designated meeting point, a key principle must be observed: these forces should not unite in close proximity to the enemy. The risk lies in the enemy potentially consolidating their own forces to obstruct this merger and subsequently defeat each of the armies individually before they can effectively join forces.

NOTE.

In the 1757 campaign, Frederick advanced toward the conquest of Bohemia with two armies, each operating along a distinct line, yet managed to unite them within sight of the Duke of Lorraine, who, with the imperial army, was positioned to defend Prague. Despite this success, such a strategy is generally inadvisable. Frederick's achievement was largely due to the Duke's inaction; commanding seventy thousand troops, the Duke failed to obstruct the Prussian armies from joining forces, an opportunity he could have used to thwart their progress.

MAXIM V.

All wars must adhere to established principles, as every conflict should pursue a clear objective and be conducted in line with strategic rules. A war ought to be waged with forces appropriately scaled to the challenges and obstacles that must be surmounted.

NOTE.

It was a saying of Marshal Villars, that when Once war is resolved upon, it is crucial to possess precise intelligence on the enemy's troop numbers, as no substantial strategy for offense or defense can be constructed without a clear understanding of what to anticipate and where potential threats lie. Marshal Villars astutely notes, "When the first shot is fired, no one can foresee the outcome of the war." Therefore, the importance of thorough contemplation before initiating conflict cannot be overstated. Yet, once the decision for war is made, the marshal advises that the boldest, most comprehensive strategies tend to be the wisest and most likely to succeed. "When we commit to war," he adds, "it should be pursued with vigor and without hesitation."

MAXIM VI.

At the outset of a campaign, deciding whether or not to advance demands serious consideration. However, once an army takes the offensive, it must pursue it relentlessly to the very end. Regardless of how skillfully a retreat is conducted, it inevitably undermines the morale of the troops, for it surrenders opportunities for victory to the enemy. Furthermore, retreats often incur greater losses in troops and equipment than even the bloodiest battles. The key distinction is that, in a direct engagement, the enemy sustains comparable losses to yours; yet in a retreat, the majority of losses fall solely on your side.

NOTE.

Marshal Saxe observes that retreats tend to fare best when they are made in the face of a sluggish or unassertive enemy, for a vigorous pursuit quickly turns a retreat into a chaotic flight. "In line with this notion, it is a major mistake," the marshal contends, "to rely on the old saying that advises leaving a 'golden bridge' for a retreating enemy. On the contrary, pursue him with energy, and he will be utterly defeated!"

MAXIM VII.

An army must be perpetually prepared—day, night, and at all hours—to present the fullest resistance possible. To achieve this, soldiers must be equipped consistently with complete arms and ammunition; the infantry should remain alongside its artillery, cavalry, and commanders; and each division within the army should always be in a state to both support others and defend itself.

Whether the troops are stationed, camped, or on the move, they should always maintain favorable positions that meet the key requirements for effective combat. This includes well-protected flanks and artillery positioned for maximum range and advantage. During marching, the army should deploy advanced guards and flanking units to thoroughly scout the terrain ahead and to both sides, maintaining a distance that allows the main force to spread into battle formation if needed.

NOTE.

The following maxims from Montécuculli's memoirs provide a wealth of strategic wisdom, expanding upon the core principles in the art of war:

1. Once the decision for war is made, it is no longer the time for doubt or hesitation. A general must cast aside scruples, embrace confidence, and trust that all potential mishaps may not materialize—that fate, strategy, or even the enemy's mistakes may yet play in their favor. Success hinges, first and foremost, on

unified command under one individual. Divided authority risks introducing contradictory opinions, which can lead to a loss of cohesion and purpose essential to victory. When responsibility is shared across many, actions often lose vigor, as personal stakes become diffused and the collective drive toward a shared outcome is weakened.

Having carefully adhered to the principles and tactics necessary for sound warfare, and taken every precaution to secure success, a commander must entrust the rest to Providence, accepting that some outcomes rest in the hands of a higher power. Regardless of the result, it is essential for a general-in-chief to remain unshaken and steady in purpose—never overly exalted by triumph nor unduly dejected by setbacks. For war's very nature entails constant shifts of fortune; it is the rhythm of military operations that periods of prosperity and adversity follow one another, each turn creating opportunities for gain or loss.

2. When a commander's own army is robust and experienced, while the enemy's forces are weak, inexperienced, or worn down by inactivity, then every means must be employed to bring the enemy into a direct confrontation. However, if the enemy's forces are notably stronger, then a head-on battle should be avoided; instead, efforts should focus on slowing the enemy's advance through defensive encampments and fortifying strategic passes along their path.

When the forces are more evenly matched, direct combat need not be avoided, but it is wise to engage only on favorable terms. To achieve this, always ensure the army's camp is positioned in front of the enemy's. Move when the enemy moves, aiming to occupy high ground or other advantageous locations along their route. By taking control of structures, roads, and critical pathways, a commander can place their army in an advantageous position, even before direct confrontation. Delaying the enemy's movements, impeding their plans, or even slowing their preparations is a strategic advantage in itself. However, if the disparity in strength is too great and tactical maneuvering offers no chance for success, then the only prudent choice is to abandon the campaign entirely, withdrawing forces to fortified positions where they can regroup and defend from a place of strength.

These principles encapsulate a strategic philosophy emphasizing preparedness, prudent action, and adapting to circumstances on the ground. They underscore the importance of unification under command, timely offensive action when advantageous, and tactical retreat when necessary to preserve one's forces.

3. In the heat of battle, the foremost concern of a general-in-chief should be to secure the flanks of his army. Although natural obstacles, like rivers or ravines, may sometimes serve as protection, these immovable features best suit a general in a defensive stance, not one advancing for attack. When offensive maneuvers are necessary, a general cannot rely on fixed positions alone and must instead employ the strategic positioning and formation of troops to secure the army from any assault on its front, flanks, or rear.

If one wing of the army is shielded by a river or impassable ravine, the entire cavalry force can be concentrated on the other wing. This arrangement allows the general to better capitalize on the cavalry's superior numbers, enveloping the enemy more effectively. Conversely, if the enemy is positioned with their flanks protected by natural obstacles such as dense woods, dispatching light cavalry or infantry to flank or attack their rear can create critical openings. An additional tactic is to target the enemy's baggage, which can deepen their disorder and further erode morale.

In a scenario where the aim is to defeat the enemy's left flank with your right wing, or vice versa, the wing designated for the attack should be bolstered with the finest units—the elite soldiers capable of the fiercest engagement. Simultaneously, the opposite wing should adopt a stance of minimal engagement to avoid full-scale combat. The attacking wing should then be advanced swiftly and with intensity, striking decisively at the chosen enemy flank. When terrain permits, it's advantageous to approach the enemy with stealth, attacking when they are unprepared. Signs of hesitation or fear in the opposing force are often detectable through erratic movements or disarray. Once these signs emerge, the general should initiate an immediate pursuit to exploit the enemy's weakness before they can recover. At this point, deploying the cavalry becomes essential; it can maneuver to intercept and sever the enemy's artillery and baggage, ensuring that their losses compound with each blow. This approach secures not only a tactical advantage but often a psychological upper hand, intensifying the enemy's sense of impending defeat.

4. In planning the movement of an army, the structure of the march should always conform to the prearranged order of battle. This preparation ensures that the army can transition smoothly from marching to combat if necessary. A march is efficiently managed when it aligns with the specific distance to be covered and the time allocated. Flexibility is key, allowing the front of the marching column to narrow or widen based on the surrounding terrain, while always ensuring the artillery remains on the main road for straightforward access and maneuverability.

When a river crossing is required, the artillery should be strategically positioned on the opposite bank to provide defensive cover for the crossing. If the river creates a natural bend or angle, or if a ford is nearby, it offers a tactical advantage. As work on the bridge progresses, infantry units should move forward to protect the engineers by maintaining fire against any potential threats on the opposite side. Once the bridge is complete, it's critical to quickly deploy a mixed unit of infantry, cavalry, and field artillery across the river. The infantry should entrench at the bridgehead to secure this vital crossing point, and additional defenses on the original bank are prudent to safeguard the bridge should the enemy attempt a counter-offensive.

The vanguard of the army must have reliable guides to navigate the best routes and be supported by a team of pioneers to enhance road conditions for smooth passage. If the army is split into detachments, each unit leader should receive a written directive with the name of the regrouping location. This spot should be chosen far enough from the enemy's reach to prevent interception before all units converge, and it's crucial that the location remains undisclosed to maintain secrecy.

As the army nears the enemy, it should align itself in the anticipated battle formation. In situations where an ambush or sudden assault is anticipated, preparations should be scaled to match the perceived threat. When traversing narrow passes or defiles, the army should halt on the far side until all units have safely exited the confined area.

To mask an army's movements, night marches are advantageous, especially through wooded areas, valleys, or secluded roads that avoid populated areas. Fires should be strictly prohibited to prevent detection, and orders should be delivered verbally to maintain stealth. If the objective is to capture an enemy-held position or relieve a besieged site, the vanguard should march within musket range of the main force to maintain a tightly coordinated structure, ready to respond immediately if engaged.

When forcing an enemy-guarded pass, deception can be valuable. A feigned attack at one point, followed by a rapid shift to the actual target, can catch the enemy off-guard. At times, pretending to retreat along the initial route can lead the enemy to relax, allowing a sudden countermarch to capture the pass before it can be reinforced. Some commanders have successfully executed this by deploying a detachment under cover, moving stealthily across elevated terrain to seize the passage undetected. Meanwhile, the main body diverts the enemy's attention, enabling the detachment to establish a fortified position in its newly acquired location. This approach not only allows the army to secure strategic points but also keeps the enemy in a state of uncertainty, yielding a psychological edge.

5. When setting up camp, an army adjusts its approach based on the level of caution required by the circumstances. In a friendly or allied territory, the troops may be divided into smaller groups, allowing for more comfortable accommodations and easier access to local resources and supplies. However, in proximity to the enemy, it is crucial for an army to always encamp in a formation that mirrors the anticipated battle order. This alignment provides readiness for immediate deployment and enhances the camp's defensive stance.

In these conditions, it becomes essential to place parts of the camp under the protection of natural defenses, such as rivers, rock formations, or deep ravines, whenever possible. Such features not only hinder enemy access but also provide a defensive advantage. The layout of the camp should also ensure that no high ground nearby could be used to command or overlook the camp, as this would expose the army to surprise attacks or surveillance from a position of advantage. Another priority is maintaining unobstructed communication lines between the different units within the camp, enabling them to provide mutual support quickly if any sector comes under attack.

If an army plans to remain in one place for an extended period, having a reliable supply of provisions and ammunition is essential, as are secure access routes for replenishment. In such cases, it is vital to establish a well-protected line of communication and avoid leaving any hostile fortress or enemy stronghold behind the main camp that could interfere with supply lines or potentially cut off escape or reinforcement routes.

During winter quarters, an army's security is maximized by fortifying the camp itself. This approach is especially effective if the camp is near a large town or close to a river, which would facilitate the transport of supplies and allow for commercial exchanges to support the troops. Another strategic option is to position the army in closely grouped cantonments. In this setup, even if dispersed across several locations, the troops remain in close enough proximity to provide mutual assistance. This organization ensures that, even in separate quarters, units are capable of coming to each other's aid in the event of an attack. These strategies, carefully implemented, enable an army to maintain both safety and readiness across seasons, whether actively engaged in campaigns or in periods of necessary rest.

Winter quarters for an army require additional defensive measures to ensure stability during the off-season, as vulnerabilities are increased in static positions. To safeguard these quarters, small covered works should be erected along all approaches to the cantonments, serving as early defensive structures. These are essential for preventing enemy access or surprise attacks. Additionally, placing advanced guards of cavalry at strategic locations offers an extra layer of security by allowing close observation of any enemy movements, enabling swift response if threats arise.

6. A battle should be pursued when there is a reasonable prospect of victory or when an army faces unavoidable ruin unless it engages. Battles are strategically advantageous when a besieged location needs relief or when blocking reinforcements from reaching the enemy becomes critical. They are also valuable opportunities if they allow forces to exploit a strategic advantage, such as gaining control of an unprotected point or attacking when the enemy has made a tactical error. If divisions or miscommunications exist among the enemy's generals, these moments are ideal for a decisive attack.

When an enemy avoids confrontation, several tactics can compel them to engage. Besieging a critical location forces them to act, while surprise maneuvers or positioning that limits their escape can also drive them into battle. Alternatively, after feigning a retreat, a rapid countermarch to catch them off guard with a vigorous assault can force them into action.

Certain scenarios call for avoiding battle. For example, if defeat poses greater risk than victory promises benefit, or if reinforcements are expected but the current forces are significantly outnumbered, holding off is often wiser. Particularly, when the enemy is well-positioned, or when errors and internal discord within their ranks naturally contribute to their decline, it's advantageous to let time erode their strength.

Securing victory in battle relies on skillfully positioning each division so that both flanking and frontal engagement are possible. Ideally, natural obstacles protect the flanks, though, if needed, fortifications can be used to create defensive barriers. Units must support one another smoothly, avoiding congestion or overlapping that could create chaos in the ranks. If any corps is forced to fall back, it's vital that they do so without disorganizing others.

A primary defensive measure is ensuring that gaps between units are small enough to prevent the enemy from exploiting these spaces to penetrate the formation. A gap would force the use of reserves and increase the risk of being overpowered. Victory can sometimes be achieved through timely diversions or by positioning troops in a situation where retreat is impossible, giving them no option but to fight fiercely for survival.

At the start of an engagement, advancing toward the enemy can encourage troops, particularly on flat terrain. However, if forces hold an advantageous position, especially with artillery in a prime location, it's best to stand firm and let the enemy approach. This tactic preserves energy while allowing artillery to inflict damage from a distance. During battle, it's critical to fight steadfastly, offer support where needed, and reserve fresh troops as a final contingency, holding back some reserves as a fallback for regrouping broken lines.

When a full-force attack is necessary, launching it in the late afternoon provides the benefit of impending nightfall, which serves as a natural break. This timing enables a withdrawal under cover of darkness if the engagement's outcome demands it. Throughout the action, the general-in-chief should be stationed at a vantage point that allows the widest possible view of the field, remaining informed of developments across divisions. He must be ready to intensify pressure with fresh troops on points where the enemy is faltering and reinforce any units that show signs of wavering.

In the event of success, the general should pursue the retreating enemy immediately, denying them the chance to regroup. Conversely, if defeat appears inevitable or the tide of battle turns unfavorably, he must manage a structured retreat, maintaining as much cohesion as possible to prevent a complete rout. This ability to adapt to the flow of battle, reinforce strengths, and mitigate losses in defeat is essential for sustaining a capable and resilient fighting force.

7. A general demonstrates exceptional skill when he brings well-prepared troops into direct conflict with those who are unprepared, exploiting the advantage of fresh troops against those who are fatigued or depleted. The advantage is even more pronounced when experienced, battle-hardened soldiers confront inexperienced recruits. To capitalize on this, a general should be vigilant for opportunities to strike at weak or isolated enemy detachments. Pursuing the enemy strategically, he should aim to confront them in terrain that impedes their ability to regroup or establish a solid defensive position, such as attacking them in narrow passes before they can organize their defenses.

8. The effectiveness of a battlefield position depends largely on ensuring that all units are positioned to engage effectively, with none remaining idle or unutilized. In situations where cavalry superiority exists, positions on open plains are most beneficial, maximizing the cavalry's maneuverability and charge potential. Conversely, if infantry strength dominates, an enclosed, wooded, or rugged terrain provides the best advantage, leveraging infantry skills in confined settings. When forces are significantly outnumbered, seeking defensive terrain such as narrow passes or chokepoints is essential, while a large, open battlefield is preferable when one holds the numerical advantage

9. To achieve maximum impact from a diversion, it's critical to first confirm that the terrain targeted is accessible, allowing for rapid penetration into enemy territory. A diversion must be executed decisively, and it should focus on areas where it will inflict the greatest disruption or harm on the adversary. Effectiveness lies in both the speed and surprise of the maneuver, applying pressure precisely where the enemy is most vulnerable or least defended.

10. Success in warfare rests on a set of core principles that, if consistently followed, offer the best chances of victory:

- Strive to maintain superiority over the enemy both in troop numbers and morale. A larger, well-motivated force is more likely to overcome challenges and succeed in engagements.

- Engage in battle not only to secure immediate tactical objectives but also to instill fear and exert control over the surrounding territories.

- Divide the army into manageable corps, balancing the need for broad strategic reach with the caution necessary to avoid undue risk. This enables simultaneous operations, creating strategic pressure on multiple fronts.

- Employ contrasting tactics to address the attitudes of those encountered: treat those who surrender with leniency to encourage compliance, while handling resistance with firm, sometimes severe, measures to discourage rebellion.

- Secure the rear of the advancing army, establishing a well-defended post that can serve as a command center for support, logistics, and reinforcements for upcoming operations.

- Guard vigilantly against desertion to preserve the integrity and strength of the force.

- Prioritize gaining control over significant rivers, mountain passes, and other critical chokepoints, which are essential for maintaining lines of communication and for safe, reliable movement of troops and supplies.

- Capture fortresses strategically to establish strongholds along your line of advance, ensuring that vital areas remain secure. Combat is often unavoidable, as battles are essential in claiming territories. However, following a successful victory, conquered lands are best held by blending firmness with fairness—balancing strength with generosity ensures stability.

Through these carefully considered tactics and strategies, a commander maximizes not only the likelihood of military success but also the sustainability of newly acquired territories.

MAXIM VIII.

A general-in-chief must continuously evaluate his position by asking himself multiple times throughout the day: "What action would I take if the enemy's army suddenly appeared in front of me? What would be my response if they advanced on my right flank? What would I do if they attacked from the left?" If he finds himself uncertain or unable to provide clear answers to any of these questions, it is an indication of a flawed position. In such a case, he should take immediate steps to adjust his strategy or reposition his forces to strengthen his defenses, ensuring he is fully prepared for any sudden engagement with the enemy.

NOTE.

In the 1758 campaign, the Prussian army's position at Hohen Kirk was flawed, as the enemy's batteries held command over all the surrounding heights. Despite this strategic vulnerability, Frederick the Great remained in camp for six days without adjusting his position, even as the corps of Laudon threatened his rear. Frederick appeared unaware of the true extent of the danger. Taking advantage of this, Marshal Daun maneuvered during the night to launch an attack at dawn, catching the Prussians off guard within their own lines and fully encircling them before they could properly mount a defense.

Though Frederick managed an orderly retreat, it came at a high cost: ten thousand men, numerous general officers, and almost all of his artillery. Had Marshal Daun pursued his victory more aggressively, Frederick would likely have been unable to reorganize his forces. In this instance, Frederick's characteristic luck compensated for his lapse in strategic judgment.

Marshal Saxe observed that there's more skill involved in turning a flawed position into an advantageous one at just the right moment than most realize. Such a maneuver can deeply unsettle the enemy, who, having made all preparations based on an expected course of action, is caught off guard if it suddenly changes. "Nothing confuses an enemy more," said Marshal Saxe, "than this tactic; for if he holds to his initial plan, he is likely to be defeated, but if he scrambles to adjust it in the midst of battle, he is equally undone."

Nevertheless, relying solely on this approach is risky. A skilled and observant opponent might exploit poor arrangements before the opportunity arises to transform them. For such a strategy to succeed, it requires impeccable timing and judgment, as well as an enemy vulnerable to surprise.

MAXIM IX.

The effectiveness of an army, much like the principles of mechanical force, is measured by the product of its mass and speed. A swift, determined march not only boosts the morale of the troops but also amplifies their capacity for achieving victory. Therefore, push forward without hesitation!

NOTE.

Montécuculli emphasizes that "speed is crucial in keeping an army's movements concealed, as it allows no opportunity for the enemy to discover the intentions of its leader. Therefore, attacking unexpectedly is advantageous, catching the enemy off-guard, surprising him, and delivering the blow before he can anticipate it. However, if excessive speed tires out your forces, while hesitation causes you to miss the opportune moment, you must carefully weigh the benefit against the cost and make the best choice."

Marshal Villars also notes that "success in war hinges on deceiving the enemy, and once this advantage is gained, not giving him any chance to regroup." Villars indeed practiced what he preached, with his daring and swift advances often leading to victory. Similarly, Frederick held that all wars should be brief and decisive, as prolonged conflict gradually undermines discipline, depletes the population, and drains the nation's resources.

MAXIM X.

When an army finds itself outnumbered, lacking in cavalry, and deficient in artillery, it becomes crucial to evade a full-scale confrontation. The shortage of manpower can be counterbalanced by swift and agile maneuvers; the absence of artillery can be mitigated through careful and strategic maneuvering; and the weakness in cavalry should be compensated for by selecting advantageous positions that minimize exposure. In these situations, much rests on the morale and determination of the soldiers, which often plays a significant role in overcoming physical limitations.

NOTE.

The campaign of 1814 in France exemplified masterful execution based on these principles. Napoleon, commanding an army far outnumbered, worn down by the disastrous retreats from Moscow and Leipzig, and further demoralized by the enemy's presence on French soil, managed to offset this overwhelming disadvantage by employing swift, well-coordinated maneuvers. Through victories at Champ-Aubert, Montmirail, Montereau, and Rheims, he began to revive the spirit and morale of the French forces. The fresh recruits in his army quickly gained confidence, following the steadfast example set by the seasoned regiments. Just as this resurgence of spirit was taking hold, the sudden capture of Paris and the dramatic turn of events it triggered forced Napoleon into an unavoidable surrender.

However, this outcome was more a consequence of the broader circumstances than an outright necessity. Napoleon could have, by leading his forces across the Loire, united with the armies stationed in the Alps and the Pyrenees, allowing him to return to the field with a reinforced army of over one hundred thousand men. With this formidable force, he could have regained a strong position in the ongoing conflict, especially considering that the allied armies would have had to operate within France while the strongholds of Italy and France lay securely behind him.

MAXIM XI.

Directing operations with different groups that are far from each other and without clear communication is always a mistake that leads to more problems. A separate group of soldiers only has orders for the first day. What they do on the following day depends on what has happened to the main army. So, in an emergency, this group might waste time waiting for new orders, or they may have to act on their own and take risks. Therefore, it should be a rule that an army keeps its groups close enough so that the enemy cannot easily slip between them. When, for specific reasons, this rule is broken, the separated groups should be able to operate independently. They should move toward a place where they will rejoin the main army, without hesitation and without waiting for more orders. Every possible measure should be taken to prevent the enemy from attacking them one by one.

NOTE.

The Austrian army, led by Field Marshal Alvinzi, was split into two groups, each meant to operate independently until they could meet up in front of Mantua. The first group, made up of forty-five thousand soldiers and under Alvinzi's command, was to advance through Monte Baldo toward the positions held by the French army along the Adige River. The second group, led by General Provéra, was assigned to operate along the lower Adige and to lift the siege of Mantua. Napoleon, aware of the enemy's movements but not fully certain of their plans, focused on gathering his forces and ordering his troops to be ready to maneuver. Meanwhile, new information assured the French commander that the group advancing from La Coronna over Monte Baldo was trying to link up with its cavalry and artillery, both of which had crossed the Adige at Dolce and were heading toward the plateau of Rivoli along the main road through Incanole.

Napoleon immediately realized that by holding the plateau, he could block this link-up and gain the advantage of the first move. So, he set his troops in motion, and by two o'clock in the morning, they had taken up this key position. Once he controlled the point chosen for the meeting of the Austrian forces, everything went according to plan. He repelled every attack, captured seven thousand prisoners, and seized multiple standards and twelve cannons. By two in the afternoon, the battle of Rivoli was already won. However, when Napoleon learned that General Provéra had crossed the Adige at Anghiari and was marching toward Mantua, he left his generals to pursue Alvinzi's retreat and took command of a division to counter Provéra's plans.

With a swift march, Napoleon again seized the initiative, stopping the Mantua garrison from joining forces with the relief army. The corps assigned to keep up the blockade, eager to impress the victor of Rivoli, forced the garrison back into the city, while Victor's division, ignoring the exhaustion of a forced march, charged head-on at the relief army. At that critical moment, a sortie from the lines of St. George struck his flank, and Augereau's corps, which had been tracking the Austrian general's movements, attacked from behind. Surrounded on all sides, Provéra surrendered. The outcome of these two battles cost the Austrians three thousand men killed or wounded, twenty-two thousand captured, twenty-four standards, and forty-six cannons.

MAXIM XII.

An army should have only one line of operation. This line must be carefully maintained and should only be abandoned in the direst situation.

NOTE.

Montécuculli says, "An army's line of communication must be clear and well-established, for any army operating far from its base that fails to keep this line fully open is heading toward disaster. It moves toward inevitable ruin, as countless examples have shown. If the route for bringing up food, ammunition, and reinforcements is not completely secure—if the supply stations, hospitals, weapon depots, and other resource points are not strategically placed—not only will the army be unable to stay in the field, but it will also face serious dangers."

MAXIM XIII.

The allowed distances between the units of an army on the march must be determined by the terrain, the specific situation, and the intended goal.

NOTE.

When an army moves a considerable distance away from the enemy, it has the flexibility to arrange its columns along the road to make room for the artillery, supply trains, and baggage wagons. This arrangement helps the army move efficiently and keep all its resources together, especially when there's no immediate threat from the enemy. However, when the army is advancing into battle, the situation changes drastically. In this case, each division must form into close, compact columns, prepared for engagement. This formation helps ensure that the different corps can support each other directly and quickly if the need arises, presenting a unified front to the enemy. The generals overseeing these columns have the important task of ensuring that each attacking column maintains its position relative to the others, preventing any from advancing too far ahead. As the army nears the battlefield, it becomes critical to keep the proper intervals between columns, allowing them the space needed for an effective deployment when they engage the enemy.

As Frederick the Great once stated, "The marches taken before a battle require the greatest caution." He emphasized that during these preparatory marches, generals must stay extremely vigilant and take careful measures to assess the terrain. By scouting the ground at regular intervals, the army can secure an advantage by taking up positions that best support a strong attack. Frederick advised that these positions should be chosen specifically for their strategic advantages, providing the army with the best opportunity to gain the upper hand when they engage the enemy. For example, occupying higher ground or areas with natural cover could offer an advantage in terms of defense and visibility.

During a retreat, the strategy shifts, but many generals believe that an army still capable of counterattacking should concentrate its forces and march in tightly packed columns. This formation keeps the army compact and ready to respond quickly if a favorable chance to strike the enemy arises. By maintaining this structure, the army can swiftly form a battle line, allowing it either to slow down the enemy's advance or launch an attack if the opposing forces are not prepared to respond. This tactic was famously illustrated during Moreau's retreat after the Austro-Russian army crossed the Adda. The French general, charged with overseeing the safe withdrawal of his forces, first focused on covering the evacuation of Milan, ensuring that his troops could withdraw without exposing themselves to immediate danger. Afterward, he positioned his army between the Po and Tanaro rivers, using the natural landscape as a defensive measure. His camp was strategically located near the fortresses of Alexandria and Valentia, two essential strongholds that provided him with defensive advantages and allowed him to control the roads leading to Turin and Savona. These routes offered potential escape paths if uniting with Macdonald's forces proved impossible. Macdonald, who had been ordered to leave the Kingdom of Naples, was urgently marching toward Tuscany to join forces with Moreau.

However, unforeseen circumstances, such as widespread uprisings in both Piedmont and Tuscany, forced Moreau to adjust his plans. Under pressure from these local revolts, he retreated to Asti, where he soon discovered that his link to the Genoa River had been severed following the capture of Ceva by enemy forces. In response, Moreau made several attempts to reclaim Ceva, but when these efforts failed, he realized that his only option for survival was to maneuver his forces into the mountains, where the rugged terrain could offer some protection from the advancing Austro-Russian army. To carry out this plan, he directed his heavy artillery and supplies along the Col de Fenestrelle toward France, securing his most critical resources. Then, with his light artillery and the smaller field equipment that could still be mobilized, he led his forces over the St. Bernard pass to Loano. This move was a testament to his strategic skill, as it allowed him to keep his lines of communication with France open while also observing the movements of the Neapolitan army. This approach facilitated a potential link-up with Macdonald's forces by concentrating his troops at the crucial points needed for their eventual union.

Meanwhile, Macdonald's actions did not align with Moreau's strategy. Although Macdonald's chances of success hinged on gathering his smaller army into a concentrated force, he neglected this key step, leading to his defeat in three consecutive battles at the Trebia. This setback delayed his march and disrupted Moreau's plans to unite their armies in the plains along the Po River. Following his determined but unsuccessful efforts at the Trebia, Macdonald's retreat further complicated Moreau's efforts to provide reinforcements, undermining the arrangements that had been carefully made for their joint operations. However, despite these challenges, Marshal Suwarrow's unexpected inactivity eventually gave Moreau the opportunity to regroup and join forces with the remaining troops from Naples. This consolidation allowed Moreau to gather his forces along the Apennines, positioning them defensively to protect Liguria's vital areas until conditions allowed for a renewed offensive.

When an army, after a decisive defeat, has lost essential resources like artillery and equipment, it is often no longer in a position to take the offensive or even slow down the enemy's pursuit. In such cases, the best strategy may be to divide the remaining forces into several smaller groups and send them along separate, distant routes toward the base of operations, with each group aiming to reach fortified positions for safety. This approach offers the highest chance of survival, as the enemy, unable to determine the exact direction of the retreating army, will not immediately know which group to pursue. It is in this moment of hesitation and uncertainty that the army gains valuable time. Moreover, smaller groups can move faster and more easily than a larger, unified force, making this strategy particularly effective for an army in retreat. By splitting into separate routes, the retreating forces have a better chance of evading capture and preserving their strength for future engagements.

MAXIM XIV.

In mountainous regions, there are always many naturally strong positions that are risky to assault. The nature of warfare in such terrain involves setting up camps on the enemy's flanks or behind him, forcing him into a difficult choice: either he abandons his position without a fight to take up a new one further back, or he has to descend from his position to launch an attack. In mountain warfare, the attacker is always at a disadvantage; even in open-field battles where one is on the offensive, the real strategy lies in defensive engagements, drawing the enemy into a position where they must attack.

NOTE.

In the 1793 campaign in the Maritime Alps, the French army, under General Brunet's command, made every effort to capture the camps at Raus and Fourches by attacking directly from the front. However, these repeated and ultimately pointless assaults only served to strengthen the resolve of the Piedmontese forces, while causing heavy losses among the elite grenadiers of the republican army. In contrast, the strategic maneuvers Napoleon employed in 1796, which compelled the enemy to abandon these strongholds without engaging in direct combat, effectively highlight the strength of these principles. This example clearly illustrates that success in warfare depends not only on the bravery and endurance of the soldiers but also on the keen intelligence and strategy of the general who directs them.

MAXIM XV.

During the 1793 campaign in the Maritime Alps, the French army, commanded by General Brunet, exerted every possible effort to seize control of the camps at Raus and Fourches through direct frontal attacks. However, these repeated, ultimately fruitless assaults only served to heighten the determination of the Piedmontese troops while causing considerable losses among the finest grenadiers of the republican army. In stark contrast, Napoleon's strategic maneuvers in 1796, which led the enemy to abandon these fortified positions without a single direct engagement, underscore the effectiveness of these guiding principles. This contrast powerfully illustrates that true success in warfare requires not just the courage and resilience of the soldiers, but also the astute planning and insightful leadership of the general in command.

NOTE.

In 1645, while the French army under the Prince of Condé was advancing to lay siege to Nordlingen, it became clear that Count Merci, leading the Bavarian forces, had anticipated this move. Merci had entrenched his troops in a fortified position that not only defended Nordlingen but also provided cover for Donawerth. Despite the enemy's advantageous position, Condé ordered an attack. The battle was intense and brutal. The infantry at the center and on the right were successively engaged but eventually routed and scattered, despite the efforts of the cavalry and reserve units, which were also swept away with the retreating soldiers. The battle seemed lost.

In a moment of despair, with no center or right flank to rely on, Condé gathered what was left of his battalions and redirected them to the left, where Turenne was still fighting. This act of determination reignited the spirit of the troops. They successfully broke through the enemy's right wing, and Turenne, with a swift shift in formation, launched another attack on the center. The arrival of night aided Condé's daring efforts. One Bavarian corps, believing themselves surrounded, surrendered their arms. Condé's relentless pursuit of victory was rewarded; the French held the battlefield, captured a large number of prisoners, and seized nearly all the enemy's artillery. The Bavarian army retreated, and the following day, Nordlingen surrendered.

MAXIM XVI.

A well-established principle in warfare is to avoid doing what the enemy wants, simply because it is what they desire. Therefore, a battlefield that the enemy has carefully studied and scouted should be avoided, and even greater caution should be exercised if they have had time to fortify and entrench themselves there. A key takeaway from this principle is to avoid launching a frontal attack on a position that can be captured by outflanking it.

NOTE.

Marshal Villeroi disregarded this principle during the 1701 campaign in Italy when, upon taking command, he recklessly attacked Prince Eugene of Savoy, who was well-fortified in the entrenched position at Chiavi on the Oglio River. Although other French generals, including Catinat, deemed the position unassailable, Villeroi pressed forward with unjustified confidence. The outcome of this otherwise minor battle was the heavy loss of the finest troops in the French army, which might have been even worse if not for Catinat's efforts.

Similarly, in 1644, the Prince of Condé failed by overlooking the same principle in his repeated attempts to break through the entrenched position of the Bavarian army. Count Merci, commanding the Bavarian forces, had positioned his cavalry skillfully on the plain near Freyberg while his infantry held a strong position in the mountains. After numerous failed assaults, Condé recognized that dislodging the enemy was impossible and shifted his strategy to threaten Merci's supply lines. Seeing this, Merci quickly broke camp and withdrew beyond the Black Mountains, maintaining his position by prioritizing mobility over direct confrontation.

MAXIM XVII.

In a campaign marked by marches and maneuvers, when seeking to avoid direct battle with a larger army, it becomes essential to set up entrenchments every night and secure a strong defensive position. Natural positions, while often available along the way, are rarely enough to shield an army against overwhelming numbers without additional fortifications and strategic reinforcement.

NOTE.

The 1706 campaign of the French and Spanish armies, commanded by the Duke of Berwick, against the Portuguese provides a valuable example of strategic maneuvering. The two armies nearly circled Spain, beginning the campaign near Badajoz and, after maneuvering through both Castiles, concluding in the kingdoms of Valencia and Murcia. Throughout this campaign, the Duke of Berwick established camp eighty-five times, and although no major battle took place, his forces managed to capture around ten thousand enemy soldiers.

Similarly, Marshal Turenne conducted a notable campaign of maneuvering against Count Montécuculli in 1675. When the imperial army planned to cross the Rhine at Strasburg, Turenne acted swiftly, constructing a bridge near the village of Ottenheim, about three leagues below Strasburg. He crossed with the French army and set up camp near the small town of Vilstet, securing it to protect the bridge at Strasburg. Through this strategic positioning, Turenne effectively blocked the enemy's access to the city.

In response, Montécuculli mobilized his entire army, posing a threat to the Ottenheim bridge, through which the French received their supplies from upper Alsace. Realizing the enemy's intention, Turenne left a detachment at Vilstet and quickly marched his entire force to the village of Altenheim. This intermediate position between the two bridges enabled him to reinforce either post before the enemy could capture it. Recognizing the futility of attacking either bridge, Montécuculli decided to attempt a Rhine crossing below Strasburg and returned to his original position at Offenburg. Turenne, closely monitoring the Austrian army's movements, returned his forces to Vilstet, maintaining control over the strategic positions and preserving his defensive advantage.

Meanwhile, this attempt by the enemy alerted the French general to the vulnerability created by his bridge's location, so he moved it closer to the bridge at Strasburg to reduce the area he needed to defend. Montécuculli, in turn, instructed the Strasburg magistrates to gather materials for constructing his own bridge and moved to Scherzheim to receive them. However, Turenne once again disrupted his plans by taking up a position at Freistett, where he occupied the islands in the Rhine and quickly built a stockade.

Throughout the entire campaign, Turenne maintained the advantage by dictating the enemy's movements and forcing Montécuculli to respond to his strategies. At one point, Turenne conducted a swift march that effectively cut Montécuculli off from Offenburg, his source of supplies. This maneuver would likely have prevented the Austrian general from joining forces with Caprara's corps if not for the tragic event that followed—a single cannon shot that ended Turenne's remarkable life.

MAXIM XVIII.

A general of average skill, when caught in a poor position and faced with a stronger force, will often seek safety in retreat. However, a truly great commander compensates for any disadvantages with bold courage, advancing confidently to meet the attack. This unexpected move can throw the enemy off balance; and if the opponent hesitates, a skilled leader can exploit that uncertainty, potentially turning the situation toward victory. At the very least, such a leader can use the day to maneuver, then either entrench for the night or withdraw to a stronger position. Through this decisive approach, he upholds the honor of his forces, which is fundamental to achieving military superiority.

NOTE.

In 1653, Marshal Turenne found himself caught off guard by the Prince of Condé in a highly vulnerable position. Although he could have safeguarded his forces by quickly retreating to the Somme, which he could cross at Peronne, just half a league away, Turenne understood that a retreat could weaken the morale of his troops. Weighing the risks, he chose to counter these disadvantages with courage, advancing boldly to confront the enemy despite having far fewer soldiers. After marching for a league, he reached a favorable position and made all necessary preparations for battle. It was already three o'clock in the afternoon, but the Spanish forces, weary from their efforts, hesitated to engage. During the night, Turenne fortified his position with entrenchments, and by morning, the enemy no longer dared to launch a full-scale assault and instead withdrew from the field.

MAXIM XIX.

The transition from the defensive to the offensive is one of the most delicate operations.

NOTE.

By examining Napoleon's first campaign in Italy, we can observe the power of genius and boldness in shifting an army from a defensive stance to an offensive one. The allied army, led by General Beaulieu, was well-equipped and formidable, with a strength of eighty thousand men and two hundred cannons. In stark contrast, the French forces numbered barely thirty thousand soldiers and had only thirty cannons. They had gone without meat for some time, and even bread was in short supply. The infantry was poorly clothed, the cavalry inadequately mounted, and most draught horses had died from neglect, forcing the artillery to rely on mules. To address these challenges, substantial funds were required, but the financial state was so dire that the government had only been able to supply two thousand louis in cash to start the campaign. In this condition, the French army had no choice but to either advance or retreat.

Napoleon understood the value of striking a decisive blow early in the campaign, which led him to focus on renewing the morale of his troops. In a powerful proclamation, he reminded them that remaining on the defensive meant facing a dishonorable death and that while they could expect little from France, victory held every promise. "Abundance awaits you in the fertile plains of Italy," he declared. "Do you lack, soldiers, in constancy or courage?" Using the enthusiasm he had inspired, Napoleon gathered his forces to unleash a concentrated assault on the enemy's scattered corps. This led to swift victories at the battles of Montenotte, Milesimo, and Mondovi, boosting the soldiers' already high regard for their leader. The army, which only days before had been camped amid barren rocks and plagued by hunger, now began to dream of conquering Italy.

Within a month of beginning the campaign, Napoleon had ended the conflict with the King of Sardinia and conquered the region of Milan. The soldiers, soon encamped in prosperous areas, quickly forgot the hardships and hunger of their grueling march. Meanwhile, a well-organized administration of local resources restored the equipment and supplies of the French army, providing the means for further victories.

MAXIM XX.

A fundamental principle in warfare is that the line of operation should generally not be abandoned. However, one of the most skillful maneuvers is knowing when and how to change this line when circumstances justify or necessitate it. An army that expertly shifts its line of operation creates confusion for the enemy, who is then uncertain about where to find its rear or which points are vulnerable to attack.

NOTE.

Frederick occasionally changed his line of operation in the midst of a campaign, but he was able to do so because he maneuvered within central Germany—a resource-rich area capable of meeting his army's needs if his lines of communication with Prussia were cut off. Similarly, in the 1746 campaign, Marshal Turenne abandoned his line of communication to the allies, yet he, too, was conducting operations in central Germany. After concentrating his forces at Rain, he took the precaution of securing a supply depot to establish a reliable base of operations.

Through a series of maneuvers characterized by both boldness and strategic insight, Turenne then forced the imperial army to abandon its supply depots and retreat into Austria for winter quarters. These examples, however, are best followed with caution. Such maneuvers should be attempted only after carefully assessing the capabilities of one's adversary and, above all, when there is no risk of an uprising in the region where the theater of war is being shifted.

MAXIM XXI.

When an army is transporting heavy artillery or large convoys of sick and wounded, it must take the shortest possible route to its supply depots.

NOTE.

This principle is especially crucial in mountainous regions and areas scattered with woods and marshes. In such terrain, convoys and transport often become entangled in narrow passes, making them vulnerable. An enemy can easily disrupt the escorts through strategic maneuvers or even launch a successful attack on the entire army when difficult terrain forces it to advance in a stretched-out column.

MAXIM XXII.

The skill of setting up camp in a secure position is similar to forming a battle line in that same location. For this purpose, the artillery must be positioned to its best advantage, with the ground chosen so that it cannot be easily outflanked or dominated by higher terrain. Whenever possible, the guns should be placed to cover and control the surrounding area.

NOTE.

Frederick observed that to confirm your camp is well-positioned, you should be able to make a small maneuver that forces the enemy into a much larger one, or if, after causing him to retreat one march, you can compel him to withdraw even further. In defensive warfare, every camp should be fortified at the front and on the flanks of its position, ensuring that the rear remains completely open. If there is a threat of being outflanked, preparations should be made in advance to fall back to a more distant position. Additionally, any disarray in the enemy's march should be used as an opportunity to target their artillery or baggage.

MAXIM XXIII.

When occupying a position that the enemy threatens to encircle, gather all your forces at once and counter by making an offensive threat. This maneuver will prevent the enemy from detaching units to harass your flanks, should you decide that a retreat is necessary.

NOTE.

This was the maneuver used by General Desaix in 1798 near Radstadt. Despite being outnumbered, he compensated with boldness, holding his position against the fierce attacks of Archduke Charles throughout the day. By nightfall, Desaix withdrew in good order and repositioned his forces further back.

Similarly, in the same campaign, General Moreau followed this principle when he engaged at Biberach to secure his retreat through the Black Mountain passes. A few days later, he fought at Schliengen with the same objective. From a strong defensive position, he threatened Archduke Charles with a sudden offensive shift while his artillery and baggage crossed the Rhine via the bridge at Huningen. Meanwhile, he was organizing his own retreat across the river.

It's worth noting that such offensive feints should generally be timed for late in the day, to avoid becoming too deeply engaged in a prolonged fight that cannot be sustained. Nightfall and the ensuing confusion will often aid a retreat, should it be deemed necessary. To further mask the movement, fires should be lit along the lines, deceiving the enemy and concealing the retreat. In such cases, gaining even a single march's advantage over the enemy is invaluable in a successful withdrawal.

MAXIM XXIV.

Always remember this rule: establish your cantonments at the furthest and best-protected point from the enemy, particularly where there is a risk of surprise. This way, you will gain the time needed to bring all your forces together before the enemy can launch an attack.

NOTE.

In the 1745 campaign, Marshal Turenne lost the Battle of Marienthal by disregarding this principle. If, instead of gathering his divisions at Erbsthausen, he had rallied them at Mergentheim, behind the Tauber River, his army would have reunited much faster. Count Merci, who had precise intelligence about French troop positions, would then have faced the entire French army, protected by a river, rather than only the three thousand men he encountered at Erbsthausen.

When someone indiscreetly asked Viscount Turenne how he had lost the Battle of Marienthal, the marshal replied, "By my own fault." He then added, "But when a man has made no mistakes in war, he has probably only been at it for a short time."

MAXIM XXV.

When two armies are positioned for battle, and one must retreat across a bridge while the other has open access around the circumference, all advantages favor the latter. In this situation, the general should act with boldness, deliver a decisive strike, and maneuver along the enemy's flank. Victory is within reach.

NOTE.

This was the situation faced by the French army at the renowned Battle of Leipzig, which ended Napoleon's 1813 campaign with disastrous results, as the subsequent Battle of Hanau had little effect on the army's desperate condition. In circumstances similar to those of the French army before Leipzig, a general should avoid relying on any fortunate turn that might come from resuming the offensive. Instead, he should focus on every possible measure to secure a safe retreat.

To achieve this, the general should immediately set up strong entrenchments to repel enemy attacks with a smaller force while his supplies and equipment cross the river. As troops reach the far side, they should take up positions to defend the crossing for the rear guard. Once the army breaks camp, this rear guard should be shielded by a bridgehead, or tête de pont. During the Revolutionary Wars, entrenchments were often neglected, which is why we witnessed large armies scatter after a single defeat and the fate of entire nations hanging on the outcome of one battle.

MAXIM XXVI.

It goes against all sound principles to have separate corps, without communication between them, act independently against a central force whose own communications are severed.

NOTE.

The Austrians lost the Battle of Hohenlinden by disregarding this principle. The imperial army, commanded by Archduke John, was split into four columns that had to march through a vast forest before joining up in the plain of Anzing, where they intended to surprise the French. However, these separate corps, lacking direct communication, were forced to engage individually with an opponent who had wisely concentrated his forces and could maneuver them easily in familiar territory.

As a result, the Austrian army, caught in the narrow passes of the forest with its artillery and baggage train, was attacked on both flanks and in the rear. Archduke John managed to rally his scattered and battered divisions only under the cover of night. The trophies captured by the French were immense: eleven thousand prisoners, one hundred cannons, several flags, and the entire baggage of the enemy.

The Battle of Hohenlinden determined the outcome of the 1800 campaign, and Moreau's brilliant and well-deserved victory elevated him to the ranks of the era’s greatest generals.

MAXIM XXVII.

When an army is forced to abandon its initial position, the retreating columns should regroup far enough to the rear to avoid any interruption from the enemy. The worst disaster is when columns are attacked individually before they can join forces.

NOTE.

One significant benefit of rallying columns at a point distant from the battlefield or prior position is that it confuses the enemy as to your intended direction. If the enemy splits his forces to pursue, he risks having his detachments defeated one by one. This is especially effective if you have acted swiftly, enabling your troops to unite in time to position themselves between the enemy’s columns, dispersing them sequentially.

In the 1799 Italian campaign, General Melas used such a maneuver to secure victory at the Battle of Genola. General Championet, commanding the French army, attempted to sever the Austrians' connection with Turin by positioning separate corps in their rear. Melas, seeing through this strategy, feigned a retreat, convincing Championet of his withdrawal, while his actual goal was to consolidate his forces at the point where the French detachments planned to converge. With superior numbers, he then defeated and dispersed these French units one by one, ultimately securing control of Piedmont through decisiveness and insight.

Similarly, by neglecting this principle, General Beaulieu, leading the Austro-Sardinian forces in the 1796 campaign, suffered losses at Milesimo following his defeat at Montenotte. Beaulieu aimed to regroup his corps at Milesimo to protect the main roads to Turin and Milan. However, Napoleon, understanding the power of recent victories on troop morale, attacked before Beaulieu could assemble his divisions. Through a series of skillful maneuvers, Napoleon successfully separated the allied armies, forcing them into a disordered retreat—one group toward Milan, the other toward Turin.

MAXIM XXVIII.

No forces should be detached on the eve of a battle, as the situation may shift overnight, either due to the enemy's retreat or the arrival of substantial reinforcements, which could enable the enemy to resume the offensive and disrupt your original plans.

NOTE.

In 1796, General Jourdan's Army of the Sambre and Meuse conducted a retreat made even more challenging by losing their line of communication. Observing that Archduke Charles's forces were spread out, Jourdan decided to secure his retreat toward Frankfort by advancing through Wurtzburg, where only two Austrian divisions were positioned. This move might have succeeded if the French general hadn't made the mistake of separating from Lefevre's corps, which he left at Schweinfurt to guard the army's only direct communication line with its base.

This initial error, combined with some delays in Jourdan's march, ultimately handed victory to Archduke Charles, who quickly concentrated his forces. The timely arrival of Kray's and Wartensleben's two divisions during the battle allowed him to amass fifty thousand troops against the French army's mere thirty thousand. Consequently, the French forces were defeated and forced to continue their retreat through the mountainous terrain of Fulda, where rough roads only added to the difficulty of the journey.

Had Jourdan not assumed he was facing only two divisions at Wurtzburg, Lefevre's fourteen-thousand-strong division could likely have turned the tide in his favor.

MAXIM XXIX.

When you decide to engage in battle, bring together all available forces. Leave nothing behind, as even a single battalion can sometimes determine the outcome.

NOTE.

It is wise to designate a specific point behind the reserve for the assembly of various detachments before the battle. If unforeseen circumstances prevent these detachments from joining before the fight begins, they could be vulnerable to enemy forces if a retreat becomes necessary. Additionally, it is beneficial to keep the enemy unaware of these reinforcements to maximize their impact. As Frederick remarked, "A timely reinforcement guarantees victory, as the enemy will always perceive it as stronger than it is and lose heart accordingly."

MAXIM XXX.

There is nothing more reckless or more against the rules than to march along the side of an army that is already in position, especially when this army is positioned on heights and you are forced to pass below them.

NOTE.

Frederick neglected this principle during the first campaign of 1757, leading to his defeat at Kollin. Despite incredible bravery, the Prussians lost fifteen thousand men and much of their artillery, while Austrian losses were no more than five thousand. This battle had even more severe consequences, as it forced the King of Prussia to abandon the siege of Prague and withdraw from Bohemia.

Similarly, the French suffered a humiliating loss at the Battle of Rosbach because they attempted a flank march in front of the Prussian army. This risky maneuver was especially careless, as Prince de Soubise, commanding the French forces, moved without advanced guards or flanking units, despite being in the enemy's presence. As a result, his army of fifty thousand was defeated by just six battalions and thirty squadrons. The French lost seven thousand men, twenty-seven flags, and a large number of cannons, while the Prussians suffered only three hundred casualties.

Thus, by ignoring the rule that a flank march should never be made before an enemy in battle formation, Frederick lost his army at Kollin, and Soubise, at Rosbach, lost both his army and his honor.

MAXIM XXXI.

When you decide to take the risk of a battle, keep every possible advantage on your side, especially if your opponent is highly skilled. For if you are defeated, even with your supply depots and lines of communication nearby, misery awaits the one who loses.

NOTE.

Marshal Saxe once said, "We should make war without leaving anything to chance, and this is where the true skill of a general lies. But when we have taken the risk of a battle, we should know how to take full advantage of the victory and not merely satisfy ourselves, as is customary, with possession of the battlefield."

It was by failing to follow through on their initial success that the Austrian army, after securing the battlefield at Marengo, found itself forced to abandon all of Italy the next day. General Melas, observing the French in retreat, left the direction of his army's movements to his chief of staff and returned to Alexandria to rest from the day's exertions. Colonel Zach, equally certain as his general that the French army was completely shattered and reduced to mere fugitives, organized the divisions into marching columns.

With this arrangement, the imperial army prepared to embark on its victorious advance in a formation that extended nearly three miles in depth.

Around four o'clock, General Desaix rejoined the French army with his division. His presence somewhat restored a balance between the opposing forces; yet Napoleon hesitated briefly, unsure whether to resume the offensive or to use Desaix's corps to secure his retreat. The enthusiasm of the troops for returning to the fight resolved his indecision. He rode swiftly along the front of his divisions, addressing the soldiers: "We have fallen back far enough for today," he said. "You know I always sleep on the battlefield!"

The army, with a unanimous shout, promised him victory. Napoleon resumed the offensive. The Austrian vanguard, struck with panic at the sight of a formidable and unbroken force suddenly appearing where they had seen only fleeing troops moments before, turned about and spread disorder through their ranks. Soon after, attacked with force both at the front and on the flanks, the Austrian army was completely routed.

Marshal Daun almost met the same fate as General Melas during the Battle of Torgau in the 1760 campaign. The Austrian army's position was ideal, with its left side secured at Torgau, its right on the Siptitz plateau, and its front shielded by a large body of water, providing significant natural defenses. Confident in his strong position, Daun prepared for the Prussian assault. Meanwhile, Frederick devised a plan to turn the Austrian right flank, intending to strike their rear with an unexpected attack. To achieve this, he split his army into two corps: one under Ziethen's command, ordered to attack head-on along the water's edge, and the other led directly by Frederick, aiming to outflank the Austrian right and disrupt Daun's position from the rear.

However, Marshal Daun, informed of the Prussian maneuver, quickly altered his battlefront with a countermarching maneuver that repositioned his forces to defend against Frederick's anticipated assault. This defensive shift enabled Daun's army to repel Frederick's direct attacks, eventually forcing the Prussians into a retreat. Throughout the engagement, the two Prussian corps had been operating independently, without coordination or communication between them. Ziethen, hearing the distant sound of gunfire growing faint, assumed the king's forces had been defeated and began moving leftward to rejoin Frederick. On his way, he encountered two battalions of reserve forces, which he skillfully incorporated into his column, seizing the opportunity to go on the offensive.

Reinforced and resolute, Ziethen launched a vigorous renewed assault, ultimately capturing the Siptitz plateau—a key position—and soon after, the entire battlefield fell into Prussian control. Night had already descended when the King of Prussia received word of this unexpected victory. He returned with all haste, taking advantage of the darkness to restore organization to his scattered and battle-weary army. By morning, Frederick's forces had taken control of Torgau, securing the field and claiming victory.

Marshal Daun, in the midst of receiving congratulations for what he believed to be his victory, was taken aback upon hearing that the Prussians had resumed the offensive. He promptly ordered a full retreat, and by dawn, the Austrian forces had crossed back over the Elbe River, suffering a loss of twelve thousand men, eight thousand captured as prisoners, and forty-five cannons left behind.

In earlier campaigns, similar outcomes followed failures to solidify initial success. After the Battle of Marengo, for instance, General Melas, despite being positioned near his fortresses and fully supplied, found himself forced to abandon everything simply to save what remained of his defeated army. Likewise, General Mack capitulated following the Battle of Ulm, even though he was in the heart of his own country with resources nearby. Similarly, the Prussian army, despite having its reserves and depots intact, was compelled to surrender after the Battle of Jena, and the French found themselves in an identical plight after the Battle of Waterloo.

These examples illustrate that the true devastation of losing a battle does not stem solely from the immediate physical losses of men and supplies. Instead, the primary damage lies in the deep discouragement that permeates the defeated army, shattering its morale and coherence. In stark contrast, the victors gain not only physical resources but also a tremendous boost in courage and confidence, which tend to rise in direct proportion to the diminishing morale of the defeated. Regardless of how vast an army's resources may be, any retreat is likely to devolve into a chaotic rout unless the general-in-chief can combine boldness with strategic finesse and persistence with strength of character to effectively restore the morale of his troops, stabilizing them for a renewed campaign.

MAXIM XXXII.

The role of an advanced guard is not simply to advance or retreat; its primary duty is to maneuver strategically. An advanced guard should be composed of light cavalry, backed by a reserve of heavy cavalry, along with infantry battalions, which are in turn supported by artillery. Such a unit should consist of elite, well-trained troops, with the general officers, officers, and soldiers chosen specifically for their skills, experience, and knowledge. Any unit lacking in training or preparation only hinders the effectiveness of an advanced guard.

NOTE.

Frederick believed that an advanced guard should include detachments from all branches of the military. The commander of this force should be highly skilled in selecting advantageous ground and should use numerous patrols to stay constantly informed of all activity within the enemy's camp.

In warfare, the primary role of an advanced guard is not to engage in combat but to closely monitor the enemy, thereby protecting the movements of the main army. However, when pursuing a retreating enemy, the advanced guard should charge with determination, aiming to capture baggage trains and isolated units. For this purpose, it should be strengthened with as much of the army's light cavalry as can be spared.

MAXIM XXXIII.

It goes against the rules of warfare to allow artillery parks or batteries to enter a defile unless you control the exit on the other side. In the event of a retreat, the guns will hinder your movements and likely be lost. They should remain in position with a strong escort until you have secured the defile's exit.

NOTE.

Nothing burdens an army's march as much as excessive baggage. During the 1796 campaign, Napoleon abandoned his heavy artillery under the walls of Mantua, after disabling the guns and destroying their carriages. By making this sacrifice, he gained the ability to maneuver his small army swiftly, securing the initiative and achieving a general advantage over the larger but scattered forces of Marshal Wurmser.

Similarly, in 1799, during his retreat in Italy, General Moreau, forced to maneuver through mountainous terrain, chose to detach himself entirely from his reserve artillery, directing it to France via the Col de Fenestrelle, rather than letting it slow his progress.

These examples are worth emulating. If we gain victory through swift marching and rapid concentration on decisive points, an army's equipment can quickly be replenished. However, if we face defeat and are forced to retreat, saving our equipment becomes difficult. In such cases, we may be grateful we abandoned it in time, sparing it from becoming the enemy's prize.

MAXIM XXXIV.

It should be established as a guiding principle to avoid leaving gaps that would allow the enemy to penetrate between corps arranged in battle formation, unless the intent is to lure them into a trap.

NOTE.

IIn the 1757 campaign, the Prince of Lorraine, defending Prague with the Austrian army, noticed the Prussians attempting a flanking movement to outmaneuver his right wing. In response, he ordered a partial shift in his front by angling the infantry of that wing to form a right angle with the main line. However, executing this maneuver in the enemy's presence led to some disorder. The front of the columns advanced too quickly, causing the rear to lag, and when the line reformed to the right, a significant gap appeared at the salient angle. Frederick saw this mistake and moved quickly to exploit it. He ordered his central corps, led by the Duke of Bevern, to occupy this opening, deciding the battle's outcome in his favor. The Prince of Lorraine, defeated and pursued, was forced to retreat to Prague, having lost sixteen thousand men and two hundred cannons.

It's also essential to note that attempting to send a corps through openings created by an enemy during battle should only be done if your forces are at least equal in strength and you have the opportunity to outflank the enemy on one side. Only then can you hope to divide his army at the center and completely isolate the wings. If you're outnumbered, this maneuver risks failure, as the enemy's wings may close in on your flanks and encircle you.

The Duke of Berwick used this maneuver to win the Battle of Almanza in 1707 in Spain. The Anglo-Portuguese army, led by Lord Galloway, had come to besiege Villena. Marshal Berwick, commanding the French and Spanish forces, left his camp at Montalegre and advanced toward Villena to lift the siege. As he approached, the English general, eager to engage in battle, moved to meet him on the plains of Almanza. The outcome remained uncertain for some time. The first line, commanded by the Duke of Popoli, was broken, and the Chevalier d'Asfeldt, leading the second line, arranged his forces with large intervals between them. When the English, chasing the first line, reached these reserves, d'Asfeldt seized upon their disarray, attacking them from the flank and routing them completely.

Seeing the success of this maneuver, Marshal Berwick opened up his front, deploying his forces to envelop the enemy's flanks while the reserves held the center and the cavalry maneuvered to the rear. This coordination achieved a decisive victory. Wounded and pursued, Lord Galloway managed with great difficulty to gather the remnants of his army and took refuge in Tortosa.

MAXIM XXXV.

Camps within the same army should always be arranged to provide mutual protection.

NOTE.

During the Battle of Dresden in the 1813 campaign, the allied camp, though advantageously positioned on the heights along the left bank of the Elbe, had a major flaw: a deep ravine cut through it lengthwise, completely isolating the left wing from the center and right. This critical weakness did not escape Napoleon's sharp observation. He immediately directed his entire cavalry and two infantry corps against the isolated wing, attacking with superior numbers. The wing was overwhelmed and defeated, with ten thousand prisoners captured before any reinforcements could arrive to assist.

MAXIM XXXVI.

When the enemy's army is protected by a river with multiple bridgeheads (têtes de pont), do not attempt a frontal attack. Doing so would split your forces and make you vulnerable to flanking. Instead, approach the river in an echelon of columns, positioning the leading column so it is the only one the enemy can directly engage, without exposing its flank. Meanwhile, have your light troops secure the riverbank. Once you have chosen a crossing point, move quickly, establishing a bridge at that location. Ensure that the crossing point is positioned some distance from the leading echelon to mislead the enemy.

NOTE.

If you control a town or village on the riverbank opposite the enemy's position, it's advantageous to establish your crossing there. In a town, it is easier to shield your transport and reserve artillery and to conceal bridge construction than in open terrain. It is also highly advantageous to cross the river opposite a village that the enemy occupies only lightly. As soon as your advance guard reaches the far bank, it can secure the village, fortify it with defensive structures, and convert it into a bridgehead (tête de pont). This preparation will make it easier for the rest of the army to cross the river.

MAXIM XXXVII.

Once you control a position that commands the opposite bank, the task of crossing the river becomes significantly easier, especially if this position is wide enough to hold a large artillery force. However, this advantage lessens if the river is more than three hundred toises (or six hundred yards) wide. At this distance, which is beyond the effective range of grape shot, the defending troops can line the bank and find cover. Consequently, if the grenadiers sent to protect the bridge manage to cross, they would be vulnerable to enemy fire, as the enemy batteries positioned two hundred toises from the landing could inflict severe damage, even while being over five hundred toises from the attacker's artillery. In this scenario, the enemy would hold the artillery advantage.

For similar reasons, crossing becomes nearly impossible unless you can surprise the enemy or have the protection of an intermediate island, or if you can exploit an angle in the river to establish a crossfire on the enemy's defenses. In such a case, the island or river bend naturally serves as a bridgehead (tête de pont) and shifts the artillery advantage to the attacking army.

When a river is narrower than sixty toises (or one hundred and twenty yards) and you control a post on the opposite side, the troops crossing gain substantial protection from your artillery. In this situation, however small the angle may be, it becomes almost impossible for the enemy to prevent the construction of a bridge. Skilled generals, when they detect the crossing plans of their adversary and position their forces at the crossing site, generally focus on blocking the bridge's completion by forming a semicircle around its end, as if surrounding the exit of a defile, and positioning themselves three or four hundred toises away to stay beyond the range of artillery from the opposite side.

NOTE.

Frederick observed that "the passage of great rivers in the presence of the enemy is one of the most delicate operations in war." Success in such complex situations hinges on maintaining strict secrecy, executing maneuvers swiftly, and ensuring each division follows its assigned orders precisely. Crossing a river while the enemy is aware—and doing so without alerting them in advance—requires not only careful planning but also flawless execution without a hint of disorder. Even the smallest misstep in such a high-stakes operation can lead to exposure, rendering the entire crossing vulnerable to attack.

An example of this precision in river crossings comes from the 1705 campaign, when Prince Eugene of Savoy sought to assist the Prince of Piedmont. To achieve this, he aimed to cross the Adda River, a point heavily defended by the French army under the command of the Duke de Vendome. Prince Eugene identified a favorable location and set up a battery of twenty cannons on a commanding height, giving him a clear view of the opposing bank. He further fortified his infantry along the slope by constructing a line of entrenchments in parallel formations, making it as defensible as possible. These preparations were intended to protect his troops as they worked on constructing a bridge, a process requiring both time and a high degree of protection against potential enemy interference.

The construction proceeded steadily until the Duke de Vendome arrived with his entire army. Initially, Vendome seemed determined to stop the bridge from being completed, appearing prepared to mount a direct assault on Eugene's position. However, after carefully examining the strategic setup Prince Eugene had established, Vendome concluded that a direct attack would be impractical and unlikely to succeed. Instead, he opted for a more cautious and strategic approach. Vendome withdrew his forces to a position out of reach of Prince Eugene's artillery, aligning his wings along the river to form a broad arc, using the Adda River as the bowstring. To further fortify his position, Vendome reinforced his lines with entrenchments and constructed barriers of felled trees, known as abattis. From this vantage, he set his troops in readiness to attack Eugene's forces as they emerged from the bridge. In this way, Vendome planned to break Eugene's troops into smaller, manageable segments as they attempted to cross, rendering them vulnerable to piecemeal defeat.

Upon examining Vendome's formation and considering the strength of the enemy's position, Prince Eugene realized that pressing forward with the crossing would likely end in failure. Recognizing that the risk was too high, he made the difficult decision to halt the bridge construction, dismantle it, and retreat his forces under the cover of night. By withdrawing discreetly, he avoided a costly engagement in an unfavorable situation, a choice that preserved his army for future operations.

A similar maneuver was executed in the 1809 campaign by Archduke Charles, who successfully forced the French to retreat back to the Isle of Lobau after they had crossed to the left bank of the Danube. Archduke Charles's approach was meticulously planned, centering his march around a coordinated, concentric advance. His forces threatened three critical points: Grosaspern with his right, Esling with his center, and Enzersdorf with his left. By establishing his position with both wings anchored firmly on the Danube, Charles's army formed a semicircle around Esling, creating a formidable barrier.

In response, Napoleon quickly ordered an attack, managing to break through the Austrian center. However, even after pushing past the Austrian front line, Napoleon's forces found themselves stopped by

Austrian reserves who were strategically positioned to counter any breakthrough. Compounding this setback, the bridges over the Danube—Napoleon's main supply line—were destroyed, leaving several corps, along with their artillery, stranded on the right bank. This disruption left his army vulnerable and unable to fully reinforce its position on the left bank. The combination of these unexpected obstacles and the Austrians' strong positioning led Napoleon to decide on a strategic withdrawal. He retreated to the Isle of Lobau, where he had prudently prepared a line of defensive fieldworks, transforming the island into a well-fortified camp.

In both cases, these river-crossing operations illustrate the level of tactical precision and caution required to execute maneuvers successfully in the presence of a strong enemy defense. Archduke Charles's concentric formation and Vendome's defensive arc demonstrate how awareness of terrain and strategic position can neutralize even a well-prepared assault. Additionally, Prince Eugene's withdrawal from the Adda and Napoleon's retreat to the fortified Isle of Lobau underscore that in war, even the most skilled generals must weigh risk and advantage carefully, sometimes choosing to avoid engagement to maintain their forces for future battles.

MAXIM XXXVIII.

It is challenging to stop an enemy equipped with pontoons from crossing a river. When the purpose of an army defending the crossing is to protect an ongoing siege, as soon as the general realizes he cannot prevent the crossing, he should act quickly to reach an intermediate position between the river he was defending and the location he aims to secure.

NOTE.

It is worth noting that this intermediate position should be scouted in advance and ideally fortified beforehand. By doing so, the enemy will be unable to launch an offensive against the corps conducting the siege until they have defeated the army positioned to observe them. The defending army, protected by its fortified camp, can then watch for a favorable opportunity to attack the enemy's flank or rear.

Furthermore, an army entrenched in this manner has the advantage of concentration, allowing it to act as a unified force. In contrast, the enemy must divide his forces to protect his bridge and monitor the movements of the observing army. This division forces the enemy to cover multiple objectives: securing his bridge, keeping track of the observing army, and preparing to attack the besieging corps without leaving his own rear vulnerable or risking the loss of his bridge.

MAXIM XXXIX.

In the 1645 campaign, Turenne found himself with his army under attack near Philipsburg by a much stronger force. With no bridge over the Rhine available, he made strategic use of the land between the river and the town to establish his camp. This instance provides a valuable lesson for engineering officers—not only for fortress construction but also for the planning of têtes de pont. There should always be a sufficient space left between the fortress and the river, where an army can form and rally without being forced to retreat within the walls, thus avoiding any compromise to the fortress's security.

An army retreating toward Mayence while pursued by an enemy is inevitably at a disadvantage because it requires more than a day to cross the bridge, and the Cassel lines are too constrained to accommodate an entire army without risking entrapment. Ideally, a buffer of two hundred toises should have been left between these lines and the Rhine. This principle is essential for têtes de pont on large rivers; if not followed, they become inadequate for covering a retreating army's crossing. The têtes de pont designed according to conventional methods are suitable only for smaller rivers, where crossing time is relatively short.

NOTE.

In the 1741 campaign, Marshal Saxe, after crossing the Moldau to intercept a detached force of fourteen thousand men attempting to enter Prague, left a thousand infantry stationed on a height opposite the tête de pont, with orders to entrench. This precaution allowed Saxe to secure his retreat and provided a safe route back across the bridge. By rallying his divisions between the entrenched height and the tête de pont, he ensured they could recross without disarray.

Are these examples unknown to today's generals, or do they consider such precautions unnecessary?

MAXIM XL.

Fortresses are valuable in both offensive and defensive warfare. While they may not completely halt an advancing army, they are highly effective at delaying, disrupting, weakening, and frustrating a victorious enemy.

NOTE.

The remarkable success of the allied armies in the 1814 campaign has led some military minds to develop a misleading view of the true value of fortresses. The formidable allied forces that crossed the Rhine and the Alps during this period could afford to send large detachments to blockade the fortresses along France's borders without significantly diminishing the numerical superiority of the main army advancing on Paris. Consequently, this army could operate without concern for threats to its line of retreat.

However, it is essential to remember that never before in military history had Europe's armies been so unified or guided by a single strategy toward one common goal. In this unique context, the fortresses surrounding France proved less effective, but it would be a grave error to assume that a frontier defended by numerous fortresses can be crossed without consequence. Nor should one believe that battles can be fought with these fortifications in one's rear without first either besieging them or, at minimum, assigning sufficient forces to contain them.

MAXIM XLI.

There are only two reliable methods for ensuring the success of a siege. The first is to begin by defeating the enemy's covering army, driving it from the field, and pushing its remnants beyond a major natural barrier, like a mountain range or a large river. Once this is achieved, an observation force should be stationed behind this natural barrier until the trenches are completed and the fortress is taken.

However, if the objective is to capture the place in the presence of a relieving army without engaging in battle, then all siege materiel and equipment must be ready from the outset, including sufficient ammunition and provisions to last for the estimated duration of the siege. In addition, defensive lines of contravallation and circumvallation should be constructed, utilizing natural features like hills, forests, marshes, and flooded areas.

In this case, communication with depots is no longer essential; the primary focus becomes containing the relieving force. An army of observation must be established to continuously monitor the enemy, effectively blocking access to the besieged location while maintaining the flexibility to intercept the enemy's flanks or rear if they attempt to approach stealthily.

It is also crucial to remember that by strategically using the lines of contravallation, part of the besieging force can be freed up to engage the approaching enemy in battle if needed.

In general, when besieging a location in the presence of an enemy army, the siege must be secured with lines of circumvallation. If the besieging force is sufficiently strong—able to leave a corps before the fortress with four times the number of the garrison and still contend with the relieving army—it can afford to operate more than a day's march from the besieged location. However, if the besieging force becomes numerically inferior after setting up for the siege, it should remain within a day's march to retreat to its defensive lines if needed or to receive reinforcements in case of an attack.

If the combined strength of the investing corps and the observation army is only equal to that of the relieving force, then the entire besieging force should remain within or close to its defensive lines, pushing forward with the siege operations as quickly and vigorously as possible.

NOTE.

"When we undertake a siege," Montécuculli noted, "we should not position ourselves opposite the weakest part of the fortress, but rather at the point most suitable for establishing a camp and executing our overall plans."

The Duke of Berwick fully grasped this principle. In 1706, when tasked with laying siege to Nice, he decided to attack from the Montalban side, contrary to the advice of Vauban and even the king's orders. With a relatively small force at his disposal, his first priority was to secure his camp. To achieve this, he constructed redoubts on the heights between the Var and Paillon rivers, which provided natural support for his flanks. This arrangement safeguarded him against surprise attacks, as the Duke of Savoy could potentially advance suddenly via the Col de Tende. Berwick needed to be able to quickly gather his forces, move promptly toward his adversary, and engage him before he could fully establish a position. Without this readiness, Berwick's smaller numbers would have forced him to abandon the siege.

Similarly, when Marshal Saxe was besieging Brussels with just twenty-eight thousand troops against a garrison of twelve thousand, he learned that the Prince of Waldeck was gathering forces to lift the siege. Lacking sufficient strength to establish an observation army, Saxe scouted a suitable battlefield along the small river Voluve. He made all necessary preparations to deploy his forces quickly to this spot if the enemy approached. In this way, he could be ready to confront his opponent without halting the siege operations.

MAXIM XLII.

Feuquière asserts that "we should never wait for the enemy within the lines of circumvallation, but instead go out and attack." However, this view is mistaken. In warfare, there are no absolutes, and it would be unwise to dismiss the idea of awaiting the enemy from within fortified lines of circumvallation.

NOTE.

A prime example of the value of this strategy occurred during the 1691 siege of Mons. The Prince of Orange gathered his army and advanced as far as Notre Dame de Halle, making a visible effort to relieve the besieged town. Louis XIV, who was personally overseeing the siege operations, called a war council to deliberate on how best to respond should the Prince of Orange continue to advance. Marshal Luxembourg recommended holding firm within the circumvallation lines, rather than leaving to confront the enemy. This advice carried the day. Luxembourg's principle was clear: if a besieging army lacks the strength to defend the full extent of the circumvallation line, it should indeed go out to meet the enemy. However, if the besieging force is sufficient to establish a double line of encampment around the besieged fortress, it is generally more advantageous to rely on well-prepared entrenchments, which allow the siege to continue without disruption and provide strong defenses against an advancing army.

A similar situation arose in 1658 when Marshal Turenne was conducting the siege of Dunkirk. Having already begun trenching operations, he received word that the Spanish army, under the command of Prince Don Juan, Condé, and D'Hocquincourt, had positioned itself on the Downs about a league from his lines. Turenne assessed the situation and saw that he held several advantages. His forces were greater in number, and the enemy had no artillery, which limited their offensive capabilities. Additionally, the unfavorable terrain hindered the enemy's superior cavalry. Given these factors, Turenne decided to leave his entrenchments and engage the Spanish army before they could entrench or bring up their artillery. This swift, proactive approach led to a decisive French victory, validating Turenne's tactical choice to confront the enemy rather than wait.

In 1733, Marshal Berwick faced a similar dilemma while besieging Philipsburg. He had reason to believe that Prince Eugene would soon arrive with the full strength of the imperial forces, potentially threatening the siege. After organizing the necessary troops to maintain the siege, Berwick established a corps of observation with his remaining forces, positioning it to counter any advance by Prince Eugene. This observation corps was tasked with keeping watch on the enemy and preventing any attempts to attack or divert forces toward the Moselle or Upper Rhine.

When Prince Eugene did arrive in front of the besieging army, some officers proposed that it would be better to meet him outside the circumvallation lines rather than waiting within. However, Berwick, aligning with Luxembourg's reasoning, believed that a well-fortified army, fully manned and positioned within secure entrenchments, had little to fear from a direct assault. Deciding to hold his position, Berwick kept his forces within the lines, a choice that proved sound. Prince Eugene, evidently recognizing the strength of the defensive positions, refrained from launching an assault on the entrenchments. His reluctance to attack indicated that he saw little likelihood of success against such formidable defenses.

These examples illustrate that defensive entrenchments can be a powerful strategic asset when managed correctly. By choosing to stay within circumvallation lines and fortifications, a besieging force can maintain its siege efforts uninterrupted and reduce the risk of being overwhelmed by a larger relieving army. The effective use of entrenchments also allows a besieging general to engage with superior positioning, rather than risking an open confrontation where the outcome may be uncertain.

MAXIM XLIII.

Those who dismiss lines of circumvallation and all the benefits that engineering science can provide are forfeiting a valuable resource that is never detrimental, almost always beneficial, and often essential. At the same time, it must be acknowledged that the principles of field fortification require advancement. This vital branch of military art has stagnated since ancient times and, in fact, is now less developed than it was two thousand years ago. It is crucial to encourage engineer officers to refine this aspect of their work, elevating it to match the progress made in other military disciplines.

NOTE.

"If we are outnumbered," Marshal Saxe once remarked, "entrenchments are useless, as the enemy will concentrate his forces on specific points. If we are equally matched, they are unnecessary. If we are stronger, we don't need them. So why bother with the trouble of entrenching?" Despite his skepticism about the value of entrenchments, Marshal Saxe frequently relied on them.

In 1797, Generals Provéra and Hohenzollern appeared before Mantua, where Marshal Wurmser was besieged, with the goal of lifting the siege. However, their advance was halted by the lines of contravallation around St. George. This seemingly minor barrier provided Napoleon with enough time to arrive from Rivoli and thwart their attempt. In the previous campaign, it was the French army's failure to fortify their positions that had forced them to abandon the siege entirely.

MAXIM XLIV.

If circumstances make it impossible to leave an adequate garrison to defend a fortified town containing a hospital and supply depots, then every effort should be made to secure the citadel against a surprise attack.

NOTE.

A few battalions scattered throughout a town may not inspire fear, but when concentrated within the compact perimeter of a citadel, they present a far more formidable appearance. For this reason, it seems that this precaution is essential not only in fortresses but also in any location housing hospitals or depots of any kind. If no citadel exists, a part of the town that is best suited for defense should be selected and fortified to offer the maximum possible resistance.

MAXIM XLV.

A fortified place can serve only to protect its garrison and delay the enemy for a limited time. Once that time has passed, and the fortifications are no longer defensible, the garrison should surrender. All civilized nations agree on this principle, with the main debate centering on the extent of defense a governor should make before capitulating. Yet some generals, including Villars, believe a governor should never surrender; rather, when all hope is lost, he should destroy the fortifications and attempt to break through the besieging army under cover of night. If blowing up the fortifications is not possible, they argue, he should at least withdraw with his garrison to save his troops.

Officers who have followed this bold approach have often succeeded in rescuing a significant portion of their garrison.

NOTE.

In 1705, the French defenders of Haguenau, besieged by Count Thungen, found they could no longer withstand an assault. Governor Péri, who had already demonstrated valor through a vigorous defense, realized that surrender on favorable terms was unlikely. Determined not to become a prisoner, he decided to evacuate and force his way through the besiegers.

To keep his plan secret and gauge his officers' resolve, Péri called a council of war and declared his intention to fight to the death on the ramparts. Then, under the pretense of an imminent, desperate situation, he ordered the entire garrison to assemble. Leaving a few sharpshooters at the breach to cover their departure, Péri quietly led his men out of Haguenau at night. This audacious plan succeeded, allowing him to reach Saverne without losing a single soldier.

Two notable examples of resilient defense in recent history include Massena at Genoa and Palafox at Saragossa. Massena, refusing all calls to surrender, held out until starvation forced him to capitulate; he marched out with his arms, baggage, and full honors of war. Palafox, in contrast, fought until his garrison was nearly destroyed, defending Saragossa block by block until famine and death left him no choice but to surrender. This siege stands as one of the most memorable in military history, a testament to both the French and Spanish forces. Palafox exemplified every resource that courage and determination can bring to the defense of a city.

Ultimately, true strength lies in the mind. For this reason, in selecting a governor for a besieged place, I believe that personal character is more important than sheer strategic skill. Essential qualities include courage, persistence, and unwavering dedication. Above all, a governor must inspire both the garrison and the local population with a spirit of resistance. Without the support of the people, even the most fortified city will be forced to surrender after only the first or second assault.

MAXIM XLVI.

The surrender of a fortress is well worth allowing the garrison to withdraw honorably, provided they only yield on such terms. Based on this principle, it is often wiser to grant an honorable capitulation to a garrison that has put up a strong resistance than to risk the losses of an assault.

NOTE.

Marshal Villars aptly noted, "No governor of a fortress should excuse his surrender by claiming a desire to preserve the king's troops. Any garrison that demonstrates courage will avoid becoming prisoners of war. There is no general, no matter how confident he is of taking a place by assault, who would not prefer offering terms of capitulation rather than risk losing a thousand men to force determined defenders into submission."

MAXIM XLVII.

Infantry, cavalry, and artillery are ineffective without one another, and thus should always be positioned in cantonments where they can support each other if an unexpected attack occurs.

NOTE.

Frederick emphasized that "a general should focus all his attention on the safety of his cantonments, ensuring that soldiers can rest securely from their exertions without worry. To achieve this, arrangements should be made for troops to quickly form on pre-surveyed ground, that generals remain present with their divisions or brigades, and that duties are carried out with precision throughout."

Marshal Saxe believed that an army should not rush to leave its cantonments but rather wait until the enemy is worn out from marching, allowing the army to strike with fresh troops when the enemy is weakened by exhaustion.

However, I would caution against following this advice unreservedly. There are many instances where taking the initiative is advantageous, especially when the enemy has been forced to extend his cantonments due to a lack of supplies. In such cases, a swift attack could be launched before the enemy has time to concentrate his forces.

MAXIM XLVIII.

Infantry formations in line should always consist of two ranks, as the length of the musket allows for an effective fire only in this arrangement. Firing from a third rank is not only unreliable but often poses a risk to the soldiers in the front ranks. When infantry is organized in two ranks, a supernumerary should be positioned behind every fourth or fifth file, and a reserve force should be placed twenty-five paces behind each flank.

NOTE.

If circumstances require infantry to form a square, I believe a two-deep line is too weak to withstand a cavalry charge. Although the third rank may seem less useful for continuous file-firing, it is crucial for replacing fallen soldiers in the front ranks. Without this additional rank, the files would need to close in as soldiers fall, creating gaps between companies that cavalry could easily exploit. Additionally, when infantry is organized in two ranks, the columns tend to spread apart when marching to the flank.

In cases where it is advantageous to keep infantry in two ranks, such as behind entrenchments, the third rank could be held in reserve and moved forward to relieve the front rank when soldiers are fatigued, or when the firing rate decreases. I raise these points because I have reviewed an excellent pamphlet advocating the two-deep formation as ideal for infantry. While the author supports this view with a variety of convincing reasons, I find that the arguments are not entirely sufficient to address all the potential issues with this practice.

MAXIM XLIX.

Mixing small units of infantry with cavalry is an ineffective practice, leading to numerous issues. The cavalry loses its mobility, becoming restricted in its movements and losing its dynamic power. Even the infantry is put at a disadvantage because, when the cavalry moves, the infantry is often left unsupported. The best way to protect cavalry is to cover its flanks.

NOTE.

Marshal Saxe shared this view, observing that "the weakness of such a formation is enough to intimidate the infantry platoons since they will be doomed if the cavalry is defeated." Cavalry that depends on infantry for support is also thrown off when a rapid forward movement takes them out of sight of their supports. Although Marshal Turenne and other generals of his era occasionally used this mixed formation, I do not believe this justifies its recommendation in a modern context, as seen in an essay titled Considerations sur l'Art de la Guerre. This formation has long since been abandoned, and with the advent of light artillery, suggesting such an arrangement now seems almost absurd.

MAXIM L.

Cavalry charges are valuable at any stage of a battle—whether at the beginning, middle, or end. Whenever possible, they should target the flanks of the enemy's infantry, especially when the infantry is already engaged from the front.

NOTE.

The Archduke Charles advised that cavalry should be concentrated in force at a decisive point when the ideal moment for its use arrives, specifically when it can strike with a high chance of success. Due to the speed of cavalry, allowing it to operate effectively along the entire battle line within the same day, the commanding general should keep the cavalry massed and avoid breaking it into smaller detachments. When terrain permits the use of cavalry across all points of the line, it is advantageous to position it in columns behind the infantry, where it can be swiftly deployed to any critical area as needed.

If the purpose of the cavalry is to defend a position, it should be stationed far enough back to meet any approaching force at full speed. When protecting the flank of infantry, it should likewise be placed directly behind, ready to respond. Since cavalry is inherently offensive, it should always be positioned just far enough from the collision point to reach its maximum speed upon impact.

Regarding the cavalry reserve, this should be deployed only in the latter stages of a battle, either to secure a decisive outcome or to cover a retreat. Napoleon noted that, during the Battle of Waterloo, his guard cavalry, which was held in reserve, was engaged contrary to his orders. He lamented that by five o'clock, he had lost access to this reserve, which, when used effectively, had so often secured him victory in the past.

MAXIM LI.

Cavalry's role is to pursue the defeated enemy and prevent them from regrouping.

NOTE.

Whether victorious or defeated, it is crucial to keep a reserve body of cavalry, either to exploit the success of victory or to secure a retreat. Even the most decisive battles lose much of their impact when the lack of cavalry prevents the victor from fully capitalizing on success and denying the enemy a chance to rally.

When pursuing a retreating army, the main force of the cavalry should focus on the flanks, especially if the cavalry is strong enough to intercept and cut off the enemy's escape route.

MAXIM LII.

Artillery is even more crucial for cavalry than for infantry, as cavalry lacks any natural means of defense by fire, relying solely on the saber. Horse-artillery was introduced to address this need, providing essential support to cavalry. Consequently, cavalry should always have artillery support, whether in attack, rally, or defensive positions.

NOTE.

Horse-artillery was first introduced by Frederick, with Austria quickly incorporating it, though not fully developed. It was only in 1792 that France adopted horse-artillery, rapidly advancing it to its current state of effectiveness. During the Revolutionary Wars, the impact of horse-artillery was immense, reshaping tactical possibilities; its mobility allowed artillery to be positioned swiftly at any point where its use could turn the tide.

Napoleon observed in his memoirs that a flanking battery, able to strike the enemy at an angle, could alone decide the outcome of a battle. Beyond this, horse-artillery provides critical benefits to cavalry by securing its flanks and clearing the way for effective charges through its destructive fire. Therefore, cavalry and horse-artillery should remain closely integrated, ready to seize strategic points where artillery is needed. In such scenarios, the cavalry screens the artillery's approach, protects its setup in position, and shields it from attack until it is prepared to unleash its fire on the enemy.

MAXIM LIII.

During marches or while positioned, most of the artillery should be distributed among the infantry and cavalry divisions, with the remainder held in reserve. Each gun should be equipped with three hundred rounds, excluding the limber ammunition, which is sufficient for approximately two battles.

NOTE.

The better-trained the infantry, the more critical it becomes to support them with artillery to ensure their sustained effectiveness. It is also vital that the divisional batteries lead the column, as this arrangement greatly boosts soldiers' morale. Troops attack with greater confidence when they see that the flanks of their column are well-supported by artillery.

The artillery reserve should be held back for decisive moments, when it can be deployed with full impact, as the enemy is unlikely to attempt an assault on such a formidable force at that point. There are very few cases where a battery of sixty cannons has been taken by an infantry or cavalry charge unless it was left unsupported or was positioned in a way that made it easily flanked.

MAXIM LIV.

Artillery should always be positioned to its greatest advantage, placed as far forward from the cavalry and infantry lines as possible without compromising the safety of the guns. Field batteries should have commanding views of the surrounding area from the level of the platform, ensuring a full range in all directions without any obstruction to the right or left.

NOTE.

A notable example is the battery of eighteen cannons that secured the Russian army's center at the Battle of La Moskwa (Borodino). Positioned on a circular elevation that provided an unobstructed view in every direction, its fire was so effective that, for a considerable time, it stalled a vigorous attack by the French right wing. Although the Russian left was twice pushed back, it pivoted around this battery, allowing it to reclaim its position. After a series of exceptionally brave assaults, the French finally overtook the battery, but only after suffering heavy losses, including Generals Caulaincourt and Montbrun. Its capture was pivotal, leading to the retreat of the Russian left.

Another impactful instance occurred in the 1809 campaign, where General Lauriston commanded a concentrated battery of one hundred cannons from the Guard at the Battle of Wagram. This overwhelming artillery fire was directed at the Austrian right, producing devastating effects that significantly influenced the outcome.

MAXIM LV.

A general should avoid placing his army in cantonments when it is possible to gather sufficient forage and provisions to support the soldiers directly in the field.

NOTE.

One significant advantage of keeping an army in camp is that it becomes easier to maintain its morale and discipline. In cantonments, soldiers can become accustomed to rest, gradually finding comfort in idleness and growing reluctant to return to the field. The opposite is true in a camp. There, the monotony of daily life, combined with stricter discipline, often leaves soldiers eager for the campaign's start, as it offers variety and the excitement of war.

Moreover, an army in camp is generally less vulnerable to surprise attacks than one in cantonments, which often occupy too large an area. When an army must take quarters, the Marquis de Feuquière recommends setting up a camp in front of the line, where troops can regularly assemble. Such gatherings, held sometimes without warning, serve both to train the soldiers' vigilance and to keep the various corps coordinated and prepared for action.

MAXIM LVI.

A capable general, a well-structured organization, clear instructions, and strict discipline, supported by effective logistical systems, will consistently produce competent troops, regardless of the cause for which they fight. However, a love for one's country, enthusiasm, a sense of national honor, and even fanaticism can positively influence young soldiers.

NOTE.

This observation seems more relevant to the soldiers than to the officers. Since war is not a natural state for humanity, those who pursue it are often driven by strong emotions or motivations. A considerable degree of enthusiasm and dedication toward the commanding general is essential for inspiring an army to achieve great deeds, particularly in a war where the soldiers may have little personal investment. The indifferent attitude of auxiliary troops often highlights this point—unless they are motivated by the inspiring leadership of their commander.

MAXIM LVII.

When a nation lacks established military structures and a comprehensive system, organizing an army becomes a formidable challenge.

NOTE.

This is an undeniable truth, particularly for an army that must operate under the demands of modern warfare, where order, precision, and rapid movement are critical to success.

MAXIM LVIII.

The first essential quality of a soldier is resilience in the face of hardship and deprivation. Courage ranks only second; the best training ground for a soldier is found in hardship, poverty, and need.

NOTE.

Valor may come naturally to both new and seasoned soldiers, but it is often fleeting in the former. Only through repeated campaigns and the routines of service does a soldier gain the moral courage to endure the strains and shortages of war without complaint. Experience teaches him how to meet his needs; he becomes content with whatever he can obtain, understanding that success is built upon endurance and determination. Napoleon aptly described hardship as the best teacher for a soldier; no army was as destitute as the Army of the Alps when he took command, yet it achieved remarkable success in Italy. The soldiers who triumphed at Montenotte, Lodi, Castiglione, Bassano, Arcole, and Rivoli had seen entire battalions in tatters, deserting due to lack of provisions only months before.

MAXIM LIX.

A soldier should always carry five essentials: his musket, ammunition, knapsack, provisions for at least four days, and an entrenching tool. The knapsack may be minimized if necessary, but it must accompany him.

NOTE.

It is fortunate that Napoleon has recognized tNapoleon's endorsement of an entrenching tool for every soldier is a decisive response to those who ridiculed the idea. An axe is as manageable for a foot soldier as the sword at his side, and far more useful. When axes are issued to companies or carried by fatigue-men during a campaign, they are often misplaced, leaving the army unprepared when it needs to cut wood or build shelters. By making the axe part of every soldier's equipment, it remains with him at all times. Whether tasked with fortifying a village or constructing huts in a camp, commanders will quickly recognize the significant benefits of this simple addition to each soldier's gear.

Once the general use of the axe is established, the value of equipping select companies with pickaxes and shovels will likely become apparent, as will the advantages of more frequent entrenchments. Entrenching becomes particularly crucial during retreats when the army reaches a strong position. An entrenched camp not only provides a rallying point for troops under pursuit but, if fortified well enough to cast doubt on the success of an enemy attack, it helps sustain the morale of soldiers during a retreat. Moreover, such a camp offers the general-in-chief opportunities to switch back to the offensive, ready to exploit any misstep by the enemy.

A memorable example of this was Frederick's campaign of 1761. Facing two combined Russian and Austrian armies that outnumbered his forces fourfold, Frederick safeguarded his troops by entrenching at the camp of Buntzalvitz, thereby averting defeat despite the overwhelming odds.

MAXIM LX.

Every effort should be made to strengthen the soldier's loyalty to his regiment. This is best achieved by showing respect and consideration for the veteran soldier. His pay should also increase with years of service; it is deeply unfair not to reward a veteran more than a recruit.

NOTE.

Some modern thinkers suggest limiting the length of military service to ensure that the youth of a nation rotates through the ranks, making the entire population trained and ready for defense in case of invasion. Though this system seems beneficial at first glance, it has significant drawbacks.

Firstly, a soldier worn out by the tedious details of garrison life may be unlikely to re-enlist after completing his term, especially since he may feel he has already fulfilled his civic duty. Upon returning home, he is likely to settle down, perhaps marry or start a trade, and as he adjusts to civilian life, his military spirit fades, making him less suited to return to war. Conversely, a soldier who serves for many years becomes deeply attached to his regiment, much like a family. Over time, he accepts the discipline, adapts to the hardships of military life, and eventually finds a certain satisfaction in it. Experienced officers can attest to the difference between seasoned and newer soldiers in terms of resilience during long campaigns, the steadfast courage displayed in an attack, and the ability to regroup quickly after being scattered.

Montécuculli noted that "it takes time to discipline an army; even more to prepare it for war; and even more to create veterans." For this reason, he advised that old soldiers be treated with great respect, provided for carefully, and maintained as a significant part of the standing army. It also seems necessary not only to increase a soldier's pay with time served but to grant him distinctions and privileges that motivate him to stay in the military long-term and, importantly, to do so with honor.

MAXIM LXI.

It is not stirring speeches made just before battle that make soldiers courageous. Veterans barely listen, and recruits often forget them at the first sound of gunfire. If talks and speeches have any real value, it is during the course of the campaign: to dispel harmful rumors, to correct misinformation, to foster the right spirit among the troops, and to provide material that enlivens camp discussions around the bivouac. Any printed orders of the day should focus on these goals.

NOTE.

The general-in-chief's opinion, strongly and clearly conveyed, can have a profound impact on the soldiers' morale.

For instance, in 1703 at the assault on Hornbec, Marshal Villars noticed that his troops were advancing half-heartedly. He threw himself to the front and shouted, "What! Do you expect me, a marshal of France, to be the first to scale the walls when I have ordered YOU to attack?" These few words reignited the troops' enthusiasm, and officers and soldiers surged forward, capturing the town with minimal losses.

Similarly, at Marengo, as the battle turned, Napoleon rode through the ranks and declared, "We have retreated far enough for today; you know I always sleep on the battlefield!" This single statement was enough to rekindle the soldiers' courage and help them forget the exhaustion of a day in which nearly every man had fought continuously.

MAXIM LXII.

Tents are detrimental to health. Soldiers fare better when bivouacking, as they can sleep with their feet toward the fire, which quickly dries the ground beneath them. A few planks or some straw provide adequate shelter from the wind.

However, tents are essential for senior officers, who need a protected space for writing and consulting maps. Tents should therefore be issued to these officers, with instructions for them to avoid sleeping indoors. Tents can also attract the attention of the enemy's observers, as they reveal the army's numbers and position. In contrast, an army bivouacking in two or three lines is only visible by the smoke rising, which merges with the clouds, making it impossible for the enemy to count the fires accurately.

NOTE.

The well-known benefits of bivouacking further support the idea of including an entrenching tool in every soldier's equipment. With an axe and a shovel, soldiers can easily construct shelters. I have seen soldiers build huts from tree branches covered with turf, which provided them with excellent protection from cold and rain, even in harsh conditions.

MAXIM LXIII.

All information obtained from prisoners should be taken cautiously and valued appropriately. A common soldier rarely knows anything beyond his own company, and an officer's knowledge is typically limited to the position and movements of the division his regiment belongs to. For this reason, a general should not rely on intelligence from prisoners unless it aligns with reports from advanced guards concerning the enemy's position and other key details.

NOTE.

Montécuculli wisely advises that prisoners be questioned separately to verify the consistency of their answers and determine if they may be attempting to mislead. Generally, intelligence sought from captured officers should focus on the strength, resources, and sometimes specific locations or positions of the enemy. Frederick even recommended threatening prisoners with immediate execution if they were found providing deceptive or false information.

MAXIM LXIV.

Nothing is more crucial in war than a unified command; thus, when fighting against a single adversary, there should be only one army, operating from one base, under the direction of a single commander.

NOTE.

The Archduke Charles remarked, "Success can only be achieved through coordinated efforts directed at a specific point, sustained with determination and carried out decisively." It is rare for a group, even when united in purpose, to agree fully on the means to reach a goal. If one individual's authority does not lead, there will be no unity in executing plans, and the desired outcome will likely remain unattained. Examples validating this principle are abundant in history.

The success of Prince Eugene and Marlborough in their campaigns was largely due to the lack of unity among the opposing armies, where internal disagreements and intrigues constantly weakened their coordination. Without such discord, their victories might have been less certain.

MAXIM LXV.

The same outcomes that have consistently followed lengthy discussions and councils of war will always prevail: they usually conclude with the adoption of the least effective course of action, which in warfare tends to be the most cautious or, if you prefer, the most "prudent." True wisdom in a general lies in decisive courage.

NOTE.

Prince Eugene once remarked that councils of war "are only useful when you need an excuse for doing nothing." Villars shared this sentiment. Therefore, a general-in-chief should avoid convening a council in moments of difficulty, instead consulting individually with his most experienced generals. This approach allows him to draw on their insights while ultimately relying on his own judgment to make a decision. Though this places full responsibility for the outcome on the general, it offers the advantage of acting on personal conviction and prevents the risk of operational secrets being leaked, as often happens when strategies are debated in a council of war.

MAXIM LXVI.

In war, only the general can truly assess specific decisions, and it is up to him alone to overcome obstacles through his superior skill and determination.

NOTE.

An officer who follows orders, regardless of the nature or scope of his command, is always justified in carrying out those orders to the letter. This is not the case for the general-in-chief, on whom the army's safety and the campaign's success depend. Continuously engaged in observation and analysis, the general-in-chief gradually develops a depth of judgment that allows him to view situations more broadly and clearly than his subordinate commanders.

Marshal Villars, for example, often acted against the advice of his generals during his campaigns and was usually successful. This illustrates that a general with confidence in his command abilities must trust his own instincts and insights if he hopes to secure victory.

MAXIM LXVII.

Allowing generals or other officers to surrender their forces under a specific capitulation, except when they are part of a fortress garrison, is a dangerous concession. It undermines the military character of a nation by opening a path for the cowardly, the weak, or even the misguidedly brave to yield too easily. In times of great adversity, extraordinary resolve is necessary. The more unyielding an army's resistance, the greater its chances of receiving assistance or finding success. History shows us that countless feats, once thought impossible, were achieved by men who faced death as their only alternative.

NOTE.

In the 1759 campaign, Frederick sent General Fink with 18,000 men to Maxen to block the Austrian army's access to the Bohemian passes. Surrounded by an enemy twice their number, Fink surrendered after a tough fight, with 14,000 men laying down their arms. This was seen as especially disgraceful since General Winch, commanding the cavalry, managed to break through the enemy lines. Thus, the full blame for the surrender fell on Fink, who was later court-martialed, stripped of his rank, and imprisoned for two years.

In the 1796 Italian campaign, Austrian General Provéra surrendered with 2,000 men in Cossaria Castle. Later, at the Battle of La Favorita, he again capitulated, this time with a force of 6,000. And the capitulation at Ulm in 1805, led by General Mack, saw 30,000 Austrian soldiers lay down their arms—an act especially disappointing given that, during the Revolutionary Wars, numerous generals had broken through enemy lines by sheer force, even when supported by only a few battalions.

MAXIM LXVIII.

No sovereign, nation, or general can feel secure if officers are allowed to capitulate on the battlefield, laying down their arms under terms favorable to the opposing party but damaging to the broader interests of their own army. To abandon danger and thereby expose their comrades to even greater risk is the height of cowardice. Such conduct should be condemned, branded as dishonorable, and punished by death. Generals, officers, and soldiers who surrender in battle solely to save their own lives should face decimation.

Those who give such an order and those who follow it are equally guilty of betrayal and deserving of the severest penalty.

NOTE.

Soldiers, generally unaware of their commander's larger plans, cannot be held accountable for his actions. If their commander orders them to surrender, they must obey, as discipline is fundamental to an army's strength, more so than sheer numbers. Therefore, in these situations, the responsibility and resulting punishment for cowardice should fall solely on the commanding officers. There are countless examples of soldiers standing firm in dire situations when led by officers of proven courage.

MAXIM LXIX.

There is only one honorable way to become a prisoner of war: by being captured individually, meaning by being completely cut off and no longer able to wield arms. In such cases, no conditions apply, as honor dictates none—we surrender solely to an overpowering necessity.

NOTE.

There is always time to become a prisoner of war, so surrender should be delayed until the absolute last extremity. Here, I would like to recount an extraordinary example of unyielding defense, as told by eyewitnesses. Captain Dubrenil, of the 37th Line Regiment's grenadiers, was detached with his company when a large party of Cossacks intercepted and surrounded him. Dubrenil formed his small force into a square formation, attempting to reach a nearby wood within musket range, and managed to do so with minimal losses. But as soon as the grenadiers saw the safety of the wood, they broke formation and fled, leaving only their captain and a handful of loyal men at the mercy of the enemy.

Soon, however, the fugitives, ashamed of abandoning their leader, decided to return to rescue him if captured or recover his body if fallen. Reforming on the edge of the woods, they fought through the cavalry with bayonets and reached their captain, who, despite seventeen wounds, was still defending himself. They surrounded him and successfully brought him back to the woods with minimal further losses. Examples like this were not uncommon during the Revolutionary Wars, and it would be valuable for a contemporary historian to collect them, as they serve to teach soldiers the heights that can be reached through determined courage and unwavering resolve.

MAXIM LXX.

The role of a general in an occupied country is fraught with challenges. If he is too harsh, he stirs resentment and increases opposition; if too lenient, he fosters unrealistic expectations, making the inevitable hardships of war feel even more burdensome. A victorious general must balance severity, justice, and leniency to manage or prevent uprisings.

NOTE.

In ancient Rome, generals attained command only after serving in various civil and administrative roles, acquiring skills that prepared them to govern newly conquered territories with the discretion and prudence that such a power required. This comprehensive training enabled Roman generals to handle the complexities of both military leadership and civil governance. Today, however, generals are typically trained solely in the operations of strategy and tactics, with limited exposure to the broader administrative or civil responsibilities that occupation demands. As a result, civil functions during wartime are often managed by lower officials outside the military command, whose actions can unintentionally escalate the abuses and frustrations that accompany military operations, causing additional hardship for both soldiers and civilians.

This issue deserves careful attention: if generals used peacetime to study diplomacy or were involved in various embassies and foreign courts, they could acquire valuable insight into the laws, governance, and cultural norms of the countries they might later engage with militarily. They would also become familiar with the foundational interests on which treaties and alliances rest, which could prove invaluable in achieving favorable terms and outcomes at the end of a campaign. This knowledge would equip generals to govern more effectively and to control all aspects of an occupied territory, enhancing their ability to manage both the military and civil spheres. Figures like Prince Eugene and Marshal Villars were renowned not only for their military prowess but also for their diplomatic skill, handling both roles with notable success.

Additionally, an occupying army that enforces strict discipline within its ranks typically faces little resistance from the local population, except in cases where injustices are exacerbated by the demands of civil administrators. Thus, the general-in-chief's attention should focus heavily on ensuring that the contributions demanded from the occupied territory are collected equitably and applied directly to the army's needs, rather than diverted to enrich those tasked with collection, as often happens. This approach can prevent the resentment that tends to build when local populations are unfairly burdened or see their resources misused, fostering greater stability in the long term.

MAXIM LXXI.

To use the expertise gained in the service of one's country to surrender its borders and towns to a foreign power is an act condemned by every tenet of religion, morality, and honor.

NOTE.

Those who, driven by ambition and their own passions, incite citizens of the same nation to take arms against each other under the misleading guise of the "public good" are even more culpable. For no matter how restrictive a government may be, long-established institutions are always preferable to the chaos and suffering that civil war brings. Civil war inevitably creates the instability that some use to justify acts of treachery and violence.

A soldier's first duty should be to remain loyal to his sovereign and to respect the established government. These are the foundational principles that define both a soldier's integrity and a man of honor.

MAXIM LXXII.

A general-in-chief has no right to use his sovereign or a distant minister as a shield for his own errors in warfare, especially when those superiors, being far removed from the front lines, may be poorly informed or completely unaware of the true circumstances on the ground.

From this, it follows that any general is at fault if he proceeds with a plan he knows to be flawed. It is his duty to present his objections, advocate for a change, and, if necessary, resign rather than become the instrument of his army's downfall. A general who engages in a battle based on orders, despite knowing he will lose, is equally responsible for the resulting failure.

In such cases, a general should refuse to obey. Absolute obedience is warranted only when a command is given by a superior physically present at the moment of action, where immediate clarifications can be provided to the executor. However, if a general receives explicit orders from his sovereign to engage in battle with instructions to yield and accept defeat, he should assess the logic or benefit of such an order. If he perceives the strategic advantage, he should comply; if not, he should refuse.

NOTE.

In 1697, Prince Eugene intercepted a courier carrying imperial orders forbidding him from engaging in a battle he had meticulously prepared and which he knew would be decisive. Judging it his duty to ignore these orders, he proceeded and achieved victory at Zenta, where the Turks suffered the loss of around 30,000 men, including 4,000 prisoners. Despite the significant benefits of this triumph for the imperial cause, Eugene faced disgrace upon his return to Vienna.

Similarly, in 1793, General Hoche, ordered to advance on Treves with an exhausted army traversing difficult, mountainous terrain, refused to obey. He reasoned that such an effort would jeopardize his troops for a minor objective, risking total ruin. Hoche chose to return his forces to winter quarters, prioritizing the preservation of his army, essential for the success of the coming campaign, over his own safety. For this defiance, he was recalled to Paris and imprisoned, only gaining his freedom after Robespierre's fall.

While these examples are controversial and not necessarily models to follow, it seems crucial that such a complex issue be examined by qualified individuals capable of weighing its implications and potential merits.

MAXIM LXXIII.

The foremost quality required in a general-in-chief is a composed and level-headed mind—one that receives impressions accurately and evaluates events and situations at their true worth. Such a leader must avoid being overly encouraged by positive news or disheartened by negative developments. Each piece of information that comes to him, whether in succession or all at once during the day, must occupy exactly the space it deserves in his mind, neither more nor less. The capacity to weigh and prioritize these impressions properly is the foundation for sound reasoning and effective judgment.

Some people, due to their physical and emotional constitution, view everything through an overly dramatic lens. They build vivid mental images out of minor events and assign undue significance to trivial occurrences. However, regardless of how much skill, talent, or courage such individuals may possess, they lack the temperament for commanding armies or managing major military operations.

NOTE.

Montécuculli once stated, "The first essential in a general-in-chief is deep knowledge of the art of war. This wisdom is not innate but the product of experience. No one is born a commander; one must become one. A true general remains calm, resists anxiety, maintains composure, avoids confusion in commands, never changes expression, and issues orders in battle with the same ease as if he were completely relaxed. These are marks of a valiant leader.

"A general must encourage the fearful, multiply the brave, rekindle the fighting spirit of his troops, regroup those who have been scattered, and lead back into the fray those who have been pushed back. He must find solutions in difficulty, success even in adversity, and be ready to sacrifice himself if necessary for the state's welfare. Such qualities earn a general true honor and distinction."

Additionally, an outstanding general must have the insight to assess character accurately and assign individuals to roles best suited to their abilities. As Marshal Villars noted, "I always focused on observing the younger generals. One, with a daring nature, was fit to lead an attacking column; another, though cautious yet courageous, was more reliable for defending a position." Only through this careful alignment of each person's unique traits with the tasks they are best suited to can true success in warfare be achieved.

MAXIM LXXIV.

The primary qualities essential for an officer appointed as head of the staff include a deep knowledge of the terrain, the skill to conduct reconnaissance effectively, the ability to ensure rapid and accurate transmission of orders, and the capability to outline even the most complex maneuvers in a clear, concise, and simple manner.

NOTE.

In the past, the responsibilities of chiefs of staff were limited to preparing for the execution of the campaign plan and overseeing the orders from the general-in-chief. During battles, their role was primarily to direct and supervise movements. However, recent wars introduced a notable shift, where staff officers were often entrusted with leading an attack column or large detachments when the general-in-chief wished to keep his plans confidential. This innovation, although initially resisted, brought significant benefits. It allowed staff officers to refine their theoretical knowledge through hands-on practice and to earn respect from soldiers and junior officers, who often regard leaders who don't fight alongside them as less capable.

Marshal Berthier exemplifies the qualities of a chief of staff, as he held this demanding role under Napoleon with exceptional skill. His long career spanned over fifty years and included warfare on four continents, leading him to participate in and oversee thirty-two campaigns. Raised by his father, an engineer officer, Berthier learned early on to draft precise plans and mastered the foundational skills of a staff officer. Beginning his military journey with Prince de Lambesq's dragoons, he developed proficiency in horsemanship and swordsmanship—vital skills for any soldier. Later, while attached to the staff of Count Rochambeau, Berthier distinguished himself in his first campaign in America with notable bravery, dedication, and skill. As he rose through the ranks within Marshal de Segur's staff corps, he visited the Prussian camps and eventually served as chief of staff under Baron de Bezenval.

Throughout the Revolutionary and Napoleonic Wars, Berthier's career mirrored the history of Napoleon's campaigns, as he managed every detail both in planning and on the battlefield across sixteen campaigns. Staying clear of political intrigue, Berthier focused solely on his military duties, demonstrating tireless commitment, sharp strategic insight, and the prudence to direct operations with clarity and precision. His discretion, modesty, and unwavering dedication to duty were coupled with a strict yet just approach to discipline. His personal example of vigilance and zeal earned him the respect and obedience of those under his command.

MAXIM LXXV.

An artillery commandant must have a thorough understanding of each branch of the service, as he is responsible for providing arms and ammunition to all units within the army. His communication with artillery officers stationed at the frontlines should ensure he is fully informed of the army's movements, allowing him to manage and position the main artillery reserves based on accurate and timely intelligence.

NOTE.

While the importance of entrusting arms and ammunition supply to a dedicated military branch is well-recognized, it is surprising that the same approach is not applied to the provision of food and forage, which is often managed by a separate administrative body. Civil establishments connected to armies are generally assembled at the onset of a conflict and are typically staffed by individuals unfamiliar with the military's rules of discipline, rules they are often inclined to overlook. These civilians are often seen unfavorably by the military because, rather than supporting the army's mission, they tend to prioritize personal profit, caring little about the means by which they achieve it. They are motivated only by self-interest in a service where they share no direct stake in glory or honor, though the success of the army can depend significantly on their efficiency.

The inefficiencies and abuses that often plague such civilian-managed services would likely diminish if these roles were filled by personnel with prior military experience, individuals whose dedication to the army would enhance their commitment to the cause. In return for their work, they would share in the honor and success achieved by their fellow soldiers, fostering a sense of unity and discipline that would benefit the army as a whole.

MAXIM LXXVI.

A skilled general of advanced posts must be able to thoroughly scout all kinds of defiles and fords, secure trustworthy guides, gather information from locals such as the parish priest and postmaster, quickly build rapport with inhabitants, deploy spies, intercept both public and private correspondence, and analyze the contents of these letters. In essence, he must be prepared to provide the general-in-chief with detailed intelligence when the full army arrives.

NOTE.

In earlier times, small foraging detachments led by junior officers provided valuable training for officers in command of advanced posts. Nowadays, however, the army is supplied through organized contributions, so it's mostly through partisan warfare that officers can gain the experience necessary to excel in these roles.

A partisan leader operates with a certain degree of autonomy, often without consistent support or supplies from the main army and relying instead on his own resources throughout a campaign. An officer in such a role must blend ingenuity with courage, balancing bold action with careful judgment, as he gathers resources without risking direct confrontation with stronger enemy forces. Constantly alert and surrounded by potential threats that he must anticipate and overcome, a partisan leader rapidly gains a level of tactical insight rarely achieved by officers in regular line service. Unlike the latter, who are typically directed by higher command, a partisan leader's skill and intuition are honed through self-reliance, fostering an independent adaptability vital for success in the field.

MAXIM LXXVII.

Generals-in-chief must rely on their own experience or innate talent to guide their decisions. While tactical maneuvers, battlefield evolutions, and the technical duties of an engineer or artillery officer can be learned from manuals, the art of strategy is grasped only through direct experience and a deep study of the campaigns led by the great military leaders of history.

Gustavus Adolphus, Turenne, and Frederick, alongside Alexander, Hannibal, and Caesar, all operated by similar core principles. They consistently kept their forces united, ensured that no weak points were left exposed, and swiftly took control of crucial positions. These are the principles that lead to victory; they inspire respect for one's forces and instill fear in the opposition, thereby securing loyalty and reinforcing authority.

NOTE.

"A great captain can only be made," said the Archduke Charles, "through extensive experience and intense study. Yet personal experience alone is rarely enough—whose life is rich enough in events to provide universal knowledge?" A general must therefore expand his knowledge by studying the achievements of others, discerning the insights of his predecessors, and using the grand military feats of history, along with their political outcomes, as benchmarks for comparison. Only through this combination of self-acquired insight and learned wisdom can one aspire to be a truly great commander.

MAXIM LXXVIII.

Study the campaigns of Alexander, Hannibal, Caesar, Gustavus Adolphus, Turenne, Eugene, and Frederick over and over. Shape yourself after their example. This is the only path to becoming a true leader in war and mastering the art's hidden intricacies. Through this close study, your own insights will deepen, and you'll gain the discernment to dismiss any strategies that stray from the core principles of these legendary commanders.

NOTE.

To support this purpose, I have assembled the present collection. By reflecting on and analyzing the history of modern warfare, I aim to demonstrate, with practical examples, how a great captain's strategies can best be integrated into one's study of the art of war. May this work fulfill its intended purpose!

Instructions to His Generals

Frederick the Great

The King of Prussia's Military Instruction to His Generals

Article I. Regarding Prussian Troops: Their Strengths and Weaknesses

To shape and maintain my troops, commanding officers must exercise the highest degree of diligence and care. Absolute discipline is essential, and attention to their well-being must be a priority. Prussian soldiers deserve a standard of nourishment superior to that of almost any other European army.

Our regiments are half-composed of native soldiers and half of foreign enlistees who join for financial gain. The latter often seek any opportunity to leave a service to which they hold no personal allegiance, making the prevention of desertion a vital concern.

Some of our generals mistakenly assume that one soldier can replace another without consequence, as long as the ranks are filled. But this view fails to recognize the unique conditions of our own army compared to others. If a deserter is replaced by a soldier equally trained and disciplined, the impact may be minimal. However, if a soldier who has two years of training deserts and is replaced by a poorly trained recruit—or left unreplaced—the effect on the regiment can be significant.

Such lapses in officer vigilance have, at times, led to regiments not only losing personnel but also diminishing in reputation. When regiments lose disciplined soldiers, the army itself weakens precisely when full strength is most needed. Without dedicated effort, you risk losing the best of your forces and may find it challenging to restore your ranks.

While Prussia has a healthy population, finding men of the necessary height for service is no simple task. Even if they are available, they cannot be trained immediately. For this reason, preventing desertion becomes one of the essential responsibilities of generals commanding armies or detachments. To achieve this:

1. Avoid encamping too close to forests unless absolutely necessary.
2. Conduct roll calls several times each day.
3. Send hussar patrols frequently to scout the area surrounding the camp.
4. Station chasseurs in crop fields at night and double cavalry posts at dusk to secure the perimeter.
5. Do not allow soldiers to stray and ensure that each unit is led to water and forage by an officer.
6. Enforce strict punishment for marauding, as it breeds disorder.
7. Keep guards stationed in villages until the troops are assembled on marching days.
8. Enforce strict orders prohibiting any soldier from leaving his rank or division while on the march.
9. Avoid night marches unless absolutely necessary.
10. Deploy hussar patrols on both flanks while infantry move through wooded areas.
11. Position officers at both ends of a defile to maintain order in ranks.
12. If a backward march becomes necessary, keep the reason concealed from the troops, or offer a

motivating explanation to maintain morale.

13. Ensure regular provision of essential supplies such as bread, meat, beer, brandy, and other necessities for the troops. Maintaining a steady and dependable issue of these is crucial for morale and health.
14. Identify the root causes of desertion if it begins to affect a regiment or company. Investigate whether the soldiers have received their enlistment bonuses and customary benefits, and determine if any misconduct by captains or officers might be a contributing factor. However, under no circumstances should discipline be relaxed. Some may believe that this is the responsibility of the colonel alone, yet the efforts of one individual cannot suffice to achieve excellence across the entire force. An army must strive collectively for cohesion and unity, giving the impression of being directed by a single, resolute mind.

An army is largely composed of individuals who, if not under consistent direction, may tend toward idleness. Without vigilant oversight from the general, who enforces a strong sense of duty, this carefully assembled force will begin to deteriorate, losing its effectiveness and ultimately becoming little more than the semblance of a disciplined army. For this reason, constant, purposeful activity for the troops is essential. Commanders who maintain such discipline will see the clear benefits, and they will also notice that numerous minor infractions often go unaddressed by those who lack the vigilance to uncover and address them.

Although this level of continuous attention may initially seem burdensome for a general, the substantial rewards make it well worthwhile. With troops of such exceptional bravery, skill, and discipline, the achievements possible are boundless. A general who may appear reckless or overly bold in other nations would, with our troops, be considered merely diligent in adhering to established standards. With a force of well-provisioned soldiers like ours, any undertaking within human capability can be approached with confidence. Furthermore, the soldiers uphold such a high standard that anyone showing signs of cowardice or hesitation would not be tolerated among them, a stance rarely seen in other armies.

I have personally observed officers and soldiers alike who, even when severely wounded, would not abandon their post or retreat to seek medical attention. With troops of this quality, almost any objective becomes attainable. Supplied adequately, they are capable of incredible feats. Whether marching at a rapid pace to gain an advantage over the enemy, storming a forest position, scaling a mountain, or engaging in cavalry charges, they exhibit unshakable courage and resilience. In close combat, they will press on relentlessly, turning resistance into rout and transforming a mere encounter into a decisive victory.

However, the excellence of the troops alone is not enough. The general's expertise is equally vital, as the incompetence or poor judgment of leadership can squander all advantages. Therefore, I will now discuss the essential qualities that a general must possess. I will also outline specific principles and guidelines, whether derived from the wisdom of experienced generals or from hard-won lessons learned through my own experience.

Article II. On Troop Subsistence and Provisioning

A notable general once remarked that feeding an army should be its foundational priority, as it sustains all operations. This crucial aspect can be divided into two sections: the first addresses where and how to establish supply depots, while the second covers the effective use and transport of these supplies.

The foremost rule is to establish large supply depots securely in the rear of the army whenever possible. During the wars in Silesia and Bohemia, our main depot was located in Breslau, strategically chosen for its access to replenishment via the Oder River. Establishing depots directly at the front lines may seem efficient, but a single setback could force their abandonment, leaving the army without resources. When depots are organized sequentially in the rear, any operational setback will only be a temporary obstacle rather than a full-scale crisis.

On the Electorate's frontiers, the most strategic locations for depots would be Spandau and Magdeburg, with the latter's position on the Elbe particularly suited for offensive campaigns into Saxony. For operations toward Bohemia, Schweidnitz would be an ideal location.

The integrity of commissaries and their deputies is crucial in this regard, as dishonest conduct directly compromises the state. Therefore, officials of reputable character should be appointed to these positions, and they should regularly conduct personal and meticulous inspections to verify accuracy in all records.

There are two primary methods of stocking depots: one is to procure grain by purchasing it from local nobility and peasants at established finance chamber rates; the other method is through requisitioning specified quantities. Commissaries are responsible for coordinating and authorizing these transactions.

Specially constructed vessels should be used to transport grain and forage along rivers and canals. However, purveyors should only be hired under the most pressing circumstances since even Jewish merchants, known for demanding high prices, are typically more reasonable. Purveyors' inflated rates drive up the costs of supplies, which they then resell at extravagant profits.

Supply depots must be prepared well in advance so that the army has everything it needs when setting out on campaign. Delaying their establishment until winter could mean that freezing conditions halt river transport, or that roads become so bogged down that transporting supplies becomes exceedingly difficult.

In addition to the covered wagons assigned to regiments, which carry an eight-day bread supply, the commissary has provisions for transporting a month's worth of supplies. The use of navigable waterways should never be overlooked; without this transport option, no army can be reliably or abundantly supplied.

Wagons used for transporting supplies should be drawn exclusively by horses. Attempts have been made to use oxen, but they proved inadequate. Wagon masters must pay careful attention to the well-being of their animals, as the loss of horses directly reduces the number of wagons, thereby diminishing the army's provisions. The general must also oversee this matter since neglected horses mean fewer wagons and potentially lost supplies on the march. Inadequately fed or exhausted horses will inevitably falter, leading to a breakdown in logistics and possibly derailing well-planned operations. Thus, the general must diligently monitor these essential factors, which are critical to the success of all military maneuvers.

When conducting a campaign against Saxony, using the Elbe River to transport provisions is highly advantageous. In Silesia, the Oder serves this purpose, while in Prussia, access to the sea is invaluable. However, in Bohemia and Moravia, land transport is the sole means of conveyance. Often, a line of depots is created, as in Bohemia in 1742, when magazines were established at Pardubitz, Nienbourg, Podjebrod, and Brandies. This chain enabled us to keep pace with the enemy and pursue him toward Prague if necessary. Similarly, in the recent Bohemian campaign, Breslau supplied Schweidnitz, which in turn supplied Jaromirez, and from there provisions were carried directly to the army.

In addition to the covered wagons carrying provisions, the army transports portable iron ovens, which have recently been increased in number. These ovens are set up during rest days to bake fresh bread. On any expedition, it's essential to carry a ten-day supply of bread or biscuits. While biscuits are an excellent ration, our soldiers are not accustomed to utilizing them efficiently and typically only enjoy them in soup form.

When marching through hostile territory, the meal depot should be kept in a secure, garrisoned town near the army. For instance, in the 1745 campaign, our depots progressed from Neustadt to Jaromirez and eventually to Trautenau. If our advance had extended further, our nearest secure depot would have been at Pardubitz. Each company has been provided with hand mills, which have proven invaluable. These mills are operated by soldiers who grind the meal, exchange it at the depot, and receive bread in return. This setup allows us to conserve larger stores and remain in camp longer than would otherwise be possible, reducing the need for large escorts and frequent convoys.

Regarding convoy security, I must elaborate. The strength of the escort should match the anticipated threat level from the enemy. Infantry detachments are stationed in towns along the convoy route, providing support points. Sometimes, large covering detachments are deployed, as was done in Bohemia. In terrain with significant cover, infantry should primarily compose convoy escorts, supplemented with hussars to scout for hidden enemy positions and survey the route.

Even in open terrain, I favor infantry over cavalry for convoy escorts, as I find them more effective in this role. For details on convoy escort procedures, I direct you to my military regulations. Securing convoys should be a high priority for the general. One reliable strategy is to deploy troops to occupy key defiles before the convoy reaches them and position the escort a league ahead of the convoy toward the enemy's position. This maneuver effectively masks the convoy, allowing it to pass securely through challenging areas.

Article III. Of Sutlers, Beer, and Brandy.

When planning any operation against the enemy, it is essential to direct the commissary to gather all available beer and brandy to ensure the army has these supplies, at least for the initial days. As soon as the army crosses into enemy territory, all nearby brewers and distillers must be requisitioned at once. Distillers, in particular, should be set to work immediately so that soldiers won't miss out on their rations, which they rely on greatly for morale.

Sutlers must be protected, especially in areas where local inhabitants have fled and where regular provisions cannot be obtained with money. In such instances, we have some leeway to avoid strict adherence to local regulations concerning the peasantry. The sutlers and accompanying women should be sent to search for vegetables and livestock to supplement rations. Attention must be paid to the prices of provisions, ensuring that soldiers can buy supplies at fair prices while allowing sutlers to earn a reasonable profit.

It's worth noting that during a campaign, soldiers receive two pounds of bread daily and two pounds of meat weekly at no charge—a privilege they greatly deserve, particularly in regions like Bohemia, where the terrain is harsh and resources are limited.

Convoys transporting supplies for the army should also include herds of cattle to guarantee soldiers' nourishment and sustain their strength throughout the campaign.

Article IV. Of Dry and Green Forage.

Dry forage includes items like oats, barley, hay, and chopped straw, which are stored in the magazine. If the oats are spoiled or musty, the horses are likely to develop mange or farcy, rendering them weak and ineffective even at the beginning of a campaign. Although chopped straw is traditionally given, it merely serves to fill the belly without providing substantial nourishment.

The initial aim of gathering and storing forage is to ensure a strategic advantage, either by preparing ahead of the enemy or by stocking up for a distant campaign. However, when horses are limited to dry forage, the army often cannot afford to stray too far from its supply magazines due to the sheer challenge of transporting enough feed; entire regions sometimes lack sufficient carriages to meet the army's needs. Consequently, this approach is usually reserved for situations lacking rivers to facilitate the transportation of forage.

During the Silesian campaign, my cavalry was entirely reliant on dry forage, but we limited our movement from Strehla to Schwiednitz (where there was a magazine) and onward to Cracau, where we were near the Brieg and Oder Rivers. For winter campaigns, cavalry should carry forage sufficient for five days, firmly bound on their mounts—particularly if action is anticipated in regions like Bohemia or Moravia, where inadequate forage would rapidly weaken the horses.

In regions with standing crops or unharvested fields, forage is gathered there first, moving to village stores only when the fields are exhausted. When the army plans to remain in one location, an inventory of available forage should be taken to ensure that rations are distributed evenly according to the intended duration of stay.

For large foraging operations, the escort typically consists of a body of cavalry sized according to proximity to the enemy and the perceived threat level. In some instances, entire wings or even the entire army may engage in foraging activities.

Foragers assemble on their designated routes, positioned on the army's wings, front, or rear as necessary. Hussars lead the advance, followed by cavalry in open terrain; in rougher areas, infantry precedes the cavalry. This advanced guard moves ahead of the main foraging column, which is divided into sections. Each section of foragers is followed by an escort composed of both horse and foot soldiers. This staggered arrangement continues, with successive detachments of foragers and escort troops. The rear guard comprises a final troop of hussars, completing the orderly formation and protecting the column's tail.

It is important to remember that all escorts should have infantry carrying their cannons and foragers equipped with swords and carbines. Upon reaching the designated foraging area, a protective chain must be set up, positioning infantry near villages, behind hedges, or in sunken paths. A reserve unit combining cavalry and infantry should be centrally located, ready to provide support at any vulnerable points where the enemy might attempt to break through. The hussars are to engage in skirmishes with the enemy to create distractions and draw them away from the foragers. Once the area is secured, the foraging ground is divided among regiments, and officers must ensure that foraged bundles are tightly bound and large enough to maximize the load.

When the horses are loaded, the foragers should return to camp in small groups, each protected by an escort. Once the foragers have vacated the area, the chain troops should gather to form the rear guard, with the hussars following behind to provide additional cover.

Foraging in villages follows a similar procedure, with the key difference being that infantry form a defensive perimeter around the village while the cavalry holds a position slightly behind, ready to act if necessary. Each village should be foraged individually to avoid overly dispersing the chain troops.

In mountainous regions, foraging becomes a challenging operation, requiring escorts primarily composed of infantry and hussars due to the rugged terrain. When camped close to the enemy for an extended period, it's essential to secure the forage located between both camps first. Foraging should then extend outward up to two leagues, beginning with the more distant fields and reserving those nearest to camp for later use. If the army doesn't plan to stay long, foraging can focus on the immediate camp area and surroundings.

When gathering a substantial amount of green forage, it's preferable to send out smaller foraging parties twice rather than spread across too wide an area all at once. This strategy keeps the protective chain more compact and the foragers safer, as stretching the chain too thinly weakens it, making it vulnerable to being breached by the enemy.

Article V. Of the Knowledge of a Country.

Understanding the geography of a country is essential and can be acquired through two primary methods. The first step is to thoroughly study a map of the anticipated war zone, clearly noting the names of significant rivers, towns, and mountains. This preliminary step helps create a general framework of the area. With this groundwork established, the next phase involves a more detailed examination to understand the layout of major roads, the locations of towns, and whether these towns can be fortified for defense or how best to attack them if the enemy occupies them. The defense requirements for these towns should also be assessed.

It's crucial to have accurate plans of fortified towns to understand their defenses and identify the most vulnerable points. Equally important is the knowledge of rivers, including their depth, navigability, and any potential crossing points, along with seasonal changes—whether rivers are impassable in spring or dry up in summer. Marshes, which could hinder movement, should also be identified.

In a flat, open landscape, fertile areas should be distinguished from barren ones, and it's important to know the possible routes connecting major cities and rivers, including how to secure camps along these routes. Flat areas are easily surveyed; however, in mountainous or forested regions, where visibility is limited, reconnaissance is more challenging. To gather essential information in such terrains, it's helpful to climb high points with a map in hand and bring along local villagers, such as hunters or shepherds, who know the area. If a single mountain stands taller than others, it should be ascended to gain a comprehensive view of the area of interest.

Familiarity with roads is critical—not only to plan marching formations but also to strategize alternative routes for reaching or flanking the enemy's camp should they establish nearby positions. Identifying defensive camps, potential battlefields, and enemy-held posts are among the most important reconnaissance goals.

Each reconnaissance should yield a complete understanding of key locations, valleys, defiles, and all advantageous sites. Every possible action should be carefully considered to create well-prepared arrangements, eliminating confusion when action is required. These preparations should be meticulous, revisited and revised as needed, until they are entirely satisfactory.

When choosing camps for either offense or defense, it is generally essential to ensure proximity to wood and water, a well-shielded front, and an open rear. If a thorough personal inspection of the area is not possible, intelligent, resourceful officers should be dispatched, under plausible pretexts or even in disguise if necessary, to gather the necessary intelligence. They must know precisely what to observe, and upon their return, their findings on potential camps and other locations should be added to the map. However, where possible, personal reconnaissance is always preferable over secondhand accounts.

Article VI. Of the Coup D'Oeil.

Understanding the coup d'oeil in military strategy can be broken down into two primary skills. The first is the ability to accurately assess how many troops a specific area can hold. This skill only develops through practice; after overseeing the layout of several camps, the eye becomes attuned to space, so estimation errors become minimal.

The second, and more critical skill, is the ability to identify immediately all possible advantages of any piece of ground. While some may seem naturally adept at this, it is a skill that can be learned and perfected. Fortification principles are the foundation of this skill, providing a universal framework adaptable to any army's position. With this knowledge, an experienced general can utilize every defile, marsh, hollow path, or slight rise in terrain to their advantage.

In a space of two square leagues, there might be two hundred potential positions to consider, yet an insightful general will quickly identify the most advantageous one. This begins with examining even small elevations to get a comprehensive view of the surroundings. Using the same fortification principles, the general can pinpoint the weaknesses in the enemy's formation. Ideally, if time allows, the general should walk over the ground to become even more familiar with the terrain.

Fortification principles also guide how to occupy heights effectively, ensuring positions are not easily dominated by higher ground nearby. These principles provide insight on how to secure the wings so the flanks are well-covered, and they also aid in distinguishing strong, defensible positions from those that would be difficult and risky to hold, even for a seasoned leader. Through this approach, a general can also recognize weaknesses in the enemy's setup, whether due to a poorly chosen position, an ill-judged distribution of forces, or limited natural defenses.

These considerations naturally lead into how troops should be arranged to maximize the benefits of their environment, which I will outline next.

Article VII. Of the Distribution of Troops.

While understanding and selecting suitable terrain is crucial, it's equally important to make full use of these advantages so that each unit is positioned where it can be most effective. Cavalry, known for its speed, should be deployed on open ground to maximize maneuverability, while infantry can handle a wider range of terrain, using their firepower for defense and bayonets for offense. Defensive measures are typically established first to ensure a camp's security, particularly in areas where an enemy engagement is possible at any moment.

Current battle formations are often inherited from earlier strategies and don't always consider the unique features of the terrain. This can lead to a misapplication of tactics. The entire army should be arranged according to what each segment of terrain demands. For example, while plains may suit cavalry, if a plain is small or bordered by woods with enemy infantry positioned there, then cavalry may need to be placed at the edges of the infantry wings to benefit from their support.

There are cases where all cavalry might be positioned on one wing or held in reserve. At other times, infantry brigades may close off their wings. Ideal locations for troops include elevated areas, churchyards, sunken roads, or broad ditches. When used wisely, such terrain features can effectively shield against attacks.

However, placing cavalry behind a swamp or marsh limits their usefulness, as they would be unable to charge effectively. Similarly, positioning cavalry too close to wooded areas could allow enemy forces to cause disarray from cover. Infantry faces similar risks when placed on open ground without protected flanks, as the enemy will likely exploit such vulnerabilities by attacking the exposed side.

In mountainous terrain, I would position the cavalry in the second line, deploying only a few squadrons in the first line for support or for flanking any enemy infantry attempting to advance. Generally, well-organized armies form a cavalry reserve on open plains, while in broken or uneven landscapes, this reserve typically consists of infantry with some light cavalry, such as hussars and dragoons.

The art of troop deployment lies in positioning each unit so it can perform optimally and contribute uniformly to the operation. Villeroi's error at the Battle of Ramillies illustrates this: by stationing his left wing behind an impassable swamp, he prevented it from supporting his right wing, thereby losing the utility of a significant portion of his force. This oversight demonstrates how critical it is to ensure that each unit's placement allows for effective maneuvering and support.

Article VIII. Of Camps.

To ensure your camp is well-chosen, assess whether a minor movement on your part forces the enemy into a more substantial shift, or if, after one of your marches, they are compelled to make additional ones. The side with the fewest necessary maneuvers is generally in the better position.

The responsibility for selecting the camp's location should rest solely with the general, as the chosen spot often becomes the battlefield, and the success of his operations hinges on this decision. Given the importance of this matter, I'll delve into it in detail, focusing solely on factors that directly impact the general and leaving the specific placement of troops within the camp to my military regulation.

Camps serve two primary functions: defense and preparation for attack. The first type includes camps where troops are gathered primarily for rest and convenience, ideally near the magazine but organized so they can quickly form a battle line. These camps should generally be positioned at a distance from the enemy to avoid disturbances. Ignoring this caution, as the King of England did by encamping along the bank of the Main opposite the French army, led to a significant risk of defeat at Dettingen.

The first essential rule when selecting a camp location is proximity to both wood and water. In our custom, camps are fortified, following the Roman example, to guard against possible surprise attacks by enemy light troops and to discourage desertion. I've noticed consistently fewer instances of desertion when the camp's defenses were solid, such as when redans were interconnected by two lines extending around the perimeter, as opposed to camps without this added security. This may seem trivial but has proven to be a substantial factor in maintaining troop integrity.

Camps of rest, intended for provisioning and observation, are another type. These camps are positioned to monitor enemy movements without being actively engaged, allowing us to respond to their maneuvers. Since relaxation is key in such camps, they are often located behind large rivers, marshes, or other natural barriers that make their front impassable. Our camp at Strehla, for instance, was of this type. When streams or rivers at the camp's front are too shallow, they should be dammed to increase their depth.

Even in camps of this nature, where the enemy threat is minimal, the general must remain vigilant. The time granted here should be used to oversee the troops closely and restore discipline. The general should verify that operations proceed according to protocol, ensuring officers on guard understand and fulfill their responsibilities, and confirm that the standards I've established for positioning cavalry and infantry guards are meticulously observed.

The infantry should undergo their drills three times each week, with new recruits practicing daily; at times, whole corps may execute their maneuvers together. The cavalry should also perform their exercises unless they're engaged in foraging, and the general, who is well-aware of each corps' exact numbers, must ensure that both the young soldiers and inexperienced horses are trained thoroughly. Regular visits to the lines are essential, where the general commends officers diligent with their troops and firmly reprimands those who show signs of neglect, as no large army can sustain itself without active supervision. Armies will inevitably be populated with idle or malingering soldiers who require the general's vigilance to stay engaged in their duties.

Camps like these yield great benefit if used as recommended, as the discipline and structure instilled in them lay a solid foundation for the upcoming campaign's success.

When we establish camp for foraging or other purposes, whether near the enemy or farther off, I will focus on the scenarios when we camp close to enemy lines. Here, choosing fertile grounds and strategically advantageous spots, either by natural terrain or fortified by human efforts, is essential.

Foraging camps positioned near the enemy should be difficult to reach, as foraging missions function like combat detachments sent against the opposition. These teams might encompass as much as one-sixth or even half the army, making it imperative that our location protects against any advantage the enemy might seize during these expeditions. A well-chosen camp can prevent these vulnerabilities.

However, even when our camp is well-positioned and appears secure, we cannot overlook further precautions. We must uphold strict secrecy about the timing and location of foraging missions, and not even the general assigned to lead these efforts should know the details until late the night before.

Sending out multiple scout parties is advisable to monitor any movements from the enemy; unless there are significant reasons against it, we might choose to forage on the same day as they do, though we must remain cautious. The enemy, learning of our intentions, might halt their own foraging and redirect their forces to attack our main group.

An example is Prince Charles of Lorraine's camp near Königgrätz, which was naturally fortified and ideal for foraging purposes. Similarly, our camp at Cholm became robust through human intervention, with abatis placed along the right wing and redoubts erected in front of the infantry camp to reinforce our defenses.

We entrench camps when preparing for a siege, defending a challenging passage, or compensating for terrain disadvantages by constructing defensive works to guard against potential enemy aggression.

When establishing entrenchments, a general should use every marsh, river, inundation, and natural or artificial obstruction to limit the width of defensive lines. It's better to construct smaller, manageable entrenchments rather than excessively large ones, as these barriers alone do not stop the enemy; it is the troops stationed behind them that prevent their advancement.

I would avoid constructing entrenchments unless I had sufficient battalions to line them continuously and a reserve of infantry that could be readily moved to any threatened point. Abbatis and other such barriers are useful only when actively defended by infantry.

The main focus should be on properly reinforcing the lines of countervallation, which typically end at a river. In such cases, the trench should extend into the river itself and be deepened enough to prevent fording; neglecting this precaution risks having your flank turned. Additionally, it's crucial to secure ample provisions before settling behind defensive lines to lay siege.

Entrenchments' flanks demand particular attention, as no segment should allow the enemy to approach without being subjected to crossfire from multiple directions. When defending mountain passes or defiles, entrenchments must be reinforced with extra caution, as support for the flanks is vital. Redoubts are often constructed on both wings, and sometimes the entire entrenchment comprises redoubts, ensuring that the defending troops are shielded from being outflanked.

Experienced generals skillfully direct the enemy to attack the most fortified points, where trenches are widened and deepened, lined with palisades, with chevaux de frise at entry points, and parapets made cannon-resistant. Additionally, pits are dug in vulnerable areas to further complicate enemy advances.

However, when it comes to covering a siege, I would always prefer deploying an army of observation over relying solely on an entrenched camp. This is simply because experience has shown that the old approach cannot be fully trusted. Prince de Condé saw his entrenchments before Arras overcome by Turenne, and if I recall correctly, Condé in turn broke through the entrenchments that Turenne had set up before Valenciennes. Since then, neither of these seasoned commanders relied on entrenched camps to cover sieges but opted instead for armies of observation.

I will now discuss defensive camps, which are naturally strong due to their position and meant solely to withstand enemy attacks. To make these positions serve their purpose effectively, the front and both flanks must be equally fortified, while the rear remains open and accessible. Ideal examples include elevated areas with extensive fronts and flanks protected by marshes, like Prince Charles of Lorraine's camp at Marschwitz, which was shielded by a marshy river in the front and lakes on the flanks, or our encampment at Konopist in 1744.

An alternative defensive measure is positioning near a fortified town, as demonstrated by Marshal de Neipperg after his defeat at Mollwitz when he took a secure position under the walls of Neiss. As long as a general can hold such a position, he remains secure from direct attack. However, if the enemy begins maneuvers to outflank him, he can no longer safely remain there. His preparations should, therefore, include fallback plans so that, if outflanked, he can retreat to another strong defensive position further back.

The geography of Bohemia, filled with naturally fortified spots, often forces us to occupy these camps, sometimes against our preference, due to the varied landscape that makes strategic maneuvering challenging.

I must reiterate the utmost importance of a general maintaining vigilance to avoid being lured into errors due to poorly chosen positions. A misjudgment in selecting posts could lead to situations where retreat is only possible through narrow, vulnerable defiles. If faced with a skillful opponent, a general could find himself so tightly confined and restricted by the terrain that he may have no option but to accept the most humiliating fate for a soldier: laying down arms without a chance to fight back.

In camps meant to defend a region, the priority should not be on the strength of the camp itself but on safeguarding the key points vulnerable to attack through which the enemy could breach. Such points should be secured by the camp's positioning. This doesn't mean occupying every possible approach an enemy might take, but rather the one route that would most likely lead to their objective. Selecting a strategic post allows us to thwart their plans, forcing them into extended detours while enabling us to disrupt their advances with minimal repositioning.

For example, the camp at Neustadt is strategically placed to protect the entirety of Lower Silesia from an army stationed in Moravia. The ideal positioning involves having Neustadt and the river in front. Should the enemy attempt to move between Ottmachau and Glatz, we only need to shift our position between Neiss and Ziegenhals, where we can secure a favorable post that blocks them from accessing Moravia. Similarly, the enemy would hesitate to move toward Cosel because positioning ourselves between Troppau and Jaegerndorff—areas with numerous excellent strongholds—would sever their connection to supply convoys.

Another essential camp lies between Liebau and Schaemberg, providing Lower Silesia with formidable defense against threats from Bohemia. In all these scenarios, adherence to the principles I've outlined is vital, though, of course, flexibility in applying them to specific circumstances remains necessary. Additionally, when there's a river before our position, it's crucial to ensure that tents remain no farther than half musket-shot from the front of the camp, keeping defensive readiness intact.

As for the Brandenburg frontier, no camp alone can cover this open terrain, which spans six leagues of uninterrupted plains. Protecting it from Saxony demands control over Wittenberg, either by setting up camp there or following the approach taken in the winter expedition of 1745. The camp at Werben, on the other hand, serves effectively to secure the flank facing Hanover.

In offensive camps, it is essential to have both the front and flanks well fortified. If the flanks, typically the weakest points of an army, are not secured, confidence in the troops will falter. Our camp at Czaslaw, before the 1742 battle, suffered due to this very oversight. Additionally, villages positioned on the wings or in the camp's front are generally garrisoned by our troops, except on combat days when these troops are withdrawn. This precaution prevents potential hazards if the enemy sets these nearby wooden buildings—typical of the region—ablaze, risking loss of men. However, an exception to this rule can be made for villages with solid stone buildings or churchyards detached from flammable structures, as these can provide a defensible position without excessive risk.

Our main principle is to always be on the offensive, not defensive. This kind of position should only be held at the front of the army or in front of its wings; in these places, it will provide a lot of cover for our troops during an attack and will also be very troubling for the enemy throughout the fight.

It's also extremely important to check the depth of the small rivers or marshes that are in front of or on the flanks of our camp. Otherwise, if the rivers can be crossed or the marshes can be passed through, you might realize too late that you've trusted a weak point for defense. Villars was defeated at Malplaquet because he thought the marsh on his right couldn't be crossed, only to find it was just a dry meadow that our troops crossed easily to attack him from the side. Every detail should be inspected with our own eyes, and no matter of this kind should ever be ignored or treated as unimportant.

The front of the first line should be protected by infantry regiments, and if there is a river nearby, guards should be stationed on its banks. The back of the camp should be guarded by guards from the second line. These guards should be protected by simple redoubts joined by light earthworks, so the camp will be defended in the Roman style. We should occupy any villages located on the wings or even half a league away if they can help secure other access points.

The cavalry guards should be set up according to the rules I've outlined in my military instructions. We rarely had more than 300 maîtres de garde among 80 squadrons, unless we were very close to the enemy, as when we marched to Schweidnitz after the Battle of Hohenfriedberg, or when we entered Lusatia on our way to Naumbourg. These advance guards should include all types of troops, such as 2,000 hussars, 1,500 dragoons, and 2,000 grenadiers. The general commanding the forward troops should be a person with good judgment, and since his goal is to gather intelligence and not to engage in combat, his camps should be chosen with care, with woods or narrow passes he is familiar with positioned at the front. He should also send out regular patrols to gather information so that he knows at all times what is happening in the enemy's camp.

Meanwhile, if you use the hussars remaining with you to patrol the rear and the sides of the camp, you've taken every possible measure to protect against any hostile actions. If a large enemy force tries to slip between you and your rear guard, you can be sure they intend to attack it, and you should rush to provide support.

To sum up all I have to say on this topic, it's essential to add that if generals who set up their troops in villages want to be safe from danger and disturbance, they should only occupy villages located between the two main lines.

Article X. In what Manner and for what Reason we are to send out Detachments.

In war, there's an old saying: "He who divides his force will be beaten in detail." This advice has stood the test of time for a reason. If you're about to engage in battle, it's essential to bring together as many troops as you can, using every effort to gather as large a force as possible. When united, these troops can serve the best purpose in the upcoming fight. History has shown repeatedly that generals who overlook this rule usually find themselves with plenty of regret.

For instance, Albemarle's detachment at Oudenarde was defeated, which cost the great Eugene the entire campaign. Similarly, General Stahrenberg was defeated in the Battle of Villa Viciosa in Spain because he was separated from the English forces, unable to coordinate in time. These aren't isolated cases. Detached forces have repeatedly caused disastrous losses, as seen in the Austrian campaigns in Hungary. Prince Hildburghausen's army suffered defeat at Banja Luka, and General Wallis was dealt a setback on the Timok River's banks. The Saxons, too, were beaten at Kesselsdorf due to their failure to unite with Prince Charles, even though circumstances allowed for it. Personally, I nearly faced defeat at Sohr; it was only the quick thinking of my generals and the courageous action of my soldiers that saved me from such a fate. Had they faltered, I would have paid the price for having fragmented forces.

This leads to an important question: should detachments never be sent out under any circumstances? My response is that detaching forces is a sensitive decision and should only be made under the most urgent necessity and for reasons of the highest importance. When conducting an offensive, sending out detachments should generally be avoided. Even in open country where you may control a few locations, only the minimum number of troops should be spared to protect supply convoys, and no more. Keeping your force unified is paramount.

However, there are exceptions, particularly in specific regions such as Bohemia or Moravia. In these areas, the need for provisions can make it necessary to send out detachments to ensure the arrival of supplies. Encampments should be set up along the chain of mountains where supply convoys must pass. These encampments should remain in place until you've gathered enough supplies to sustain the army for several months. Additionally, securing a strong position within the enemy's territory as a supply depot becomes crucial. Once these detachments are deployed, the main army should move into advantageous camps and wait for their safe return.

An advanced guard, however, should not be considered a detachment. The purpose of an advanced guard is to stay in close proximity to the main army. Under no circumstances should it be stationed too close to the enemy, as its function is not to be exposed to undue risk.

In some cases, particularly when on the defensive, there may be no choice but to send out detachments. For instance, when I deployed detachments in Upper Silesia, they were relatively safe because they kept to the areas near fortified places, as I previously advised. This closeness to strongholds provided them with a safe haven if threatened by the enemy.

Officers tasked with leading detachments should be men of sound judgment and strong resolve. Although they receive general orders from their commanding officer, they must be prepared to independently decide when to advance or retreat, based on their specific situation. If the enemy's force is too powerful, they should pull back strategically. Conversely, if they have the upper hand, they must recognize this advantage and seize the moment. Such decisions require an officer to be flexible and responsive to changing circumstances, knowing that each choice could turn the tide of battle.

If the enemy approaches by night, these officers may sometimes find it prudent to feign a retreat. In some cases, while the enemy believes they're in retreat, the detachment can suddenly regroup and launch a surprise attack, catching the enemy off guard. This tactic can be effective in breaking the enemy's formation and morale. Light troops, however, need not be a concern in these maneuvers.

The primary duty of an officer in command of a detachment is to ensure his own safety and that of his men. Once this is achieved, he can turn his focus to planning and executing attacks against the enemy. Keeping his adversary on high alert by frequently taking the offensive will ensure the enemy is unable to rest. If this officer can succeed in two or three such instances, the enemy will eventually be forced onto the defensive, a position that will grant his forces an advantage.

If these detachments are close to the main army, they should establish communication lines using either a nearby town or forest as a conduit. This connection is crucial for relaying information, coordinating movements, and ensuring that both the main force and the detachment can offer support if either comes under attack. Maintaining such a link enhances the detachment's effectiveness, keeping it as an extension of the main force rather than an isolated unit vulnerable to enemy strikes.

In a defensive war, we often find ourselves needing to make detachments. Generals with limited experience tend to worry about preserving everything, while a skilled and daring leader focuses only on the main objective, aiming to strike a significant blow. Such a leader accepts smaller setbacks if they help prevent a larger disaster.

The enemy's army should be our primary focus. We must work to uncover their plans and counter them with as much force as possible. In 1745, we chose to leave Upper Silesia exposed to Hungarian raids so that we could better interfere with the plans of Prince Charles of Lorraine. We refrained from making any detachments until after we defeated his army. Once that victory was secured, General Nassau cleared Upper Silesia of the Hungarians in just fifteen days.

Some generals have a habit of making detachments before launching an attack, intending for these forces to strike the enemy from the rear during the battle. However, this approach is risky because the detachments often lose their way and end up arriving either too soon or too late. For example, when Charles XII sent out a detachment on the night before the Battle of Poltava, they got lost, which contributed to the army's defeat. Similarly, Prince Eugene's plan to surprise Cremona failed when the Prince of Vaudemont's detachment arrived too late to attack the Po Gate as planned.

Detachments should never be made on the day of battle unless it's done with careful strategy, like Turenne's maneuver near Colmar. There, he presented his first line to the army of Elector Frederick William while his second line moved through narrow passes to strike the enemy's flank, leading to their rout. Another example comes from Marshal de Luxembourg at the Battle of Fleurus in 1690, where he hid a group of infantry in tall corn on Prince Waldeck's flank, and this tactic won him the battle.

Only after a victory, and never before, can troops be detached to protect supply convoys. Even then, they should not move farther than half a league from the main army.

In conclusion, detachments that weaken an army by half or even by a third are extremely dangerous and should be firmly avoided.

Article XI. Of the Tricks and Stratagems of War.

In war, the skill of a fox can sometimes be just as essential as the strength of a lion, because cleverness and subtlety may accomplish what sheer power cannot. Since brute force can, at times, be countered by equal force, or even bested by clever strategies, we must be thoroughly skilled in both methods. This knowledge enables us to use either force or cunning as the situation demands, ensuring we can adapt and succeed in the face of different challenges.

I won't attempt to recount the countless strategies that have been used in warfare, as they all share a common goal: to mislead and exhaust the enemy by making him move or prepare unnecessarily. When we effectively conceal our true intentions, we keep our enemy guessing, preventing him from countering our actual plans and positioning our forces to advantage. Therefore, it is vital to lead the enemy to believe that we are planning moves that we have no intention of executing. In doing so, we force him to respond to phantom threats, weakening his position and creating opportunities for us to strike effectively.

When we are gathering troops, we often march them in various directions, creating confusion to keep the enemy uncertain about where we truly plan to assemble. By keeping our destination ambiguous, we prevent the enemy from reinforcing his defenses in the area we actually aim to attack. In regions where there are fortresses or strongholds, we choose a campsite that appears to threaten multiple locations at once. By doing so, the enemy may feel compelled to divide his forces, reinforcing several of these areas at the same time. This division weakens his main body of troops, making it easier for us to attack when the right moment arises. However, if he chooses to focus on just one location, this also serves us well, as we can then concentrate our efforts on laying siege to whichever fortress appears most vulnerable.

If our goal is to cross a river or seize a position of particular importance, we begin by withdrawing to a considerable distance from both the crossing point and the position we intend to capture. This maneuver lures the enemy away from our actual target, leading him to believe that he no longer needs to guard it closely. Then, when our troops are fully prepared, and our movements remain hidden, we return quickly to the pre-determined location, seizing control of it before the enemy can reposition.

When we desire a battle, but the enemy shows a clear reluctance to engage, we employ tactics to make him believe we are fearful of his strength. For instance, we may spread rumors that our own forces are weak, diminished, or in disarray. This tactic was effectively used before the Battle of Hohenfriedberg, when I ordered roads to be repaired as though I planned to retreat to Breslau in four columns, at the approach of Prince Charles. His overconfidence worked in our favor, as he pursued us onto the plain, and we were able to achieve victory.

At times, we even shrink the size of our camp to give the appearance of having a smaller force. By keeping detachments out in the open, we make the enemy believe they're of greater importance than they truly are. Such tactics lead him to underestimate us, causing him to overlook chances to attack when they arise. For example, during the 1745 campaign, if my goal had been to take Königgrätz and Pardubice, I would have needed only two marches across the Glatz region toward Moravia. This would almost certainly have alarmed Prince Charles, prompting him to rush to protect the areas from which he drew his supplies after leaving Bohemia, thus leaving other positions vulnerable. By merely threatening locations linked to his supply routes or those connected with the capital, we can create a sense of vulnerability and sow doubt within the enemy ranks.

If we have no intention of engaging in battle, we make an effort to present ourselves as a formidable and confident force, spreading rumors of our strength and readiness. Austria has mastered this approach, turning it into a refined art form where they appear stronger than they are, intimidating their opponents with mere appearances.

By keeping up a bold and determined front, we project the image that we are eager for battle and that we have a daring plan in place. Such a display encourages rumors that we are about to launch a bold, risky maneuver, which often makes the enemy hesitant, fearing the consequences of an engagement. By leading him to believe we have some bold or daring plan in mind, we keep the enemy on edge, making him wary and defensive. Often, this bold appearance alone is enough to make him stay on the defensive, avoiding any confrontation altogether, and ensuring our troops maintain their advantage.

In a defensive war, one of the most important skills is choosing strong positions and holding them until the very last moment. When forced to retreat, the second line of defense should be the first to begin moving back, followed gradually by the first line. With natural barriers, like defiles, in front of you, the enemy will find it difficult to take advantage of your retreat, keeping your forces protected as they withdraw.

Even during the retreat, it is crucial to select positions that are angled and unclear, making it hard for the enemy to understand your intentions. The more the enemy tries to interpret your movements, the more uncertain he will become, while you indirectly achieve your desired objective without giving away your true strategy.

One effective tactic in warfare is to present a broad front, creating an illusion of a large-scale engagement. If the enemy mistakes this feint for an actual attack, he will be caught off guard and will likely suffer defeat. Through these deceptive maneuvers, you can prompt the enemy to send out detachments, taking advantage of his divided forces to strike with precision.

One of the best stratagems is to lull the enemy into a false sense of security, particularly as winter approaches and troops prepare to disperse and settle into winter quarters. By retreating under the guise of ending the campaign season, you can prepare to reassemble your forces quickly and catch the enemy off guard. To do this effectively, troops should be distributed in a way that allows for swift regrouping, enabling a surprise advance on the enemy's quarters. If successful, this strategy can undo the setbacks of an entire campaign within a matter of weeks.

A careful study of Turenne's last two campaigns provides an excellent example of such tactics; they are considered masterpieces of stratagem from this era. Our ancestors' techniques for warfare have largely been relegated to light troops, who still use ambushes and feigned retreats to draw the enemy into narrow spaces where they can be surrounded and defeated. However, generals today rarely fall for such basic traps, having become wise to these older tricks. Yet even skilled leaders can be vulnerable to betrayal; for instance, Charles XII was misled at Poltava due to the treachery of a Cossack chief, and Peter I faced a similar fate on the Pruth due to the failure of a local prince who could not provide the promised supplies.

As for the methods of conducting warfare through parties and detachments, these are detailed extensively in my Military Regulation. Anyone who wishes to refresh their memory on these tactics should refer to that document, as there is little else I need to add on this subject here.

To understand how to compel the enemy to make detachments, we need only examine the brilliant campaign of 1690, led by Marshal de Luxembourg against the King of England. This campaign, culminating in the Battle of Neerwinden, is a prime example of how to keep the enemy divided and vulnerable through strategic maneuvers.

Article XII. Of Spies, How They Are to be Employed on Every Occasion, and in What Manner We Are to Learn Intelligence of the Enemy.

If we could know the enemy's intentions ahead of time, we would always have an upper hand, even with a smaller force. This advantage is highly sought by generals but rarely obtained. The use of spies is essential in this regard, and they fall into several categories: 1) ordinary individuals who volunteer for this work; 2) double agents; 3) high-value spies with access to important information; and 4) those forced into this unpleasant line of duty.

The first type, ordinary individuals like peasants, artisans, priests, and others who enter the enemy's camp, can only be used to locate where the enemy is stationed. Their reports, however, are often vague or contradictory, which can increase our uncertainty rather than reduce it.

The intelligence gathered from deserters is usually no more reliable. A soldier may know what's happening within his own regiment but is unlikely to have insight into broader plans. As for hussars, who are frequently dispatched ahead and spend much time away from the main army, they may not even know where the army is camped. Despite these limitations, we still commit all reports to writing, as that is the only way to derive any potential benefit from them.

Double agents, on the other hand, are spies used to feed false information to the enemy. For example, an Italian at Schmiedeberg acted as a spy for the Austrians. When we told him that we intended to withdraw to Breslau if the enemy approached, he hurried to report this to Prince Charles of Lorraine, who came close to being deceived by this misinformation.

High-ranking spies, or those with direct access to critical intelligence, are invaluable assets. The postmaster at Versailles, for instance, worked secretly for Prince Eugene. This unfortunate man would open letters and orders sent from the court to the generals, copying their contents and forwarding them to Prince Eugene, who often received these messages even before the French commanders did. Similarly, Luxembourg managed to win the loyalty of a secretary to the King of England, who then informed Luxembourg of sensitive information. The king discovered this betrayal, turning it to his advantage. He forced the traitor to write to Luxembourg with a report that the allied army would go out the next day on a major foraging mission. This nearly led to the French being ambushed at Steenkerque, and they would have been destroyed if not for their exceptional defense.

Securing such spies in a war against Austria, however, would be highly challenging. This isn't because Austrians are less susceptible to bribery, but because their army is surrounded by a swarm of light troops who inspect all who pass through their lines thoroughly. This challenge led me to consider persuading some of their hussar officers to join our side, allowing us to establish a line of communication in the following way: when hussars engage in skirmishes, they sometimes agree to a brief truce. Such occasions could provide an opportunity to exchange messages discreetly.

In cases where we want to gather intelligence on the enemy or mislead him about our circumstances, we can send a loyal soldier from our camp to theirs to spread whatever information we want them to believe. This soldier might carry handbills encouraging desertion, return by a roundabout route, and bring back any information he can gather.

There is another, harsher way to gather intelligence when less severe measures fail, though I admit it is a cruel method. We identify a wealthy citizen with a large family and considerable property. Then, we assign him a person fluent in the enemy's language, disguised as his servant. This "servant" accompanies him to the enemy's camp under the pretense that the citizen is there to complain of injustices he has suffered. To ensure his cooperation, we threaten that if he does not return within a set time, bringing his servant with him, we will burn his house and harm his family. I had to resort to this tactic once, and it worked as I hoped.

Finally, it's worth noting that when paying spies, we must be generous, even to the point of extravagance. A person who risks his life to provide valuable information deserves to be well-compensated for his courage.

Article XIII. Of certain Marks, by which the Intentions of the Enemy are to be discovered.

Understanding where the enemy has established his main depot for provisions is one of the most reliable ways to anticipate his intentions before the campaign begins. For instance, if the Austrians set up their supply depots at Olmütz, it's almost certain they plan to launch an attack on Upper Silesia. If they place them in Königgrätz, it's a strong indication that the region around Schweidnitz may be targeted. Likewise, when the Saxons aimed to invade the Electorate's border, the locations of their supply depots—Zittau, Görlitz, and Guben—revealed their intended path, as these towns lie along the route to Crossen.

Therefore, the primary objective in gathering intelligence should be identifying where the enemy has decided to place their supply depots and understanding the positions in which they are established. The French, for example, used a cunning tactic by setting up supply depots on both the Meuse and the Scheldt rivers to obscure their true plans, giving them flexibility and creating uncertainty for their adversaries.

The Austrians, on the other hand, often give away their movements through certain customs. For example, when they are preparing to march, they usually cook early in the morning on the day of departure. If significant smoke is observed in their camp around five or six in the morning, it's a reliable sign that they intend to break camp and move out that day.

Moreover, when the Austrians are preparing for battle, they tend to recall all of their strong detachments of light troops, consolidating their forces in preparation for the fight. If this is noticed, it is a clear signal to stay vigilant and prepare for immediate engagement.

If you are attacking a position defended by Hungarian troops and find it highly resistant to your assault, this may indicate that the main Austrian army is nearby, ready to provide reinforcement. Similarly, if the enemy's light troops maneuver to place themselves between your main army and one of your detached forces, it's a strong indication that the enemy has targeted that detachment, and you should make the necessary preparations to counter this move.

If you consistently face the same general on the opposing side, his tactics and intentions will eventually become apparent. Over time, his strategies and habitual methods will grow familiar, allowing you to anticipate his actions more easily.

After carefully evaluating the terrain of the war theater, the current condition of your army, the security of your supply depots, the strength of your fortified positions, and the potential strategies the enemy might use to capture these resources, it's essential to consider the risks posed by the enemy's light troops. These troops may position themselves along your flanks, rear, or other vulnerable spots or be deployed for diversionary tactics. Taking all these elements into account, you can reasonably assume that an intelligent enemy will pursue an operation that promises to disrupt you in the most damaging way. At the very least, this will likely be his intent, and you must focus all your efforts on countering it to protect your position effectively.

Article XIV. Of Our Own Country, And That Which Is Either Neutral or Hostile; of The Variety of Religions, And of The Different Conduct Which Such Circumstances Require.

War can be conducted in one of three types of territories: our own lands, those belonging to neutral powers, or the land of the enemy. If my sole aim were glory, I would only wage war within my own country, due to the numerous advantages it provides. Every inhabitant becomes a potential informant, making it nearly impossible for the enemy to move undetected.

In our own country, we can safely send out large detachments that can perform any military maneuver with confidence. When the enemy gains an advantage, the local population often takes up arms to resist, just as they did after the Battle of Fehrbellin. At that time, Elector Frederick William saw more Swedes fall to the hands of the peasants than on the battlefield itself. Similarly, after the Battle of Hohenfriedberg, I saw the mountaineers in Silesia capturing and delivering fleeing Austrians to us in large numbers.

When war takes place in a neutral country, both sides have an equal footing, and the main focus shifts to winning the favor and trust of the local population. Achieving this requires strict discipline among the troops, banning any form of looting or theft, and enforcing such rules with severe penalties. It might also help to suggest that the enemy has harmful intentions toward the country, thereby turning the locals against them.

If the country is Protestant, we can pose as protectors of the Lutheran faith, stirring religious fervor among the lower classes, who are often susceptible to our persuasive tactics. In a Catholic country, we promote tolerance and moderation, blaming religious animosities on the priests, who we claim are responsible for much of the existing tensions between different groups. Despite their conflicts, people of different sects often agree on core tenets of faith, which we can use to our advantage.

The size of any detachment we send out must reflect the trustworthiness of the local populace. In our own country, we can take almost any risk, knowing we have widespread support. In a neutral country, however, more caution is required, at least until we're certain that the majority of the population harbors no hostility. Once their trust is secured, detachments can be dispatched with more confidence.

In a thoroughly hostile country, such as Bohemia or Moravia, we must take no risks, sending out no detachments for the reasons previously discussed, as the inhabitants cannot be trusted beyond what we can directly observe. Here, most light troops are best employed to guard convoys, as it's unrealistic to expect any positive sentiment from the population. The Hussites around Königgrätz are the only ones who might offer assistance. Those of influence may appear friendly but are traitorous at heart; nor are the priests or local magistrates any more reliable. With their interests tied to Austria, whose objectives do not entirely align with ours, we should neither trust nor rely on them in any capacity.

Our remaining option in such places is to appeal to religious zeal, stirring up passion for religious liberty and subtly suggesting to the population that their priests and noble leaders keep them under oppressive rule. This, one might say, is a matter of invoking powerful forces to serve our interests.

Since I recorded these thoughts, the Empress-Queen has significantly raised taxes in Bohemia and Moravia. This change could be used to gain the goodwill of the people, especially if we imply that they would be treated more favorably should we take control of the region.

Article XV. Of every Kind of March, Which It Can be Necessary For an Army to make.

An army moves with specific purposes in mind: advancing into enemy territory, securing a strategic campsite, joining with reinforcements, preparing for battle, or retreating before the enemy. Once the camp is well-fortified, the next priority is to scout the surrounding area and all roads leading into and out of the camp. This reconnaissance allows for precise planning in response to various scenarios.

To achieve this, large detachments are sent out under various pretexts, accompanied by engineers and quartermasters who examine every location that could potentially be occupied by troops. Their job is to analyze the terrain and survey the roads that the army might need to use. Following them are several chasseurs, whose task is to study these roads in detail so they can effectively guide the columns should the general decide to march along those routes.

Upon returning, these officers provide a thorough report on the camp's location, the roads leading to it, the characteristics of the land, and the nearby woods, mountains, and rivers. With this information in hand, the general is equipped to make informed decisions. When the camp isn't too close to the enemy, a specific marching order can be implemented as follows:

Imagine that the camp can be accessed by four different routes. The advance guard, which consists of six battalions of grenadiers, one infantry regiment, two dragoon regiments (each with five squadrons), and two hussar regiments under the command of Mr. N. N., will depart at eight o'clock this evening. All of the army's encampments will follow this advance guard, which will carry only its tents and leave the heavier baggage with the main army.

These troops will march four leagues ahead, securing any important features they encounter—such as defiles, rivers, hills, towns, or villages—until the main army arrives. Once the main army reaches them, the advance guard will then enter the camp that has already been designated.

The following morning, the main army, arranged in four columns, will advance behind the lead of the advance guard. Soldiers stationed as guards in villages along the route will rejoin their respective regiments.

The right-wing cavalry, split into two lines and marching on the right, will form the first column. The infantry of the right wing, also in two lines and marching by the right, will create the second column. The infantry of the left wing, filing by the right as well, will establish the third column. Finally, the left-wing cavalry, likewise filing by the right, will constitute the fourth column.

The regiments N. N. of the second line, along with three hussar regiments under General N. N., will escort the baggage, which will follow behind the two infantry columns. Four aides-de-camp will supervise this escort to ensure that the carriages proceed in a well-ordered line with minimal gaps between them.

If the rear guard general requires additional support, he must immediately alert the commander in chief. The chasseurs who initially scouted the roads will guide the four columns to ensure they follow the intended paths accurately.

In advance of each column, a team of carpenters will travel with wagons carrying beams, joists, and planks to construct bridges over smaller rivers as necessary. Column leaders must ensure that each column progresses at an even pace, without moving ahead of one another, and with controlled spacing. Division officers need to monitor their distances carefully, maintaining cohesion.

When crossing a defile, the heads of each column should march slowly or pause intermittently to allow the rear to maintain alignment. This steady pace ensures the entire march remains well-coordinated.

The march continues with this order in mind. When the army encounters mountains, forests, or defiles, the columns should split, allowing the infantry to lead, followed by the cavalry, which will close the march and provide additional protection from behind.

If a plain lies at the center of the area, it should be designated for the cavalry, while the infantry, organized into columns at both ends, should move through the woods. However, this setup applies only when the march is taking place at a safe distance from the enemy. When closer to the enemy, it's sufficient to place a few battalions of grenadiers at the head of each cavalry column to help maintain the battle order.

The most reliable way to ensure a reinforcement reaches us safely is to march along a challenging road to meet it, simultaneously distancing ourselves from the enemy to avoid any confrontation. The advantage gained from the arrival of reinforcements will soon allow us to retake any ground temporarily conceded to the enemy.

When circumstances require marching parallel to the enemy, it should be conducted in two lines, either to the right or left, with each line forming a column and accompanied by an advance guard at the front. The same principles I previously outlined can also be applied here.

All of our marches from Frankenberg to Hohenfriedberg were organized in this manner, consistently moving to the right. I favor these arrangements over others because the army can be easily organized into battle formation by a single movement to the right or left, which is the quickest way to assemble them. This method would always be my preference when engaging the enemy if I had the option, even though I lost the benefit of it at Sohr and Hohenfriedberg. In this style of march, it is essential to ensure that the flank never exposes itself to the enemy.

When the enemy begins a march indicating preparations for battle, it is important to offload all heavy baggage and send it with an escort to the nearest town for safekeeping. The advance guard should then be formed and sent forward to a distance of roughly half a league.

When marching directly toward the enemy, special care must be taken to prevent columns from advancing too far ahead of one another. As they approach the battlefield, the columns should spread out in such a way that the troops occupy precisely the amount of ground they will need in battle formation. This task is challenging, as some battalions often find themselves too crowded, while others end up with too much space.

Marching in lines presents no particular disadvantage, which is why I have always preferred it.

When a battle is expected during the march, extreme caution is required. The general must remain vigilant, surveying the terrain cautiously from one vantage point to another without overexposing himself, in order to develop a clear understanding of different possible positions should the enemy attempt an attack.

Church steeples and elevated areas should be used to gain a view of the terrain, and any paths leading to these vantage points should be cleared by light troops dispatched from the advance guard.

Retreats are typically organized as follows: one or two days before departure, the heavy baggage is assembled and sent off under a strong escort.

The number of columns in a march should be carefully chosen based on how many usable roads are available and, equally importantly, on the nature of the terrain. In open plains, where space is abundant, it is most effective to have the cavalry lead the advance guard, as their mobility and speed make them well-suited for this task. However, if the landscape is more varied, with mixed fields, woods, and potential obstacles, it becomes safer to assign the advance guard duties to the infantry, as they can adapt more readily to varied terrain. When marching in open country, it's typical for the army to be organized into four columns.

In such an arrangement, the right wing's second line of infantry, filing by the right and followed by the cavalry of the same wing, will form the fourth column. Similarly, the first line of the right-wing infantry will also file by its right, followed by its cavalry, forming the third column. On the left wing, the second line of infantry, accompanied by its corresponding cavalry, will make up the second column. Finally, the infantry of the left wing's first line, followed by its cavalry, will compose the first column.

With this formation, the entire rear guard is made up of the cavalry, which provides flexibility and, if necessary, can be reinforced by hussars for added security. The rear guard plays a vital role in ensuring the protection of slower-moving troops and equipment, giving the main body of the army time to maneuver as needed.

During a retreat that requires crossing a defile, it's critical for the infantry to secure the passage the evening before departure. By positioning themselves strategically, they shield the rest of the troops, ensuring that the defile remains open and accessible. In this way, if any resistance or unexpected challenges arise, the infantry can provide cover, allowing the rest of the army to move through safely.

If circumstances require the army to move in only two columns, this will alter the arrangement somewhat. In such a case, the cavalry of the right wing will file to the left, with the second line moving first and taking the lead in the second column. Following this, the second line of infantry will fall into place, with the first line of infantry filing behind them to complete the formation. On the left wing, the second line of cavalry will also file by the left, moving first and taking the lead of the first column. This first column is then completed by the infantry of the left wing, with the second line moving first, followed by the first line.

The rear guard in this arrangement is strengthened by six battalions from the rear of the first line, accompanied by ten squadrons of hussars. These battalions and squadrons position themselves in a two-line formation at the front of the defile, adopting a checkerboard pattern to secure the area as the army moves through. While the main force passes through the defile, these rear guard troops use their positioning to provide cover fire, protecting those troops still on the other side.

Once the army has fully crossed, the advance guard's first line moves into the defile, passing through openings in the second line. After this first line is through, the second line follows under the cover of the rear guard, which remains stationed on the opposite side to maintain protection until the last units have safely passed.

One of the most challenging maneuvers is to cross a river while in retreat, especially when the enemy is close. An excellent example of this complex operation is our retreat across the Elbe at Kolin in 1744, where careful planning and disciplined execution enabled a successful crossing under pressure.

However, suitable towns or strongholds are not always nearby to support such maneuvers. In cases where two bridges are the only available crossing points, a large entrenchment should be constructed to secure both bridges, with small openings left at the heads of each bridge. Once this entrenchment is in place, several artillery pieces and a designated number of troops should be positioned on the far bank of the river. This opposite bank should have a moderate slope—steep enough to provide a height advantage but gentle enough to permit maneuvering. This elevated position enables these troops to control the crossing area, keeping enemy forces at bay.

With the entrenchment manned by infantry, the main force can proceed with the crossing, beginning with the infantry. The cavalry remains behind, forming a checkerboard arrangement within the entrenchment to act as the rear guard, providing cover for the crossing. Once the majority of the army has crossed, the infantry positioned at the heads of the bridges can take up positions to cover the last stages of the withdrawal.

If the enemy attempts a pursuit, they will be met by concentrated fire from troops positioned at both bridgeheads as well as from the forces stationed across the river. This setup provides a layered defense that can significantly hinder the enemy's advance.

When the entrenchment's infantry has crossed the river, the bridge itself should be dismantled or destroyed, preventing the enemy from following. Those troops who had been stationed at the bridgeheads can then cross by boat, shielded by supporting troops on the far side who are ready to advance and assist if needed. Once the pontoons are loaded onto their carriages, the remaining troops can begin their movement, completing the withdrawal.

At the angles of the entrenchment, fougasses (explosive traps) can be strategically placed. The last grenadiers to cross the river will ignite these fougasses to disrupt any pursuing forces, giving the army time to establish a safe distance.

Article XVI.
On the Precautions Necessary to Be Taken in A Retreat Against Hussars and Pandours.

Hussars and pandours may seem terrifying to those who aren't familiar with their methods, but their courage is often superficial. They're brave only when they're driven by the promise of loot or when they can harass others without risking their own safety. Their tactics mainly involve two types of aggression: one directed at convoys and baggage trains, where they seek easy plunder, and the other aimed at troops forced into retreat, where they attempt to annoy and hinder the soldiers' withdrawal.

While our regular troops have little to genuinely fear from these forces, the skirmishing methods of the hussars and pandours can delay our marches. Their attacks are inconvenient, especially since we inevitably lose some men—often at critical moments. For this reason, I will explain the most effective way I know to handle these opponents.

When retreating through open plains, we can typically drive off the hussars with a few well-placed cannon shots, while the pandours can be kept at bay with our dragoons and hussars, who inspire significant fear in them. However, the most challenging retreats occur when our path takes us through forests, narrow passes, or mountainous terrain, as these areas give pandours ample opportunity to inflict damage. In such situations, it is almost unavoidable that we will suffer some losses.

In these difficult environments, the heights should first be secured by our advance guard, positioned with their front facing the enemy. At the same time, we should detach troops to the flanks of the marching column, allowing them to traverse the heights and woods alongside the main body. Additional squadrons should be kept ready to engage wherever the ground allows.

In these scenarios, it is crucial to maintain steady movement without halting, as a stop would only expose some of our men unnecessarily, leading to preventable casualties. The pandours typically lie flat as they fire, keeping themselves well hidden, and when our army's advance forces the rear guard and small detached units to abandon their positions, the pandours quickly occupy these vacated spots. From these concealed positions, often behind trees or on higher ground, they pick off retreating soldiers with relative safety.

Neither musket fire nor cannon loaded with cartridges can effectively target them, as they remain dispersed and hidden behind terrain features like hills and trees.

I faced two retreats under these conditions in 1745: the first through the valley of Liebenthal en route to Staudenitz and the second from Trautenau to Schatzlar. Despite every possible precaution, we lost sixty men killed and wounded in the first retreat and over two hundred in the second.

In cases where we must retreat along difficult paths, our marches should be kept very short, allowing us to stay vigilant and prepared. No march should exceed two leagues, or roughly one German mile. This measured pace reduces strain on the troops, enabling us to respond more effectively to any pandour attacks. If the pandours are careless enough to take refuge in a wood, we sometimes have the advantage of turning their position, forcing them to either flee or face us directly.

Article XVII. Of the Method in Which the Light Prussian Troops Conduct Themselves When Engaged with the Hussars and Pandours.

When we aim to dislodge enemy light troops from a position, our approach is to launch a swift and forceful attack. Given that these light troops tend to scatter in their fighting style, they are poorly equipped to withstand a direct assault from our disciplined forces, who are trained to engage with full commitment and without hesitation.

To execute this plan, we first detach a few units to secure the flanks of the main force advancing against the light troops. With the flanks protected, we then attack with vigor, ensuring a high chance that the enemy will break and flee.

Our dragoons and hussars, advancing in tightly formed ranks with swords drawn, engage these light troops directly. This type of close combat is something light troops are generally unprepared for and incapable of enduring. In every instance, this approach has proven effective, allowing us to drive them off without concern for any numerical advantage they might possess.

Article XVIII.
By What Movements on Our Side the Enemy May Also be Obliged to Move.

It is a grave mistake to think that merely moving an army will compel the enemy to respond by moving as well. Forcing the enemy into action isn't achieved simply by movement; it requires a deliberate and calculated approach in how that movement is executed. An intelligent adversary won't be easily swayed by superficial maneuvers you may employ. Instead, you must take up strategically significant positions that will compel the enemy to think deeply about his options and eventually force him to abandon his own camp.

To execute this effectively, you need a thorough understanding of the terrain, the capabilities of the opposing general, the locations of his supply depots, the towns that provide him with resources, and the areas from which he gathers forage. Only after carefully analyzing these factors can a solid plan be formulated. A general who employs a creative and determined approach to unsettle his enemy will, in time, earn the distinction of challenging his opponent in both skill and reputation.

At the onset of a campaign, the general who promptly gathers his forces, advances to seize a town or occupies a key position will immediately set the pace, forcing his opponent into a reactive, defensive posture. However, there should always be sound strategic reasons behind any attempt to force the enemy to move during a campaign. This may include securing a nearby town close to his encampment, driving him into desolate territory where sustaining his forces becomes difficult, or creating conditions that favor a decisive engagement. With such clear objectives in mind, you begin to develop a plan that considers both the risks and benefits of each maneuver.

It is vital that the marches you undertake and the camps you occupy do not create greater challenges for you than for the enemy. For example, drawing too far away from your depot may expose it to attack by enemy light troops, especially if it is inadequately fortified. Similarly, taking up a position that disconnects you from supply lines or communications with your own country could lead to shortages that force a retreat.

After carefully evaluating these considerations and calculating the potential actions of the enemy, you can then determine your approach. This may include setting up camp on one of the enemy's flanks, moving closer to the regions that provide his sustenance, cutting off his access to his capital, threatening his supply depots, or choosing a position that disrupts his access to essential provisions.

A concrete example of such a strategy, well-known to many of my officers, occurred when I planned to force Prince Charles of Lorraine to abandon Königgrätz and Pardubitz in 1745. Upon leaving the camp at Dubletz, our route should have taken us leftward, skirting the Glatz region and advancing near Hohenmauth. This maneuver would have pressured the Austrians, who relied on supply depots in Teutschbrod and mostly drew their provisions from Moravia, to move to Landscron, effectively conceding Königgrätz and Pardubitz to us. The Saxons, being cut off from their homeland, would have been forced to leave the Austrians and return to defend their own territory.

I ultimately refrained from executing this maneuver because, even if I had secured Königgrätz, it would have been of limited benefit. I would still have needed to send detachments to support Prince of Anhalt if the Saxons decided to return home. Additionally, the supply depots at Glatz could not sustain my entire army for the length of the campaign, rendering such a position unsustainable.

Creating diversions by dispatching troops to separate areas can also pressure the enemy into breaking camp. Generally, any unexpected operation that catches the enemy off-guard has the potential to disrupt his plans, forcing him to abandon his current position. Such operations include crossing mountains that the enemy believes to be impassable or fording rivers without his knowledge.

The campaign of Prince Eugene in 1701 provides valuable insight into these tactics. The disarray of the French army when Prince Charles of Lorraine unexpectedly crossed the Rhine serves as a well-known example of how such maneuvers can unsettle an enemy force.

In conclusion, the success of these operations lies in ensuring that the execution aligns with the intent. As long as the general's plans are carefully crafted and based on solid strategic principles, he will be able to dictate terms to the enemy, forcing him to remain on the defensive. By maintaining this strategic advantage, the general keeps control of the campaign, always a step ahead of his adversary.

Article XIX. Of the Crossing of Rivers.

When the enemy remains on the opposite side of a river that we aim to cross, brute force alone is futile; instead, strategic deception becomes essential. To understand how to execute a successful river crossing, we need only examine Caesar's crossing of the Rhine, Prince Eugene's crossing of the Po, or Prince Charles of Lorraine's crossing of the Rhine. These generals used detachments to mislead the enemy, obscuring the actual crossing point. They prepared bridges in locations where they had no intention of crossing, thus misleading the enemy, while the main body of the army marched under cover of night to a significant distance away, allowing them time to cross the river before the enemy forces could organize a defense.

Rivers are generally crossed at points where there are small islands, as these natural features provide valuable support for establishing a foothold. It is also preferable to encounter woods or other natural obstructions on the opposite bank, which hinder the enemy from launching an immediate counterattack, giving us time to organize our troops once across.

Such operations demand meticulous planning and vigilance. Boats, pontoons, and all other necessary equipment must be in place by the designated time, with each boatman thoroughly briefed on the typical demands of night operations. Once every component is in order, the troops proceed to cross and secure a position on the opposite bank.

In any river-crossing operation, it is crucial to fortify both bridgeheads, placing ample troops to hold these positions. Nearby islands should be fortified to reinforce the bridgehead defenses and prevent the enemy from seizing or damaging the bridge during the crossing.

For narrower rivers, it is advantageous to select crossing points where the river creates natural angles or bends, with slightly elevated banks that provide a vantage over the opposite side. At such locations, we position as many cannons as the terrain permits, along with a proportional number of troops, to cover the construction of bridges. As the angle creates a narrower stretch of land, we advance carefully and gain ground gradually as the troops cross.

If fords are available, the approach should be smoothed to facilitate the cavalry's crossing, ensuring an effective and coordinated river passage.

Article XX. Of the Manner in which the Passage of Rivers is to be defended.

Defending the crossing of a river, especially when the area to be covered is vast, is one of the most difficult tasks in warfare, if not altogether impractical. Successfully defending a river crossing requires specific conditions. The section of the river to be defended should not exceed eight German miles in width, as a broader front would be impossible to cover effectively. Additionally, two or three well-placed redoubts must be established along the riverbank within this range, and there should be no fords available elsewhere that might allow the enemy to bypass these defenses and cross unimpeded.

Assuming these conditions are met, adequate time is crucial to properly prepare for the enemy's crossing attempts. The preparations should follow a precise defensive strategy to cover all vulnerabilities.

To begin, gather all available boats, barges, and any other watercraft from the river and relocate them to the redoubt areas. This prevents the enemy from using these vessels to cross the river or otherwise aid in their approach. Next, conduct a thorough reconnaissance of both riverbanks to identify and obstruct any potential crossing points. Every possible location where the enemy might find cover during an attempted crossing must be given special attention, as these areas can offer them protection from our defensive positions.

Once the crossing points are identified, preparations for defense must consider the terrain's specifics. Roads wide enough to support multiple columns should be constructed along the entire defensive front, ensuring that troops can move rapidly without congestion. These roads allow our forces to reposition and reinforce different areas of the defense line without delay, maintaining a flexible but robust defense.

With the defenses in place, the main army should camp at the center of the defensive line, reducing the distance to either end to just four miles, allowing quick access to all points of defense. From this central position, form sixteen mobile detachments commanded by the most diligent and alert officers among the dragoons and hussars. These officers should be handpicked for their intelligence and adaptability. Split the detachments equally: eight assigned to cover the right flank of the defense line and the remaining eight to guard the left flank, each group under the command of a capable general officer.

These detachments serve dual roles. They constantly monitor the enemy's movements, detecting any signs of an attempted crossing, and report any significant activity or shifts in the enemy's positions. During the daytime, guard posts are strategically positioned along the riverbanks to observe any preparations the enemy might be undertaking. At night, patrols should be sent out every fifteen minutes, advancing to the river's edge and remaining there until they have a clear view of the enemy's bridge-building efforts or detect the leading edge of an attempted crossing.

The generals overseeing these detachments, along with the officers in command of the redoubts, must send reports to the commander in chief four times per day. To expedite communication, a relay of fresh horses should be placed between the front lines and the main army to ensure messages reach the commander as swiftly as possible, giving him immediate awareness of any enemy activity at the river. The general must be prepared to respond to a breach in defenses at a moment's notice; for this reason, his baggage should be sent ahead to avoid any delay in his movements.

Each segment of the defensive line should have specific, pre-planned countermeasures ready for activation when the enemy's crossing attempt begins. The commander in chief assigns experienced generals to manage the defense at key points along the river. Upon receiving notice of the enemy's attempt to cross, the army should advance swiftly, with the infantry leading the columns, as it is presumed that the enemy will immediately begin entrenching once they establish a foothold on the other side. Speed and decisiveness are crucial upon arrival at the crossing point; a rapid, forceful attack is the best chance of successfully repelling the enemy and preventing them from establishing a secure position.

Defending the crossing of smaller rivers, though seemingly easier, presents its own set of challenges, often making such defenses even more difficult. If the river contains fords, every effort should be made to render them impassable by blocking them with felled trees or other debris to prevent enemy cavalry from advancing. However, if the enemy's bank is elevated above ours, resistance becomes nearly futile, as they will have the advantage of height for both cover and attack.

Regarding the surprise capture of towns, a successful surprise relies on several favorable conditions. A town susceptible to surprise is often poorly guarded and lacks strong fortifications. If the town's ditches are water-filled, a surprise attack can only succeed during winter, when a hard frost makes the water a negligible obstacle.

Surprises can be conducted by an entire army, as demonstrated by the capture of Prague in 1741. Alternatively, they may result from a prolonged blockade that leads the defenders to a false sense of security, as in Prince Leopold of Anhalt's capture of Glogau. In some cases, smaller detachments suffice for a surprise, as illustrated by Prince Eugene's attempt at Cremona or the Austrian success at Cosel.

The primary rule when planning a surprise attack is to obtain accurate intelligence regarding the town's fortifications and interior layout. Such knowledge allows for a focused assault on specific weak points, increasing the chance of success. The surprise at Glogau stands as an exemplary model of such an operation; it is widely regarded as a masterstroke and provides a worthy example for anyone considering similar endeavors. In contrast, the surprise of Prague, although effective, succeeded largely due to the scale and variety of attacks, which overwhelmed the garrison by forcing them to defend an extensive perimeter. Cosel and Cremona, however, were secured through betrayal: Cosel fell when an officer defected and informed the Austrians that a section of the ditch had not been completed, allowing them to enter and capture the position.

For smaller fortifications, surprise attacks can be directed at the gates. Mortar fire should be used to batter specific gates while detachments are positioned at others to prevent the garrison from escaping. If cannons are employed, they must be strategically positioned to avoid exposure to enemy musket fire; otherwise, the artillery risks being overrun and captured, jeopardizing the entire operation.

Article XXII. Of Combats and Battles.

The Austrian camp is so densely surrounded by light troops that mounting a surprise attack would be exceptionally difficult. Such vigilance and defensive positioning create formidable barriers against surprise maneuvers. When two armies are in close proximity, a decisive encounter is almost inevitable, unless one side holds an elevated or fortified position that discourages direct engagement and guards against surprise—a scenario that is rare for entire armies but occasionally seen with smaller detachments.

For a successful surprise on an enemy encampment, several conditions must be met. First, the enemy must be overconfident, perhaps relying excessively on the strength of his own troops or assuming his position is too secure to be threatened. He may place undue trust in reports from his scouts or spies or feel assured by the extensive patrols and alertness of his light troops. All these factors create a foundation for complacency, opening the door to a surprise attack. Before forming any concrete plan, however, it is essential to understand the terrain, the enemy's precise location, and the general layout of their camp. Each road leading toward the camp must be thoroughly scouted, allowing us to assess the best approach points and develop a structured strategy tailored to the situation.

Select only the most experienced chasseurs, especially those familiar with the roads, to lead each column. This local knowledge will be indispensable in guiding the troops accurately and avoiding any errors that could expose our movements prematurely. Above all, the operation's success hinges on maintaining complete secrecy; secrecy, as always, is the essence of all surprise maneuvers. To prevent any deserter from betraying our plans, the light troops should lead the march. Beyond ensuring loyalty within the ranks, these light troops will also keep the enemy's patrols at a safe distance, reducing the risk that they will detect our advance too soon.

It is crucial that all subordinate generals receive clear, detailed instructions regarding possible scenarios and know precisely how to respond to unexpected developments. If the enemy's camp is positioned on an open plain, the advanced guard should consist of dragoons. Once these dragoons are joined by the hussars, they can charge into the camp at full speed, creating immediate chaos and cutting down anyone in their path.

The entire army should closely support this initial wave, with the infantry at the forefront. Their primary objective is to target and disrupt the wings of the enemy's cavalry, weakening their defensive cohesion. The advance guard should initiate the attack roughly thirty minutes before dawn, creating maximum confusion at the break of day, while the main body of the army should remain no more than eight hundred yards behind, ready to reinforce immediately.

During the entire approach, absolute silence must be observed. Soldiers should be strictly forbidden from speaking unnecessarily, and all smoking should be banned, as the smallest spark could betray our location in the darkness.

Once the assault begins and dawn breaks, the infantry, organized into four to six columns, should advance directly into the heart of the enemy's camp to support the efforts of the advance guard. No firing should take place before dawn, as the risks of friendly fire in the dark are too high. However, as soon as daylight allows, artillery should target areas where the advance guard has yet to penetrate, especially focusing on the wings of the enemy cavalry. The goal here is to force the enemy cavalry to abandon their horses, especially if they haven't had time to prepare properly, which will throw them into further disarray.

The pursuit should continue beyond the enemy's camp, with the entire cavalry force released to chase the fleeing troops and take full advantage of their panic and confusion. If the enemy has discarded their weapons in their haste to escape, leave a detachment in charge of securing the camp while the rest of the army continues the pursuit, avoiding the temptation to halt for plunder. Pressing the attack to its fullest potential is crucial, as such opportunities to completely rout an enemy are rare. Taking advantage of this moment can allow us to dominate the campaign, dictating the terms of engagement for the foreseeable future.

I encountered a near-perfect opportunity of this kind shortly before the Battle of Mollwitz. We approached Marshal de Neipperg's army undetected, as his forces were scattered across three villages. With the benefit of hindsight, I realize I should have deployed two columns to surround the village of Mollwitz and initiated an assault there. At the same time, I could have sent dragoons to the other two villages, where the Austrian cavalry was stationed, to create confusion and prevent the cavalry from organizing. Following these dragoons, I would have deployed infantry to block the cavalry from mounting. I have little doubt that, with these tactics, we could have effectively annihilated their entire force.

I have already discussed the essential steps for securing our own camp and protecting it from enemy incursions. However, if despite all precautions the enemy manages to approach, the immediate response should be to organize the troops in battle formation on their assigned positions. The cavalry should hold firm, maintaining its position and firing by platoons until dawn. As daylight breaks, the generals should assess the situation, determining whether an advance is advisable based on the condition of the cavalry and the overall state of the field.

In these critical moments, each general must be prepared to act independently, making decisions without waiting for direct orders from the commander in chief. Personally, I am committed to avoiding night attacks due to the inherent confusion that darkness brings. Most soldiers need the oversight of their officers and the motivation provided by discipline to perform their duties effectively, and darkness can undermine both.

Charles XII of Sweden provides an instructive example of the perils of night attacks. In 1715, he launched a night assault on Prince of Anhalt immediately after landing on the island of Rügen. The King of Sweden had specific reasons for this tactic; daylight would have revealed the limited size of his force—only 4,000 men—against the 20,000 troops of his enemy. Despite the element of surprise, this numerical disadvantage ultimately led to his defeat, underscoring the risks of such endeavors.

An unchanging principle of warfare is to secure your flanks and rear while attempting to turn those of the enemy. This strategy can be executed in several ways, but they all share the same underlying goal: to outmaneuver the opponent and place them in a disadvantageous position.

When faced with the need to attack an entrenched enemy, the assault should be launched without delay to prevent the enemy from completing their fortifications. What may be an advantage today could turn against you by tomorrow if the enemy has time to strengthen their defenses.

However, before committing to the attack, it is essential to personally survey the enemy's position and determine its strengths and weaknesses. This close inspection will help you assess whether your initial plan is feasible or whether the task will require considerable effort and resources. A firsthand reconnaissance ensures that your approach is grounded in accurate knowledge of the terrain and enemy positioning.

Often, the main reason entrenchments are breached is due to inadequate support. Historical examples illustrate this well: the fortifications held by Turenne were captured due to insufficient support, as was another notable entrenchment because Prince of Anhalt could outflank it. Similarly, at the Battle of Malplaquet, the allied forces managed to breach Marshal Villars' left flank by utilizing a wooded area. If the allies had recognized this vulnerability sooner, they could have spared their army a loss of fifteen thousand soldiers.

If a river that can be forded provides support to an enemy entrenchment, then that side of the defense becomes the logical target for an attack. For instance, the Swedish fortifications at Stralsund were overcome because the attack was directed from the sea, where the defenses were vulnerable due to shallow waters.

When the enemy's fortifications are extensive, stretching their forces thin across a broad front, the best approach is to attack at multiple points. If our plans can be concealed from the enemy, preventing them from reinforcing any one area sufficiently, we increase our chances of penetrating their defenses. Such a strategy, when executed well, disrupts the enemy's defensive cohesion and enhances the likelihood of capturing key positions.

Consider the following hypothetical formation for an assault on an entrenched position. Picture a line formed by thirty battalions, with the left wing fortified by the river N. N. The primary assault will focus on the left, where we intend to break through with twelve battalions, while a supporting attack will be carried out on the right with eight battalions. The troops assigned to these attacks will form in a checkerboard pattern, ensuring adequate spacing between units for flexibility. The remaining infantry will form a third line, positioned at the center to reinforce as needed. Four hundred yards behind this line, the cavalry will be stationed, ready to exploit any weakness in the enemy's defense.

The presence of these infantry lines will serve to keep the enemy occupied and prevent them from reinforcing threatened areas. Additionally, the cavalry positioned in the rear will be prepared to seize upon any missteps made by the opposing forces, such as an overextension or shift in defense.

Each attacking force should be closely followed by a contingent of pioneers equipped with shovels, pickaxes, and fascines. Their task is to fill in ditches and clear paths, creating access points for the cavalry once the entrenchment is breached. These support units play a crucial role in ensuring the attack's success by enabling the cavalry to move through the enemy's fortifications smoothly.

The infantry designated for the assault should refrain from firing until they have overtaken the enemy's fortifications and are properly arrayed on the parapet in battle formation. Maintaining silence and restraint during the approach can provide the advantage of surprise and limit the enemy's awareness of our exact position and strength.

Once breaches are made in the entrenchments by the pioneers, the cavalry should enter through these gaps and engage the enemy with force. Timing is critical here—the cavalry must wait until a sufficient number of troops have penetrated the enemy lines and consolidated their position within the entrenchments. Then, with the pioneers' groundwork complete, the cavalry can deliver a decisive blow, exploiting the vulnerabilities created by the infantry's assault.

By executing each phase of this plan with precision and coordination, the assault on an entrenched enemy can disrupt even the most fortified positions, using the advantages of surprise, careful planning, and concerted force to overcome resistance.

If the cavalry is forced to retreat, they should regroup under cover from the infantry's fire, maintaining their position until the rest of the army has moved in, and the enemy has been fully routed. I must emphasize here that I would generally avoid entrenching my army unless a siege is underway or anticipated. Even then, I am inclined to believe it may be more advantageous to advance before the arrival of a relieving force rather than fortify too heavily.

However, if there is indeed a need to entrench, the following approach would be the most effective. In constructing a fortified position, we would establish two or three substantial reserve units positioned to deploy rapidly to any point where the enemy mounts a strong attack. These reserves serve as mobile support, reinforcing sections of the line under the greatest pressure.

The main parapet should be lined with battalions, with a reserve force stationed immediately behind them to provide support when needed. Positioned further back, the cavalry should be organized in a single line behind these reserves, ready to respond swiftly to any breach or weakness in the defense.

The entrenchments themselves must be thoroughly fortified. If there is a river along one side of the line, the ditch should extend into the river, preventing the enemy from easily outflanking the position. Where the fortifications border a wooded area, the defensive line should end in a redoubt, and a thick abatis (a barricade of felled trees) should be created within the forest to further reinforce that side.

Particular attention must be paid to the flanking capabilities of any redans (angled fortifications). The ditch should be dug as wide and as deep as possible, while the entrenchments should be improved daily. Reinforcements to the parapet, palisades at barrier entrances, deepened pits, and chevaux de frise (spiked barricades) around the entire camp all serve to strengthen the position incrementally.

The most significant advantage in defensive entrenchments lies in selecting the appropriate structure and adhering to sound fortification principles, which will force the enemy to attack from a narrow front and focus only on the key points of the defense line. For example, an illustration on Plate 7 shows an entrenched army positioned near a river. Here, the layout angles the front line outward toward the approaching enemy, creating a natural projection. Batteries positioned at the far end of the right flank prevent attacks from that direction, as these batteries would rake the enemy's flank, while a central redoubt would hit the attackers from the rear. Consequently, the center redoubt becomes the only feasible target for assault, but even here, the enemy must cut through a thick abatis before they can engage.

Given these defenses, the fortifications of the center redoubt should be reinforced heavily. By concentrating our attention and resources on one key point, we ensure that this critical part of the defense is as solid and secure as possible.

Alternatively, Plate 8 demonstrates a different fortification style, with alternating projecting and recessed redoubts linked by entrenchments. This configuration requires fewer but strategically positioned redoubts, making it possible to complete the defenses in less time while maintaining strength at the crucial points of potential attack.

In such projecting redoubts, the musketry fire should be planned so that it crosses, creating overlapping fields of fire that trap the enemy in a deadly crossfire. To maintain this coverage, the redoubts should be spaced no more than six hundred yards apart.

Our infantry, defending the entrenchments, should rely on battalion volleys, with each soldier supplied with one hundred rounds. This ammunition supply is complemented by artillery, as many cannons as possible positioned between the battalions and within the projecting redoubts.

When the enemy is still at a distance, we use solid shot, firing to weaken them before they come within effective range. Once they close to within four hundred yards, we switch to grapeshot and canister, intensifying our defense as they near the entrenchment.

If, despite the strong defenses and steady, intense fire, the enemy manages to press forward and make a dent in our line, the infantry reserves must advance to push them back. Should this line of defense falter, the final counterattack rests with the cavalry, who charge forward as a last effort to drive the enemy into retreat.

Entrenchments typically fall for a few critical reasons: poor adherence to established fortification rules, a failure to effectively cover flanks, panic within the ranks, or the enemy's ability to outmaneuver the defenders. The attacking force often benefits from greater freedom of movement and confidence, which gives them a distinct advantage in overcoming fixed defensive positions.

Historical examples have demonstrated that once an entrenched position is breached, the entire defending army can quickly become demoralized and may even retreat in disarray. While I have complete faith in the resilience of my troops and their willingness to rally and repel the enemy, such determination would be wasted if the entrenchments themselves prevent us from exploiting any advantages gained. Entrenchments, while seemingly beneficial, can often impose limitations on an army's freedom of movement, making it challenging to capitalize on unexpected breakthroughs and limiting the possibility of strategic counterattacks.

Given these inherent disadvantages, it stands to reason that continuous defensive lines covering a large front are even more ineffective. These long lines of defense, although popular in recent military tactics, serve more to create vulnerabilities than to offer substantial protection. The style currently in vogue follows the approach of Prince Louis of Baden, who first implemented such defensive lines along the Briel. Later, the French employed a similar approach in Flanders, hoping that extensive lines would deter invasion. I maintain, however, that such defensive lines are more detrimental than beneficial. They require a broader span than the troops can realistically defend, creating gaps and weak spots where the enemy can easily break through. Instead of creating a secure front, these lines tempt the enemy into aggressive attacks and increase the likelihood of failure. Rather than protecting territory, they expose our forces to reputational damage should the line falter under pressure.

In warfare, numerical disadvantage need not lead to defeat, especially when sound tactics and intelligent maneuvering are employed. When facing a larger enemy force, a smaller army should aim to position itself in difficult, mountainous terrain where narrow passes and limited space neutralize the advantage of larger numbers. By restricting the enemy's ability to spread its forces and fully utilize its wings, we effectively level the playing field, making the numerical disparity less relevant. Such terrain provides natural choke points, creating opportunities to ambush the enemy, slow their movements, and limit the effectiveness of their formations. In close, hilly regions, we gain the added benefit of strengthened flanks, a distinct advantage compared to open plains where there is less natural cover. In fact, we secured victory at the Battle of Sohr largely due to our favorable positioning. Although the Austrian forces vastly outnumbered ours, they were unable to break through our flanks, as the terrain kept their superior numbers from becoming an insurmountable threat.

Choosing the most advantageous ground is my first priority, as the right terrain can fundamentally shift the odds in battle. Following the selection of ground, my focus turns to arranging the battle disposition itself. Here, my preferred tactic is the oblique order of battle, an approach that offers a means of both defensive and offensive maneuvering. In this arrangement, we refuse one wing to the enemy, keeping it out of the main engagement, while reinforcing the other wing, which is tasked with leading the attack. Concentrating our forces on a single point enables us to turn the enemy's flank and launch a decisive blow where they are weakest.

An army of even ten thousand men, if its flanks are turned effectively, will find itself rapidly encircled and at risk of collapse. The maneuver centers on the actions of the right wing, where all our offensive power is directed. First, a body of infantry is sent forward to infiltrate the wooded area on the flank, striking at the enemy cavalry from the side and creating a gap for our own cavalry to exploit. Meanwhile, a regiment of hussars charges into the enemy's rear, further destabilizing their line and causing confusion. As the enemy cavalry is broken and begins to retreat, our infantry advances from the woods, flanking the enemy's infantry, while the rest of our forces press the attack head-on.

Meanwhile, the left wing remains stationary, preserving its strength until the enemy's left wing is fully routed. This coordinated approach achieves multiple strategic objectives. Firstly, it enables a smaller force to hold its own against a much larger opponent, as the focus is on exploiting weaknesses rather than matching strength with strength. Secondly, it allows us to concentrate our attack on a single, decisive point that, once breached, has the potential to unravel the enemy's entire formation. Thirdly, if our attacking wing is repulsed, the remainder of our forces remains intact, with three-fourths of our troops still fresh and available to cover a strategic withdrawal, should it become necessary.

When confronting an enemy holding a naturally advantageous position, it is critical to carefully assess both strong and weak points before making any move. The goal should always be to identify the area of least resistance and direct the attack there, maximizing efficiency and minimizing unnecessary losses. Attacks on fortified villages, for example, are often unreasonably costly. Such actions typically result in high casualties among our best infantry, which weakens the overall force. For this reason, I avoid attacking villages unless it is absolutely unavoidable. Villages often serve as a trap, consuming resources and soldiers in a battle for limited gains while risking significant losses.

Some military theorists suggest that the center of the enemy's position is the most effective target, arguing that a successful penetration there will cause the enemy's entire formation to buckle. For instance, if an enemy position includes two large towns and two villages on its wings, then capturing the center will cause a ripple effect, leading to the inevitable fall of the flanks. Plate 10 illustrates such a situation, where a break in the center exposes the wings, leading to their eventual collapse. This approach, when properly executed, has the potential to yield a complete and sweeping victory by exploiting the inherent weakness in the enemy's structure.

Once a breach is made in the center, the attack should be intensified, pressuring the enemy to retreat from both the right and left sides. There is no greater asset in such an assault than the concentrated fire of artillery loaded with cartridges, which devastates the enemy's battalions. The powerful effect of artillery fire was evident during the battles at Sohr and Kesselsdorf, where attacks on well-defended batteries taught me valuable lessons in the complexities of capturing fortified gun positions. For example, let us imagine attempting to capture a heavily fortified battery with fifteen cannons that cannot be outflanked. In such situations, a frontal assault would likely result in devastating losses, as the combined fire of artillery and infantry makes it nearly impregnable. Capturing such a position often depends more on enemy error than on brute force.

In these cases, as our infantry mounts an attack, they are often repulsed, prompting the enemy's defenders to abandon their posts temporarily in pursuit. This movement leaves the artillery momentarily undefended, creating an opportunity for our forces to regroup and push forward. The defenders, realizing their mistake, then attempt to return to their guns, only to find our troops seizing control alongside them.

To improve our chances in such scenarios, I devised a specific maneuver based on experiences from these engagements. The attacking forces are arranged in two lines with a checkerboard formation, supported by a third line of dragoons. The first line advances with a light attack, designed to draw a response without engaging fully. Once contact is made, this line falls back through gaps in the second line, feigning retreat and enticing the defenders to abandon their position to pursue. At this point, we launch a vigorous, coordinated assault, using the defenders' momentary lapse to overrun the position.

This tactic aligns with a guiding principle: never place undue reliance on any single position unless it is unequivocally secure against all foreseeable threats. The primary strength of our troops lies in their offensive capability. Ceding this advantage without sufficient cause would undermine our fundamental tactical approach.

When occupying defensive positions becomes necessary, the priority should be to secure high ground, as elevation offers inherent strategic value. Additionally, reinforcing the flanks is essential to prevent the enemy from finding weak spots. If there are villages situated at the head or on the flanks of our position, it would be prudent to burn them, provided the wind direction does not drive smoke into our own camp. Destroying these villages prevents the enemy from using them as cover and disrupts any planned approach, further strengthening our position and enhancing the defense's overall effectiveness. By adhering to these principles and maintaining flexibility in both offensive and defensive operations, we can maximize our chances of success in any engagement, regardless of the size or positioning of opposing forces.

If there are any solid stone buildings situated in front of the main line, I would station infantry within them to harass and impede the enemy during the engagement. Such structures offer natural defensive benefits and can serve as strong points to delay or disrupt the enemy's advance.

It is critical, however, to avoid placing troops on terrain where they cannot effectively operate. Our position at Grotkau in 1741 was rendered nearly useless because the center and left wing were posted behind impassable bogs. The only usable ground, where any maneuvering could take place, was occupied by a portion of the right wing. This misalignment cost us strategically, limiting the effectiveness of our formation. Similarly, Villeroy's defeat at the Battle of Ramillies occurred because his right wing was positioned in such a way that it became ineffective, leaving the entire French force vulnerable when the enemy concentrated their attack against the unsupported right flank.

While I encourage Prussian troops to occupy advantageous positions as other armies do, these positions should serve a temporary purpose. Once these positions have been used to favor a movement or secure artillery support, the troops must vacate them promptly to engage the enemy directly. Rather than allowing the enemy to initiate an attack, we turn the tables, attacking them instead and thwarting their plans. Any unexpected movement we make in the enemy's presence is almost certain to yield positive results, particularly when directed against a weak or exposed point.

I consider battles fought in this manner to be among the most effective engagements. On these occasions, I would order the infantry to refrain from firing as it only slows their advance. Victory in these encounters is not measured by the number of casualties inflicted but by the extent of ground gained. The surest path to victory is to march forward swiftly and in tight formation, continuously advancing and pressing the enemy. When moving through challenging, broken terrain, it is customary to allow an interval of fifteen yards between squadrons. However, on even ground, the line should be unbroken, forming a solid front.

For the infantry, the spacing should be just wide enough to allow room for the artillery. Exceptions are made only in certain scenarios—such as assaults on entrenchments, batteries, or villages, and in forming the rear guard during a retreat—where cavalry and infantry are arranged in a checkerboard formation. This pattern allows the second line to immediately fill any gaps in the first, providing support and enabling an orderly retreat, with each unit able to cover the other as they withdraw. This principle is fundamental and should never be overlooked.

This discussion provides an opportunity to outline some core principles for arranging an army in battle formation, regardless of the terrain. First, select prominent landmarks as reference points for aligning the wings. For instance, the right wing might align itself with a particular steeple designated as point N.N. The commanding general must exercise extreme caution in ensuring that the troops do not establish their positions incorrectly, as even a slight misalignment can disrupt the entire formation.

It is not always necessary to delay the attack until the full army is ready to engage. At times, opportunities arise that can be exploited swiftly, and hesitation could result in losing a strategic advantage. While a large portion of the army should generally be engaged in the battle, the first line should receive primary consideration when establishing the order of battle. If any regiments in the first line are unavailable, they should be replaced with an equal number from the second line to maintain continuity.

Special attention should be given to the wings, especially those expected to bear the brunt of the engagement. In open terrain, where the enemy is free to maneuver, it is essential to maintain a uniformly strong order of battle throughout the line. The enemy may hold back a reserve force, which they could deploy to disrupt our formation, so all parts of the line must be equally prepared to respond to potential threats.

If one wing lacks adequate support, the general commanding the second line should immediately dispatch dragoons to extend and reinforce the first line, without waiting for formal orders. Meanwhile, hussars from the third line can take the place of the dragoons, ensuring that the reinforcement does not weaken the second line's overall integrity.

This maneuver is critical because, should the enemy attempt to flank the first line's cavalry, the dragoons and hussars will be in position to counter the enemy's move and return the threat, ensuring that our forces remain adaptable and resilient in the face of unexpected developments.

To support the left wing, I recommend positioning three battalions in the interval between the two lines, as this will provide additional security. In the event that our cavalry is repulsed, these battalions will serve as a barrier, preventing the enemy from advancing directly onto the infantry—a tactic that proved effective during the Battle of Mollwitz.

The general in command of the second line should maintain a distance of three hundred paces from the first line. If he notices any gaps or intervals forming in the first line, he should promptly deploy battalions from the second line to fill them. This proactive approach ensures continuity in the battle formation, preventing weaknesses that the enemy could exploit.

In an open plain, it's advantageous to station a reserve cavalry unit behind the center of the infantry battalions. This reserve should be led by a capable officer who can operate independently, either reinforcing a pressured wing or flanking the enemy in pursuit if they manage to disorder one of our wings. This reserve gives the cavalry a moment to rally and reorganize while protecting the main force.

To initiate the engagement, the cavalry should charge at full gallop, while the infantry advances briskly toward the enemy. Commanding officers must ensure their troops penetrate and break through the enemy lines entirely. It is crucial that no one fires until the enemy is clearly routed, as premature firing can disrupt the momentum of the attack. Should any soldiers fire without orders, they must be immediately commanded to shoulder arms and resume their march without pausing. Once the enemy begins to falter, we can allow firing by battalions, which, when coordinated, can bring the engagement to a swift conclusion.

This formation includes a unique feature where small bodies of infantry are positioned at the extremities of the cavalry wings. These battalions provide support by using their own cannons, along with those on the cavalry wings, to target the enemy's cavalry from the outset, giving our cavalry an advantage as they prepare to charge. Additionally, if our wings are forced to retreat, the enemy's pursuit will be deterred by the risk of being caught between two fires—our main line and these supporting battalions.

When our cavalry appears to have gained the upper hand, this supporting infantry should advance toward the enemy's infantry. The battalions positioned in the intervals between the cavalry units should then quarter-wheel, moving to the flanks and rear of the enemy infantry, allowing us to surround and decisively engage them.

The victorious cavalry wing must prevent the enemy's cavalry from regrouping, pursuing them in orderly fashion and cutting them off from their own infantry. As confusion overtakes the enemy, the commanding officer should dispatch hussars to pursue the routed troops, supported by our main cavalry force. At the same time, dragoons should be sent along the roads the enemy infantry is using to retreat, capturing as many as possible and disrupting any organized escape.

This order of battle introduces another element—integrating dragoon squadrons with the infantry of the second line. In past engagements with Austrian forces, I observed that after approximately fifteen minutes of musket fire, Austrian soldiers tend to gather around their colors in small, dense formations. During the Battle of Hohenfriedburg, our cavalry exploited this tendency by charging these clusters, capturing many prisoners in the process. With the dragoons positioned nearby, they can immediately charge into these groups when the opportunity arises, leading to effective captures and disrupting enemy cohesion.

Some may argue that I appear to rely heavily on artillery over small arms in these dispositions. My response is that one of two outcomes is nearly inevitable: either our infantry will fire despite orders not to, or they will hold fire, waiting for the enemy to waver. In either case, the moment confusion is observed among the enemy, the cavalry should be ordered to charge. Facing flanking attacks on one side, a frontal assault on the other, and a cut-off line of retreat, most enemy troops will inevitably surrender or be captured.

In such a situation, the battle becomes less a contest and more a complete rout, especially if no natural obstacle, such as a defile, exists to shield the enemy's retreat.

In marching to battle, whether advancing by the right or left, the battalions or divisions must remain closely aligned, ensuring they are ready to engage as soon as they deploy. If advancing in a broad front, careful attention must be paid to maintain appropriate spacing, so that units are neither too tightly clustered nor too far apart.

There is also a distinction between positioning heavy artillery and field pieces attached to battalions. Heavy cannons should be stationed on elevated terrain, while the battalion field pieces should be set fifty paces ahead of the infantry. All artillery, regardless of type, must be well-aimed and consistently fired to maximize impact.

As the line advances to within five hundred yards of the enemy, field artillery should be moved by hand, allowing for uninterrupted firing. Once the enemy is in full retreat, the heavy artillery should also advance, firing a few more rounds as a parting blow to ensure their departure remains chaotic.

Each piece of artillery in the first line should be manned by six gunners, along with three regimental carpenters to maintain and operate the equipment efficiently. At approximately three hundred and fifty yards, artillery should switch to firing cartridges for maximum effect as the enemy is within critical range.

Victory in battle requires more than defeating the enemy in the immediate sense; it demands understanding how to capitalize on that victory fully. To spill blood needlessly, without securing a strategic advantage, is wasteful and inhumane. Pursuing a retreating enemy to heighten their fear and capture prisoners not only determines the current engagement but influences the course of future encounters. However, practical limitations—such as a shortage of provisions or troop exhaustion—may sometimes prevent a full pursuit. These factors must always be weighed carefully to balance immediate gains against the needs of sustaining the campaign over time.

It is ultimately the responsibility of the commanding general if an army finds itself lacking in provisions. When he chooses to engage in battle, he does so with a specific purpose in mind; and having such a purpose obliges him to ensure that all necessary preparations are in place to achieve it. This includes having a sufficient supply of bread or biscuits to sustain the army for eight to ten days. Such planning is essential to maintaining momentum and avoiding logistical setbacks that could undermine the success of the campaign.

As for the physical demands on the soldiers, any hardships they endure should not be given undue consideration if those exertions contribute to the attainment of victory. In times of exceptional opportunity, it is expected that the troops will be called upon to perform extraordinary feats, accepting the rigors of such efforts as part of their duty.

Once victory has been decisively secured, I recommend dispatching a detachment from among the regiments that have suffered the greatest losses. This group's mission would be to care for the wounded, prioritizing our own but extending basic care to enemy casualties as well. These soldiers should be transported to the hospitals, which, ideally, have already been set up in advance, demonstrating foresight in caring for the casualties.

Meanwhile, the main army should not hesitate to press on and pursue the defeated enemy to the nearest defile. In their state of panic, they are unlikely to maintain control of such positions if they are immediately pursued. The pursuit must be relentless to prevent the enemy from catching their breath and regrouping; otherwise, they might turn these natural defenses to their advantage.

After securing this initial victory and attending to the aftermath, it is time to establish the camp. When doing so, strict adherence to established rules and security measures is essential; overconfidence can be a grave miscalculation. Even when the victory appears complete, we should not assume that the enemy has no fight left. They may still have the resources or cunning to seize upon any negligence or error in our ranks, and vigilance is crucial to prevent this.

In cases of an absolute victory, additional steps can be taken to maximize the gains. Detachments may be dispatched to intercept the enemy's retreat routes, seize their supply depots, or even lay siege to multiple towns simultaneously. Here, specific strategies depend largely on the situation at hand, as circumstances beyond control often influence the best course of action. One must remember that as long as there is more to accomplish, the task is not finished. A sharp-minded, defeated enemy will seize any opportunity to exploit lapses in our conduct.

I earnestly hope the Prussian forces will never know defeat and am confident that, with sound leadership and rigorous discipline, they will avoid such a fate. However, should such a misfortune befall them, there are specific actions that can help mitigate its impact and restore the army's footing.

When it becomes evident that a battle is lost and that the enemy's advances are unavoidable, immediate steps should be taken to secure a controlled retreat. First, the second line of infantry should be sent to any nearby defile to establish a defensive position, utilizing the principles outlined in the section on retreats. Along with the infantry, as many cannons as can be spared should be stationed at this point to strengthen the line.

If no such natural chokepoint is available, the first line should retreat through the intervals in the second line, reforming into battle formation approximately three hundred yards behind. This spacing allows for an orderly fallback, providing a buffer for regrouping. The remaining cavalry must be consolidated and, if desired, can be arranged into a square formation. Such a formation offers greater defensive resilience, shielding the retreating forces from enemy incursions.

History offers notable examples of this tactic. After the Battle of Frauenstadt, General Schullembourg used a square formation to lead his forces across the Oder River without interference from Charles XII. Similarly, after the first Battle of Hochstädt, the Prince of Anhalt deployed his forces in a square to withdraw across a two-league plain, deterring the French cavalry from engaging them. These cases illustrate how, even in defeat, maintaining composure and using strategic formations can protect an army's integrity during retreat.

Finally, I emphasize that a defeat does not necessitate a long and frantic retreat of forty leagues or more. Rather, the army should withdraw only to the nearest advantageous position, rallying there to regain cohesion and morale. By taking up a defensible position and projecting confidence, the army can gather its scattered ranks and provide reassurance to those who are disheartened. This immediate regrouping prevents an initial setback from devolving into a complete rout and keeps the army poised for future engagements.

Article XXIII. Of the Reasons Which Should Induce Us to Give Battle, and in What Manner it is to be Conducted.

Battles shape the fate of nations. It is essential that they be decisive, whether the goal is to free ourselves from the ongoing burdens of war, place the enemy in a disadvantaged state, or resolve a conflict that might otherwise persist indefinitely. A wise commander will not make any movement without a sound reason, and a general should never engage his forces in battle unless he has a strategic objective of considerable importance. If he finds himself forced into battle by his opponent, it is likely due to previous errors that have allowed the enemy to dictate the terms and place him at a disadvantage.

Reflecting on my own experience, I do not claim infallibility. Out of five battles fought by my troops, only three were intentionally planned, while in two instances, circumstances forced me into conflict. At Mollwitz, for instance, the Austrians had positioned themselves between my army and Wohlau, where I kept my provisions and artillery, necessitating a battle to maintain access to essential resources. Similarly, at Sohr, the enemy had cut off my route to Trautenau, leaving me no choice but to fight or risk the loss of my entire force. The contrast between battles we choose and those imposed upon us is striking. The premeditated battles of Hohen-Friedberg, Kesselsdorf, and Czaslau yielded brilliant victories, with the engagement at Czaslau even leading to a negotiated peace.

In setting forth these guidelines for battle, I do not deny that I have made my own share of errors through oversight. However, I expect my officers to learn from these mistakes, and they can be assured that I am committed to rectifying them through diligent study and improved tactics.

There are instances when both armies may desire engagement, leading to a swift and decisive resolution. However, the most advantageous battles are those in which we compel the enemy to fight against his will. It is a fundamental principle of warfare to force the enemy into actions he would rather avoid. Since our interests and the enemy's are naturally opposed, it is unlikely that both of us desire the same outcome from a confrontation.

Numerous factors might compel us to engage in battle: the need to force the enemy to lift a siege on a strategically valuable location, to drive him from a province he occupies, to penetrate further into his territory, to gain the upper hand in a siege, to press him toward peace negotiations, or to capitalize on any mistake he has made. For example, if we maneuver to threaten a town of importance to him or sever his lines of communication, the enemy may be forced into a confrontation to protect his interests.

In conducting such maneuvers, however, we must be cautious not to place ourselves in a similar predicament, as overextending our forces or occupying a position vulnerable to counterattacks could give the enemy the same opportunities against us. Engagements targeting an enemy's rear guard often carry the least risk, as they can disrupt his movements without exposing our own forces to undue danger.

If such a strategy is pursued, the most effective approach is to encamp near the enemy and wait for an opportunity when he attempts to withdraw through defiles or narrow passages. At that moment, we can strike his rear guard, potentially securing a decisive advantage with minimal risk. Small-scale engagements like these can yield substantial gains and often produce outcomes disproportionate to their scope.

There is also the tactic of harassing the enemy to disrupt his ability to consolidate scattered forces. The purpose of this strategy is justified by the objective at hand, although a skilled enemy may counter it with a rapid forced march or by positioning himself in an advantageous spot to avoid interception. On occasion, we may also find ourselves drawn into battle by the enemy's missteps. When the opposing force makes an error, it is our duty to capitalize on it, as every fault in the enemy's plan presents an opportunity to punish his lack of prudence.

Moreover, it is essential to keep in mind that our wars should be as brief and decisive as possible. Prolonged engagements are not in our interest, as they gradually weaken discipline, deplete the population, and exhaust the nation's resources. Consequently, Prussian generals should strive to conclude campaigns with a balance of prudence and urgency. Success should not tempt us to delay; instead, we must act efficiently to secure a quick and strategic conclusion.

The Marshal de Luxembourg's response during the Flanders campaigns is a cautionary tale. When his son suggested that they could capture yet another town, Luxembourg replied dismissively, "Hold your tongue, you little fool! Would you have us go home to plant cabbages?" Such complacency risks prolonging conflict without purpose. Rather, we should adopt the philosophy of the Hebrew leader Sennacherib, who believed it better to sacrifice one man than to risk the well-being of an entire people.

There are instances in military history that illustrate the principle of exploiting an enemy's mistake. In the Battle of Senef, the Prince of Condé seized the opportunity to engage the rear guard of the Prince of Orange (or possibly Prince of Waldeck) when he failed to secure the entrance to a defile, making his retreat vulnerable. The battle accounts of Marshal de Luxembourg's unnamed victory, as well as the Battle of Raucoux, provide further examples of how adept generals have capitalized on enemy errors.

In sum, battles are complex affairs with far-reaching consequences, and every engagement must be approached with purpose, preparation, and a readiness to exploit any advantage. By understanding and applying these principles, we can increase our chances of achieving not only victory in battle but also a swift and favorable resolution to the larger conflict.

Article XXIV. Of the Hazards and Unforeseen Accidents Which Happen in War.

This discussion would become unmanageably lengthy if we delved into every possible mishap a general might encounter in war. To summarize, a general needs both skill and good fortune to succeed. Generals face far more challenges and scrutiny than most people realize. Their actions are judged by the public, often based on nothing more than a brief report in the gazette, while the very readers passing judgment may lack even the basic experience to lead a small detachment, let alone command an army.

I don't aim to excuse generals who have made errors—my own campaign in 1744, for instance, had its share of missteps. But while I've often made mistakes, I have also undertaken successful operations, such as the siege of Prague, the defense and retreat at Koelin, and another strategic retreat in Silesia. I won't detail these campaigns further here, but it's important to acknowledge that some misfortunes cannot be avoided, no matter how well-planned or carefully considered the strategy may be.

Since these notes are intended for my generals, I'll focus on lessons from my own experiences rather than other examples. At Reichenbach, I planned a forced march to reach the Neiss River, intending to cut off

General de Neuperg's communication by positioning my forces between his army and the town of Neiss. All preparations were in place, but heavy rain turned the roads to mud, stalling our advance guard and preventing the pontoons from moving forward. A dense fog compounded the issue, leaving village guards lost and unable to rejoin their regiments. The conditions were so poor that, rather than arriving at 4 a.m. as planned, we reached the river at midnight. By that time, the element of surprise was lost; the enemy had already prepared for our approach, and the opportunity slipped away.

Disease can also derail the best-laid plans. During our campaign in Bohemia in 1741, poor provisions led to sickness among the troops, forcing us into a defensive position. In another instance, at Hohen-Friedberg, I dispatched an aide-de-camp to instruct Margrave Charles to command the second line, as General Kalckstein had been detached to lead the right wing against the Saxons. Unfortunately, the aide misunderstood and instructed the Margrave to reorganize the first line into the second, a miscommunication that could have thrown our lines into complete disarray had I not discovered it in time to correct the error.

These examples underscore the importance of staying vigilant and recognizing that a single poorly executed order can disrupt an entire strategy. If a general commanding a critical detachment falls ill or is killed, it can create substantial complications for the overarching battle plan. Offensive maneuvers, in particular, demand generals of both sound judgment and unwavering courage, qualities that are rare; in my entire army, I count no more than three or four such individuals.

Even with the best precautions, losing a critical convoy to the enemy can ruin a plan, requiring either a significant pause or a complete reevaluation. Should circumstances necessitate a retreat, the troops may become demoralized. While I have fortunately not experienced such a setback with my entire army, I observed this effect at the Battle of Mollwitz. After a setback, it took considerable effort to revive the spirits of the troops, especially the cavalry, which was so shaken that they seemed resigned to defeat. To restore their morale, I sent out small detachments to give them a manageable task and gradually ease them back into combat readiness. It was not until the Battle of Hohen-Friedberg that our cavalry regained the confidence and effectiveness they continue to exhibit today.

The discovery of a significant spy within the enemy's camp can deal a severe blow to one's intelligence efforts. Without such informants, a general must rely solely on personal observation, a limitation that restricts insight into the enemy's movements and intentions.

The carelessness of officers tasked with reconnaissance can also create distressing complications. Marshal de Neuperg, for example, was taken by surprise when a hussar officer, assigned to keep watch, neglected his duties, allowing our forces to approach undetected. Similarly, an officer from the regiment of Ziethen failed to conduct his night patrol properly, enabling the enemy to build bridges at Selmitz and surprise our baggage train.

War is fraught with unpredictable challenges, and while one must be prepared for setbacks, many factors remain beyond a general's control. That said, by anticipating potential issues, staying alert to changing conditions, and instilling responsibility in subordinates, we can better navigate the many hazards of command. Through these reflections, I hope to equip my officers with the resilience and adaptability necessary to mitigate the effects of unforeseen setbacks, maintaining both the integrity of the army and the momentum of the campaign.

This illustrates the importance of my belief that the security of an entire army should never rest solely on the vigilance of a single officer. Entrusting such a consequential responsibility to one man, particularly a lower-ranking officer, is an unwarranted risk. Remember carefully the guidance I have given on this matter under the topic "Of the Defence of Rivers." It is essential to rely not solely on patrols and reconnaissance parties, but on strategies that provide stronger, more reliable safeguards.

Of all the disasters that can befall an army, treason is the most perilous. A notorious example occurred in 1733 when Prince Eugene was betrayed by General St. . . ., who had been bribed by the French. I, too, have felt the sting of betrayal; the fortress of Cosel was lost due to the treachery of a garrison officer who defected and led the enemy directly to it. Such examples serve as a stern reminder that, even when fortune seems firmly on our side, we should be wary of complacency and refrain from letting success breed overconfidence. Instead, we should remain mindful that any skill or foresight we claim is, at best, subject to the whims of unforeseen events—forces beyond our control that seem determined, for reasons unknown, to humble even the proudest of human plans.

Article XXV. If It Be Absolutely Necessary That the General of an Army Should Hold a Council of War.

Prince Eugene once remarked that "if a general does not wish to fight, he only needs to hold a council of war." His point is well-proven, as councils of war tend almost universally to vote against engaging. In these settings, secrecy—so essential to military operations—is often lost, as too many opinions and details are shared openly.

A general, entrusted by his sovereign with command of the army, should act independently and decisively. The confidence placed in him by his king justifies such an approach. Yet, while a general must lead firmly, he should not disregard the counsel of even the lowest-ranking officer. In matters concerning the nation's welfare, a true patriot sets aside personal pride and considers all suggestions, valuing advice that may lead to the successful outcome they all strive for.

Article XXVI. Of the Manoeuvres of an Army.

The principles outlined in this work shed light on the theory behind the maneuvers I have instilled within my troops. These tactics are designed with the primary goal of maximizing every possible moment, enabling us to resolve engagements more swiftly than has been customary, and ultimately to overwhelm the enemy through the relentless momentum of our cavalry's charge. This intense, impetuous force ensures that even the most reluctant soldier is swept along, compelled to perform his duty alongside the bravest, making every trooper an active participant in the assault. Success relies heavily on the vigor of the attack.

With this in mind, I am confident that each general, fully appreciating the necessity and benefits of strict discipline, will prioritize its preservation and enhancement, both during wartime and in periods of peace. I am often reminded of the inspiring words of Vegetius regarding the Romans: "And finally," he declared, "Roman discipline triumphed over the hordes of Germans, the strength of the Gauls, the cunning of the Germans, the vast barbarian hosts, and conquered the entire world." Such is the importance of disciplined forces to the flourishing and security of a state.

Article XXVII. Of Winter Quarters.

When a campaign concludes, the focus naturally shifts to organizing winter quarters. This requires careful planning and must align with the unique circumstances at hand. The first priority in establishing winter quarters is to construct a robust protective chain around these positions. Such a defensive line can be created in several ways, depending on the available natural and constructed defenses: positioning the line behind a river, leveraging mountainous terrain for added security, or taking advantage of nearby fortified towns to serve as protective barriers.

During the winter of 1741-42, for example, when my forces wintered in Bohemia, we set up behind the Elbe River, with our protective chain beginning at Brandeis and extending through key points, including Nienbourg, Koelin, Pojebrod, and Pardubitz, eventually ending at Konigingraetz. However, it is important to remember that rivers are not impenetrable barriers. When frozen, they can be crossed at numerous points, which highlights the need for constant vigilance. For this reason, hussars should be stationed along the full length of the chain to observe the enemy's movements carefully. These hussars are responsible for patrolling frequently, monitoring for any unusual activity or signs of enemy troop gatherings in the area.

Beyond the infantry chain, additional brigades of both cavalry and infantry should be stationed at strategic intervals. This arrangement ensures a rapid response and provides reinforcement to any section that might require immediate assistance. In the winter of 1744-45, we secured our quarters by establishing a defensive line along the mountain range separating Silesia from Bohemia. We guarded this line meticulously, aiming to maintain peace within our quarters. Lieutenant-General de Trusches, for instance, oversaw the front of Lusatia up to the Glatz region, covering crucial posts from Sagan to Schmiedberg, extending to Friedland, where redoubts were fortified for additional defense. Additional fortified posts were constructed along the vital routes of Schatzlar, Liebau, and Silberberg, bolstered by a reserve unit, ready to assist any post that might come under attack.

To add further strength, abbatis were set up in the surrounding forests, creating blockages on all routes leading into Bohemia and thereby limiting enemy movement. Every post was also equipped with hussars, assigned specifically for reconnaissance duties, ensuring that any attempt by the enemy to advance would be immediately detected. General Lehwald similarly protected the Glatz region with his own defensive arrangements, fortified positions, and prudent precautions. He and General Trusches coordinated their efforts to provide mutual support. Thus, if the Austrians moved against General Trusches, General Lehwald could counter by advancing into Bohemia from the rear, and General Trusches would do the same if Lehwald's forces were threatened. This network of mutual defense ensured that neither general's position could be easily overwhelmed.

Tropau and Jagerndorf were significant posts in Upper Silesia, and the main line of communication with Glatz ran through Zeigenhals and Patchskau, while another route through Neustadt connected to Neiss. It is also prudent to avoid excessive reliance on mountainous terrain for security, as we must remember the adage, "Where a goat can pass, a soldier can follow." For those winter quarters that benefit from proximity to fortresses, Marshal Saxe's arrangements provide an excellent model. Yet, we cannot always choose the ideal positions, as our defensive lines must adapt to the geographical realities of the terrain we occupy.

It should be regarded as a fundamental principle that we are never to consider any location entirely safe from enemy incursions. A constant state of readiness is required to maintain security within our winter quarters. Another important practice is to assign regiments by brigades, keeping them under the direct supervision of their respective generals. Where possible, generals should remain close to their own regiments, providing oversight and ensuring that discipline and readiness are maintained. However, exceptions to this rule may be necessary at times, depending on the broader strategy and the army's needs, which the commanding general is best positioned to assess.

There are also logistical considerations to be addressed regarding the upkeep of troops during winter quarters. If circumstances demand that we take winter quarters within our own territory, captains and subordinate officers should be compensated to match what they would typically receive in occupied winter quarters. Additionally, the soldiers should be provided with bread and meat at no cost to them, ensuring that their needs are met without imposing undue strain on their resources.

If, however, our winter quarters are in enemy territory, resource allocation follows a distinct structure. In this scenario, the commanding general receives an allowance of 15,000 florins, while generals of cavalry and infantry receive 10,000 florins each. Lieutenant-generals are allocated 7,000 florins, major-generals or camp marshals receive 5,000, cavalry captains are given 2,000, infantry captains 1,800, and subaltern officers between 1,000 ducats and 400-500 florins. Soldiers are provided with bread, meat, and beer without charge, though they are not issued money directly, as this could increase the risk of desertion.

The commanding general must closely monitor this allocation to prevent looting and to maintain order. Some leniency may be afforded to officers if they can secure small, fair gains, but plundering should be strictly controlled to maintain discipline and prevent resentment among the local populace. When stationed in enemy territory, the general must also ensure that an adequate number of recruits are obtained. The distribution process should be organized so that each district, or "circle," supplies a certain number of regiments. Ideally, each circle should be subdivided to match our cantonment arrangements, thereby streamlining the recruitment and training process.

If local authorities willingly supply recruits, that arrangement is preferable. If not, firmer methods may be required to meet recruitment needs. The early arrival of recruits is crucial, as it allows sufficient time for them to undergo training and become combat-ready by the spring. Captains should still send out additional recruiting parties if necessary to meet the numbers required.

The general must oversee all logistical aspects, such as securing artillery horses and other necessary supplies, either directly from the region or through compensation. Equipment maintenance is vital, and all military gear, from baggage wagons to basic supplies, should be repaired or replaced at the enemy's expense. This includes specific attention to the needs of the cavalry, whose officers must ensure saddles, bridles, stirrups, and boots are maintained in peak condition. Infantry officers, meanwhile, should ensure their men are supplied with adequate shoes, stockings, shirts, and gaiters for the next campaign. Soldiers' blankets and tents must be repaired, and cavalry swords sharpened, while infantry arms should be inspected and readied.

Additionally, artillery teams must prepare ample ammunition, especially cartridges for the infantry, to ensure our forces are fully equipped for the spring campaign. By attending meticulously to these logistical details, we can enter the next season with a well-prepared, well-provisioned, and confident army, ready for whatever engagements may come.

It remains essential for the general to ensure that all troops assigned to form the defensive chain are adequately supplied with powder and shot, and, indeed, that no essential provision is lacking for the entire army. Should time permit, it is highly advantageous for the general to visit various quarters himself. By doing so, he can assess the condition of the troops firsthand, ensuring that officers are diligently overseeing both the training and welfare of their men. Such oversight is vital, as regular drilling is necessary not only for recruits but also for seasoned soldiers to keep them sharp and ready for the demands of combat.

At the start of each campaign, the arrangement of cantonments is adjusted to align with the expected order of battle. Typically, this involves positioning the cavalry on the wings and placing the infantry at the center. These cantonments often extend nine to ten leagues (or about four to five miles) forward, with a depth of approximately four leagues (or two miles). As the time for encampment approaches, it becomes necessary to draw these cantonments inward slightly, consolidating the positions in preparation for rapid deployment.

A well-organized structure within the cantonments can significantly enhance the efficiency of command. I have found it highly practical to assign command responsibilities to the six senior-most generals. For instance, one general should oversee the cavalry on the right wing of the first line, while another commands the left. Similarly, two additional generals can command the cavalry of the second line, each responsible for a wing. This approach facilitates swift communication and execution of orders and enables the troops to assemble into columns for camp or combat with greater ease and precision.

Concerning the subject of winter quarters, I must once again advise great caution in entering them prematurely. It is imperative to confirm beyond doubt that the enemy's forces have fully disbanded before settling into winter positions. Let the misfortune of Elector Frederick William serve as a reminder: he was caught off guard and surprised in his quarters in Alsace by Marshal de Turenne, suffering a setback that might have been avoided with greater vigilance.

In sum, these strategies are not mere formalities but are fundamental to preserving the army's readiness, security, and overall effectiveness, ensuring that our forces are always prepared for rapid mobilization or engagement should the need arise.

Article XXVIII. Of Winter Campaigns in Particular.

Winter campaigns are particularly taxing on troops, not only due to the illnesses they often bring but also because they demand constant movement, preventing soldiers from being adequately clothed or reinforced. Such campaigns also strain the transportation of ammunition and provisions. Even the best-trained army cannot sustain prolonged winter campaigns without severe consequences. For these reasons, winter campaigns should generally be avoided, as they are among the most punishing and challenging forms of warfare. Yet, circumstances may arise where a general has no choice but to undertake them.

Reflecting on my own experience, I believe I have undertaken more winter campaigns than any general of this era, and it may be useful to outline the motivations behind these decisions. In 1740, following the death of Emperor Charles VI, Silesia held only two Austrian regiments. Determined to assert my family's rightful claims over this duchy, I launched a winter campaign, aiming to capitalize on the advantageous conditions and quickly advance toward the Neiss. Had I waited until spring, the war front would likely have settled between Crossen and Glogau, necessitating three or four grueling campaigns to accomplish what we achieved with a single, well-timed march.

Another example is my winter campaign of 1742, when I attempted to protect the region from the Elector of Bavaria. That endeavor fell short, but not due to the season itself; rather, it failed because the French acted foolishly, and the Saxons proved untrustworthy. My third winter campaign, in the winter of 1741-42, became necessary when the Austrians invaded Silesia, forcing me to drive them back during a time of year when most would avoid warfare. In the winter of 1745-46, both the Austrians and the Saxons aimed to invade my hereditary lands, intending to wreak havoc. As was my custom, I decided to act preemptively and initiated a winter campaign within the heart of their territory, seizing the advantage by taking the war directly to them.

If I were to face similar conditions again, I would not hesitate to repeat such actions, and I would commend any of my generals who chose to follow this example. However, I must caution that without compelling reasons like these, a winter campaign should never be undertaken lightly.

For the logistics of winter campaigns, certain precautions are essential. Troops must be stationed as closely as possible in their cantonments, concentrating their strength in larger villages or towns whenever feasible. Ideally, two or three regiments of cavalry, mixed with infantry, should be housed together if the village is large enough to accommodate them. On some occasions, as when the Prince of Anhalt quartered his forces at Torgau, Eilenbourg, Meissen, and several other small Saxon towns, all infantry regiments may be gathered within a single town to maintain a more cohesive force, with the general remaining nearby in an encampment.

When we approach enemy territory, a rendezvous point should be established for all troops, who will then proceed in multiple columns. At the moment of any critical movement, whether preparing to storm enemy quarters or advancing to confront the enemy directly, the troops should arrange themselves in battle formation. In such circumstances, they may remain in open fields overnight, each company lighting large fires to endure the cold. Yet, these maneuvers demand great endurance, and their duration must be minimized. Swift, decisive action is key in winter warfare. Hesitation is a luxury we cannot afford; plans must be formed with boldness and executed with unwavering resolve.

If possible, winter campaigns should be avoided in regions dotted with fortified towns, as the season's constraints prevent a prolonged siege. Attempting to take well-defended positions by surprise is often doomed to fail, as the logistical challenges of winter make it nearly impossible to sustain such efforts.

In the ideal scenario, troops should be allowed to rest as much as possible during the winter months. This time can be used to strengthen the army and make any necessary preparations so that when spring arrives, our forces can move out with a renewed advantage over the enemy.

These principles outline the key aspects of large-scale maneuvers in winter warfare, as comprehensively as I am able to explain. I have endeavored to make these guidelines as clear as possible. If any part seems ambiguous, I welcome you to communicate these concerns to me, so that I may either elaborate further or acknowledge if your insights exceed my own.

Through my experiences, limited as they may be, I have come to understand that war is a complex art, one that can never be fully mastered. It continually rewards those who study it with dedication, offering fresh insights to those who remain attentive. If this account encourages my officers to deepen their understanding of military science, I shall consider my time well spent. Such knowledge opens the surest path to glory, allowing men to lift their names from obscurity, achieving renown, and securing a legacy of immortal fame through bold and distinguished deeds.

Thank You for Reading

Dear Reader,

We hope this timeless classic has sparked your imagination and enriched your literary journey. Now that you've turned the final page, we want to share a vision for the future of reading—one where every classic you've ever wanted to explore is at your fingertips, in a format that best suits your life.

We'd like to invite you to gain immediate, unlimited digital & audiobook access to hundreds of the most treasured literary classics ever written—along with the option to secure deluxe paperback, hardcover & box set editions at printing cost. Together, we can spark a new global literary renaissance alongside our small, independent publishing house called "The Library of Alexandria."

Thousands of years ago, the Library of Alexandria stood as a beacon of knowledge—until it was lost to history. We aim to reignite that spirit of preservation and discovery right now, in the modern age—only this time, it's accessible to all, in every language and every format.

Picture a world where every timeless classic, novel, poem, or philosophical treatise is not only available to read but also updated for today's readers—modernized, translated into any language or dialect, and ready to enjoy in any format you choose, whether that is in an eBook, audiobook, paperback, or deluxe hardcover & box set version a printing cost.

By joining our movement to rebuild the modern Library of Alexandria, you become part of an unprecedented mission to offer:

- **Unlimited Audiobook & eBook Access to the Greatest Classics of All Time**

  Instantly explore thousands of legendary works, from Plato and Shakespeare to Jane Austen and Leo Tolstoy. All are instantly ready to read or listen to, giving you a complete literary universe at your fingertips.

- **Paperback & Deluxe Editions at Printing Costs:**

  Purchase any title in a paperback, deluxe hardbound, or deluxe boxset edition at printing costs, shipped right to your doorstep. Curate your personal library of Alexandria with editions worthy of display—crafted to last, designed to captivate, and delivered straight to your door.

- **Modern translations for Contemporary Readers in all languages and dialects**

  Discover a vast selection of classics reimagined in clear, current language—no more struggling with outdated phrases or obscure references. Next to the original versions, we aim to offer translations in as many languages and dialects as possible.

  As we continue our translation efforts and add new languages, readers everywhere can connect with these works as if they were written today. By bridging linguistic divides, you're contributing to ensuring that these timeless stories become more meaningful, accessible, and inspiring for people across the globe.

- **Your Personal Library of Alexandria:**

  Over the months and years, you'll curate a unique physical archive of classics—each volume a testament to your taste, curiosity, and love of knowledge. It's not just about owning books—it's about curating a cultural legacy you'll cherish and pass down for generations to come.

- **Join a Global Literary Renaissance:**

  Your support fuels an ongoing mission: allowing us to reinvest in offering deluxe print editions (including special boxsets) at their true cost, broaden the range of available formats and translations, and extend the reach of these works to new audiences worldwide. By joining today, you're not just preserving a legacy of masterpieces; you set in motion a powerful wave of literary accessibility.

  We are more than a publisher—we're a movement, and we can't do it alone. Your support lets us scale our mission, preserving and reimagining history's greatest works for tomorrow's readers.

Become a Torchbearer of knowledge.

Thank you for picking up this book and allowing us into your literary journey. As you turn the pages, know that you're part of something larger: a global effort to keep these stories alive, share their wisdom across borders and generations, and spark a true cultural revival for the modern era.

If this resonates with you—please consider taking the next step by visiting:

www.libraryofalexandria.com

With gratitude and a shared love of knowledge,

The Modern Library of Alexandria Team

Visit:

www.libraryofalexandria.com

Or scan the code below:

www.ingramcontent.com/pod-product-compliance
Lightning Source LLC
Chambersburg PA
CBHW081322090726
47907CB00010B/2343

* 9 7 8 1 8 0 6 2 9 4 5 7 2 *